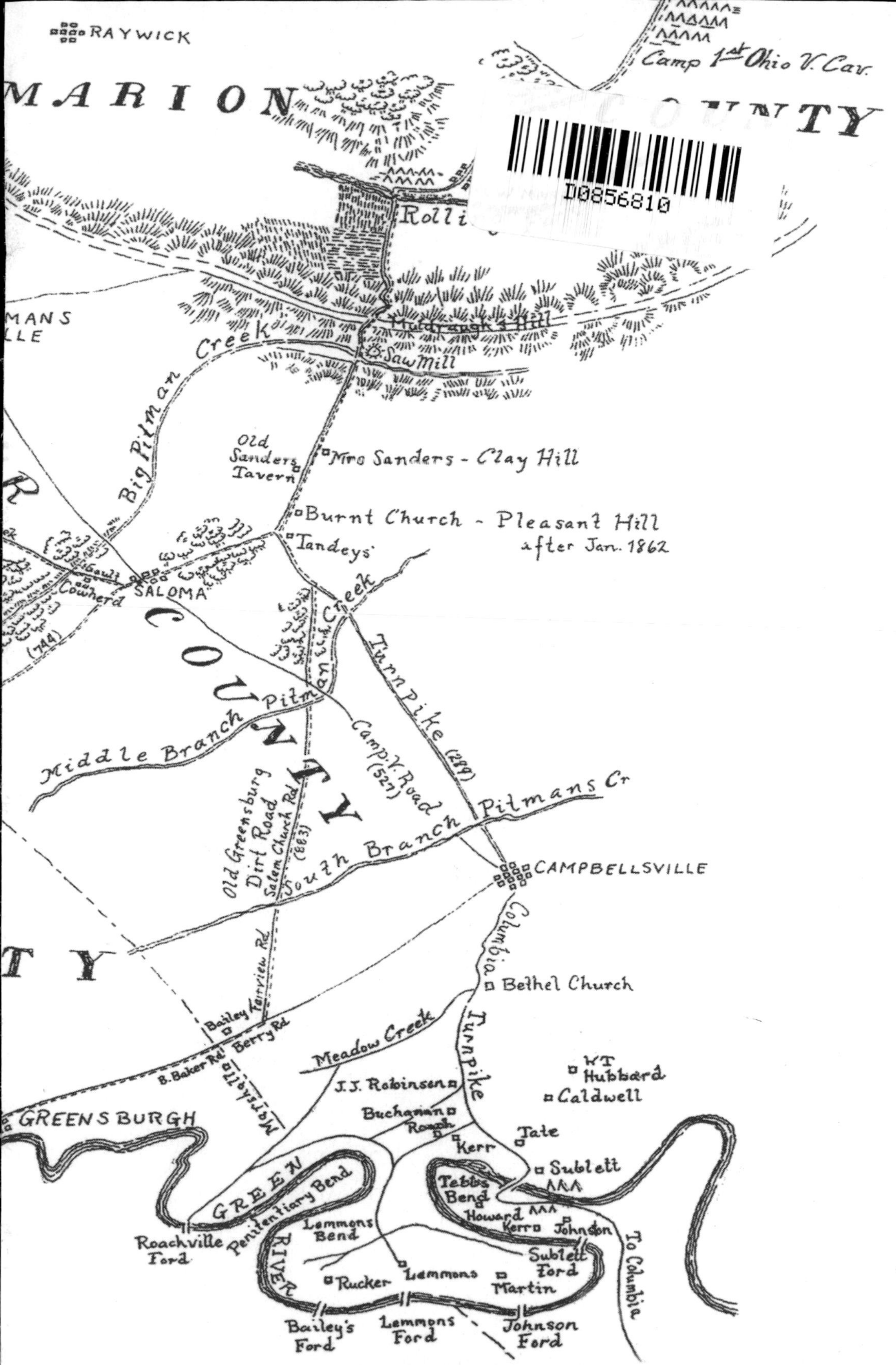

RAYWICK
MARION
COUNTY
Camp 1st Ohio V. Cav.
Rolli
MANS
LLE
Big Pitman Creek
Muldraugh's Hill
Saw Mill
Old Sanders Tavern
Mrs Sanders - Clay Hill
Burnt Church - Pleasant Hill
after Jan. 1862
Tandeys
SALOMA
Cowherd
(744)
COUNTY
Creek
Turnpike (289)
Middle Branch Pitm
Camp. V. Road (527)
Old Greensburg Dirt Road
Salem Church Rd. (883)
South Branch Pitmans Cr
CAMPBELLSVILLE
TY
Columbia
Bethel Church
Turnpike
Bailey
Fairview Rd
Berry Rd
B. Baker Rd
Meadow Creek
J.J. Robinson
W.T. Hubbard
Caldwell
GREENSBURGH
Buchanan
Roach
Kerr
Tate
Sublett
Tebbs Bend
Howard
Kerr
Johnston
GREEN
Penitentiary Bend
Lemmons Bend
Roachville Ford
RIVER
Sublett Ford
To Columbia
Rucker
Lemmons
Martin
Bailey's Ford
Lemmons Ford
Johnson Ford

"Morgan Is Coming!"

Confederate Raiders in the Heartland of Kentucky

General John Hunt Morgan

"Morgan Is Coming!"

Confederate Raiders in the Heartland of Kentucky

By Betty J. Gorin

To Kenny Bennett,
distinguished businessman,
good citizen, and
long-time friend -
Best wishes,
Betty J. Gorin
23 Feb 2006

Harmony House Publishers—Louisville

Harmony House Publishers
P.O. Box 90
Prospect, KY 40059
502-228-2010

Design: Laura Lee

Printed in Canada

ISBN: 1-56469-134-9

Library of Congress Number: 2005934268

Dedication

to Gordon E. Smith,

my husband and editor,

and my children,

Mark and Beth

Contents

Maps

Prologue

MORGAN IS COMING! This cry of alarm rang out through the heartland of Kentucky during the Civil War. The mere sound of that name evoked fear and spread panic among its citizens. In Taylor and surrounding counties, the legendary Confederate cavalry commander, John Hunt Morgan, came to represent in people's minds everything that happened in the war—the loss of loved ones in battle, the pillaging of their homes, farms, and businesses, the confiscation of their horses and foodstuffs. Since he came to the area six times, it was all seen as Morgan's doing.

Today, if someone asks, "Who burned the Taylor County Courthouse during the Civil War?" the answer is, "Morgan!" even though he had been in his grave for three months when the courthouse was set ablaze. After the war ended, all this began to change. Morgan's name conjured up the image of a dashing, romantic, and fearless horseman. His defeats and the destruction his men wrought were forgotten. With the return home to Kentucky of heroic Rebel commanders, a romantic view of the "lost cause" began to replace wartime sympathy for the Union with its policies of emancipation, arming of African Americans, and violation of civil rights. During the postwar years, former Confederate leaders dominated Kentucky's political leadership.

When Taylor County citizens research the history of family members who fought in the war, anticipating stories of Rebel triumphs, they find that their kin fought for the Yankees and played a significant role in Union victories. The truth is that almost all the men from Taylor and surrounding counties who served in the war were on the Northern side. In this heartland of loyalty to the Union, I, too, was curious to see if I had a Confederate ancestor. But an ardent native Virginian great-great-great-grandmother was my only Confederate find. She was Mary Sheldon Rucker who remarked, "The Yankees better bring their shirttails full of dumplings, for they're going to get hungry before they beat the secesh."

This book is not intended to be a biography of Morgan. It is an attempt to gather information about the events that took place in Taylor County and its contiguous areas: Marion to the north, Green to the west, Adair and Cumberland to its south, that is, Kentucky's heartland in south central Kentucky. This work provides the first detailed account of the Battle of Tebbs Bend–Green River Bridge, one of the bloodiest small battles in the western theater.

The road to accomplish any kind of meaningful research for Taylor County is fraught with difficulty. The index for circuit court suits which cover the Civil War period is missing. The county order book for the Civil War hardly mentions the war. The county did not have a newspaper until the 1880s and those editions, for the most part, have been destroyed.

My writing is based on the *Official Records of the War of the Rebellion*, the Orlando Moore Collection at Kalamazoo Valley Museum in Michigan, Kentucky newspapers, and interviews with people who remember stories told to them by grandparents. I have relied heavily on the works of Morgan's biographers, Basil Duke and James Ramage.

A special note of appreciation is extended to Steven Wright of Elizabethtown, whose newspaper collection on Kentucky and Tennessee from the Civil War period, has been invaluable. Richard Skidmore, Ruth Perkins, and Barbara Wright and her historical library have also been helpful. The libraries and museums of Michigan, particularly the Kalamazoo Valley Museum, Kalamazoo Public Library, Bentley Library at Ann Arbor, Hope College at Holland, Calvin College Library, Detroit Public Library, and the State Museum at Lansing deserve special recognition for their assistance. A collateral descendant of Col. O.H. Moore, Grif Cook, and his wife, Barbara, of Niles, Michigan, shared information. Don Elmore did credible research on Tebbs Bend in the 1970s.

Almost all of the pen and ink sketches were drawn by Gerald Myers of Campbellsville with one sketch by Jim Hoffman of Frankfort. The maps were produced by Judy Ross of Bowling Green and Maria Brent of Versailles. Joe Brent of Versailles, Porter Harned of Louisville, John Sickles of Merrillville, Indiana, and Al McGeehan of Holland, Michigan were helpful in securing photographs. Dr. Smith Powell of Berea provided data on the phases of the moon in 1862 and 1863. James A. Ramage, Lowell H. Harrison, Stuart Sanders, and Gary Osborne kindly read the manuscript and offered suggestions.

To the people who have accompanied me on out-of-town trips—Carol Settle and Pat Durham, to acquaintances who kindly showed me sites in surrounding counties—Joe Barbee, Randy Flowers, Vonnie Kolbenschlag, David Arms, Nash Hayes, Gypsie Jones, and Rick Johnston, or allowed me to stay in their homes near the National Archives and libraries in Michigan and Kentucky—Tony and Jonna Mendez, Grif and Barbara Cook, Al and Marsha McGeehan, David and Kay Howell, Ed and Joan Loy, and Barbara Whitlock, thank you for your hospitality.

The many wonderful people who have shared stories with me through the years are credited in the notes.

I have tried to make this dramatic period in our local history vivid through the observations of the people who actually participated in the events I describe. Almost no diaries of Taylor County citizens for this period have been located, but the letters and diaries of soldiers, particularly Curtis Burke, James B. McCreary, Robert Alston, John Sprake, John Wilterdink, Johannes Van Lente, and Dirk Van Raalte, are frequently quoted. John Hunt Morgan, the dashing and enigmatic cavalryman, the Battle of Tebbs Bend, and his antagonist, Union Col. Orlando H. Moore of Michigan, remain at the center of this account.

It is hoped that this modest work will help its readers separate myth from reality concerning what happened in the Heartland of Kentucky during the Civil War.

The Morgan Legend

Morgan was a partisan Confederate commander with no formal military education, fulfilling assignments in the rear of Federal lines in Kentucky and Tennessee. Union commander U.S. Grant wrote in his *Memoirs*: Morgan "had no base of supplies to protect but was at home wherever he went. . . . Morgan was foot-loose and could operate where his information . . . led him to believe he could do the greatest damage. During the time he was operating in this way, he killed, wounded, and captured several times the number he ever had under his control. He destroyed many millions of dollars of property; in addition, places that he did not attack had to be guarded as if threatened by him."[1]

The *Louisville Journal*, whose editor declared a journalistic war against Morgan, acknowledged that "unscrupulous" Morgan had been "immensely effective." He became "the terror of the Federals and the boast and glory of the rebels."[2]

Morgan inspired such a depth of loyalty that a bond of mystique developed among his officers and men. Popular with both men and women, it was said: "Maidens worshiped him; and young men died for him."

The Morgan Presence

Six feet tall, hundred eighty-five pounds, with blue-gray eyes, he wore a neatly trimmed goatee. His hair, mustache, and beard were dyed black, a common practice at the time. His hairline was beginning to recede.[3] Col. Thomas Berry, a cavalryman in Morgan's troop, made these observations about his commander:

> Morgan on horseback was a striking figure. There were few men in either army, who possessed the easy graceful poise and striking proportions. His

> easy management of his horse, made him appear almost a harmonious part of the animal itself. . . . His was the air and manner of a polished gentleman, the noble bearing of a born leader, and a soldier. Straight as an Indian arrow shaft, always neatly and tastefully dressed, elegantly mounted, he was superb, the ideal cavalry officer.[4]

Morgan endured long days in the saddle with little sleep. Generous and gracious to subordinate officers and men, he cultivated and maintained close friendships. Duke commented that only one other cavalryman, Nathan Bedford Forrest, was Morgan's equal.[5]

His love of great horses and a good game of cards, gracious attention to women, and military accomplishment fit into the Bluegrass's demands for a gentlemanly lifestyle.

Morgan and his Methods

Oftentimes, in order to disrupt the Union supply line, Morgan struck at the stockades, bridges, and trestles of the Louisville and Nashville Railroad. This happened in Marion County, but not in Taylor, since the railroad spur from Lebanon to Campbellsville and Greensburg was not completed until 1879, years after the war was over.

As Morgan and his cavalrymen gained experience and their numbers increased, the following tactics served them well in their raids in Taylor County and south central Kentucky:

1) They sometimes traveled in Federal uniforms or in civilian clothes.

2) They used parallel roads when riding through the country, causing exaggerated reports of the number of troops in the press, Federal telegraph messages, and rumors in the civilian population that he was here, there, everywhere.

3) The cavalrymen usually fought dismounted as infantrymen, using their horses only for approach and getaway. Firing dismounted insured greater accuracy and they became less a target. They rode in fours and, when they dismounted to fight, one man stayed in the rear to hold the horses. Sometimes, the horse-holder was the youngest or one who did not have a weapon. Other times, the men simply took turns.

4) Morgan used reconnaissance extensively, sending scouts out five miles ahead and on the flanks. Men were also posted at crossroads to receive reports from the scouts and make sure advancing forces knew the locations of fords on the rivers and streams ahead. Local men were sometimes conscripted to serve as guides.

5) Morgan's telegrapher tapped into telegraph lines to procure information and send false messages to the enemy. Cutting the wires became part of the game.

6) Southern cavalrymen were expected to live off the land, finding food for themselves and forage for their mounts wherever they could.

7) The men often stole horses to replace their worn-out mounts, which were left behind or taken with them on leads.

8) Morgan obtained information and support from fellow Masons, sometimes granting them favors, even if they were his adversaries.

9) Morgan usually employed hit-and-run tactics, avoiding direct frontal assaults on strongly defended enemy positions, thereby more likely assuring victory. One writer said: "He struck like a thunderbolt their weakest point, and was away before they could look beneath the smoke."[6]

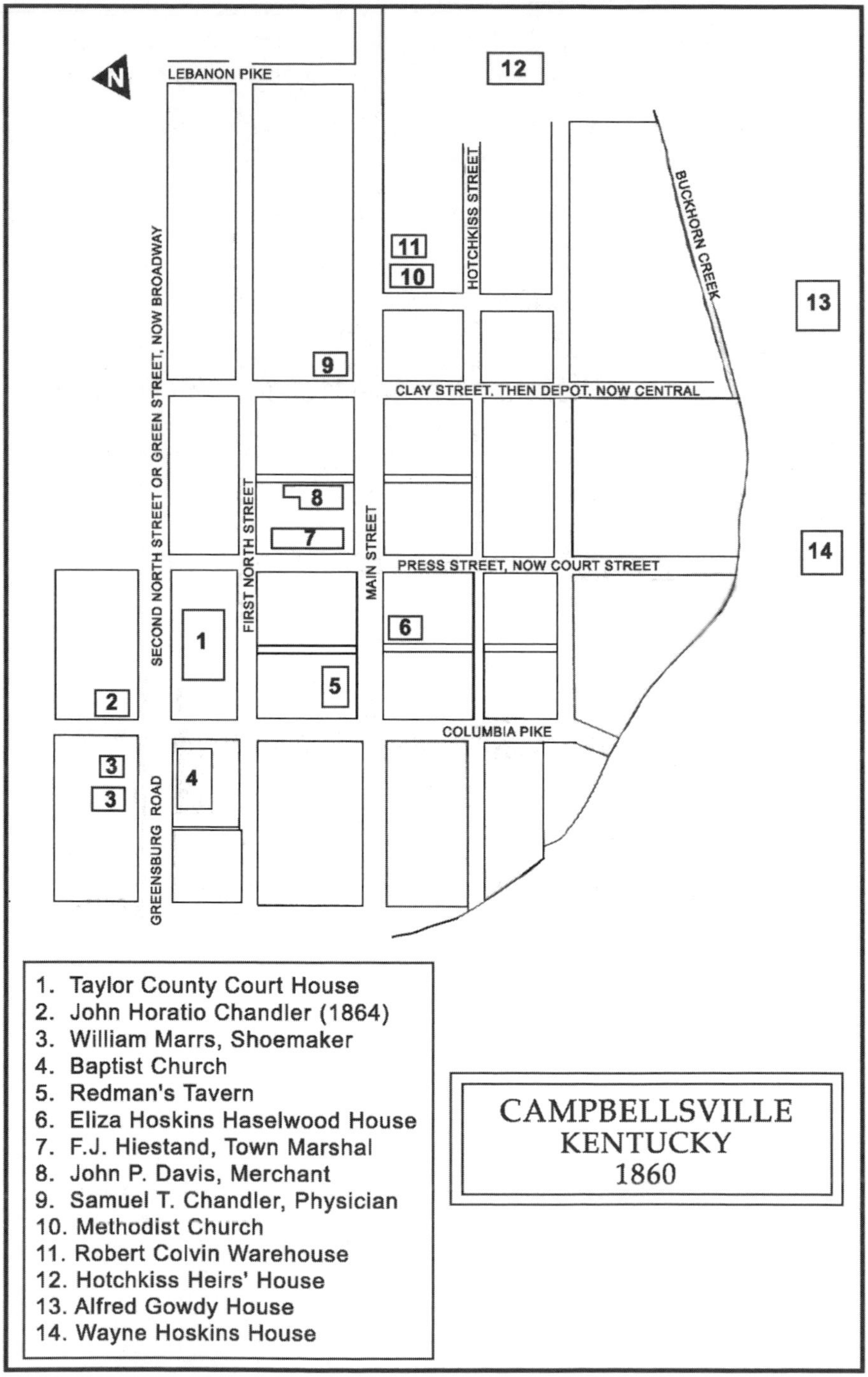
LEBANON PIKE
N
SECOND NORTH STREET OR GREEN STREET, NOW BROADWAY
FIRST NORTH STREET
MAIN STREET
HOTCHKISS STREET
BUCKHORN CREEK
CLAY STREET, THEN DEPOT, NOW CENTRAL
PRESS STREET, NOW COURT STREET
COLUMBIA PIKE
GREENSBURG ROAD
12
11
10
13
9
8
7
14
1
6
2
5
3
3
4
1. Taylor County Court House
2. John Horatio Chandler (1864)
3. William Marrs, Shoemaker
4. Baptist Church
5. Redman's Tavern
6. Eliza Hoskins Haselwood House
7. F.J. Hiestand, Town Marshal
8. John P. Davis, Merchant
9. Samuel T. Chandler, Physician
10. Methodist Church
11. Robert Colvin Warehouse
12. Hotchkiss Heirs' House
13. Alfred Gowdy House
14. Wayne Hoskins House
CAMPBELLSVILLE
KENTUCKY
1860

Map by Judy Ross

Part One

Campbellsville, Kentucky
1860

"A place of several log houses"
William R. Plum, Union telegrapher

The people of Campbellsville never tired of hearing about how the Civil War affected the lives of those who lived through it. As late as the 1890s, citizens were still gathering around old soldiers to listen to tales about their exploits under the shed in front of Chandler's Store on Main Street.[1] There Dick Archie Webster, who had fought with Morgan, held crowds spellbound with vivid accounts of his all-night rides, his capture at Buffington Island, mistreatment and escape attempts in the Allegheny prison.

Many men from Kentucky's Union regiments returned home from southern battles, heroic in victory but broken in health. However, staying home as a civilian, or serving as a member of the Home Guard, did not guarantee that one would escape the dangers of the battlefield.

* * *

By 1860 Campbellsville had been the county seat of Taylor County for twelve years. Its one-story brick courthouse stood in the center of the public square.[2]

On Saturdays and court days, crowds of people coming and going to town in wagons created clouds of dust on the dirt streets. Log and frame houses, barns, small board-and-batten sheds occupied the lots around the square, on First North, Second North, and Main streets. The town had a somewhat "ragged, tumble-down appearance," its buildings not having seen paint or repair since its founding some fifty years earlier. Horses were watered in Buckhorn Creek and at two cisterns behind stores on Main Street.[3]

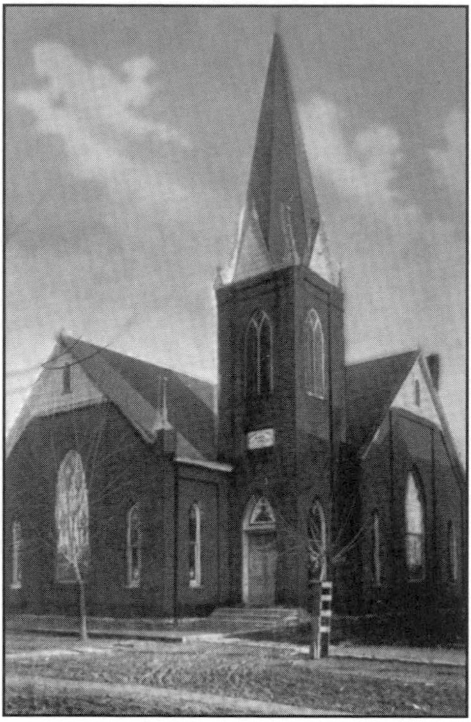

Methodist Church

James Campbell-Hotchkiss Home, Campbellsville

John H. Chandler Home, Campbellsville

Alfred F. Gowdy Home, Campbellsville

Wayne Hoskins Home, Campbellsville

Across Buckhorn Creek on a hill overlooking the town lived two wealthy merchants in elegant Greek-revival houses: A.F. Gowdy and Wayne Hoskins. Benoni Hotchkiss's descendents lived in the Federal-style brick built by a town-founder and Virginian, James Campbell, on the upper end of Main. In the central part of downtown, merchant John P. Davis and Eliza Hoskins Haselwood owned brick houses on opposite sides of the street.[4] In 1864 John Chandler's family built a new two-story frame house, across from the courthouse on the northeast corner of Second North Street and North Columbia Avenue.[5]

There were four churches in the downtown area. A simple white frame Baptist Church, with double front doors, looked out on the Courthouse Square. A brick Methodist Church sat adjacent to postmaster Robert Colvin's warehouse on the south side of upper Main Street. A log Christian Church was located in the midst of the cemetery on the west side of town, and the African-American Baptist congregation met on the town's northeast side. Sunday schools were usually held weekly, but preaching services were conducted once a month, since ministers often served several congregations.[6]

The town burial ground on the Greensburg Road, which was said to look more like a briar patch than a cemetery, was about ten years old. The town school was located below the cemetery on the south side of Buckhorn Creek. Across the Greensburg Road from the "old school on Buckhorn," the town's founder, Andrew Campbell, had operated a saw and grist mill and, in 1816, had the first voting precinct for the northern section of Green County in his house. By 1860, Campbell had lain in his grave by Buckhorn Creek for almost forty years.[7]

George W. Redman's tavern was often the busiest place in town. A sign, which read "The Golden Horse," hung out in front of the frame-over-log building on 101–109 East Main Street. In 1861, before the stringing of the military telegraph, Gen. George Thomas in Lebanon and Gen. Jeremiah Boyle in Columbia used it as a place for their couriers to meet and exchange information and orders. In early February 1862, Union telegrapher William R. Plum and telegraph superintendent W.G. Fuller spent the night in two of Redman's twenty beds at the Campbellsville tavern. Plum remembered that the room was poorly lit and its door bolted from the inside. But Redman's "table" was exceptional and it was reported that a guest was treated like a lord.[8]

The bonds to pay for the extension of the rail line from Lebanon through Campbellsville were sold at Redman's. By 1863, visitors who came to town on the stagecoach were being charged 40 cents for their meals, 20 cents for a drink of whiskey, and 20 cents for a night's lodging. If a guest wanted his horse fed, an extra 40 cents was charged. Government taxes were raised on liquor to pay for the war; therefore, the rates were raised again in 1864. Redman, a large landown-

George W. Redman

Redman's Tavern, Campbellsville

er with eighteen slaves, also operated a tannery on Buckhorn Creek, a business which had been started by Swiss German settler Jacob Hiestand some forty years before.[9]

In earlier years, at 203 East Main, a second tavern-boarding house was operated by Ferdinand Jacob Hiestand. The 1850 census listed Ferdinand as "landlord" with a merchant, two physicians, and two lawyers as guests. He and his brother, Josiah Landis Hiestand, served as postmasters of the town and ran the office out of the tavern from 1846-1850. By 1860, F.J. Hiestand's occupation had changed to town marshal and his brother, Dr. J.L. Hiestand, had moved to Texas; therefore, it appears that Redman was the only hotel keeper in Campbellsville at the start of the war.[10]

As the war progressed and more and more troops passed through Campbellsville, the granting of the right to sell spirits proliferated. The requests of Edwin Rice, George W. Asper, William F. Chandler, L. McClelland, Mr. McWhorter, and the firms of Gowdy & Turner and Chandler & Davis were granted by the court.[11]

In 1860, the state's population was 1,155,651. Taylor County had the smallest population of the counties in the Heartland: 7,481, including 1,597 slaves, as well as 129 free blacks and mulattoes. Its population, however, had increased by 230 from the preceding decade. Marion County, with its railway link, had by far the largest number of people: 12,593 including 3,479 slaves. Adair with 9,509, including 1,602 slaves, and Green with 8,806, including 2,372 slaves, were only somewhat more populous than Taylor. Taylor County had twice as many free blacks as Adair County, and more than Green and the much larger Marion County.[12]

In order to enforce the Fugitive Slave Law of 1850, whereby citizens were required to return runaway slaves to their owners, county courts appointed slave patrollers to apprehend escaping slaves or those visiting other farms at night without their owners' permission. No concrete evidence has been uncovered concerning any Underground Railroad activity in Taylor County; however, there was one operating in Green County and it may have had some connections in Taylor.[13]

In 1860 Campbellsville was a very small place with a population of 446, an increase of only ten over the preceding decade. It would be surprising if there were more than 85 able-bodied men in town, excluding slaves. Some ten stores, including Chandler and Mourning, Gowdy & Turner Company, Hoskins, Davis and Asper, as well as three blacksmiths, several carpenters and wheelwrights were located in the downtown area of Campbellsville. The town also had a cabinetmaker, a carriage maker, a wool carder, two shoemakers, two saddlers, three lawyers, five physicians, a hotel owner, a barkeeper, a butcher, and three stage drivers. William Cloyd was county judge, Henderson J. Colvin, county sheriff, and George W. Montague, county clerk.[14]

The nearest railway line, which reached Lebanon in 1857, was twenty miles away. Campbellsville was connected to Lebanon, Columbia and Greensburg by stagecoach, some running every day and some on alternate days of the week.[15] At one o'clock in the afternoon in Lebanon at the Harris Hotel, on the corner of Market and Main streets, Nace Harris, the hotel's slave, cried out in his melodious voice: "All aboard for Campbellsville and Columbia, with intermediate stops at New Market, Pinchem [Saloma], Peola, Tampico and Cane Valley."

On the way to Campbellsville, the stage changed its four horses twice, at Schooling's stable, just over the Rolling Fork Bridge past New Market, and at Tandy's Stage Stand. As the stage approached its stopping place, the driver blew his bugle, the vehicle accelerated, and then rattled over the stony road to a halt. At Tandy's, passengers could make a connection to Saloma. After a brief stop, the coach proceeded on to Campbellsville.[16]

Because of the threat from guerrillas, the Taylor County Court allowed the stage company to build a shed for the safekeeping of the coach next to the courthouse in the Public Square, with the company providing the lumber.[17]

Since the closest bank was ten miles away in Greensburg, A.F. Gowdy and F.J. Hiestand extended credit to county residents, taking mortgages on their property.[18] Before Taylor County was formed out of Green County in 1848, Greensburg served as the county seat. Even when Campbellsville became the

Ken Pierce

Hiestand House, outside Campbellsville

Joseph Harrison Chandler

new county seat, many people continued to have close ties to Greensburg, using its attorneys and sending their children to its boarding schools. It remained a convenient place to do business because of the river trade and its developed commercial community. With the coming of the railway to Lebanon, Campbellsville's business links to Greensburg weakened and ties to Lebanon strengthened.

Some years before the outbreak of the Civil War, Aaron Harding, a Taylor County native and son of Revolutionary soldier Thomas Harding, moved to Greensburg to practice law. He was elected to the U.S. Congress from the Fourth Congressional District, which included Green and Taylor counties in 1861. Harding, a strong Democrat and opponent of abolition and Lincoln's war policies, was easily reelected in 1863. Attorney Joseph H. Chandler, a fellow Democrat and state representative, supported Harding enthusiastically. Chandler lived in a stone house, built by his father-in-law Jacob Hiestand, at the edge of Campbellsville on the old Greensburg Road.[19]

Taylor County Voting Patterns

Even though the Kentucky General Assembly named the county after Mexican War hero Zachary Taylor, its citizens rejected him when he ran for president as the Whig Party candidate. In the election of 1848, Taylor Countians gave Democrat Horace Greeley 59.1% of the vote and Taylor 40.9%, even though every county surrounding Taylor voted for the general. Unaffected by Henry Clay's nationalist

Zachary Taylor

Stephen A. Douglas

George B. McClellan

tradition in the Whig Party, they voted Democratic by wide margins in the elections of 1852 and 1856, 66.6%, and 67.9%.[20]

In 1860, most people in Kentucky, including Taylor Countians, wanted to remain in the Union and, at the same time, retain their slaves. The county had 288 slave owners, fourteen of whom owned twenty or more slaves. Naturally, they would vote for a candidate protecting their interests.

In the election of 1860, almost 50% of Taylor County voters cast their ballots for Stephen A. Douglas of Illinois, the Northern Democrat Party candidate for president, who supported maintaining the right to own slaves in the slave states and to allow people of the western territory to choose for themselves whether or not to permit slavery. But 33.9% of the county's vote went to John Bell, the Constitution Union candidate and 16.4% went to Kentucky-born John C. Breckinridge, the Southern Democratic candidate. Only one person in Taylor County voted for Abraham Lincoln, the Republican Party candidate. Less than 1% of Kentucky voters voted for him; in Lexington, his wife's hometown, Lincoln received only five votes.[21]

Through the war years, the Democratic vote in Taylor County increased dramatically. In 1864 the Democratic candidate, Union Gen. George McClellan, who was frequently in conflict with President Lincoln, received 94% of the vote in the county, with Lincoln receiving only 30 votes. Although large crowds in Campbellsville greeted Union soldiers and applauded patriotic speeches, they did not vote for Lincoln, even though he was born in neighboring Larue County. The vote in Taylor County reflected the highly negative views of its citizens toward the Emancipation Proclamation and the administration policy of providing military training and arming of freed slaves.[22]

Lebanon-Columbia Turnpike Road

By 1860, practically all the roads in Kentucky, including the Lebanon-Columbia Turnpike, were privately owned. Counties subscribed to the stock of private turnpike companies which built and maintained the roads. Tollgates were usually located about every five miles, with the toll for a horse and rider being five cents. The state set the toll charge, but revenue from tolls went directly to the turnpike companies.[23]

The Lebanon-Columbia Turnpike was the main corridor to the outside world from Campbellsville. Mail, newspapers, and goods from Louisville, Lexington, and eastern cities as far away as Cincinnati and Philadelphia came to Campbellsville over the pike. During the Civil War, Federal supply columns moved along this road from the Lebanon military depot through Campbellsville into southeastern Kentucky and to towns along the Cumberland River such as Burkesville. Much of what happened in Taylor County during the Civil War was directly related to this strategically important route.[24]

The turnpike was described as a "macadamized" road, i.e., its roadbed consisted of layers of crushed stone. By May 1863, it was recognized as an important military route by the U.S. Army Chief Engineer, Capt. T.B. Brooks, who reported that the road was well located but that the "metaling" [broken stone] was considerably worn and needed repair before the winter rains came. He commented that, since the turnpike company had received tolls from the U.S. military, it should either repair the road or open its tollgates.[25]

After leaving Lebanon, the pike passed the village of New Market on the Rolling Fork River in Marion County, and, in a serpentine-fashion, ascended Muldraugh's Hill into Taylor County. One soldier wrote that "the crossing of Muldraugh's Hill is a tortuous road and so steep as to make it quite an undertaking." To this day this set of curves is referred to as the "Turkey Foot." At the top of Muldraugh's Hill, for a short way in Taylor County, the pike followed an older route, the Lexington-Nashville Road. The pike ran past the 1835 brick James Sanders house on the Lebanon Road, the old brick Sanders Tavern which had started operating in 1797, a tollgate house which was located across from the Pleasant Hill Meeting House, the log Tandy farm house, and then on into Campbellsville.[26]

At the Tandy house, the Lexington-Nashville Road, often referred to as "the great road" in court records, made a right turn toward Saloma, a thriving community sometimes known as Pinchem. It was possible to avoid going through Campbellsville by using this older and shorter route from the top of Muldraugh's Hill to Greensburg via Saloma and Summersville. John Hunt Morgan became familiar with this road, using it on his first three forays into Taylor County.[27]

After the Lebanon-Columbia Turnpike left Campbellsville, it ran through the G.W. Redman farm, by a tollgate house, and past the meeting houses of Bethel Presbyterians and Liberty Cumberland Presbyterians, and by Ireland Seminary, a school founded by Scot Presbyterian settlers. Further along, the pike passed the lane to James Caldwell's Willowdale, an imposing Greek revival frame home, early settler Isaac Tate's Federal brick house, then owned by his son, Robert, and yet another tollgate house, and James Allen Sublett's cabin overlooking the river bottom just before the road crossed Green River.

On the river, downstream from the bridge, was the Tate-Sublett Landing where hogsheads of tobacco were, in the early days, loaded on flatboats and shipped to market in New Orleans. The bluffs skirting Green River across from the landing have been compared to Kentucky River palisades. An Illinois artilleryman who was there during Morgan's Christmas raid commented: "The south bank of the Green River is . . . a high, rocky hill, and even harder to ascend than Muldraugh's. Water was not often found on this road, and it was really a great treat whenever we came to a good spring. The whole distance was heavily wooded except where it had been cleared for farms."[28] The road continued along the top of the bluffs, winding through Tebbs Bend, through the villages of Coburg and Cane Valley, to Columbia.

Kentucky's Dilemma

After the outbreak of the Civil War at Fort Sumter in April 1861, the administration in Kentucky attempted to stay neutral. This strategy lasted for a few months, but soon both Northern and Southern forces were being actively recruited within the state. Taylor County listed 988 men on its 1861 Militia List as eligible for military service. Some of them, however, had enlisted in the Confederate Army by September 1862.[29]

To meet the emergency, Rodophil Jeter, one of Green County's finest citizens, stepped forward to organize a camp and recruit 130 Home Guards under Kentucky's armed neutrality. Jeter, a cabinet-maker, was the grandson of a Virginia legislator and a Revolutionary War colonel and the son of a captain in the War of 1812. The fact that Jeter owned slaves did not interfere with his loyalty to the Union. He managed to secure arms from Gen. Lovell Rousseau's Camp Joe Holt in Jeffersonville, Indiana. He paid for the shipment of some of the arms himself. These were reported to be some of the first "Lincoln guns" ever allowed to enter the state. He also furnished ammunition, drums, and other equipage out of his own pocket. These Home Guards, who proved to be loyal Union men, drilled in Adair County, not far from the Taylor County line at Cane Valley.[30]

Col. Thomas E. Bramlette

Col. Frank Wolford

There seems to be little doubt about the political sympathies of Taylor County's courthouse officials. At a citizens' meeting on county court day, May 8, 1861, State Representative Joseph Harrison Chandler spoke for the Federal cause. Afterward, a resolution was moved by E.L. Barbee, son of Revolutionary War soldier and state legislator Elias Barbee, recommending native son, attorney Aaron Harding, as the candidate to represent the Fourth Congressional District in the U.S. Congress. Chandler said that Harding was qualified because of his "great ability, patriotism, and devotion to the Union" and that "he will stand the more firmly by the Union when it is in great danger." The resolution supporting Harding was approved and signed by Judge Cloyd and County Clerk Montague. Thus, the descendants of the men who had formed the nation who resided in Taylor County demonstrated their support for maintaining its unity.[31]

The summer of 1861 was an uneasy one throughout the Commonwealth of Kentucky. Rumors of ominous plots, real and imagined, attributed to both sides, flew about. Newspapers fanned the apprehension. While Kentucky men were enlisting at Union camps Joe Holt and Clay across the Ohio River, not far to the south, just over the border in northern Tennessee, other young Kentucky men were pledging their allegiance to the Confederate flag at Camp Boone near Clarksville.

In July 1861, Navy Lt. William Nelson, with Lincoln's blessing, was sent to

Rebecca Bruce Morgan

Rebecca Morgan's Grave, Lexington

the southeastern part of the state to raise three Kentucky regiments in which lawyers Thomas E. Bramlette, practicing in Columbia, and Frank Wolford, practicing in Liberty, quickly obtained commissions. Bramlette organized the 3rd Kentucky Infantry and Wolford, the 1st Kentucky Cavalry, at Camp Dick Robinson in Garrard County. Federal troops began arriving at Camp Nelson in Jessamine County. Federal arms and more "Lincoln guns" were distributed to Home Guard units.[32]

On the other hand, a throng of Bluegrass men, including John Hunt Morgan's brother Tom, enlisted for the Confederacy at Camp Boone.

On July 21, 1861, John Hunt Morgan's life was dramatically changed when his wife, Rebecca Bruce Morgan, died after a lingering illness. She was buried next to her stillborn son, born years earlier, in the Lexington Cemetery.[33]

Morgan was now thirty-six years old, a young widower with no children. The death of Becky meant that he was no longer linked to the pro-Union Bruce family. His wife's brother and his former business partner, Sanders Bruce, was captain of the Lexington Chasseurs, a pro-Union State Guard. Morgan, a Captain of the Lexington Rifles, a pro-Southern unit of the Kentucky State Guard and a rival to the Chasseurs, was free to demonstrate his natural military ability.

University of Kentucky Archives

Young John Morgan

Gerald Myers

Morgan Imprisoned at Pleasant Hill, Taylor County

Part Two

Morgan Held Captive at Pleasant Hill
September 1861

"Captured by a man of a very bad character"
John Hunt Morgan

After Fort Sumter, President Lincoln proclaimed the cessation of commercial trade by Union states with the Confederacy. However, for some months, tons of contraband goods, including arms, flowed freely through Kentucky into the rebel South. Lincoln demonstrated great patience with Kentucky's ignoring the embargo because the president wanted to keep the state in the Union. The governors of Illinois, Indiana, and Ohio were outraged by Kentucky's flagrant disregard of Federal law, and Northern newspapers chafed at the situation. However, by August, the Mississippi River blockade had become more strictly enforced and contraband traffic to the South through Louisville almost ceased.[1]

The blockade was not popular with many business-minded Kentuckians. One of the Lexington companies owned by John Hunt Morgan and his brothers began to have a difficult time shipping the gray cloth it produced for its Confederate customers. In August, the company received an order from Memphis for jeans "as stout & as well colored as the other lot." The next month, even though it was risky business, Morgan and four companions decided to transport three loads of jeans through the blockade. They were intercepted on the Old Nashville Road near Saloma in Taylor County by Home Guards, led by Captain John W. Neville of Lebanon and Lieutenant Short of New Market.[2]

Neville and Short imprisoned Morgan and his wagoners in the nearby Pleasant Hill Meeting House, a solid log building across from the tollgate house on the Lebanon Pike. They confiscated his three loads of jeans.

Short requested support and thirty Home Guards responded, holding a disgruntled and angry Morgan for three days. Obviously displeased with his treatment, he later described Short as "a man of a very bad character." A Louisville newspaper reported that the Rebel force, which had collected to attempt to rescue Morgan, was somehow prevented from carrying out its mission.

Details are sketchy concerning this incident. It was only after an order came from the officer of customs at Danville that Captain Neville released Morgan. It was reported that Morgan had permits and passes from Federal authorities in his possession which Neville apparently did not accept. The *Louisville Journal* commented that "professed Union men in our very midst have done more to aid the rebellion than those who have openly avowed their sympathies for the traitors."[3]

Morgan returned to Lexington after his humiliating experience in the heartland of Kentucky, and he grew increasingly alarmed over the state of affairs. On September 3, 1861, a Confederate force commanded by Gideon Pillow, under orders of Gen. Leonidas Polk, had succeeded in establishing a Rebel foothold in deeply divided Kentucky by occupying Columbus, a small but important city in far western Kentucky. Union forces, led by Gen. Ulysses S. Grant, promptly occupied Paducah to protect the NO&O railroad.

Candidates of the Union Party had been victorious over the Southern Rights Party in the August elections. After the General Assembly showed its support for the Union, the state militia leaders called in the arms of the pro-Southern State Guard, which included Morgan's Lexington Rifles. Lexington was occupied by troops from Union Camp Dick Robinson. Morgan defiantly ran up a Confederate flag over his business and his allegiance to the Southern cause was no longer a secret.[4]

Upon learning that the authorities were planning to seize the weapons of his rifle company, Morgan took action. On Thursday, September 19, 1861, he and a friend took a buggy ride to Shryock's Ferry on the Kentucky River with fishing poles dangling out the back. He arranged for the ferryman to take wagons over the river late the next evening. On Friday, while most of his men were drilling noisily in the Lexington Rifles armory on the northeast corner of Main and Upper, some of them loaded weapons onto two wagons, covered them with hay, and left the city. Morgan later joined them on Versailles Pike. As planned, they crossed at Shryock's into Anderson County, and traveled to what became known as Camp Charity, near Bloomfield, in Nelson County. After a rest, they rode on to Woodsonville, a village near Munfordville, in Hart County. There he and eighty-four men were sworn into Confederate service, on the steps of Green River Baptist Church, on October 27, 1861. This company of men became the nucleus of the 2nd Kentucky Cavalry, CSA.[5]

★ ★ ★

Joe Brent

Brig. Gen. William T. Ward

Joe Brent

Col. Edward H. Hobson, later Brig. Gen.

Transylvania University

Col. Ethelbert L. Dudley

Filson Historical Society

Col. Charles D. Pennebaker

September was the month of decision for south central Kentuckians on the Federal side as well. Just twenty-four miles away from Woodsonville in Greensburg, William Thomas Ward, a Mexican War veteran and former state legislator, made a trip to Camp Dick Robinson and on to Washington, D.C. There President Lincoln appointed him Brigadier General. Ward also secured commissions for field officers of three regiments and set about organizing them: the 13th, 21th, and 27th Kentucky infantries.[6]

The 13th Kentucky Infantry was commanded by banker-businessman Col. Edward H. Hobson of Greensburg, the 21st Kentucky Infantry by Col. E.L. Dudley, a physician from Lexington, and Lt. Col. Basil A. Wheat of Columbia, and the 27th Kentucky Infantry by Col. Charles D. Pennebaker of Louisville. Hobson's nephew, William E. Hobson of Bowling Green, was made a major in the 13th and Brig. General Ward's son, John H. Ward, was named Lt. Colonel of the 27th.

Civil War Camps

There were at least five Civil War camps in Taylor County: Camp Andy Johnson, Camp Ward, Colonel Dudley's Camp, Colonel Pennebaker's Camp, and Camp Hobson at Green River Bridge. Camp Andy Johnson served as the recruiting station for the 13th Kentucky Infantry and was named in honor of U.S. Senator Andrew Johnson, Union loyalist from Tennessee. The camp was first located at the Courthouse Square in Greensburg and later moved to Campbellsville.[7]

Fairgrounds in towns, such as Lexington, Bardstown, and Springfield, were commandeered for campsites by Union troops. The fairground in Campbellsville became Camp Andy Johnson and it was probably located on a site, now part of

Taylor County Historical Society

J.R. "June" Smith

Miller Park, on the Old Lebanon Road near Little Pitman Creek. Young J.R. "June" Smith sold pies and newspapers to the troops camped by the creek as well as on Main Street.[8]

September 27, 1861, a Louisville newspaper reported, "General Ward will open a camp near Campbellsville immediately."[9] Its exact location is unknown, but General Ward was highly regarded by the local citizens. In October, a correspondent from Campbellsville to the *Louisville Journal* wrote: "Ward possesses the fullest confidence of his whole command; indeed, the energy and ability he has displayed in the difficult and dangerous duties devolving on him . . . has exacted the admiration of the whole community."[10]

Colonel Dudley's 21st Kentucky established a camp on the land of Mrs. Sarah Campbell. It is possible that this site was the Adam and Sarah Campbell farm on the Greensburg Road, which had access to water.[11] The campsite of Colonel Pennebaker's 27th Kentucky remains unknown.

The courthouse and the courthouse square served as a temporary campsite for troops passing through town. Buckhorn Creek was nearby and horses were watered there.

Another reported location for a campsite was on a hill overlooking the town in the High Street area. Since there was no water nearby, it is unlikely a camp of any size was set up at that place. At any rate, local lore reports that troops drilled there and on land which is now the Meadowbrook Subdivision. If several regiments were camped at Camp Andy Johnson on Little Pitman in the Miller Park area, this seems plausible.[12]

Outfitting Union Recruits

From the very beginning, General Ward found it difficult to secure arms for all his newly enlisted men. He had only 545 muskets for his regiments and no horses for his pickets. Colonel Pennebaker's regiment, still without tents, was quartered in and about Campbellsville in private homes. The paper reported that Colonel Hobson's 13th Kentucky had adequate tents and their campsite just outside the town of Campbellsville "presented quite a military appearance." His troops seemed to be more adequately supplied with weapons.[13]

Drilling went on daily. A reporter was pleased with the response of the local citizens: "The Union ladies (God Bless Them!) are attentive to the wants of the soldiers—feeding the sentinels placed near their dwellings, and making all as comfortable as possible."[14] A loyal newspaper predicted that the "secesh" were in for "hot times" soon.[15]

Saving the Bank Deposits

Colonel Hobson, President of the Branch Bank of the State of Kentucky, became concerned about the safety of the deposits, about $140,000 in gold, silver, and currency in the Greensburg bank. He called on Rod Jeter's mounted Home Guards, to escort him at night to Lebanon to catch the train. Hobson then delivered the money to the cashier of the Bank of Kentucky in Louisville for safekeeping. Jeter mustered into Hobson's 13th Kentucky Infantry, September 21, 1861, as Captain of Company C, at Hobson's Greensburg camp.[16]

Campbellsville

For the first time in its history, Campbellsville was humming with commercial activity. Soldiers were wandering its streets, patronizing its few businesses and Redman's Tavern. Neighing horses were tethered in front of stores. Wagons pulled by mule teams cut ruts in its dirt streets. Expletives from the drivers of balking mules could be heard by the crowd of onlookers.

Gowdy and Asper were selling pots and pans. J.A. Tresenriter was busy making pot hooks, ladles, and repairing a cannon swab. Outside the blacksmith shops of William Cloyd and Blandford and Smith, the coals were hot and one could hear horseshoes being hammered into shape. William Davenport was repairing guns. R.D. Hackley mended saddles, bridles, and stirrups for the troops in his shop, smelling of leather. Space in store buildings was rented by the government as supply depots and, in the late fall, buildings were taken over for hospitals.

Teams of wagons brought supplies into the camps from Louisville via Lebanon. For a trip to Louisville and back, teamster J.D. Williams was paid $18.50. Thomas

Taylor County Historical Society

Main Street, Campbellsville, 1889. In 1889, the town of Campbellsville still looked much the way it did during the Civil War. Redman's Tavern is the frame building in the foreground in left of photo.

S. Purdy was paid $12 for four days of hauling with a four-horse team from Lebanon to Green River Bridge, making each trip cost $3. A two-horse team was less expensive, $2 a trip, paid to Newton Smith, Isaac Blakey, and D.J. Hotchkiss. A load of straw "for bedding troops" was provided by J.F. Richeson for $1.[17]

Receipts for supplies and services that were requisitioned by the 13th Kentucky and paid for by the Kentucky Military Board provide information about how well the regiment was being equipped:

> Copies of US Army and Infantry Tactics, coffee pots, coffee mills, 72 kettles, 572 plates, 570 cups, skillets & lids, 846 spoons, pepper box, knives and forks, ovens, buckets, butcher knives, salt sets, pot hooks, sifters, rope, barrels, frying pans, bread tray, 10 tons of straw, box stoves, 30 bushels of lime, 52 lbs. of nails, 161 pans, rice, corn meal, soap, bushels of potatoes, sugar, 321 lbs. pork, 586 lbs. beef, 2 kegs rifle powder, 6 bars lead, 44 Bell tents, 26 officer tents & flies, 1 hospital tent, 1 store tent, 1 Colonel's tent.
>
> 75 yds. of Domestic, tea chambers, bed ticks, cotton, brooms, linen, brandy, Osnaberg for hospital cots, 409 blankets, 130 pr. shoes, 135 cups, 135 infantry jackets, 135 pr. pants, 985 pr. drawers, woolen socks, "Army shoes," 135 overcoats, 135 knap sacks, 434 lbs. hay, 105 bbls. corn, 4,569 bundles oats, 400 bushels shelled oats, 380 bundles fodder.

Elijah Berry received 60 cents a day for work on other buildings; Patrick Ford and George W. Sullivan were paid 40 cents a day for working on public buildings, one a hospital. Black men were paid 31 cents a day; black women 12.5 cents a day for chores at Camp Hobson at Green River.

When the sick troops began dying, coffins and wooden planks to cover the vaults were provided for $5.50 each by one of the town's carpenters, H. Greenwood.[18]

Neighbor against Neighbor

Communities with families on opposing sides began to feel the effects of the war. Calloway Underwood and William Sprowles came to town from the Mt. Carmel area to visit relatives and neighbors in the Federal camp in Campbellsville. They imbibed too much on the way home and began to feel "frolicsome" deciding to call on their neighbors, Lewis and Sally Bell, who had sons in the Confederate army. They passed around the bottle, but a comment by the visitors offended Sally, who ordered them to leave. Apparently, departure was not speedy enough, for Sally "took a gun from the rack, and shot through the door at them." Underwood and Sprowles were fined $10 each for breach of the peace. Governor Bramlette ignored their appeals for clemency.[19]

Kentucky Prepares

When Brig. Gen. George Thomas replaced William "Bull" Nelson as commander at Camp Dick Robinson, Thomas's primary goal was an invasion of East Tennessee through the Cumberland Gap. As a first step, he chose the community of Lebanon as a supply depot for the armies of southern Kentucky and northeastern Tennessee. Lebanon was the last stop on a branch line of the L&N Railroad into south central Kentucky, and soon "cars" loaded with uniforms, tents, ammunition, and camp equipment were making regular runs, sometimes as many as eight trips a day, to the little town.[20]

In the fall of 1861, troops, such as the 9th Kentucky Infantry recruited from Monroe County and commanded by Col. Benjamin C. Grider of Bowling Green, marched through Campbellsville on the way to Lebanon to secure supplies. The regiment depended on patriotic citizens along the way to feed them. After an unhappy experience with the food in Cane Valley, they were elated with the reception in Campbellsville. Evidently, Campbellsville was not a "secesh" town. Cpl. Marcus Woodcock described the scene:

> Late in the evening we approached Campbellsville, and were apprised of the fact by being met by an immense throng of citizens for so small a place who welcomed us to their really loyal town by lusty cheers . . . and

> hearty shaking of the hands. . . . We were met by a band of music and escorted by the citizens through the most prosperous part of the city to the Public Square and then there was a feast indeed prepared for us. We had "Corn-pone," common biscuit, baker's bread, a variety of vegetables, meats of all kinds, coffee and tea and in fact the supper was not wanting in anything.[21]

The troops were quartered in the Taylor County Courthouse. After a speech by Joseph H. Chandler, the men slept, without blankets, on the brick floors of the building. The next day a detail was sent to Lebanon to secure supplies. Haversacks, canteens, rifles, and accouterments were issued to the guards of the wagon train. Two squads, one in advance and one in the rear, were ordered to guard the train of nineteen wagons. Departing Lebanon at three in the afternoon, they arrived at Campbellsville some hours after dark.[22]

Disease Strikes the Camps

Ominously, Pvt. Marcus Woodcock entered a note in his diary: "first case of measles in our camp, October 8." Throughout the following four months, many of these young men would engage in the greatest battle of their military life: disease in the camps. It would send as many as one third of some regiments to early graves. Measles, smallpox, and typhoid fever seem to be most often listed as the cause of death in late 1861, but pneumonia, dysentery, and meningitis were also rampant in some units during the war.[23]

Schools, boarding houses, and public buildings of any kind were commandeered to become hospitals for the sick. Seldom in American history had so many men been in such close proximity and so vulnerable to the spread of disease. Except for smallpox, vaccination against childhood diseases was unknown, and few in the hinterlands of Kentucky had access to this vaccine.

When disease broke out in Taylor County's Camp Andy Johnson, Camp Ward, and Camp Hobson, the commanders first sought help from the local citizens. On November 10, 1861, James Mason, a blacksmith in Campbellsville, was paid $16.66 for feeding and lodging five sick soldiers from the 27th Kentucky Infantry for ten days. James Allen Sublett cared for soldiers in his home near Camp Hobson on Green River. Soon illness became so widespread throughout the camps that the commanders turned to local churches for help.[24]

Surprisingly, Campbellsville had few churches in 1861. The Bethel Presbyterian and the Catholic churches were still located out in the county. Only the Methodists had an early church in the town. Even though the Baptists had had a congregation in the county since 1791, they did not move from their

Saloma Road site into town until 1852, when the trustees purchased a lot bordering the town square on North Columbia and built a frame church.[25]

This Baptist "town church" was one of the sites chosen by General Ward to use as a hospital for his Kentucky volunteers. On December 16, 1861, a group of citizens, not members of the church, was called upon to assess damages done to the building. Forty dollars was the sum agreed upon and General Ward signed the document. By December 28, 1861, the trustees of the church received the money.[26]

A large brick building in town which housed Pitman Lodge No. 124 was also rented for the sick troops. It was then located on East Main Street on Town Lot #73, across from the present-day Methodist Church. About 1852 the Methodists and the Masonic Lodge built a two-story brick building on this plot of ground. The Methodists met on the first floor and the Masons on the second floor. Although no photograph of the church remains, it is remembered for its low ceilings and two large front doors. When they built their new church on an adjacent lot, they sold the building to Robert Colvin, and he leased it to the U.S. Government for a warehouse. From November 1 to December 31, 1861, and possibly longer, the Masonic Hall portion of the building was rented as a hospital. For two months rent, the Kentucky Military Board paid $25.00. This building, however, was not the "small pox hospital."[27]

The "small pox hospital" was three miles from Camp Andy Johnson, somewhere out in the county. Thomas M. Johnson, a veteran of the Mexican War, was paid $180.40 for 55 days service to attend the ill men. "His services were necessary—he having had small pox and being well acquainted with its treatment. The attending physicians of the regiment had never waited on small pox cases." More explanation was added by Dr. William L. Turner and Dr. J. C. Green: "While Dudley's Regmt. [21st Ky] was encamped at Campbellsville a number of cases of Small Pox broke out in the Regiment and caused great uneasiness for fear it might spread extensively among the Troops. Upon consultation among the Physicians it was decided to remove them as fast as the cases occurred to a House 3 miles from Camp."[28] The exact location of this "house hospital" is unknown.

A "measles hospital" was located in the Red Fern area of the county in a large two-story house with a center hall, now the front lot on the north side of Hollybrook Subdivision. 27th Kentucky Capt. Tom T. Fisher and many others lay sick there.[29] The early Christian church located in what is today the Brookside Cemetery was reported to have been used as a hospital and so damaged that it could never again serve as a church. At least 52 deaths occurred among the soldiers in the camps and hospitals of Taylor County in the fall of 1861 and early 1862. A list of the deceased appears in Appendix C.[30]

Because Lebanon had thousands of soldiers occupying its town, it is not surprising that 1,700 men were in the hospitals in Lebanon in March 1862. Every available building, church, school, home was being utilized there. Mrs. Malvina Robinson and "the loyal ladies of Campbellsville" sent two boxes of articles for sick soldiers to Lebanon; therefore, it may be assumed that these same ladies were helping the soldiers here in Campbellsville hospitals. Malvina was the wife of Capt. John R. Robinson of the 27th Kentucky, but her brother, Dr. Ben Scott was a physician in the Rebel army.[31]

When the troops moved from Campbellsville to defend Green River Bridge, arrangements had to be made for ill soldiers to be cared for in private homes. The James Mayes house, adjacent to Bethel Presbyterian Church on the Columbia Road, was called "Camp Lizzie Mayes" after Mayes' daughter. It was opened alongside Henry Botts' house-hospital. In both of these, men with typhoid fever were placed. Pneumonia, which was often fatal, accompanied typhoid attacks, but antibiotics to fight infection were not known at the time.[32]

The arrangement of hospitals varied according to the housing available. If in a church, patients lay in the seats, aisles, pulpit area, and the balcony. Sometimes benches were moved, straw beds placed on the floor, and arranged in rows wide enough for two persons. Blankets were placed over the straw and tacked to the floor. Since high fever was associated with measles, typhoid, pneumonia, and smallpox cases, hospital stewards spent much of their time giving water to men who were delirious with fever.[33]

"Noble hearted women," such as the ones who brought medical supplies from Louisville to the ill men in Lebanon, helped by preparing soups and soft food for sick soldiers, boiling their laundry, and hand feeding weak men who were too dehydrated to hold a spoon.[34]

The Rebels are in Greensburg!

Needing more volunteers to fill his regiment, in October 1861, Col. E.H. Hobson came to Campbellsville to recruit. Confederate sympathizers made Hobson's officers' task more difficult by running off the property of anyone who joined the Federal army. On October 18 Hobson directed his wife, still in Greensburg, to send their slaves to Campbellsville for safe-keeping.[35]

That same month Confederates, commanded by Brig. Gen. William J. Hardee, were reported to have 4,000 men and 13 pieces of artillery at Munfordville. Looking for a fight, some of Hardee's men were guided to the vicinity of Greensburg by James Moss and A. Monroe Adair, two local CSA leaders. Adair had served as county attorney for Taylor County for two terms and was a brother to Union officer Edward H. Hobson's wife, Katie Adair. Rumors around Greensburg of an impending Rebel attack abounded.[36]

Steven L. Wright

James Moss

Carl Howell

Green County Courthouse Square, Greensburg

General Ward, Union commander in Greensburg, sent for help from Col. Benjamin Grider in Columbia. On October 19, 400 men of Grider's 9th Kentucky left nineteen lightly guarded wagons behind and followed their commander to Greensburg. He stationed his small force outside the town and rode with two officers into Greensburg to gain information about the strength of the enemy. Grider told the residents of Greensburg to prepare for the arrival of a force of 3,000 Federals who would set up camp outside the town. He then departed indicating that he was going out to meet them. The ruse worked for a brief time.[37]

Confederate Cavalry Major C.W. Phifer left Cave City on the morning of October 25 with 180 troops and was joined by 75 more men from Major Cox's cavalry. They moved in the direction of Greensburg. Their objective was to acquire the army supplies being stored there.[38] A party of ten was then sent out under Confederate Lieutenant Owens to scout Greensburg and report the strength of the Union forces.

Detecting Confederate forces approaching, General Ward withdrew to Campbellsville. He did not feel that his green recruits were drilled or outfitted adequately to take on the enemy. He marched his men, numbering about 1,200 from two regiments, the 13th and the 27th Kentucky, to Campbellsville arriving on Friday night, October 25.[39]

Fortunately for General Ward and the Federals, high waters from a flooding Green River saved Greensburg from a full fledged Southern attack. The Rebel forces were sighted on the far side of Green River at Greensburg on Saturday, October 26. Fewer than fifty Rebels swam the swollen river and invaded the town, and, according to a Louisville newspaper, they retreated in "great confusion on being told that General Ward would return that evening."[40] Confederate correspondence told a somewhat different story: the Rebels had succeeded in taking control of half of Greensburg and advised that, if a brigade moved on Campbellsville, it "would drive the enemy beyond Muldraugh's Hill" and secure the area for Southern forces.[41]

Ward's withdrawal from Greensburg to Campbellsville was the cause of some comment by Louisville editorial writers. Ward had acted prudently, but rumors in Louisville hinted that Ward had run at the sight of the enemy. An editorial expressed concern that Ward's troops had not been properly equipped by the Quartermaster's Department and that Camp Andy Johnson was being overrun by fleeing Union sympathizers seeking protection from the secesh troops.[42]

From Louisville, Brig. Gen. William T. Sherman cabled Ward in Campbellsville: "I trust to you to prevent the passage of any force between Muldraugh's Hill and Green River in that direction."[43] Still not completely equipped, Ward asked for wagons, teams, arms, and ammunition. Sherman ordered him to gather arms from the citizens and added that he would see that the debt was paid.

The Rebels remained interested in the size of Ward's command. One report stated that Ward had a force of 2,300 at Campbellsville. By November 3, the Confederate cables had increased the number to 7,000, and Federal forces were reported moving out to Columbia. Confederate Col. Pat Cleburne was probably more realistic when he reported on November 11 to Maj. General W.J. Hardee that there were 3,000 Federals in Campbellsville, between 2,500 and 3,000 at Columbia, and 3,000 at Lebanon.[44]

Both Union and Confederate sympathizers reported deprecations of property: houses broken into, crops laid waste, and families forced to flee for safety. A sizable number of Confederate troops remained in Green and Taylor counties throughout the last days of October. Home Guards, trying to follow orders from Hobson and Ward to report Confederate movements and to arrest suspicious people and spies, were particular targets of the Rebels. If the guards arrested anyone, they often had to endure a lawsuit from the culprit in the local court. The verdicts rendered by juries were unpredictable, depending on whether the jury was dominated by Confederate sympathizers or Union men.[45]

Congressman Aaron Harding became so fearful for the safety of his family that he sent some of them to Meadville, Pennsylvania. When he was in the area, he stayed in Green County with his daughter Mat and his Irish-born son-in-law, Rev. Henry McDonald, a noted Baptist minister. In a letter dated October 31, 1861, McDonald reported that secession pickets had visited his farm.[46] Harding particularly wanted to protect one of his prized possessions. He told his friend, Allen Rogers, "I fear they are coming this same day and burn me out and I'd hate much

Ray Perkins

Daniel M. Williams Home, Green County

to see that Steinway go up in smoke... My father paid $1,000 for that piano—it is solid rosewood."[47]

Four hundred Southern cavalrymen, reported to be Simon B. Buckner's men, came through Summersville and into the edge of Taylor County in October 1861 bivouacking on the farm of Unionist Lloyd Thurman and robbing him of a rifle and a pistol. The Rebels were "swearing they would burn his valuable residence, together with his outbuildings." He and his family, including his slaves, fled to Camp Andy Johnson for protection.[48] The paper reported that there were many other families seeking shelter at the camp, leaving their property to the ravages of the Rebels.

Runaway slaves also sought refuge at Camp Andy Johnson. Colonel Hobson, a slave owner himself, held them in the camp and notified their owners to retrieve them. He wrote, "I am not engaged in this War to deprive men of their Slaves, but to afford protection and Sustain the best Government on Earth."[49] It was not uncommon for senior Union officers in Kentucky to hold pro-slavery views.

On the other hand, Southern-leaning Kentuckians, particularly those involved in selling goods to the enemy, were often arrested and sometimes imprisoned by Federal authorities. Daniel Motley Williams lived in Green County, just two miles from Thurman's home in Taylor County. Both were large land owners, with adjoining farms. Thurman surely suspected that his neighbor was allowing the Rebels to use Williams' farm as a safe haven. Elizabeth Price's great-grandmother Marshall lived across from Williams. She grew so suspicious and anxious about the number of troops around Williams' house that she took the carpet up off the floor, took the boards up, and buried jewelry and valuables in the ground.[50]

A suit in Taylor Circuit Court reveals that indeed Daniel Williams was one of the citizens targeted by General Ward. Josiah Mitchell, brother-in-law to Union loyalist Rod Jeter, and neighbor of Williams, was accused of warning Williams of his impending arrest. Ward told Mitchell that if Williams did not stop making big knives in his blacksmith's shop for men going to the Southern army that he would be arrested.

Indeed, Williams, in company with other men, left with the Confederates. At the request of the family in late October, 1861, Confederate Major Phifer took away Williams' niece and daughter and six young slaves to safety. That same day, Ward's men came to Williams' home with a warrant to arrest him, his blacksmiths, and his tools. They were informed that Williams had fled. Ward's men proceeded to take his horses and mules, nine slaves, household furniture, some of his stock, and a wagon and buggy. The troops, according to Williams' wife, spoiled the crops and robbed the smokehouse.[51]

Again, in December 1861, Williams' residence was raided by a Union detachment of twenty-five men of the 10th Indiana, a company which was encamped on top of Muldraugh's Hill in Taylor County. Upon investigation, the Federals found out that Williams had allowed 140 Texas Rangers to camp on his property on the night of December 12, 1861, and that they had captured Captain Payne, one of General Ward's scouts. Consequently, the Yanks went to Williams' barn, took three horses, three mules, and two colts from the farm and delivered them to Captain Carroll, 10th Indiana company commander at Finley.[52]

From the *Official Records* we can ascertain that a number of other citizens were being arrested. In November 1861, General Sherman advised Ward: "When prisoners are received have the papers all handed to Judge Bullitt, a good Union man. . . . We cannot imprison and keep in custody all suspected persons. . . . The cases you mention are certainly such as the safety of the community would justify in having imprisoned, and I will caution Judge Bullitt on the point." There was some fear that the Northern jails could not hold all the Southern sympathizers, if all were detained.[53]

At the start of the war, troops were frequently enlisted and sent to a post without being fully equipped or trained. They often did guard duty and went on patrols. Some fought skirmishes with the enemy. Confederate General Hindman reported that Ward's troops were doing picket duty near Bowling Green in late October. But it was not until December that the troops enrolled by General Ward were officially mustered into the Union Army.[54]

Beginning December 1, 1861, General W.T. Ward was placed in command of troops at Camp Hobson, defending Green River Bridge. The camp was in a heavily wooded area on Green River halfway between Campbellsville and Columbia.[55]

On December 30, 31, 1861 and January 2, 1862, the troops of the 13th

Green River Stockade. Stockades of the period were constructed of squared timber posts, butting upright against each other, and set solidly in the ground. The walls were tall enough to prevent the enemy from scaling them.

Kentucky Infantry and some companies of the 21st Kentucky Infantry were mustered into service at Green River Bridge. One campsite was on the north side of the bridge, on the James Allen Sublett farm, between the Sublett home and the river.[56] Other camps south of the river occupied the hilltop overlooking the bridge. One of the regiments camped there was responsible for constructing the Federal stockade guarding the approaches to the bridge and for keeping the roads in good repair.[57]

The Green River Stockade, square in shape, provided protection for a company, 80–100 men, sheltering in tents located at the stockade's corners. Its gated entrance was only wide enough for men to pass through in single file. Two-foot high vertical slits, flaring outward, were cut in the stockade walls and gave the defenders excellent fields of fire.[58]

Confederate Challenge in Southeastern Kentucky

During the first week of December 1861, a Southern force under Brig. Gen. Felix K. Zollicoffer completed crossing the Cumberland River near Logan's Cross Roads, Kentucky, and set up camp on the north bank of the river opposite Mill Springs.[59]

The 1st Brigade of the 1st Division of the Department of the Ohio, commanded by Brig. General A. Schoepf, was ordered to Somerset to check Zollicoffer's

Brig. Gen. Jeremiah T. Boyle

Brig. Gen. George H. Thomas

Col. Mahlon Manson, later Brig. Gen.

Joe Brent

Col. Robert McCook, later Brig. Gen.

advance. That same month, the 11th Brigade under Brig. Gen. Jeremiah Boyle, a Kentuckian from Boyle County, was ordered from Lebanon to Columbia. Marching through Taylor County came the 1st Kentucky, 9th Kentucky, 2nd Ohio, and the 59th Ohio infantries. Their fifty creaking wagons of supplies lumbered over the roads, muddied by December rains.

Gen. George H. Thomas, at Lebanon since November, was ordered to Somerset to join Schoeph's 1st Brigade in checking Zollicoffer. On December 31, 1861, Thomas left Lebanon with the 2nd Brigade under Col. (Acting Brig. General) Mahlon D. Manson. On January 1, 1862, the Third Brigade, under Col. (Acting Brig. General) Robert L. McCook, followed the 2nd. The 2nd Brigade was made up of the 4th Kentucky, 10th Kentucky, 10th Indiana, and the 14th Ohio; the 3rd consisted of the 2nd Minnesota, the 9th Ohio, who were mostly all German speakers from the Cincinnati area, and the 35th Ohio, who were already in Somerset, and the 18th US, who remained in Lebanon. With McCook's Brigade was Battery C, 1st Ohio Light Artillery, and three companies of the 1st Regiment Michigan Engineers and Mechanics. Schoeph's Brigade had marched via Danville to Somerset, but the 2nd and 3rd Brigades traveled south from Lebanon on the Campbellsville-Columbia Turnpike.[60]

By January 1, 1862, Thomas's forces had begun to cross into Taylor County. Each of the regiments of the 2nd Brigade had at least thirteen wagons "loaded to their roofs." An observer standing at New Market in Marion County looking toward Muldraugh's Hill would have seen an unbroken line of wagons stretching for miles. Hour after hour the train crawled up Muldraugh's Hill. Eight mules were required to pull the wagons' heavy loads up the hill. The 14th Ohio adjutant recorded that 92 mules, 8 horses, 15 wagons, and 3 ambulances accompanied his regiment.[61]

The next day in Lebanon, the 3rd Brigade started on its way south "with bands playing and colors displayed.... Each soldier carried a musket and accoutrements, with four rounds of ball and cartridges, knapsack with all his personal property, overcoat, blanket, canteen and haversack with three days' rations in it, in all forty-five pounds."[62] Two regiments of the brigade were retained so that its passing would have taken somewhat less time than that of the 2nd Brigade.

On the eve of the New Year, the 2nd Brigade camped near Big Pitman Creek, eleven miles from Lebanon, possibly on the Clay Hill farm property. While some of the troops were in the Big Pitman Creek area, others, such as the 10th Indiana, were camped atop Muldraugh's Hill.[63]

On New Year's Day night, the 3rd Brigade camped 14 miles from Lebanon, probably at the confluence of Owl Creek and Middle Pitman on the Old Lebanon Road. In all, five thousand men and hundreds of wagons made their way down the pike.[64]

As the men marched, their feet developed blisters, and they began tossing away some of their equipment. The weary soldiers emptied their knapsacks of superfluous items: extra clothes and shoes, books, bottles, cards. Stragglers fell to the rear, rested along the roadside, and grumbling was common in the ranks. The band's music grew fainter as it drifted to the back. It was said about them, "'Here comes the band, first they play, then they play out.'"[65]

After Manson's Brigade's first night camp, they marched to the Tandy House and turned toward Saloma and then into Campbellsville on the Saloma Road. They passed through Campbellsville, "a village very dilapidated" and camped that second night one mile outside the town on the Columbia Road.[66]

Because there were reports of a large Rebel cavalry force near Greensburg, Manson's and McCook's brigades were ordered to remain in Campbellsville. After a fruitless march to Greensburg by several companies of the 10th Indiana on January 3, Manson's Brigade continued on to Columbia.[67]

During that first week of January, wet winter weather became a significant factor in Thomas's march from Campbellsville to Mill Springs. Pvt. James H. Price, Company C, 10th Indiana, wrote in his diary: "We went to Campbellsville and we lay there two days and then we went to Greensburg rained all day and we lay there over night and marched back to Campbellsville rained all day and then we started for Columbia and it rained on us all the way there and we stayed over night and crossed the river next morning and marched on our way to Mill Spring and it rained all the way there."[68] For ten days, it rained.

A drummer boy of the 2nd Minnesota Infantry, William Bircher, marched through Taylor County with a new blue uniform and "forty pounds on his back." Some companies of the regiment camped in Campbellsville for four days, beginning on January 2. While teams returned to Lebanon for more commissary stores,[69] Bircher recorded observations of his trip from Lebanon to Campbellsville in his diary.

He commended the "good turnpike road on which to travel on" and the natural resources, such as the abundance of rivers in the state and streams "that gush from every hill-side" in the county. But Bircher was critical of the social and economic level of development:

> The land was nobly covered with timber of a very good quality. We also passed many good mill-sites, which in some spots, particularly New England, would be very desirable property. Here they were wholly unimproved, partly from the want [lack] of means to erect mills, but mostly from a lack of energy on the part of the settlers.
>
> The land along the streams is very productive and yields large crops of corn and hay. . . . Cultivation is good for the production of fruit, while the climate is particularly adapted for fruit raising. Notwithstanding all these advantages, settlers along the road were reduced to great straits, sometimes to obtain a bare subsistence. Log houses were the rule, and framed were the exception. School-houses languished and ignorance flourished, and the mass of the people were but tools in the hands of the educated few. . . . There must have been some powerful agency at work to hold so large a tract of country in a state of nature, as it were, while other States, with poorer soil and a colder climate, had made such rapid advance in wealth and productiveness.[70]

While some thought the pike to Columbia was a good road, by the time the 10th Indiana used it, James Birney Shaw said it was "shoe-mouth deep in limestone mortar." At Columbia, the Minnesota regiment turned off onto a mud road, "which was well named, for the mud was unfathomable." Bircher had kind words for Columbia, labeling it a "smart little village" and stated that the 14th Ohio Infantry under Col. James B. Steedman was camped there.[71]

As the winter rain poured down on the troops, the dirt road from Columbia to Russell Springs that Bircher found so unfathomable, brought comment from another soldier. Thomas M. Small, a black-haired 20-year old private, a member of the 10th Indiana, camped atop Muldraugh Hill on the Taylor-Marion County line New Year's Eve, 1861, left camp at 9 o'clock on the morning of January 1, 1862. After five hours of marching over ten miles, the regiment arrived in Campbellsville and started setting up camp at two in the afternoon. Private Small refrained from making any comments about his stay in Campbellsville, but the condition of the roads south of Columbia caused considerable comment:

Saturday Jan 11th 1862: marched 8 miles over the worst Roads in the Union

Sunday Jan 12th 1862: Roads near 40 feet deep and through a god-forsaken country

Monday Jan 13th 1862: marched only 5 miles and camped in Russell Co. Ky[72]

While eight thousand troops were engaged in battle around Nancy, Kentucky, at the Battle of Fishing Creek or Mill Springs, John Hunt Morgan was planning vengeance for his earlier humiliation at Pleasant Hill Church in Taylor County.

Harper's Weekly, September 24, 1864

PLEASANT
HILL RAID
JANUARY 1862
OHIO
CINCINNATI
INDIANA
KENTUCKY
Ohio River
LOUISVILLE
FRANKFORT
Kentucky
River
Rolling Fork
Rolling Fork
LEBANON
Pleasant Hill Church
Saloma
SUMMERSVILLE
CAMPBELLSVILLE
Montgomery's
Ferry
Green
River
Barren
River
CAVE CITY
GLASGOW
BOWLING
GREEN
Cumberland
River
N

Map by Judy Ross

Part Three

Morgan's Pleasant Hill Raid
January 31, 1862

Morgan: "*What do you think of Morgan?*"
Civilian John Feather: "*I think burning is too good for him.*"

As the war progressed into Kentucky, the need for quick and accurate communications became apparent. A new invention, the telegraph, used for the first time in warfare, worked to fill that need.

Expansion of the Federal telegraph system into central and southern Kentucky was deemed essential. William Greenleaf Fuller, who would construct more miles of telegraph than anyone before the war was over, was placed in charge of building and operating the United States Military Telegraph south and southeast of Lebanon, Kentucky. Fuller sent to Ohio for a work crew. His foreman, William L. Tidd, broke twelve wild horses to use in constructing the system. Usually the wires were strung alongside rail routes, but when these were unavailable, the workers used main roads along which to string the wire. Soon telegraph poles were in place from Lebanon to Danville to Stanford into Somerset.

As soon as the battle of Mill Springs secured a Union victory on January 19, 1862, telegraph superintendent Fuller was ordered to extend the line south from Lebanon along another route—through Campbellsville, Columbia, Jamestown, to Somerset.

In less than two weeks, by the end of January, he and his crew ran the line from Lebanon over Muldraugh's Hill into Taylor County. They stored their supplies in Pleasant Hill Baptist Church, the same meeting house in which Morgan had been held prisoner just four months earlier.[1]

Telegrapher stringing wire, Taylor County

William G. Fuller

Morgan Strikes

On January 28, 1862, Morgan, with nine men, one of whom was his nephew, 3rd Lt. Samuel D. Morgan, and a guide, left Camp Ash near Bowling Green and crossed Barren and Green rivers that night. Almost all the men accompanying him were members of Company C, 2nd Kentucky Cavalry.[2] Traveling by night and sleeping in sympathizers' homes during the day, eventually they were within ten miles of Greensburg. Heavy rains fell. On Thursday night, January 30, the drenched men made it to the home of Daniel M. Williams, who had earlier evaded arrest by General Ward's men.

Williams' house served as an inn on the old Lexington-Nashville Road. It was located ten miles north of Greensburg, about twelve miles west of Campbellsville, and ten miles from the top of Big Muldraugh's Hill. Until General Ward took his slaves and confiscated his horses and furniture, it had been a fine establishment.[3] On the way, Morgan had tried to cross Big Pitman Creek, which was lined with steep, rocky banks. During the crossing, the creek was so high that Morgan was almost swept off his horse and drowned. The squad reached Williams' house for the night.

Morgan's destination was the Clay Hill plantation of Mrs. James Sanders in Taylor County. Morgan knew that she was a Southern sympathizer and that he would receive a friendly reception and gain valuable information from Widow Sanders, who was then in her sixties.

Big Pitman Creek

When they left on Friday morning, January 31, his men were wearing Yankee uniforms. Morgan met a slave owned by Lloyd Thurman, whom they asked to guide them across the dangerous ford at Pitman Creek.[4] On the other side, they stopped at Lloyd Thurman's house, and pretended to be U.S. government troops carrying dispatches from General Don Carlos Buell.

Thurman, the son of an Indian fighter in the American Revolution, was loyal to the Union.[5] When Morgan asked for a guide around Saloma, Thurman obliged and offered one of his slaves who knew the route.

Still impersonating Yankee troops, the Rebels stopped by the house of John T. Nelson, a private in Company F, 13th Kentucky Infantry. The brick home of the Nelsons was near Saloma, and Nelson was away. His wife and children locked themselves in the front part of the house, but left the kitchen open. Everything edible was taken from the pantry, including all the cornbread and even a pig-tail left from killing hogs. Had the Southerners not been in such a hurry, they might have found fine mounts in the woods and a coin-silver pitcher that John Nelson was awarded at the Kentucky Society of Agriculture Fair. In 1859, Nelson placed his tobacco on a flatboat at Gleanings and floated it to the contest in Louisville. There, he was judged to have the second best hogshead of tobacco in the state. He walked back from Louisville with the pitcher awarded him in his hand.[6]

The Rebels traveled the Sanders-Pleasant Hill Church Road until it meets the Lebanon-Columbia Turnpike, along which, Morgan wrote, all Federal troops and transportation passed.[7]

Pleasant Hill Church was located directly opposite the junction of the two roads. During the late 1840s the deacons had enlarged the church, replaced the board roof with a shingled one, put glass in the windows, ceiled the walls, and put a fence around the grounds. It had become a relatively substantial building for the backwoods of antebellum Kentucky.[8]

In Morgan's Official Report, he described what they saw when they arrived at the church:

> The building had a large quantity of stores and telegraph implements, and a large quantity of mess pork, beans, crackers, flour, soap, sugar, coffee, candles, and stores of various kinds; close around the building were three United States wagons filled with provisions.[9]

At this crucial moment, luck was on the side of the Confederates. It was 10 A.M. and Captain Fuller had already left the church to go to Lebanon, twelve miles away, to get money to pay his men. Before departing, Fuller sent a detachment of twenty-four men to continue stringing the telegraph line. A small camp squad was left in charge of the three wagons and nine horses. Fuller left his navy revolvers, new boots, fur cape, gloves, and a fine field glass in their care. He directed the squad to pack up the supplies and start out at 11 A.M. to the next campsite with the wagons, horses, and his personal belongings. They were to feed the crew stringing the telegraph line on the way.

The day before the workers had strung wire four miles ahead. Therefore, by 10 A.M., they were at Bear Tract Road, almost to Campbellsville's Courthouse with their work.

Just as the camp squad was preparing to leave Pleasant Hill, Morgan's cavalrymen "pounced" upon them. William C. Olney, A. Wells, Sylvester M. Bartlett, George McCadden and a hired slave were taken prisoner. The nine horses, four of them belonging to Dr. Michael Shuck of Lebanon, the wagons, and stores were Morgan's. The booty included all of Fuller's possessions, including $190 and his prized field glass, with which Morgan was delighted. The telegraph builders were left with only the clothes on their backs. The camp squad was forced to accompany Morgan all the way to Murfreesboro, Tennessee.[10]

For a few moments, Morgan visited with Widow Sanders at Clay Hill. He heard from her that there were many sick Union soldiers in Campbellsville, that there were two regiments at Greensburg, and a large force at Columbia, and that the bridge over Rolling Fork near New Market was well guarded by Federal forces. Captain Morgan took a guide with him from Sanders' and crossed the Muldraugh's Hill to within six miles of Lebanon to investigate the Union forces himself. Using the field glass he had just captured, Morgan stood on Finley

Gwynette Sullivan

James Edward Tandy Home, Taylor County

Ridge on the border of the Taylor-Marion line, a post from which he could have a vista over three miles to the Rolling Fork River and watched the force there.

Captain Morgan was accustomed to risk-taking and his gambling instincts were part of his psyche. His biographer, James Ramage, calls it a teasing, taunting vitality that would become his trademark. With enemy forces to his north, south, and west, Morgan returned to the log church and had a meal with his prisoners.[11]

At least a portion of the food for his men was prepared by an unhappy slave on the nearby James Edward Tandy farm, at the mail stage stand, located just 300 yards south of the church. In spite of Tandy's hospitality, Morgan abducted his son and a slave and stole three of his horses.[12]

According to storyteller R. Towler Parrott, soldiers burst into the kitchen cabin of the Tandy home. Richard Emmett, Tandy's 5-year old son, was curious and followed the soldiers into the kitchen. The men told the black woman to cook them something to eat.

The black lady had a small baby with rompers on who was lying in his cradle crying. She told them she had to tend the baby. One of the soldiers turned to Richard and said, "Rock that baby, boy." Richard refused. One of the soldiers whipped out a pistol. His willful nature broken, Richard then began rocking with enthusiasm while the woman prepared the meal, supposedly adding a little of her spit to the biscuits.[13]

After they had finished their meal at the church, Morgan prepared to set the church and the supplies he could not transport afire.

Capture of John Feather, Taylor County

Catherine Feather

John Feather

There is a traditional account of what happened next, which adds another dimension to the story.

Morgan and two Confederates, still disguised in Union overcoats, met 53-year-old John Feather, who came riding up Little Muldraugh's Hill on his fine black horse. Feather, a native Virginian, settled in the beautiful valley along Big Pitman Creek and began a milling operation. Soon that section of the creek became known as "Feather Creek."

At the time of the incident, Feather's son, John, was serving in the Union army. As Feather came up the hill, he met Captain Morgan. They exchanged pleasantries and then Morgan turned his horse and they rode back toward the church together. Morgan noticed that Feather's horse had a Union army halter on it.

Morgan asked Feather, "What do you think of Morgan?" Feather replied, "I think burning is too good for him." Morgan called to his men and ordered Feather to dismount. He was captured and so was another citizen, who was subsequently released.

"Burning is what we will do to you," said Morgan when Feather questioned why he was not being released.[14] Morgan continued his game of teasing and frightening "Lincoln men," which he played until the end of the war.

It was now 2 o'clock in the afternoon. The men with Morgan put John Feather in the church, loosely bound his hands, and set fire to the building, the wagons,

Gerald Myer

Morgan Burns Pleasant Hill Church, Taylor County

and the stores. Morgan reported that they "remained until all the wagons and house were consumed."[15]

Inside the church with the doors bolted, Feather managed to get his wrists free and began stacking the log pews under a window. Through the shutters, he could see the smoke unsettling the horses tied some distance away from the meeting house. When the Rebel on guard left his post to run to calm the horses, Feather saw his opportunity, leaped out the window, and hid in one of the empty barrels that had rolled off a wagon, which had been pulled close to the church so it would burn. When darkness fell, Feather escaped into the woods behind the building, where he stayed hidden for three days. And then he walked home.

The neighbors were convinced Feather was dead and circulated the report three miles down the road and up the creek to Polly, his wife, and to other members of the Feather family. During the fire, Feather's horse had broken loose from his tether and galloped home.

When Feather himself stepped out of the woods, his 12-year-old son, Rial, and his wife were splitting wood to cook breakfast. Startled at seeing him, his wife fainted. However, the story has a sad ending. Within three months of this incident, Feather and his wife lost their son in the Federal service to disease.[16]

The pro-Southern Sanders family may have had mixed feelings about the burning of the church. The father of James Sanders, Henry Sanders, Jr., gave the land for the meeting house twenty-five years previous and named the church, Pleasant Hill. Now it was gone, and would not be rebuilt until 1867.

The *Louisville Journal*, whose editor George Prentice had two sons in the Confederate army and whose wife was a Southern sympathizer, but whose editorials reflected his strong Union feelings, condemned the "infamous outrage" of the church burning.[17]

Morgan and his group again passed Tandy's and turned west on the Old Nashville Road.[18] There he took Sanders, Richeson, Schooling, and his old enemy, Lieutenant Short, prisoners. The latter is the same man, along with the Home Guards, who had held Morgan prisoner for three days in the church just four months earlier. Captain Morgan placed his captives on the wagon horses and they were forced to accompany his squad. His men soon acquired horses and saddles for the telegraph crew. The group stopped for a few minutes at the crossroads in Summersville and, while there, captured one of Hobson's 13th Kentucky infantrymen.

By 5 o'clock the Rebel force was at Green River, which was running out of its banks. At the river, Morgan released Sanders, Richardson, and Schooling in that they were "States rights" men, but it is unclear what happened to the unfortunate Lieutenant Short.

Still wearing Federal overcoats, they persuaded a Union man, David Montgomery, to ferry them over the flooded river. While transporting them, Montgomery discovered he had been deceived and ran the boat into trees leaning into the river. One of the horses was raked into the water and lost; the boat had to be caught and then reused to bring the rest of the men and horses across. Road weary and uneasy about riding with no moonlight, the group stayed at Barnett's near the river. The next day, they crossed the Barren River at Brewersburg, near present-day Pierce, and reached Glasgow, exhausted, the evening of February 2, 1862. By the time the group reached Glasgow, Morgan had fifty new horses. After this visit to Taylor County, Morgan's reputation as a horse thief began to have real credibility.[19]

The Captured Field Glass

The story of the field glass took on a life of its own. After Morgan and the group remained in Glasgow a few days, the telegraph party was escorted to Nashville where they were confined in a small room for seventeen days. Then they were taken to Murfreesboro and on February 27, 1862, released by order of Gen. Albert Sidney Johnston and escorted to Federal lines. On the trip up from Murfreesboro, they saw Morgan fifteen miles south of Nashville. Morgan had in his hand Fuller's fine field glass, which he said he "couldn't spare at the time, but would return after the war was over, if he was not killed."[20]

Superintendent Fuller never quite got over the loss of his field glass. Gen. Jeremiah T. Boyle, known for his short temper, was now in command of the post at Columbia. General Boyle was not concerned about the field glass, but really angry that Morgan had taken every telegraph key the crew had. He threatened to shoot him. Ingenious, Fuller sent Boyle's messages by using the wire ends as a key and his tongue as a sounder. As Fuller worked his nimble fingers, an enraged Boyle changed his mind about Fuller and said he was "too useful to be shot."[21]

Knowing how Fuller valued his field glass, Confederate George "Lightning" Ellsworth, the Canadian-born, witty, cagey telegraph expert of Morgan, pretended to be Fuller, playfully sent and received the following messages over the telegraph six months later:

George "Lightning" Ellsworth

From Barbourville, Ky.
To General John H. Morgan, Somerset:

General: I am informed that you have my field glass and pistols, captured in my camp on the pike between Lebanon and Campbellsville, Kentucky, January 31. Please take good care of them.

W.G. Fuller

— — —

From Somerset, Ky., July 22 [1862]
To W.G. Fuller,

Glad to hear that you are well. Yes; I have your field glass and pistols. They are good ones, and I am making good use of them. If we both live till the war is over, I will send them to you, sure.

John H. Morgan.[22]

Pursuit of Morgan

Two companies of the 1st Ohio Cavalry, who were stationed at New Market at Camp Spring Garden, were sent in pursuit of the Confederate party, but, as usual, were unable to overtake Morgan. They followed their trail as far as Vaughn's Ferry, south of the community of Gabe in Green County, and then gave up the chase.[23]

Notified that Morgan was in the vicinity, Capt. Rod Jeter, 13th Kentucky, was ordered by Gen. Boyle through Col. E. H. Hobson, to accompany a detachment of Lt. Col. John I. Scott's 5th Kentucky Cavalry in search of the Rebels. Jeter was chosen because he had lived in Green County and was familiar with the country.

As Jeter related the story, they were riding on a very dark and rainy night two miles north of Summersville on the Lexington-Nashville Road. Colonel Scott ordered Jeter to take a squad and go back to make sure Morgan had not gotten in behind them on their rear. Jeter argued for going back alone, without the squad, because he was afraid that Morgan's men would be alerted. Jeter and his horse traveled through brush and when the horse's hooves hit rock, Jeter thought he had reached the old road. But when he spurred his horse, it slipped down a hill, rolling over on his right leg and hip, seriously injuring him. After he regained consciousness, Jeter managed to get to the house of his brother-in-law, Josiah Mitchell.

After Jeter reported to Colonel Scott the events of the previous evening, Scott sent the regiment through a "nighway," and being a physician, Scott went home with Jeter the next night in order to treat him. Jeter never completely recovered from this accident.

Traveling into Tennessee with the 13th Kentucky in a wagon and an ambulance, Jeter was in such pain that he had to resign before the battle of Shiloh. He was appointed the provost marshal for Taylor, Green, and Adair counties. In an editorial mailed to the *Louisville Journal*, his military abilities were touted, and evidently, he was very respected by his men. When the Federal draft began in 1864, Jeter continued to serve as provost marshal for Taylor County. At the end of the war, he eventually was able to resume, in a limited way, his lumber and stave business and became a skilled builder.[24]

Clay Hill and the Southern Connection

Being large slave holders, it is not surprising that the descendants of Henry Sanders, Jr., owner of Sanders Tavern, were Southern sympathizers. One of the sons, James Sanders, the owner of Clay Hill across the road from Sanders Tavern,

Richard A. Sanders, II

Cary Ann Sanders

Ken Pierce

Clay Hill, Home of Widow Sanders, Taylor County

died before the war began, in 1858, leaving his widow, Mary Ann Griffin, daughter of Revolutionary Soldier Sherrod Griffin, to care for the plantation.[25]

Some of the Sanders men traded in mules, horses, and sometimes, slaves. Robert Page Sanders, one of the sons of James, believed in the cause of the South and he and Morgan are likely to have had business dealings together. At any rate, it was rumored that he was staying at Clay Hill. Early in the war, a squad of Union soldiers, possibly from the General Ward's camp or from any number of units camped around New Market Bridge, came to Clay Hill searching for Robert P. Sanders.

With much ado, a squad of soldiers came riding up to the house. They burst into the parlor of the widow Sanders' home and asked the daughter, Cary Ann, the whereabouts of her brother. Standing by and frightened, the black maid Aunt Cisely said, "Miss Cary, tell them; tell them anything."

This made the Yankee soldiers think that Cary knew where he was. The officer said to his men, "Well, men, 'A bird that can sing and won't sing, must be made to sing. Charge bayonets.'"

Continuing to threaten her, one of the soldiers backed Cary up against the wall on the left side of the fireplace in the parlor. Angered by her silence, he threw his bayonet and pinned her dress sleeve to the wall. A shaken Cary Ann still remained silent. Disgruntled, the unhappy soldiers departed.

For over 130 years the hole, not quite the size of a thimble, has remained in the plaster.[26]

Morgan at Shiloh

In February 1862, Forts Henry and Donelson in Tennessee surrendered to Northern General U.S. Grant. Confederate Gen. A.S. Johnston moved his forces from Bowling Green to a point south of Nashville. To keep from being outflanked, Morgan's men left Kentucky for Tennessee.

Southern forces were assembling around Corinth, Mississippi, to effect a surprise attack on Grant's forces at Pittsburgh Landing, called Shiloh by Southerners. April 4, 1862, while on his way south, Morgan received news that he had been promoted from captain to colonel. His squadron was attached to John C. Breckinridge's Reserve Corps, in Robert Trabue's 1st Kentucky Brigade.

At 1:00 P.M. on the first day of the battle, he led a cavalry charge in support of a Kentucky infantry attack on Union troops in the woods. Morgan's cavalry, accustomed to fighting dismounted, charged "at full gallop, with sabers drawn." Ramage observed: "The attack resembled a wild horse race more than a military movement. In the confusion all line was lost; it was a crowded mass that converged on the Federals. . . . Some of Morgan's men attempted to use the saber and failed ridiculously." This charge, in which four of his men were killed, and several, including Duke, were wounded, was Morgan's contribution to the battle of Shiloh. It convinced him that this was not the way to fight battles. This would be the last time Morgan acted in concert with other commanders. His talent lay in independent command.[27]

His men did not fight with sabers anymore. Kelion Peddicord, a Morgan trooper, wrote, "Any member . . . who attempted to carry [a saber] would be forever after a laughing stock for the entire command."[28]

Elsewhere at Shiloh, men from Taylor County marched into battle under the Union flag of the 13th Kentucky Infantry. Under Col. E.H. Hobson's leadership, they were engaged in the fight on the afternoon of the second day, leaving behind sixteen dead and several wounded. "Its unwavering ranks were repeatedly assaulted by the enemy, but without effect. In this struggle the regiment established a reputation for bravery which it gallantly sustained throughout the whole rebellion."[29] See Appendix D for a list of casualties.

Capt. Elijah Fisher Tucker, born at Arista in Taylor County, received a slight gunshot wound across the forehead, but the same bullet killed a soldier by his side.[30]

A soldier from Lebanon arrived at Pittsburgh Landing on the steamboat *Izetta* on the night of April 12, five days after the battle. His letter home described the aftermath:

> There are a great many men still lying on the field unburied, and as you pass along you can here and there see a leg or an arm lying severed from

Capt. Elijah F. Tucker

> the body. Guns are scattered in every direction. Trees two or three feet thick are torn to pieces, the cannon balls passing entirely through them. Our loss has been very great.[31]

At Shiloh, the death of Southern Commander Albert Sidney Johnston on the first day, and the subsequent Northern victory on the second day, bode ill for the Southern cause.

These Southern reverses set the stage for Morgan's kind of fighting. The long North-South supply line was the Louisville & Nashville Railroad. As the Northern lines stretched deeper into Southern territory, Morgan saw it as an opportunity for him to do what he did so effectively—go into enemy-held territory and cut the rail lines running into the South's heartland.

He went to General P.G.T. Beauregard, who had assumed command after the death of Johnston, with a plan for his cavalry to interrupt the Northern supply line and attack the communication system in Tennessee and Kentucky. Morgan received approval for his plan, several thousand dollars to purchase equipment, and another company for his command.

In a skirmish with a large party of soldiers working on the telegraph line, Morgan captured 268 and paraded them victoriously through the town of Pulaski, Tennessee. Morgan's men then made their way to Lebanon, Tennessee, where Morgan took over the town's hotel for the night. They were 30 miles from Federal-occupied Nashville and 170 miles from Confederate support.[32]

The Fight at Lebanon, Tennessee

On the cold, wet night of May 4–5, 1862, Morgan's pickets abandoned their positions when lured into a house to have a drink and warm themselves by the fire. Morgan's sleeping troops in Lebanon were surprised by an early morning attack. Brig. Gen. Ebenezer Dumont, later posted as commander of Lebanon, Kentucky, with his 9th Pennsylvania Cavalry, was the Federal commander in the attacking force.

It was Kentuckian against Kentuckian. Wolford and Morgan were friends from service in the Mexican War. Wolford, leading the advance for Dumont, was wounded and captured in the melee, but he refused Morgan's offer of parole and safe-keeping in a hotel. As the fighting progressed around the town square, Morgan lost 108 men, six killed and over 100 captured and had to make a quick getaway.

Morgan, with about twelve men, raced Black Bess thirty miles down to the Cumberland River, followed closely behind by Capt. Jesse Carter of Wolford's Cavalry. Morgan's men commandeered a river ferry and frantically rowed across. Morgan had to abandon his horse on the banks. There was no room for her on the ferry. Tom Quirk jumped into a canoe to return to get her, but the enemy started firing at him. He, too, had to give up going back for Bess.[33]

This means that on Morgan's later raids across Taylor County, he would be riding a horse named "Glencoe" instead of beautiful "Black Bess." And he would soon retaliate against the 9th Pennsylvania Cavalry, too.

Thomas Henry Hines

Kentucky Building, Western Kentucky University

John M. Porter

Morgan Sends Out Scouts

After he captured a train in Cave City, people and the press forgot about Morgan's debacle in Lebanon, Tennessee. He started making plans for more Kentucky raids. During the latter part of May 1862 Morgan sent three men of the 9th Kentucky across the state, journeying through Warren, Barren, Hart, Green, Taylor, Marion, Boyle, Jessamine, Fayette, and Clark counties, to scout Yankee troop positions. As part of this reconnaissance, the fearless spy-genius, 140-pound Thomas Henry Hines arrived in Columbia where he caught the stage for Lebanon. Eventually he linked up with John M. Porter and Andy Kuykendall. Dressed in civilian clothes, they passed themselves off as stock traders or agents purchasing supplies for the Federal Army. The information they gained would be most useful in the following months.[34]

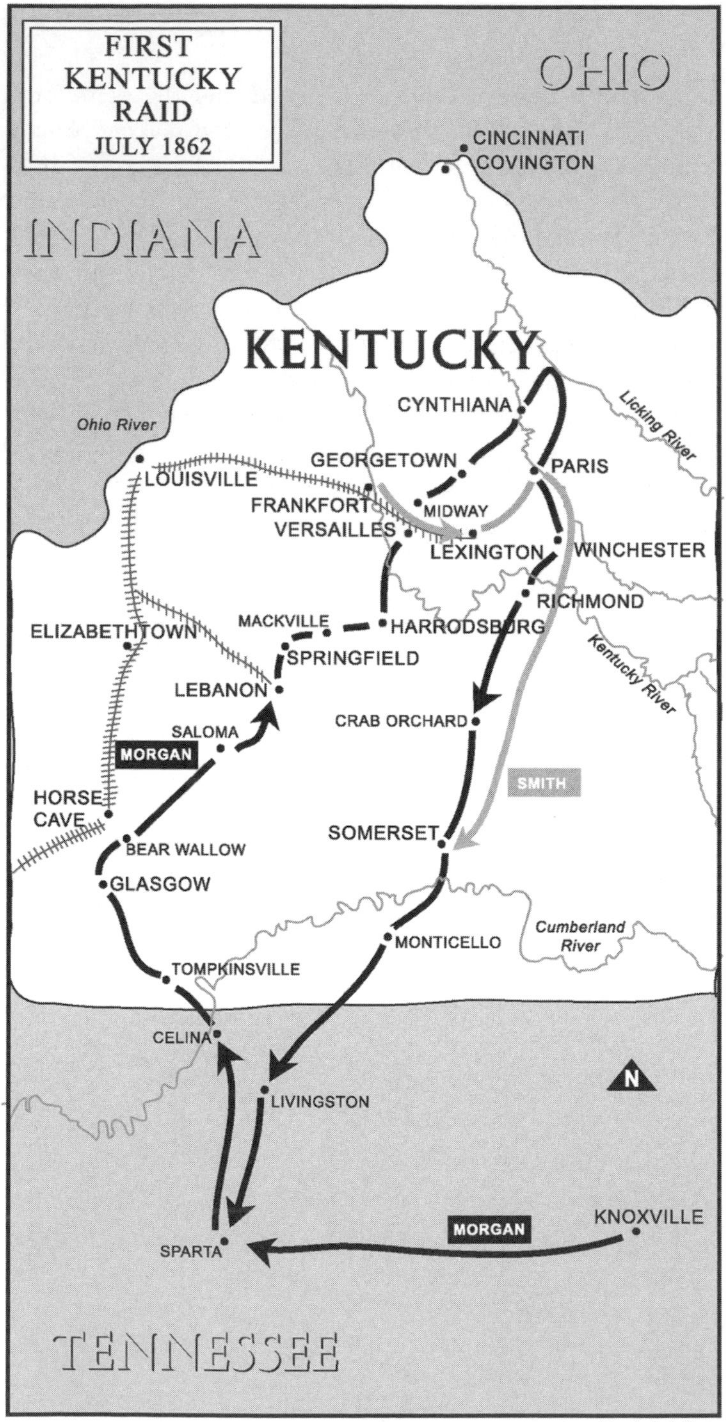
FIRST KENTUCKY RAID JULY 1862
OHIO
INDIANA
KENTUCKY
TENNESSEE
CINCINNATI
COVINGTON
Ohio River
Licking River
Kentucky River
Cumberland River
LOUISVILLE
CYNTHIANA
GEORGETOWN
PARIS
FRANKFORT
MIDWAY
VERSAILLES
LEXINGTON
WINCHESTER
RICHMOND
MACKVILLE
HARRODSBURG
ELIZABETHTOWN
SPRINGFIELD
LEBANON
CRAB ORCHARD
SALOMA
MORGAN
SMITH
HORSE CAVE
SOMERSET
BEAR WALLOW
GLASGOW
MONTICELLO
TOMPKINSVILLE
CELINA
LIVINGSTON
N
KNOXVILLE
MORGAN
SPARTA

Map by Judy Ross

Part Four

Morgan's First Kentucky Raid
July 1862

"You had auter be on the look out. The guerrillas are in the neighborhood of Pinchem [Saloma] and it is said they are after you and all officers they can find."
J.H. Thomas to Union Gen. Edward H. Hobson[1]

Leaving Knoxville, Tennessee, with 900 men in his force, Morgan crossed the Cumberland River and entered Kentucky south of Tompkinsville in July 1862. Revenging his earlier defeat at Lebanon, Tennessee, Morgan captured 30 members of the 9th Pennsylvania Cavalry, 20 Federal wagons and 90 mules and horses at Tompkinsville. Going north, his forces raided Glasgow and rode on toward Horse Cave.

Morgan was headed to Lebanon, a town lightly defended and brimming with Federal supplies. He took his cavalrymen up the road with which he was already familiar: the old Lexington-Nashville Road.[2] The road was used so often that Marion County citizens would soon learn to prepare for a Rebel attack, when the courthouse bell tolled and the cry went out, "The Rebels have taken Greensburg."[3]

As the cavalrymen crossed the Green-Taylor county line, Lloyd Thurman, unwilling to be duped as he was six months earlier, sent two of his slaves to Lebanon to warn its citizens. The Home Guard of Lebanon, under Lt. Col. A.Y. Johnston, and one company of the 28th Kentucky under Capt. George W. Barth, hastily worked to defend the town.[4]

When some of the raiders were riding up a parallel road, the old Summersville Road, they passed Archibald Webster's large frame house which sat on a high hill overlooking Pitman Creek.[5] Elizabeth, a daughter of Archibald, was married to John A. Marshall, and for a while during the war, the Marshalls lived with her widowed mother. Elizabeth's brother, Dick Archie Webster, was an officer in the Morgan's 6th Kentucky Cavalry. Elizabeth left the Webster home for a day or two to visit a neighbor.

Archibald Webster Home, Taylor County

The appointed time came for her to return home, and one of her sons started after her astride her favorite horse. On the way, he met some Southern soldiers, who were, as usual, looking for fine horses and forage. The argument that his uncle was one of Morgan's Men made no difference. According to a grandson, R. Towler Parrott, "They took the horse, and gave him an old horse, that was dead tired, skinned all over, half-starved. . . . They changed saddles. The soldiers didn't need a side saddle." Crying, the son went on after his mother. They brought the horse on home. "They greased up his skinned places. He turned out to be a better horse than the one the soldiers took!"[6]

A Stop at Saloma

On Thursday night of July 11, some of Morgan's troopers reached Saloma. The men crowded around the village well and walked across Main Street to the social center of the village, Durham Tavern.[7] The "tavern stand," which included a general store, was operated by James Samuel Durham.[8]

Although in his thirties, Durham joined the Union Army when the war first broke out. His great-grandfather, Samuel Durham, was a Revolutionary War veteran, his grandfather served in the War of 1812, and James Samuel and his son, John Samuel, followed in their family's footsteps in service to the Union. Since the evacuation of Corinth, Mississippi, military life had taken its toll on James Samuel and he was too ill to continue with the troops. He was sent to the Louisville Military Hospital. Eventually, he came home to Saloma on furlough.[9] Now the Rebel leader, John Morgan, was outside his place of business and his cousin, James Elijah Durham, was riding with Morgan.

It was not long before the men in grey found out that Durham had fought against them just months before at Shiloh. Outraged, a Rebel captain gave the order to burn Durham's Tavern. The troops started throwing hot coals on the

Durham Tavern, Saloma, Taylor County

George St. Leger Grenfell

beds of the inn. Hastily, Durham, a Master Mason, ran over to Morgan and gave the Masonic sign of distress. Colonel Morgan commanded the men to stop the destruction, moved the men away from the tavern, and paid for the damage.[10]

While the Rebel troops milled around the Main Street stores of Saloma, some Taylor Countians compared the casually dressed Southerners with smartly dressed Yanks they had observed. They could see two howitzers being drawn, by two horses each, with limbers full of ammunition. The "bull pups," as they were called, would see action in a few hours up the road at the covered bridge at New Market.[11]

And, if the citizens of Saloma were listening carefully, they may have heard the English accent of Morgan's Adjutant General George St. Leger Grenfell, a British soldier of fortune, who joined Morgan's troops and carefully trained the men in the finer points of cavalry warfare. This graying, six-foot Englishman with a chequered past had experienced warfare in India, Morocco, and Turkey. After witnessing Morgan's marriage later in the year, he left Morgan's command. Before the war was over, Grenfell was captured and sentenced to death for his alleged participation in a plot to free Confederates at Camp Douglas. His sentence was commuted by President Andrew Johnson and he spent twenty-six months in prison at Fort Jefferson off the coast of Florida in the Dry Tortugas. He was a cellmate of Dr. Samuel Mudd, who had the misfortune of setting the broken leg of John Wilkes Booth. In 1868, after courageous service in the yellow fever epidemic on the island, Grenfell met a tragic end. He and four others escaped from Fort Jefferson and set out in a boat and were lost at sea.[12]

Rolling Fork Bridge at New Market, Marion County

Morgan had men from some of the best Bluegrass families riding with him, many of whom were highly educated and others students of the law. But the good people of Saloma would have been frightened to know that the infamous Dick Davis, one of Morgan's men, was walking their streets. Davis, a Kentuckian from Maysville, would later earn the reputation of a brutal and lawless renegade. Evading capture on Morgan's Great Raid of 1863, he and his gang road south to West Tennessee where he terrorized and murdered citizens known to be Union sympathizers before he was hunted down and hanged in December 1864.[13]

Rolling Fork Fight at New Market

In the evening of July 11, Morgan's forces left Saloma. The slaves of Thurman's had reached Lebanon in time to warn the town about the Confederate approach. A few men of the Home Guard rode out to New Market to fight a delaying action.

About midnight, Morgan's men approached the covered bridge over the Rolling Fork at New Market. Morgan, "who was riding with his staff in front with the advance guard, was fired upon as he entered the bridge." One of the few Yankee bullets that were shot whizzed through his hat![14]

One of the cannoneers went to work by moonlight and fired at the Northern squad across the bridge. One shot fell too low and went into the bridge's wood-

Ben Spalding Home, Lebanon

en support beams. The Rebel gun's aim was adjusted and soon, after more Rebel cannon fire illuminated the night, the overpowered Yank defenders fell back to Lebanon, losing one of their men.

This little affair, however, was almost deadly for Morgan. His narrow brush with death changed the way Morgan and the command rode in the succeeding raids. Accustomed to riding up front, Morgan was placed in behind a protective shield of the advanced guard.

At New Market, Morgan's men set to work replanking the bridge so that all their force could cross the Rolling Fork and continue the march to Lebanon.[15]

Lebanon, July 12, 1862

After a brief skirmish with Morgan's men, the small Union force of the 28th Kentucky and Home Guards surrendered. By this time, most of the citizens of the town had fled. Morgan took possession of the railroad depot and his troops began enjoying the Union supplies stored in the town. "Guns were bent by hard licks over rocks; powder, cartridges, and caps were thrown into the creek."

In Morgan's Official Report, he recounts how he "burned two long buildings of commissary stores . . . a very large amount of clothing, boots . . . the hospital buildings . . . together with about 35 wagons and 53 new ambulances." According to the newspaper, the sick were turned out into the street. His men were rearmed with the U.S. weapons found there and took with them what they could load into one wagon and destroyed the rest. While in Lebanon, Morgan made his headquarters at Ben Spalding's house on Spalding Avenue, now called Myrtledean. It is said that his horse left his hoof prints on the stairs.[16]

The clever Ellsworth got on the telegraph wire, tricked the agent in Lebanon Junction, and confused any Union troops coming to help. Morgan's exploits appalled many but appealed to some. About fifty men from Marion County joined the Rebels during this raid, including Dr. W.W. Cleaver. It was estimated that Morgan left with at least 250 Marion County horses.[17]

After Lebanon

After striking Lebanon, the men rode to Springfield, Harrodsburg, and took 300 horses and mules between Lawrenceburg and Versailles. The troopers tore up railroad tracks in Midway and destroyed rail bridges around Georgetown. The Rebels fought their way into Cynthiana before turning southward. Morgan struck Winchester, Richmond, Crab Orchard, Somerset, and Monticello, before returning to his headquarters in Sparta, Tennessee.

Morgan's men covered 1,000 miles between July 4 and July 26. The colonel left Tennessee with 857 men and returned with 1,200, captured 17 towns, hundreds of horses and destroyed thousands of dollars of Union supplies.[18]

The Federal telegraph wires and Northern newspapers were frantic with excitement in Louisville, Lexington, Covington, and Cincinnati. It was during this raid, on July 13, that Lincoln issued his often quoted telegraph message to General Henry Halleck: "They are having a stampede in Kentucky. Please look to it."[19]

It may have been that Morgan's July Raid prompted Capt. Edmund Penn of Mannsville to form "I" company of the 6th Kentucky Cavalry to support the Union cause. The men were mostly from the eastern part of Taylor County. Capt. George W. Craven of Raywick recruited "H" company whose men were from northwestern Taylor County and the edge of Marion and Larue counties. The men were enrolled and sworn in for three years service by the end of September, 1862.[20]

Bragg and Kirby-Smith

Mindful of Morgan's success in Kentucky, General Braxton Bragg and General Edmund Kirby-Smith decided on a two-prong invasion of Kentucky to re-establish Confederate control in the state. Kirby-Smith was to bring his army from Knoxville and enter the state through the southeast while Bragg was to sweep around the eastern flank of the Federal army under Buell in Middle Tennessee and enter Kentucky through Scottsville and Tompkinsville. Their forces were to link up in Kentucky.

Will Henry Cowherd Home, Beech Woods, Taylor County

To help keep Buell's forces occupied in Nashville, Morgan led an audacious raid at Gallatin, Tennessee. Twin railroad tunnels between Gallatin and Nashville were destroyed. These tunnels were not reopened until December 1862, hindering Union efforts to supply their troops for 98 days.

Morgan's men came from the South and stopped near Columbia to camp for two days in late August 1862. Capt. John Porter, 9th Kentucky Cavalry, CSA, stated that the purpose of the Adair County encampment was to wait for the artillery to come up from Knoxville.[21]

Meanwhile, Thomas E. Bramlette, colonel of the 3rd Kentucky, was home in Columbia with Mary Adelia, his little three-year-old daughter who lay desperately ill. Young James Baker saw a squad of Morgan's cavalry approaching and ran across the field to warn the colonel of the proximity of the Rebels, but Bramlette chose to stay. Henceforth, the Confederates rode up to capture him at his house on the south side of Burkesville Street. Bramlette told them that he had been warned already and had chosen not to escape. The Southern officer decided to leave him alone. Mary Bramlette died September 28, 1862 and was buried in the Columbia City Cemetery.[22]

Bragg's army moved north up the Louisville Road to the east of the L&N Railroad through Munfordville and Hodgenville and continued along the Green River-Bardstown Road that ran through New Haven, now 31E. A story handed down in the Will Henry Cowherd family of Bengal, some twenty miles from Hodgenville, says that General Bragg and his staff stopped at the Cowherd farm on the Old Lexington-Nashville Road and that Cowherd's wife, Mary Marshall, served them cake and coffee. There can be no doubt that the

Cowherds were Confederate to the bone. They named a child born in 1863 Robert Lee and called him "Dixie" all his life. However, whether any of Bragg's staff came through Taylor County on their way to Perryville is doubtful, but possibly his cavalry scouted the area and some of those officers stopped there.[23]

In Kentucky, the months of August, September, and October 1862 were some of the driest months on record. From the front window of her house overlooking Hardin's Creek in Lebanon, Maria Knott watched the vast Union camps in the woods and fields in front of her home on Bradfordsville Road.[24] She was convinced that the great battle between the North and the South in Kentucky would occur in her hometown. A letter written on the night of September 1, 1862, to her son Proctor, later governor of Kentucky, and his wife Sallie, revealed her fears:

> My dear Children,
>
> I am sitting alone in my room after 10 o'clock, all the family having retired and the most of them sleeping as soundly as if there were no danger nigh—But as for me sleep is banished for the night at least—
>
> There are more than a thousand men encamped before our door, and in all probability before twenty four hours more shall have passed, many of them will be in eternity, or writhing in excruciating pain on the field of battle—
>
> 'Tis thought by many that the biggest fighting of the war will be done now pretty soon here in Ky—and no doubt Lebanon will be one of the battle grounds—If you live a little longer, you in all probability will hear of its being entirely demolished, the country around laid waste, and the citizens, if any are left alive, turned out to starve—
>
> The immense armies that are now in the state, and still coming in, are enough to use up the most of the provision and forage and if there should be any left, as a matter of course it will be wantonly destroyed, as has been in other states where the fighting has been done. God only knows what is to be our fate, and that pretty soon—From every indication we will hear, and see sights very soon—
>
> Now while I am writing I can hear the clatter of the hoofs of the Cavalry horses in all directions going to and from scouting, and occasionally the crack of a gun—Truly we are fallen on evil times—
>
> We have had very dry weather now for some weeks, water is very scarce

> and quite bad so if we should have a fight here now there would be great distress for want of water—
>
> O! God is there no way to avoid the coming contest—My heart almost ceases its throbbing at the thought of our perilous condition. Midnight

Federal forces evacuated Lebanon just six days later, on September 7, and the town was occupied by Col. John Scott, commanding the 1st Louisiana Cavalry, CSA, the next day. The announcement of Lincoln's Emancipation Proclamation proved helpful to Confederate recruiters in filling their ranks. Just as abruptly, on October 5, Confederate forces left.

Perryville, not Lebanon, proved to be where the largest Civil War battle in Kentucky occurred. The armies of Kirby-Smith and Bragg did not join as planned. The Northern army of Don Carlos Buell, with 58,000 on or near the battlefield, fought Braxton Bragg's 16,000 Confederates throughout the day of October 8, 1862. Even though the Rebels had fewer combatants, they won a tactical victory. Realizing that they were greatly outnumbered, however, Bragg pulled his force from the area and lost Kentucky, forever, for the South.

Taylor County escaped most of the immediate effects of the Confederate attempt to retake Kentucky. All the towns around Perryville were filled with casualties. In Lebanon, practically every church, public building, and warehouse—up to 20 buildings—were filled with wounded and dying men.

Withdrawal from Perryville

After Perryville, both Northern and Southern troops moved south. Bragg's army withdrew to the southeast toward Cumberland Gap. Buell ordered the First and Third Corps to concentrate at Bowling Green and then move to Nashville; other forces were ordered to pursue Bragg.

Taylor County would never see as many troops throughout the Civil War as they witnessed after the battle of Perryville. Buell's army used at least four routes to withdraw from Perryville and move south: 1) Bardstown-Green River Turnpike through New Haven, which did not pass through Taylor County;[25] 2) Lexington-Nashville Road; 3) Lebanon-Columbia Turnpike to points southeast; 4) Lebanon-Campbellsville Turnpike. From Campbellsville, they marched west to Greensburg and south to Glasgow.

Maj. Gen. Alexander McCook, Commander of the First Corps, and his Federals passed through Taylor County using the second route. The 16th United States Infantry camped at Saloma from October 24 to October 26, remaining there until their baggage wagons caught up. On the night of October 24, uncommonly low temperatures caused five inches of snow to fall and the men had to sleep on the ground without shelter. Capt. James Biddle observed that it was "fine country, but the weather generally too cold at night for comfort." Finally, on the 26th, the wagons arrived with their tents. Biddle was grateful for a tent and great-coat.[26]

The men of the 10th Indiana marched the same route as the 16th US Infantry. Starting from Crab Orchard, they made a "hot and dirty march" to Lebanon, and on to Rolling Fork at New Market where they camped. Suddenly, the temperature dropped dramatically. They, too, had no tents and they made shelters of cedar brush to keep out of the freak October snowstorm. On October 25, the soldiers received four months pay and celebrated. After the 10th Indiana completed their march from New Market through Saloma, Greensburg, Glasgow, to Bowling Green, the troops were given a new flag by their Governor, Oliver Morton.[27]

On the way, some of the Indiana men felt that General Buell was doing too little to catch Bragg. Thomas Small wrote in his diary: "No forward moving for us untill Bragg is Safely cared for." After days of marching in zigs and zags with little result, Small wrote in exasperation, "Some one tell us whare Bragg is pleas."[28]

Withdrawing from the Perryville area on their way south the men of the 2nd Minnesota returned to Taylor County. On this occasion they bypassed Campbellsville, but they made their way from Danville to Perryville and Lebanon, and then Saloma and Cave City. [29]

On October 29, Wolford's 1st Kentucky Cavalry was on the march through Saloma to Summersville. At a place along the road, the cavalry halted and a resident asked Wolford himself to be shown where the famous Wolford was. At the time Wolford was dismounted, wearing a dusty beard, and dressed as a private. Wolford looked around and found a smart looking captain mounted on his horse and pointed to him.[30]

The orders to the troops give one a sense of how far infantrymen were expected to march in a day. On October 30, 1862, the line of march of the 101st Indiana and the 123rd Illinois was from Lebanon to five miles past Saloma the first day, and through Summersville to Green River where they had to cross at Vaughn's or Montgomery's ferry the second day. They were expected to arrive at Woodsonville in Hart County on the third day. They were supplied five days' rations and had to purchase forage along the road. Accompanying each of these regiments were 12–18 wagons, each pulled by 4–8 horses. Being some of the last regiments to use this route, it was extremely difficult to find any forage for their horses, as the forage for the local horses to winter on had already been taken by earlier units.

Ken Pierce

Winlock-Barbee-Gaddie Home, Beech Woods, Taylor County

Some of the soldiers camped near the Winlock-Barbee House as they went south. The 1822 brick plantation home was located on the Lexington-Nashville Road and Andrew Jackson had watered his horses along Locust Lick Branch that flowed in front of the house in 1832. Later in the war, after John G. Gaddie bought the place, more Yankee soldiers were in the neighborhood. One day, as the family sat down to dinner and John was just starting to slice the ham, a big burley soldier burst into the room, reached over and picked up the ham and started to the door. Margaret Willet Gaddie was so angry that she said, "That was a Yankee trick! And he replied, "Yes, and it is a damn Yankee that played it."[31]

A third route away from Perryville used by Buell's army was the Lebanon-Columbia Turnpike. From Campbellsville, Union troops in Crittenden's Corps marched to Mt. Vernon and then down the Wilderness Road trying to catch Bragg.

Eben Sturges, 1st Ohio Lt. Artillery, in Crittenden's Corps, stopped at Campbellsville's Redman's Tavern at noon November 1, 1862, and "fared well." He found other parts of Crittenden's corps encamped along the road before he got to Columbia, where he reported to the Headquarters of Brig. Gen. William S. Smith. There he slept on the ground in front of the fire. Contrary to the soldier who thought Columbia was a smart little village, he rode around the square and made the assessment in his diary that Columbia contained about 800 people and was "like a great many Kentucky county seats, had a decayed appearance."

When the macadamized road stopped at Columbia, the roads further south were an abomination to many a Northern soldier. Sturges wrote: " Marched 8 miles through a poor country and over a rough road & encamped in a last year's cornfield. Went to bed at dark on a rough bed." The forebears of the Yankees who pour into Kentucky today to visit Lake Cumberland and Green River Lake decried Kentucky's roads in the 1860s.

A fourth route used by Buell's army moving south was through Campbellsville and Greensburg to Glasgow. Union divisions, the Third, [1st Army Corps] under Brig. Gen. L.H. Rousseau, the First [3rd Army Corps] under Brig. Gen. Albin Schoepf, moved along this road. While General George Thomas, second in command to Buell, was camped near Campbellsville on the night of October 30, 1862, he sent a message to Washington expressing his frustration about Buell being replaced by Rosecrans, an officer his junior.[32]

The 17th Ohio Infantry marched from outside Lebanon to New Market, crossed the Rolling Fork Bridge, and camped in the lowlands on its south side. They joined in target practice with troops stationed at New Market because of a rumor that Morgan was close by. Diarist John Inskeep reported that it was "an imaginary foe." On October 30 the regiment came through Campbellsville and camped near a creek three miles from Greensburg. Inskeep remarked upon arrival, that, because of his tight boots, he was "played out." His company finally got their tents after they crossed Green and Little Barren rivers.[33]

General Rosecrans continued supplying Tennessee with Union troops, with regiments pouring through Campbellsville through the middle of November 1862. Maj. Gen. H.G. Wright informed Rosecrans that three regiments of infantry, one regiment of cavalry, and four pieces of artillery were due to reach Campbellsville on November 14 and Columbia the following day.[34]

Confederate Recruits of Capt. W.S. Edwards of Greensburg Visit Taylor County

"I recognize the knife and boots and coat as that of my brother." Robert Scott

Even though the heartland of Kentucky had dozens of Federal regiments marching through it during October and November 1862, the Confederates were not deterred from making forays into the area, where antipathy to Lincoln's war policies and admiration for Morgan's ability to roam at will in Kentucky encouraged Confederate sympathizers.

Capt. William S. Edwards

Morgan CDV given to Miller Family

In September, eighteen Nelson County Rebels, supposedly on their way to join Morgan, attempted to capture U.S. Congressman Aaron Harding in Greensburg.[35]

William S. Edwards of Greensburg recruited a company of Confederates in late summer and fall of 1862 from Taylor and Green counties. They were sworn into service at Camp Reed, near Danville in September 1862 and became Company E, Grigsby's 6th Kentucky Cavalry, CSA. Edwards and some of his men were detached to return home to continue recruiting.[36]

It was around this time that a small group of Rebels came to the John Miller farm on the Trace Fork of Pitman Creek, near the Green-Taylor line. Miller agreed to help them and, while pretending to feed his hogs at dusk, left food for them on a rock near where they were hiding in a cave. At night, they slipped out and gathered the food. When they departed several days later, their leader presented John Miller with Morgan's calling card with his picture on it. This gesture so pleased Miller's family that the card has been passed from generation to generation and is now in the hands of a descendant, Frank Wilcoxson.[37]

About the same time, William S. Warren of the Union 26th Kentucky Infantry, came home to visit his father. During his stay, Edwards' Confederates burst into his house and shot William four times. He was severely wounded, but after a long period of convalescence, returned to service as a wagon master for General Ward. He survived the war but suffered from a severe limp for the rest of his life.[38]

Some thirty men of Captain Edwards' Company were involved in another dramatic incident when they were hunting down Union Home Guards. On October 6, 1862, they captured A.H. Scott of Green County, questioned him, and forced him to lead them to his brother Marshall's house. The Rebels, convinced that Marshall was a member of the Home Guard, rode off with him, leaving A.H. behind.

Later that night a small party of Rebels arrived at Samuel Durham's Tavern in Saloma with two prisoners, Marshall Scott and a mulatto man, had an evening meal, and spent the night.

The next day Rebels—Frank Smith, Andy Gumm, and Wilson Bailey—left, taking Scott mounted on a bay pony, saying they were escorting him to Captain Wade in Lebanon. On route, in the evening, they stopped at the farm of Jeremiah and Emily Sanders, cursed their children for wearing Lincoln caps, and departed. Some time later, Mrs. Sanders heard shots and screams in the distance. That night the Rebels returned to Durham's without Marshall Scott, and leading the bay pony.

Marshall Scott's body, in torn clothing, was found by Jeremiah Sanders, William and Nathan Farmer, not far from Sanders' house. His skull had been shattered by a musket ball and his arm was badly broken. The body was buried in a shallow grave.

At the Coroner's Inquest convened in Taylor County on November 5, 1862, before Judge Albert N. Green and Justice of the Peace B.C. Hord, to investigate the manner of Marshall Scott's death "upon the view of the body... then and there lying dead." Drs. Alexander Shively and Samuel Bass testified that Scott had been a victim of violence. James and Robert Scott identified their brother's body. A man named Angel said that he had been captured by this group also and had heard them say they meant to kill every member of the Home Guard they could catch.

The twelve citizens of the county who were asked to act as jurors concerning the manner in which Marshall Scott met his death decided that Smith, Bailey, and Gumm using "guns or pistols . . . did inflict . . . wounds of which he then and there died."[39]

On October 8, 1862, the *Louisville Journal* reported that Rebel recruiting was being led by Richard A. Webster, "a meek Christian of the Methodist persuasion, and a convert to secession under the Rev. Thomas Bosley," and that he had gathered a company from the Beech Woods community, known as Bengal today. In addition, a Southern camp was claimed to be forming at the site of the burned Pleasant Hill Church. It further stated that the Confederates had captured Union-leaning citizen Martin Cure in Campbellsville and had tied his limbs to four stakes set in the ground and had left him there overnight. A few days later, Cure joined the 20th Kentucky Infantry. The local loyal citizens were much alarmed, were losing their horses, and some had taken to the woods to avoid the Rebel conscription act. The people of the area were asking for protection from these Rebel bands.[40]

The government answered their plea for help. In November, a company of the 10th Indiana set up Camp Carroll on Muldraugh's Hill in the Finley area. The camp was commanded by Capt. William B. Carroll of Company E. It remained in operation in November and December, 1861, and then the regiment moved south.[41]

Map by Judy Ross

Part Five

Morgan's Christmas Raid 1862–1863

"There was not a good horse left in town."
Louisville Daily Democrat, January 13, 1863

University of Kentucky Archives

John and Martha Ready Morgan

On **Sunday, December 14, 1862,** the much-sought-after widower John Hunt Morgan married Martha Ready in a candlelight evening wedding in Murfreesboro, Tennessee. Martha, just 21, wore a lace dress with a veil, and Morgan, his dress uniform. Performing the ceremony was Episcopal Bishop Gen. Leonidas Polk. Attending were generals of the Army of the Tennessee—Braxton Bragg, William Breckinridge, William J. Hardee, and Benjamin F. Cheatham. In the streets outside the Ready mansion, bonfires were lit, bands were playing, and men were cheering. Morgan's cavalrymen were celebrating the wedding and their brilliant victory over the Yankees at Hartsville, Tennessee, for which Morgan was promoted to Brigadier General.[1]

A week later, Morgan launched his Christmas Raid from Alexandria, Tennessee, into Kentucky. Bragg ordered Morgan to destroy the L&N train trestles in the Muldraugh Hills four miles north of Elizabethtown in order to stop supplies from reaching Rosecrans' Federal army in Tennessee. By this time, the Federals had built and garrisoned stockades to protect the railway line. The task of destroying the North's rail link to the South was not to be carried out as easily as in earlier raids.

On Sunday, December 21, 1862, Morgan assembled his forces for the task. "As company after company moved forward into line with sabers jingling, horses prancing, firearms glistening, bugles blowing, and flags waving, with our artillery on the right flank . . . it formed a grand and imposing scene," wrote Maj. J.B. McCreary in his journal. They set off with three days' rations and each cavalryman carrying two horseshoes, a dozen nails, ammunition, one blanket, and an oil-cloth or overcoat.[2]

Morgan's newly organized company of scouts was in the advance, 400 yards in front of the 2nd Kentucky Cavalry. It was led by Irishman Tom Quirk, owner of a candy store in Lexington before the war. The regiments of horsemen, in columns of four, were strung out along the road for seven miles. The men sang "Cheer, Boys, Cheer" as they trotted along. John and Tom Morgan, and many of the cavalrymen had fine voices; some, including Basil Duke, wrote martial lyrics for familiar tunes.

Morgan organized his command of seven regiments with a total of 3,900 men into two brigades, each supported by its own artillery, for the Christmas Raid.

Morgan's Organization for the Christmas Raid

1st Brigade:	**Col. Basil Duke, commanding**
2nd Ky. Cav.	under Lt. Col. John B. Hutchinson
7th Ky. Cav. (3rd)	under Lt. Col. John M. Huffman*
8th Ky. Cav.	under Col. Roy S. Cluke

Capt. Baylor Palmer's 4 piece battery:
2 12-pounder howitzers
2 6-pounder guns

Total: 2,100 men, including Palmer's battery

2nd Brigade	**Col. W.C.P. Breckinridge, commanding**
9th Ky. Cav.	under Lt. Col. Robert G. Stoner
10th Ky. Cav.	under Col. Adam Rankin Johnson
11th Ky. Cav.	under Col. David Waller Chenault
9th Tenn. Cav.	under Col. James Dearing Bennett**

Capt. B. T. White
1 3-in. Parrott
Lt. Christopher C. Corbett
2 mountain howitzers

Total: 1,800 men, including White's and Corbett's batteries[3]

* This regiment is called by three names: 3rd, 7th, and Gano's, after Col. Richard Gano, who recruited the men, even though he was transferred to the Trans Mississippi Department and was not present.

** Bennett became ill with typhoid, died, and was replaced by W. W. Ward at Elizabethtown in December 1862.

Col. Basil Duke, later Brig. General

Col. W.C.P Breckinridge

Tim Heath

Maj. Robert G. Stoner

Tim Heath

Col. James D. Bennett

Col. Richard A. Gano, 7th (called 3rd) Ky. Cav.

Tompkinsville to Elizabethtown

Tompkinsville in Monroe County was the first town in Kentucky raided by Morgan's men. They spent Christmas Eve below Glasgow in Barren County after driving out the 2nd Michigan Cavalry which was occupying Glasgow.

On Christmas Day, the raiders moved on toward the L&N railway line through Bear Wallow. In a skirmish there, Captain Quirk, wounded by two minie balls, bandaged his head and continued on along the old Lexington Road to Cave City and Munfordville.[4]

Green River Railroad Bridge, Munfordville, Hart County

Gen. E.H. Hobson, now at Munfordville, knew that his main duty was to protect the railroad bridge over Green River. The 13th Kentucky, one company recruited in Campbellsville, the 25th Michigan commanded by Col. Orlando H. Moore, and other regiments stood guard through the night, anticipating Morgan's attack. The 27th Kentucky, with Capt. John R. Robinson's Company E, recruited in Taylor County, guarded roads and fortifications south of Green River. These deployments were in vain because this bridge was not Morgan's strategic objective on this raid. It was the L&N trestles north of Elizabethtown.[5]

Raid on Sutler's Wagon, Hart County

Near Munfordville the Confederate raiders overtook a sutler's wagon with Christmas supplies for the Union Army and stripped it of its contents, including a box of women's shoes. Taking advantage of this lucky find, they knocked on the doors of nearby farms and presented shoes to the ladies who answered. The men long remembered the Christmas pies they received in return.[6]

A few miles north of Munfordville, near where Bonnieville is now located, the raiders destroyed, for the third time, the L&N trestle at Bacon Creek and its stockade, defended by the 91st Illinois. Its garrison of ninety-three men surrendered after a five-hour artillery bombardment. As Morgan's troops moved north along the rail line, they burned the ties, tore up the rails, and twisted them into bows. This practice, which the *Louisville Journal* called, "a most wretched business," became Morgan's signature action.

Bacon Creek Trestle, Hart County

Morgan's next objective was the stockade at Nolin, between Sonora and Glendale. Once the Union officer in charge saw the strength of the Confederate artillery, he surrendered without a fight. Rebel telegrapher Ellsworth was sowing confusion among the Federals by sending messages which wildly exaggerated the size of Confederate forces.[7]

When Union troops in Elizabethtown stubbornly refused to surrender, a Rebel artillery barrage of over one hundred shells from the town's cemetery hill changed their minds. The battle won, Morgan's men entered Elizabethtown singing "Southern Yankee Doodle."

Twisted Rails of the L&N

That evening, Quirk's Scouts camped in the Main Square, forced open stores, and gathered up pants, boots, hats, handkerchiefs, and combs. An immigrant merchant stood outside his store and glared at the Federal prisoners under guard nearby. Shaking his fists, he shouted, "You tam Yanks, vat you leta de rebbles in for and takes all mine goods; I wish dey shoots you, tam you." Meanwhile, Rebel cavalrymen came upon stores of munitions, seized 600 rifles, and filled their cartridge boxes with Yankee ammunition.[8]

Burning the Muldraugh's Hill Trestles

The 500-foot long, 80-foot high trestles at Muldraugh's Hill, protected by the 71st Indiana, were Morgan's next target. At each trestle, Morgan's artillery shelled the Yankees until they surrendered. Colonel Duke's 1st Brigade set fire to the upper trestle, and Colonel Breckinridge's 2nd Brigade destroyed the lower.[9] Sitting on the slope beside the upper trestle's burning timbers, one of Quirk's Scouts from Lexington, Pvt. Curtis Burke, took notes by the fire's light:

> We all went to work, some carrying wood, and others building fires along under the trestle supports and posts. We soon had fires around every upright. While they were burning, some of the boys fired the stockade. Then we sat down and rested. It was then after dusk. Waiting awhile and seeing that the trestle was not burned enough to fall, we were ordered to go to carrying rails. We tore down the shanties in camp

> to build up the fires. We soon had the fires burning brightly again at the trestle. We again waited a little while, then our company took one end of the trestle and the other two companies the other, with axes and set to work knocking the half burned braces down. They all worked hard, but our boys' end fell first. It fell panel after panel like a dead fall. It was the grandest sight I ever witnessed. . . . The ground around was strewn with huge rough rocks to build abutments under the trestle. On one of these rocks stood John H. Morgan, hat in hand, fairly shouting with the excitement. He remarked to us that we would not be apt to see such a sight soon again. . . .
>
> I went into the burning stockade. I saw about a wagon load of cartridges piled up in the middle of the floor. Roof all on fire above, so I got out of there in double quick. The stockade was nearly square. The sides were made of heavy upright logs. The roof was flat, two layers of heavy logs. A ditch around the whole. We then burned the tents and a wagon filled with arms. . . .[10]

The *Louisville Journal*, reporting on the incident, fumed:

> The grand trestle-work at the Muldrow's Hill was destroyed without the firing of a gun. [not true] Where in the name of gunpowder and bayonets were the troops that should have defended it?[11]

Muldraugh's Hill Trestles, north of Elizabethtown

Now, the "Scouts Song," written by Curtis Burke and often sung by the men as they marched, took on new meaning:

In John H. Morgan's Army
There's a company of Rebs
Formed out of the old Squadron
Of which so much was said.

Chorus:
So its boys pass the liquor long
Up and down the line
For we're the boys that likes the noise
Or burning trussels down.

Now the name of this company
Is well known as Morgan's Scouts
And the Yankee pickets hate us
For we make them all clear out.

The Morgan Scouts were organized
In Eighteen Sixty-two
And they will never disunite
Until the war is through.

Tom Quirk is our Captain
And a gay one he does make
But when he get scared
You may look to see him shake.

George Owen is First Lieutenant
And Frank Brady's Third
We obey all commands
And never say a word.

And for our Orderly Sergeant
We have kind Peddicord
The men all seem to like him
Yes, all with one accord.

And when we take up line of march
We're always in the lead
We always get the best to eat
And the best of all to feed.

We number eighty rank and file
No merrier can be found
But we're always very careful
And not to run aground.[12]

Rolling Fork to Bardstown

The raiders then turned southeast toward Bardstown. In typical Morgan fashion, three detached forces were sent out to destroy other bridges and then rejoin the main force in Bardstown. Chenault's Regiment was ordered to destroy the stockade and trestle at Boston. Major McCreary commented, "I stopped at Boston to parole prisoners and destroy a bridge and was near being captured." McCreary would be called upon to destroy the Green River Bridge in Taylor County just three days later.

Morgan commandeered the Hamilton house, about 600 yards from the Rolling Fork, to hear court-martial charges against Texan Lt. Col. John M. Huffman that he had granted paroles that were too liberal to Federal prisoners at the Bacon Creek stockade. At the time, Huffman was recovering from a shattered left shoulder suffered in the Battle at Hartsville. After a short trial, Huffman was acquitted and he will command the 7th Regiment at the Battle of Tebbs Bend in Taylor County six months later. Morgan's officers, relieved that the proceedings were finally over, were startled to discover that the Yanks were upon them.[13]

Joe Brent

Hamilton House, Rolling Fork River near Boston

The Yankee Challenge

Col. John Marshall Harlan, later a U.S. Supreme Court justice, commanding several infantry regiments, some cavalry and a section of artillery, caught up with the Southerners at the mouth of Beech Fork on the Rolling Fork River near Boston, just off Highway 62. On the left flank of Harlan's force, the 13th Kentucky, commanded by General Hobson's young nephew, William E. Hobson, arrived from Munfordville, and once again, faced Morgan.[14]

Col. John M. Harlan

Steven L. Wright

Col. William E. Hobson

Porter Harned

Capt. Tom Quirk

Some Southern troops had already crossed the Rolling Fork into Nelson County before Harlan arrived. Col. Roy Cluke's detached regiment, with two pieces of artillery which had been sent on an operation to destroy another bridge over the river, was ordered to return. The Confederate force on the west side of the river under Duke came under Harlan's artillery fire. Colonel Duke and Captain Quirk stayed in the rear to insure that all the Southern troops got safely across the Rolling Fork River. In the meantime, Cluke's detachment was able to get across the river at a newly discovered ford. Most of the Southern raiders had, once again, escaped unscathed.

At the end, as Union cannon shells were flying over the heads of the men, the Federal gunners adjusted their sights and a shell fragment hit Colonel Duke, knocking him to the ground. Captain Quirk lifted his commander's limp body onto his horse in front of him. Holding Duke steady in the saddle, Quirk urged his horse across the ford, cannon shells splashing all around them, and rode three miles for help. He commandeered a carriage, padded it with blankets, and conducted the colonel to Bardstown where he found a friendly doctor.

Word spread that Duke had been killed. Burke said: "We felt that if it was true, we had sustained a loss too great to count." Colonel Breckinridge, with tears streaming down his cheeks, rode over the field, urging the last four companies of the 9th Kentucky Cavalry to hold their positions until Duke had been carried to safety.[15]

Dixie Hibbs

Dr. Gus Cox Home, Bardstown

Upon arrival at Bardstown on December 29, Duke was taken to an upstairs bedroom of Dr. Gus Cox's home. Rev. J. V. Cunningham bent over to examine him and saw that the skin was torn and bone exposed above Duke's ear. "That was a pretty close call," whispered Duke. He recovered enough to return to the carriage and accompany Morgan's force as it moved south.

Harlan's force, mostly infantry, having marched 43 miles in 31 hours, was exhausted and did not pursue. Instead, he busied himself with routine matters—seeking rations and ordering shoes and socks for his troops.[16]

With Harlan to his rear and with his mission of torching the L&N trestles completed, Morgan turned south to Bardstown and proceeded toward Tennessee, where Mattie, his new bride, was awaiting him.[17]

Meanwhile, in Bardstown, Morgan's men broke into the post office, read the papers to learn the latest news, tore open the mail looking for information about troop locations, scattering the paper over the area. They looted stores and "compelled" the merchants to take their Confederate money.

Mortified at the latest Morgan exploits, the *Louisville Journal* claimed that the "notorious John Morgan, at the head of his band of sneaks," had made a dash on Bardstown defended only by men in hospitals.[18]

On to Springfield

On December 30, 1862, Morgan's men moved out of Bardstown, singing "Lorena," wearing hats and shoes looted from a general store, and reached Springfield by late afternoon. There Morgan learned that the Federals had moved all their forces into his line of march from the southern part of the state to Lebanon. The 34th Brigade, made up of the 50th, 98th, 121st Ohio and 80th Indiana infantries, commanded by Col. W. P. Reid, had been called to Lebanon from Columbia, leaving behind a storehouse of supplies in Campbellsville. The brigade reached Lebanon on December 28.[19]

At Springfield, Morgan's men built a fire in the center of town and gathered around it, some dropping to the ground and sleeping. A light drizzle was falling and the temperature dropped precipitously.

On the wet, cold evening, Federal 6th Kentucky cavalrymen Maj. William H. Fidler of Marion County and Capt. Edmund Penn of Mannsville rode toward Springfield on a scouting mission for the Union forces under Hoskins, trying to discern the direction of Morgan's approach. They made their way into town down East Main Street to the vicinity of the courthouse, and came within fifty yards of the Rebel artillery battery. They opened fire directly into the Southern artillery position, killing two. Miraculously, amid the confusion, they escaped. In Hoskins' Official Report, he said that Fidler had performed a feat of daring which was "worthy of the highest praise."[20]

The Union commander at Lebanon, Col. William A. Hoskins with about 6,000 troops and reinforcements expected from the Cumberland, waited to "bag" the Rebels. Morgan, with the enemy to his front and rear, was certain he faced defeat and capture. He commented, "My position was now sufficiently hazardous."[21]

Morgan realized he had to move quickly to avoid a fight and ordered a night march for the late evening of December 30. He forced Springfield hotel keeper, J.C. Rawlins, to guide him over the countryside. His men mounted and rode south out of Springfield on the Lebanon Road and turned west on the old Elizabethtown-Loretta road.[22]

Steven L. Wright

Maj. William Fidler

Annetta Penn Harding

Capt. Edmund Penn

Johnson Distracts the Yankees

Morgan ordered Col. Adam R. Johnson to lead three hundred men, under McCreary's command, to make a feint by riding directly down the Lebanon Road toward the city while his main force took a circuitous route around Lebanon. McCreary made contact with the enemy a mile from Springfield, drove them back, fighting continuously for two miles. As the Rebels moved south, they sent their scouts to set fire to fence rails and leave them glowing against the black sky.[23] John A. Wyeth, who rode with Quirk's scouts, wrote in his journal:

> We were ordered . . . to drive in the pickets there and build fires in order to give the foe the impression that we were up in force and were only awaiting daylight to attack. We piled rails and made fires until late at night, while Morgan was making a detour along a narrow and little-used country road around Lebanon.[24]

McCreary's men continued to fight the reinforced enemy, which pressed him on all sides. The feint had succeeded because the Union force was heavily involved fighting McCreary's men.

Morgan's orders had stated that he would send a courier giving instructions to abandon the feint and rejoin the main force. This order was slow to come; the men were freezing cold and wanted to get close to the fires they had set for warmth. But McCreary warned them that standing in the firelight was certain death with the enemy so close. Before the order came, McCreary's men had repulsed more Yankee attacks. Finally about one o'clock, the courier came with orders for McCreary to rejoin the main body at the double quick. After a tortuous two-hour march to catch up to the main body, McCreary's exhausted men were assigned to serve as rear guard until the dawn.[25]

A Remarkable Night March around Lebanon

December 30, 1862, was remembered by the soldiers for the hardest march of their lives. The temperature was below zero. The troops struggled forward in the dark and rain, which was turning into sleet and freezing the manes of their horses. Bennett Young said:

> Icicles . . . dangled from their nostrils. Ice coated the beards and moustaches of the men. Half the time they walked by their steeds, stamping their feet, swinging their hands and beating their bodies to drive away the stupor which extreme cold imposes upon flesh and blood.[26]

Night March around Lebanon, December 30, 1862

They rode in silence. The road became slippery, and the horses and men could hardly maintain their footing. Colonel Johnson said that they took on a ghostly appearance. In his diary, Wyeth described their difficult situation:

> Between the bitter, penetrating cold, the fatigue, the overwhelming desire to sleep, the numerous halts to get the artillery out of bad places,

> the impenetrable darkness, and the inevitable confusion which attends the moving of troops and artillery along a narrow country road, we endured a night of misery never to be forgotten.[27]

When contact within the column was lost, McCreary had to assume leadership of the Second Brigade and find a guide to lead his men back to the rest of the troops. He remembered the Lebanon march as the "roughest, riskiest work I have ever encountered."[28]

Burke recorded that the "road got so bad the artillery had to leave half of their caissons sticking in the mud and the ammunition wagons had to throw away whole boxes of cartridges. The horses were giving out. . . . Daylight still found us plodding through the mud."[29]

The force regrouped at dawn, went through St. Mary's, crossed the Rolling Fork at the fords in the "Lagoons," and looked up at Muldraugh's Hill, seeking the pike between Lebanon and Campbellsville. A carriage carrying the wounded Colonel Duke moved with the column.[30]

Hoskins' Response

In Lebanon, Union commander Hoskins had established a strong defensive position with Company A of the 16th Kentucky, supported by two artillery pieces, atop the steep bluff overlooking Springfield Road at Cartwright's Creek. All during the day of December 31, he anticipated Morgan's attack. For the preceding two days Hoskins' scouts had been desperately seeking some trace of Morgan.

Concerned that Morgan would try to bypass the Union position in Lebanon, Hoskins dispatched a courier to Col. Frank Wolford at Greensburg recommending that he move his force to Saloma or Muldraugh's Hill at Finley. Good fortune was once more with Morgan. The messenger was captured, and Wolford did not receive the order. In the late afternoon of December 31, Hoskins was dismayed to find out that Morgan had, once again, slipped away.[31]

In her January 1, 1863 diary entry, Maria Knott reflected the feeling of the people in Lebanon that Morgan was invincible: "The troops . . . left to try and overtake Morgan, they had better saved their time and wind for they can't overtake him."

Halisy Incident on the Way to Campbellsville

During the flanking move to the west of Lebanon, Lt. George B. Eastin, Lt. Alexander Tribble, two of Morgan's trusted officers, accompanied by Pvt. S.D. Bristow, desperate to obtain footwear, being "well nigh barefooted" dropped out of the line of march near New Market.[32] When they tried to return to their unit, still without the boots, the Confederate rear guard was already gone.

The Bluegrass men—Eastin from Lexington, and Tribble from Madison County—observed that they were being pursued by a party of three Union officers. Instead of getting away as quickly as possible, the Confederates decided to do battle. Eastin took cover on the right, behind the fence corner in a lagoon near the Rolling Fork, but Tribble's horse overshot the corner and he was left in a more exposed position in the middle of the lagoon where the water was only about two feet deep. The private, wanting no part of this game, rode off.[33]

Lt. George B. Eastin

Leading the Federal chase to catch the Rebels was 33-year-old Col. Dennis J. Halisy, who before the war was a scholar, linguist, teacher, and respected physician in Washington County. As he came upon Eastin, Eastin fired his English Adams revolver and missed; Halisy returned fire, also missed, and then threw up his hands as if to surrender. Eastin approached him, with a lowered weapon, but Halisy reached for his gun and fired another shot at Eastin. At this, Eastin raised his gun and shot Halisy through the head, killing him instantly, his body ending up in the lagoon.[34] The shot was at such close range that Halisy's eyebrows and eyelids were singed.

While Lieutenant Eastin was confronting Halisy, another Federal exchanged shots with Tribble. Neither hit their target. Tribble then rode toward the Federal, "threw his arm around him, and dragged him from the saddle" into the lagoon. "Tribble fell on top, and strangled his foe into surrendering." A third Federal, Turner W. Bottom, then rode up, saw the fate of his fellow officers, and threw up his hands.[35]

Tribble survived this encounter, but his bravery at Tebbs Bend six months later cost him his life. What actually happened here is debated to this day. The Federals claimed Halisy was murdered, but the Southerners maintained Eastin was acting in self-defense.

The Confederate troopers scurried up Muldraugh's Hill, using the old Dug Road, also called Old Hill Hollow Road.[36] At 1 P.M. December 31, Morgan was looking for the pursuing Federals through Fuller's field glass. He could see their pickets in the fields below, but he need not have worried.[37]

When on the pike, the men in gray and butternut discovered a U.S. army wagon full of crackers, left behind by Reid's brigade as it moved toward Lebanon three days before. They devoured the crackers and then cut the telegraph wire.

Peter Sapp lived at the foot of Muldraugh's Hill and was a neighbor of John Feather's. Peter, leaving his wife and family at home, and the eldest Feather son, John H., went to Lebanon to join the Union 10th Infantry, Company C, in the fall of 1861. Typhoid fever broke out in the camp and Peter caught it and died in Nashville on March 28, 1862, and was buried in the National Cemetery there. Feather died a month later. Mary Sapp was left a widow in her thirties with seven children—five boys and two girls—to raise. When Morgan came through on the Christmas Raid, the raiders took Mary Sapp's horses and left some jaded ones. The older son, Greenberry, found his daddy's old gun and stuck it out the window to shoot the men at the stables, but his mother followed him into the room and stopped him. After the war was over, widow Mary received a Federal pension until all the children were grown.[38]

The Rebels rode by Pleasant Hill Church, which Morgan had burned a year earlier. When they came to James E. Tandy's Stage Stand, they helped themselves to his corn, chickens, horses, and some fence rails. Their officers told the soldiers, "Just take the top rail. Don't take anything but the top rail." Well, it didn't take long to figure out that, when they took the top one off, the next one was the top, so soon the whole fence was carried off.[39]

New Year's Eve in Campbellsville, 1862

McCreary encamped in "lonely" woods outside Campbellsville, after forty-eight hours in the saddle. His men had found "an abundance of corn, hay, molasses, crackers, and ham," and he was happy to have a "good supper."[40]

Some of Morgan's regiments camped outside the town but others stayed in the village. New Year's Eve was an uproarious affair for Morgan's men as every Rebel not on picket turned up to celebrate.[41]

The *Louisville Democrat* ran a report on Morgan's visit to Campbellsville:

> No one was warned of his approach until the town was occupied. He began his usual work of robbery immediately. There was not a good horse left in town. The stores were inundated, post office robbed, etc. Mr. W.F. Chandler, one of the merchants in the village, was damaged to the amount of several thousand dollars. Mr. Redman [owner of Redman's Tavern] who keeps hotel and a tan yard, lost about two thousand dollars' worth of leather, and his hotel was taken over by Morgan and made headquarters.
>
> Nearly every citizen was damaged to some extent, and some were rendered almost destitute.... Some say 'Morgan himself is a gentleman,'... but now they all admit that he is as much a rogue as any man in his command.
>
> He did not discriminate between Union and Secesh, but just took things wherever they could be found. He destroyed government property, but I think not a great deal.[42]

The Union 34th Kentucky Brigade had left military supplies behind in Robert Colvin's tobacco warehouse on Upper Main Street when all the Union forces withdrew. The Rebels broke into the building and confiscated whatever they needed. Colvin was also postmaster; therefore, in true Morgan fashion, it is certain that the mail was captured.[43]

Curtis Burke and his company of scouts camped in a stable, sleeping in the loft. Auburn-haired Burke, a member of the Lexington Rifles and a third-year student at Transylvania University before the war, would soon celebrate his 21st birthday. He described the scene at Colvin's Warehouse and the activity on the upper end of Main Street:[44]

> A crowd of us got into a room where there were four large boxes full of new cavalry overcoats, pants, and boots. I got an overcoat, a pair of pants, and a pair of boots. Not seeing but one of the [Quirk's] scouts in the crowd, I concluded to take as much as I could carry to give to the boys. So I added three overcoats and three pairs of pants to my loot.

Several blocks away, William Marrs (1813–1872), one of two shoemakers in the town, was hard at work in his cobbler shop at 103 West Second Street, now Broadway, across from the Courthouse Square, when some of Morgan's men set up camp in his yard and took possession of the log cookhouse in its left rear corner. The Rebels left evidence of their night of New Year's revelry in its loft—bullet holes completely through its logs, which remained there until the cookhouse was torn down in the 1940s. Ironically, Marrs was left bootless when the raiders departed.[45]

Iris Summers

William Marrs Home, Campbellsville

Sam Moore, Sr., historian and raconteur from Green County, told of Morgan's troops breaking into stores, running out with bolts of calico, tying them onto the pummels of their saddles, and riding up and down Main Street until late in the evening. Duke observed, "They did not pilfer with any sort of method or reason; it seemed to be a mania, senseless and purposeless." What a New Year's Party the Southern troops must have enjoyed![46]

Thursday, January 1, 1863, was a clear, crisp day without a cloud in the sky. Buglers playing "Boots and Saddles" awakened the sleepy Rebel force. Quirk's Scouts came out of the stable in search of Yankee whiskey to fill their canteens for the return trip to Tennessee. Some, however, still needed shoes. They went to a tan yard, probably Redman's, to get leather to make boots for themselves.[47] The soldiers' problem of the morning was that they had no way to transport all their booty back to Tennessee. To prevent the rations remaining in Colvin's warehouse from being used by the Federals, Morgan's men made preparations to burn it. The townspeople became very alarmed because they knew that any fire could easily spread through the town's wood buildings. The Methodist Church, sitting adjacent to the warehouse, would also be in danger.

In response to the citizens' pleas, the Confederate commander, probably Major McCreary, permitted supplies to be dragged out of the warehouse and stacked in a heap in the center of Upper Main Street before giving the order to set them afire. People watched in dismay as "thousands of pounds of bacon and a hundred gallons of molasses, together with bushels of crackers" went up in smoke.[48] Pvt. Sid Cunningham, of the 11th Kentucky Cavalry, recalled:

> Our regiment was left to finish the work of destruction commenced the night before and a grand bonfire did we raise.... Shoulder to shoulder and ham to ham stood the meat piled mountain high in the streets and ... the crackers went into the crackling flames. We boxed the boxes about and it seemed hard to burn the hard bread.[49]

The fires were still burning when Union forces arrived.

Gerald Myers

Robert Colvin's Warehouse, Main Street, Campbellsville

Ruth Ford

Robert Colvin

Federal Pursuit from Lebanon to Columbia

The Union force, after some confusion as to who was in command, moved out of Lebanon on December 31, 1862, at 6 P.M. It was made up of squadrons of the 6th Kentucky Cavalry under Maj. Louis A. Gratz, 9th Kentucky Cavalry under Maj. George W. Rue, 258 men of the 7th Tennessee Infantry, 650 men of the 16th Kentucky Infantry, and 425 of the 12th Kentucky Infantry, Battery M, Illinois 1st Field Light Artillery, and the 34th Brigade under Col. W.P. Reid.[50]

Aware that Morgan's cavalry would be impossible to catch with infantrymen, wagons were emptied of baggage, and filled with foot soldiers so that they could stay close to their cavalry. The proud men of the 16th Kentucky refused to ride in the wagons claiming they would have no trouble keeping up with the rest. This caused no difficulty because the column often halted on account of broken wagons and harnesses. "We had made such a noise as to keep Morgan . . . well posted as to our progress," commented a soldier.[51]

Even though Reid's 34th Brigade had just been ordered to the area, the territory was not new to many of the troops. The battery had been through Campbellsville just days before, and on the night of November 14, 1862, the artillerymen had camped on South Columbia Avenue, outside the town, noting that it was a "rich district." The men had immediately set to work gathering chickens, potatoes, and apples at a Rebel house for their supper. They made use of the cider press on a plantation and took the rest of the apples back to camp.

The next day the battery moved on to Columbia, which they called "a hotbed of secession," and camped to the west of the town. After a useless expedition to Millerfield, "two houses and a stable," they moved their camp to the north bank of Russell Creek outside Columbia, which they named Camp Gilbert, after Brig. Gen. Charles C. Gilbert. It was later known as Camp Reid.[52]

Camp Boyle-Gilbert, Russell Creek, Columbia

As late as December 1862, the Illinois battery conducted gunnery drills firing into a "high, almost perpendicular hill" to accustom the horses to the noise of cannons. Infantry small arms target practice took place nearby.

Gen. J.T. Boyle telegraphed them they could anticipate a Rebel attack within ten days. The battery, helped by the infantry, started building a defensive position, a fort and log shanties for quarters.

In spite of these preparations, Reid's whole brigade, including the artillery, was called back to Lebanon to confront Morgan. On December 22–25, the brigade stopped in Campbellsville and again camped south of town, near its old quarters on South Columbia Avenue. On Christmas Day, the men feasted on turkeys, geese, chickens, mutton, sweet potatoes, Irish potatoes, and apples. An abundance of peach brandy and apple jack, probably secured at Joseph H. Chandler's Distillery, now the Hiestand House Museum, made the meal festive. In the early morning hours of December 27, the brigade formed in line of battle, anticipating that Morgan might appear.

Nothing happened so the full brigade continued on to Lebanon on December 29, as ordered. "All felt confident we could bag Johnny very easily," commented an artilleryman.[53]

The left section of Battery M was ordered to the Springfield Road to guard the approach to Lebanon, where they could clearly see the fires of the Rebels. The Federals were ordered to extinguish their fires while, they complained, the "Johnnies enjoyed good, warm fires."[54]

When Morgan eluded them in Lebanon, Reid's Brigade with its artillery set out for Columbia, its winter camp. Somewhere before New Market, news arrived that Colonel Halisy was dead. Federal scouts reported that the Rebels were to their west on the Rolling Fork. Incredibly, the command called a halt. Major Rue's 9th Kentucky Cavalry was sent forward to guard the Rolling Fork Bridge at New Market. Fearing that Morgan might get in his rear and attack Lebanon, Hoskins dispatched a cavalry picket to his rear to guard St. Mary's Road at the junction of Highways 68 and 426. The Brigade staff, still confident, met at a house in New Market, probably the old brick Robertson House which overlooked the mill, the ford and bridge over Rolling Fork, and discussed their plans to capture Morgan. An order went out for the column to rest, but no fires were allowed that night.[55]

Elizabeth Bridgwater Hamilton

Robertson House at New Market, Marion County

In contrast to the riotous, reveling of the Rebel troops in Campbellsville, the Federals celebrated New Year's Eve quietly under the stars: "The night was intensely cold.... We laid down in fence corners, but soon had to rise and walk for exercise, otherwise we would have frozen. Noiselessly we watched the old year die."[56]

A little after sunrise on New Year's Day, 1863, the Yanks began to climb Muldraugh's Hill in search of the Confederates. But, much to their chagrin, Morgan's men were nowhere to be seen.[57]

As soon as the leaders of the Union brigade realized they had again let Morgan slip away, they concluded that his next target would be Green River Bridge. It was obvious that they had to "push on with all possible speed" to save the bridge. However, as they approached Campbellsville on the Lebanon Road, friendly citizens told Colonel Hoskins that Morgan's men were still in town.

Still two miles out, Hoskins hurried his men to Campbellsville. He ordered a charge. And forward dashed the cavalry and artillery down Main Street. Around the courthouse they circled. The Union hospital stewards waved as they watched from doors and windows. The troops advanced with such speed that "the road was soon lined with Federal blankets, kettles, sabers," and everything that could fall off the saddles of cavalrymen.

Supplies that had been set afire at Colvin's warehouse were still burning, the "streets were filled with crying women and children, the stores were all gutted, and such things as could not be carried along had been thrown into the street.... The road was strewn with ribbons and gewgaws Morgan's men had stolen."[58] The Yanks had missed Morgan's rearguard by an hour. Only a few lagging Confederates were captured.

The Burning of Green River Bridge

On New Year's morning, 1863, the Confederates left Campbellsville riding down the Columbia Turnpike toward Green River Bridge, eight miles away.

Out in the Lone Valley community, William Wesley Johnson, hearing that troops were coming down the Columbia Pike, rushed to hide his horse and stock in the woods. His wife, Virginia Steger Johnson, was left alone in the log house, tending to the little girls, Elsie and Martha, aged three and one. Her body, heavy with another child, was weary as she was due in two weeks. When twenty of Morgan's men galloped up to her door demanding that she cook them a good meal, she had little choice. She killed the few chickens that they were left on the place, dressed them, and prepared fried chicken and gravy in a black iron skillet.[59]

Frances Davenport

Virginia Steger Johnson

When Morgan's troops arrived at Green River, they saw that the stockade built in late 1862 was not garrisoned, the troops from Reid's Union Brigade having been diverted to Lebanon leaving the bridge completely undefended. Morgan's 3,900 troops rode across Green River Bridge unopposed.[60] A detachment of Pioneers was sent to block Green River Ford below the bridge. They used their axes to fell trees onto the trail to the river, thereby making the ford almost unusable.[61]

Four companies of the Rebel 11th Kentucky Cavalry, commanded by Major McCreary, which usually served as rear guard for Morgan, were given the job of burning the bridge, stockade, and Federal supplies and corncribs in Sublett's bottom. McCreary's Journal, January 1, 1863, recorded in a matter of fact way: "Burnt two very large pens of U.S. corn, bridge across Green River; burnt Green River Stockade, which was a tough job."[62]

Burning the bridge was also no easy task. Axes were taken out of saddles and used to shave the dry rafters of the bridge for kindling. Straw, taken from a nearby barn and stuffed between the trusses, was set ablaze. Soon the raging fire caused the supports to break, and the bridge fell into the river.

Francis Mendon Barnes, a young trooper from Wayne County, was the last one across the bridge before it collapsed. James Madison Griffin and his family stood on their front porch some distance down the road and watched the smoke curl up behind the hills.[63]

January 1, 1863, the date the Emancipation Proclamation went into effect, was remembered by the residents of the Columbia Road for the bridge over Green River being burned by Morgan's Men.[64] This cut off the supply route between the railhead in Lebanon and the Union camps in Columbia and to the towns south of it. "The destruction of the bridge across Green river between this place and Columbia is a serious blow to the city," commented the *Louisville Democrat.*

Gerald Myers

Green River Bridge, Taylor County, January 1, 1863

Burning the Stockade

Morgan's men had real difficulty burning the stockade because the wooden uprights were wet from the sleet and snow. To get the fire started, they went across the field to Pleas C. Howard's house to get kindling and firewood. Soon the walls of the stockade were ablaze.[65]

Since the bridge had been destroyed, Morgan's troops did not have to rush back to Tennessee. They had significantly delayed the pursuit troops, who would have difficulty crossing Green River.

Federal Pursuit: January 1, 1863

Leaving the slower infantry regiments in Campbellsville, the Union cavalry and the battery went down the Columbia Road at a gallop. When they came to a clearing less than a mile from the river, they could see smoke billowing in the distance. The

Gerald Myers

Green River Stockade, Taylor County, January 1, 1863

bridge over Green River, the Federal stockade on top of the bluff, and two large corn cribs in Sublett's bottom were ablaze. Everything there seemed to be on fire.[66]

Major Rue's cavalry raced ahead to reconnoiter the bridge. On a hill in Robert Tate's field about 600 yards from the bridge, the right section of Battery M opened fire. One shell exploded near the Federals' own cavalry, three shells hit the burning bridge, two struck the sheer face of the palisades, and the rest of the sixteen rounds fired fell in various places in the area. One of them wounded a Confederate trooper, who was later found being cared for in a neighborhood house a half mile away from the gun position. The gunners were told that their barrage had killed or wounded fourteen Rebels. The Federal commanders hoped that the echo of their cannon would signal other forces in the region to come and reinforce them.[67]

One of the shells burst near the home of Joseph and Mary Katherine Howard Hubbard, shaking the house. She grabbed the children and thrust them under a feather bed, while she waited for another round to drop. Mrs. James Allen Sublett was walking a sick soldier and was almost struck by one of the fragments from a shell which landed near her.[68]

While the Yanks rested and ate supper, Hoskins ordered a squad of Pioneers to begin removing the debris and felled trees blocking the Green River Ford. While there, he received news that Wolford's 1st, 7th, and 11th Kentucky cavalry were at Greensburg, just ten miles away, expecting an attack from Morgan.

Morgan's Men at Columbia: January 1, 1863

The early evening of January 1, Morgan placed a section of artillery on the high ground covering the approach to Columbia down the Campbellsville Road, probably the Lindsey Wilson or cemetery hill. Then he slept for a few hours at Timoleon Cravens' large colonial home on Burkesville Street.

Still celebrating a rainy New Year's Day, the raiders camped around town, fed their horses, and found their supper at any house they could. Storekeepers opened their shops for Morgan's men and Scout Burke bought winter underwear for $3.

On right: Champ Ferguson, Confederate Guerrilla

While in Columbia, Champ Ferguson, who was riding with Morgan and had a reputation as a vicious Confederate fighter, set out from camp with his men to settle a personal grudge. They rode to the home of Elam Huddleston, a former captain in Wolford's Cavalry, and surrounded it. As Ferguson broke down the front door, Huddleston grabbed his rifle and shots were exchanged. Huddleston fell, mortally wounded. Ferguson shot him three more times and stuck a knife in his chest. Then he returned to camp to boost his exploit and display the bloody knife. Colonel Duke, who was lying in his carriage, recovering from his wound at Rolling Fork, said that the incident sickened him. At the end of the war, Ferguson, a native of Clinton County, was charged with murder of twenty men and sentenced to be hanged.[69]

Later in the evening, Morgan's men were ordered to saddle up and move out the Burkesville Road. They rode until after midnight. Curtis Burke fell asleep on his horse, his hat dropping off and waking him up. After arriving in the town square of Burkesville, he and ten others found an empty room where they bedded down for the rest of the night. Burke commented that the town that bore his name was a "lonesome looking" place.

At Burkesville, in the early morning hours of the January 2, Morgan penned a letter to "My dearest wife," in which he recounted his destruction of the L&N trestles:

> They were the finest works in this Country & it will be impossible to reconstruct them in less than two months. The [rail]road is completely destroyed from Bacon Creek to near Sheppardsville.... Col Duke was very dangerously wounded but [we]have him along in a carriage & he will recover.... No time will be lost in reaching you.... My friend Gen Hardee thought it impossible for me to burn the trussell work above Elisabethtown. We determined to succeed and have done so.[70]

The morning of January 2, "shopping" by Morgan's men resulted in their having "a good many things that never got paid for," commented Burke. The *Louisville Democrat* made a report:

> I suppose they carried from this country 250 or 300 horses and mules, for which they did not pay one cent, even in confederate trash; yet they had it in abundance. They took from poor widows their only horse. Yes, and fed their last ear of corn. It would have made you heartsick to have seen that crowd with bed quilts, counterpanes, blankets, prints, brown muslims, leather boots and shoes, and indeed, all manner of articles that were portable. They remained here until about two o'clock P.M. during which time a great many applications were made for the restoration of horses.

It seems that the owners of the horses would be promised that they could see General Morgan, and then be told that he was fatigued and sleeping, with orders not to be disturbed. By the time they saw him, the horses were out of town. Parson Martin Baker lost six horses, appealed to the men for their return, only to have the one horse they had left him be taken while he was making his appeal. It seems the secesh fared as poorly as the ordinary citizen. It was estimated that $8,000 of goods were taken from the merchants paid for with $5,500 in Confederate money.[71]

Morgan's men moved out of Burkesville in a column, "with glittering arms and wearied horses, winding far in front and far back in the distance like an immense anaconda," noted McCreary. They forded the Cumberland, and rode to the Tennessee line where they stopped at Embry's, a Confederate staging place and mail drop, where the men and their horses always fared well, only a short distance from the safety of their camp in Tennessee.[72]

Wolford Joins the Pursuit

On January 1, in response to a message from Hoskins, Wolford set out from Greensburg to join him in the chase. At eight o'clock in the evening, the column started moving across Green River at Roachville, continued along present-day Meadow Creek Road, and linked up with Hoskins' regiments. They made a night march until 4 A.M. when they bivouacked. At 10 o'clock the next morning, Hoskins and Wolford's forces entered Columbia and found out that Morgan had been gone for six hours. Wolford pursued Morgan three miles down the Burkesville Road until ordered to give it up by Gen. Speed Fry. Wolford's men would ultimately be successful in capturing Morgan, but not on this raid.[73]

The 11th Kentucky Cavalry stationed at Greensburg departed from there before daylight on January 2 and rode at the doublequick to Columbia and five miles further south, before, they too, "gave it up."

Gen. Joseph J. Reynolds, with 5,000 infantrymen, 600 cavalrymen, and 12 pieces of artillery, was positioned in Glasgow, ready to move to Burkesville. The 7th Kentucky Cavalry came north from Tennessee and joined Reynolds' efforts to overtake Morgan in Columbia, but all were too late. As a result of the arduous journey from Tennessee, 7th Kentucky Cavalry's horses were so fatigued that they were taken to the camp at Green River Bridge to recover before returning to Tennessee.[74]

Morgan had again slipped away from thousands of Union troops pursuing him.

Rumors of Another Rebel Threat to Campbellsville

Battery M of the Illinois Artillery, with the rest of Reid's Brigade, spent the night of January 2, 1863, at Camp Gilbert in Columbia. Early the next morning, they left and arrived in Campbellsville that evening about 8 P.M. and sent for their tents and luggage from Lebanon.

Although Morgan had returned to Tennessee, news arrived on January 4 that the famous Rebel cavalryman, Gen. Nathan Bedford Forrest, was in Kentucky. Reid's Brigade was again placed on alert to deal with him. Battery M had its guns positioned on a high hill, maybe today's Wilson Heights, where they could cover the Columbia Road. On January 5, the artillerymen did without breakfast, were told they could only whisper as they lay in wait for the enemy, who was supposed to appear before daylight. But, when their baggage train arrived from Lebanon in the afternoon, its teamsters "reported that there was no such thing as an armed Rebel within fifty miles." The battery was then ordered to move out the Summersville Road and make camp twelve miles from Campbellsville, probably somewhere in today's Bengal community. "The country through which we passed on this march was the best we found in Kentucky," wrote the battery historian.[75]

On December 29, 1862, the *Louisville Journal* had run an article on the fine fort being built at Camp Gilbert.[76] However, Morgan had been able to bypass it because the troops who were supposed to garrison the fort had been dispatched to Lebanon. The lackluster showing of the Federals at Columbia was keenly felt, and the newspapers delivered scathing criticism of Morgan's being able to roam about Kentucky virtually untouched:

> There has been much and just complaint of the slow Federal operations in this war. We all the while hear of Rebel cavalry making bold and impetuous dashes, capturing our troops, here, there, and elsewhere, carrying off or destroying arms, army stores, and camp equipages, burning bridges, breaking up railroads, etc, etc, etc, but not a word about Federal dashes upon the Rebels. If would seem as if our troops everywhere were half asleep, or half paralyzed, just waiting in a sort of stupefaction, wondering where the next Rebel blow would fall.... It is certainly high time that this constantly repeated John Morgan game upon the theater of Kentucky be brought to a close.[77]

A letter from a Campbellsville woman which appeared in an Akron, Ohio newspaper added to the Morgan legend:

> Old Morgan has been through here again with 7000 cavalry, tearing up railroads, burning bridges etc. He went into Campbellsville on Wednesday and left on Thursday morning. He took every horse and mule in town; all of Redman's leather, and robbed all the stores, taking hats, caps, boots, shoes, and every piece of dry goods that could be made wearable.... He took $4000 from William Chandler alone.... He took horses from J. [James Allen] Sublette, 21 from three adjoining farms, burned 300 bushels of government corn, and a large quantity of Sublett's and then burned the bridge.[78]

The debate over the laggardly pursuit of Morgan from Lebanon through Columbia, 9th Kentucky Cavalryman Col. John Boyle's attitude toward obeying infantry orders, and Hoskins' leadership continued for weeks in the *Louisville Journal*. Finally on March 7, 1863, the *Journal* said it hoped it would hear no more on the matter.

Maj. Louis A. Gratz

It seems clear that Col. John Boyle, commanding the 9th Kentucky Cavalry, against Hoskins' orders, had stayed asleep at New Market on the evening of December 31 instead of leaving immediately to go after Morgan. He had received the order to pursue Morgan at ll P.M. that night and did not leave until 9 A.M. the following day. On the evening of January 1–2, Boyle decided to halt the pursuit between Campbellsville and Columbia without any consultation with his subordinate officers, Maj. L.A. Gratz or Maj. William Fidler. Fidler refused to dismount his men until specifically ordered to do so by Boyle. Later Boyle defended himself by claiming that he had received information from men returning from Columbia that Morgan had already left there the evening of January 1. Boyle maintained that it would have been useless for him to pursue Morgan at 2 A.M. when the Rebel commander had a six-hour lead.

When Lt. Thomas Mahoney, 9th Kentucky Cavalry, came to Colonel Hoskins' Headquarters at a house at Green River [probably Tate House], to report on Boyle's failure to act, he found that Hoskins was fast asleep. Hoskins and Mahoney proceeded to Boyle's headquarters and found Major Gratz, commander of the 6th Kentucky Cavalry, sitting by a fire, evidently in no rush to chase Morgan. Gratz explained his inaction by stating that he had orders to wait for infantry support, adding that Capt. Ed Penn's company of his regiment, was armed with only pistols and sabers. Confusion reigned at Colonel Boyle's headquarters between Green River Bridge to Columbia, and Morgan was soon over the Tennessee border.[79]

The Christmas Raid is considered to be Morgan's most successful. His men destroyed the L&N trestles, thereby stopping supplies for the Northern armies being carried on the Louisville and Nashville Railroad for five weeks. Everything needed by them had to be shipped down the Ohio and up the Cumberland River to Nashville. It kept 7,300 soldiers of Maj. Gen. William S. Rosecrans committed to protecting transportation and communications lines. The raid resulted in the capture of 1,877 prisoners and the destruction of much Federal government property while providing arms and ammunition to 400 of Morgan's men. According to Morgan's Report, the Southerners lost two killed and 24 wounded.[80]

On New Year's Day, as the Rebel troopers were on the crest of a high hill around the Green River Stockade at Tebbs Bend, they heard the sound of big guns to the south, cannon fire from the Battle of Stones River in Murfreesboro. Morgan's forces were supposed to serve as Bragg's cavalry, but Morgan had not returned in time to help Bragg fight the Northern army of Rosecrans. Bragg withdrew to Tullahoma and formed a new defensive position, and Mattie had to abandon her home in Murfreesboro.[81]

Would the outcome of Stones River, in which Rosecrans defeated Bragg, have been any different if Morgan's forces had arrived earlier? Not so, thinks James Ramage, Morgan's biographer. In his opinion, Bragg did not know how to use cavalry effectively. Too, Ramage feels that the raid ought to have occurred in November or early December to have the maximum effect on the supplies coming down the L&N.[82]

General J.T. Boyle, commander of the Military District of Western Kentucky, headquartered in Louisville, reporting the destruction of the Green River Bridge to his superior officer, Maj. Gen. Horatio G. Wright, commander of the Department of the Ohio, commented, "Green River Bridge, on the Columbia Pike, is important. Shall I have it rebuilt?"[83] Wright must have answered in the affirmative, because in the spring, reconstruction of the bridge began.

Southern Sympathizers

By 1863, Kentucky was, for the most part, under Union control, except for the territory south of the Cumberland, along the Tennessee border. However, there was almost no part of Kentucky that did not have Southern sympathizers and marauding guerrilla bands.

In May of 1863 Union Order #18, calling for the wives and families of Confederate soldiers to be arrested and sent south, was promulgated. The vise was tightening around Kentucky Southern-sympathizer families from its Union government, and many left the state to escape harassment.

A soldier posted in Columbia reports that he had received orders to arrest all who are not good Union men.[84] This may have precipitated the incident that took place on Lone Valley Road and which was typical of what was happening in other places in Kentucky:

Walker T. Hubbard was a loyal citizen-farmer living in a sizable log house, with a son serving in the Union army. One of his close neighbors, James Caldwell, a slave holder living in a two-story Greek revival home just across the field, made no secret of his Southern sympathies.

Ken Pierce

James Caldwell Home, Taylor County

A squad of Federal soldiers came down the Lone Valley Road and told Hubbard that they were on their way to arrest Caldwell. Hubbard made a deal with the officer in charge that, when the corn was ripe, later in the year, he could bring his men and horses back and have all the corn they needed in return for not bothering his good friend and neighbor. The deal was struck, and Caldwell escaped arrest. Other Southern sympathizers in Kentucky were not as fortunate as Caldwell.

Walker T. and Rachel Watson Hubbard

Hubbard would lose his son, John Wesley, fighting with the 3rd Kentucky Infantry, at the Battle of Missionary Ridge. Hubbard, a school teacher before the war, was a sergeant and experienced much hard combat. After listing the casualties from his company in his last letter home, he said, "Tell Pa he need not buy me a horse" as if he had a premonition of death. Hubbard's letters home appear in Appendix S.[85]

Guerrilla Activity

Unexplained, senseless, and violent actions on the part of both Union and Confederate soldiers occurred when they moved through Taylor County. Civilians E.M. Durham and John Mayes, farm laborers in their twenties, were awakened from their sleep one night by two hundred Federals firing their muskets. The soldiers surrounded the house in the Lone Valley neighborhood and apparently planned to kill them.

Durham and Mayes armed themselves with pistols, and Mayes ran out of the house shooting off his side arms with good effect and secreted himself in the woods. Durham decided that his best chance was inside the house. The attackers rushed inside and shot through the door of the wardrobe where he was hiding. When all got quiet, Durham emerged, unscathed, but the soldiers beat him over the head with their weapons until he was unconscious and left him for dead. Durham never fully recovered from his injuries.[86]

Even being a loyal county official was a dangerous job during the Civil War. On August 22, 1863, the *Louisville Journal* reported that George W. Montague, clerk of both county and circuit courts in Taylor County during the early part of the war, was robbed by the Rebels of his wagon and four horses. Since he was not a man of wealth, this loss created a considerable financial burden on him. He resigned as clerk, and his brother took over his duties.

Susan B. Saufley

Lt. M.C. Saufley, Morgan's Men, dressed in cavalrymen's attire

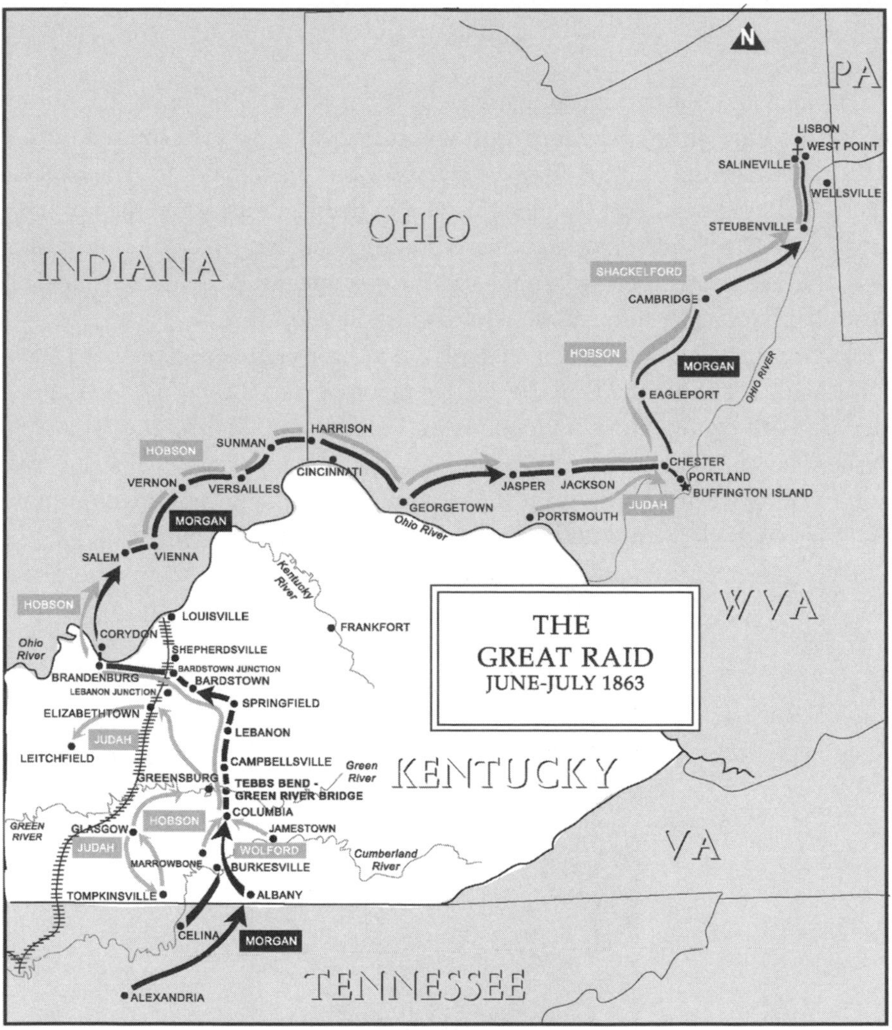
THE GREAT RAID
JUNE-JULY 1863
INDIANA
OHIO
PA
WVA
VA
KENTUCKY
TENNESSEE
LISBON
WEST POINT
SALINEVILLE
WELLSVILLE
STEUBENVILLE
SHACKELFORD
CAMBRIDGE
HOBSON
MORGAN
OHIO RIVER
EAGLEPORT
HARRISON
SUNMAN
HOBSON
CINCINNATI
VERNON
VERSAILLES
GEORGETOWN
JASPER
JACKSON
CHESTER
PORTLAND
BUFFINGTON ISLAND
JUDAH
PORTSMOUTH
Ohio River
MORGAN
SALEM
VIENNA
Kentucky River
HOBSON
LOUISVILLE
FRANKFORT
CORYDON
Ohio River
SHEPHERDSVILLE
BARDSTOWN JUNCTION
BRANDENBURG
BARDSTOWN
LEBANON JUNCTION
SPRINGFIELD
ELIZABETHTOWN
LEBANON
LEITCHFIELD
JUDAH
CAMPBELLSVILLE
Green River
GREENSBURG
TEBBS BEND - GREEN RIVER BRIDGE
COLUMBIA
GREEN RIVER
GLASGOW
HOBSON
JAMESTOWN
JUDAH
WOLFORD
Cumberland River
MARROWBONE
BURKESVILLE
TOMPKINSVILLE
ALBANY
CELINA
MORGAN
ALEXANDRIA

Map by Judy Ross

Part Six

Morgan's Great Raid into Kentucky, Indiana, and Ohio *July 1863*

The Great Indiana and Ohio Raid was the "grandest enterprise he [Morgan] ever planned, and the one that did most honor to his genius." Basil Duke[1]

Chapter One: January–June

In January 1863, General John Hunt Morgan's forces returned to Tennessee from the Christmas Raid into Kentucky. From January to June, the east central Tennessee area around Liberty, Alexandria, and Lebanon and the southeastern Kentucky counties south of the Cumberland River, Wayne, Clinton, and sometimes Cumberland, were the domain of Morgan's forces. Morgan was guarding the 150-mile front from McMinnville and Murfreesboro on Bragg's far right wing.[2]

In the early months of 1863, Morgan's men were engaged in only one big battle, that of Milton, Tennessee, where Morgan lost 15% of his force, including thirteen officers. Morgan seemed unconcerned, writing Mattie that "while in the hottest of the engagement was I thinking of my dear beautifull Mattie." The *Louisville Journal* taunted him, saying that "the fair Delilah has shorn him of his locks."[3]

While Morgan was playing the role of a devoted husband, his subordinate, Col. Roy S. Cluke, led a raid into Kentucky in early 1863. He, with 750 men, some of whom were from Chenault's Cavalry from Wayne and Clinton counties, crossed the Cumberland at Stigell's Ferry in Somerset and captured Mt. Sterling. John Wesley Badgett, who lived on the Garrard-Lincoln County line, hearing of the approach of the legendary raiders, swam the Dix River on a cold winter night to hide his cherished horses in the woods. He saved his horses, but caught a cold which progressed to pneumonia, and in April 1863, died at the age of 27. His wife delivered a baby boy after his death whom she named John Wesley, Jr.[4]

Colonel Cluke slipped away from his Federal pursuers in a march from Salyersville to Slate Creek that, some say, surpassed Morgan's maneuver around Lebanon in the severity of the weather and terrain. His raid lasted seven weeks destroying property worth a million dollars, and he returned to Tennessee with fresh mounts and a keen spirit.[5]

Conditions for Morgan's men in northern Tennessee were particularly difficult. There was no forage for the horses and little food for the men. The men grew disheartened and the horses started to die. Even though the Southern top brass entrusted the cavalry with essential military duties, the men were expected to provide their own arms and horses, as well as food for themselves and forage for their horses. Generals, observed Basil Duke, were aghast if the cavalrymen asked for anything. Consequently, cavalrymen took what they needed whenever or wherever they found it.[6]

Therefore, most of the men left Tennessee and camped in southern Kentucky in April and May. The headquarters of Duke's 1st Brigade was at Albany, the 2nd Brigade's was first at Albany, then at Monticello. By April 28, this Rebel camp had moved back to a site near Albany.[7]

"They are devouring everything," reported Thomas Bramlette to Gen. J.T. Boyle.[8] Often they not only demanded food, but "asked" that it be prepared for them. April 9, 1863 at Monticello, J.D. Sprake wrote in his diary: "She didn't like to cook for us but had it to do. She was Union to the backbone. Sons and son-in-law in the Yankee army." When cavalry regiments camped in neighborhoods for an extended time, the ladies grew weary of the soldiers' demands. Later near McMinnville, Tennessee, he wrote: "Old Mrs. Goss told us she never would cook for another soldier while she lived that they were all a low and unprincipled set of men and she hoped never to see another one."[9]

Drill and work were the daily routine, but camp life had a lighter side, which is reflected in jottings in soldiers' diaries:

> Played a trick on Fletcher Ellmore. Stillhouse half a mile, boys frequent it pretty often. Card playing, horse racing, stealing bee gums, courting girls and everything for fun. Going fishing tomorrow. Having a good time, get breakfast at young Norman's, had couple sisters, good looking, some of the boys there all the time. Some playing town ball. All got breakfast at Mr. Davis' a Southern man, had six grown daughters, all wanted to marry Billy McCann, carry on high with them. Made the acquaintance of Miss Lilly Gilliland, pretty girl. Robinson, desperately smitten. Heard old time music on the guitar.[10]

The Kentucky raids of 1862 had established the raiders' reputation as horse-thieves. Horse-pressing was particularly disruptive to citizens' lives. Not only did the horse or mule provide a person with transportation and communication, they were essential to a family's livelihood. Horses were given names and special care was given to these valuable animals. Whenever a horse was taken, the owner implored its captor to take good care of it. Sometimes Morgan's men left an exhausted horse in place of the one they pressed, making the loss less serious. Ironically, that horse sometimes turned out to be better than the one taken.

These tactics were heralded in the South as heroic, but condemned in the North as pure banditry. A poem by Jacob Cox of Ohio described their apprehensions about Morgan:

> John Morgan's foot is on thy shore
> Kentucky! O Kentucky!
> His hand is on thy stable door,
> Kentucky! O Kentucky!
>
> He'll ride her till her back is sore
> And leave her at some stranger's door
> Kentucky! Oh Kentucky![11]

While camped in southern Kentucky, Morgan's men crossed and re-crossed the Cumberland River scouting in all directions. After long rides in the wind, rain and snow, the soldiers huddled together around the fire trying to dry out. As in the winter of 1861–1862, measles and typhoid fever struck the exhausted men. Then an epidemic of meningitis began taking its toll.[12] Col. Chenault, commander of the 11th Kentucky Cavalry, described what was happening:

> We have been here [Albany] for seven weeks and leave this point tomorrow for Monticello. . . . We have lost three men by death since our arrival here. The disease of which they died was inflammation of the brain and spine. . . . All that take it die.[13]

By April, the troops in Kentucky were holding their own. However, Morgan's main headquarters in McMinnville, Tennessee, was overrun in a surprise attack from Gen. J. J. Reynolds' Federal cavalry which had become more effective in recent months. Morgan barely escaped capture, when Maj. Dick McCann pretended to be Morgan and allowed himself to be captured. Morgan's wife Mattie was taken prisoner, but released. Maj. Gen. Joseph Wheeler, commander of cavalry for the Army of Tennessee, who had little confidence in Morgan, relieved him from screening the right flank.[14]

With the coming of spring, Morgan's men regained their health, and it was time for battle. The Federals in Lebanon were aware of the Rebel presence and decided it was time to check it. The first of April, Gen. Manson sent a reconnaissance squad of six "in citizens dress" to southeastern Kentucky to scout the Rebel position. At that time, "one Rebel regiment was camped in the bottoms of Cumberland river, about seven miles from Jamestown—on the south side of river. Two regiments were camped in the streets of Monticello, and some other regiments in the neighborhood—supposed to be thirty five hundred strong in all."[15]

This report prompted the sending of 150 Federal cavalrymen, commanded by Col. William E. Riley of the 11th Kentucky, to Burkesville. On their way, they camped at Clay Hill and arrived at Columbia on April 18. Colonel Riley left 50 men to guard wagon trains and proceeded to Creelsboro with 129 of his own and 30 of the 12th Kentucky Cavalry.

As they came over the hill to descend to the town, they caught a Rebel detachment rifling a store and detached a squad to deal with it. The Federals were fired on from houses and stables on each side of the road as they pushed the Southern troopers back toward the river. One wounded Confederate was left with their surgeon, Dr. J.H. Peyton, another was wounded, and twelve were captured. "Calico, jeans, shoes . . . were strewed on the road to Burkesville by the fleeing Rebels for three miles."[16]

Creelsboro, Russell County

In May 1863, Morgan's forces were engaged at Greasy Creek and Monticello. Chenault and Cluke were attacked by Col. Richard Jacob's 9th Kentucky Cavalry, which moved south across the Cumberland River after them. Chenault's men fell back slowly toward Monticello where they were reinforced by Morgan. The 8th Kentucky, under Maj. Robert S. Bullock, advanced and forced the bluecoats to retreat on May 9. At Greasy Creek, also called Horse Shoe Bend, on May 10 the Federals were finally driven back across the Cumberland. "During the greater part of the day, Chenault's and Bullock's regiments were without ammunition, and lay patiently under fire," but when ammunition arrived, the Rebels charged the enemy and drove them back toward Columbia.[17]

But the victory came at a price. Confederate J.D. Sprake's diary reveals that Capt. Joseph Chenault and two others were killed at Horse Shoe Bend on May 9 and that Ans Harris and seventeen more were killed and 30–40 wounded on May 10.[18]

The Rebels rejoiced when they heard about the Southern victory at Chancellorsville in May 1863 but were saddened by Stonewall Jackson's mortal wounding. The South was embarrassed by Yankee Col. Benjamin Grierson's penetrating raid across Mississippi to Louisiana, deep into the Confederacy. It got Morgan's attention and he dreamed of implementing the offensive plan he had been considering for months.[19]

Gen. Braxton Bragg and Morgan had disagreed about the conduct of operations in the past, and it was no secret among Morgan's officers that they believed that "Bragg's talent seems to all be on the retreat." But Bragg sent Morgan a letter thanking him for obtaining a good Kentucky horse for his wife, so relations seemed to be improved.[20]

By the summer of 1863, the Confederate position in Kentucky and Tennessee had become precarious. Bragg's force was camped near Tullahoma, a city in south central Tennessee, posting cavalry to cover his front and both flanks.[21]

Union Brig. Gen. William Rosecrans, commanding the Department of the Cumberland, with a force of nearly 60,000 men, was in Murfreesboro with his army, and was preparing to strike Bragg's force of 20,000. Bragg was hoping for enough time to move his army below the Tennessee River near Chattanooga before Rosecrans attacked.[22]

Confederate General Simon B. Buckner was camped in east Tennessee near Knoxville with about 3,000 men, anticipating an attack from Gen. Ambrose Burnside, commander of the Department of the Ohio. Bragg was unable to support Buckner and neither could Buckner further weaken his meager forces to help Bragg.

Gen. William S. Rosecrans,
USA

Joe Brent Collection

Gen. Henry M. Judah,
USA

Gen. Ambrose E. Burnside,
USA

Gen. Braxton Bragg,
CSA

Gen. Simon B. Buckner,
CSA

Gen. Joseph Wheeler,
CSA

Between the Union armies of Burnside and Rosecrans was Union Gen. Henry M. Judah, commanding the 23rd Corps, a force variously estimated from 7,000 to 12,000 troops, headquartered in south central Kentucky at Glasgow. His assignment was to keep communications between the two Northern armies open, protect the railroad, and prevent raids from the Southern cavalry.[23]

On June 13, Morgan sent a message to Wheeler requesting authority for the raid. On June 14, Wheeler called on Bragg, and that same day, Wheeler wrote a message to Morgan reporting that Bragg approved the raid. Morgan was to take 1,500 men, not his entire command.[24]

Morgan's earlier successful raids in 1862 gave him every confidence that his even grander scheme could be implemented. When Bragg gave him permission to provide a diversion into Kentucky, Morgan was delighted. However, Duke reported that he was disappointed that Bragg ordered "him to confine himself to Kentucky." Duke also said that Bragg had encouraged Morgan to take Louisville, which was lightly defended at that time.[25]

New uniforms were issued to the men. Shedding their mix-and-match clothes used on the early raids, the men took on a more military look. By mid-1863, many had been able to capture their weapon of choice, the short or medium-length English Enfield, noted for its accuracy at long range and ease of carrying on a horse. The muzzle-loading Enfield could be fired at a rate of three shots a minute, and its dependability gave the user confidence. For close range firing, their favorite revolver was the Colt. 44 caliber, Model 1860, which Morgan himself carried.[26]

Mosgrove recalled that the cavalryman desired "a good horse, a Mexican saddle, a pair of big spurs with bells on them, a light long-range gun, a brace of Colt revolvers, a good blanket, some form of oil cloth, and a canteen of brandy sweetened with honey." Many of them wore large black or brown felt slouch hats, with the brim of one side turned up and pinned with a silver crescent or star.[27]

Morgan's Men would soon be coming home.

Morgan's Organization for the Great Raid of 1863

1st Brigade:	**Col. Basil Duke, commanding**
2nd Ky. Cav.	commanded by Major Thomas C. Webber
5th Ky. Cav.	commanded by Lt. Col. D. Howard Smith
6th Ky. Cav.	commanded by Col. J. Warren Grigsby
9th Tenn. Cav.	commanded by Col. William W. Ward
14th Ky. Cav.	commanded by Col. Richard C. Morgan
Total: 1,460	

2nd Brigade	**Col. Adam Rankin Johnson, commanding**
7th Ky. Cav. (3rd)	commanded by Lt. Col. John M. Huffman
8th Ky. Cav.	commanded by Col. Roy S. Cluke
10th Ky. Cav.	commanded by Col. Adam R. Johnson & Lt. Col. G. Wash Owen
11th Ky. Cav.	commanded by Col. D. Waller Chenault
Total: 1,000[3]	

Artillery

Kentucky Battery, Major Edward P. Byrne

2 3-inch Parrots (attached to the 1st Brigade)

2 12-pounder howitzers (attached to the 2nd Brigade)

Great Raid

Tom Jeffries

General John Hunt Morgan
Division Commander

First Brigade

Col. Basil W. Duke

Maj. Thomas C. Webber

Lt. Col. D. Howard Smith

Col. J. Warren Grigsby

Col. William W. Ward

Col. Richard C. Morgan

Second Brigade

Don Elmore

Col. Adam R. Johnson

Major Highley, Alabama

Bragg's Commissary Train

Maj. Edward P. Byrne, Artillery

Col. Roy S. Cluke

Lt. Col. G. Wash Owen

John Sickles

Col. D. Waller Chenault

Chapter Two: Taking the War to the North

General Morgan had an aggressive plan: go on the offensive; march across Kentucky; threaten Louisville; and cross the Ohio River into Indiana and Ohio. In short, seize the initiative, take the war to the North.[1]

Since he had already settled on his strategic plan, Morgan decided to disregard Bragg's orders. Long before he had permission for the raid, he sent his trusted scouts, Tom Hines and Sam Taylor, a nephew of Zachary Taylor, to reconnoiter the fords on the Ohio River, including the one at Buffington Island.[2]

The channel of the Ohio River has broadened through the years, but in 1863 when the water was unusually low, it could be easily forded, even walked across in places.[3] Still, the idea of moving an army of men and horses across a river such as the Ohio stuns people to this day. General Burnside observed, "I can scarcely believe that Morgan has crossed the river with his whole force."[4] Morgan was a risk-taker, and he was gambling that the weather and the gods would be on his side and he would be able to re-cross the Ohio on his return.

Colonels Duke and D. Howard Smith had misgivings about Morgan's grand scheme, but Morgan remained confident of its success. Smith pointed out that the plan called for two crossings of the Ohio, the success of which was wholly dependent on whether the Ohio was flooded or not. Union gunboats on the river might also prevent a re-crossing.[5] Colonel Johnson, however, favored the plan, stating in a letter to Morgan that he would be "willing to share any part of the blame attached to crossing the river" and that he approved it "then and will do so again if the opportunity offers."[6] Smith commented that if it worked, it would be "the most brilliant achievement of the war."[7]

Morgan reasoned that the raid into the North would not only cover Bragg's retreat, but it would also cause such excitement among the citizens along the invasion route that a Federal force would have to be diverted to pursue Morgan. As a result, Burnside's expected move to Tennessee to deal with Buckner would have to be delayed.

Morgan would prove to be correct in his assessment of the situation. Bragg completed his retreat to Chattanooga, and, instead of reaching Knoxville by July 9, Burnside did not arrive there until September 9.[8]

To carry out his grand strategy, Morgan needed more than the 1,500 troops authorized by General Bragg. Without revealing his true plans, Morgan convinced Wheeler that he needed additional troops. Morgan somehow secured more men than he had been allotted and soon had under his command 2,460 "of the best mounted and most effective men" in the Confederacy.[9]

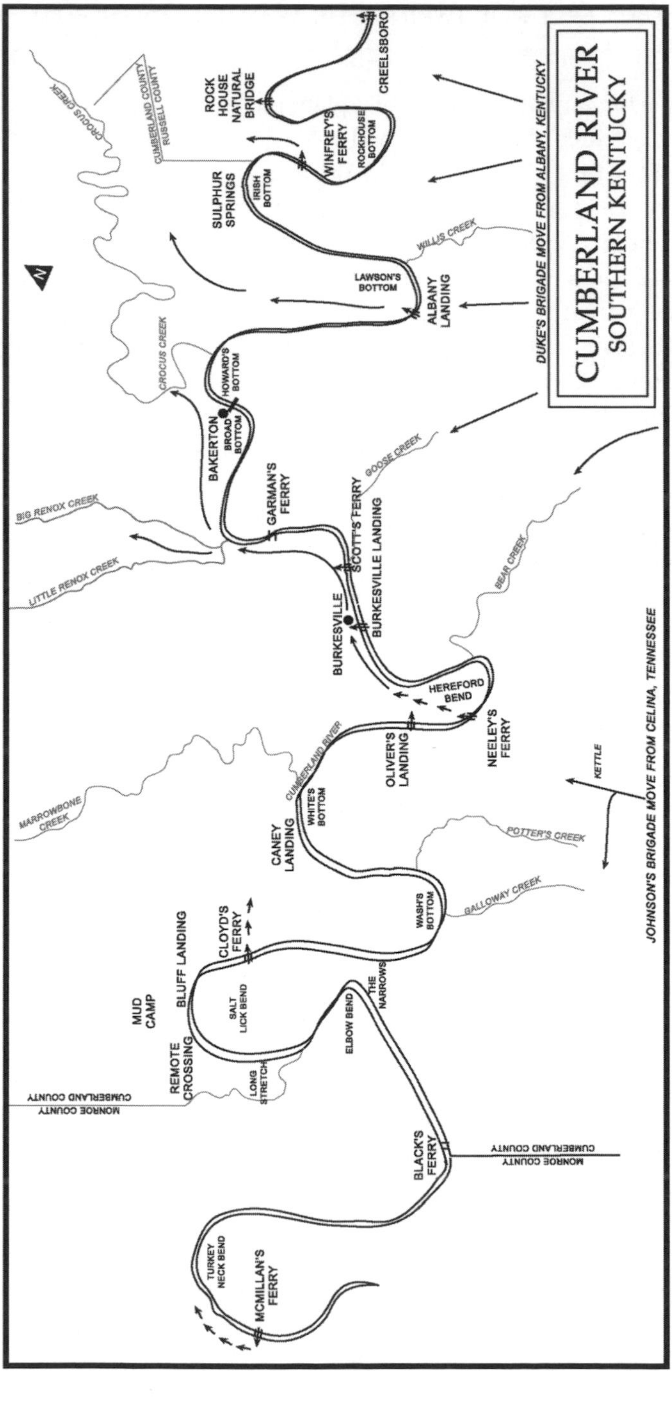

Map by Judy Ross

Cumberland River in Southern Kentucky, 1863

Bragg assigned a commissary train of six wagons to obtain food supplies for Morgan's troops and forage for his horses in Kentucky.[10] The train was supposed to rejoin Bragg's army in its withdrawal south into Tennessee, accompanied by an escorting regiment. In true Morgan fashion, he retained the commissary wagons and kept control of the regiment.[11]

All of Morgan's brothers, except young Key—Calvin, Richard, Charlton, and Tom—served with him on the Great Raid. Morgan created the 14th Kentucky for Richard, who had been on the staff of his brother-in-law, Gen. A.P. Hill, before this raid. The 14th was made up of three or four understrength companies including Major O.P. Hamilton's company of Tennessee and Kentucky conscripts, and, most important of all, Quirk's Scouts.

Colonel Dick's new regiment was beset with internal conflicts. The Scouts were generally unhappy with their reassignment, did not want to be reined in by their colonel's disciplinary measures, such as having to show up for roll call five times a day. They were gleeful when Hamilton's men left the command, had no regard for the conscripts, and still proudly referred to themselves as "Quirk's Scouts."[12]

Only a small detachment of the 9th Kentucky Cavalry, commanded by Col. W.C.P. Breckinridge of the 2nd Brigade, participated in this raid, often playing a prominent role as scouts. The diaries of Sgt. Henry L. Stone and Lt. Leeland Hathaway of this detachment are excellent sources of information about the Great Raid. The main body of the regiment initially remained at McMinnville. It was expected to join Morgan at the Ohio River, but failing to arrive on time, did not take part in the raid.[13]

Morgan recognized that his troops would face four difficult problems: crossing the Cumberland River, crossing the Ohio River, bypassing Cincinnati, and re-crossing the Ohio.[14]

First Brigade (Duke's) Delayed

Morgan's force set out from Alexandria, Tennessee, on June 11, and crossed the Cumberland River on June 20, while a detachment captured a mail train and a sutler's wagon. Unexpectedly, Bragg ordered Morgan to intercept Union Col. William P. Sanders' troops entering East Tennessee from Kentucky. Duke's 1st Brigade was dispatched to Monticello to stop Sanders. The roads between Carthage and Monticello were paths running atop curving ridge lines and through narrow creek valleys. The torturous roads and torrents of rain in late June in southern Kentucky and Tennessee made the advance painfully slow and difficult, particularly for artillery. Duke arrived at Albany three days late to learn that Saunders and his troops had already slipped into East Tennessee.[15]

2nd Brigade (Johnson's) Moves to Kentucky

Tuesday, June 23, Morgan ordered the regiments to move toward Burkesville using parallel roads. Chenault's 11th Kentucky Cavalry left Tennessee, marching on the Celina Road into Cumberland County, Kentucky. They crossed the Tennessee-Kentucky state line at Embry's and turned west into Monroe County. By evening they had encamped in their old quarters in Turkey Neck Bend of the Cumberland River. Chenault again established his headquarters at the Andrews' farm. Major McCreary declared of Mrs. Andrews, who welcomed them, that there "was no better, truer, or kinder woman" and described the area as "a fertile and pleasant valley, flowing with milk and honey."[16]

This level bottom land had been lived in by the Coe family for generations. Turkey Neck Bend Baptist Church, with large forsythia bushes, sat as a sentinel on the hill overlooking the farms. On the southern side of the horseshoe-shaped bottom, the ferry over the Cumberland was operated by McMillan, a Southern sympathizer and father of Benton McMillan, a future governor of Tennessee. Colonel Johnson sent Capt. Fielding Helm's scouts to reconnoiter the crossing there and obtain boats.[17]

On Saturday, June 27, more of the 2nd Brigade moved from its Tennessee campsites toward Kentucky. They passed through Livingston, Tennessee, and camped on the Johnston and Armstrong farms on the Obey River, which flows into the Cumberland in northern Tennessee.[18] On June 28, the Obey, a half-mile wide when flooded, was too high to ford.[19] Rebel scout Burke described the difficult crossing, which fortunately met no enemy opposition:

> The first company [of Quirk's Scouts] took the saddles off of their horses and drove them into the river and made them swim across and the saddles and men were taken over in a canoe. The other companies followed suit . . . . I crossed with a detail near the first to catch the horses

Bottomland of Turkey Neck Bend

McMillan's Ferry, Monroe County

Obey River, northern Tennessee

> and tie them up as they crossed. Capt. [Thomas] Quirk and a lot of the boys went in swimming. As soon as all of our company got across and saddled up, we moved up apiece and dismounted in the woods to await the arrival of the balance.[20]

Colonel Cluke's 8th Kentucky Cavalry camped with the 11th Kentucky in Turkey Neck Bend, but after a few days, moved their camp to Salt Lick Bend.[21] From there they crossed the Cumberland.

Scouting for the Second Brigade, Curtis Burke traveled further north into Cumberland County and turned into White's Bottom of the Cumberland River. The land there, much like Salt Lick and Turkey Neck bends, is a wide, level bottom with high hills surrounding it. The Scouts split up into small groups and went to different houses to secure food. It is reported that some of them raced through the center hall of a house near Oliver's Ferry, smearing grease from the meat confiscated there on the walls and furnishings. They also feasted on dewberries from Ferryman Richards' fine patch.[22]

Not far from the Confederate camps and the ferry crossings of the Cumberland in Turkey Neck, Salt Lick, and White's Bottom, there was a large Federal encampment at Marrowbone, probably on Hominy Creek.[23]

Crossing the Cumberland River

"Heard that the Comd was camped up and down the Cumberland for 20 miles." J. D. Sprake, 8th Kentucky Cavalry, CSA

"It is my understanding that Morgan's Men crossed all up and down the Cumberland, using many different ferry crossings." Randolph Smith, Cumberland County historian

Neeley's Ferry Crossing, Cumberland County

Cumberland River at Neeley's Ferry

The Cumberland River, the headwaters of which are in Letcher County, Kentucky, snakes through the middle of Cumberland County southwest to Tennessee. Its fertile lowlands are flooded after heavy rains.

In the early evening of June 30, Col. Dick Morgan's 14th Kentucky moved toward Burkesville and began crossing the Cumberland.[24] Three miles below Burkesville at Neeley's Ferry, the scouts moved across the river and placed beacons on the opposite bank. The difficult crossing continued all through the night, but only the first two companies of the regiment got across. The Cumberland, like the Obey, was one-quarter mile to one-half mile wide in places. Scout Burke wrote:

> We had to take our horses some distance above the regular entrance to the river, so that the swift current would not wash the horses too far below the landing on the other side. We would unsaddle our horses, lead six or eight of them to the edge of the water, then let them loose and the boys would get around them and rive them in with sticks, clods of earth, and rocks. If one started across the balance would follow, but most of the time we had to holler and pelt them a good deal before they would make the trip. The bank was steep and rocky. Some felled down and skinned their

> legs badly. Several canoe loads of the boys were over on the other side catching the horses as they crossed.[25]

Captain Quirk, with Company C, decided to wait until the morning of July 1 to complete their crossing. The scouts already across the river joined the rest of the 14th Kentucky camped in a stable yard four miles west of Burkesville on the Glasgow Road.[26] Burke reports that they had been warned to anticipate attack at any moment.[27]

Gen. Henry Judah, at Paces Cross Roads in Metcalfe County, was convinced that the river was too high to be crossed by the Confederates. He only ordered light pickets at the fords.

1st Brigade Crossing, July 1–2

In late June, Duke's 1st Brigade, with the artillery of both the 1st and the 2nd brigades, as well as Bragg's commissary train, departed from Albany. They camped south of Burkesville, from White's Bottom to Irish Bottom. Most of the men were Kentuckians and excited to be going home.

A squad of troops arrived at Caleb Radford's farm on Brush Creek and asked his wife Elizabeth to cook for them. Elizabeth had already prepared meals for Union troops, now she was using her last chickens to cook for the Rebs. A lover of fine horses, Caleb wanted to keep the raiders at the house instead of letting them wander around his farm. He tried to protect his horses by hiding them in a specially built pen in the hollow far away from the house.[28]

Only Morgan's senior officers were aware of his complete plan for the raid. While waiting for Morgan's return from McMinnville where he was getting ammunition and six more wagons of supplies, the troopers, knowing there would soon be a battle, checked their weapons, equipment, and rations.[29]

In order to get his brigade across the Cumberland as quickly as possible, Duke divided it into three groups. The first was to use the ferries in the Irish Bottom area at Bakerton and Winfrey's. The second, together with the artillery, was to move through Forest Cottage and cross at Scott's Ferry, just above Burkesville. Here they were watched by the Thrasher children, Emma and John, from a hayloft in which they were hiding. The soldiers came to the Thrasher place in late afternoon, camped there during the night, and left the next morning, taking horses and all the food they could carry. The third group was to move from Albany to Burkesville via Green Grove and Modoc, and along Bear Creek [today Hwy 90] to cross at Burkesville and Neeley's ferries. This group, which included most of the 2nd Kentucky, camped in White's Bottom for a couple days before crossing at Neeley's.[30] According to a story handed down in the Rush family for generations, General Morgan stayed at the Rush House on Bear Creek at this time.[31]

Pvt. William A. Milton of Company A, 2nd Kentucky, told what happened on July 1: "We broke camp and reached the McNealy's ferry about noon. Our company and a portion of Co. B crossed by dark." He added that the rest of the regiment made it across by 8 o'clock in the morning of July 2.[32]

Duke observed: "The first brigade had, with which to cross the men and their accouterments and artillery, only two crazy little flats, that seemed ready to sink under the weight of a single man, and two or three canoes." Fortunately for the 1st Brigade, they met only light opposition from Wolford's cavalry pickets in and around Burkesville.[33]

No man who made these crossings ever forgot it. Henry L. Stone crossed with twelve others in a canoe, taking their saddles with them. About the experience, he wrote: "The surging waves came lapping up to within three inches of the edges of the canoe. . . . The two men at the oars were inexperienced . . . but finally landed us safely on this side. I breathed much freer when I got out."[34]

Henry Lane Stone

Pvt. John Weathered, 9th Tennessee Cavalry, reported that about one hundred cavalrymen at a time, together with their blankets and saddles, crossed in an old flatboat. He said that the horses swam the river and then were held on the far bank until their owners claimed them.[35]

At Scott's Ferry, Pvt. Bennett Young, a member of Quirk's scouts, vividly described the crossing:

> The saddles, guns, ammunition, cannon and clothing were placed in the ferryboat, and regiments one at a time were brought down to the river. The horses with their bridles and halters were driven into the stream and forced to take their chances, not only with the rapid current, but with the driftwood, which was very abundant and large. At some places it covered almost the entire surface. The stream was five-eighths of a mile wide. Many of the men clung to the ferryboat and thus swam across. Some held to the canoes and floated by their side, while others swam with their horses, holding to their manes or tails to prevent being swept down stream by its fierce tides.[36]

Bennett Young

He also recounted the first detachment's encounter with the Yankees on the far side of the river:

> The Confederates who were in the ferryboat and canoe with their clothes on, rushed into line, while those who swam, unwilling to be laggard, not halting to dress, seized their cartridge boxes and guns[already on the bank after being brought across in canoes] and rushed upon the enemy. The strange sight of naked men engaging in combat . . . amazed the enemy.[37]

According to Sgt. John W. Shely's Memorandum Book, Smith's 5th Kentucky also crossed at Scott's.[38]

As soon as Morgan came into the town square at Burkesville, he dispatched Company E under Capt. Mike Salter, 7th Kentucky, and a few other volunteers, up river to destroy the telegraph wire. They rejoined the main force at Green River Bridge. The company departed and was near the line at Jamestown when they ran into enemy fire that scattered the men. It is not clear if these men accomplished their mission, but before the day was over, the line was cut.[39]

Back at the Burkesville Landings, wagons had to be offloaded, disassembled, loaded on the makeshift rafts, then reassembled and the cargo reloaded on the other side.[40] While waiting in Burkesville for provisions to be brought up from the boats, the men heard skirmish fire to the west of town on the Marrowbone and Glasgow Road. Some of the 14th Kentucky had come into contact with enemy pickets.

Morgan ordered Captain Quirk and fifteen men from various companies to reconnoiter enemy strength. By mid-afternoon of July 2, Ward's 9th Tennessee and Grigsby's 6th Kentucky with two artillery pieces had got across and could be deployed. By this time Morgan was aware that a serious situation might be developing to the west of town. He ordered Colonel Ward and his men, supported by Colonel Grigsby's regiment, to deal with it. Led by Morgan, they dashed out the Glasgow Road to help the scouts who were exchanging fire with the enemy.[41]

Skirmish at Norris Branch—July 2

In the Norris Branch area of the Marrowbone-Glasgow Road, Morgan hid his men in an ambush and surprised the head of a 300-man Yankee cavalry column with rifle and artillery fire. The Yanks quickly turned their mounts and spurred them back down the road. With a whoop, the Rebels tore after the bluecoats. Scout Kelion Peddicord wrote:

> When the enemy realized the smallness of the force that was chasing them, they halted in a strong position, and showed fight, but our General . . . was too shrewd for them.

Norris Branch Skirmish, Cumberland County

> Quickly detaching a single scout around to their left flank secretly, with orders to fire his gun [rifle,] and navies [pistols] in rapid succession into their line. . . . Back they flew again, using their spurs . . . [42]

Morgan, on Glencoe, rode behind the scouts, "hat in hand, cheering the boys with 'Charge them, boys, charge them!'"[43]

The ensuing rout raised such a cloud of dust that the Southerners could not see a regiment of Northern infantry which had formed in line of battle. One of Quirk's scouts, spotting the enemy through the haze, grabbed the reins of Morgan's horse and the charge was stopped. At that moment the Yanks fired a volley into the Rebels at short range. The shots surprised Maj. William P. Elliott knocking him off his horse. In the exchange of fire that followed, Morgan's men sustained two mortally wounded and two others slightly wounded. Federal losses were five killed, fifteen wounded.[44]

Capt. Tom Quirk received a severe wound in his left wrist and his rein arm was broken. He had to be taken to Tennessee to recover. He may have lain for a while under a tree at an old red brick house on Norris Branch, which still has bullet holes in its walls.[45]

This encounter with the Yanks took Morgan's chief scout out of action for the Great Raid. Morgan would begin his thousand-mile incursion into Kentucky, Indiana, and Ohio without his "eyes and ears." Quirk, who had rescued Colonel Duke from the Rolling Fork River during the Christmas Raid of 1862, would be

Old Brick House on Norris Branch, Cumberland County

sorely missed. Two days later, Morgan will pay a great price for the poor scouting of the strong Union position at Tebbs Bend of Green River.

P.H. Burns, 22nd Indiana Battery, reported that this had been their "first experience to face the enemy" when "a little skirmishing was had in some of the ravines as he [Morgan] came over, but the old fox slipped around us, and then began the race."[46]

2nd Brigade Crossing the Cumberland, July 2

"We were in Turkey Neck Bend and were expected to cross at that point, which we did under many difficulites."[47] Pvt. L.D. Hockersmith, Co C, 10th KY Cavalry, CSA

Porter Harned

Lorenzo D. Hockersmith

At McMillan's Ferry, Private Hockersmith saw a large force of Federals on the opposite side of the river. From his report, Colonel Johnson anticipated that the 2nd Brigade's crossing would be strongly opposed. He directed his regiments to cross at various other points, retaining the plan of taking the 10th Kentucky across at McMillan's Ferry from their camp at Turkey Neck Bend.

The men had very few adequate boats at their disposal here, but the ready use of McMillan's ferryboat to carry troops and their equipment may have encouraged them to attempt the crossing. Johnson wrote that "no boats were large enough to carry a horse."[48] Besides this, Federal General Hobson's large force was camped at Marrowbone, just eight miles away.

Captain Helm of the 10th Kentucky, on return from a scouting mission, reported to Colonel Johnson that the road they would have to take was heavily picketed. Johnson dispatched Captain Tipton's Company of the 8th Kentucky, Capt. J.R. Bennett's Company of the 10th Kentucky, together with Helm's scouts, to drive in the enemy pickets.

After crossing the river on July 2, the 10th Kentucky set off in a heavy evening fog which provided cover for their movement. Since they had camped in the area for months at a time, they had no trouble finding a familiar road along the river, following it for some distance, and soon arrived in Burkesville.[49]

Salt Lick Bend, Cumberland County

Durning the night of July 1, continuing into the day of July 2, Rebel troops crossed the Cumberland River at the Burkesville Ferry Landing. A full moon aided the operation.

Cluke's 8th Kentucky started crossing the Cumberland at Salt Lick Bend, using what today is called Cloyd's Ferry on the morning of July 2. Its advance guard almost immediately came in contact with enemy pickets about one mile from the river and fought them during the day, while the rest of the troops continued to cross throughout the day and into the night. Trooper John D. Sprake of the 8th Kentucky, wrote that they "slept on arms all night" after crossing the river.[50]

The 11th Kentucky camped in Turkey Neck until ordered to cross at the Burkesville Ferry. McCreary wrote: "We swam the horses and many of the men. The command has fought the enemy and driven them out of the way. We are rear guard and got the whole Regiment across at 1 P.M."[51]

Having dealt with Union resistance, the 1st and 2nd Brigades concentrated in Burkesville. Some soldiers rode around the courthouse square, others made small purchases in the stores, but most waited for rations to arrive. The hungry soldiers had been told that six wagons of crackers were crossing the Cumberland with Colonel Duke's forces and expected to arrive at any moment. Unfortunately, no rations appeared because the boats were in use transporting the troops and military supplies.[52]

The resistance that the Rebels encountered around Burkesville came from Col. Frank Wolford's cavalry force made up of components of the 1st Kentucky

Cavalry, the 45th Ohio Mounted Infantry, and Ohio 2nd Cavalry stationed at Jamestown. Wolford reported to Brig. Gen. Samuel P. Carter at Somerset.

Lt. A.T. Keen of Company I, 1st Kentucky Cavalry, and some of his men, joined a detachment of the 45th Ohio which was involved in the skirmish with Morgan's troops after their crossing at Scott's Ferry. A wounded scout from this detachment was left in the care of a woman who, at his request, rode to Somerset and informed General Carter that the Rebels were already across the Cumberland.[53]

On the afternoon of July 2, the two brigades set off for Columbia, Duke's brigade taking the shorter route along Crocus Creek, and Johnson's traveling the longer route, up Little and Big Renox Creeks. These parallel routes, covering about 30 miles, were dirt roads, crossing sizeable hills. Familiar with the terrain, McCreary wrote that the troops had the prospect of a dark, rough march before them.[54] A Union soldier hid in a closet under the pie-shaped stairway of a brick 1818 house on Allen Branch while the Rebel troops rode past.[55]

Even in 1940, the roads were so poor, it took three and half hours in a car to drive from Burkesville to Columbia via Crocus Creek. The road up Renox was even worse.[56]

Maj. Gen. George L. Hartsuff, 23rd Corps

The Federal Response: Lost Opportunity

Major General George Lucas Hartsuff, commanding the newly formed 23rd Army Corps, had responsibility for guarding railroads and Union supply depots in Kentucky. Its 3rd Division, commanded by Judah, occupied Bowling Green, Glasgow, Columbia, and other points along the Cumberland. Judah's corps consisted of three brigades: the 1st at Glasgow, commanded by Gen. Mahlon Manson; the 2nd at Columbia, commanded by Gen. Edward H. Hobson; and the 3rd at

Carthage, Tennessee, commanded of Gen. J.A. Cooper. Gen. James M. Shackelford's brigade, of the 2nd Division, was stationed at Russellville.[57]

Although equal in rank, General Judah had seniority over General Hobson, a Greensburg banker and businessman whose military experience came from his service in the Mexican War. Judah, a native of Maryland, was a West Point graduate and a career military man.[58]

Knowing the area, Hobson wanted to close the gap in the Northern defense along the Cumberland River at Burkesville. Judah was not convinced by Hobson's reasoning that Morgan would attempt to cross the Cumberland there. He ordered Hobson to Glover's Creek, ten miles southeast of Glasgow, where he remained until June 28. While there, Hobson scouted the area and gained intelligence that Morgan's men were moving their regiments from Tennessee toward the Cumberland. On June 30, Hobson, with the 12th Kentucky Cavalry and some of the 9th Cavalry, went to Tompkinsville. While there, Hobson learned that Rebel Colonel Johnson's Brigade was in Turkey Neck Bend, just eight miles away. Hobson rode out to a point on a high bank of the river where he could observe Johnson's position, some 300 yards away.

On June 30, Judah arrived and was briefed by Hobson, who asked permission for a night attack on Johnson's brigade. Hobson also suggested a brigade might be sent to Burkesville to hold the road from Columbia and to prevent the Confederates from crossing at Scott's Ferry. Judah denied both these requests and ordered Hobson to depart for Marrowbone, ten miles west of Burkesville, at 6 A.M. the next morning. He was to block all roads leading to Marrowbone from the Cumberland River except the one from Burkesville and to defend that by some means, permit his advance, if necessary.[59] In the meantime, Shackelford's brigade was ordered to Ray's Cross Roads, called Smith's Crossroads today, in Metcalfe County, to support Hobson at Marrowbone. General Manson was ordered to Tompkinsville. All were to be controlled from Judah's headquarters in Glasgow.

Judah telegraphed Hartsuff: "This disposition protects all west of Columbia. . . . I presume Carter to be at Jamestown and that he can protect Columbia from any advance." It seems he considered Burkesville and Columbia out of his territorial command.[60]

Union telegraphic messages reveal that Hartsuff was receiving information from May 30 to June 30 that Morgan's forces were mainly camped opposite Rowena, Creelsboro, and in Long Bottom of Cumberland County, territory of General Carter. Judah's report to Hartsuff then proceeded to give contradictory intentions. He said that he could "attack at Burkesville moving on concentric lines." Hobson had reported that a drunk telegraph operator at Columbia had been giving contradictory messages for two days. It seems the condition was contagious.[61]

Troops Moving out of the Federal Camp at Marrowbone, Cumberland County

Not to be outdone, on July 2 Hobson sent a force out from Marrowbone to catch Morgan, led by Lt. Col. James H. Holloway, with a detachment of the 3rd and 8th Kentucky cavalries. They were followed by the remainder of Col. Benjamin H. Bristow's 8th Kentucky Cavalry, Col. William A. Hoskins' 12th Kentucky Infantry, Lt. Col. Mehringer's 91st Indiana Infantry, Captain Denning's 22nd Indiana Battery, and Captain Hammond's artillery section, Company K of the 65th Indiana. They had just begun their march when the unfathomable happened. Three miles out the Burkesville Road, Hobson received an order from Judah, his superior officer, to halt and return to Marrowbone![62]

Hobson then dispatched Col. Richard C. Jacob, commanding the 9th Kentucky Cavalry, to overtake and bring back the Federal cavalrymen.

Rebel Ride between Burkesville and Columbia, July 2–3, 1863

The troops in Duke's 1st Brigade rode along Crocus Creek, fully aware that Wolford's Cavalry was headquartered at Jamestown, some forty miles away on their right flank. Fronting the Crocus road to Columbia, Dr. Thomas Baker's two-story Greek revival house was an easy target. The troops "borrowed" one of the family slaves and forced him to guide them all the way to Columbia. The white and the black families of the Bakers were so upset that Doctor Baker saddled up the only horse that Morgan had left him and rode off after the troops toward Columbia. He found the offending regiment there and brought the slave, a valued family member, home.[63]

Some of Quirk's Scouts had not accompanied the 1st Brigade, remaining in Burkesville, anticipating the early arrival of the supply wagons. When their crossing was delayed, the scouts set out from Burkesville "riding lively," [drinking whiskey] caught up and passed Capt. Jim Murphy's small squad of scouts, and rejoined the brigade.

One of Duke's regiments was already six miles up the road to Columbia and had camped in a bottom at a schoolhouse near the present location of Jones Chapel Church. General Morgan came to the camp with the news that Captain Quirk had been wounded in the arm and would not be returning to his unit.

Although disheartened by this information, Private Burke rode out looking for something to fill his empty stomach. It is not surprising that the men had difficulty securing meals in this thinly populated and hilly country. Burke commented: "I saddled up and went down a creek a mile stopping at several houses to get my supper and get something for the mess, but every house was full of soldiers." Finally, his lot changed. He rode up another creek and bummed three pones of cornbread and some fried bacon for a dollar.[64]

After darkness fell, the regiments moved up the road two more miles and "camped in a lot near a large white house." Since family members of the Elliott and Rowe plantations tell that Morgan's troopers raced across their land, it is probable that some of the men camped there for the night of July 2.[65] Heavy pickets were on the roads and, as usual, Chenault's regiment was protecting the rear.[66]

Friday, July 3, opened cloudy. Scout Burke spent his early morning looking for forage for his horse. A crib at a nearby farm solved this problem. But then, as hundreds of others, he rode off looking for food for himself. After several miles, he was able to buy two biscuits, some meat, and rye coffee for a dollar. The search for food required so much time that, when he returned to the main road, his regiment had left him behind. Burke hurried on ahead and "came upon several yoke of oxen at the foot of a long steep hill waiting to pull the artillery up."

After Burke ascended the Dug Hill, he found most of the 1st Brigade resting, some sleeping, and some shoeing horses. It started sprinkling rain which cut the heat of the hot day. Later the troops were drenched. It was then about 10 A.M.[67]

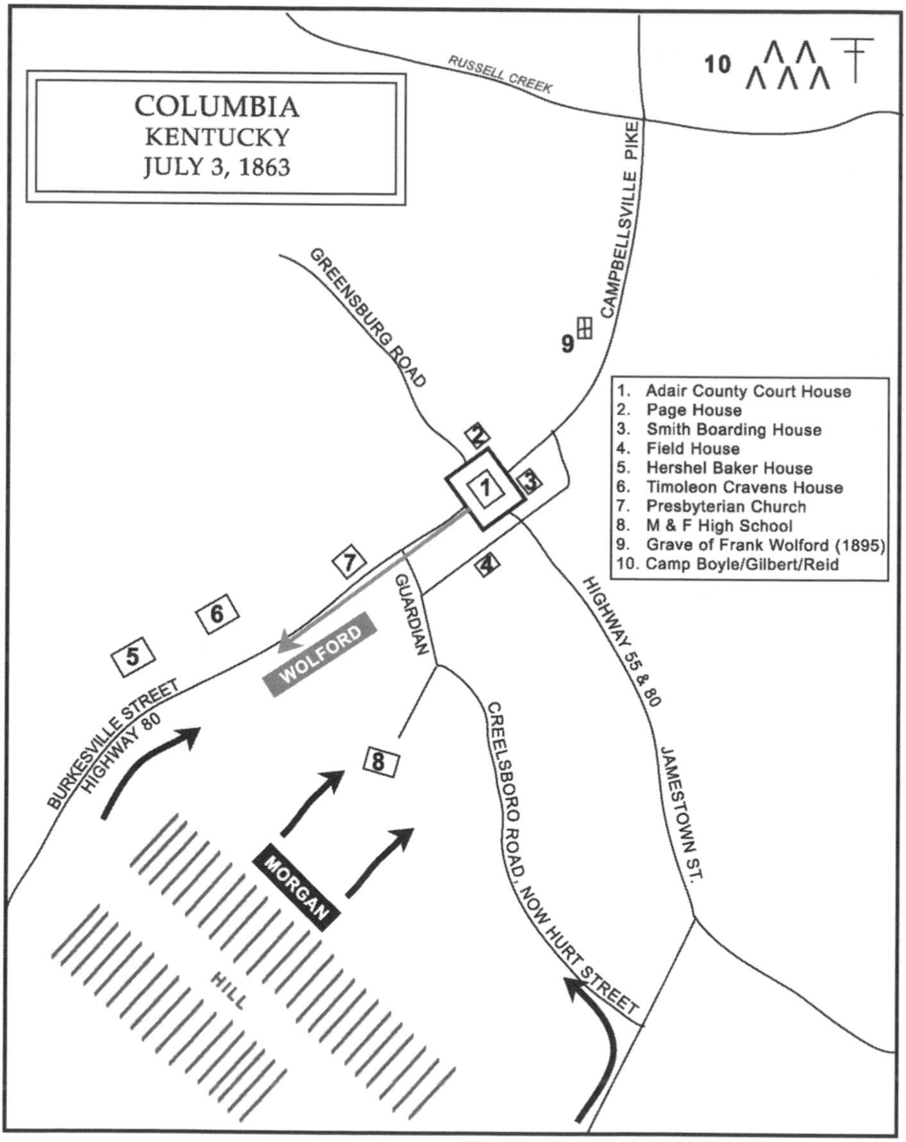
COLUMBIA
KENTUCKY
JULY 3, 1863
RUSSELL CREEK
CAMPBELLSVILLE PIKE
GREENSBURG ROAD
GUARDIAN
WOLFORD
BURKESVILLE STREET
HIGHWAY 80
HIGHWAY 55 & 80
JAMESTOWN ST.
CREELSBORO ROAD, NOW HURT STREET
MORGAN
HILL
1. Adair County Court House
2. Page House
3. Smith Boarding House
4. Field House
5. Hershel Baker House
6. Timoleon Cravens House
7. Presbyterian Church
8. M & F High School
9. Grave of Frank Wolford (1895)
10. Camp Boyle/Gilbert/Reid

Map by Judy Ross

Skirmish at Columbia, July 3

For weeks Wolford's cavalry had been patrolling the Cumberland and exchanging shots with the enemy across the river. On July 2 they were alerted by patrols at Burkesville that Morgan was approaching. On July 3 Capt. Jesse Carter, with 150 men, was sent to defend Columbia. His detachment included men from the 1st Kentucky Cavalry, 45th Ohio Infantry (mounted), and 2nd and 7th Ohio cavalry. Carter had been a leader in the chase to capture Morgan at Lebanon, Tennessee, and now the opportunity to seize him presented itself again.[68]

About 1 1/2 miles from Columbia, Morgan's videttes, led by Lt. Winder Monroe, came in contact with Wolford's pickets, Sgt. R.T. Pierce and Texton Sharp, and fell back under "close and well sustained" Union fire, pursued by the Yankees. Both sides sent couriers to the rear: Morgan's men to request support from the advanced guard and the Federals to inform Captain Carter that fifteen Rebels had been encountered on the Burkesville Road.[69]

In response, Morgan's advance guard, led by Colonel Dick Morgan, dashed forward at a gallop until they came under fire from Federal cavalrymen. The advance guard and scouts halted, returned fire, and then charged. The Yanks withdrew to Columbia and rejoined their comrades around the Main Square.

Capt. Jacob T. Cassell, commanding Quirk's Scouts, was severely wounded in the thigh while leading a charge. Leeland Hathaway, known for his indifference to danger and coolness under fire, took charge and saw that Cassell was carried to the rear, put in an ambulance wagon, and given treatment. Cassell accompanied Morgan's men as they advanced through Kentucky and crossed the Ohio with the troops, luckily evading capture in Ohio. Cassell was replaced as leader of Quirk's Scouts by Capt. Tom Franks.[70]

In response to a request for help and hearing the sound of gunshots, Duke's regiment hurried forward with its artillery, with the 7th Kentucky in support. The Rebels, who now greatly outnumbered the Federals, concentrated behind Guardian Street Hill and prepared to attack, dismounted. Some of the scouts, including Burke, Henry Allen, and John Wilson, were left behind the old M&F School to hold the horses. Burke managed to place himself where he could see the progress of the fight. Lt. Ben Drake of 2nd Kentucky, Company L, was overheard saying to his men, "There is only half a Yank apiece and I want you to go for them."[71]

When the war broke out, Jesse Carter of Burkesville had gathered a company of loyal Union men together and they were sworn in as part of Wolford's 1st Kentucky Cavalry. Carter, highly respected for his courage and as a leader of men, was made captain.

Old M&F High School, Guardian Street Hill, Columbia

Leeland Hathaway

Alerted by the courier, Captain Carter left the Public Square and led a squad up the Burkesville and Glasgow Road, today's Burkesville Street. Leaning forward in his saddle, he passed Union Col. Thomas Bramlette's residence on the left, the brick Presbyterian Church on the right, and the large white frame home of Timoleon Cravens, where Morgan had stopped during his Christmas Raid, further along on the right.

Near the Baker House, Carter came upon Sergeant Pierce, who had been slightly wounded in the skirmish out the road and was riding a severely injured horse. From Pierce, Carter learned that Morgan's men were just over the hill in considerable strength. He ordered Pierce to return to town for reinforcements.[72]

Near a persimmon tree in the front yard of the Cravens House near the street, a shot rang out and struck Carter in the chest.[73] Barely clinging to his saddle, he turned his horse back toward the square, stumbled into the town hotel, his headquarters [maybe the Page House], and collapsed. Sergeant Pierce followed him to his room, where the captain was lying on his face in great agony.[74]

Hershel Baker was awakened from an afternoon nap by the shots. Looking out the upstairs window of his house on Burkesville Street, he saw a lone horseman being pursued by a squad of pistol-firing Rebels. Now fully awakened, he remembered what his neighbor, Timoleon Cravens, had told him, "We will have Confederate troops here very soon."

Continuing to watch, Hershel was astonished to see hundreds of Rebel soldiers positioned just under the brow of the hill from the old Creelsboro Road [Hurt Street] to the Burkesville Road. He watched them take cover in the apple orchard near the two-story frame Rosenfield House, now Angel Manor. He

Page House, Columbia

Baker House, Columbia

Hershel Baker

watched as Captain Carter came up the hill, completely exposed to the enemy, in the middle of the road, while his comrades were creeping up the street taking cover behind snaked rail fences. Another squad of Federals rode up Guardian Street toward the M & F High School, now Adanta. He felt helpless, unable to warn Jesse Carter, of his hazardous situation. He could see Federals taking positions behind the Cravens house and others creeping under his window and across his yard.

With a wild yell, the Rebels began pouring over Guardian Street Hill and in behind Baker's house coming down into the yard of his neighbor, Timoleon Cravens. He watched the Federals taking cover behind the wooden fences and houses along the street, firing their weapons as they withdrew through the back-yards, hiding behind stables, barns, and outbuildings, moving toward the Public Square.[75] As Hathaway described it, the men in grey were met by "galling fire from troops stationed behind the houses." He claimed that he "led the regiment into the streets, dismounted, and drove the Yankees out of the houses and had complete possession of the town and a squad of prisoners before [Capt. A. A.] Norris or Lt. Col. Huffman . . . came up."[76] Burke reported that the "firing was brisk for half an hour."[77]

Young Baker was still at his window when he saw Rebel soldiers move past, some crossing Burkesville Street and surrounding his house. Soon there was pounding on the front door. The family kitchen at the back of the house was surrounded by Rebels.

Baker, a graduate of Centre College in Danville, realized that he could be conscripted into Morgan's army. He unlocked and opened the door cautiously. The soldiers rushed in, with pistols out, and questioned Baker, "Where are the soldiers in this house?" He assured them that he had locked the door and that no one had fired at them from the house. Not satisfied, they continued to badger him. One of the soldiers knew Baker from Centre and urged his fellow Rebels to put their pistols away. "I know him, and whatever he says is true." Relieved, the two college friends shook hands.[78] Baker was asked, possibly by Tom Morgan who was known for his musical ability, "Can you sing?" Baker replied, "I am the only tenor in the Presbyterian Choir." That seemed to please the men. They let young Baker go free.[79]

After the fight, Baker went out into his yard. He saw one of the Federals who had passed under his window lying near their side gate with a seriously wounded leg. He saw three or four Rebels lying beside the road, now Burkesville Street, on improvised stretchers made of boards.[80] Others were brought to Cravens' porch that ran alongside the house.[81]

Old Adair County Courthouse

Wolford's Cavalry, in the previous months, had occupied the Adair County Courthouse and issued commissary supplies from there.[82] Columbia was no longer theirs.

Realizing that they could not engage Morgan's entire force, they kept up the firing as they withdrew. They headed out the Jamestown Road. An Ohio cavalryman reported, "We thought it might be a small force we could crush. But when we fired musketry we were answered with grape and canister; when we fired a few rifle shots we were answered with whole volleys of musketry. We speedily beat a hasty retreat, going as fast as our horses would carry us to Jamestown."[83]

It is uncertain if Wolford himself participated in this skirmish, but hearing that Morgan was heading north, he directed his family to hide in Todd's Cave. They stayed there for nine days, until the threat of Morgan was gone.[84]

Lt. Col. R.A. Alston, Morgan's adjutant, recorded that the Rebels lost two killed and two wounded, one of the wounded being Cassell. Curtis Burke, while a horse holder, saw one of the bodies of Captain Drake's men being returned to Company L, with a blanket wrapped around it. Burke gave Yankee losses as four killed and six to eight wounded.[85] The Presbyterian Church was reportedly used as a temporary hospital.[86]

Presbyterian Church

Columbia's Public Square became the site of the Confederate victory celebration. The Commissary issued "buttercrackers and bacon" and "liberated" whiskey from the stores got some of the boys "pretty jolly."[87]

General Morgan was informed of the theft of goods from merchants, and he ordered that everything be paid for. Colonel Alston was ashamed of the behavior of some soldiers: "These outrages are very disgraceful, and are usually perpetrated by men accompanying the army simply for plunder. They are not worth a ——."[88]

Captain Carter, lying mortally wounded in the town hotel on the corner of Greensburg Street after having fallen into Confederate hands, could hear the clamor and uproar through the shuttered windows of his room. Peddicord, a Quirk scout, recorded that, as Carter lay dying, he was visited by the Southern soldier who had wounded him. Carter consoled the man, saying that "he shot him in self-defense and while in the service of his country." Peddicord adds that "the gallant Captain sure met his fate soldierly."[89]

It is also reported that a Union detachment of 150 men, led by Lt. Col. Silas Adams, returned to the edge of Columbia during the night and that Lt. Keen slipped into Columbia to see Captain Carter, but it must have been quite late. Hershel Baker reported that his good friend, Captain Carter, whom he described as "brave as the bravest," died around midnight. Carter's body was taken back home to Burkesville and buried on a high hill overlooking the Cumberland River.[90]

Silas Adams, USA

Kel Peddicord, CSA

The story is told that Morgan wanted to burn the Columbia Courthouse since it had been a Federal outpost. A widow lady, Mrs. Lillie Smith, ran a popular boarding house directly across the street on the Public Square. A great cook, she also had the power of persuasion. She begged Morgan not to set the courthouse ablaze for she was afraid it would spread to her rooming house. Apparently she got out her handkerchief to demonstrate the direction of the wind, showing that her rooming house would be doomed if a fire were started. Morgan obliged her.[91]

Randy Flowers

Pvt. Creed Hood, CSA

Pvt. Creed Hood, Co H, 2nd Kentucky, riding with Morgan, thought this would be a good time to visit his parents in Cyclone, a community north of Columbia. Alas, he stayed too long and the pursuing Yankees captured him. He paid dearly for being a good son, spending the next twenty-one months as a prisoner at Camp Douglas.[92]

Some Confederates did not come through Columbia. They had crossed at upper fords of the Cumberland and they were crossing Adair County riding through an area known as Egypt. The Dillinghams were ready, however. Their daughter, Audra, had taken her show horses to the back of their farm and hidden them in a clump of trees.[93]

At Columbia nimble-fingered Ellsworth followed a different path north. He rode to Greensburg, Hodgenville, New Haven, and Lebanon Junction where he tapped into the telegraph lines to confuse the Yanks about Morgan's troop disposition.[94]

In the late afternoon of July 3, Morgan's regiments began filing out of Columbia, with the 2nd Brigade in the advance. The exception was the 11th Kentucky, which did not get through Columbia until 3 A.M., the morning of July 4.[95]

Colonel Chenault wrote home in March 1863 that Morgan had great faith in his regiment:

> We have the confidence of the General, and when anything dangerous is to be done Chenault's Regt. is called out. If the rear is to be protected on a March, we have our full share to perform. In our retreat from the state this winter after pushing around Lebanon, Ky, where there was a very superior Yankee force, we were on the rear. A report went up the lines

> that there was firing in the rear. General Morgan rode back until he met Colonel Breckinridge, "Who is on the rear today?" said Morgan. "Chenault's regt.," was the reply. "Then all will be right," was the answer and he rode back to the head of the column.[96]

As Morgan's men left Columbia, they rode by Camp Gilbert where thousands of Federal troops had been encamped. It was now abandoned. Its troops had been moved south to guard the Cumberland crossings. And Morgan had slipped right past them.

Evening and Night of Friday, July 3: Cane Valley

"Morgan . . . done a grat deel of develment in this section"
Mary Christie to her brother, Lt. Norman Christie

Some of Morgan's men stopped in the field in front of the old brick Page house, then owned by Elijah Sublett, four miles out of Columbia, and fed on wheat while there. General Morgan passed by and the troops cheered him as they fell in behind him.

Curtis Burke was detailed to go with Capt. Tom Berry to find forage. They went up the road to where it forked at Cane Valley, near a large white house, found some hay and corn in a stable, and watched others raiding a milk house. The regiment camped in a lot opposite the house. Scout Burke slept outside on the grass.[97]

As the road between Columbia and Campbellsville and the villages of Cane Valley and Coburg filled up with Morgan's troops, the president of the Greensburg

Page-Sublett House, Cane Valley, Adair County

Independent Bank, J.M.S. McCorkle became increasingly frightened. Cane Valley was only a few miles from Greensburg. Following the example of Colonel Hobson early in the war, McCorkle decided to transport the funds of his bank to Louisville for safekeeping. He placed the gold coins in saddle bags for the trip, but he still had to find a way to disguise the paper money. He followed the practice common in spy networks of the period—using women as carriers with messages and money hidden in their clothing. His daughter, Flora McCorkle, sewed the paper money in her linen petticoat and started the ride from Greensburg toward Louisville.[98]

At the James Page home in Cane Valley, a little girl with dark curls and big eyes named Sally Jane Rice, swung on the gate, watching the soldiers march by her grandfather's home.[99] She never forgot the scene.

Keith Humphress

Stephen Humphreys

Steven Humphreys owned a large farm on a side road that entered the main turnpike near Cane Valley. He was a slave owner and a pro-Southern man, but his farm was pillaged along with the others. The raiders emptied his smoke house of its hams and took his horses.[100]

A mile east at Beechtop in Adair County, William and America Edrington hid their silver and hams under the strawberry vines in their garden. When their farm was searched by hungry soldiers, they found nothing. Martha Revis, aged five when she heard the family story from her grandmother Grant, decided she would hide a beautiful gold bracelet given to her by her godmother, Winifred Moore, in her grandmother's garden at Cane Valley. She dug a hole and hid the bracelet. For years, Thomas and Annie Edrington Grant searched their garden for Martha's bracelet, but never found it.[101]

The families near the town well in Cane Valley had soldiers billeted in their houses. Sophie Dudgeon Sublett, who owned a grocery store at Cane Valley,

Janice Wilkerson

Sophie Dudgeon Sublett

remembered that the soldiers paid for their goods in Confederate money, which, of course, had no value in that part of the country.[102]

On the night of July 3, Morgan established his headquarters in John F. Bridgewater’s house. After consultation with Lt. “Dick Archie” Webster from the local area, Morgan sent out Capt. Franks’ scouts to reconnoiter Tebbs Bend and Green River Bridge. That was the first time Franks was in charge of reconnaissance.

After a nice dinner, Morgan went to sleep at Bridgewater’s, confident that the Federal commander at Green River would put up little resistance. He asked that his breakfast be prepared early the next morning, July 4.

On a high bluff overlooking Green River, Colonel Orlando H. Moore of the 25th Michigan, who had a reputation for courage and stubbornness, was preparing his defenses against the attack that he anticipated the following morning. He was fully aware that his “fresh fish” had no experience of fighting. In Moore, Morgan may have met his match.

John F. Bridgewater House, Cane Valley, Adair County

University of Kentucky Archives

Brig. Gen. John Hunt Morgan, CSA

USAMHI

Col. Orlando Hurley Moore, USA

Chapter Three: Two Dauntless Commanders: Morgan and Moore

"This being the fourth of July, I cannot entertain his proposition to surrender."
Col. Orlando H. Moore, 25th Michigan Infantry

Both commanders at Tebbs Bend were in their thirties. They were born two years apart: John Hunt Morgan, June 1, 1825; Orlando Hurley Moore, July 13, 1827. Morgan was born in Huntsville, Alabama, and when he was five, moved with his parents, Calvin and Henrietta Hunt Morgan, to Lexington, Kentucky. Moore was born in Wilkes-Barre, Pennsylvania, and when he was eight, moved with his parents, Andrew Young and Elizabeth Baldy Moore, to a two-story brick house in Schoolcraft, Michigan.[1]

John grew up in a large two-story house on a 300-acre farm on Tates Creek Pike in Lexington, Kentucky. He was the eldest of ten children. John's father, called Colonel Morgan because of his militia rank, was farm manager for his father-in-law, John Hunt, overseeing slaves, crops, livestock and horses. Calvin was one of the first in Fayette County to use a wheat thresher.[2]

The boy was tutored by his father, who had scholarly and literary interests. John attended Transylvania University for a short while until suspended for participating in a duel. He decided not to return to school but tried to secure a commission in the United States Marine Corps.

Orlando, called Hurley by his family, grew up on a large farm in Prairie Ronde, Kalamazoo County, Michigan. His father, Andrew "A.Y." Moore, was a highly respected and innovative farmer, who introduced the Hiram Moore combine which cut, threshed and sacked grain at the same time. A.Y. was the first president of the Michigan Agricultural Society and was one of the founders of Michigan State College. He, as Morgan's father, had literary interests. Orlando was a precocious, intellectual child, whose education included the classics, arts, and music. He demonstrated remarkable talent as a violinist. He later studied portrait painting in New York City and operated portrait studios in New York and Kalamazoo. On October 3, 1855, at age 28, he married 16-year-old Sarah Abigail Haynes, daughter of David and Ann Eliza Haynes.[3]

John Morgan grew up in Lexington with all the privileges of the Southern aristocratic tradition, with at least a nominal connection to the Episcopalian church. His family had ample slave help in the kitchen and on their farm, where hemp, grain, and hay were grown and livestock raised. A slave named Aunt Betty, whom the children adored, helped his mother with the children.

Even though ownership of slaves was declining in Kentucky by 1860, John and his brothers, Calvin and Richard, owned slaves, working them in their hemp and woolen factories, as well as hiring them out as laborers on steamboats. Slaves, in addition to being valuable property, continued to confer status and contribute to their masters' self-esteem.[4]

The breeding and raising of horses was important in the antebellum Kentucky Bluegrass. There were many fine thoroughbreds and harness horses in the barns of the Morgan family. John and his brothers loved to ride and hunt in the forests of Fayette County. They raced their mounts, bet on the races, gambled at cards, and rarely refused a drink. This was a "gentlemen's life" in the South and the Morgan boys reveled in it.[5]

In contrast to the Morgan family, Orlando Moore's family were staunch Presbyterians, held strong views against slave-holding, and were appalled at the idea of slave-trading. Moore is said to have entertained his troops with stories about helping his father guide escaped slaves on the underground railroad that ran through Schoolcraft, Michigan.[6]

Like John Morgan, Orlando learned to ride early in life, and by his late teens, was considered to be an extraordinary equestrian. His father took fine horses and cattle with them when they moved from Pennsylvania to Michigan. One of his favorite mounts was named Bucephalus, after Alexander the Great's horse. Orlando often drove the sixteen-horse team required to pull his father's combine.[7]

A military tradition was common to both the Morgan and Moore families. Both had ancestors in the American Revolution: Morgan's great-grandfather, Gideon, served as a corporal in a Connecticut regiment; Moore's grandfather, Stephen, served in John Phillips' Company, 3rd Regiment, Hunterdon County,

New Jersey militia. Orlando's father and his five brothers were members of the local militia, the Columbia Guards.

The war with Mexico gave John Morgan an opportunity to fulfill his military ambition. When Col. Humphrey Marshall formed the 1st Regiment of Kentucky Mounted Volunteers, John Morgan enlisted, with his brother Cal, as privates in its Company K, commanded by Capt. Oliver Hazard Perry Beard. Morgan was elected second lieutenant and soon promoted to lieutenant. After being officially called to duty, the "Fayette Mounted Men" formed up "in line of march" and set out from Lexington for Louisville on June 4, 1846.

After enduring an arduous journey, on which he suffered a severe illness, Morgan, in a detachment of dismounted cavalry, exchanged fire with Mexican infantry at Buena Vista. He also survived a cavalry charge by Santa Anna's men and a savage battle in which "the opposing horsemen clashed head on and fought hand to hand." In spite of being outnumbered, the Americans won a decisive victory, but sustained heavy losses, including Morgan's Uncle Alexander and Henry Clay, Jr. Green County men carried Clay's body from the field. Only half of Marshall's Kentucky regiment returned to a hero's welcome in Lexington in 1847.[8]

Zachary Taylor's victory in the battle of Buena Vista made him a state and national hero. When a new county was formed out of Green in 1848, it was given the name Taylor. The village of Mannsville became Buena Vista and kept its new name on maps for fifty years, even after it had been incorporated as Mannsville in 1864.

In contrast to Morgan, at the time of the Mexican War, Orlando Moore was pursuing other interests and did not volunteer.

After the Mexican War, John Morgan and a young friend, Sanders Bruce, entered into a partnership. They purchased slaves to be rented out to local industries, bred and trained racehorses. John began to spend time with Sanders' sister, Rebecca, an attractive, intelligent, and cheerful girl. After a brief courtship, they were married on November 21, 1848, in Christ Church Episcopal in Lexington, when John was 23 and Rebecca only 18. Since her father was dead, John and Rebecca moved into the Bruce family home with her mother on North Mill in Gratz Park. The house was just across Mill Street from his grandfather Hunt's home, Hopemont.

In 1852, Morgan organized an artillery company of the Kentucky militia and became its Captain. When Kentucky officially abolished the militia in 1854, Morgan's company became inactive. In 1857, there was a revival of interest in the militia and Morgan organized the Lexington Rifles and dressed its sixty men in elegant green uniforms and stylish plumed hats, bearing the seal of Kentucky. The state armed them with new long-range rifles. The well-drilled company with its dashing commander soon became a popular attraction, marched in parades, and put on drill displays for the guests at mineral spring resorts. His men idolized Morgan, and romantic myths soon surrounded his name.

Soon after Beriah Magoffin was elected governor of Kentucky in 1859, he established the State Guard, a pro-Southern militia, and the Lexington Rifles immediately joined it.[9] Morgan's brother-in-law, Sanders Bruce, became commander of another militia company, the Lexington Chasseurs, which Union supporters joined.

In 1854, Moore's military career began when he became a paymaster in the Michigan Militia, with the rank of Captain, and was soon appointed aide-de-camp to the Adjutant General by the governor of Michigan. In 1856, he was commissioned Second Lieutenant, 6th United States Infantry, and posted to Kansas during the troubled period prior to its statehood. Moore vehemently supported the new state's being free of slavery. This earned the enmity of many fellow officers, who later enlisted in Confederate service.

In 1857, Moore took part in an expedition against the Cheyenne Indians, led by General Edwin V. Sumner, during which he marched 1,800 miles over difficult terrain, at times, suffering a severe lack of food and supplies.[10]

In June 23, 1858, his regiment left Fort Leavenworth, Kansas, and marched through Utah over mountains and through deserts to Benicia Arsenal, California, a distance of 2,100 miles, arriving in the middle of November. Participants claimed it was "the greatest continous march on record." Moore and his officers were on horseback, his wife rode in an army ambulance, but his men were on foot. After he arrived, conflict arose between Moore and local garrison officers with secessionist sympathies, which led to his being challenged to two duels. He avoided the duels, apparently by exacting terms which discouraged his opponents from fighting him. The fact that he was reputed to be a superb marksman may have been a factor.[11]

Moore himself, and through his daughter as his biographer, claimed that he was given a "secret mission" which was to investigate a secessionist movement seeking to establish a "Pacific Republic" involving California, Oregon, and Nevada. This claim has been supported in newspaper editorials by Gen. George O. Cress and Lt. Col. L.A. Nickerson and Republicans in California. Whether his boast is true or not, Moore sincerely felt he had played a significant role in preventing 60,000 stands of arms [a set of arms for one soldier consisting of a rifle, bayonet, cartridge box, and belt] at the Benicia Arsenal from falling into secessionist hands.

Gen. Albert Sidney Johnston, commander of the Pacific Department from January 1861 until he resigned in April 1861, seems to have been one of the men Moore distrusted most. Johnston was subsequently replaced as commander by

Gen. Edwin V. Sumner. It is true that Johnston made no secret of his divided loyalties, particularly of his loyalty to Texas; but Johnston's biographer, Charles P. Roland, presents a strong case for Johnston's never having been a party to the conspiracy: "There is not a shred of evidence that Albert Sidney Johnston was involved in that plot."[12]

At any rate, the "Pacific Plot" never came to fruition. It is probable that Moore worked with Republican leaders in California and Washington to defeat the plans of the conspirators.[13] Three officers at the post at that time did indeed join the Confederacy: Generals Albert S. Johnston, Richard Brooke Garnett, and Lewis Addison Armistead.

Moore's first child, Allen Young, was born in 1860 at the army post in San Diego.[14] In May, 1861, Moore's rank was Captain. He became eager to return to the east and become involved in the action of the Civil War. Restless at a desk job in Chicago, he was appointed Lt. Colonel of the 13th Michigan Infantry in December 1861.[15]

Both Moore and Morgan were at the battle of Shiloh in April 6–7, 1862, but neither played a significant part in the fighting. Moore was, by then, on the staff of Brig. Gen. James A. Garfield, whose brigade arrived at the Shiloh battlefield in the afternoon of the second day of fighting. Garfield positioned some of his force in the line about 440 yards from the batteries of the enemy, but they arrived too late to be engaged. Moore's antagonist in California, Gen. A.S. Johnston, had been killed there the previous afternoon. Gen. Jeremiah T. Boyle, Moore's future commander in Louisville with whom he will have many unpleasant exchanges, led a brigade at Shiloh.[16]

Morgan's dashing, commanding appearance before his troops has already been addressed. Michigan's Colonel Moore had many of these same traits. He was described as "tall and commanding, genial and cordial in manner."[17] For the most part, his men adored him, seldom writing negative comments about their commander in their letters home. Pvt. Benjamin Van Raalte wrote to his minister father, "We like our Colonel and will do for him whatever is possible to do."[18]

By 1863, Morgan's risk-taking adventures were legendary. There was no doubt that Moore was also fearless in the face of danger. Charles Woodruff described his actions while hunting for guerrillas near Owenton, Kentucky:

> Our Colonel is very brave and might also say reckless of himself. I had been sent to the left to act as a scout and was riding slowly along, my horse stumbling over logs and stumps, keeping my eyes open for "secesh" when suddenly I saw through the bushes a horse and the next moment came full upon the colonel, he alone and half a mile from the rest of the

> party. I expressed my surprise and told him I thought it would be very unpleasant business if a colonel should be taken prisoner by guerrillas. He seemed to have no fear but rather liked the excitement.[19]

Nelson Ogden, drummer for the 25th Michigan, later killed in the war, wrote to his sister: "I expect that we will have some pretty hard fighting here; . . . if we do, we have got a good commander."[20]

Moore and the 25th Michigan

In August 1862, Moore was posted to Kalamazoo, Michigan, where he was made Colonel of the 25th Michigan Infantry, formed from companies that were surplus to existing regiments in several newly organized Congressional Districts. For the most part, the men were from Berrien, Calhoun, Cass, Ionia, Kalamazoo, Kent, Ottawa, and St. Joseph counties in southwest Michigan. Moore immediately undertook training the regiment in Kalamazoo. A bronze marker on Egleston Avenue there marks the location of the regiment's camp. The 25th Michigan was officially mustered into the United States Army on September 22, 1862.[21]

Company I, from Holland, Michigan, with 84 men, was made up of "genuine imported Dutchmen, straight from the Netherlands," many of whom knew little or no English and had to have orders interpreted for them.

The regiment was outfitted with frock-coat uniforms with brass buttons and buckles, and white gloves, as well as new Enfield rifles. The ladies of Kalamazoo presented the regiment a silk regimental flag bearing the inscription: "This flag is given in faith that it will be carried where honor and duty lead." In October, the regiment with 896 men left Kalamazoo by train and disembarked at Louisville, Kentucky.[22]

While in Kalamazoo and Louisville, Colonel Moore trained his men and his horses, Rob Roy and Old Lion, to respond to bugle commands. The regiment soon gained the attention of senior commanders because of their excellent turnout and precision marching. It became known as the "White Gloves" Regiment and was much sought after for ceremonial parades. In October 1862, the regiment acted as escort to the remains of Brig. General James S. Jackson, Lt. Col. George P. Jouett, Maj. William P. Campbell, Col. Lucius C. Polk, and other general officers. The 25th men fired the 21-gun salutes during burial ceremonies at the gravesides in Cave Hill Cemetery. After the regiment's return to Louisville from the field in the spring of 1863, it again received accolades for its deportment and precision drill.[23]

After being stationed in Louisville and performing scouting duty for two months, the regiment left for Munfordville, arriving there in the middle of December 1862. The Post Commandant at that time was Col. E.H. Hobson. The

25th Michigan, along with other regiments, was assigned to guard the long L&N railroad bridge over Green River. "Our troops built strong fortifications in order to be able to defend ourselves," wrote a Dutch private. It will be here that the 25th Michigan will again become imbued with the fear of Morgan's guerrillas. By December 23, they were forming a line of battle at 4 or 4:30 A.M., expecting Morgan. This was "to teach us to fall in quickly and not be half asleep in case the old boy should come as he has the habit of attacking at daylight." Before the war was over, John Morgan made so many raids on the railroad that the Editor of the *Louisville Journal* named him "Superintendent of the Railroad."[24]

At Munfordville on Christmas and the following day, the 25th Michigan had its first encounter with Morgan's cavalry. At 4 A.M. Christmas morning the men were turned out by bugle call with rifles in hand and remained in line of battle until daylight. There was no more sleep for anyone that early morning. During Christmas Day the men worked in the trenches or slept in their clothes. Scouts brought in fifteen captured prisoners later that day. At 2:00 A.M. on the 26th, firing was heard and 25th Michigan's pickets came riding in shouting, "The enemy is upon us." Every man came running out, took up battle positions in the trenches, and loaded their rifles.[25]

Pvt. John Wilterdink described the same events in a letter dated December 28. He said that four companies of the 2nd Michigan cavalry came into camp after being attacked by Morgan's troops. They suffered one dead and 17 wounded. He says that "the camp was in turmoil" and that he "was glad there was not a big battle." He described how he "had to fall in line in haste" while preparing the noon meal "because the enemy was only one-half mile away." He commented on the seventeen Confederate prisoners in their guardhouse: "*THE DEVIL SEEMS TO SHINE IN THEIR EYES*".... What Morgan wanted to do was to get the railroad bridge that stands 135 feet above the water.... Between Louisville and Munfordsville he burned a railroad bridge.... If I have been informed correctly, Morgan is nothing but a robber."[26]

Charles Woodruff reported what Morgan had done. "He has torn up the track for some two miles, cut the telegraph wires and done what other mischief he could.... It appears that a company of "secesh" dressed in the uniforms of union troops had approached to within about one hundred yards of the pickets when they [Morgan's men] suddenly fired a volley upon them—and then turned and fled... This is another of Morgan's tricks."[27] Benjamin Van Raalte wrote home, "We must teach the Rebels a lesson they will never forget."

By the end of December, B, F, and I companies, 25th Michigan, were moved to Bowling Green to serve as provo-guards, under Lt. Col. Benjamin Orcutt, who was made Provost Marshal. Illness broke out in the camp, even infecting their regimental Doctor Barnum, in January 1863, seriously affecting the regiment's readiness for duty.[28] Their 12-year-old drummer boy, "the pet of the regiment," died. In February and March, the men grew stronger and most recovered their health.

For a few days in March and early April, the regiment was posted to Lebanon. Dirk Van Raalte thought the land was beautiful for farming there, but that the citizens were mostly secesh in sympathy. While there, they marched to Hall's Gap hoping in vain to find Cluke's Rebels. Upon returning, they had fun with the Dutch boys of the 8th Michigan. Little did they know that their paths would all meet at Tebbs Bend a few months later.[29] In April, the 25th Michigan was ordered back to Louisville on provost duty, replacing the 34th Kentucky Infantry.

Moore's wife and child had been living in a boarding house in Louisville, even while the regiment was in Bowling Green, and Moore often spent time there.[30] It is known that Moore, when in Louisville, attended the theater often.[31] The *National Tribune* reported that he attended "Seven Sisters," at Wood's Theater, at the corner of 4th and Jefferson, between March 16 and March 30. In the performance was Pauline Cushman, born Harriet Wood in New Orleans. There is a story that Southern sympathizers asked her to propose a toast on stage to Jefferson Davis and that she told Colonel Moore about the request. He is credited for giving her permission to "Hurrah for Jeff Davis" so that he could "sniff out" Confederate supporters in the audience when they cheered and clapped.

Pauline Cushman

The story continues. It was reported that Colonel Moore recruited Miss Cushman for a spying mission in Tennessee. It is said that she contacted General Braxton Bragg and gathered key information about the disposition of Southern units while socializing with Confederate officers. Apparently she succeeded in sending this intelligence North but was arrested and then made a daring escape. Whether true or not, Pauline Cushman profited for the rest of her life from her tales of adventure as a spy during the Civil War. She is buried in a cemetery near the Presidio in the San Francisco area, where her gravestone credits her with being a Union spy. Even though this story is consistent with Colonel Moore's interest in spying, he never mentioned this incident in any of his writing about his career.

Moore Challenges General Boyle

On April 7, 1863, Colonel Moore was appointed Provost Marshal of Louisville. The city was a thriving manufacturing and commercial city able to provide everything needed by the more than a hundred thousand soldiers who passed through the city during the war. It was surrounded by Federal campsites and its streets were crowded with soldiers on furlough or parole. Louisville did not lack for brothels, bars, and gambling joints, one of the most notorious being Mayfield's, at 11th and Walnut.

Moore's responsibilities included issuing passes on the railroads and roads; policing all the places frequented by soldiers and maintaining military order in the city; guarding supplies in transit and depots; guarding Rebel prisoners while they were being processed at the military barracks and escorting them to their destinations in Northern prisons. Moore used the men of the 25th Michigan in these routine tasks and maintained that being Provost Marshal was more difficult than serving in the field.[35]

Louisville's citizens were divided in their loyalties. Many of its leading citizens, while pretending to be loyal to the North, were secretly, and sometimes openly, sympathetic to the Confederacy.

The city's strategic position on the Ohio River made it the staging area for supplies pouring in from the North to be shipped south down the Ohio and Mississippi rivers or by the Louisville-and-Nashville Railroad. Columns of troops, with their baggage wagons pulled by six mules, and provision trains continually moved through the city's muddy streets. When Buell passed through Louisville in September 1862, before the Battle of Perryville, his baggage train of 1,800 wagons was 24 miles long.[36]

The Union army maintained huge stockpiles of war material at Louisville: hundreds of cannons, thousands of rifles, and tons of ammunition, as well as large

Louisville during the Civil War

quantities of salt beef and pork, beans, and rice. Supply depots held boots and shoes, denim for uniforms, medicines and bandages, saddles and harnesses, sufficient for thousands of soldiers. A large military prison which processed Southern prisoners of war and several military hospitals were located there.[37]

The 25th Michigan and its colonel strove to meet the demands of its new assignment. Even though the work was arduous, the 25th Michiganders enjoyed their privileged status because of the perks that went with it, particularly using the housing in the barracks surrounding the prison yard. This was much preferred to tent life. Letters home reflected pride in their commander, Colonel Moore. Still, sometimes the work was dangerous. In May 1863 there was a shooting incident involving a soldier resisting arrest.[38]

By mid-April Moore again showed his zealousness in ferreting out Confederate sympathizers in an incident at Wood's Theater. While Bella Golden was singing the *Star Spangled Banner,* two men got up and tried to leave. Moore intercepted them in the lobby, learned their names, and ordered them to remain until the song was finished. It was reported that similar incidents were occurring during entertainments at the Masonic Temple. Prentice, owner of the *Journal,* advised the secessionists to "grin and bear it."[39] Dirk Van Raalte commented on the situation in the city: "Louisville is filled with Secesh but our Colonel Moore knows how to deal with them. He arrests them at once as soon as they talk the least bit in the Secesh way."[40]

To add to Moore's travails, his valuable horse, Rob Roy, lost its footing, fell on a curbstone, and died. The horse, trained to the bugle, had been with him at Shiloh, and was his mount in all ceremonial parades. It had served him well and was a favorite with the troops. The *Louisville Journal* reported that "his loss will be severely felt by the Colonel."[41]

Louisville was the gathering place of many "contrabands," that is, runaway slaves, who were sometimes returned to their masters, resold, made servants of Union officers, or made to work on roads and fortifications. Sometimes freed slaves were arrested and resold into slavery.[42]

After the Battle of Shiloh, Gen. Jeremiah Boyle was made Commander of the District of Kentucky, Department of the Ohio. His headquarters were in Louisville. He was a fiery, slave-owning Union officer from Boyle County who learned that he had to play a balancing act between keeping Kentucky in the Union while, at the same time, assuaging the feelings of Kentucky's many Southern sympathizers. Historian Merle Coulter called it Kentucky's "peculiar situation." During the first months of his "regime," Boyle vigorously enforced the policy, arresting Southern sympathizers until he was ordered by Secretary of War to make no further arrests except upon orders of the Governor, who at that time was James F. Robinson.

At first, Boyle forbade any slaves to enter military camps but then, realizing that he needed their labor, reversed his order and put slaves to work on military fortifications, roads, and railroads.[43]

By 1863, discontent over the Lincoln administration's policies ran very deep in Kentucky. When the Emancipation Proclamation went into effect in January 1, 1863, Kentuckians initially ignored it because it only applied to the seceding states. George Prentice referred to the government's policy as "exceedingly odious." Earlier, the General Assembly had declared that emancipation was unconstitutional and void in Kentucky. Taylor County's state and national representatives were openly vocal against Lincoln's policies. Many Unionist Kentuckians were slave-holders and hoped that, by staying loyal to the Union, they would be able to retain their slaves.[44] Many of them were influential people in Louisville who were becoming increasingly incensed by rumors that African-Americans were to be armed and allowed to serve in the Union Army. Into this heated atmosphere stepped Colonel Orlando Moore.

At the beginning of his tour of duty as Provost Marshal, Colonel Moore and his men received favorable comments from the *Louisville Journal*. It reported that the people frequently watched their "soldier-like movement of a squad or company on the street" with admiration.[45] Citizens approved of Moore's men clearing out brothels and breaking up fights. But Moore appeared at the Jefferson County

Courthouse during a slave sale in April and gave notice that four of the Blacks were "free Negroes" under the Emancipation Proclamation and that "he would hold them responsible if the said Negroes were sold." The crowd was warned not to bid on them. The buyer disregarded Moore's orders, and the case was eventually appealed to the Federal district court.[46]

Moore was now treading on dangerous ground, both from the viewpoint of General Boyle and the local media, as well as from the Kentucky General Assembly. After January 1, 1863, "freed slaves" were escaping from their masters in the South and filtering into Louisville. General Boyle was putting them in jail and then allowing them to be resold into slavery.[47] In doing this, he was supported by an act passed by the Kentucky General Assembly in March 1863. It forbid any Negro claiming to be free under the Emancipation Proclamation from entering the state, and if one were found, he could be jailed. If the runaways were not picked up by their owners in one month, they could be resold.[48]

Moore was not to be intimidated. He ignored the Kentucky law and was determined to implement the Federal law instead. Without consulting Boyle or any higher authorities, Moore issued the following order which appeared in the *Louisville Journal*:

> Headquarters Provost Marshal
> Louisville, Ky., May 1, 1863
>
> *Special Order* No 12:
>
> Hereafter all unlawful interference with the authorized negro servants of officers of the United States Army, and Negroes legally entitled to their freedom, passing through Kentucky to Indiana is prohibited; and while the legal rights of the citizens of Kentucky *shall be strictly guarded*, parties will be held responsible for such unlawful interference.
>
> Orlando H. Moore
> Col. 25th Mich. Inf. and Provost Marshal[49]

When General Boyle read the order, he immediately revoked it and relieved Moore as provost marshal.[50] He went to Cincinnati to consult with General Burnside about it, accusing Moore of breaking the state law. Colonel Moore also went to Burnside to tell his position on the matter. Three days later, after some heated exchanges, Boyle revoked his order relieving Moore and Moore returned to his job.[51] In order to resolve the problem, a Commission of Contraband Negroes, with D. C. Fitch, Adjutant of the 25th Michigan, as its head, was established to have the cases properly dealt with.[52]

On June 5, 1863, Indiana Governor O.P. Morton entered the fray with a heated letter supporting Moore to General Hartsuff, Commander of the 23rd Army Corps, declaring that Moore was a "gentleman of high character" and that he was "carrying out the war policy of the administration with reference to negroes, declared free, by the President's proclamation."

Colonel Moore continued to persist in standing up to his superior, General Boyle, and to Louisville newspaper editors. No sooner had Moore been returned to duty, he wrote the following letter to the editor of the *Louisville Democrat*, published on June 10, and carried the following day in the *Louisville Journal*. In it, Moore directed his comments to editors who, in his opinion, had failed to support U.S. government policy:

> Headquarters Provost Marshal
> Louisville, Ky., June 6, 1863
>
> Editors *Louisville Democrat*:
>
> Gentlemen:
>
> I have the honor to most respectfully request that you discontinue your attacks and reflections upon the war policy of the Administration and the war measures of the Government.
>
> I am, gentlemen, very respectfully, your obedient servant,
>
> Orlando H. Moore
> Colonel and Provost Marshal.[53]

Moore's letter did not stop Prentice from continuing to write his opinions. His earlier support for Moore as Provost Marshal ended. Prentice suffered the same conflict of loyalties as many of his kind in the state. His Federal loyalty did not include acceptance of equality for African Americans. After Blacks were recruited to fight in the Union army, he supported McClellan for president against Lincoln. He also published a long response to Moore's letter:

> It is too silly and absurd a thing to get angry at. We wonder what under the moon can be the matter with Col. Moore. He dumbfounds us. . . . He has seemed to us a courteous and intelligent gentleman and officer, but this thing of his, which was sent upon his sole responsibility, beats the devil. . . . He seems to have a good heart; perhaps his heart can't be beaten; but one would think his head had been beaten all hollow. His notification to us, we presume, was the last act of his Provost life, for he was superseded even before it reached us—his second super-session within a few weeks. . . . As he has been ordered to the head of a

> part of a regiment, we suppose we may now venture to do a little free talking, unless he thinks that, as Colonel of half a regiment, he has the same right to govern newspapers that he had as Provost Marshal and shall march his half regiment against the Journal office for the first supposed offence.

Prentice went on to point out that the war policy of the administration was opposed by the Union candidates for the legislature and the U.S. Congress. He ended the article by saying, "We have seen a great many official asses, and now we see one in Moore. Let all small officials be careful lest, in trying to kick newspapers, they by mistake kick the bucket."[54]

There was more occurring than was discussed in the newspapers. Wilterdink writes that "Boyle is, according to hearsay, angered at our Colonel because he was helping slaves across the Ohio River. Our Colonel knows what he must do. He is for right and justice." If it is true that Moore watched the Underground Railroad at work when he was young, it is not surprising that he was issuing passes to slaves and free Blacks for the ferry across the Ohio when he was an adult.[55]

Moore Posted to Green River Bridge

As Moore's dismissal indicated, General Boyle had had enough of this upstart subordinate. With no consideration of the fact that Moore had a personal concern, that is, his wife was due to have her second child at any moment in a strange city, with no family nearby to help, he posted Moore to Green River Bridge, eight miles from Campbellsville and twelve miles north of Columbia. Boyle also divided the 25th Michigan in half: Companies D, E, F, I, and K, commanded by Col. Moore were to go south by rail to Green River Bridge; Companies A,B,C,G, and H, commanded by Lt. Colonel Benjamin Orcutt, remained in Louisville. Major Dewitt Clinton Fitch of the 25th became the Provost Marshal of the city.[56]

George D. Wood, a Michigan resident, wrote to Asa and Chester Slayton in June, 1863: "Your Col is not of the right stripe to suit Kentuckians. He thinks and acts too much for himself. I think he will make his mark in the field."[57] Members of the 25th Regiment, once heralded, now were being humiliated and subjected to ridicule in Louisville. They were called "half a regiment" and some of their letters home expressed dismay at their fate. Adjutant Charles H. Brown, popular and highly regarded by the troops, was disheartened by Moore's actions and tendered his resignation.[58]

On June 11, 1863, the "marooned" companies got on "the cars," and departed for south central Kentucky. The rail line stopped at Lebanon, where the men disembarked, gathered their weapons, and marched twenty-eight miles to Green River Bridge in Taylor County. By the evening of June 13, they arrived at the campsite there, so weary that they slept on the ground in the moonlight.[59]

When the column was marching out of Lebanon, Lt. Travis noticed a young person in uniform following along behind them and occasionally talking to some of the soldiers. After some conversation with him, Travis reported, the boy said, "I'm a girl and have come along as the doctor's waiter." Travis added that although he had made no comments about her to the other men, he believed that they knew that the "boy" was really a girl. After they arrived at Green River, Travis reported the incident to Colonel Moore. He interviewed the girl and discovered that her name was Lizzie Compton and that she claimed to be from Tennessee. Evidently, Moore decided to deal with the matter later and the evening of the 13th, Lizzie slept under the sky with the men.[60]

☆ ☆ ☆

All spring, rumors had been in the air that General Morgan, camped in Tennessee, was planning to come north.[61] If Morgan, with thousands of troops available to him, chose to come through Columbia to Green River Bridge, Moore would be in a perilous situation, his closest reinforcements being at Lebanon, Glasgow, or Munfordville. Lt. Travis observed, "If Col. Moore could be captured, it would seem to satisfy his superior officers, who would then be rid of him for a time."[62] Dirk Van Raalte indicated in a letter that General Boyle got into difficulty with General Burnside when he heard that Moore's regiment had been split. "Now Boyle is in trouble . . . Boyle has to give an account to Burnside why he sent the Colonel away with five companies. It is not allowed to send off a regiment unless a major general has given permission."

Western Theological Seminary Collection, Jt Archives of Holland, MI

Pvt. Dirk Van Raalte, 25th Michigan

Gerald Myers

Camp at Green River

Colonel Orlando Moore's 25th Michigan Camp at Green River Bridge

Co D	1st Lt. John Gilchrist
Co E	Capt. Edwin Childs & 1st Lt. Benjamin Travis
Co F	Capt. Spencer S.Lansing & 2nd Lt. Arthur Twombly
Co K	1st Lt. John Tennant & 2nd Lt. Frank Weaver
Co I	Capt. Martin M. DeBow & 1st Lt. John Kramer

Lt. Edward Prutzman, Adjutant

Capt. Edwin Childs

Lt. Benjamin Travis

Kalamazoo Valley Museum

Capt. Martin DeBow

Al McGeehan

Lt. John Kramer

Kalamazoo Valley Museum

Adj. Ed Prutzman

News of Moore's continual insubordination to Boyle had reached the highest levels among the staff on the western front. Moore was placed directly under the authority of General Hartsuff, instead of General Boyle. Moore telegraphed Hartsuff asking him to suspend any action as to the disposition of his regiment until he could talk to him. On June 18 Burnside telegraphed Hartsuff to not move the Michigan regiment until he talked to him, but the deed was already done.[63]

Green River Bridge had retained its strategic importance since the beginning of the war. When Morgan burned it and the adjacent stockade on New Year's Day, six months earlier, he destroyed a vital transportation link for the Union armies. Federal regiments, batteries, and government wagons regularly moved along the road which crossed the bridge. There was also a campsite at the bridge which served troops on marches between Lebanon and Columbia. With the bridge out, military, civilian, and postal traffic had to be ferried across the river, involving lengthy delays.

Although danger was imminent, the 25th's "half-a-regiment" seemed to enjoy its camp on the knoll north of the bridge. Pvt. Van Raalte commented: "It is nice camping here close to Green River. . . . It is just beautiful out here." Pvt. John Wilterdink said, "We have good water to drink and the river to do the washing. . . . It is a lazy life, except for the cooks, but it is nice under the shade trees."[64] The men had been issued "dog" tents before leaving Louisville, which were set in five company rows, with arms stacked in front of the tents.[65]

Al McGeehan

Pvt. John Wilterdink

Adjutant Edward Prutzman's was dismayed when he learned that Colonel Moore had taken no action concerning the presence of Lizzie Compton in their camp. Prutzman's inquiries revealed that she was passing herself off as a volunteer with experience in the eastern theater. The regimental historian of the 25th, Benjamin Travis, tells that she "tented with two of the soldiers," and she "frequently went in swimming in the river."

Later, Colonel Moore became determined to be rid of her and she, herself, gave him good reason. She was in possession of one of the men's pistols. Capt. Spencer Lansing of Company F headed a sham court martial at which she was tried, found guilty of the theft, and ordered to leave camp. She, however, did not obey and remained somewhere not far from the camp.

Under Colonel Moore, camp life followed a normal regimental routine:

5:00	Reveille and Roll Call
5:30–7:30	Breakfast
8:00	Guard Mounting
9:00–11:00	Drill by Company
11:00	Orderly Call
12:00	Dinner
2:00–4:00	Drill by Battalion
4:00	Surgeon's Call
4:30	Dress Parade
5:30	Supper
9:00	Tattoo
9:30	Taps-Extinguish lights

Daily five or six men from each company were chosen for guard duty: two hours on, followed by four hours off. The mounted men had additional duties of feeding and watering their horses. When the bugle sounded "Assembly," companies assembled on their respective parade grounds; when it sounded "To the Colors," the companies formed to the right and left of their colors in line of battle.[66]

After being stationed at Green River a while, the boys began to have mixed feelings. One man had typhoid; another had rheumatism so bad he was on crutches. Some longed to return to Louisville. Van Raalte observed:

> I do hope that we can go . . . we are stationed in the middle of the wilderness. You hardly see a living soul around here. Four farmers live around here, and they ask anything they want whenever one wants to buy something from them. For a peck of potatoes they ask a dollar, and a dozen of eggs costs twenty-five cents. . . . The camp is situated in thick woods, and we can always sit in the shade if we want to.[67]

Bridge Builders: 8th Michigan and 79th New York

The 25th Michigan was not the only unit assigned to Green River Bridge. The 8th Michigan, together with the 79th New York Highlanders, were ordered there from Lebanon on April 26 and 27, 1863 to defend the site and rebuild the bridge.

The movement of the 8th Michigan by itself would have been commonplace, but the lively New Yorkers attracted attention on the march. The 79th New York Cameron Highlanders' uniforms—kepis, dark blue Scottish tailcoats with red piping and cuff guards, dark blue or tartan pants—were traditional. A Scotch piper accompanied them, dressed in kilts. It is likely that the skirling of his bagpipes brought many onlookers as the Highlanders marched by.

They halted outside of Campbellsville the night of April 28, probably on Trace Fork of Pitman. Before departing from camp on the 29th, the men feasted on beef-steak, broiled on ramrods over the fire, coffee and crackers.[68] When the 8th Michigan and the 79th New York arrived at Green River, they had to ford the river to reach the flat land on the bluff and set up their camp.

Lt. Col. Ralph Ely, commander of the 8th Michigan, who had arrived a day early, pitched his tent inside the old stockade. He recorded in his diary:

> May 1, 1863—Commenced to rebuild the bridge across the Green River, which the Rebel General Morgan burned in January last. . . . We are ordered to hold this Pass at all hazards.[69]

Col. Ralph Ely, 8th Michigan

The 8th Michigan worked for a month felling timbers and cutting stones to strengthen the bridge's abutments. The 79th also set to work as soon as their tools arrived. On some days, both regiments held company and battalion drills and occasionally Capt. George B. Fuller, his wife, and some other officers spent "jolly" evenings at the Johnstons, neighbors across from the stockade.[70]

The 79th had been there but a short time, when it was ordered away on a scouting mission to Jamestown and the Cumberland River on May 11.

The 8th Michigan continued with the bridge building and, by May 21, had completed a temporary bridge, an uncovered structure, its floor made of split logs put down crosswise. Two days later, the men began work on the permanent covered bridge. On Sunday, May 24, the regiment held a dress parade in celebration and the officers finished the evening back at the Johnstons with food and drink.[71]

Gerald Myers

Temporary Green River Bridge, Taylor County

During the latter part of May, Capt. T.B. Brooks, U.S. Military Engineers, made a report on the state of "the important military route" from Lebanon to Columbia:

> The Green River Bridge burned by the Rebels has been replaced by a temporary structure which is in turn being replaced by a permanent bridge built by the troops.[72]

But most of the 8th Michigan was not to stay long at Green River. After an uneventful regimental scout to Jamestown, they left Green River Bridge on June 5 to return to Lebanon. They then went by train from Lebanon to Louisville to Cairo, Illinois, where the regiment was put on board a steamer to Vicksburg, Mississippi.[73]

On special orders from General Boyle, 8th Michigan Lt. Michael A. Hogan, an experienced bridge builder for the Milwaukee Railroad, and 42–44 men were ordered to remain behind on detached duty to complete the covered bridge.[74] Col. David Morrison, commander of the 79th New York, placed a number of men to remain under Hogan's command to also help build the bridge. Hogan also hired civilians, some from Michigan, with bridge-building experience.[75]

Other military units camped there for brief periods during the time the bridge was being reconstructed. One hundred ninety men of the 11th Kentucky Cavalry stayed for an extended period. Their camp was on the bluff south of the river, on the west side of Tebbs Bend Road, opposite the Federal Stockade. The 11th Kentucky was responsible to defend the site of the damaged bridge, the bridge builders, and the fords over Green River, as well as send out scouts to the Cumberland River valley, looking for evidence of any Confederate approach. Supply trains from Lebanon to Columbia and on to southeast Kentucky had to be protected from roving guerrilla bands, especially Champ Ferguson's.[76]

John Humphress

An early morning mist rises from Green River as it did in 1863.

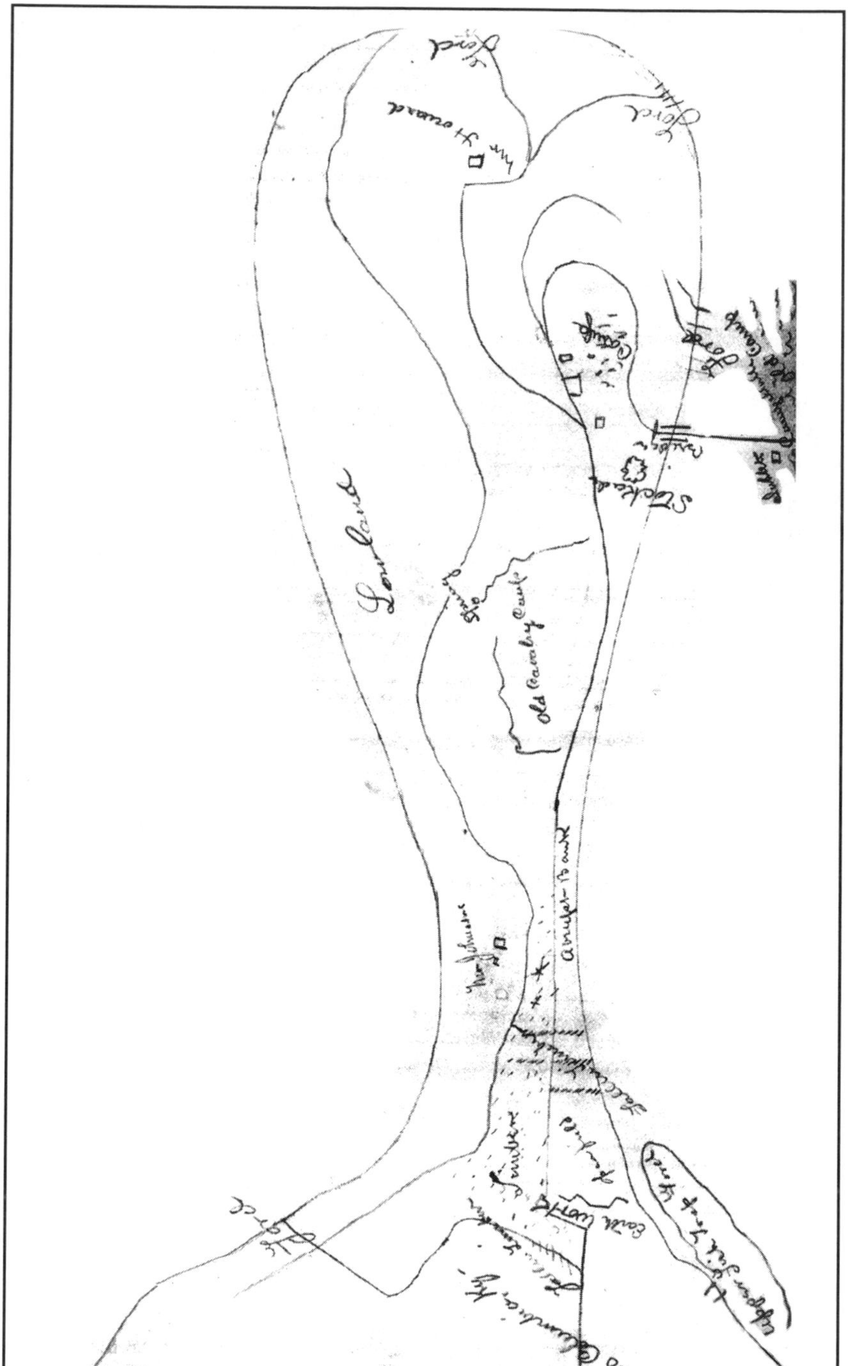

Lt. M.A. Hogan's Map of Tebbs Bend, July 4, 1863, National Archives

CHAPTER FOUR: MOORE PREPARES FOR MORGAN

Gen. Edward H. Hobson, headquartered at Glasgow, ordered Moore back to Louisville for five days the middle of June. The purpose of this trip is unclear, especially in light of the impending invasion from the south. It may have been personal desire to be with his wife who was awaiting the birth of their second child; Dirk Van Raalte said it was to try to get the regiment back together again.[1]

At any rate, when Colonel Moore arrived in Louisville on June 19, he read in the paper General Order No. 5, issued on June 18, requiring all officers to register at the Assistant Adjutant General's Office at Boyle's Headquarters when they came into the city. Moore ignored the order.[2]

When General Boyle discovered Moore was back in Louisville, he was furious. When he found out that Moore had ordered the arrest of Lt. Col. Benjamin Orcutt for some trivial thing, Boyle immediately released Orcutt. Discovering that Moore had not reported in and registered in accordance with regulations, Boyle ordered Col. Marc Munday, commandant of Louisville, to arrest and detain him in Barracks No. 1, and then send him back to his post. Consequently, Moore had to plead to keep from being returned to his post under armed guard. Only after much discussion, the contrite Moore was allowed to board the train to Lebanon and return to his unit on horseback. His baby daughter, Jessie, was born that evening, June 23, in Louisville, after he had left the city to return to duty at Green River Bridge.[3] Soon the rains began. Nothing, it seemed, was going well for Moore.

Saturday, June 27: Green River Rising

This was the fourth day of rain on the Green River countryside. The usual dust on the turnpike had turned into a limey mire. The river rose ten feet over its banks and was spilling out into the bottomlands.

The day was brightened by the taking of two of Morgan's cavalry as prisoners. They turned out to be from the squads of scouts Morgan was sending throughout the counties as far north as Neatsville in Adair County and Springfield.[4]

A wagon master of the 12th Rhode Island departed from his camp at Jamestown on June 21 and headed to Columbia for supplies. None were available so he set out for Lebanon. After loading his wagon train with supplies at the U.S. Supply Depot there, he got to Green River Bridge and encamped. He departed the next day and was within four miles of Columbia when he heard about a Rebel force there. He turned around, re-crossed Green River, brought the news about the enemy's approach, and camped in the lot below James Allen Sublett's house.

Beginning June 24, day after day, heavy rains fell and the rivers in southern Kentucky continued to rise. By June 29, the Cumberland River at Nashville had risen 13 feet. The Rhode Island wagon train had to remain at Green River Bridge.[5]

Sunday, June 28: Bridge Washes Away

Heavy rain was still falling early in the morning when Adj. Ed Prutzman rose. After listing the names of those assigned to picket and camp duty, he left Green River to go to Lebanon to turn in reports.

At 9 o'clock the bridge over Green River collapsed. When the strong current dislodged the temporary log supports of the trestle bridge, it broke loose from its abutments and began floating down the river. Lt. Travis watched as it "slid quietly along the rocky bed, as easily as if it had been greased to smooth its passage."[6] Even though it was recognized that the bridge had to be rebuilt as soon as possible, the men decided to build a ferryboat so they would be able to cross the river. Lt. John Tennant started on the task, but soon found out that the rope needed to keep a ferry boat on course was on the opposite side of the 100-feet wide, raging stream. Travis volunteered to swim across the river to get the rope. He walked a considerable distance upstream on the north side of the river and jumped into the water. The current was very swift, but he managed to swim across the river and land where the old bridge met the road on the south side. There he located the rope, with a cord attached to it. He put the cord between his teeth and swam back to the north side of the river. Work on building the ferry continued, and in a day or two, it was in operation.[7]

With the enemy so near, one would expect that Colonel Moore and Lieutenant Hogan would be cooperative with each other. But it was a rocky relationship indeed. Complicating the matter was the fact that Hogan reported directly to General Boyle, while Moore reported directly to General Hartsuff, the new 23rd Army Corps Commander and fellow Michigander.

After the bridge floated away, Hogan apparently asked for help from Moore. When he declined, Hogan contacted Boyle's headquarters. Boyle's adjutant telegraphed Hartsuff to ask him to order that all carpenters in the 25th Michigan be ordered to report to Hogan. This confrontation set the tone for Hogan's future relations with Moore.[8]

Moore, recognizing that an attack from Morgan was imminent, had no time to be concerned about the bridge. He increased the number of men on picket duty from six to twenty-five. One post was a half mile north of his camp and two were in Tebbs Bend, on the Columbia Turnpike and at the Lower Fishtrap

Ford. Moore extended the pickets placing them one and a half miles from the camp and posting mounted videttes further, a half mile to a mile beyond infantry pickets. Moore managed to find ten mounted infantrymen to serve as videttes and issured rifles of convalescing soldiers to them.[9]

Anticipating that Morgan might come this way, Moore and Dr. J.N. Gregg rode out to inspect the pickets before midnight. There is disagreement on the number of men in each picket, Hogan reporting three and Tennant six.[10]

Monday, June 29: Strained Relations between Moore and Hogan

Colonel Moore paid a visit to the camp of the bridge-building crew on the early morning of June 29. He gave orders to Lieutenant Hogan to spike, stack, and burn his tents and have his men fall in with the 25th Michigan. Hogan refused to obey Morgan's orders, stating that the 8th Michigan would stand and fight until he, Hogan, decided that it was necessary to leave.

After this incident, Hogan left for Columbia. Moore returned to Hogan's camp at four o'clock in the afternoon and ordered Pvt. Malvenus Colby of the 8th Michigan to take all the 8th Michigan's equipage over the river. Colby was in a dilemma and, knowing that Hogan would not want him to obey Moore's order, delayed doing anything until Hogan's return, which was quite late in the night. Clearly, even in the face of the enemy, Hogan and Moore's relationship was an uneasy one.[11]

At midnight on June 29, a man from Columbia named Suddarth, came to Hogan's camp to deliver the message from Capt. Silas G. Adams of Wolford's Cavalry, that the enemy was scouting heavily around Columbia and his regiment needed reinforcements.[12]

Tuesday, June 30: Decision to Stand at the Narrows of Tebbs Bend

At 2:30 A.M. Hogan and Suddarth crossed the river after bailing out a flooded boat. At 3:00 A.M. they woke up Moore, exhausted and ill tempered. When told of the request from Adams, he at first refused to send any men to support Wolford. Then he changed his mind and agreed to send 40–50 men if Hogan would go with them. They returned before July 4.

Heavy showers continued to fall, making the bridge repair slow and hazardous.

Moore had to make a decision on what to do about Morgan's approach. On his many trips riding around the defended area in the Green River valley, Moore had made himself knowledgeable of the terrain. From his military experience in the West, Moore, more than anyone else, realized how important terrain could be in the location of a defensive position. He had also learned that concealing one's forces was a great advantage and that an abatis fronted by fallen trees would slow any attack.

He was well acquainted with the Green River, having guarded the long railroad bridge across the Green at Munfordville. His troops had been to Hall's Gap where the stream begins. At the southern tip of Taylor County, the river makes one of its many sweeping horseshoe bends, forming a peninsula of land called Tebbs Bend. Where the river returns to almost meet itself is called the Narrows. The land here is shaped like an hourglass. The narrows are only about 100 yards wide with the Green River flanking both sides. The land drops precipitously on the north side of the ridge 150 feet into the river. On the south side of the narrows, the land drops, but more gradually, to the river. Both sides are heavily wooded. Duke later described it as "one of the strongest natural positions I ever saw." Here Colonel Moore chose to make his stand.[13]

The turnpike road ran through the narrows, and this was the road up which Morgan chose for his advance into Tebbs Bend. Moore knew that the campsite north of the bridge would not be defensible, nor would the stockade on the bluff south of the bridge. He had no artillery and the Confederates were reported to have four pieces. Moore knew his small force could be easily shelled in either of those locations.

Wednesday, July 1: Digging the Rifle Pit

Morgan is coming! Confederates are crossing the Cumberland, fifty miles away.

On the evening of July 1, Moore set his men to work, detailing seventy-five men to cross the river and construct a temporary forward line in a rifle pit, about a 100 yards in front of his main position. The pit was to be buttressed by fence rails and barbed wire, and could receive covering fire from the higher ground in the rear. After the battle, Adam Johnson and Basil Duke understood that the rifle pit had been "only a blind," or a "slight" earthwork. This forward line, however, had a

Maria Brent

Left to right: Moore's main defensive position, ditch, fallen timber, forward Union rifle pit.

Rebel Attack at the Narrows of Tebbs Bend, Brown Farm. The turnpike made a sharp "S" curve to the left behind the double trees. In front of the present dwelling was the Union Rifle Pit.

number of supplementary trenches built on its flanks, providing for the swift withdrawal of Moore's men to the main defended line once their delaying mission was complete. Approaching from the south, the turnpike road ran toward the center of the rifle pit and then made an almost ninety-degree left turn across the front of the pit.[14] Hogan's map labeled the rifle pit, "earth work."

While the rifle pit was being prepared, Moore assigned a second detachment to fell trees at the west end of the six-acre cultivated field to provide timber to reinforce the main defense line. They worked until almost midnight, keeping their weapons close by, and then slept where they worked.[15]

The wagon train of the 12th Rhode Island, which had returned to the safety of the camp at Green River Bridge, pulled out in the morning. The party, including a guard detachment of 28 men, hoped that it could get to Jamestown safely by going through Neatsville.[16] Alas, the slow-moving wagon train did not reach Jamestown without a skirmish with Morgan's troopers the following day. It fought well, although attacked by 65–70 of the Rebels. Confederate casualties were one killed, two wounded, and seven captured.[17]

Thursday, July 2: Further Defensive Preparations

Morgan is coming! The Confederate force has almost completed crossing the Cumberland River near Burkesville, fifty miles away.

Capt. Edwin Childs, of Company E, brought in a relief crew to work on the Tebbs Bend defenses this morning. They felled trees around the chosen defended position to clear fields of fire. They dug a trench, set "fair-sized logs" on end, and threw dirt in front of them to form breast works. According to Rebel Pvt. Green

Keller, who charged the emplacement during the battle, it was a "ditch filled with water outside the earthwork" and "beyond this were felled trees with sharpened branches pointing toward the enemy." This arrangement was called an abatis.[18] Other participants referred to the defenses as a stockade.

Sara Wells Sherrod

Green Keller, CSA

Friday, July 3: Final Preparations

Morgan is coming! Morgan reaches Columbia, 12 miles away, by 10:00 A.M. and defeats a detachment of Wolford's Cavalry. Capt. Jesse Carter lies dying at the hotel.

Lt. Benjamin Travis, officer of the day, alerted the men on guard that Morgan's men were massing not far away. Moore's men continued to fell trees and prepare their defenses, all through the day into the night. They cut trees south of the rifle pit and along the road. More sharpened stakes were placed in two zigzag rows in front of the abatis.

The families along the road and in Tebbs Bend were warned by the Michigan troops to vacate their homes to avoid being hit by shellfire. The Edmond Burress family and the John Johnston family, who lived near the Federal camps, both decided to flee. The Burresses were taken in by the Robert S. Tates, who lived further north on the Columbia Road.[19] The Mary and John Johnston family, who had entertained the Federal troops, began gathering their belongings in saddlebags to flee. Husband John was sick, so Mary waited until late afternoon to depart when she managed to get him on horseback, with one-year-old Eliza in front and four-year-old George behind him.

Mary and son Thomas, aged 11, set off on foot walking south down an old wagon road leading to Sublett Ford of Green River, leading the horse. At the ford, they called out to William Branch Sublett, who lived across the river, to come help them. He came across the river on his raft to pick up the family. They continued their journey through Lemmon's Bend on their way to the Ebenezer community.

It was getting late. Mary Johnston took down the rails of a fence, led the horse into some woods and left it with Thomas holding the reins. She then returned alone to replace the rails. After completing the task, Mary sat on the fence to rest. While there, her bonnet was pierced by a bullet and her face grazed. She fell to the ground as if dead and lay there for some time. Then she got up and ran into the woods.[20] Another version of the story has this happening at the ford. William Branch Sublett took her across the river and returned for her husband. While waiting on the bank, a bullet tore into her bonnet.[21]

When she returned home after the battle, Mrs. Johnston found a Union soldier seated on her front doorstep guarding the house. The young man said, "Mrs. Johnston, I got a Rebel yesterday evening. I know I got him, for I saw him drop off the rail fence when I shot." Mary replied, "I guess I'm the Rebel you got," showing her wounded cheek and the bullet hole in her bonnet.[22]

Night of July 3: Morgan Sets Order of Battle

Late in the day, Morgan, at his headquarters at the Bridgewater House in Cane Valley, was finalizing preparations to capture the Yanks and burn the bridge again. The forces available to him were much larger, more experienced, and better trained than the ones defending the bridge under Moore's command.

Morgan, accustomed to victory, did not anticipate serious difficulty with defeating the untried Moore. At his side was 25-year-old, wiry Colonel Duke, his brother-in-law and "managing man." A native of Scott County and a young attorney, Duke had helped train the men and was responsible for many of Morgan's innovative tactics and maneuvers.[23]

Morgan decided to use only three regiments in a direct attack against the Union position and hold two regiments in reserve. He also planned to send two regiments on a wide flanking maneuver north of the bridge to cut off Moore's communications, to prevent reinforcements from Lebanon, and to block the retreat of the defeated enemy.[24] In the language of the day, the Rebels planned to "gobble up" the Yanks.

Morgan chose the 8th Kentucky, commanded by Col. Roy S. Cluke, and several companies of the 10th Kentucky, usually commanded by Col. Adam R. Johnson, to make the left flanking maneuver. Since Johnson was to be in the main assault, Lt. Col. Wash Owen assumed command of this action.

The Confederates were well led. Cluke, in his 40s, 6 feet 4 inches tall with sandy brown hair and a mustache, from Winchester, was a veteran of the Mexican War. He would later die in a Northern prison of diphtheria. Owen, from Henderson, had a reputation as a "dashing, daring, cavalryman, admired for his courage and high honor by all who knew him." He was well organized and in complete control of his troops at all times.[25]

The fords across Green River to the west of the bridge—Johnson's, Lemmon's, Bailey's—were reached by the dirt road which passed by Ebenezer Presbyterian Church. These fords provided crossings to Lemmons Bend, where the troops could then proceed to Morgan's objective—the bottomland north of the bridge.[26]

One of the guides was Lt. Dick Archie Webster, a native of Taylor County, who as a boy knew the fishing holes, riffles, and fords of Green River. It is said that he took a stick and drew the roads to the fords in the dust. The Roach boys, John and William from Green County, who also served as guides, knew that the ford at Roachville could be reached from Penitentiary Bend.[27]

Porter Harned

Lt. Richard A. Webster

Some of Captain Franks' scouts departed first from Cane Valley, riding down the Columbia-Campbellsville Turnpike and turning off to the west on Ebenezer Road. There they rode past the farm of Revolutionary soldier-settler Sherrod Griffin and the cemetery where he and his brother Burgess, an overseer of Poplar Forrest, one of Thomas Jefferson's plantations, were buried. About a mile down the road, the scouts turned north down a wagon road through the Johnson farm and descended the wooded river bank to Johnson Ford, where the drop was gradual and easy on the horses.[28] They crossed the river there.

After a brief rest, they pressed on through the late evening, aided by the moonlight. Encountering no enemy, they made excellent progress and camped by a big spring on land owned by Merritt Martin. Some rode on through the bottomlands and saw the campfires of the 25th Michigan, on the north side of the river.[29]

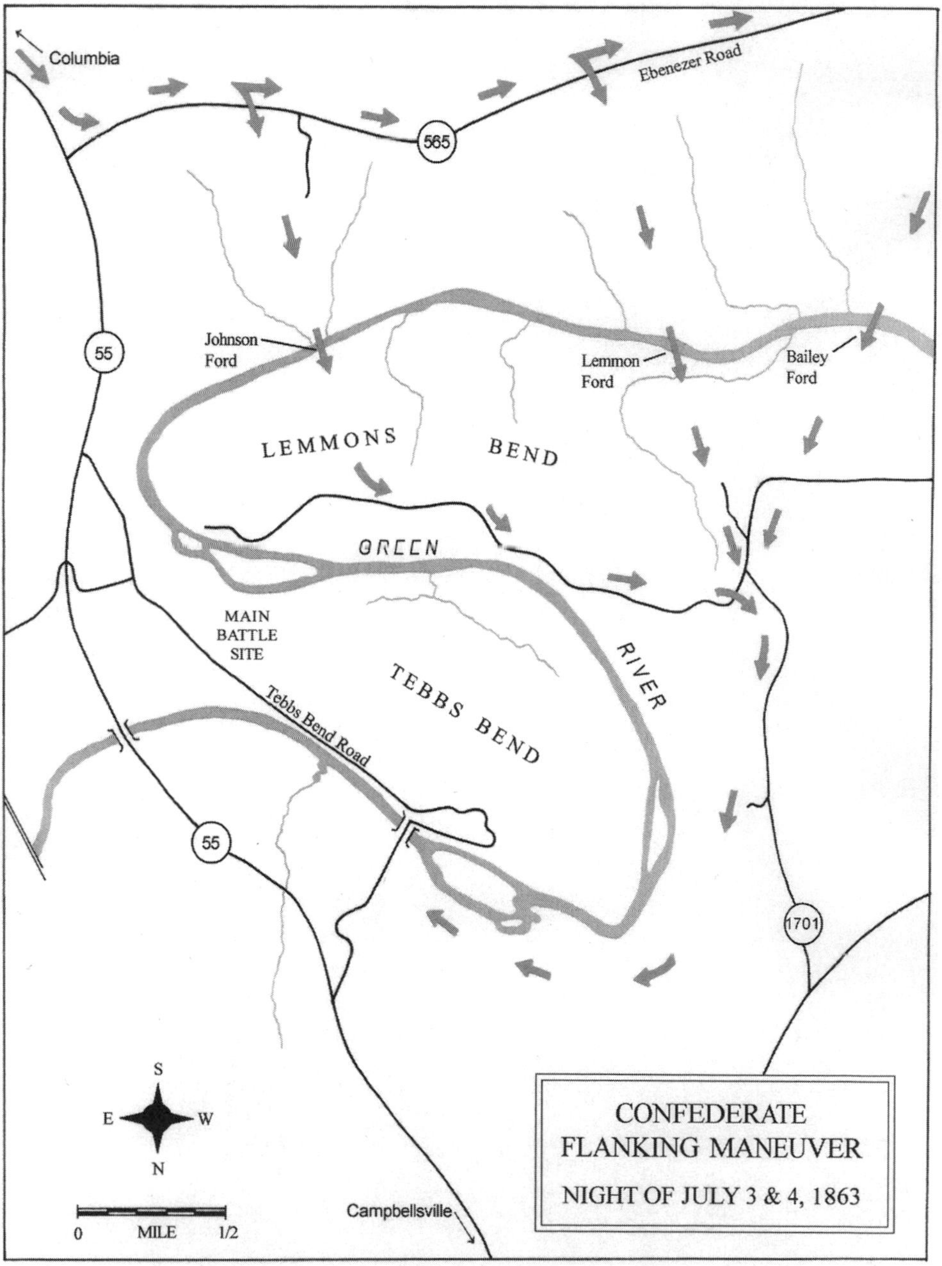
Columbia
Ebenezer Road
565
55
Johnson Ford
Lemmon Ford
Bailey Ford
LEMMONS
BEND
GREEN
RIVER
MAIN BATTLE SITE
TEBBS BEND
Tebbs Bend Road
55
1701
S
E
W
N
0
MILE
1/2
Campbellsville
CONFEDERATE FLANKING MANEUVER
NIGHT OF JULY 3 & 4, 1863

Map by Maria Brent

Approach to Johnson Ford

Johnson Ford, Taylor County

Cluke's and Owen's forces followed in the path of the scouts, but did not begin crossing the fords until after midnight, moving quietly so as not to alert the Federal pickets on the bluff above them. The horses had to be led over the slippery rocks in the beds of the streams which emptied into the river. Green River had receded and the crossing in the moonlight at Johnson's Ford went well.[30]

Saturday, July 4: In Lemmons Bend, Taylor County

Morgan is here!

On the other side of the river, Cluke's and Owen's troops rode through the corn and grain fields of Lemmon's Bend, passing log houses, one of which had been built with the help of Federal soldiers the previous summer.[31]

Log House built by Union soldiers, Lemmons Bend, Taylor County

Lemmons Bend was named for early settler Jacob Lemmon, whose descendents still had their home in the bend at the time of the Civil War. In the intervening years the Subletts, Martins, Kerrs, and Stubbs established farms there. The fertile bottomland is surrounded by palisades of limestone rock, where Indians are buried in caves on the cliffs.

The view from the Griffin farm on the bluff overlooking the valley is one of the most picturesque in south central Kentucky. In the spring, white dogwoods and pink redbuds bloom against the backdrop of trees not yet fully in leaf. In July, the fields become a carpet of emerald velvet. The rugged bluffs above the curving river, home to copperheads and rattlesnakes, are steep and rarely climbed.

Lemmons Bend viewed from Green River Bluff. The Johnson Ford road into Lemmons Bend runs from the river on the left behind the silos in the center of photo.

Another of Morgan's regiments, the 2nd Kentucky, rode further down the Ebenezer Road and then turned north toward the river. After crossing at Lemmon's and Bailey's fords early in the morning of July 4, some of the hungry men stopped at William A. Rucker's log house in Lemmons Bend. As the mounted men approached the house, his boys, William Joseph, aged nine, Robert Fields, aged seven, and Richard Thomas, aged five, crawled under the bed. The soldiers dismounted, stepped up on the porch, and asked for food. William's wife, Letitia Bratton Rucker, cooked breakfast for the rough and rowdy cavalrymen, using up "everything in the house," while she watched toddler John and held the hand of her four-year-old daughter, Sarah Frances. From their hiding place, the boys could only see mud-spattered boots with spurs. "When the boys came out from under the bed, there was nothing left for them to eat." When the family went to the barn, their fresh horses had been swapped for Morgan's tired ones.[32]

Gracie Jeter

William A. Rucker Home, Lemmons Bend

Jewell Reynolds

Jake Lemmons House, Lemmons Bend, Taylor County

Other Rebels found breakfast further up the road, at Jake Lemmon's house, where they "stole all the eggs, chickens, horses, or anything else they could find."[33]

By daylight, Cluke's and Owen's forces had reached their objective, the bottomland on the north side of the bridge. But by that time, the reported Federal camp on the north side of the bridge was no longer there. From the deserted spot, they looked back toward the river for enemy troops on the high bluffs overlooking the bridge.

At the river, they captured Sgt. Norris H. Merrill, 25th Michigan, who told them that reinforcements were on the way, a deliberate fabrication. This news was quickly related back through the lines to the Confederate command.

Friday, the Night before the Battle, July 3–4: Federal Position

Moore's pickets on the bluff observed scouts and forward elements of Cluke's forces moving through Lemmon's Bend below them. This led to the hope that the Confederates might be bypassing their main position, giving rise to the feeling that the anticipated battle might not happen. The "green" young soldiers might not "see the elephant" after all.

This hope soon passed. The videttes Moore had posted on the Columbia-Campbellsville Turnpike rode into Moore's camp and reported that the Rebel army was now only six miles away and moving rapidly toward them.[34]

Moore wanted the Rebel scouts to believe that his camp was still north of the river and vulnerable. He had delayed moving it as long as possible so as to create the illusion that he was receiving reinforcements.

BATTLE OF TEBBS BEND - GREEN RIVER BRIDGE JULY 4, 1863

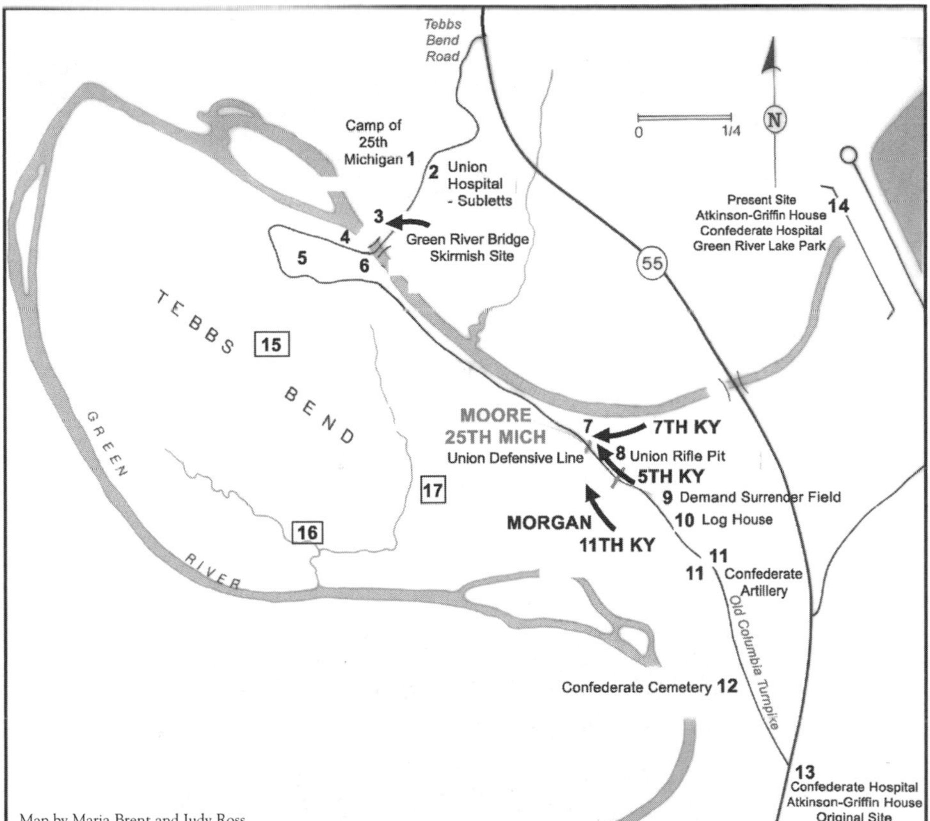

Map by Maria Brent and Judy Ross

1. Camp of the 25th Michigan
2. Union Hospital - Subletts
3. Green River Bridge Skirmish Site - Ford
4. Soldiers' Spring
5. Union Field Hospital & Temporary Graves
6. Green River Stockade
7. Union Defensive Line
8. Union Rifle Pit
9. Demand Surrender Field
10. Log House
11. Confederate Artillery
12. Confederate Cemetery
13. Original Site Confederate Hospital
14. Present Site Confederate Hospital
15. Pleasant Howard House
16. William Kerr House
17. John Johnston House

Approach to Green River Bridge with Sublett's Field in the foreground. Site of the burning of U.S. government corn by Morgan's Men on the Christmas Raid and of Col. R.S. Cluke's skirmish on the Great Raid. Sublett's house is out of photo on the left of the road.

At 8:30 P.M. videttes reported that the Rebel force was only two miles away. At that point, Colonel Moore decided to move his camp equipage from the north side of the Green River to the south side. The wagon masters started fording the river and pulling their wagons to the flat land on the top of the bluff near the stockade. They worked slowly and deliberately all through the night by the light of the full moon, knowing that the sound of the wagon wheels rumbling over the macadamized road could be heard by neighbors and enemy scouts.[35]

Green River Iron Bridge, built 1907, replaced the 1863 covered bridge. The 8th Mich. & 79th New York set up a defensive position behind a rock wall on the south end of the bridge, July 4, 1863.

The sky was clear and the moon was rising as Moore's men readied themselves for the move. Everything but the barest essentials had been placed on the wagons. Anticipating the next day's fight, each man made certain that his Enfield was in perfect order and his cap pouch and ammunition was in place. An advance party of about 185 set out down the road past Sublett's log house toward the temporary bridge over the river. The roadside was lined with wild ditch lilies and Queen Anne's lace. The marchers paid little attention to their surroundings, thinking only of what awaited them on the morrow.

Sublett Home—Union Hospital, Tebbs Bend Road

Watercolor by Billie Young, Hendersonville, Tenn.

A few sick Yankees were at Sublett's, being taken care of by James Allen Sublett and his wife. Before the night was over, other ill soldiers, Rebels, would join them, the Subletts keeping the Rebs and Yankees in separate rooms.[36]

Moore's troops broke ranks and walked over Lieutenant Hogan's temporary bridge in single file, those in I Company, whispering in Dutch. As they gazed at the river, muddy from the rains, none foresaw that in a few hours bodies would be floating downstream in its reddened waters. At least one company then turned, walked back over the bridge, and returned again and again to make it appear to enemy scouts listening that there were reinforcements arriving. Some mounted horsemen did the same, with hooves clattering over the wooden planks.[37]

The men stopped at the "soldiers' spring" to fill their canteens as they marched up the road to the summit of the bluff. They entered the open ground of Tebbs Bend of Green River and passed beyond the dilapidated stockade that had guarded the bridge earlier in the war. A hospital tent was already set up nearby.[38]

Colonel Moore had never considered making his stand at the stockade.[39] He had no intention of giving Morgan a second chance to burn it.[40] Now the stockade only had a few tents belonging to the 8th Michigan and the 79th New York bridge builders.

The men could look out over the land and see a flickering light from the log house of William B. Kerr. The house, with the river at its back, had happy memories for the soldiers. Some of them had gotten water from the Kerr spring. Many had talked with Lucinda Bratton Kerr, as she stood over a hot fire cooking meals for them, which she had done for the hundreds of troops camped there. When she had to go deliver babies, she would call "her boys" to ferry her across the river."[41]

The rich land in this bend of Green River had been claimed by Destin Tibbs as early as 1799. Tibbs' son died in the War of 1812 and his daughters married and did not carry on the family name. After the following day's battle was reported by Colonel Moore in the Official Records, Tibbs Bend will be remembered forever in its misspelled form, Tebb's or Tebbs Bend.[42]

The troops marched on past the John Johnston house where no one was at home. When the family returned, little was bothered in the house; only the linen, bed clothes, needles and thread, had been taken. They were grabbed by desperate hospital stewards to bandage and suture wounds at the Federal field hospital up top of the bluff.[43]

With twenty-five men, Lieutenant Travis stayed behind at the campsite on the north side of the river to complete the move to new campsite on the bluff above the bridge. Men from each company were detailed to load tents, cooking utensils, extra rations, and ammunition into wagons and transport them to the new site.

Dirk Van Raalte, hospital steward, told his parents in a letter how difficult it had been to get the hospital "material" across the ford. The temporary bridge could not sustain the weight of the heavily loaded wagons, which were pulled by as many as four horses. Travis wrote: "The water had subsided and we were able to ford the river just below the bridge, which was very opportune in the present emergency." They had to take the old road down to Sublett Landing and cross at the "riffle" where there was a sand bar. Wilterdink tells that "it took the whole night with hard labor."[44]

Travis realized how precarious their position was. A few Confederates could easily capture his little contingent. He posted a "vigilant guard" one third of a mile north of where they were working, probably at the Thomas and Jane Caldwell Buchanan House, which was just being constructed.[45]

Colonel Moore formed up his men and gave them final instructions for the upcoming battle: "Don't be afraid, my boys. Be quiet, men. Let your guns speak for themselves. No shouting. No colors are to fly so the enemy will not know our numbers." He advised them to be as "cool as cucumbers." Moore assured his men of his confidence in them: "We can take on thousands."[46]

Undoubtedly there were prayers on the lips of the untested boys of Co. I, remembering the words of Dutch minister A.C. Van Raalte as the company, including his sons, departed from Holland, Michigan: "You may return wounded, maimed, crippled, or dead—but never as cowards."[47] They felt that their

Ken Pierce

Federal Lookout: Thomas Buchanan Home, Columbia Road, Taylor County

cause was "just;" some felt they were on a holy crusade and petitioned God to be on "their side."

Moore looked forward to the battle, expecting to redeem himself in the eyes of the officers who had "bullraggled" him in Louisville. His wife and new-born daughter, whom he had never seen, were also in his mind. It is likely that he did not doubt that his strong position would repel Morgan's attackers, and anticipated putting his faithful bugle to his lips in the midst of battle.

Little did he know that his California adversaries, Generals Garnett and Armistead, had fallen in Pickett's charge and lay dead on the great battlefield at Gettysburg.

Moore's sharpshooters, many of whom were farmers accustomed to hunting squirrels, quail, and rabbits, were well trained for their task of taking out the artillerymen and were confident in their skills. One of the sharpshooters was an Indian, noted for his keen eyesight. They, however, certainly must have been apprehensive, knowing how critical their role was in the impending conflict. Moore knew the Confederates had four pieces of artillery and predicted where they would be sited. His sharpshooters had been trained to make use of cover, take careful aim, and fire at the gunners as they served their cannons.

Throughout the night and into the early morning of July 4, seventy-five men of the 25th Michigan lay in wait in the rifle pit, thinking of home and family, with their Enfields at the ready. Many months had passed since they first waited in battle line at Munfordville anticipating an assault from Morgan, whose exploits were legendary. Now, at last, they were going to do battle with him.

About 100 yards to the rear of the rifle pit, the rest of the men behind the abatis looked out over the breastworks, stumps, and sharpened branches of the felled trees. No one slept.

Green River, Taylor County

Daybreak, Saturday, July 4: Narrows of Tebbs Bend

The day dawned hot and steamy. The Green River was running fast against bended boughs of sycamore and water maples. The river often has a mist that hangs over it that lifts with the sun. When streaks of light started illuminating the sky, Lieutenant Travis and the men could hear, as they finished moving the camp over the river, the melancholy calls of the wood thrush and the great blue herons squalling.

The men assigned to guard duty came in and helped get the last wagons through the mist and across the ford below the bridge. Twenty men of Moore's, in addition to twenty of Hogan's bridge-builders of the 8th Michigan and the 79th New York, were assigned to defend the bridge on the south side of the river from a lightly defended position next to the bluff and at the south end of the bridge. To their rear was a path up the bluff to the stockade that could be used to withdraw from an attacking force.

Among the defenders at the bridge were sharp shooters. Because of the heavy tree cover, the regiments of Colonel Cluke and Owen in the bottomland were hidden to them. The trees across the river on the north side along the bank had been cut, however, so that the defenders would have clear fields of fire on anyone attempting to take the bridge or cross at the ford.

After the wagons of the 25th Michigan climbed the long hill with their last load and were nearing the old stockade, Travis heard the first gunshot from a picket echo across the still dark southern skies. He could see his watch. It was 4:35 A.M. It would soon be daylight and the skirmishing was about to begin.[46]

Daybreak, Saturday, July 4 — Confederate Position: Cane Valley

Before dawn at Cane Valley, the Bridgewater servants were up early preparing breakfast for General Morgan and his staff. After a hearty meal, they mounted their horses and galloped up the road. In his haste, one of the officers, maybe Morgan himself, left a long, heavy overcoat, which remained in the Bridgewater family for years.[47]

The boots-and-saddles bugle call rang out early in the morning in the Confederate camps from Cane Valley to Ebenezer Road. It alerted one regiment as it was coming up from Columbia, and awakened another after a hard night consuming "spirits" looted in Columbia. Many of the men called to duty were exhausted from their harrowing experiences crossing the Obey and the Cumberland. Some had fought in Columbia. Every cavalryman fed and watered his horse, grabbed what food he could, and moved out as the rays of the dawn lit up the sky in the east.[48]

Captain Tom Franks' scouts had reported hearing the sound of axes and the crash of falling trees through the night at Tebbs Bend. The sound of horses' hooves clattering across the bridge had also been heard. A slave had told that he had heard "the rumbling of wagons all night long." Lt. Xenophon Hawkins, Company A, 2nd Kentucky, was on picket duty that night, and reported that Michiganders were cutting the trees a quarter mile away from where he stood.[51]

General Morgan was certain that Colonel Moore had no artillery, and according to Louisville newspapers, less than a regiment of troops. In spite of indications that Moore had been preparing a defensive position, Morgan anticipated that Moore would see the fruitlessness of his situation and, after token resistance to uphold his honor, would retreat, or surrender. Morgan expected that Cluke and Owen's forces would soon be in position to cut off any attempt by Moore to withdraw. He resisted his subordinates' recommendation that they just bypass Tebbs Bend because he did not wish to have a Union force to his rear and was accustomed to easy victories. Therefore, he ordered his troops forward to this ill-fated encounter.

The men in Morgan's two brigades were battle-hardened and superbly led. The attack force was commanded by Col. Adam Rankin "Stovepipe" Johnson, who had used stovepipes as fake cannon in his victory at Newburgh, Indiana in 1862, and deceived the Yanks with his bonfires at Lebanon.

Two regiments of Johnson's 2nd Brigade were committed to battle: 7th (often called the 3rd) Kentucky Cavalry, commanded by thirty-one year old Texan Lt. Col. John M. Huffman, and the 11th Kentucky Cavalry, led by thirty-seven year old, bearded Col. David Waller Chenault of Madison County. Capt. J.C. Bennett's company from the 10th Kentucky also fought with the 2nd Brigade.

Duke's 1st Brigade included the 5th Kentucky, commanded by Col. D. Howard Smith of Scott County, loved by his subordinates and recognized everywhere by his long, white beard that flowed over his chest, as well as companies of Grigsby's 6th and Cluke's 8th Kentucky.

Two regiments—Col. J. Warren Grigsby's 6th Kentucky and Col. William W. Ward's 9th Tennessee—were held in reserve on the pike.[52] At least some elements of Col. Dick Morgan's regiment were also in the rearguard.[53]

Major Ed Byrne's battery of two Parrot 3-inch rifled guns and two 12-pounder howitzers supported Morgan's force. Byrne only recruited "the better class of men" as his first gunners in Greenville, Mississippi in 1861/1862. He sought similar men when he reconstituted his unit after the battle of Shiloh.

Artillerymen required more technical and mathematical skills than infantrymen and were often fascinated by their field pieces which could wreak such havoc on the battlefield. A single cannon required seven men to serve it and sixteen horses to pull the gun and its caisson. After Shiloh the battery was broken up, and Byrne accepted a promotion to major and command of an artillery battalion from his friend General Morgan.

Byrne's reorganized battery retained many of its leaders—Lieutenants Elias D. Lawrence, John Joyes, Jr., Frank Peak, and Sergeant-major A.G. Talbott. Several cavalrymen from the 2nd, 3rd, and 9th Kentucky were assigned to the battery in late 1862.[54]

Chenault's men of the 11th Kentucky were weary from all-night marches and little sleep. The regiment included the four sons of Oliver Wingfield Cosby, an Irish wheelwright, James William, Austin Dunn "Ausey," John, and Oliver, whose mother was a cousin of Henry Clay. One of the Cosby daughters, Amanda, married Peter Dozier, a cavalryman of this unit. Also with the group was E.G. Baxter, who enlisted when he was 12, turned 13 by the time of the Christmas Raid, the youngest on this raid. The 11th had been rear guard in Columbia and its men had been on duty until 3 o'clock in the morning, getting only two hours sleep. As they moved into position at Tebbs Bend and waited to go into battle, the men, including the four Maupin boys, who had shared a single musket on enlistment until captured Federal weapons became available, could hear the ominous ringing of axes.[55]

Maj. Thomas Y. Brent, Jr., 5th Ky. Cavalry, CSA

Probably no one looked finer on a horse than Major Thomas Young Brent, Jr., who would soon lead the 5th Kentucky with reckless courage in the face of enemy fire. His wife, at home in Bourbon County, feared that the blood she had discovered on her dress at a party might prove a bad omen. While others were thinking of the fighting that lay ahead, Brent may have wished that he could slip away home and embrace his baby girl and pregnant wife. Three brothers of Lt. Tom Jeff Current had served in the war, one had died and his aged and deaf father had been shot in early 1863 by a Federal soldier when he had not responded to the command "Halt."[56]

As Morgan's regiments rode down the road, they passed the double-pen log house of Virginia Griffin Atkinson, widow of Joel Atkinson. Griffins and Atkinsons were slave holding families. They felt that their family fortune depended on Kentucky returning to Confederate hands. Close to the road, they were often visited by soldiers on both sides. Virginia hid the silver in the well and kept the horses in the back woods. Although it was dangerous to show sympathy for the South, they gave Virginia's grandson, born in 1863, the name Jefferson Lee, but referred to him as "Brother" until the war was over.[57]

From where they stood in front of their house on the east side of the pike, the Atkinson-Griffin family, together with their slaves, watched the cavalrymen. Not one of them would ever forget the superb horses, the pungent smell of their sweat, their neighing and pawing, with tails swishing. Eyes remained fixed on the men as they halted, checked their Navy Colt revolvers, and counted their scarce ammunition with anxious expressions on their faces, with the clinking of the tin cups in the background. The watchers later reported that, in those moments, they had felt the immediacy of that morning's battle, sensing and sharing the men's apprehension and confidence.

Original site of Atkinson-Griffin House was the Columbia Road, Taylor County; now the house is a museum at Green River Lake Park.

James Madison Griffin, with beard seated in left center of photo, at family home, 1908.

Later reports indicate that ammunition was short, each man in the 10th having only seven rounds for his musket. Maybe some thought that this would do since they were about to face very few Yankees. Standard issue was 60 rounds, 40 in the cartridge box and 20 somewhere in the clothing.[58]

Pickets Exchange Fire

Between the Atkinson house at Tampico and the next log house on the pike to the north, the Southern advance guard from Company C, 10th Kentucky, moved down both sides of the road, exchanging fire with the Union pickets, who, as they were driven back, scurried from tree to tree returning fire, until they came in range of covering fire from their own forward positions.[59] Mounted Federal videttes had long since ridden in and reported on the strength of approaching enemy forces.

Nineteen-year-old Pieter VerSchure, a Northern picket, took a musket ball in the belly and lay on the battlefield, gravely wounded, with entrails exposed, until the morning's fighting ended. Hours later, John Wilterdink, his friend in Company I, found him. As he and three other men carried him toward the hospital, Pieter called out, "Oh John, give me water," and then said, "Just keep it for yourself." Pieter kept his eyes fixed on Wilterdink and murmered, "John, can you pray for me?" John replied, "Yes, Piet, with my whole heart." Pieter's last words were, "I will die before I reach camp." And so he did.[60]

Pieter, one of six children born in the Netherlands, was a tanner by trade in Holland, Michigan and enlisted in Captain Martin DeBow's Company I, 25th Michigan, in Adamsville. He was described as a "good faithful boy and steady in his work," who brought his wages home to his family and continued to send his pay home as a soldier. His father, Andries, a gardener by trade, suffered a stroke when he learned of Pieter's death at Tebbs Bend.[61]

As the Rebels rounded the curve in the pike, they came upon a small rise on terrain suitable for placing the artillery. To their front, they could see the side of a story-and-a-half log house close to the road. A stable stood about one hundred yards behind the house toward the rifle pit. The buildings and the terrain offered some cover for the dismounted troops forming up for the coming attack and allowed horses to be sheltered from the fire of Northern sharpshooters.

Log House Lookout: Narrows of Tebbs Bend

The Rebels quickly moved forward and seized the log house, as it provided an excellent observation post.[62] They scurried up the pie-shaped stairway to a second-floor room with sloping ceilings and a window looking out toward the enemy's forward defenses. The chinking and interstices between the logs were removed with knives and bayonets.[63]

About 400 yards in the distance across an open field, they could see the earthwork Moore had thrown up as a forward defensive position, which became known as the Rifle Pit. It consisted of a trench about 120 feet long, fronted by a parapet of earth, tree branches and fence rails, designed to delay the Rebel advance. It was manned by 75 men, plus the pickets who had withdrawn into it. Moore's plan was to have the rifle pit defenders withdraw to the main defensive line after putting up a brief fight.[64]

Major Ed Byrne was ordered to pull his battery into position on the overlooking ridge. This was exactly where Moore predicted the Confederate guns would be placed, where they could bring fire on his rifle pit.[65]

Log House, commandeered by the Confederates, Tebbs Bend Road, Taylor County, torn down in 1979

Gerald Myers

Rebel Artillery, Tebbs Bend

Chapter Five: Confederate Attack at the Narrows of Tebbs Bend, July 4, 1863

Rebel Artillery Shot, 6:30 A.M.

Byrne's Parrotts fired one or two shells into the rifle pit, 530 yards to their front, "crashing through the works, which were too slightly built to withstand the use of artillery, being intended only as an outer defense." The sound of splintering wood could be heard as the fencing around the rifle pit was torn to bits. Two Federals were wounded. George Hicks had an arm torn from his body and a leg shattered. Hicks, a handsome 21-year-old blue-eyed farmer, died from his injuries on July 22, 1863, in Campbellsville, leaving a widow and an 18-month-old son, William.[1]

Roy Olson

George Hicks, 25th Michigan

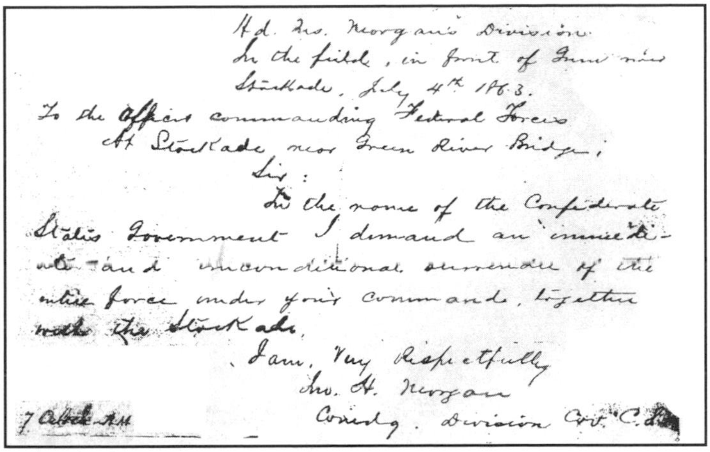
Hd. Qrs. Morgan's Division
In the field, in front of Green River
Stockade, July 4th 1863.
To the Officer commanding Federal Forces
At Stockade near Green River Bridge;
Sir:
In the name of the Confederate States Government I demand an immediate and unconditional surrender of the entire force under your command, together with the Stockade.
I am, Very Respectfully
Jno. H. Morgan
Comdg. Division Cvt. C.S.A.
7 o'clock AM

Original note, Bentley Historical Society, Ann Arbor

Morgan's Demand for Surrender, July 4, 1863

Georgia Dept. of Archives

Lt. Col. Robert A. Alston

Porter Harned

Lt. Col. Joseph T. Tucker

Steven L. Wright

Maj. William P. Elliott

Morgan Demands Surrender

Immediately after the guns had fired on the Union forward position, General Morgan followed his usual practice in this situation and sent officers forward under a flag of truce to demand that the enemy surrender. Lt. Colonel Robert A. Alston, his chief of staff, formerly of the 2nd Kentucky, now of the 9th Tennessee, Lt. Col. Joseph T. Tucker, of the 11th Kentucky, and Major W.P. Elliott, quartermaster of Morgan's Division, and possibly Col. Basil Duke, rode out with the following note:[2]

> Hd. Qrs. Morgan's Division
> In the field, in front of Green River
> Stockade, July 4, 1863.

To the Officer commanding Federal Forces
At Stockade, near Green River Bridge

Sir:

In the name of the Confederate States Government, I demand an immediate and unconditional surrender of the entire force under your command, together with the stockade.

I am, Very Respectfully,
Jno. H. Morgan
Comdg. Division Cav. C.S.A

7 o'clock A.M.[3]

Federal Capt. Spencer S. Lansing, Company F, in command of the front, rode out and met the bearers, and took the written message back to Colonel Moore. Mounted on Lion, Moore rode forward to meet the delegation in the open field between the log house and the Federal rifle pit. After a handshake and another careful reading of the demand, Moore smiled, as confirmed by Col. Tucker, and replied:

> Present my compliments to General Morgan, and say to him that, this being the fourth day of July, I cannot entertain his proposition [to surrender.][4]

The flag bearer, Lt. Colonel Alston, described as very outspoken, urged Colonel Moore not to fight, pointing out part of Morgan's force was already in his rear and that retreat was impossible, adding "I hope you will not consider me as dictatorial on this occasion; I will be frank with you. You see the breach we have made in your work with our battery; you cannot expect to repulse Gen. Morgan's whole division with your little command. You have resisted us gallantly and deserve credit for it, and now I hope you will save useless bloodshed by reconsidering your message to Gen. Morgan."[5]

With a determined look on his face, Colonel Moore replied: "Sir, when you assume to know my strength, you assume to know too much. I have a duty to perform to my country, and the presence of this day supports me in my decision; therefore I can not reconsider my reply to General Morgan."

Once again shaking hands, Colonel Alston replied with a touch of gallantry: "Goodbye, Col. Moore, God only knows who may fall first."[6]

Moore turned Lion toward the rifle pit and the Confederates turned their mounts toward the log house. Aware that the fatal decision had been taken and that they may not be alive on the morrow, the Confederate and Union parties galloped to their respective sides.[7]

Battle of Tebbs Bend as portrayed in Harper's Magazine, *August 1865.*

Clash of Men and Arms

And so, Colonel Moore, with inexperienced troops, no reinforcements for thirty miles, and no artillery, was surprisingly confident about defeating Morgan. Moore's force numbered about 266, including Hogan's 20 men. He had approximately 170 on the field, 26 at the fords—including the 10 mounted men, 40 back at the bridge—20 of Hogan's and 20 of Company I, and 30 unarmed men, serving as teamsters and hospital stewards. General Morgan's three regiments plus several companies from other regiments, as well as the artillery battery, totaled 800-1,000, not including the two regiments being held in reserve. Thus, Colonel Moore was outnumbered 4 or 5 to l. Colonel Tucker said that the 11th Kentucky alone had 500 effective troops before the battle.[8]

Again the Southern cannons flashed. Deadly fire poured in among the seventy-five Federals, lying side by side in the rifle pit. The shot into the bank protecting the men knocked out more of the fence rails, turning the rifle pit into dust. The field was momentarily blanketed with smoke.[9]

The Michigan regiment had come under serious enemy fire for the first time in their lives. Now, they had seen the "elephant." The cannoneers were in the midst of reloading their pieces.[10]

More shots were fired. The deafening shriek of the shells shook the earth. On this high bluff, it seemed as if the world stood still, waiting for the next burst of fire. Six miles from the field, a gentleman was sitting on a stump and listening to the explosions.[11]

Colonel Moore ordered his men, who had been lying on the ground during the cannon attack, to fire: "Now boys, rise up and take deliberate aim. Shoot those Rebel gunners." As the sharpshooters in the trenches rose to their feet, they waited for the smoke to clear. Now, they could see the guns of the enemy shining in the early morning sunlight.[12] They squinted their eyes against the sun's rays and carefully sighted their Enfield rifles at the artillerymen. Dressed in gray uniforms, trimmed in scarlet, the men of Byrne's Battery were outlined against the morning sky. Moore's men took deliberate aim and fired by rank. Yankee Minie bullets spattered off the cannons.[13]

Bentley Historical Library, Ann Arbor

Adj. Charles Woodruff, 25th Michigan

"After the first fire Morgan was unable to work his artillery as our men would shoot down every gunner that came out from behind the trees. In fact the wheels of the gun carriage were so riddled by ball as to be entirely useless," Adj. Charles Woodruff wrote to his father.[14]

At first only one piece of artillery was brought to bear on the Michiganders. With the disabling of the first, other pieces were brought forward and more shells were fired. Travis commented that the well-directed fire of the Enfields made it impossible to work the Southern artillery with safety.[15]

In all, eighteen Confederate artillerymen were picked off by the sharpshooters, reported the historian of the 25th Michigan. One of Morgan's men wrote that four cannoneers were killed and seven wounded. Whatever the truth, standing on the little rise behind the artillery on that sunny morning loading those pieces was fraught with great peril. When Colonel Moore wrote his report in the *Official Records*, he simply stated: "The Confederate artillery was silenced."[16]

At this point the entire nature of the battle changed and Morgan's hope for a quick victory evaporated. He could little afford to lose any more trained artillerymen or have his cannon disabled so early in his campaign. Morgan now faced the same dilemma that Lee experienced at Gettysburg: should he withdraw without any more losses or make a frontal assault in force. It would not be difficult to retreat two miles down the turnpike road, turn west on the Ebenezer Road, and follow the path of Cluke and Owen, bypassing the fortified position above Green River Bridge. Clearly, colonels Johnson and Smith thought that this was the best option.[17]

On the other hand, the bypass was not without difficulty. The skies threatened rain and it would take precious time for the rest of the regiments, artillery, and Bragg's commissary train to ford Green River. Significant delay would derail Morgan's overall plan of threatening Louisville, crossing the Ohio River, and invading Northern territory. It might allow time for reinforcements to arrive and block his path. And this was not the way "the Thunderbolt of the Confederacy" fought battles.

If Duke disagreed with or discouraged Morgan in this endeavor, he did not record it. Colonels Johnson and Smith seem to have played the Longstreet role at Gettysburg, cautioning against frontal assault in front of such a strategically located and strongly fortified position.

As Lee, Morgan had a very high opinion of his men's ability and courage. Surely, the untested Michigan boys would give way; and surely, after a few volleys of minie balls, Colonel Moore would reason that his boys had made their best effort and surrender.

Morgan made the fateful decision to take the rifle pit first and then mount a frontal assault with all his forces on the formidable position 120 yards to its rear. He was falling into Colonel Moore's trap.

When he constructed the rifle pit just north of the narrows, about 33 yards wide, Moore ordered that dirt be taken from the northern side and heaped on the southern approach leaving the northern side open and in view of his forces. The rifle pit was built with the anticipation of its capture by the Confederates. It was situated "a little down the slope of the field, so that when it was in possession of the enemy, it would be useless," exposed to musket fire from Moore's main second line of defense."[18]

As the Confederates advanced through the narrow gap in front of the rifle-pit, they came under withering fire, took many casualties, and were forced to regroup by pulling into the woods near the stables. The Union force in the rifle pit provided Moore the disruption and delay he had anticipated.[19]

The fight in the rifle pit, however, was not as easy as Moore anticipated. His men came under fire during the first Confederate assault that they remembered for the rest of the war: "It was too hot for us to stay in the trench, so we fell back. I hadn't time to find my own company, so attached myself to another one. I tell you it did not make any difference with me as to what company I fought with as long as I didn't get a Rebel bullet through me . . . so I loaded and fired my musket as fast as I could," said Pvt. John Frick.[20]

Kalamazoo Public Library

Pvt. John Frick, 25th Michigan

Moore had divided the seventy-five men into two groups left and right: half were to run along the trench on the left side and half on the right side, and then withdraw quickly up the far sides of the field to join their comrades in the main defended position to the rear. In this way they would leave the advancing Federals open to fire from along the battle line behind the abatis.[21]

As the Federals withdrew, their fellow soldiers, behind the felled trees and breastwork in their rear, directed galling fire on the advancing Rebels.

Forward Movement of Artillery Halted

Johnson and Morgan could now see clearly Moore's main defended position. The Confederates now realized the difficulty they faced.

Moore had placed his main force, behind the formidable abatis with the fallen large trees distended toward the Southern position. The 100 men behind the abatis were joined by the pickets and the men from the rifle pit.[22]

The Rebels assaulting the Federal line would have to charge across an open field, then fight through sharpened tree branches, and cross a ditch filled with water to reach the fortification. During the charge they would be exposed to direct fire. The woods on the edge of the steep bluffs provided little cover, especially on the right flank.

Johnson saw that the use of artillery was essential to securing a Southern victory. Colonel Johnson wrote: "I was moving my artillery [forward] with the intention of opening fire on the fortifications, when General Morgan joined me in the Federal earthworks, [rifle-pit, no longer under fire] and gave orders not to use the artillery...." A Federal newspaper in Grand Rapids also reported this incident. Morgan saw that the terrain was such that the Rebel gunners would put themselves in more danger as they moved the cannon forward, that the cannoneers would be, again, in range of the Yankee rifled muskets. Therefore, Morgan ordered Johnson to remove the guns from the field.[23]

When the frontal assault was being discussed, Colonel Johnson reminded Morgan that his troops had only seven rounds of ammunition per man. Johnson insisted that this short supply of ammunition would be critical in the frontal assaults on the heavily defended position they faced.

Johnson asked the general not to attempt the direct attack and to bypass the position. But Morgan had made up his mind.[24]

Attack on the Federal Abatis

Johnson's men moved forward on the main defensive line. They came out of the rifle pit and ravines flanking it, trying to form an orderly attack force. Having left their mounts with horse holders in the rear, Chenault's 11th Kentucky massed on the left and Huffman's 7th Kentucky on the right. The troops formed "in infantry line of single rank with two yards of space between each man, the left and right flanks were thrown slightly forward."[25] They advanced on the double-quick, 165 steps a minute, screaming the Rebel yell, Yai-i, yai-i-i, yai-i-i-ih. Dirk Van Raalte commented on the charge: "The Rebels were as thick as hair on a dog."[26] J.C. Bennett's Company A of the 10th Kentucky moved forward on the Confederate right to set up enfilading fire on the left flank of Moore's position.[27]

Men lunged and leaped over the brush in front of the abatis, swore as they slipped in the mud, and struggled through the ditch before the hastily-built structure. As they fought their way forward, minie bullets whizzed past or thumped into flesh and bone.

Yankees, like Rebels, usually yelled during a battle, but on this day Colonel Moore specifically instructed his soldiers not make a sound and to hold their fire until they had taken careful aim at every Rebel that showed his head. He urged his men to let their guns make all the noise, warning them that their cheers would reveal the 25th's weakness in numbers.[28]

Morgan then ordered Duke to send the 5th Kentucky to support Johnson. Colonel Smith's men were in line behind its regimental flag, a red Latin cross on a blue field on one side and the words, On to Victory, on the other. The bearded Smith led his dismounted troops from behind the stables, through the narrow gap and past the rifle pit at the double-quick. From there they charged across the open field toward the main Union defensive position. As the men pushed forward, they kneeled to fire, and while doing so, came under deliberate fire from the fortification. More and more men fell and companies moved to the edge of the woods to regroup and charge again. A Confederate reported that as he "looked at the fortress, he could see no men but only rifle muzzles protruding out of port holes and little puffs of smoke rising from them." More fearless Rebs reached the abatis which fronted the Union defensive line.[29] Its "sharpened limbs or branches cut into their flesh" as the men crawled and slashed their way over it, struggling forward to the stockade."[30]

Moore's men, quiet in their ranks, but intensely in earnest, took sure aim and fired with devastating effect. The hours of practice and drill by their meticulous commander served the men of the 25th Michigan well. Usually, green troops under fire have trouble even reloading their weapons after firing their first shot. But Moore had seen to it, through practice and drill, that his men could bite the end off the paper cartridge, ram it and the ball down the barrel efficiently and automatically.

Pvt. John Frick offered another explanation for why his comrades fought so well. "Every boy in Co. I and the whole regiment, in fact, was a squirrel hunter and not used to wasting ammunition, so every time the Rebs made a charge we took our time and picked off a few dozen of them."[31]

As charges were renewed the Confederates had to leap over the bodies of their comrades, hearing the cries of the wounded. Only a few minutes elapsed between charges, with surviving Rebels regrouping where the east end of the field made a slight descent and screened them from view and returning for yet another futile assault. Through the smoke and din of musket fire, the men of the 25th could hear the curses of Confederate officers urging their exhausted men to foment another charge.

Morgan's men, unaccustomed to such desperate fighting, had seldom experienced such losses. Finding that they were certain to be shot if they reloaded their weapons standing up, many lay down on the ground, in the midst of the firing, rolled over on their backs, and rammed fresh cartridges home before getting to their feet and continuing to advance.[32]

Johnson does not record how many charges were made, but wrote: "By the time we reached the abatis our ammunition was exhausted and fifty of my men were killed and wounded."[33] Basil Duke, confirmed that the second brigade had insufficient ammunition and that their fire "slackened on that account."[34]

"Morgan's men, forced to retreat, rallied time after time in the woods beyond the open field, and then came forward again yelling their . . . defiance." Abbott wrote in *Harper's:* "The fight now became terrible. The men fought with a desperation I never saw equaled."[35]

There were sharply sloping banks with heavy undergrowth on the Confederate left flank, but Moore had cleared the field and forest near the main defensive line for easy observation and clear fields of fire.

At the height of the battle, Moore was riding up and down behind the line, signaling his orders by the bugle, and shouting, "Hurrah boys, give it to um!" He was mounted on Lion, "a horse of almost human intelligence," and at times, Moore would order Lion to the ground. At the order, Lion would lie down and remain motionless until the colonel gave the bugle call to advance. Then, "in the thick of the fight, a Rebel bullet wounded Harvey C. Lambert, an officer from Marcellus who lived to tell the story, and then hit Lion," mortally wounding the horse. The loss of Lion created "a real sorrow to each one of the regiment for the boys almost worshipped him."[36] Moore was soon remounted and was "back cheering his men again, apparently oblivious of the danger and of the narrow escape he had."[37]

1st Sgt. Harvey C. Lambert, 25th Michigan

Colonel Moore, photo made c1875

Later Moore had another close call. Travis reports the incident: "Col. Moore seeing a rebel standing near a stump capping his gun, turned to a group of our men saying, 'There's a man getting ready to shoot me; if one of you has a loaded gun, take care of him.' A member of Co. D leveled at him, put a bullet through his head."[38]

During the battle, Col. Moore used his bugle to convince the enemy that reinforcements with a band were coming up. He knew it would be discouraging to the foe, during the heat of the battle, to hear an inspiring march coming from Union lines.[39]

In his Official Report, Colonel Moore stated that "the conflict was fierce and bloody with three and a half hours of hard fighting." Much of the time the forces

Orla Loper

Pvt. Henry Phillips, 25th Michigan

Sgt. Joseph Gault, Co E, 25th Michigan, severly wounded, Tebbs Bend

were within a few feet of each other, with only the fallen timber separating the Northern from the Southern forces, in "almost a hand-to-hand fight."[40] Southerner Sprake recorded in his diary that "the fight was desperate" and pointed out that his detachment got within twenty paces of the enemy. "The bullets flew everywhere," wrote Dirk Van Raalte to his parents. And again in a later letter Dirk wrote: "The bullets flew from all sides. Sometimes we and the Rebs were only six or eight feet from each other." A soldier writing about combat recalled the "shouts, cheers, the hissing shot, dull heavy thuds of clubbed muskets,... groans and prayers." When Van Raalte wrote, he mentioned three bayonet charges of the Rebels. Another Michigan paper stated that the Confederates fought with clubs attached to their right hand. If this is true, these may have been men who had run out of ammunition.[41]

By this time, dead and wounded men were lying on the field. Pvt. Henry Phillips observed that the "Confederates would become entangled in the network of fallen trunks and branches and were shot while trying to climb over or push through . . . The ground was strued with dead Rebels. It looked as every shot of our toled."[42]

Mary Christie wrote to her brother Norman, a lieutenant with the 3rd Kentucky Infantry of the Union army, that the men of the 25th "fit like willcats."[43]

The Confederates were losing their men and especially their officers at an alarming rate. The men of the 5th Kentucky suffered the most casualties. Killed were Lt. Tom Jeff Current of Company C, Lt. James H. Ferguson of Company A, Lt. George W. Holloway of Company B, Sgt. Weston Threlkeld of Company

B; Privates A.J. Boggess, Brockenbury Fisher, James A. Headley, James Hockensmith, Alexander "Alec" Hockersmith, S.T. Johnson, Samuel Miles, Jr., Dennis O'Nan, and Norton Stoughton. Wounded were Adjutant Joseph Marshall Bowmar, Capt. Martin Van Gudgell, Lt. James Ferguson of Company B, Cpl. George Agee, Cpl. Robert Jones, Pvt. Thomas Gormley, and Pvt. John R. Moreland. Wounded, but able to continue on the raid, was Pvt. Tom Jeff Williamson. Privates James Jones and James Orr were captured. Major Brent had not yet become a casualty. After the battle, Col. D. Howard Smith commented, "I lost 17% of all my command present."[44]

Lt. James H. Ferguson, 5th Ky. Cav.

Lt. George W. Holloway, 5th Ky. Cav.

The 7th Kentucky under Huffman lost Lt. Robert H. Cowan of Company I, Lt. C.N. Kirtley of Company K, Cpl. John Hudson of Company K, Cpl. Henry Goodloe of Company I, and Sgt. Dock Nelson from Company C. Privates Josh Turner and John Wood were also killed. At least three were wounded: Henry Clay Buford, Jim Cowan, and J.C. McQuerry, who was left on the field. Many were captured: Sgt. John Kastenbine and privates John Canter, E.A. Hansbrough, Gabriel Jennings, J.H. Jennings, John A. Jennings, John R. Jordan and Joseph Scott.[45]

Pvt. John Branham of the 9th Tennessee was shot in his wrist. Grigsby's 6th Kentucky had three captured—privates Philip Beswick, Michelberry Stephens, and William H. Tevis. The list of those taken prisoner included privates Frederick Cook and Stephen Masterson from Cluke's 8th Kentucky.

The 11th Kentucky still had its sacrifices to make. The worst was yet to come for the regiment.

Colonel Tucker, in command of four companies of the 11th, was ordered to set the Union fortifications on fire. His men tried to ignite the fallen timber and brush in the abatis, but to no avail.[46]

The seventh Confederate charge brought extreme pressure on the flank of the Federal position. A few men of Bennett's company managed to break through the defenses on the top of the river bank on the left of the Union position and direct enfilading fire along the line of defenders. The Federals quickly returned fire killing or wounding the Rebels, whose bodies tumbled down the steep bluff into Green River.

Mary Christie, who lived nearby, reported seeing bodies clad in gray, floating down the river. C.H. Taylor confirmed that there were 12–14 bodies caught in the trap at a ford down river.[47]

Pvt. John Weathered of the 9th Tennessee, whose horse had broken down at Columbia, secured permission to obtain a horse from the enemy when the battle was over. During a lull in the fighting he cautiously moved forward, came under fire, and ran into the woods, where he hid behind a tree until General Morgan ordered the attack to stop. Dismayed by the confusion and carnage on the battlefield, he made his way back to his unit. Six hours later, a mount was found for Weathered. He rode it happily through the rest of the campaign in Kentucky.[48]

Chenault's Left-Flank Assault

Seeing that he was losing heavily, especially in officers, Morgan decided on one final desperate effort. With a view of ending the affair, he called on Colonel Chenault, with his crack regiment of Kentuckians, to attack the Federals' right flank in force by leading his men down into the ravine, along the river bank, and up the steep bank to a position where they could pour enfilading fire into the Union trenches behind the abatis. Morgan hoped this would so disrupt the defenders that his main assault could swarm over the abatis and drive the enemy from the fortifications, securing victory.

To prepare for this attack, while the fighting was raging on the field above, the weary 11th Kentucky, in sweltering heat, was making a reconnaissance and clearing out the fallen trees and underbrush that protected Colonel Moore's right flank.[49]

Colonel David Waller Chenault and the 11th Kentucky had never failed Morgan. He was an experienced, courageous commander and his men idolized him; they would follow him anywhere. He had served as rearguard in Morgan's operations for months. Morgan knew that, when Chenault was in the rear, he was safe.[50] At the Battle of Hartsville, in December of the previous year, Chenault had played a key role in Morgan's stunning victory. In March, two companies of the 11th had endured the Cluke Raid. In April, part of Chenault's regiment took part in a skirmish at Mill Springs and then withdrew in an orderly manner before a large Federal force. In May, the 11th Kentucky had done much of the fighting in the Monticello area where they were under fire for ten hours without food and water. Now, in this desperate situation, Morgan called on Chenault's 11th to gain the victory.

The Confederate lines were longer and fuller than the Federals, and they began to outflank and lap around the Federal defensive line. It was said the Confederates swarmed up the ravine like locusts. Colonel Moore, realizing that all would be lost if his right were crushed, called up Company I, under Capt. Martin DeBoe, which had been held in reserve 200 yards in the rear, and deployed them as skirmishers, down the side hill, to meet Chenault's assault.

At this point, Moore summoned Travis's squad from his position with Hogan's party, which was guarding the bridge. Moore needed some indication that reinforcements had arrived.[51]

"The Confederates came crowding through the ravines, yelling shrilly, Chenault riding at their head. They gained the Union line, and its defenders actually commenced to fall back, when the reserve arrived and checked them. The notes of Colonel Moore's bugle, as he signaled his orders, and the shouts of the men as they saw help coming, caused Morgan to believe a large reinforcement, had arrived for the defenders."[52] Wilterdink reported the conditions on the Union right flank:

> They [the Confederates] started heavy firing and the enemy thought they could encircle us. Some of our men had to retreat from the stronghold into the woods. We were soon in line for action. Our men had fallen back considerably in the last charge, and the Rebels had gained a slight foothold in the edge of the timber, doing their best to move forward. I noticed that Captain Edwin Childs of Company E and Capt. John Tennant of Company K and all the others were making every effort to start their men forward and regain the lost ground.[53]

DeBoe of the Dutch Co I, a Mexican war veteran, climbed to the top of a fence and urged his men to push the Rebels back. With faces black from biting off ends of paper cartridges, the Federals rallied. "When the rebels were within reach of a pistol-shot of us, we began to shoot and every shot from our men was deadly for the enemy. We lost very few."[54]

Jim Hoffman

Death of Colonel Chenault Charging the Abatis at Tebbs Bend

Chenault's Grave, Richmond Cemetery

On this last charge Colonel Chenault, still on horseback, was hit in the forehead with a minie ball, only paces from the fortress. He fell dead at Major McCreary's feet. The Rebels, stunned, pulled the line back a bit. When McCreary assumed command of the regiment as Lt. Colonel, he passed along the line to designate Capt. Alex Tribble his second in command. Captain Tribble threw his hand up to accept the promotion and then grabbed his sword in one hand and his pistol in the other, charged the works, "aided by all the expletives he could command, and called for his men to follow him." He got to the edge of the fallen timber before a bullet fired by Pvt. John V. Hardy of Company E crushed his skull. He, too, fell at McCreary's side. Dudley Tribble, brother of Alex, then assumed command of the company.[55]

Sensing that something was amiss, Major Thomas Y. Brent, Jr., of the 5th Kentucky, dashed across the field to see what had happened and he, too, was killed. Dr. Theophilus Steele of the 7th rode up to learn what was happening on the flank, and his horse was killed as he leaned over to hear the report from McCreary.[56] This ravine was where the "Rebel dead lay thickest on the field."[57]

A Michigan soldier reported an incident that happened in the midst of the fighting. He came upon a wounded Rebel officer who cried out to him: "I wish you'd drag me there under the shade of that tree." So he hooked his arms under the shoulders of the officer and pulled him out of the sun. He muttered, "I need

Lt. Col. James B. McCreary, 11th Ky. Cav.

Capt. Alexander Tribble, 11th Ky. Cav.

James Neal, Jr.

Dudley Tribble, 11th Ky. Cav.

a drink of water." The Union soldier took off his canteen, placed it in the wounded man's hand, then grabbed his gun and ran back into line just as the bugle call for reinforcements sounded. After the battle, when he went back to find the Confederate officer, he was dead, but half the water in the canteen was gone.[58]

The three Baldwin brothers and their father from Winchester had joined Chenault's regiment at the beginning, but on that fatal day, one of them, Lt. William W. Baldwin, was killed instantly by a minie ball. Another officer, Lt. Frank West, was mortally wounded and died on the battlefield.

Just before the last Confederate charge, Oliver, one of the four blond Cosby brothers, was sent as a runner to another regiment. His brother, John, charging up the hill in the front line, took a shot in the head, and was killed instantly. Pvt. Cyrus Newkirk, climbing the hill directly behind John, moving from tree to tree, saw him fall. Seconds later the third brother, Ausey, was mortally wounded by a minie ball. Oliver returned to his unit, which had retreated and was reforming, and then went looking for his wounded brother Ausey, found him, and carried him back through the woods, tree to tree, up the steep hill, and to the Atkinson-Griffin House down the road, which had been secured as a Confederate hospital. He stayed behind a while to nurse him but, fearing he would be captured, left and rode through the dark night to catch up with his regiment before it crossed the Ohio. Ausey died slowly, and on July 9, was buried in the apple orchard on the Griffin farm.[59]

By 1864, Oliver and Amanda Wingfield Cosby lost three children, two sons in the war, Ausey and John, and a daughter from illness and had a son, James, and a son-in-law, Peter Dozier, in prison at Camp Douglas.[60] Oliver avoided capture by fording the Ohio and returning to Confederate service via West Virginia.

Gypsie Cosby Jones

Oliver Cosby, 11th Ky. Cav.

Gypsie Cosby Jones

James Cosby, 11th Ky. Cav.

Sherman Dozier

Peter Dozier, 11th Ky. Cav.

Pvt. Isham Fox went over to where Colonel Chenault's body lay, gently lifted his dead commander's body and placed it over his shoulder, and carried him from the woods to the rear.[61] With Chenault's death and the sounding of the bugle apparently signaling Union reinforcements, the demoralization of the Rebels was complete, and another charge impossible. The Federals caught and took prisoner eleven of Chenault's Rebels still in the woods, exhausted from trying to climb the steep hill and return to their lines. Captured were Lt. Edmund Baxter, Lt. James H. Tevis, Sgt. Squire Turner Tevis, Sgt. Milton Vivian, Cpl. John Ryan, privates John Benson, James C. Browning, James Wesley Huguely, Squire Huguely, John M. Judd, and W.S. Young.

Colonel Moore, after a quick assessment of the situation, signaled an advance with his bugle. He, however, reconsidered and, before his men had begun to move forward, bugled a halt. Moore, an old Indian fighter, feared that he was being drawn into an ambush. He also knew that he had too few men to risk a rash pursuit, even against a demoralized enemy. Moore concluded that victory was already his and stayed behind his fortifications.[62]

The Confederates were also considering their situation. Colonel Smith reported to General Morgan that he had "made a close and thorough reconnaissance" and gave his opinion that "the enemy could not be dislodged."[63]

☆ ☆ ☆

An incident which occurred on the battlefield caused Morgan to overestimate Moore's strength and contributed to his decision to give up the fight. Sergeant Merrill, 25th Michigan, had become ill and was sent to a log house, possibly James Allen Sublett's, to recover. The morning of July 4, he heard gunshots and walked over to the abandoned camp and down to the ford on the north bank of the river. There he encountered the advance guard for Col. Roy

Cluke's forces and was taken prisoner, quickly mounted on a horse, and taken back to Morgan's headquarters where he was questioned. He was asked about Colonel Moore and the size of his force, and threatened with his life if he did not answer truthfully. Merrill responded that the Rebels were fighting a force that had been reinforced with "two regiments of infantry, but a battery of six guns and the 2nd Michigan Cavalry would soon be there." He was then taken down the road to the battlefield where General Morgan and Colonel Duke were and repeated his testimony. Merrill later reported that Morgan and Duke expressed "signs of uneasiness." Soon, General Morgan began withdrawing his forces from the field.

Norris H. Merrill, 25th Michigan

Col. Moore announced to his men that the Rebels were completely whipped. Lieutenant Travis started creeping from tree to tree on the west side of the road to find out if enemy forces were still in the rifle pit. The abandoned earthworks were soon reoccupied by Michigan men. About a half hour later, horsemen were seen moving in their direction at the further bend of the road, and it was thought "the prelude of another onset." However, it turned out to be defeated Rebels carrying a flag of truce, seeking permission to bury their dead. It was now 10:30 A.M., four hours since the first cannon shot.[64]

Stretcher bearers moved amid the dead and wounded in the carnage of the battlefield. Cries of pain and calls for water were heard. Rifles, pistols, ammunition pouches, spent shot, and blankets littered the ground. Pvt. John Wilterdink picked up a six-shot pistol from a dead officer. Years later, he still had the weapon.[65]

Skirmish at the Bridge

By 10:00 A.M. the last gun had been fired on the main battlefield. Colonel Cluke took this to mean that Morgan had gained an easy victory on the bluff above and that defeated Yankees would soon be retreating in disarray. Anticipating little resistance, he ordered his cavalrymen to cross Green River Ford west of the bridge and take up positions where they could intercept and capture the fleeing, demoralized enemy.

Ten of Hogan's men had taken cover behind a stone wall that they had constructed near the south end of the bridge. Others were concealed in woods on the bluff. As the Rebel cavalrymen charged at the ford, Lieutenant Hogan's sharpshooters of the 8th Michigan and 79th New York "unseated two or three of them." The disappointed Confederate troopers quickly withdrew under fire, rode off, and rejoined the Confederate forces bypassing the position.[66]

Morgan's Sends Flag of Truce, 10:30 A.M.

The message carried forward by the party bearing Morgan's flag of truce read:

> To the Commandant of Federal Forces
> At Battle Ground Near Green River Bridge
>
> I have sent under Flag of Truce Dr. J. F. Keiser, The Rev Mr. Moore, Chaplain of 5th Ky Regiment, other attendants to recover the bodies of our dead & wounded who are left on the field.
>
> Resp Yours,
> D Keller, Surgeon
> lst Brigade, Ky Cavalry C.S.A.
> 10 1/2 o'clock[67]

Colonel Moore, uncertain of Morgan's motives, agreed on the condition that Moore's men carry any Confederate bodies within Union lines out to the front of the Union defenses. He wanted to be certain that Morgan would never know how few men he actually had. Moore's men, under Martin DeBoe, cleared Confederate bodies from the battlefield, carried them to the west side of the rifle pit, and laid them out along the road.

Pvt. Bennett Young came to the front to see the long line of bodies of his comrades and wrote:

> None of those who saw these dead brought out under the flag of truce, and the wounded carried in blankets from out of the woods and from the ravines and laid along the turnpike road from Columbia to Lebanon, will ever forget the harrowing scene. When they looked upon the dead, with their pallid faces turned heavenward, and their pale hands folded across their stilled breasts, poignant grief filled every heart.[68]

Porter Harned

Sid Cunningham, Morgan's Adjutant

Sidney P. Cunningham, Morgan's Adjutant, commented: "Indeed, this was the darkest day that ever shone on our command, eleven commissioned officers were killed, and nine wounded." *Richmond Enquirer*, August 1, 1863.[69]

Lt. Leeland Hathaway eloquently wrote about their loss that day:

> Here fell Col. Chenault—a man fashioned by nature in one of her lavish moments—brave, generous, noble and kind, he was the pride of his regt & the favorite of his friends. Maj. Brent, too, offered up his life upon the altar of his country on this memorable day. He was a chivalric gentleman, a brave & skillful officer, giving promise of a brilliant future. The gallant Tribble fell at the head of his company while nobly leading them in the fruitless charge . . . Nobly did they die and sincerely do we mourn them.[70]

The Kentuckians who gave their lives at Tebbs Bend represented some of the finest families of the Commonwealth; their talents and their leadership were lost to the state forever.

In the camp of the 11th Kentucky that evening, McCreary, then a lieutenant colonel and later twice Governor of Kentucky and U.S. Senator, listed the names of his fellow officers killed at Tebbs Bend and wrote in his diary:

> It was a sad, sorrowful day, and more tears of grief rolled over my weatherbeaten cheeks on this mournful occasion than have before for years. The commencement of this raid is ominous.[71]

The Confederates took away the bodies of Colonel Chenault, Major Brent, and Lieutenants Baldwin and Cowan to be taken home for burial. They, however, left the rest of the dead where they lay at the side of the road, to be buried by others. Because there were still rumors of further Confederate attacks, Moore did not detail his men to burial parties until he was sure no more Rebels were in the area. He kept them on alert in the rifle pit and behind the abatis until the rumors proved to be a ruse.[72]

Colonel Moore's Official Report

As soon as time allowed, Colonel Moore dictated his Official Report to Lt. Col. G.B. Drake, a staff officer of Major Gen. Hartsuff. It has been used throughout the narrative concerning the battle, and the complete record is included in Appendix E.

In the report, Moore complimented Hogan's "gallant" defense against a Confederate cavalry charge at the bridge. Years later, Moore circled that paragraph and pointed out that the information in it was inaccurate. Travis agreed and said that Moore had written the report quickly without examining all the facts. Hogan claimed a significant role in the victory and became so boastful and obnoxious that he and Moore almost came to blows. Travis supports Moore's revised version of events and denies that Hogan had been the hero he claimed to be.[73]

In June before the battle, Hogan had reported that he and three mounted men dashed into Columbia, encountered Rebels and killed three, took two prisoners, and dispersed the Rebels occupying the town. On July 16 Moore discovered that Hogan had fabricated the entire incident and reported to General Hartsuff that Hogan's report was untrue and that he "made it up for effect," adding that Hogan was a "rascal." Later, Hogan sought revenge, allied himself with General Boyle, and became one of Moore's antagonists.[74]

A short time after the end of the battle, Moore issued Special Order No. 42 from the field, commending his officers and men:

> My brave, my noble men! It is with pride and pleasure that I congratulate you upon the great victory won to-day. While you numbered but 200 men, the enemy numbered thousands. Being advised of their strength, and of their advantage in having artillery bearing upon me, their demand for a surrender was answered with a response that echoes the feelings of the gallant little band of the Twenty-fifth Michigan Infantry, that was about to engage them.
>
> The engagement was long and bloody; charge after charge was successfully repelled, and after three and a half hours' hard fighting, the enemy was defeated and victory crowned our efforts. Our brave companions who fell, fell gallantly fighting for their country and in defense of the starry flag; their names, deeply inscribed on the pages of memory, will be wreathed

ever in bright laurels of fame, and though tis hard to part with our noble dead, we know tis sweet in the cause of our country to die. Although no marble slab have we placed o'er their heads to mark their last resting place, although no monumental pile have we erected over their graves, yet in the hearts of the people of our own peninsula State will be erected a monument that will perpetuate their names to all eternity.

By order of Col. O.H. Moore;
Ed. M. Prutzman, Lt. and Adjutant.[75]

Federal Congratulations to Moore and His Troops

Major Gen. Hartsuff commended Moore and his men from Headquarters, 23rd Army Corps, Lexington, July 17, 1863:

General Order No. 12

The General commanding the Corps hereby extends his thanks to the two hundred officers and soldiers of the 25th Michigan Regiment under Colonel O.H. Moore, who so successfully resisted by their gallantry and heroic bravery, the attack of a vastly superior force of the enemy, under the Rebel John Morgan, at Tebb's Bend on Green River, on the 4th of July, 1863, in which they killed one fourth as many of the enemy as their own little band amounted to, and wounded a number equal to their own.[76]

Major Gen. Burnside also wrote from Cincinnati on July 10 to congratulate Colonel Moore on his victory:

I desire to thank you and your command for your gallant fight on Green River. I intrust to you the holding of your present [place] with your force and the mounted men now with you. Have you any artillery? Your position may be changed by orders from General Boyle.[77]

A reporter for a Louisville newspaper wrote that "the battle of Tebbs Bend was evidently one of the finest planned and best fought battles of the war." He reached this conclusion after a speech delivered by Col. George T. Wood of Hart County who related the story of the battle before the Kentucky House of Representatives. Wood offered the opinion that Morgan's repulse had "saved the city of Louisville from sack and pillage by the rebel hordes," and said that "this fight was without a parallel in the history of this war." The Kentucky Legislature, duly impressed, acknowledged the services of Col. Moore and his command in two joint complimentary resolutions:

> Whereas, Col. Orlando H. Moore, in command of Green river stockade with a detachment of two hundred officers and soldiers of the 25th Regiment Michigan Volunteers, received from the rebel General John Morgan, on the 4th of July, 1863, in command of a vastly superior force, a demand for the immediate and unconditional surrender of the stockade, and its forces; and whereas, Col. Moore replied that "the 4th day of July was no day for him to entertain such a proposition," and whereas, the battle of Tebbs Bend immediately ensued, ending in three and a half hours in the retreat of Gen. Morgan, with a loss of fifty of his command killed and two hundred wounded—now therefore,
>
> 1. *Resolved by the General Assembly of the Commonwealth of Kentucky,* That the thanks of this Assembly be presented to Col. Orlando H. Moore, and the two hundred officers and soldiers of his command, who in the language of Major General Hartsuff, "so successfully resisted by their gallant, and heroic bravery, the attack of a vastly superior force of the enemy, in which they killed one-fourth as many of the enemy, as their own little band amounted to, and wounded a number equal to their own."
>
> 2. *Resolved,* That a copy of this preamble and resolution be transmitted by the Governor of Kentucky to Col. Moore with a request that he cause the same to be read to the officers and soldiers of his regiment, and that the Governor do also transmit a copy of the same to the Governor of the State of Michigan.[78]

Needless to say, nothing was heard from General Boyle. It may be presumed that he retained his dislike for Moore and could not bring himself to say anything positive about the former Provost Marshal of Louisville. Boyle's silence only confirmed Moore's officers' speculations that Boyle had sent Moore to Tebbs Bend hoping that he might be captured in any encounter with Morgan.[79]

Significance of the Battle

The battle of Tebbs Bend was "one of the most outstanding small victories in the Civil War. It was unusual for a small Union force to resist Morgan, and to fight so fiercely and effectively," observed historian James Ramage.[80]

In this brief encounter, 200 untested recruits of Moore's 25th Michigan withstood repeated assaults by 800–1000 battle-hardened and confident dismounted cavalrymen from Duke's and Johnson's brigades.

The battle, which lasted under four hours, is regarded as one of the bloodiest of the war in the Western Theater, even though relatively small numbers were involved, with the Rebels suffering by far the most casualties, losing twenty experienced officers which included a colonel, a major, four captains, and nine lieutenants.

Morgan's decision to make a frontal attack against an entrenched and fortified enemy position, which could have been bypassed, was uncharacteristic and opposed by his senior commanders, D. Howard Smith and Adam R. Johnson. Morgan considered his troops invincible. He also underestimated the strength of his enemy's defensive position, the difficulty of the terrain, and the quality of Moore's leadership.

Morgan's resolve to continue the assault while withdrawing his artillery after many of its gunners had been shot by Union snipers from the rifle pit, seems a more doubtful, even rash decision. Hockersmith commented that Morgan's decision to fight this battle was "one of the few, very few mistakes that was made by General Morgan during his whole military career."[81]

Faulty Confederate intelligence concerning the terrain leading up to and surrounding the Union main defensive position on high ground, flanked by steep bluffs may have been a factor in Morgan's defeat. On the Union left, the bluff could not be scaled, and on the right it could only be climbed with great difficulty. His experienced and trusted chief scouts, Quirk and Cassell, had been wounded just prior to the battle, and it was the first day for Tom Franks to be in charge. Colonel Smith recorded that a scouting party had been sent out by Morgan the night before, but its report must have been unconvincing. The fact that he sent Colonel Tucker forward to reconnoiter the Union defenses on the early morning of July 4 indicates that Morgan was uncertain about what his men would face.

In spite of his limited battle experience and almost no engineering background, Moore's preparations for the upcoming battle were meticulous and complete. He also took great care to keep information from the Confederates and to create the impression that his force was much stronger than it was. He stopped all civilian traffic on the road to the bridge and nearby fords. Even the few people living in the area knew little about the defense works Moore's men were erecting. They had only heard the ringing of axes.

Moore had, however, observed the importance of defended positions out West and at Munfordville, and the 25th Michigan had gained some experience digging in when an attack was anticipated at Munfordville. Asa and Chester Slayton of Company B built fortifications there and probably passed on information about this in conversations around the campfire.

In addition to their good training, there is another element that helped the Michigan men fight: many were imbued with a sense of great patriotism and of "doing God's duty." The religious upbringing is evident in the letters of the men, particularly Company I, the Dutch regiment. "It is clearly seen that God fought for us. I see a higher hand in it because that is the first time John Morgan's been beaten so badly," wrote Wilterdink, a devout soldier." Van Lente thanked God for delivering them from death, as He had at Green River.[82]

Moore has been credited with delaying Morgan thirty hours and giving Louisville time to prepare its defenses. Since Morgan had already planned to meet Hines' squad at Brandenburg and had scouted the river crossing there, apparently he never seriously intended to attack Louisville. However, he wanted Union forces to believe that he was coming there.

General Morgan hoped for Moore's surrender at Tebbs Bend, the capture and parole of his men, and a march to Lebanon by early afternoon of July 4. Instead, the rearguard of his battered force did not leave Campbellsville until dusk and rode long into the night to reach New Market.

This site demonstrates how crucial it is in battle to occupy the ground that dominates the surrounding terrain with fields of fire covering enemy approaches. The Northern forces, well dug in and protected by an abatis and the steep banks of Green river on both flanks, defeated the much superior Southern force with artillery, losing only six that day. It was an axiom in the Civil War that to capture a strong defensive position one needed at least 3 or 4 to 1 odds in the attacker's favor. In this case, Morgan had 4 or 5 to 1. It was a brilliant victory, indeed.

Maps of the Battlefield

The maps of Michael Hogan and Benjamin Travis on the end page are key to understanding the Battle at Tebbs Bend. Hogan's map indicates that there may have been defensive lines in depth. Travis does not mention this, not does his map indicate it, and he wrote his history based on his personal diary. However, Hogan's map was drawn in 1863 while Travis' map was published in 1897.

There is a third map in a Michigan 1894 newspaper. The strength of that map shows where the Federals first buried their dead—between the Union field hospital and the stockade, the uncovered bridge over the river, and the heavy woods around the site. But it has so many other distortions, particularly the shape of the road and the inaccurate placement of the artillery position, that it loses its value as an authentic piece of evidence.[83]A fourth map exists in the *National Tribune*, but it adds no new information, except to show the abatis coming across the road down into the woods on the Federal right flank.

The Tebbs Bend Battlefield Today

View from Rebel Artillery Position looking toward the Rifle Pit. Log house, captured by the Rebels, was located in front of the Brockman brick house facing the Old Columbia Turnpike.

Morgan's Demand for Surrender and Moore's Rebuff site in the Brockman field

A meadow with a house garden is the Main Battle Site. The Main Union Defensive Line was located just past the Williams' brick dwelling.

Chenault's Flanking Maneuver involved clearing a path and ascending the hill in right of the photo.

James Allen Sublett log house, built 1849. Officers and men from both the Northern and Southern forces sat on this porch. The Sublett family cared for many ill soldiers here.

Steep bluffs drop from the tree line, in left of photo, to Green River. Tebbs Bend's bluffs on its south side are gradual in this location, but become more steep at the Narrows, past the house in this photo. This field was a Union cavalry camp.

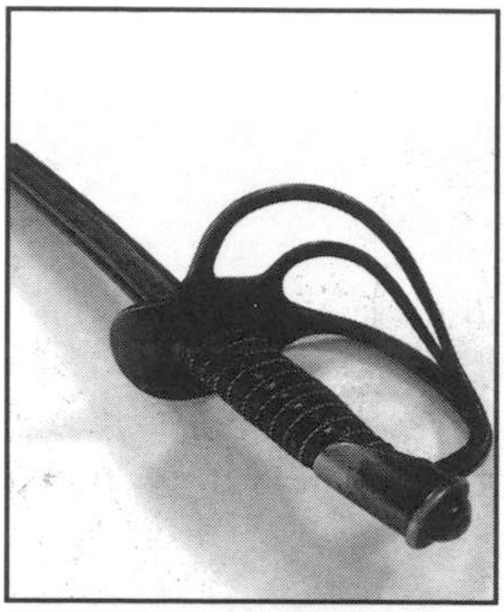
George Freund

Saber found by John Steger, Tebbs Bend

Holland City Museum

Nelson Odgen's Drum, 25th Michigan, used at Tebbs Bend

Holland City Museum

Canteen inscribed with battles, Tebbs Bend on top left

Joel Smith House, Cane Valley

James Neal, Jr.

Pvt. James P. Tribble, 11th Ky. Cav., CSA

Shellie Kendall Nunn

Pitcher sent by the Tribble family to Joel Smith

Chapter Six: Aftermath of the Battle

People living in the area went to view the battlefield soon after Morgan's men had departed. Among them were John Steger, a boy of twelve, and his black friend. They had to cross the bridge over the river in order to reach the scene, and the sentries at both ends of the bridge allowed them to pass. Once on the battlefield they saw the dead on the ground all about them. The boys saw a saber on the body of a cavalryman, unfastened it, and started home. Once again they were passed through by the sentries on the bridge, who allowed the boys to keep the saber. Later it was confirmed that the sword, with the name John scratched on it with a knife, was a Model 1840 Heavy Cavalry (Dragoon) saber, imported from Germany, originally issued to a Federal noncommissioned officer or enlisted man, evidently captured or taken on another battlefield by the Confederate who wore it. Because Morgan's men seldom carried sabers, it may have belonged to one of Morgan's officers. The saber and its scabbard are still in the possession of the descendants of John Steger.[1]

Clara Burress, just a little girl, remembered that the bodies of the men were covered with branches when she walked down the road to get back home after the battle.

On July 5, Joel Smith of Cane Valley, driving his team of horses pulling a buckboard, was traveling down the turnpike road toward Campbellsville. He reached the battlefield, when he noticed some movement in the woods. He investigated and found a severely wounded Rebel soldier trying to pull himself up to rest his back on the side of the tree. Joel quickly carried him from the woods, loaded him on the bed of the wagon, and returned to his large white Greek revival home away from the main road.

At first, the soldier was so weak, he could hardly speak. As he grew stronger, he started asking questions, "Where am I," and "What territory is this, North or South?" The Smiths told him that he was in Union territory, to just stay quiet and out of sight when anyone came around. He told them that his own family was "well-off" and they would reward them for being so good to him. Joel and his wife told him "not to worry about it." The Smiths took excellent care of him, and finally he was well enough to make the return trip home to Richmond. The Smiths gave him a horse to ride home on, hoping that he would evade capture by Union forces.

Back in Madison County, James Polk Tribble's parents were thrilled that their son, who had been missing, was able to return home. Another son, Alex, had been killed at Tebbs Bend, and another, Dudley, was wounded later on the raid, captured, and was sitting in a Northern prison. They tried to think of a way they could reward the Smith family.

In the winter of 1863, a traveling drummer came to the Smith farm and knocked on the door. He was delivering a double wall pitcher to the Smith family from the Tribble family. On its bottom was marked "Meriden Brit'a Co. LYMANS Patent June 1856." The pitcher remains a prized possession of Smith descendants today.[2]

When James Polk Tribble married and parented his first child, he named him Joel Smith Tribble, after his benefactor.[3]

Burying the Confederate Dead

On July 6, when the 22nd Indiana Artillery came up the road from Columbia toward Campbellsville in pursuit of Morgan, the Confederate casualties still had not been buried. "We saw the first dead in battle, which were still lying stretched alongside the road—some sixty or more of Morgan's men."[4]

When Moore was sure that no more Confederates were on their way, he detailed Capt. Martin DeBoe to bury the dead. Neighbors from up and down the road made their way to the battlefield to help with the grim task. Patrick Bridgewater, who buried twenty-three bodies, remembered it vividly. Will Henry Sublett reported seeing twenty-eight bodies lying beside the road, most of them shot "square in the forehead," and said that it was an "awful sight," and that "the center of their head on the back was all gone." C.H. Taylor, from Company D, 25th Michigan, confirms Sublett's number and said that he helped bury twenty-eight "in one trench dug beside the road." He also reported that when Union Cavalry rode up, "one of the men pointed out his brother whom we were burying."[5]

Sgt. Harvey Lambert said that he buried 40. Pvt. Wilterdink said he buried 47. Possibly the 12–14 bodies caught in the fishtrap ford in the river were not counted in Taylor's count of 28.

Will Henry Sublett

All the men were buried in a single trench, "with nothing to distinguish one from another."[6] The trench was on the west side of Tebbs Bend Road, on the Steve Cure farm in 2005, across from the Russell Williams property.[7]

General Morgan had a reputation for taking great care for his wounded and dead but, in this instance, he left Colonel Moore in charge of his dead on the field. After the war, Basil Duke complimented the Yankee colonel, writing that the surgeons and chaplains "received every assistance" that Colonel Moore could furnish and that he "proved himself as humane as he was skillful and gallant."[8]

As is readily apparent, estimates of the number of Confederate casualties varied according to the source. Duke reported 71 casualties, 36 dead and 45 wounded. Colonel Moore estimated 50 Federals killed and 200 wounded.

Duke and Alston said they expected to hear of Colonel Moore's promotion for defeating Morgan.[9] But nothing concerning any promotion was mentioned in commendations on Colonel Moore's victory.[9]

Federal Field Hospital

At the Federal Field Hospital

In the lulls between Confederate charges, the Federal wounded were led or carried to the field hospital in the rear. Pvt. Van Lente, Company I, remembered what happened as they were moving forward into battle: "We received orders to march forward, which we done courageously, and also in good order. But when we had only marched a little ways, the wounded met us. Oh, what a sight that was.

Pvt. Johannes Van Lente, 25th Michigan

Dr. J.N. Gregg, 25th Michigan

There was one who was being led by 2 men with his arm torn off [George Hicks] and another who was shot through his hand. Too much to mention."[10] Travis saw Lt. Twombley, wounded in the leg, lying beside the road.[11]

Even when it became quiet on the battlefield, surgeon John N. Gregg's field hospital on the bluff above the bridge was a busy place. Dr. Gregg was aided by hospital steward Pvt. Dirk Van Raalte and nurse Pvt. Nathan Schofield. A hospital steward covered a patient's face with a chloroform-cloth while the surgeon amputated a limb, torn apart by a minie ball. The doctor treated torso wounds in any way he could, even though he knew the patients would probably die of infection.

Two Michigan soldiers, Hicks and Nott, had their arms, riddled with bullets, amputated. Dr. Gregg performed Pvt. George W. Hicks' surgery in the field hospital. Pvt. Arbuth Nott, who was shot in the arm and taken prisoner, had his arm amputated by one of the Southern surgeons, and was later exchanged.[12]

Some of the wounded were transported by wagon over the bridge to James Allen Sublett's house. Feather ticks were confiscated from the neighborhood and placed on the wagons to make the trip more bearable. By July 12, all but the most seriously wounded, who could not be moved, had been sent to a temporary hospital in Campbellsville or to the Louisville Military Hospital.[13] Capt. Jeter took George Hicks into his home at Campbellsville and his wife took care of him.

Wounded Federals:

Company D	
1 Sgt. Harvey C. Lambert	elbow joint; sent to hospital in Louisville
Cpl. Simon Young	severe shoulder wound; sent to hospital in Louisville; transferred to Invalid Corps
Pvt. Bruce Beebe	hand, side; hospital, Louisville
Pvt. Gillespie M. Parsons	thigh; hospital, Louisville
Pvt. Samuel Stecker	instep; hospital, Louisville; disch. because of wounds
Pvt. Jonathan Walburt	chest; hospital, Louisville
Pvt. Henry Beebe	thigh; died Aug 22 at Lockport, MI*
Company E	
Sgt. Joseph Gault	arm; discharged Dec 7, 1863
Pvt. Richard W. Baxter	shoulder; rejoined troops
Pvt. Thomas W. Presto	ear; rejoined troops
Pvt. Orin White	arm; transferred to Invalid Corps
Pvt. George W. Hicks	arm, knee, & leg; arm amputated; died of wounds July 20, 1863, Campbellsville
Company F	
2 Lt. Arthur M. Twombly	ankle; discharged on disability
2 Sgt. Irving Paddock	hips; hospital, Louisville
3 Sgt. Henry Bond	right arm; hospital, Campbellsville
1 Cpl. Henry F. Garmon	thigh, arm; hospital, Louisville; discharged Dec 7, 1863, for gunshot wounds at Tebbs Bend
7 Cpl. Julius C. Webb	forearm; hospital, Louisville; rejoined troops
8 Cpl. George Bement	right ankle; hospital, Louisville; rejoined troops
Pvt. Arbuth M. Nott	forearm amputated; in hospital in Louisville discharged for wounds at Tebbs Bend
Pvt. Isaac Smith	ankle; hospital, Louisville; transferred to Invalid Corps
Pvt. Marcus Tuttle	hand; hospital, Louisville; transferred to Invalid Corps
Pvt. Thomas Woods	cheek, mouth; hospital, Louisville; transferred to Invalid Corps
Company I	
Pvt. Jan Veen	slightly wounded
Company K	
Pvt. Hiram H. Dunham	taken to hospital in Louisville; transferred to Veteran Reserve Corps

Source: Letter, Surgeon Boliver Barnum to A.J. Shakespear, Niles, Mich., *Republican*, August 1, 1863.
*Another source says he died in Campbellsville, Sept. 30, 1863.

Van Raalte wrote home to his father, July 12, 1863, from Campbellsville: "We are now here with the wounded and are waiting for the ambulances. Then we will go to Lebanon." A large training camp, as well as Federal hospitals, were located in Lebanon. From there the wounded were transported by rail to one of the Louisville Military Hospitals.[14]

The three Union dead were carried back to the field hospital. Three more died before morning. Near the hospital was a grove of trees and underneath them, graves were dug for the men. Wooden head-boards were made and the names of the men and the date of death were carved in the wood.[15]

After the war, the U.S. Government gathered many Federal soldiers from scattered cemeteries throughout the area and reinterred them in the National Cemetery in Lebanon, Kentucky. Marble stones replaced the wooden head-boards. Today six of Federal soldiers killed at Tebbs Bend are buried there.

Gerald Myers

Temporary Graves of Federal Soldiers

Lebanon National Cemetery

Federal Dead

Company D	
3 Cpl. Roswell Beebe	Grave No. 311 *
6 Cpl. Morgan L. Wallace	Grave No. 313
Pvt. Southard Perrin	**
Company F	
2 Cpl. Peter G. Cuddeback	Grave No. 349, Died July 5 ***
Company I	
Pvt. Peter VerSchure	Grave No. 347
Company K	
4 Sgt. James L. Slater	Grave No. 314

* Beebe was wounded in his abdominal cavity and subsequently hemorrhaged to death, July 5, 1863.

** Perrin's body is in a grave, marked as "Unknown" in the Lebanon Cemetery records, Death Date July 4, 1863. A poem in his honor appeared in the *Grand Rivers Reporter*, Dec. 5, 1863.

*** In Lebanon Cemetery records, the name is listed as Cuddyback.

25th Michigan Soldiers Who Died Later as a Result of the Battle

Company D	
Pvt. Henry Beebe	
Company E	
Pvt. George W. Hicks	Died at Capt. Rod Jeter's Home, Campbellsville; Jeter was Provost Marshal.

According to John Wilterdink letter home, July 14, 1863, another boy from Company D wounded in the abdomen died in Lebanon. Henry Beebe's death was reported to be at home in Michigan as well as Campbellsville.

Pvt. Dirk Van Raalte stayed behind to help nurse the wounded after the battle. He wrote home August 2, 1863: "Those that were mortally wounded were very quiet and said to the other fellows: 'Tell my folks that I have fought and that I did not die as a coward.'"

Just as today, personal effects of someone killed in battle were sent home to the family. An inventory of one of the Federals demonstrates how little a soldier had in the way of personal items.

Inventory of Personal Effects of Morgan L. Wallace:

1 blanket	1 pr. Gloves
1 dress coat	13 sheets of paper
1 great coat	14 envelopes
2 shirts	1 hat band

1 pen case & holder	2 gold pens
1 fine comb	1 acct. book
1 pocket book containing $1.00	1 knapsack

The above articles were sent to his wife who resided in Leonidas, St. Joseph County, Michigan.[16]

Lizzie Compton

There are two quite different stories about what happened to Lizzie Compton.

Story #1: Lizzie Compton, as reported in the *New York Herald* was from London, Ontario, and somehow managed to enlist and fight in the battle of Fredericksburg. She was wounded in that battle, her identity was revealed, and was dismissed from the Union army. Later, however, she showed up again, this time as a volunteer with the 25th Michigan. Supposedly she fought in the Battle of Tebbs Bend and was again wounded. The story continues that when Dr. Gregg was cutting the uniform off a soldier with a shoulder wound, he was shocked to discover the body of a woman, Lizzie Compton. Allan Keller, in *Morgan's Raid*, tells us that Colonel Moore sent her under escort to Bardstown to recover from her wound and then to be mustered out of the service.[17]

There is little evidence to support this version. She was never listed as a casualty even though her wounding was reported in a Louisville newspaper.

Story #2: Lizzie Compton, according to some accounts, served at the Federal Field Hospital, helping Dr. Gregg with the wounded. If she had been fraternizing with the men, it makes sense that she was there doing what she could and also trying to find a safe place to be in the small neck of land. Travis reported that he had never seen her render any assistance, but Travis was not at the field hospital, but was on the field. He did not approve of her and accused her of robbing the dead.

This is somewhat supported by a neighborhood story concerning the fact that a woman brought a Southerner's pistols and boots to James A. Sublett's house. She took a knife, and ripped open the lining. Sublett's son, Will Henry, asked, "What are you doing cutting those man's boots up?" She said, "Well, I'll show you." And she got $180 dollars in gold out of the lining of the boot. She said, "You can have part of it." Then Will Henry said, "No, I don't want no dead man's money. But I'd love to have one of those guns."[18]

We know that she remained with the soldiers after the battle. When the regiment went back to Lebanon, Lizzie hid among the baggage in the army wagons in order to accompany the men. The teamster reported her to Adjutant Prutzman, who felt she was a nuisance, "drew his pistol, and ordered her out of the wagon immediately, with the assurance that, if she did not get out in quick time, he would shoot her on the spot." She scrambled off the wagon, and she was never seen again.[19]

At the Confederate Hospital

Virginia Atkinson's house 440 yards south of the battle site, served as the Confederate hospital. Virginia's husband, Joel Dupuy Atkinson, had died before the war, leaving Virginia a widow. A daughter, Martha Rebecca, married James Madison Griffin in 1858 and they came to live with her mother during the war.

Many received their first treatment there, everything from cleansing and dressing of wounds to amputation. They were brought to the house on wagons and carts requisitioned from local farmers.

"Blood flowed from the yard plum down to the turnpike road," said John Griffin to E. W. Quinn.[20] The most seriously wounded were on the porch; holes were drilled in the porch to let the blood escape; more than thirty were in the yard. If the doctors thought they could be saved, they were carried upstairs to the bedroom over the parlor. Mary Elizabeth Griffin, only four and a half years old, went from patient to patient, lifting the white handkerchiefs from the faces of the men "to see if she recognized any of the soldiers."[21]

Everyone helped. Slaves were summoned, relatives and neighbors came to do what they could, to tear cloth to fashion bandages, serve water, and aid the three doctors, Edwin M. Sheppard, 7th Kentucky Cavalry, J.F. Keiser, 10th Kentucky Cavalry, and W.B. Anderson, 14th Kentucky Cavalry, who were left with the large number of casualties.

Some were treated and returned to duty. When the wounded died, Virginia Atkinson directed that the bodies be buried on her farm atop the bluff overlooking Lemmon's Bend. One was buried in the Faulkner family burial plot near the Griffin house.[22]

Later the surgeons were taken prisoner and sent, along with the remaining wounded, to Northern military prisons.

In 1979 Virginia Atkinson's home, today called Atkinson-Griffin House, was donated by Bonnie and E. W. Quinn to the Taylor County Historical Society and the society donated it to the U.S. Army, Corps of Engineers. An organization was formed called the Friends of the Log House, co-chaired by Dr. and Mrs. Richard Allen Sanders, Jr. and the author, which raised money to move the house to Green River Lake Park, where visitors can view it. The bloodstains of the soldiers still remain on the floor in an upstairs bedroom.[23]

Many people living in the area fled during the battle, but James Marshall Wilkerson stayed put. A mile from the battlefield, on July 3, he and his neighbors were placing the plate and sleeper logs on the foundation stones and cutting corner notches for his new log house. As they pulled up the logs to raise his house on July 4, "rifle fire sounded like cane reeds popping in a brush fire."[24]

Noon, July 4: Rebel Crossing of Green River

It was the middle of the day now. The sun was hot on the backs of the men. The command, five regiments in all, withdrew south on the Columbia Turnpike for two miles and then turned west on Ebenezer Road to the fords that the 2nd, 8th, 10th, and 14th Kentucky used to cross Green River. As the men in gray rode down the road, they passed an ox-cart pushed by slaves bearing the bodies of Colonel Chenault and Major Brent. Hard showers of rain began to fall. The wagon roads to the fords became muddy and the horses hooves began to slip. As they forded the river, the water was up to their saddle-skirts.[25]

Skiffs were commandeered for the wagons to cross. "Axes to the front" was called out. Trees were quickly cut and roped together to raft the artillery across. Ropes were tied to trees on the opposite bank so that the rafts could be pulled across the river.

Curtis Burke wrote: "We traveled slow.... We were in the advance as usual. The artillery got along slow through the mud and we had to halt ten or fifteen minutes several times to let all get up." After crossing into Lemmons Bend at Johnson Ford on to the Merritt Martin farm, a shell fell off a caisson in Martin's yard to be found in 1932 as Myrtle Rucker Martin, the wife of Tom Martin, and her daughter Gracie who were sweeping the yard with a brush broom. The shell, sticking up in the mud, was an Archer-bolt shell, considered unreliable by some military experts.[26]

Cavalryman Burke continued: "Details were out in every direction searching every stable and field in sight, pressing fresh horses for the boys that were on foot and on broken down horses."[27] After the shooting ceased and the first wave of troops had passed, 17-year-old Joseph Thomas Martin, son of the Merritt Martin mentioned above, thought he would get some plowing finished. But, alas, one of Morgan's Men rode up, unharnessed the horses where they stood, leaving him two rather dilapidated ones in exchange.[28]

Captured Sgt. Norris H. Merrill of the 25th Michigan continued to ride along with Morgan's command. Along the way to Campbellsville, Morgan closely questioned the dark-haired, 22-year-old farmer about the forces occupying Louisville. Merrill, who had been stationed in that city since April, was in a unique position to give Morgan information. He, however, courageously continued to feed Morgan misinformation, stating that "enough troops had arrived from Ohio, Indiana and Illinois, to enable the city to withstand any force that could be brought against it." If Morgan had seriously entertained any notions of capturing Louisville, this conversation may have squelched them.

Young J.T. Martin lost his team of horses to Morgan

Merrill was paroled in Campbellsville by Colonel Duke and made his way to Lebanon. When his regiment went to East Tennessee, he took the train back to Buchanan, Michigan, and recruited for the army, while awaiting notification of his exchange. In October of 1863, he read in the paper that he had been exchanged, and eager to return to service, quickly rejoined his regiment. On August 6, 1864, at the Battle of Utoy Creek, near Atlanta, Merrill, then a lieutenant commanding Company K, was wounded in the face and lost his left hand to a gunshot shell, which led to his arm being amputated just below the elbow.[29]

The troops traveled through the neck of land out of Lemmons Bend and made a semi-circle westward sweep around the Federal position. On the road before it intersected with the Campbellsville-Columbia Pike, Thomas Roach owned a fine brick residence. He still had six children at home, including several daughters. A native Virginian, the owner of twenty-five slaves, Roach was considered a planter, owning land all the way down to the Roachville Ford. Morgan's men justifiably expected that he would be a Southern sympathizer. However, he was completely unwilling to give his horses to Morgan. He directed his daughters to mount them and encouraged them to use their feminine charm to keep their animals. It worked![30] Burke wrote: "We saw a house where there was [sic] several horses saddled up and ladies on them and around them to keep the pressing detail from getting them. Several of the detail were at the gate but would not take the horses, because the ladies objected."

As the troops re-entered the turnpike road, they saw James Caldwell's Greek revival home in the distance, where they saw a figure moving in the yard. A rogue soldier took a shot which hit one of the upright posts of a ladder-back chair where Mary Caldwell, aged 12, was sitting. Fortunately, she was terrified, but unhurt.[31]

Some of the troops used the Roachville Ford to cross the river. This meant that they would travel six miles down Ebenezer Road before crossing Green River and would come out on today's Meadow Creek Road at Hatcher.

On Meadow Creek in Green County, but near the Taylor County line, James Scott Buchanan lived in a two-story brick with extended weather boarded ells. On this day the family received an unwelcome visit. A granddaughter, Virginia Buchanan McKinley told the story:

> They [the Rebels] raided the smokehouse and took what they could find; they took eggs and chickens, and the milk and butter from the springhouse. They left their tired horses and took all of Grandfather's horses and hay and corn for the horses.

James S. and Mariah Louise Smoot Buchanan had had their first child, Thomas William, in 1858. He was so small at birth that Mariah put him in a carpetbag and hung it on the pummel of her saddle while she rode to church. When the soldiers came, he was still sleeping in the cradle. "Grandmother would not be outdone. She hid a side of meat underneath the baby in the cradle. While the men ransacked the house and barns, she sat calmly rocking the cradle with her foot, singing a lullaby, and piecing a nine-patch quilt square."[32]

Thomas Campbell, 8th Michigan, a blue-eyed, brown haired 35-year-old lieutenant, who along with Hogan was responsible for the bridge building crew, was away from his regiment between Campbellsville and Green River Bridge the morning of July 4. When he heard cannon fire to the south, his walking pace quickened. The Rebel advance guard met him on the road, shot him, wounding him in the arm. He was made a prisoner and accompanied the Confederate troops to Lebanon. During the military engagement there the next day, Campbell made his escape to Camp Nelson in Jessamine County. His arm would heal, but just a year later, he was mortally wounded at Petersburg, Virginia, by a fragment from cannon shell.[33]

By this time, most people in Campbellsville knew that serious fighting had occurred at Green River Bridge. They heard the cannonading, and troops were beginning to file into the village.

July 4: Campbellsville

That Saturday was to be an eventful day in Campbellsville's history, but not as planned.

U.S. Congressman Aaron Harding, running for re-election in August, was scheduled to speak in Campbellsville on Saturday, July 4, at 1:00 P.M., as part of the patriotic ceremonies. Harding supported the Union although he disagreed with Lincoln's war policy, believed in states' rights, and accepted slavery, but was not a slave holder. He was to be introduced by State Representative Joseph H. Chandler, who had similar views to Harding's.[34]

Although both men's opinions could be considered as somewhat sympathetic to the southern cause, they knew they would be regarded as enemies by Morgan's men. Both Harding and Chandler realized that they were in great danger and probably would be harshly treated if captured.

Harding arrived in Campbellsville on the evening of July 3 and passed the evening making contacts with family and friends. On the morning of July 4, news swept the town that Confederates had it surrounded. His buggy-horse was taken by a friend to the woods less than a mile from town, and hid there along with the horses and cattle of other townspeople. Harding also hid in the woods. While the Confederates were combing the woods for horses and frightened slaves, they came within twenty steps of Harding, without detecting that he was there. He did, however, lose his horse. After staying there through the day and night, Harding departed the Campbellsville area. There were no speeches delivered that July 4.[35]

Most of the Rebel troops came into town by the Columbia Road. Those who used the old Greensburg Road, crossing at the Roachville Ford, had to pass the lane leading to Chandler's stone house. Chandler decided not to return home, believing that his house was more likely to be set afire if he were found there. He trusted that his wife, Araminta, could take care of herself and the five children.[36]

On this hot afternoon, with the windows and doors wide open, Araminta Chandler heard a squad of troops tearing through the cornfields. She took the shotgun down from above the door and made sure it was loaded. Her father, a colonel in the 99th Kentucky Militia, had trained his children how to handle a gun. As the troops came near the house, smelling the food being prepared in the stone kitchen out back, they undoubtedly were relishing the prospect of a good meal.

The reception they received, however, must have shocked them. Araminta stood in the doorway, pointing a shotgun directly at their heads, announced, "You can have corn for your horses and vegetables from the garden, and food from the kitchen, but do not come near this house or my children."

Startled at her demeanor, but respectful of her demands, they got the hot meals at the back kitchen, fed their horses, and headed for the meal barrel. Remembering that there were coins hidden there, Araminta she again lifted her shotgun and ordered, "It is time to leave now." Deciding that she was too formidable to be trifled with, the Rebs departed![37]

Burke's account in his Civil War Journal supports this family story: "We struck the pike and went to the suburbs of the town of Campbellsville and camped in a lot. We had to carry our corn a quarter of a mile from a crib. Some of the boys went to the nearest houses and got something for their messes. I bummed a snack for myself."

Gerald Myers

Raid on the Hiestand House, Campbellsville

Mark Chandler

Araminta H. Chandler

Other houses in Campbellsville, such as Heritage Hall, were also approached by the hungry men. After the troops watered their horses in Buckhorn Creek and filled their canteens with water from the spring on South Court Street, they would not have missed visiting the kitchen and outbuildings of the Alfred Gowdy home, the largest house in Campbellsville. It stood as a sentinel on the hill above Buckhorn Creek.

In the years following the Civil War, it became very fashionable to be a member of the Daughters of the Confederacy. Emma Gowdy Collins, daughter of A.F. and Sarah Lois Hotchkiss Gowdy, sent in her papers, declaring that she had aided the Confederacy "both personally and financially." Since her father had been loyal to the Union, a member of the state legislature and county clerk before the war, she was probably remembering as a nine-year-old how the Rebels came to their house and took their food.[38]

As the vanguard of Morgan's men moved north out of Campbellsville through the county in the late afternoon of July 4, they came to a meandering creek, called Middle Pitman, beside the turnpike. This was a good place to water their horses on this hot day, and it gave them an opportunity to "visit" the neighborhood. Turning up to the right was a little dirt road that passed by the William Linsey Miskell place.

Miskell and his fifteen-year-old son prided themselves on keeping good horses. He and "Little Billy" rode into Campbellsville that Saturday morning to go to the "horse trading lot" on the east end of Main Street. There, local farmers met and often spent the day discussing the war, their crops, and the weather. They exchanged local news, but mostly, examined horseflesh. Miskell, like most of his farmer friends, had wanted to hear Congressman Harding speak.

When Miskells saw the Rebel cavalrymen riding through town, they knew it was time to give up horse-trading, head for home, and try to hide their precious mounts in the woods. But they arrived too late. Their best horses were gone and replaced by exhausted, broken-down nags. The country hams in the smokehouse and the chickens in the yard had vanished. Every morsel of food in Mary Polly Miskell's kitchen had been wolfed down by the hungry raiders.[39]

Stealing horses

Chester Blakeman

Billy Miskell, Taylor County

Another farmer, Jonathan Milton Rafferty, who lived down the Springfield-Neatsville road, took his three horses through Saloma to the Beechwoods where he hid them in a wooded gully and cut brush for a shelter. He brought three days' food for himself and forage for the horses.

In his absence, Morgan's scouts burst into their house, searched it and the barn. Obviously in a hurry, their captain confronted Mrs. Rafferty and gruffly asked, "How many of our men can you feed tomorrow? She replied that she really didn't know. "We think you can feed a hundred. Have it ready by 11 o'clock," their leader ordered as they left the house and galloped off toward Lebanon.

Uncertain if her hundred hungry "guests" would turn up the next day, she decided to take no chances, went to the cellar and gathered up her canned goods. Next, she went to the smokehouse and brought in every shoulder of meat that they had. Rising early, she cooked all morning. At midday, troops arrived and ate it all.[40]

At Jonathan and Mariah Lively Richeson's farm in the Arista community, Morgan's troops commandeered their wagon, laid the body of a Tennessee soldier (probably either 1st Lt. Charles N. Kirtley or Pvt. John Hudson, both casualties at Tebbs Bend) in it, and ordered 16-year-old James Mark Richeson to take him home for burial.[41]

At the Washington Colvin home, Mollie, a hired girl, was forced to cook for several of the men. She is said to have spit in the dough as she kneaded it for biscuits. The men were described as "filthy" by Jane Colvin, the Colvins' 17-year-old daughter.[42]

Fuller Harding

Jane Colvin

Just down the road, over the Marion County line, the men in Jessietown, a village over big Muldraugh's Hill, decided to make a common sense move against the mighty Morgan. Maybe they could do what the Federal commanders had failed to do since the war started. They headed to the woods of the "Turkeyfoot," the set of curves around the big hill, with their crosscut saws and cut through several large trees. Just a push would fell the trees in Morgan's path. Then they waited.

Morgan came to the top of Muldraugh's Hill, the peak of which marks the county line. Alas for the men of Jessietown, Morgan's scouts had discovered the plan and evaded their trap by turning west at today's Finley community and took the same route, the old Hill Hollow Road down the Muldraugh's Hill, just as Morgan had done in the Christmas Raid. After the raiders had passed, the men of Jessietown spent the day felling the trees on an empty pike and rolling them over the bluffs.[43]

Night, July 4: New Market, Marion County

Apparently some regiments did not tarry long in Campbellsville, while others stayed several hours. Burke wrote that his regiment was ordered to saddle up at dusk, and then sat there in line until after dark. He told that they sang "John Morgan, Here's Your Mule" as they trotted through Campbellsville and again halted just outside the town on the Lebanon pike. A detail was sent back to the town for food. It is reported that Colonel Dick Morgan asked the Old Scouts to sing again. Then the regiment rode through the night and caught up with the others a few miles beyond New Market in the wee hours of the morning. Burke reported that the boys dismounted, lay down at the side of the pike, and immediately fell asleep. Burke himself slept on a pile of cracked rock with his horse tied to his foot.[44]

If Morgan's men felt betrayed by a lack of good intelligence from the scouts before the Battle of Tebbs Bend, they did not mention it in their diaries. To the contrary, William Davis wrote later that Franks was an "accomplished soldier and skillful officer . . . and a brilliant scout."[45]

Somewhere between Muldraugh's Hill and New Market, Morgan's men captured a local citizen and held him for the night to make sure that he did not give the Federals at Lebanon information about their camp and strength.

Alston recounts an incident involving two officers of the regiment. After the widespread looting in Columbia, there was an effort made to enforce more discipline, with the officers being ordered to set the example. Consequently, Captain Murphy, "by direction of General Morgan, ordered Captain Magennis to return a watch taken from a prisoner." Weathered's diary indicates that the prisoner was a storekeeper from Campbellsville. Alston vividly describes the enraged Murphy's reaction and subsequent murder of Magennis, "I . . . heard the report of a pistol . . . saw Captain Magennis falling from his horse, with blood gushing from his mouth and breast."[46] Murphy was put under guard, but before he could be court-martialed, escaped at Garnettsville. Colonel Duke minced no words in referring to the officers involved: "The wrench [Murphy] ought to have been butchered in his tracks . . . Captain Magennis was highly regarded . . . no officer in the entire Confederate army, perhaps, so young as he was . . . had evinced more intelligence, aptitude and zeal." Duke adds that General Morgan deeply regretted this incident.[47]

The David Shuck House within two miles of Lebanon is, by tradition, the house in which Morgan and his bodyguards spent the night of July 4.[48] With heavy hearts after losing so many comrades at the Battle of Tebbs Bend, Morgan's troops camped along the Campbellsville Road, and in the woods, fields, lots, and houses around New Market to within four miles of Lebanon. Disheartened soldiers asked Tom Morgan, a lieutenant who seemed much younger than his 19 years, to sing for them. He responded with all the verses of "We Sat by the River, You and I." Hathaway commented, "So plaintive and sweet were the notes that it would have been a fitting requiem for the dead."[49]

There was much more bad news that Morgan and his command were not yet aware of. On that very day General Robert E. Lee's army was enduring a terrible

David Shuck House, Campbellsville Road, Marion County

rain storm as it retreated from its defeat at Gettysburg, after the bloodiest battle in American history and the turning point for the North on the eastern front. In Scott County, Martha Buford Jones, a staunch Rebel, wrote in her diary, "the rumor is that General Lee's forces took a beating at Gettysburgh, but I don't believe it."[50]

Nor did Morgan know that General Pemberton had surrendered to Union commander U.S. Grant at Vicksburg, Mississippi that same day. Morgan just knew that he had been defeated by a shrewd Yankee and that he had lost many fine officers. He will not learn of these Confederate disasters until after he has crossed the Ohio River.

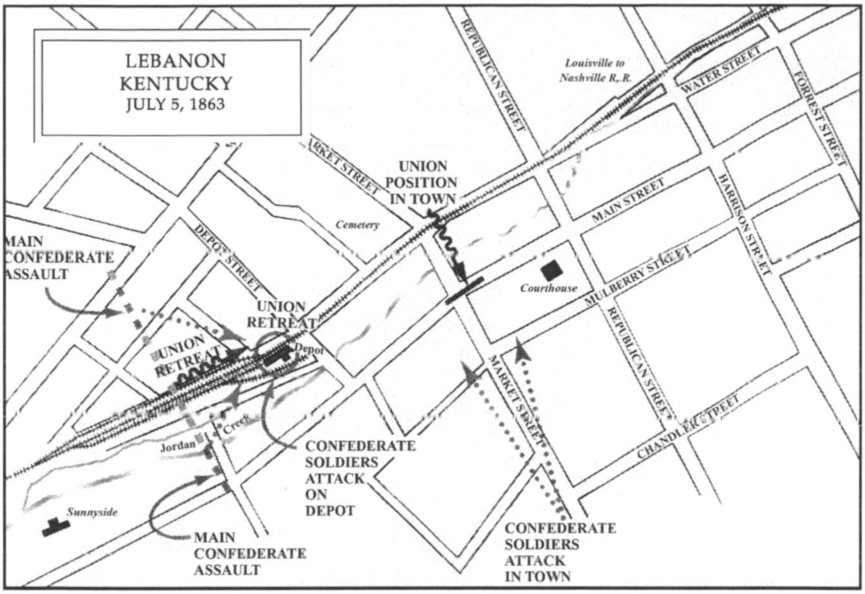

Maria Brent

Lebanon, Kentucky

Chapter Seven: Morgan Completes His Mission in Kentucky

Sunday, July 5: Battle of Lebanon

The morning dawned foggy and Morgan's men began to encircle Lebanon, stationing troops from St. Mary's Road to the Bradfordsville Road, placing Duke's 1st Brigade on the right of the Campbellsville Road and Johnson's 2nd Brigade on the left. Morgan's artillery, commanded by Lt. E.D. Lawrence, was positioned on Bricken's Hill.[1]

Union Col. Charles Hanson had occupied Lebanon, with about 360 infantrymen of the 20th Kentucky and detachments from three other regiments. He set up a defensive position at the L&N Train Depot, where, Hanson had a 24-pounder gun covering the approaches to the station. His troops occupied public buildings and several houses in the town. Hanson had also established an outer defensive position, including a barricade of wagons manned by a squad of infantry, blocking the Campbellsville Pike.[2]

Col. Charles Hanson, 20th Ky. Inf.

Morgan employed his usual tactics in his assault on Lebanon. After a short artillery bombardment at 7:00 A.M., he sent Colonel R.A. Alston, under a white flag, to demand that Hanson surrender. Hanson declined but did apologize for his men firing on the flag of truce. The tall, handsome Union commander, who was from Winchester, had many acquaintances among Morgan's men and his brother Roger, a Confederate general, had been killed at Stones River earlier that year. Anticipating the arrival of reinforcements—two Michigan regiments from Danville—Hanson sought to delay decisive action. Morgan replied by advising Hanson to evacuate the women and children and ordered Lawrence to open fire with his guns.

The Confederate artillery shells that fell on the town did considerable damage. Most of them struck the roof of the second floor of the depot; others riddled the Presbyterian Church steeple and landed on the south lawn of L.A. Spalding's stately plantation home. The Federals on the outer defensive line stationed in the fields and houses outside the southern end of town were driven back toward the depot.[3]

According to Morgan's Adjutant Leeland Hathaway, the day was very hot and Capt. Tom Franks was already drinking heavily. He was in charge of the advance and he volunteered to lead a charge to take the supply depot, formerly Christopher Beeler's store, where it was known that small arms were stored. Hathaway argued that these were ineffective guns and not worth the sacrifice and that this fight would be Kentuckian against Kentuckian, some of whom were neighbors and friends. Franks, a Mississippian, replied, "Those who did not fancy the job could stay behind."

Lebanon Depot

The assault by one hundred fifty mounted men of Cluke's 8th Kentucky began with Franks in the lead. Many of the Rebels fell from their horses dead or wounded, others quickly dismounted and sought cover in the ruts of a ploughed field. Hathaway heard Franks cry out, "I am killed." Hathaway himself was unscathed, even though he had seven bullet holes in his clothes, the top of his hat shot entirely off, and his body grazed by two balls. Lt. Pat Gardner and Dick Worsham had been killed and dead and wounded horses lay over the field. The temperature was nearly 100 degrees.

Dick Worsham

Privates Walter Ferguson and Tom Logwood were pinned down by fire in some high weeds. Logwood was wounded and carried to safety in the rear by Ferguson even though enemy fire had not ceased. Ferguson will have only a few months to live, being one of those Confederates selected at random to be shot during the arbitrary rule of Brig. Gen. Stephen Burbridge over Kentucky in retaliation for alleged Rebel crimes.[4]

Confederate Vincent Eastham, a cattle drover along the Wilderness Road, was mortally wounded. After his girlfriend married someone else, he joined Cluke's regiment at Somerset. Eastham had become fast friends with Bennett Young. He left his black horse, Bobtail, with a horseholder, and joined the charge toward the depot. He was hit by a minie ball and his friend Young carried him to the surgeons. Young reports that, as he lay there, Eastham "took my hand and pressed it to his lips while his large black eyes were filled with tears. He looked up at me and said he would see me no more." Young kept flowers on his grave for years.[5]

Some Union soldiers were firing from buildings in the town at Rebels in the streets below. Leaning out a second-story hotel window of Harris House on Main Street, John House ignored advice from his comrades to be more cautious; he was hit by a minie ball, which shattered his left arm. He later died. Dr. John C. Welch gathered his personal effects for safe-keeping. His brother, Benjamin House, who was on the ground, taking cover behind a chimney corner, was grazed in the back of the neck by a bullet. Fortunately for him, he had on every shirt he carried, which may have saved his life. He and the rest of Hanson's men ran over to the depot to help in its defense.[6]

Men from Rebel Grigsby's 6th Kentucky and Ward's 9th Tennessee cavalries kept up fire on the right side of the depot, while Cluke's 8th Kentucky and Chenault's (now Tucker's) 11th fired into the left side of the depot. Federals later claimed that the depot was hit by artillery fire 26 times. Lawrence moved one of his Parrott guns closer to the depot, in order to have more effect, but Federal sharpshooters, armed with Enfield rifles, kept the battery at bay. Hanson then ordered the burning of the commissary building, located near the depot, in order to deny its supplies to the Southern foe.[7]

Morgan, considering that he had a victory, again sent forward a demand for surrender under a flag of truce, this time with Rev. Thomas Cleland, a Presbyterian minister, and threatened to "fire the town" if the offer were rejected.

Hanson, still expecting his promised support, declined. Morgan, believing he had wasted enough time, ordered his men to renew the attack. Hathaway described his commander as offering a truce while he held "a torch in one hand and the musket in the other."[8]

Col. D. Howard Smith's 5th Kentucky, which had engaged in heavy fighting the previous day at Tebbs Bend, was ordered to assault the barricaded depot, dismounted, and on the double-quick. Under severe Union fire, the men rushed forward, led by the Colonel Smith, on horseback with hat in hand, keeping up sustained fire on the depot. Major Tom Webber, leading the 2nd Kentucky Cavalry, moved up to support Smith and the "heavy volley it poured into the windows of the depot, drove the defenders away from the windows."

Captain William S. Edwards shouted out, "I'll burn the town," and began to set nearby houses on fire.[9] When this happened, Colonel Hanson threw out a white flag and surrendered to Colonel Smith in person. It was now about 1:30 P.M.[10]

As Duke's men of the 2nd Kentucky moved forward in the final assault on the depot, Tom, Morgan's younger brother, "ran forward and cheered the men with all the enthusiasm of his bright nature. At the next Union volley he fell, pierced through the heart."[11] Picked up by his brother, Tom whispered, "Brother Cally, they have killed me."

Tom, a first lieutenant of Company I, 2nd Kentucky, at the time of the battle, was serving on Duke's staff. His rush to the front of his regiment in the midst of the battle was very much in character as he "habitually sought and exposed himself to danger, seeming to delight in the excitement it afforded him." Tom's commanders, including General Morgan, had repeatedly remonstrated with him "regarding his reckless exposure of his person." When the news of his death became known, "there was not a dry eye in the command." Many felt that "he was stricken by the fate that his friends feared for him."[12]

University of Kentucky Archives

Lt. Tom Morgan, 2nd Ky. Cav., CSA

This event has traditionally been thought to have occurred near the depot. According to a contemporary source, Rose Cleland Grundy, Tom's body was brought to the Cleland house by her brother Bob, who requested that the soldier take him back to the site where Tom fell. Bob determined that he was killed at a gate of a plank fence, northwest of their home, a spot several hundred yards from the depot.[13]

During the surrender proceedings, the atmosphere was very emotional. Colonels Smith and Hanson were childhood friends. Colonel Smith grasped Hanson's hand in friendship, and asked, "Charlie, is that you?" But then Tom's older brother, Charlton, came forward and grabbed Hanson by the whiskers, and threatened, "I'll blow your brains out, you damned rascal." Another account reports that Morgan said, "Charles, when you go home, if it is any source of gratification to you, tell Mother you killed brother Tom."[14] Alston observed that the death of Tom put the men in a state of frenzy. Colonel Smith and Levi Wheeler, Hanson's brother-in-law, tried to calm the men's tempers.[15]

Levi Wheeler

Tom Morgan's body, accompanied by a guard, was taken to Sunnyside, now Hollyhill, and laid out in Rose Cleland's brothers' clothes. A carpenter set to work to make the wooden coffin at the Cleland home. That night several visitors, both Federal and Confederate, came to Sunnyside to view Tom's body, grieving and weeping. Tom was buried in a rose garden to the west of the Cleland house.

Later Charlton Morgan made arrangements to have Tom's remains moved to Lexington. When he wrote his mother asking if Tom's body had been returned home, he was very emotional: "None knew him but to *love* him, none named him but to praise." His body was buried in Lebanon and remained there until 1868, when it was reinterred in the Hunt-Morgan family plot in Lexington.[16]

Sunnyside, now Holly Hill Manor, Lebanon

After Hanson's men left the depot, the Rebels set it ablaze. Its flames spread to the nearby Beeler house and consumed it. Morgan's men then set fire to the office of the *Central Kentuckian*, and some twenty buildings, including barns, stables, but mostly the houses of known Union supporters. The usual looting of stores occurred with boots, uniforms, and medicines being carried off.

The burning of the county and circuit clerks' offices, located south of the courthouse was one of their most destructive actions. Records of deeds, wills, marriages from 1834 until 1863 were lost. The offices may have been burned because the county clerk was James M. Fidler, a strong Federal supporter and former lieutenant of the 10th Kentucky Infantry. His brother was William Fidler of the 6th Kentucky Cavalry. James Fidler had resigned from the military to become county clerk, but he continued to serve in the Home Guards. The circuit clerk was Capt. F.B. Merimee, a former officer in the Home Guard. Pro-Southern Dr. W.W. Cleaver despised Fidler and Merimee and, indeed, had left Lebanon earlier with the Confederate force. The Confederates may have also believed that the records included indictments against Southern sympathizers, which needed to be destroyed.[17]

Federal losses were 6 killed and 16 wounded. Confederate losses were 9 killed and 22 wounded, 2 dying later of their wounds. See Appendix O for the names of the casualties at Lebanon. The Confederates took over 400 prisoners, and seized many wagons and horses, as well as the Union's 24-pounder cannon.[18] Included among the casualties was Tom Franks. Morgan had lost three Chief Scouts in four days: Quirk at Marrowbone, Cassell in Columbia, and now Franks in Lebanon.

Burning Lebanon

Burke's Diary: Sunday, July 5th, 1863

Curtis Burke did not participate in the fighting but observed the day's happenings from vantage points to the rear. His vivid account reveals much about Morgan's independent, and sometimes rowdy, cavalrymen:

> Weather pleasant. Before sun up we were ordered to mount. . . . I was among the detail for the rear guard of our regiment. We moved up in sight of Lebanon, Ky and formed a line in a lot. There were a few shots fired ahead of us. Then we moved down the [Campbellsville] pike a few hundred yards nearer and the regiment dismounted to fight and deployed forward. The horses and the rear guard went into a field on the right. There was some firing in front. Three or four of our field pieces were planted in the fields on both sides of the pike.
>
> We shifted our position to the other side of the pike to get out of the way of a long line of our advancing horsemen. The line was or seemed to be half a mile long closing in towards town. We were sheltered by a hill. A few shells were thrown into town. Then we were ordered to mount. We moved down the pike on double quick. Several regiments were in front of us. They charged into the suburbs of town and we with them. The firing became fierce. We captured a brass 24-pounder and drove the Yanks from their camp to the shelter of the houses and the brick depot from which they gave us a lively volley.
>
> Our regiment crossed the Railroad about two hundred yards from the

depot and dismounted to fight. Part of the horses were exposed in plain view, the rest were sheltered behind a rise. The Yanks opened a heavy fire from the doors and windows of the depot on the regiment. Lieut. Pat Gardener was shot instantly in the head and killed. Then the boys or most of them took to the nearest houses as they could make no impression on the depot. The balance lay on the ground.

The rearguard was ordered to stay with the horse holders. I wanted to get a shot so I left my horse in care of John Gravis and crept to a tree over the rise. The balls flew thick and close to the ground. The Yanks were firing at some of our men farther down. I fired into the open end door of the depot with my old musket, but I do not believe I hurt any person.

A ball struck a limb of a tree near me and glanced downward to where the horses were in my rear and wounded a horseholder slightly. Another ball struck my tree a few inches from my head knocking bark in my face. The Yanks were cracking away from the doors and windows like fury doing but little damage. If they had not had plenty of ammunition they could not of held out long at the rate they were firing. Our artillery got a position pretty close on my left and commenced battering at the walls of the depot and several other houses where the Yanks were. I heard that Lieut. Thomas Morgan was killed.

After striking the depot several times and burning one of the buildings the Yanks not surrendering, Gen. Morgan gave orders to commence firing the town and burn them out that he had no more time to waste on them. Several out houses were fired. Our boys came to their horses scattering or in small groups. Part of them had been laying flat on the ground under a heavy fire from the depot, so that they dare not reply or try to get away. Thomas Logwood, William Jones and several others were slightly wounded. We just learned that Dick Worsham was killed acting as a messenger. He was shot from his horse by a Yankee vidette. Our regiment mounted and rode about two hundred yards to the rear to a small grove. The firing ceased and word came that the Yanks had surrendered.

I and several others slipped off from the regiment and went into town. We found the streets full of our men from the different regiments. Some of the stores were open, others were being opened. The men were helping themselves to whatever they needed.

An officer came up rearing and charging because some Yanks had fired on his men from a house after the surrender and still refused to surrender. The officer took a squad of men with him swearing that he would fire the house and kill off every man if they did not surrender immediately, which they thought it prudent to do.

I went up town and saw a Confectionary store opened. I went in with the crowd and got a large paper of candy, four cans of cove oysters, two bottles of wine, two bottles of lemon syrup and some nuts which I wrapped up in my gum cloth. I got two saddle girths, a pair of shoes and several others things.

Then I went down to the depot and found my regiment. Ben Young, [later author of *Confederate Wizards of the Saddle* and president of the Sons of Confederate Veterans] gave me a new hat. The boys had their hands full of all kinds of tricks. I had more cheese and cake given me than I could eat.

The prisoners were at the depot. Our Colonels were getting their regiments together and leaving town. My regiment left while I and Henry Beach were at the depot window looking for some Yanks from Lexington that we knew. Joseph Reid and Henry Breman came to the window and we shook hands with as good grace as if we were old friends, although I and Joe Reid had not spoken for the last four years before we joined the army. I only had time to say a few words when the prisoners were taken away.

I started after my regiment. Stopping at a little store room where some of our men were carrying off and destroying a lot of army stores, I got two cap boxes, a pair of heavy boots and a Sharp's rifle. The rifle would not work and I threw it away, keeping my old musket. The Yanks were reported coming in town on the road we came in [Campbellsville Road] causing a considerable stir in town among the stragglers. I mounted my horse and pushed on after the regiment.[19]

July 5: From Lebanon to Springfield

During the confusion at Lebanon, 25th Michigan Sgt. Norris Merrill was able to slip away from his captors and fled to Camp Nelson near Nicholasville to receive orders.

Rose Cleland was sitting on a fence watching what was happening. She saw Morgan come dashing up on his horse, and heard him cry out, "Line up there. The damn-Yanks are coming, fly like hell."

The number of prisoners taken by the Confederates constituted a real problem for them. Having no time to carry out the paper work necessary to parole the

Yankees because a Federal force was approaching, the Rebels force marched their captured Yankee infantrymen to Springfield. Hanson's weary men tried to keep up, at double quick, with the cavalry column, but the heat and the pace were too much for some. Pvt. Ben House watched his friend Sgt. Joseph Slaughter being hit over the head with a gun butt, collapse, and die. Even though House was wounded and exhausted, he was enraged and his adrenalin kept him moving. Fortunately, a heavy rain provided some relief for the prisoners. House remembered leaning over and scooping up the water in his hands and its rivulets running down over his wounded neck. Two captives who could not keep up were run over by the wheels of the artillery caissons; Pvt. Samuel Ferguson died but Pvt. Martin Cure survived.[20]

Maj. T.B. Waller, one of the captured Yankees who survived the march, wrote his father that the Rebels "took our hats off our heads, our shoes off our feet, and run us to Springfield, nine miles in one hour. Those that gave out on the way they knocked in the head with their guns and kicked them out of the road. This I saw with my own eyes. . . . They took everything I had, $750 in money, two fine horses and bridles, two fine Colt's revolvers, one sword worth $40, and my gold watch. They took my coat and boots off me, and then knocked me down after I surrendered."[21]

As Morgan's cavalry rode into Springfield, 12-year-old Will McChord, rode out to greet them on his pony Flash. He looked up at Colonel Duke and asked, "Are you Morgan?" Duke replied, "No, General Morgan is riding in the back now." Duke did not tell the boy that the general and his brothers were grieving the death of their brother Tom.

Washington County Courthouse, Springfield

William C. McChord, Springfield

The troops captured at Lebanon followed the raiders into Springfield passing Elmwood, the headquarters of Buell before the Battle of Perryville. Colonel Alston and Capt. William Davis established their headquarters for issuing paroles at Clelland T. Cunningham's house, on East Main Street. While the Federals were ordered to line up around the rock wall of the Washington County Courthouse at Springfield, where they were issued their paroles, William C. Davis struck up a lasting friendship with Frances, one of the Cunningham daughters. They were married in 1866, moved to Louisville, where they made their home after the war.[22]

Since many of the Federal parolees were from the Bluegrass, they started walking home. Ben House got all the way to Camp Nelson and was at the covered two-lane bridge over the Kentucky River, when he was met by his brother Samuel, driving the horses of the family spring wagon. Samuel was on his way to Lebanon to retrieve his brother John's body. Ben climbed up on the wagon and together, they made the sad journey back to Lebanon to retrieve John.[23]

Colonel Alston, who had carried the flag of truce to Moore at Tebbs Bend and again at Lebanon, was too weary to move on before taking a nap on a front porch between Springfield and Bardstown. Waking up, he rode out to join the rear guard. Instead, he found himself among the pickets of the Yankees. He was taken to Lexington to prison, where he wrote Henrietta Morgan a note to tell her the details of Tom's death.[24]

Hopemont, Home of Henrietta Morgan, Lexington

On July 7, 1863, Union sympathizer Frances Peter, who lived across the street from the Morgan family in Lexington, recorded the shrieks and wailing from the Morgan house. A servant said one of his young 'marsters' had been killed.

Mrs. James B. Clay visited Henrietta and wrote, with great sadness, to her husband, a son of Henry Clay in exile in Canada, about Tom's death. She also reported taking food to Colonel Alston who was captured, paroled, but still imprisoned in the "horrid" Black jail on Short Street, while the prisoners he had just paroled were staying in the Phoenix Hotel.[25]

Because of cut telegraph lines, it took four days for Burnside to report to Maj. Gen. Henry Halleck the events in Kentucky.

> July 6, 1863
>
> Morgan got through our lines last Friday with three brigades and moved up toward Lebanon, by way of Columbia. He got several hours' start on our people, and before they could be concentrated to follow him the roads and streams became almost impassable, in consequence of heavy rain. In the mean time he reached Columbia, from which point the roads are good. He was checked at the crossing of Green River by five companies of the Twenty-fifth Michigan, leaving some 30 killed and as many wounded. Among the killed was Colonel Chenault. He made a detour and reached Lebanon, capturing a garrison of 350 men before re-enforcements could be got up. . . . It would not do to move our mounted force into East Tennessee, and leave him in Kentucky to break up our railroad communications and capture our wagon trains.[26]

It appears Morgan's raid was having its desired effect: it was delaying any Union move toward Confederate forces in Tennessee.

Gerald Myers

Union Standoff, Stable at Bardstown

From Springfield, Bardstown, to Brandenburg

On the morning of July 6, Morgan's men continued through Bardstown, where they forced a small squad to surrender at a livery stable on North Third Street. Morgan turned west. The evening of the 6th, the raiders seized a train on the L&N Railroad and, while at Bardstown Junction, Ellsworth tapped the telegraph and sent out false messages all over the lines to confuse the enemy. In true Morgan fashion, feints were made toward Lexington, Frankfort, and Harrodsburg. A detachment of about a hundred men under Captain Davis went to the east of Louisville on a risky mission to cross the Ohio at Twelve-Mile Island. All this kept the Federals mystified as to Morgan's true intentions.

Louisville, and eventually Covington and Cincinnati, were placed under martial law and businesses were closed. Men, young and old, were enrolled in Home Guard units and drilled in the streets. Newspaper headlines were alive with Morgan exploits.

On the night of July 6, the men camped at Garnettsville in Bullitt County, now on the Fort Knox reservation. On July 8, after a stunning capture the day before of a steamboat, the *John B. McCombs,* and a mail boat, the *Alice Dean*, the main force started crossing the Ohio River at Brandenburg. Captain Byrne's cannon, positioned on a hill in the town near the courthouse, fired across the river and took out opposition from Indiana's Home Guards.

As the troops waited to board the boats, they socialized with citizens in Brandenburg. Pvt. Samuel Joseph Campbell, of Company C, Cluke's 8th Kentucky Cavalry, camped on the farm of William Pike and caught the eye of his daughter, Mary Jerusha. After being captured on the raid in Ohio and subsequently released from Camp Douglas, Campbell returned to court and marry her. They operated a farm at Stithton and were the parents of eleven children.[27]

John Karel

Samuel Joseph Campbell Family, Brandenburg

Buckner House, Morgan's Headquarters while in Brandenburg

All day and into the night of July 9, the men crossed the great river. Just as the last of the Raiders boarded the boats, the advance of the pursuing Federal troops came over the hill. McCreary's 11th Kentucky, acting as rear guard as usual, held off Hobson's force. "[We] hardly had time to get on the boat before the Yankees was right on [our] heels—but the fog was so thick, could hardly see anything," remembered Morgan trooper Nathan Deatherage. When the last troops got to the Indiana side, Morgan ordered the *Alice Dean* to be burned. Deatherage returned to the boat to get a remembrance, a little blanket embroidered with the ship's name, that he carried with him across Indiana and Ohio. Oliver Cosby helped set the boat afire.

View across Ohio River, Brandenburg

Alice Dean

Scout Tom Hines joined Morgan after his own Indiana expedition and was made chief of the scouts for the Indiana Raid.[28]

Federal Pursuit

General S.P. Carter, commander for the 9th Corps stationed in Somerset, had the duty to protect the Burkesville-Columbia Road. Wolford's force, which as noted before, reported to Carter, had responsibility to guard the Cumberland. But on July 1–2, the Cumberland River was so high that Wolford did not anticipate that Morgan's army would be able to escape by crossing the river before water levels lowered.

Hobson, who had been captured by Morgan on the First Raid at Cynthiana, respected Morgan's ability to slip by an enemy force. But his warnings to Judah, Hobson's superior, had been disregarded.[29]

Judah realized that he had misjudged the situation and decided to concentrate his forces for "immediate" pursuit, but he was delayed for thirty-six hours on the old Lexington-Nashville Road on the south side of Green River at Vaughn's Ferry, near Gabe in Green County. Evidently, he lacked Morgan's ability to commandeer boats and make rafts.[30]

At Lebanon, General Burnside gave Hobson overall command of the pursuit of Morgan. Wolford's Brigade, including the 1st Kentucky Cavalry, 2nd Ohio Cavalry, and 45th Ohio Mounted Infantry, left Jamestown and Columbia to join the pursuit force. Hobson and Shackelford took their troops from Ray's Crossroads [Smith's Crossroads today] and Marrowbone to Edmonton through Greensburg to Campbellsville to Lebanon, where they concentrated. They departed from Lebanon, continuing through Springfield and Bardstown to Brandenburg, arriving at the Ohio too late to take any effective action. As has been noted, when Hobson's scouts rode up, they caught sight of last Rebel raiders completing their crossing of the Ohio.

After crossing the river, the Union force pursued Morgan's raiders across Indiana and Ohio, riding for days in the saddle, seldom having a full night's sleep. Maj. Sam Starling vividly described the pursuit to his daughters in a letter dated July 11, 1863:

> We followed him [Morgan] from Burkesville steadily, gaining nothing on him, for his scouts took literally every horse within miles of the road, leaving none for us to recruit from, his way was sprinkled with broken down horses, left on the road. Men & women were standing on the road & complaining of their losses. "Catch him if you kin," "Has took every horse I had," "Kill the last one of them" were frequent expressions. I cant give all the events of course of our tedious pursuit, it has been conducted night & day for 14 days, & when it will end we cant tell. We rode last night until ll P.M. & started at 2 A.M. and have just got here, where the streets are lined with all sorts of people with baskets of provisions. I positively have not averaged 3 hours of sleep in the 24 for 2 weeks & have not taken off my boots & spurs during the whole time. I have on the same clothes I had on when I started. The weather has been intensely hot, and all the men myself included have a dog kennel sort of odor, that is very unpleasant.... Morgan is burning depots & bridges on all the rail roads he crosses.... I have a single blanket which I spread in a fence corner, or under a tree & snatch a few minutes rest at a time.[31]

On July 19, the Union force, consisting of Hobson's 3,000 and Judah's 3–4,000 men, caught up to Morgan at Portland, Ohio, as he was attempting to cross at Buffington Island Ford to West Virginia. The Federals fired on the Confederates from the south and west. The shelling from the Federal gunboat *Moose* from the river was particularly effective. Rebel regimental commanders Duke, Ward, Smith, Huffman, Webber, Tucker, Richard Morgan, and 700 troops were captured. All of Morgan's artillery, wagons, buggies, and a hearse were seized. Confederate casualties numbered 57 killed and 63 wounded. Morgan himself and 1,000 men, eluding the Union pursuers, escaped along a ravine into northern Ohio. Under Hobson's direction, the cavalry of General Shackelford and Colonel

Wolford, had started the chase 800 miles back in Marrowbone and Jamestown, Kentucky.[32]

Artillery commander Byrne and about fifty men swam their horses and successfully crossed the flooded Ohio on flatboats into West Virginia, coming under fire of the *Moose* and cannon on the ferry *Allegheny Belle*.[33]

On July 19, Morgan could have escaped near Reedsville, Ohio, but returned to be with his men. Two hundred seventy-one of the raiders got across to West Virginia successfully but, when Morgan got to the middle of the river and, seeing that the remainder of his men could not cross without being shelled, chose to return and join them and suffer their fate. He told Lightning Ellsworth, "Save yourself if you can do so."[34]

Slaves accompanied Morgan's forces all the way, some as personal servants to the officers and men, and others as teamsters, farriers, blacksmiths, and horse-holders. A few of these names are known: Morgan's personal servant was Box; Colonel Chenault's were Abe and Charley; Capt. Ben Terry had Ike Campbell; Col. D. Howard Smith had Will Johnson, who was captured with his colonel and retained as a servant by a Union officer, later escaped, and returned to Colonel Smith; another officer had Sam who stayed with a Northern family for two years and then moved to Detroit. At Buffington Island, McCreary looked for his slave, Ruben, in order to see that he got back safely to Madison County.

Slaves also played a part in the campaign. On the Christmas Raid, Col. James Dearing Bennett's body was borne home to Tennessee by his slave. The slaves of the four Baldwins serving with Chenault's 11th Kentucky surely took Lt. W. W. Baldwin's body home to Winchester for burial after he was killed at Tebbs Bend. Col. Chenault and Maj. Brent's slaves probably also provided this final service for their masters. Slaves were silent members of Morgan's Raiders, whose stories would be fascinating if we knew them.

On Sunday, July 26, Elizabeth McIntosh watched the remnant of Morgan's force ride by her house near Monroeville, Ohio. She described them as the "dirtiest lot of fellows I ever looked at," saying that "they nearly all wore slouch hats, were hungry, but acted gentlemanly when they came to her house." She reported that Morgan rode up in a carriage pulled by two white horses, accepted some food, and continued on his way. She also saw Union General Shackelford's forces just a half hour later and commented, "They looked as dirty as the Confederates."[37] When Morgan's abandoned carriage was searched, a loaf of bread, two hard-boiled eggs, and a bottle of whiskey were found.[37]

Morgan, now mounted on Sir Oliver, together with Colonels Cluke and Owen, reached Columbiana County, Ohio, the northernmost point of any Confederate raid in the war. Racing against time, Morgan left some of his wounded to be cared for at a farm and accepted a clean shirt.[38]

Morgan turned east, trying to again reach the Ohio River and cross into West Virginia. Between Salineville and West Point, Morgan's troops rode with Wolford's 1st Kentucky in pursuit on the left flank and Rue's 9th Kentucky Cavalry on the right. Deciding that capture was inevitable, Morgan surrendered to Captain James Burbick, New Lisbon Home Guard, whom he had pressed into being his guide. He then ordered Burbick to attach a white handkerchief to a riding stick, find Shackelford, and inform him that Morgan had surrendered. Morgan hoped that this would stop Shackelford's forces and allow his men to reach the river unmolested.[39]

James M. Shackelford

As Morgan's troops crested a hill, they saw Rue's force in the distance. Realizing that they could not see Burbick's white flag, Morgan sent Maj. Theophilus Steele out with a flag of truce. First he demanded that Rue surrender, but when Rue recognized this as a ruse, Steele informed Rue that terms of surrender had already been worked out with Captain Burbick. Rue, a Kentuckian, refused to accept this surrender to a militia officer, and met Morgan under a shade tree two miles from West Point to work out terms. He gave his horse to Rue.

General Shackelford and Colonel Wolford were three miles back having dinner at a farmhouse. They quickly rode up to the surrender scene. Shackelford was adamant that the surrender be unconditional, but Wolford argued that the surrender terms agreed to by Rue should be honored. Shackelford would hear none of it. Morgan's men, now numbering about 400, were ordered to stack their weapons. The Great Raid, which had started with such promise for the Confederates, came to an ignominious end.[40]

Wolford, who had been well treated as Morgan's prisoner, saw to it that Morgan had a private room and a good meal of chicken and dumplings in a hotel in the river town of Wellsville, Ohio before he was placed under guard on a train for Cincinnati.

Upon reaching Cincinnati, Morgan, elegantly attired in a linen coat, black pants, white shirt, and a light felt hat, and his officers were paraded through the streets of the city on their way to temporary incarceration in the city jail.[41] Later Morgan and sixty-seven of his raiders, including colonels Duke and D. Howard Smith, their heads shaven, were imprisoned in the Ohio State Penitentiary at Columbus, Ohio in cells that measured 3½ x 7 feet. Other officers and men were held at camps Chase, Morton, Douglas, and Johnson's Island.

The 25th Michigan was still in Lebanon on July 26 when the news of Morgan's capture was telegraphed over the country and celebrated in Northern newspapers. The sleepy-eyed soldiers of the 25th, summoned from their quarters by the bugle, fell into line, expecting to be sent into battle. Instead, they heard about Morgan's capture and cheering swept the ranks. Burnside was elated that now he could concentrate on his grand strategy of attacking Buckner and Bragg in Tennessee. But Morgan would not remain in prison and Taylor County had not seen the last of him.[42]

Chapter Eight: Events at Tebbs Bend

The Bridge

Throughout the Civil War in Taylor County, the main concern for Union forces was to keep the strategically placed Green River Bridge in operation. After the battle of Tebbs Bend and the subsequent pursuit of "Morgan and his horse thieves" by most of the Union regiments in the area, Lt. Michael Hogan resumed his work constructing the permanent wooden bridge over the river.[1]

Hogan also assumed another role, that of quasi-correspondent to the *Detroit Free Press*. On August 8, 1863, he sent a letter to the paper in answer to inquiries about the safety of the civilian workers during the battle. He listed the names of the carpenters and reported that the men were "all in good health . . . none of them were taken prisoners, and none of them were in the battle of Tebb's Bend on the 4th." Hogan went on to say that "being civilian citizens, none of them are expected, or required, to take part in any action with the enemy."

By September, the bridge was in working order and the political leaders and people of Taylor County were elated. The *Louisville Journal*, September 9, 1863, ran the story:

Flag Raising at Green River Stockade

> In honor of the completion of the splendid new bridge over Green River, under the supervision of the worthy soldier and untiring workman, Lieut. M.A. Hogan, on Thursday, the 10th inst, the citizens of Taylor and the adjoining counties will assemble for the purpose of witnessing the raising of the beautiful flag presented by the Government to the gallant soldiers of Green River fame, as a reward for their heroic deeds and indomitable courage. The staunch patriot, Mr. [Joseph H.] Chandler, of Campbellsville, and others, will be present on the occasion and address the assemblage. The loyal ladies of the vicinity will give a large dinner to the noble boys who have left their home to fight, and if need be, die, in defense of our glorious Union.

A subsequent article in the *Louisville Journal* stated that the oversized flag measured 20 feet in length by 10 feet in height.[2]

Hogan and his men also rebuilt the Green River Stockade. The stockade and the bridge had never been defended with artillery. Unlike Colonel Moore, Lieutenant Hogan got along with and took orders from Headquarters in Louisville. He arranged for General Boyle to send a 24-pounder to Green River. Hogan was proud of it, and its arrival was reported in a news story, November 4, 1863, in the *Detroit Free Press*.

From Kentucky

> Under the supervision of the brave and energetic officers, Lieut. Hogan and Campbell, the stockade was speedily repaired and many improvements made in it. Lt. Hogan, on receipt of our huge "bulldog" (a large 24-pounder), designed a neat and serviceable port hole. It can be opened with ease by a child and closes itself at the rebound of the gun.[3]

A campaign was begun locally to honor the Federal heroes at Tebbs Bend. William M. Spencer of Greensburg, on behalf of Green, Adair, and adjoining counties, proposed that the bodies of the Federal soldiers, "the fallen heroes," be allowed to remain in their "soldiers" graves upon the battlefield. Surrounding the graves, Spencer proposed that a stone wall be erected with an iron railing. In the center of the cemetery, he wanted a "marble column of exquisite workmanship" inscribed with the names of the "heroes of the Twenty-fifth Michigan." The families of the dead men buried there were asked to send word concerning their wishes. The *Detroit Free Press* commended Kentuckians "for the measures they have taken to perpetuate the memories and do honor to the courageous heroes who so gallantly defended their homes."[4]

Paradoxically, just the opposite occurred. In 1868, most of the bodies of the Michigan soldiers were reinterred in the National Cemetery, Lebanon, Kentucky. Five of the soldiers' names—Slater, R. Beebe, Wallace, Cuddeback, and Verschure, and one unknown—appear on gravestones in that cemetery. The final resting place for George Hicks and Henry Beebe remain unknown. In 1872, the Confederates rather than the Federals erected a stone wall around their soldiers' bodies and placed a granite monument in the center of the cemetery. It has been said that Kentucky became a Confederate state after the war was over which this incident confirms.

Confederate Monument at Green River

All that is known about the Confederate Memorial is from a news article that was sent from the *Columbia Spectator* to the *Lebanon Standard*, April 17, 1872.

Honor the Dead

> The Confederate dead who fell at Green river in the furious contest between John Morgan and the Federal troops stationed at that point during the late Civil War, have been disinterred and removed to the Griffin farm, a short distance this side of the scene of conflict. The spot chosen for the last resting place of these fallen braves is upon a beautiful elevation near the [Campbellsville to Columbia] pike, and the lot

Green River Bridge Confederate Monument, 1872

was a donation by Mr. [James Madison] Griffin, the owner of the premises. The grounds are to be tastefully ornamented with shrubbery, the whole to be enclosed by a handsome iron fence, which, we learn has been donated by John D. Fogle, Esq. of Lebanon.

Mr. R.S. Kember, one of the prime movers in the final and honorable disposition of these soldiers, informs us that a suitable monument is to be erected to the memory of the slain Confederates who shall sleep beneath it, at a cost of about $500, the same to be paid by subscriptions. Subscription papers in aid of this movement have been left in the hands of Mr. Sinc Wheat and J.W. Suddarth, of this place [Columbia], to whom persons should apply who wish to contribute money in aid of the monument fund. The monument will be furnished from the marble works of T. Joyce, Louisville, and will be manufactured from pure Scotch Granite.

The neighboring counties assumed the leadership in securing the Confederate monument. Wheat and Suddarth, from Adair County, collected the subscriptions and Fogle resided in Marion County. When the Atkinson-Griffin family took care of the Confederate wounded in 1863, some of them died and were already buried on their farm. Therefore, in 1872 when the bodies were taken up from the mass grave along the Columbia Road and moved to the cemetery, they joined their comrades under the maple trees on the cemetery's grassy peak.

The iron fence promised by Fogle never materialized. In 1911, another citizen from Lebanon promoted the idea that a fence be placed around the monument and that the lot be sewn in grass. He ended his letter, "The work should not longer be neglected." Sad to say, in 1938, an editorial in the *Louisville Times* echoed the same theme: "Picturesque Confederate Burial Ground In Southern Kentucky Neglected; Memorial In Ruins."[5]

The bodies were placed inside a stone wall that is still visible surrounding the monument on Tebbs Bend Road. Sources vary as to how many bodies are buried there. Private Wilterdink recorded that he helped bury 47, while Bridgewater remembered 23. At the Confederate Memorial Day celebration in 1911, the mound of ground enclosed by the wall was said to have 24 bodies there.[6]

The Confederate Monument was erected with a memorial ceremony in 1872. The Museum of the Confederacy has no record of this monument, nor do any of the Confederate organizations that were formed after the war. It is, however, known to be one of the earliest of the Confederate memorials erected in Kentucky.[7] Inscribed on the monument are the words:

> In memory of the Confederate soldiers of General Morgan's command who fell in battle of Green River Bridge, July 4th, 1863. They have not been forgotten by their countrymen.

Confederate Monument through the Years

On Saturday, June 3, 1911, the citizens of Adair and Taylor counties participated in one of the last Confederate Decoration Day celebrations at the Confederate Monument. The invitation went out to all old soldiers, "Yanks" or "Johnnies." Even though many were deceased, about sixty veterans attended that year. Caravans of covered wagons filled the road. People brought picnic lunches and went into the beech woods located across the road from the monument in the shade to eat. Huge washing tub barrels of lemonade were offered to the public for a nickel. The seller would take a dipper which hung on a tree and fill one's glass. Music was played by a string band, old war songs were sung, and short speeches were made by the old soldiers. Two former Union officers, Capt. A. Offutt of Lebanon and Capt. Elijah F. Tucker of Greensburg, affirmed convincingly that every Confederate was now a friend. Ladies decorated the monument with flowers. The newspaper reported 4,000 in attendance, "the largest and most orderly gathering ever assembled in the Green River section." Attorney W.M. Jackson, of Campbellsville, son of a Confederate soldier, delivered the address.[8]

Fred Faulkner, Jr.

Fred and Sallie Fannie Faulkner, Sr. visiting the decorated monument on their Wedding Day, 1911.

As far back as 1919, 72/100th of an acre of land began being excepted out of deed transactions for the "Old Confederate Burying Ground." By 1961, 1.0 acre was excluded for the Confederate Burial Ground. For years, volunteers mowed the cemetery. Today the members of the Tebbs Bend Battlefield Association, aided at times by members of the Taylor County Road Department, are the caretakers of the grounds.[9]

At some point in the 1930s, the original monument toppled over and the urn on its top was lost. In May 1940 McKinley Monument Company erected a concrete base on which to place the monument, thereby elevating it several feet. The American Legion again repaired it in the 1960s before the Centennial Program there.[10]

In 1972, at the Re-enactment of the Battle of Tebbs Bend, Frank Rankin, president of the Louisville Civil War Round Table and active in Confederate memorials, delivered the address at the Confederate Monument.

In 1988, the stone wall in front of the monument was lengthened and repaired by a group of volunteers.[11] The names of the soldiers who died there were researched by the author and money was raised to erect marble markers to their memory. On August 8, 1999, the markers and the monuments provided by the U.S. government were dedicated. The search continues for a complete list of the men killed and wounded there.[12]

Confederate Monument, Dedication of Memorial Markers, August 8, 1999

Dedication Ceremony, August 1999

The Confederate Monument was entered in the National Register of Historic Places in 1998, and the battleground was added in 1999. The Tebbs Bend-Green River Bridge Battlefield Association was formed in 1997 to protect and promote the battlefield's preservation. By 2004 a three-mile battlefield tour of Tebbs Bend included ten interpretive wayside markers and two Kentucky Highway Historical Markers, one at the Confederate Cemetery and one at the battle site.

Aware that there was no marker of any kind at the battlefield honoring the Michigan soldiers, in 1988, the author contacted Willard Wichers of the Michigan Historical Commission. Within two weeks, permission was granted to place a Michigan Highway marker at the site, only one of two markers outside the state of Michigan. Through the efforts of Al McGeehan, John Noe, and

Harold Woltman, the marker was financed by the Holland-Zeeland Civil War Roundtable, Holland Chapter, Disabled American Veterans, and VFW Post #2144 of Holland. A ceremony, presided over by Gary Osborne, was held July 3, 1988 to dedicate the Michigan Marker.[13] The Michigan Legislature passed a special resolution to commemorate the 125th Anniversary of the Civil War Battle at Tebbs Bend, Kentucky, House Concurrent Resolution No. 879.

Kentucky Historic Highway Marker, Tebbs Bend

Michigan Highway Marker, Tebbs Bend

Courts-Martial, a Murder, and a Painting

Even though Colonel Moore soundly defeated General Morgan at Tebbs Bend, General Boyle was still embittered. Colonel Moore and his troops were ordered to Lebanon where they stayed until August 19, 1863. All the companies of the 25th Michigan were reunited and were sent south into East Tennessee. Moore was made commander of the 2nd Brigade, 23rd Army Corps, which consisted of eight regiments of infantry, one of which was his old regiment, the 25th Michigan, and two batteries of artillery. Another of the regiments under Moore was the 13th Kentucky, raised in central Kentucky. They engaged the enemy often and fought in a hard battle at Mossy Creek, Tennessee, on November 26, 1863.

Moore's family may have remained in Louisville while he was in the field in Tennessee. At any rate, he returned to Louisville in October of 1863 on sick leave and was living at a boarding house with his wife. He was carrying a letter from the regimental physician stating that he was suffering from consumption [tuberculosis] and was accompanied by the assistant regimental physician, Doctor Oakley.

Pvt. J.S. Carlisle wrote home to his mother: "Our Col. has gone home sick and has the consumption. We all feel sorrow to part with him. We think there are but few who can fill his place and the prospects are poor for him to join us again. Mis Moore said she is going to get him out of the service if she can." It was no secret among family members that Mrs. Moore was frail and her health continued to be worrisome throughout his career.[14] Many of the times that Colonel Moore got in trouble with his superiors, it was over his need to be with his family.

Moore's return to Louisville in October gave Boyle an opportunity to snare him. Again, Moore had stubbornly refused to register at Headquarters under Order No. 5. Boyle ordered his arrest and, in the process, Moore called General Boyle and Colonel Munday, both "damn fools." It is not surprising that Moore was placed under ninety days of house arrest and soon court-martial charges were brought against him. One of the charges involved leaving his camp unguarded at Tebbs Bend. A witness for the prosecution was Lieutenant Hogan, the bridge builder. [See Appendix N for the charges and Moore's defense.]

Hogan's testimony was taken in court on December 24, 1863. Then Hogan returned to Green River where he entertained a painter named Edward Henry, a soldier in the 79th New York, whom he had invited to return to the site to paint the new covered Green River Bridge, which Hogan considered to be "his handiwork."

Pvt. Edward Henry had been stationed here during the spring of 1863 with the rest of his regiment. When the regiment was sent south, he was posted to the Department of the Ohio Engineer's Office in Cincinnati. Hogan wrote the office to request that Henry be allowed to return to Green River on "urgent business."[15] Henry completed the painting, presented it to Hogan, and returned to the engineering office in Cincinnati.

The motive for having Henry come to Green River to paint the bridge and the stockade is conjecture on the part of the author. He may have wanted to impress General Boyle with his self-supporting 160-foot-long, Burr-arch-truss, multiple-king-post bridge. Or he may have thought about taking it home to show a future employer after the war.[16]

Whatever the truth, he took Henry's canvas from Green River to Lebanon where he left it with Miss Elizabeth Chandler, whose father operated a rooming house.[17] While there, he met the wife of Capt. Samuel M. Crandell of the 13th Kentucky Cavalry, who was in a dilemma. A small, frail woman, described as an invalid, she came by train to Lebanon from their home in Russellville and was planning to catch the stage to Greensburg to visit her husband, who was posted there. However, the train was late and she missed the stage, and she was looking for accommodation in Lebanon. Upon learning her story, Lieutenant Hogan offered to take her in his buggy as far as Campbellsville and take care of her as if she were his sister.

After leaving Lebanon on the Campbellsville Pike, Hogan's demeanor changed. He tried to make the horse run away; then he turned the buggy into a deserted, dilapidated farm house, pulled out his pistol, and forced a sobbing Mrs. Crandell out of the buggy and inside the house, where he "ravished" her. After the incident, she was forced back into the buggy, and they rode on to a farm house where Hogan secured accommodations for the night, threatening to kill her if she did not stay silent. He entered the room, and again, at gun point, forced her to allow him to her bed. The record is unclear how she got away from Hogan and how she eventually got to Greensburg to her husband.

Upon arrival, she told her husband the whole story. After hearing the details, Crandell was so enraged, he could not eat or sleep. Admired and respected by everyone who knew him, Crandell set out in search of Hogan, who had been transferred from Green River Bridge to Camp Nelson in Jessamine County.

At Camp Nelson, on the evening of February 2, 1864, Hogan was on his horse headed in a northerly direction. Captain Crandell, accompanied by two privates, all mounted, was coming from Camp Headquarters and headed south, to the camp of the 26th Kentucky Infantry. By accident, he met a lieutenant in the road, and asked him if he were Lieutenant Hogan. Hogan answered in the affirmative. Crandell then asked him if he remembered accompanying a lady from Lebanon to Campbellsville. Hogan claimed that he did not. Crandell said that he did and it was useless for him to deny it. Crandell said, "Did you treat her like a dog?" Hogan replied, "Yes, I treated her like a dog." Hogan was not contrite; he was laughing and smiling, as if it were of no consequence. At this point, Crandell pulled his pistol and shot Hogan. After he fell, Crandell shot him a second time. The killing was witnessed by W.M. Grubbs, Chaplain of the 26th Kentucky, who happened upon the event as he was returning to camp from the post office. Hogan's remains were sent home on a train to Michigan to his family.[18]

Crandell surrendered to authorities in the 26th Kentucky camp and was held there two days before being transferred to the Louisville Military Prison. Crandell caught a 10 A.M. train from Lexington to Louisville. A telegram was sent to Louisville instructing that Crandell be met. He was described as 5'10" tall, with a black moustache, dark complexion, with jean pants. Because of the circumstances, he was allowed special visitation rights for his friends.[19]

Crandell's court martial lasted only a few days in February 1864. He was defended as upholding his honor. It was said that such monsters as Hogan deserve to die. When the citizens of Greensburg heard about the "affair," as it was labeled in the paper, they petitioned the court asking that Captain Crandell be set free. They said that Crandall had been stationed in their midst for several months in the winter of 1863 and that he was the best guerrilla fighter that had been posted in Greensburg and that he kept the peace. It may have helped his cause. Crandall was voted not guilty in the court martial trial and released to return to his regiment.[20]

In 1871, the widow Mary Hogan and the children came into court asking for a pension as a widow of a war veteran. The record said that she was in dire need, virtually living on the streets, and the pension was granted.[21]

☆ ☆ ☆

Back in Louisville, Colonel Moore was kept under house arrest by General Boyle until February. The court martial, chaired by Col. Sanders Bruce, a former brother-in-law of John Hunt Morgan, continued for days, beginning on December 7, 1863. In January 1864 the last testimony was taken. The court voted Moore guilty of most all the charges and stripped him of his command.

John Sickles

Col. Sanders Bruce, 20th Inf.

The Lt. Colonel of Moore's regiment, Benjamin Orcutt, had been allowed to sit as one of the court martial judges, which, of course, was an infraction of military law. Moore promptly appealed the judgment to Headquarters in Cincinnati, where the political climate was more judicious, and no one could profit in rank from his conviction. The court martial conviction was promptly overturned on appeal by Maj. Gen. Foster, Judge Advocate, on February 2, 1864, according to General Orders No. 7, and Moore was ordered to reassume command of his regiment.

The *Louisville Journal* supported Moore in the overturning of his conviction. Editor Prentice took the local court martial members to task in regard to accusing Moore of not having his camp properly guarded at Tebbs Bend. He said, "It will be well for you to be careful how you conduct yourself, and be content with the competent, impartial, and just decision of the Headquarters of the Department of the Ohio."

Stubbornly, Moore disregarded the order to return to his regiment because he was on sick leave, with a military certificate stating bronchitis as the cause. Capt. C. J. Wilson, 33rd Kentucky, who had sat on his court martial and had been vilified by Moore in a published pamphlet that Moore circulated after his conviction, reported to Col. Sanders Bruce that Moore was lounging around the city drunk. This letter added more poison to the pot.

Moore's wife was very sick and he had planned to take her home to Michigan where family members could help. In the middle of these plans, on February 25, he was summoned to appear as a witness in the Court Martial trial of Capt. Samuel Crandell, who had killed Hogan, his former antagonist. Feeling that his presence was unnecessary and desperate to seek some remedy for his wife's illness, he walked into the court and voiced his displeasure to Crandell's defense lawyer and his old antagonist, Col. Marc Munday, in a loud enough voice that it was overheard. He said, "I will not submit to it," meaning his detention as witness, "and if my leave of absence is interfered with, by God, I'll make it a personal matter with you."

The next day, he had started home, when he was ordered to be put under arrest by Brig. Gen. S.G. Burbridge, Boyle's successor. He negotiated a leave on condition of an immediate return after taking his family to Michigan. On reporting back, Moore found that he had been discharged from the army for physical disability, Special Order No. 88! This was followed by an amendment to the order to being discharged for "conduct unbecoming an officer and a gentleman and for habitual drunkenness."[22]

Moore set about trying to set the record straight, going into battle on all fronts. He had already made a printed copy of his defense that he gave at his court martial trial and distributed it to the public, further incurring the wrath of his accusers. From Louisville, A.J. Ballard wrote Judge Advocate General Joseph Holt explaining his case. Moore went to Tennessee and met with Brig. Gen Mahlon Manson, the Division Commander. He spoke to the troops and said, "While you have been fighting the enemy in the front, I have been fighting the enemy in the rear.... I am sorry to say I am no longer your Colonel." With tears in his eyes, he said that he was "nothing but a citizen of America."[23] General Manson made a speech on his behalf. On March 25, his officers and men in the field signed a petition seeking the return of their commander.

Moore traveled to Washington, D.C. where he prepared his case. Michigan Senator Jacob M. Howard wrote Secretary of War Stanton asking that the case be investigated. Finally, on June 29, 1864, President Abraham Lincoln sent a memo to the Judge Advocate General requesting that Moore's case be looked into. Lincoln wrote: "His dismissal was based upon his conduct in Ky. And Gen

Boyle has had something to do with it." After reviewing the report from the Judge Advocate General, written July 14, 1864, Lincoln wrote in Moore's record,

> Order of dismissal revoked.
>
> A. Lincoln.

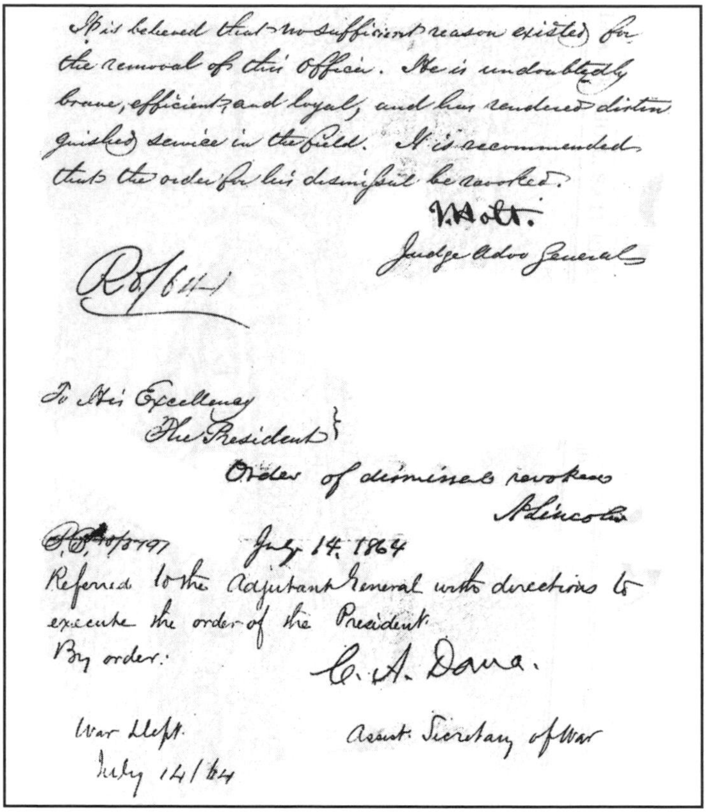

It is believed that no sufficient reason existed for the removal of this Officer. He is undoubtedly brave, efficient and loyal, and has rendered distinguished service in the field. It is recommended that the order for his dismissal be revoked.

J. Holt.
Judge Advo General

R.O./64

To His Excellency
The President

Order of dismissal revoked
A. Lincoln

R.O. 10/3797 July 14. 1864
Referred to the Adjutant General with directions to execute the order of the President.
By order: C. A. Dana.

War Dept.
July 14/64

Asst. Secretary of War

National Archives

Lincoln's Intervenes in Moore's Case

Finally, in November 1864, Moore was returned to his command of the 2nd Brigade, Schofield's 2nd Division in Tennessee.[24]

Colonel Moore led his troops in the hard fought battle of Franklin, Tennessee. He was said to be out in front, fearless and courageous, just as he was at Tebbs Bend. "As he swept along brandishing his sword over his head, he spoke to us as cheerfully as though sitting in safety at home.... Such a general as is Col. Moore in every emergency, we never had." Again, at Fort Anderson, North Carolina, he led a successful charge to take the fort.[25]

In August 1865, efforts were made by A.J. Ballard and by T.S. Bell, head of the Kentucky Branch, U.S. Sanitary Commission, to secure a promotion for Colonel

Moore. He credited him for saving the U.S. Arsenal at Benicia, California, his action at Tebbs Bend, "being one of the finest in the war," and his brigade at Franklin "never gave one inch of ground during the fight and Moore was conspicuous in handling his troops and in personal bravery." It was added that, at Fort Anderson, Moore planted the flag of the 26th Kentucky with his own hands on the ramparts. "The officers and men of the 26th Kentucky idolize Col. Moore." But the promotion that Rebel Colonel Alston said he deserved as early as July 1863 never materialized.[26]

At the end of the war, he was posted to South Carolina to help with reconstruction. In Columbia in 1867, his third child was born, whom he named Edward Prutzman Moore, after his adjutant who was killed at Resaca. The child lived only three days. That same year, when he was Officer for the Day, he gave his sword to a junior officer and left his post at the Citadel one evening for two hours, to go home to eat, for he lived very near the post. While there, he discovered that his little girl was dangerously ill and stayed longer than he had planned. Again, he had to endure another court martial trial on a frivolous matter. He was found guilty of leaving his post, but only reprimanded.

Moore continued his regular army career, lowered in rank after the war to a Captain of the 6th United States Infantry. He was posted out West and commanded forts and posts at Gibson, Arbuckle, Sill, Camp Supply, Buford, Stevenson, Snake River, White River, Douglas, and Lincoln.[27]

His family could remember sleeping through winter storms with snow coming into their tent and his dealing with many Indian tribes, some friendly, some fiercely dangerous. Moore had many close escapes. He was only thirty miles from General George Custer's massacre. When the Ute Indians became troublesome, Colonel Moore was sent to Fort Douglas, Utah. With the Sioux uprising, he was ordered to the Dakotas where he was involved in almost continual warfare. In a fight with Indians, his watch was hit by a bullet and fell into his boot. Another time, his lip was grazed by a bullet.[28]

Still a musician, Moore entertained friends on lonely posts with his 200-year old violin, but he never painted again. He held a counsel to explain to the Indian chiefs why the railroad was being put through their land and that it would be to their advantage not to resist the government. He never broke their faith in him. Kind to peaceful Indians, his relations with inept authority figures remained crusty to the end.

While on an expedition in the Rocky Mountains between Rawlins, Wyoming, and White River, Colorado, where he had been sent to deal with hostile Indians, he suffered a severe sunstroke. Because of continuing ill health, he retired from service in 1884, after a career of twenty-eight years, with the rank of lieutenant colonel of the 17th Infantry.

Moore died October 31, 1890, in Dearborn of a cerebral hemorrhage and a private funeral was held in Detroit. His body was placed on a train to California, where one of the largest attended funerals in memory was held in the Congregational Church, Tulare, California, on November 9, 1890. The Gettysburg Post, G.A.R., helped with the arrangements. He was laid to rest beside his wife, who had died in 1878 of tuberculosis.

Today his name is engraved on a dignified obelisk above his grave, with "Liberty, Love and Humanity" on the stone above his name. An American flag flies over his grave.[29]

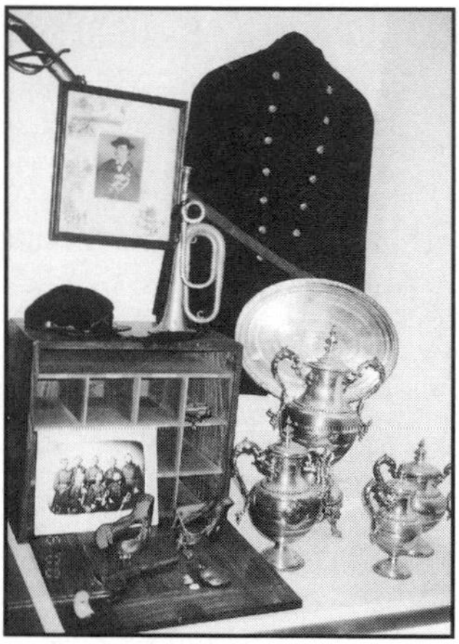

Kalamazoo Valley Museum

Moore's Headquarters Desk and Uniform

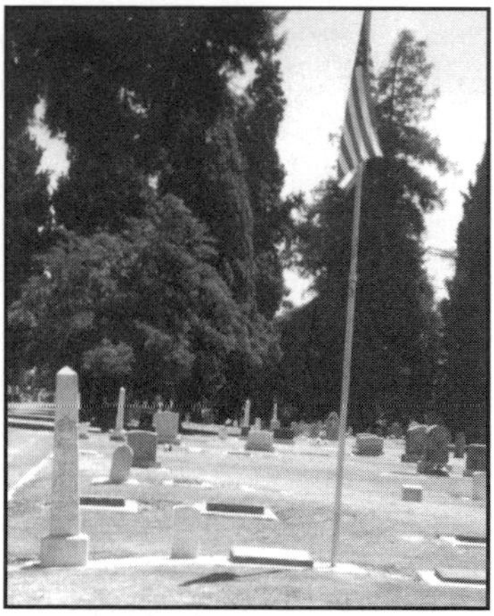

Moore's Grave, Tulare, California

Moore's two sons preceded him in death. He was survived by his daughter, Jessie Moore Loveridge of Coldwater, Michigan. She was the lady who was born in Louisville and was not seen by her father until after the Battle of Tebbs Bend. She faithfully attended all the reunions of the 25th Michigan and was named "Daughter of the Regiment." She and her husband are buried in Oak Grove Cemetery, Coldwater, Michigan.

The Painting

Henry's oil painting of Green River Bridge passed from the Chandler family to Dr. Robert Caldwell McChord. His daughter, Eliza Lisle McChord McElroy, left it to her daughter, Alice McElroy Whitehouse. In 2000, except for needing to be cleaned, it was in good condition after being exposed to oil and gas lamps for decades. The Tebbs Bend Battlefield Association was allowed to make prints of the painting, a copy of which appears on the book jacket.

Michigan Remembers

On July 4, 1864, the churches of Holland, Michigan, observed a special day of prayer for the men who fought at Tebbs Bend.[30] Years later, a Civil War Monument was erected in Holland's town cemetery and Peter Verschure's name was placed upon it. In the Kalamazoo Valley Museum, Colonel Moore's uniform, camp desk, bugle, and sword are on display. Photographs, a canteen, drum, and cup from Tebbs Bend are displayed in Holland's City Museum. In the State Museum of Michigan at Lansing, the 25th Michigan's regimental flag with battle honors "Battle of Tebbs Bend, July 4, 1863" is positioned prominently. In Three Rivers, Michigan, a Civil War monument lists "Tebbs Bend" on its obelisk along with other major Civil War battles involving thousands of men. Clearly, Michigan is proud of her moment at Tebbs Bend as well she should be.

Civil War Monument, Holland, Michigan

25th Michigan Regimental Flag with Battle Honors

Michigan Capitol Battle Flag Collection

MORGAN & HINES'
ESCAPE ROUTE
NOVEMBER-DECEMBER
1863

Source: Southern Bivouac, June 1885

Part Seven

Morgan's Escape from Ohio State Penitentiary
November 1863

On Friday night, November 27, 1863, Morgan and six companions—Tom Hines, L. D. Hockersmith, Sam Taylor, Ralph Shelton, G.S. Magee and Jake Bennett—escaped from the Ohio State Penitentiary in Columbus, Ohio. The escapees were only a few of the officers who had helped dig a tunnel down to an air shaft leading into the prison yard behind a twenty-foot wall. They made a rope to get over the inner wall and planned their escape during a rain so that the dogs would be in their houses. Morgan bribed one of the guards, paying him in gold, to get a train schedule.

The night of the escape John Morgan and his brother Dick, who stayed behind, changed places in their cells. After the group made their way down the tunnel and scaled the walls, they separated into pairs. Morgan and Hines made it to the railway station just as a train was departing for Cincinnati.[1]

Morgan, with his usual bravado, sat next to a Union officer, and soon they were sharing some brandy. As the train rolled by the prison, the officer remarked about Morgan being there. Morgan said, "I sincerely hope he will make up his mind to board there during the balance of the war for he is a great nuisance."

The train was delayed arriving in Cincinnati, and Morgan and Hines were afraid that the guards might have alerted the railway officials. As the train was slowing down, they jumped off, rolled down the embankment, and walked to the Ohio River. There they paid a young boy two dollars to row them across in his boat. Morgan was hoping to make it home before Mattie's confinement was over. But, unknown to Morgan, his newborn baby girl died that day.[2]

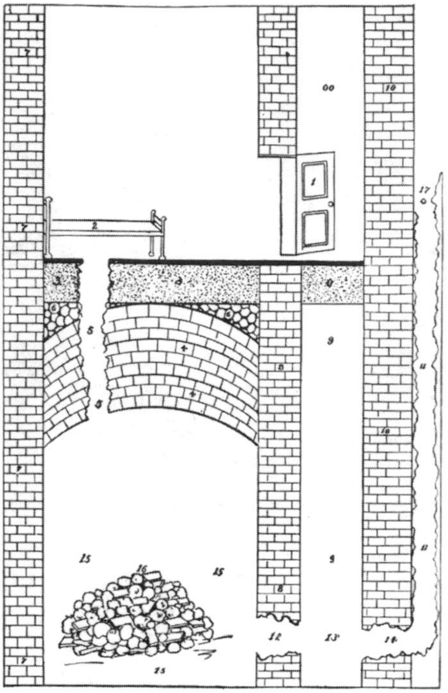

L.D. Hockersmith, "Morgan's Escape," in Davis, *Partisan Rangers*

Ohio State Penitentiary Cell

KEY

0. *Hall floor*
00. *Hall way*
1. *Door way to cell*
2. *Bedstead*
3. *Concrete floor*
4. *Arches*
5. *Hole cut through to air chamber*
6. *Filling between arch and concrete*
7. *Wall between convicts and prisoners*
8. *Wall of prison cells*
9. *Between outer and inner walls*
10. *Outer wall*
11. *Hole dug upward as escape*
12. *Opening made from air chamber*
13. *Tunnel from wall to wall*
14. *Cut through outer wall*
15. *Air chamber*
16. *Rock removed from No. 11*
17. *Where men came out from under prison*

Across the river, Hines and Morgan went to "friendly" houses in which they were sure they could be hidden. From Mrs. Ludlow's house in Ludlow, a river town west of Covington, they were taken to Dr. W.R. Thomas's in Fort Mitchell, where the doctor dressed a wound on Morgan's hand. There they secured a change of clothes, and Thomas's son escorted them through fields and along back roads to the next safe house. It is thought that Morgan rode by night and slept during the day on this trip.[3]

They are reported to have come through Lawrenceburg, Chaplin, Bloomfield, to Bardstown. George Blanford preceded Morgan and Hines from Lawrenceburg to Bardstown and arranged for Morgan to stay with Judge Felix Grundy Murphy, who lived three miles from Bardstown on the Springfield Road. "He was to come within a mile or two of Bardstown and then be guided to the residence of Judge Murphy." [The storyteller, Ben Johnson, did not include Hines in the tale, but he must have accompanied Morgan.] Morgan was to reach Bardstown before daylight, but was delayed, and it was too late for him to pass through the town to reach Murphy's house. William Johnson and Alex H. Stuart met him about a mile out of town. Instead of traveling to Murphy's, they took down rail fences and crossed the fields and into a thicket about a quarter of a mile back of the Johnson house. Confident that he would be safe there, they tied Morgan's horse to a buckeye tree and left Morgan there.

Johnson went on to his house and sent all the slaves to the opposite side of the farm. Then he went back and took Morgan to the house where Mrs. Johnson prepared breakfast for him. Morgan spent that day, that night, and the next day in the northwest room of the upstairs at the Johnsons. That night he left to go toward Hodgenville.[4] Local lore relates that Morgan and Hines came to Holy Cross, just over the Marion County line, and asked for a meal before slipping away into the night.[5] It is said that Morgan and Hines stayed with secessionist Thomas McCormick outside Howardstown on the Rolling Fork.[6] They continued south, possibly to Gleanings, may have come down Salt Lick Creek to Taylor County, and used connector roads to Summersville and Greensburg.[7]

In Green County it is known that Morgan and Hines, stayed at the home of Richard Aylett Taylor, Jr. Because he was a slaveholder and Southern sympathizer, his house was watched closely by the Federals. His brick home in 1863 was on the Ralph Vaughn Road on the south side of the Taylor Cemetery near Sartin's Ford of Green River, southeast of Greensburg. His neighbor, John Cox, lived close by in a large frame-over-log house overlooking the Green River valley. According to oral tradition, a cave behind the Taylor house hid the family silver.

In the margins of *Duke's History*, 1909 edition, a book owned by C.C. Darnell, son of Richard Darnell who was one of Morgan's cavalrymen, C.C. noted the names of the farms that hid Morgan while he was in Green County. It reads: "Morgan and Hines stoped at Aylett Taylors & crossed the river at Caldwell Place then owned by Uncle *John Cox*. The[y] ate their supper at Uncle John's. He took them to Moses Blakemans who took them to Columbia that night."[8]

This is supported by a note written by Barbara Simmons, while interviewing her mother, a descendant of Taylor's who had lived in the Taylor House: "John Hunt Morgan stayed one day and night in the back room where Uncle Ernest stayed. R.A. Taylor took him at night to Mr. Blakeman's."[9]

Margaret Perkins

R.A. Taylor Home, Green County

Cox Home, Green County

From there they crossed into Adair County. By the morning of December 7, Morgan and Hines were about a mile below Bluff Landing, Mud Camp Creek, nine miles below Burkesville. From there they returned to Tennessee.[10]

The escape of Morgan and Hines was a major topic in the newspapers. "$1,000 Reward" was emblazoned on broadsides. Secretary of War Edwin Stanton increased the reward to $5,000. Staying hidden on his route between Kentucky and Columbia, S. C., on Christmas Eve, Morgan telegraphed Mattie in Danville, Virginia: "Just arrived. Will make no stop until I reach you." He was finally back with his Mattie on Christmas Day, 1864. Parades and banquets greeted the hero of the South. Richmond papers sung his praises and an Italian composer wrote "Genl Morgan's Grand March."[11]

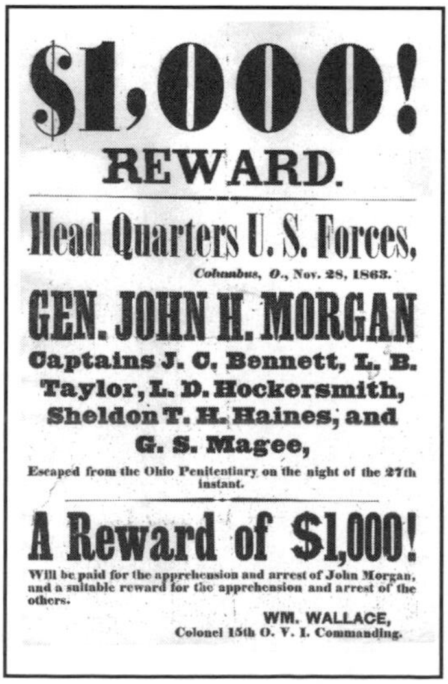

$1,000!
REWARD.
Head Quarters U. S. Forces,
Columbus, O., Nov. 28, 1863.
GEN. JOHN H. MORGAN
Captains J. C. Bennett, L. B. Taylor, L. D. Hockersmith, Sheldon T. H. Haines, and G. S. Magee,
Escaped from the Ohio Penitentiary on the night of the 27th instant.
A Reward of $1,000!
Will be paid for the apprehension and arrest of John Morgan, and a suitable reward for the apprehension and arrest of the others.
WM. WALLACE,
Colonel 15th O. V. I. Commanding.

University of Kentucky Archives

On the order of Major John A. Boyle, Citizen W.E. Goff, a resident of the Bengal community in Taylor County, was arrested on December 5 at Bardstown on charges "suspected of being a rebel." By the next day, his name appeared on the Louisville Military Prison Roll. The author cannot find any disposition of the case, but one wonders if it were thought that he had something to do with hiding or transporting Morgan to safety.[12] The records of additional Taylor County citizens being arrested are scarce, but in June 1863, a Virginia-born citizen of Taylor, Thomas G. Thompson, was charged with engaging in contraband trade with the South.[13]

Back in Tennessee in 1864, Morgan organized another cavalry command and set out on his last raid into Kentucky. In the heartland, Col. J.W. Weatherford was ordered to send forty of his 13th Kentucky cavalrymen to protect the Green River Bridge. Military telegraph operators were called back from Burkesville and Columbia to the bridge, abandoning the line until the Morgan threat abated. General Hobson was ordered to Columbia with the advice to remember the position of Moore's for defending the bridge "where Morgan was whipped in 1863."[14]

Without Grenfell and Duke and a host of other good officers, Morgan's last raid was clouded in controversy. Beside his dependable officers and good men were "other sorts of men," including a group of freebooters. Morgan was greatly troubled on this raid by the conduct of these men.[15]

One of Morgan's faithful officers, Alston, who had been exchanged after a stay at Camp Chase, and Col. H.L. Giltner, disapproved of the lack of discipline among the troops. The Confederate authorities, where Morgan had strong friends and as many strong enemies, set a date for a Court of Inquiry to take place on September 10, 1864, into some bank robberies, a source of great embarrassment to Morgan.

In Greenville, Tennessee, he headquartered in a brick mansion on Main Street, the home of Mrs. Catherine Williams, and Federal troops were alerted that he was there. In the early morning hours of Sunday, September 4, they surrounded the house and a young private, Andrew Campbell, saw someone running through the yard toward a fence. Campbell ordered the man to halt and when he did not, shot him in the back. The bullet went through his body, striking his heart.[16] The fleeing man turned out to be Morgan. News of Morgan's death reached his wife, who was two months pregnant, the next day in Abingdon, Virginia.

On September 6, Morgan's funeral was held in St. Thomas Episcopal Church in Abingdon, Virginia, and the body was first placed in a vault above ground in Sinking Spring Cemetery. Morgan's brother Cal took the body by train to Richmond where it lay in state at the Virginia House of Representatives, and then it was reburied in the peaceful Hollywood Cemetery there.

Morgan's Grave, Lexington Cemetery

In 1868, Tom's body was moved from Lebanon and John's body was moved from Richmond to Lexington, Kentucky. A service was held at Christ Church before their final interment on a beautiful April day in the Lexington Cemetery.

Today all the brothers lie side by side. Also beside them is Morgan's sister, Henrietta called "Tommie," and her husband, General Basil Duke. Across a little cemetery drive lies Rebecca Bruce Morgan and her stillborn son. In Augusta, Georgia, Morgan's second wife, Mattie Ready, bore his child after his death and named her Johnnie. Mattie later married Tennessee Judge J.H. Williamson. In 1883, Johnnie came to a reunion of veterans in Lexington and shook many of their hands. At twenty-three, Johnnie married a Presbyterian minister and died soon thereafter of typhoid fever, leaving no direct John Hunt Morgan heirs.

In 1911, a statue of Morgan was unveiled before a throng of several thousand onlookers in the Fayette County Courthouse Square. Morgan's mystique was still alive then as it is today. The 623rd Field Artillery, of which the Campbellsville National Guard is a part, called itself, "Morgan's Men." Hundreds of descendants of the raiders still roam the roads of Kentucky, Indiana, and Ohio following the trails of their ancestors and are amazed at the endurance it took to survive life as one of "Morgan's Men."[17]

Morgan Statue, Fayette County Courthouse Square, Lexington

Gerald Myers

Magruder Raid in Downtown Campbellsville

Part Eight

After Morgan: Confederate Guerrillas in Downtown Campbellsville *November 20, 1864*

Henry C. Magruder

Guerrillas, such as Tinker Dave Beatty, who supported the Union, and Champ Ferguson, who supported the South, operated almost at will in counties lying south of Taylor, particularly along the Cumberland River. North of Taylor County, Confederate guerrilla Henry C. Magruder headquartered himself near Bloomfield, in Nelson County.

By 1864, Magruder and his men had their guerrilla raiding techniques down to an art. An excellent horseman, Magruder was trained as one of CSA Brigadier General Simon Bolivar Buckner's Guards. That group prided itself in picking up a dollar bill off the ground going at full gallop and getting on and off the saddle while the horse maintained speed.

The guards were left at Bowling Green when General Buckner went to Fort Donelson. After Buckner's surrender to Federal forces there, General Albert Sidney Johnston came to Bowling Green and watched the Buckner Guards drill. Impressed with their skills, he transferred the group to become his bodyguard. In a year's time after joining the Southern army, Private Magruder found himself in a prestigious position, guarding one of the South's most important generals.

After watching the fatal wounding of General Johnston on the first day of fighting at Shiloh, Magruder made his way across a dark, rainy, battlefield on horseback to deliver dispatches to General John C. Breckinridge. By the dim light of surgeons' lanterns and amid the groans of the wounded, Magruder robbed the dead. He also murdered an African American boy and emptied his pockets. By the time he returned to camp, he was $3,200 richer.

With the death of Johnston, Magruder was given the option of joining any command of his liking. He chose to fight with fellow Kentuckian and cavalryman, John Hunt Morgan. He remained with this command until 1863. A man with a combination of great luck and agility, Magruder escaped capture on Morgan's Great Raid into Indiana and Ohio. He was a member of Company D, 2nd Kentucky Cavalry, a squad selected to serve under Captain William J. Davis, which was sent by Morgan around Louisville on its eastern edge and across the Ohio as a diversionary tactic. Most of the members of that group were captured or killed, but not Henry Magruder. Left with no commander, he and about 15–20 followers operated mostly on their own initiative, living off the land with friendly support and campsites readily available from farmers near Bloomfield. Capturing trains and stages, robbing banks, stores, and citizens became the Magruder gang's way of life. They did not hesitate to commit cold-blooded murder, particularly if full of whiskey.[1]

Magruder is described as five feet, six inches, with long hair, whiskers, and rosy cheeks. He was frequently observed on the streets of Bloomfield wearing a fancy suit, with a red or black velvet jacket and pants, high-topped boots, and large spurs. The jacket had fancy gold braids and lace. He always carried four to six pistols, some navy, several large-sized. He always possessed fine horses and sometimes wore a large black ostrich feather in his hat. However, on occasion, he would appear in a Union uniform or civilian clothes. In the winter, the gang would wear overcoats to enable them to pass for Federal soldiers.[2]

In the summer and fall of 1863, guerrilla activity exploded in southern Kentucky. Gowdy, Davis, & Chandler, of Campbellsville, and Hobson, Marshall, & Carlile of Greensburg moved their businesses to Lebanon for safety. Col. James W. Weatherford's 13th Kentucky Cavalry, organized at Columbia, stayed busy monitoring activity in Cumberland, Monroe, Adair, and Green counties, and made considerable progress capturing several bands and driving many back into Tennessee. Their vigilance may have contributed to Campbellsville's relative peace.[3]

However, most of the 13th Kentucky Cavalry was sent to Saltville, Virginia, in the fall of 1864, leaving south central Kentucky vulnerable. The Lexington-Nashville Road, the trail used by Morgan on some of his raids, was the same path that Henry Magruder followed when he rode between Green River and New Market in the summer of 1864. Daniel Williams' farm was the camp known to be safe for Southerners on these trips. Fortunately for the local citizens, a visit to the town of Campbellsville was not on their itinerary on this trip. The peace was not to continue, however.[4]

On November 17, accompanied by guerrilla Sol Thompson, Magruder murdered Frank Crady, a Union veteran wounded in the battle of Perryville, in Larue County. While there he became aware that Campbellsville was lightly defended, its Yankee guards having been decreased from fifty to twenty. On Sunday, November 20, before a heavy snow fall, Magruder's gang of guerrillas, about seventeen in number, headed south entering Taylor County. They stopped at the home of 67-year-old William Handley in the Colesby Community in the northern section of the county. It was noon and the family was having dinner. Handley's nephew, Cpl. Samuel Williams, Company L, 13th Kentucky Cavalry, happened to be visiting his uncle. Magruder quickly took him prisoner, forced him to mount his horse and ride down the road about one-half mile with his gang, and then shot Williams to death.[5]

The group then passed a farmhouse and "pressed" a slave to guide them to Campbellsville. They probably entered the town from the Saloma Road. It was now about four in the afternoon, just before sunset in the winter months. They surprised two 13th Kentucky cavalrymen on Main Street. Hopelessly outnumbered, Pvt. James C. Blankenship threw up his hands to surrender. In clear violation of military law, one of Magruder's men shot him, and Blankenship fell on the street, mortally wounded. A fellow soldier from Company L, was also shot and seriously wounded.[6]

The guerrillas fired off their weapons up and down Main Street, aiming at startled citizens. After shooting the cavalrymen, they began their work in earnest. The *Louisville Journal*, frustrated that the guerrillas were not being caught, had pointed out to its readers and the military officials that "if Billy Magruder goes to water his horse, he goes to Bloomfield."[7] The paper made the following report:

> They broke into the stores of Messrs. Gowdy, Turner & Co., and Chandler and Mourning, obtaining $75 in money from the former and nothing from the latter. Every citizen they met was relieved of pocket-books and watches. In an incredibly short space of time they robbed the

citizens of at least $2,000 in money, watches, etc. Mr. [Ferdinand] Hiestand was robbed of $1,485, mostly Kentucky bank notes. James Blandford [saddler] lost a valuable gold watch and overcoat; Jeter & Haskins, $100; E.[Edward] Rice, $100; Frank Hackley, $15; Billy Marrs, $15; John H. Chandler, gold watch, and $40 in money. Several other citizens were robbed.

Ferdinand J. Hiestand

Alfred F. Gowdy

Some people and businesses were on Main Street, such as Hiestand, corner of Main and Court, merchant John Horatio Chandler, but some were not. William Marrs' shop was at the corner of Second, now Broadway, and Columbia, but the guerrilla force was large enough to cover more than one area of town. Provost Marshal Col. Rodophil Jeter, a former infantryman himself, must have been particularly upset at being powerless to fight off the Rebel renegades. By the time of their departure, some Home Guards did have time to mobilize.[8]

With the sounding of gunshots in the lower downtown, the residents on upper Main Street quickly became aware of what was happening in the town.

Not having any warning about the disturbance, a large stagecoach from Lebanon pulled into the upper part of the village. Unfortunately for the thieves, among its many passengers were several discharged Federal soldiers, members of Battery B, 1st Kentucky Light Artillery, who had mustered out in Louisville, just days before, on November 16, 1864. Quickly informed by a lady about what was happening in the town, they ran into one of the houses, gathered weapons, and trained them on the coach. When the guerrillas discovered a valuable stage and its horses sitting empty on the street, they at once surrounded it. From the house the soldiers leveled their guns and opened fire, injuring one of the guerrillas. Quickly the thieves skedaddled, leaving behind one carbine and one blanket.

Located near the action, on the corner of Main and Depot [now Central], was the large home, barns, chicken houses and doctor's office of Dr. Samuel Thompson Chandler. Long-haired Samuel and Eliza Jane were Southern sympathizers, but afraid of guerrillas. He gathered his newborn son, Samuel Alfred Franklin, into his arms, got in the bed, pulled a shawl over his face, and pretended to be ill. The family escaped being robbed or injured.[9]

An hour after the incident on Main, Major George W. Sweeney, with more members of the 13th Kentucky Cavalry, arrived and dispatched Capt. Thomas Watson with a pursuit squad. Magruder's men were followed for several miles until the trail was lost in the hills of Salt Lick, the northeastern section of the county.[10]

After marauding in the area around Burkesville and northern Tennessee, where at least four were murdered, Magruder's band returned north through Greensburg, then up the Nashville-Lexington Road, where they ate and camped at Daniel Williams' farm. They continued along through Saloma and over to the Rolling Fork. This was the last time Magruder was in Taylor County.[11]

The gang continued into Washington County where they murdered, in the arms of his wife, Lt. Col. Hall of the county militia, two more discharged soldiers, Sam Green and John Foster, and M. Britner. The paper called Magruder a "full disciple of hell."[12]

Before Magruder was captured, he linked up with two more infamous guerrilla leaders, none other than Marcellus Jerome Clarke, alias Sue Mundy, and William Clarke Quantrill. In February, 1865, he was involved in a raid at New Market in Marion County with Quantrill and Frank James. In that incident, at least three soldiers were killed, mail wagons were burned, stores at New Market were robbed, and several mules killed.[13]

Finally on March 3, 1865, in Hancock County, Sue Mundy, Henry Metcalf, Sam Jones, and Magruder were surrounded. Sam Jones was killed and Magruder was severely wounded with a shot in his left lung. Sue Mundy and Metcalf somehow rode away with the injured Magruder. Brig. Gen. John M. Palmer, who had replaced Burbridge as commander of Kentucky, received a tip on the location of the guerrillas. He dispatched Maj. Cyrus J. Wilson, 26th Kentucky, to lead fifty men of Company B, 30th Wisconsin Infantry, to capture the two. On Sunday, March 12, at Webster, ten miles from Brandenburg, in Meade County, a log tobacco barn where they were hiding was surrounded by the soldiers who secured their surrender.[14]

On September 15, 1865, a sickly Magruder was carried into a military courtroom lying on a cot. After a thirty-day trial, he was declared guilty on seven counts of murder in Bullitt, Nelson, and Larue counties and was hanged in the Louisville prison yard on October 20.[15]

Confederate Guerrillas in Green County

In October 1863, at least one hundred guerrillas, reportedly led by Littleton Richardson, robbed the stores of Columbia and then hit Greensburg's bank and its stores. They also "stole a number of good horses."[17]

John Sickles

Littleton T. Richardson

In the fall of 1864, Lt. J.H. Smith of the 13th Kentucky Cavalry, USA, wrote General Hobson that the citizens of Greensburg were asked "to enroll their names for the defense of the place against Guerrillas," but that the "Rebel Sympathizers failed and refused positively to do so." He asked the general if he had the authority to compel them to obey.[16]

W.N. Vaughan reported that a gang, one of whom was a former member of Morgan Captain W.S. Edwards' Company, had come to Summersville and robbed Peter Richardson, Nat Tinny, and W. R. Noe. Vaughan asked native son, Gen. E.H. Hobson, for a squad of soldiers to protect the citizens.

Evidently, the lawlessness in Green County, and particularly on Brush Creek, lasted until the very end of the war. Even after Lincoln's death and Lee's surrender, on April 24, 1865, D.T. Towles reported to Hobson that "Brush Creek has been pillaged from head to mouth." Esquire McCubbins lost over $700 and "the people are in a perfect state of alarm." Worth and Theodore Goalder, some Darnells, Fidella Warren and his brothers, Jim S. Underwood and Bule Perkins were the named culprits. Towles asked Hobson to station forty men at Jim Elkins' or F. Beachamps' "with instructions not to molest Union men."

Some of these "culprits" had served in the Rebel army and found it natural to continue foraging and attacking Union soldiers when they returned home.[18] William Wallace reported that the guerrillas had stripped him of almost all his personal property and that he had lost one son and another had lost a leg in the Union army. He said he had to provide someway for the wives and children of his two sons-in-law serving in the Union army.[19]

In Marion County, men testified that the Raywick area was infested with guerrillas and the people were living in a "reign of terror." Governor Bramlette remitted the fines of J. Young and John Lampkins, of allowing gaming for drinks or money at their guest houses during the time the Federal forces could render no protection to that portion of the county. Home guards Joseph Short and John C. Harding, who fought Morgan at Rolling Fork Bridge in July 1862, made an attempt to arrest John R. Redman, a suspicious businessman they regarded as a spy. Redman then accused them of taking his pocketbook, which they had already given over to military authorities. This was only one of many cases reaching Governor Bramlette from all over the state asking for relief from false charges made about the Home Guards.[20]

In Taylor County, not far from Brush Creek, the John G. Gaddie family tried to hide their horses and cattle from the Southern guerrillas who made it a habit to stop by their house. One of the family's tactics was to take their cows and young calves into the grapevine thicket between their big brick house and slave cabins on Locust Lick and tie them up so they could not escape. But alas, one of the calves got out in the opening between the house and the thicket. Of course, the cow broke after the calf. Immediately the soldiers killed the calf. Soon they had set a fire, cooked the meat, and devoured her. The family was more successful in hiding its bacon. They sliced it, placed it between newspapers, and stored it in the attic.[21]

During January 1864, Company M, 12th Kentucky Cavalry, was stationed at the Green River Stockade to help stem the guerrilla onslaught. Rebels Littleton Richardson, Champ Ferguson, and his ally Hughes, had still not been captured; therefore, Federal troops were stationed at Green River Bridge, but more often at Columbia and Burkesville to protect the civilian population from the Rebels coming north from their Tennessee outposts. Periodically, scouts were ordered over the countryside looking for the outlaws.

ROUTE OF GENERAL HYLAN B. LYON
DECEMBER 9, 1864 to JANUARY 3, 1865

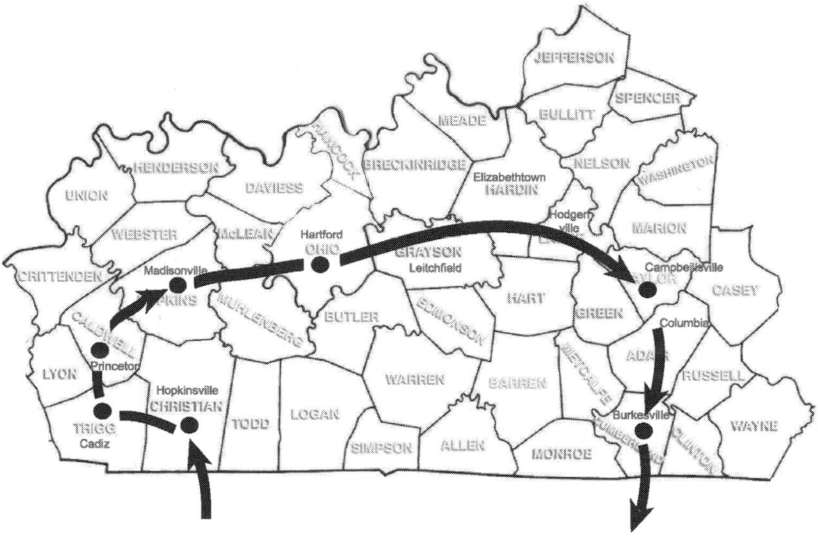

● Courthouses Burned on Lyon's Raid

Information provided by Kentucky Historical Society

Part Nine

Lyon Visits Taylor County
December 25, 1864

On **Thursday, December 22,** after Union Gen. William T. Sherman's march through Georgia had been completed, he telegraphed President Lincoln: "I beg to present to you as a Christmas gift, the city of Savannah." The Confederacy was in its last days, but one west Kentuckian, H.B. Lyon, was not giving up.

Gen. Hylan B. Lyon

Confederate Brig. General Hylan B. Lyon came to be known as the "Court House Burnin'est General in Kentucky." Besides burning the Taylor County Courthouse in Campbellsville on this raid, he ordered his men to set fire to six others in Christian, Trigg, Caldwell, Hopkins, Ohio, and Cumberland counties. In Lyon's Report, he claimed he burned eight fortified courthouses. He may have been including Hardin County where he burned buildings around the courthouse, but he did not burn that particular building. Therefore, he burned seven, few of which were "fortified."[1]

The *Louisville Journal* called Lyon "the degenerate son of a noble sire." His father was state senator Matthew Lyon, Jr., and his grandfather, U.S. Congressman Matthew Lyon. Hylan was orphaned at age eight and reared by a family friend.[2]

A West Point graduate, Lyon had had a variety of experiences in his military life. He fought against Seminole Indians and was on frontier duty in California and Washington State from 1857 to 1860. He resigned from the U.S. Army in 1861, joined the Confederacy, and organized a company of field artillery, supplying it with his own funds. It was known as Lyon's battery until it was turned over to Capt. Robert Cobb, when it became one of the best in the South.[3]

Subsequently, Lyon was elected lieutenant colonel of the 8th Kentucky Infantry, taken prisoner at Fort Donelson, and exchanged. His command escaped without surrendering at Vicksburg. During the spring of 1864, he rode with Nathan Bedford Forrest during his Middle Tennessee Campaign and also played a key role in Forrest's victory at Brice's Cross Roads, Mississippi. When General Adam Rankin Johnson was severely wounded and blinded at Grubbs Crossroads in late 1864, Lyon replaced him as Commander of the West Kentucky District.

Brig. Gen. P.G.T. Beauregard ordered Lyon's force on the raid to destroy the Union rail lines bringing reinforcements and supplies coming from the North to reinforce Gen. George Thomas, whose Federal forces were occupying Nashville. The raid was designed to support John Bell Hood, the one-armed, one-legged Confederate General, who had to be strapped to his saddle to ride. Lyon was also directed to put the grist mills in Clarksville back in operation to supply Hood's dwindling army.

Much as Morgan had done in the past, Lyon succeeded in burning a trestle and stockades on the L&N Railroad near Elizabethtown. The raid, however, came too late to help Hood. After the battle of Nashville, Confederate soldier Sam Watkins observed that General Hood was "agitated and affected, pulling his hair with his one hand, and crying like his heart would break."[4] Lyon did not know about Hood's defeat by Thomas until days into the raid.

Lyon left Tennessee on December 6, 1864, to begin his raid across Kentucky. He had 800 men, half of whom were newly recruited unwilling conscripts, and two twelve-pounder howitzers, under Capt. F.P. Gracey. The cavalrymen departed Paris, Tennessee, and headed to Clarksville, but that city proved to be too heavily fortified to attack. Instead, they cut telegraph lines. Lyon's men continued to Hopkinsville, Cadiz, Eddyville, Princeton, Madisonville, Hartford, Leitchfield, Elizabethtown, Hodgenville and Campbellsville. The weather was bitterly cold, and along the way, many of the men were captured or deserted, and some were killed.

At Elizabethtown, Lyon's men learned that Confederate General Hood had been defeated at Nashville and many of them lost heart. By the time Lyon galloped into Campbellsville on a rainy Sunday, December 25, he had only 250 men remaining, an ambulance, and one gun.[5]

The details have disappeared with time. Lyon and his men left Hodgenville early on Christmas Day and arrived in Campbellsville around noon. No Federal troops were in town and the few Home Guards were unprepared to handle such a force. Women were coming home from church to prepare Christmas dinners, general stores and trade shops were closed, and the men enjoying a day of rest. Lyon and his men met no resistance. The *Nashville Daily Press* reported the story:

> They broke into stores and robbed them of a large amount of goods. The principal sufferers were Messrs. Chandler and Mourning, D.G. Taylor and Gowdy, Turner & Co. . . . There were no Federal troops at Campbellsville when they entered. No citizens interfered with them whatever, as . . . resistance would have been useless.[6]

When it became known that Lyon intended to fire the courthouse, the townspeople begged him to let them save the records. Lyon cooperated, as he had done in other towns, and allowed three women and a boy, J.R. Smith, to carry the books to safety. One of the ladies was Lou Cowherd Taylor, who was the mother of attorney Henry Robinson's first wife. Then Lyon's men took the benches of the courthouse and split them into kindling, which they used to set fire to the building. They stood guard while it burned to the ground.[7] They stayed the night, robbing civilians and taking "all the horses in the county that were of any service."[8]

Lyon's cavalrymen then set out down the Columbia Road. They claimed to have burned the bridge over Russell Creek before entering Columbia, and then they rode on to Burkesville.

Lyon and His Men Burn Taylor County Courthouse, December 25, 1864

Lyon's troops were said to have been there on December 27, but the courthouse was not burned until January 3, 1865. The Cumberland County Courthouse at Burkesville was a two-story, sixty-foot-square brick building completed in 1858, but Lyon showed it no mercy, claiming it had been used by the 13th Kentucky Cavalry as a depot for commissary stores. Again, he allowed the citizens to save the records, but his men stayed in the square until the brick building was completely razed.[9]

Since many of Lyon's cavalrymen remained without warm coats or blankets in the cold temperatures, they plundered the town, taking the heavy clothing and celebrating the New Year in fine style. While the courthouse was burning, they set a storehouse ablaze, but accepted $200 to put it out. The post office was robbed, and when Lyon's men departed, there were not enough horses left in town "to go to mill on." The *Louisville Journal* reported that several of Morgan's former officers were present, such as Colonels Chenoweth and Cunningham, Captains Lovell and Page from Allen County. The Morgan tradition continued.[10]

Gen. George H. Thomas ordered two brigades of the 1st Cavalry Division, commanded by Gen. Edward McCook, to "push Lyon to the wall." The roads were so covered with ice that the Union cavalrymen had to lead their horses to keep them from losing their footing. McCook's troops became so exhausted that they gave up the chase. After Elizabethtown, few Federal troops were continuing to pursue in Kentucky. Brig. Gen Eli Long of the Second Division, Cavalry Corps, was ordered to destroy Lyon's force.

After he entered Tennessee, Lyon himself barely escaped capture when his quarters were surrounded. He answered the door in his nightclothes and asked permission to dress before surrendering. In his dark bedroom, he managed to draw his revolver from under his pillow, shoot the Union soldier at the door, and escape through the back entrance into the night.

Lyon's 700-mile raid through three states ended in Tuscaloosa, Alabama, January 20, 1865. Lyon reported that he had captured steamers and courthouses, destroyed railroad bridges, depots, stockades, and blockhouses, and that he had taken many prisoners. Like Morgan and Forrest, Lyon diverted enemy troops from where they were really needed. He caused McCook's division of cavalry to leave Nashville and kept Wilder's Cavalry Brigade in Louisville, thus depriving Thomas of 4,500 men for his defense against Hood. Lyon's Raid disrupted Union supply lines and caused general confusion. But as Morgan, Lyon had no influence on the ultimate outcome of the war. The Confederacy was in its last days.

After the war, Lyon served as Warden of the Kentucky Penitentiary from 1868 until 1875. Then he became Commissioner of Kentucky Penitentiary Construction. He died suddenly on his farm near Eddyville, Kentucky, in 1907. Even though General Lyon caused much needless destruction to Kentucky courthouses, an elegant monument to him at Mineral Springs, Kentucky, was erected in 1931.[11]

Questions remain as to why General Lyon ordered his men on this Kentucky Raid to burn courthouses. It was said that some courthouses held indictments against Confederate sympathizers. Some, such as Cumberland County's, were depots for commissary and quartermaster stores for the Union army. A few, such as in Trigg and Ohio counties, were used as Union headquarters or for sleeping quarters for traveling regiments. Lyon was particularly agitated at the idea of Negro troops in the Union Army being quartered in courthouses. In Trigg County, his men killed an ill Black soldier left behind in the courthouse by occupying troops and then set it afire, claiming that the soldier had smallpox. Sources state that the use of the Taylor County Courthouse as a Federal supply depot and temporary hospital may have been the reason Lyon targeted it.[12]

At any rate, in 1864, the little brick building which occupied the center of the Taylor County's Courthouse Square was only 15 years old. The county clerk's office held the fiscal court minute books, deeds, wills, marriages, tavern licenses, road overseers, and probate records since the county's formation in 1848. The circuit clerk held records of criminal indictments and civil suits over land, slaves, and bad debts. There were no noteworthy indictments against Southern sympathizers in Taylor County, however.

The court, whose members were Thomas M. Wright, Thomas E. Cowherd, Benjamin C. Hord, William Dearen, M.O. Robinson, Abel Weatherford, Lewis Grinstead, and James O. Mercer, had voted two months previously to pay the bill for a stove and for building a fence around the courthouse yard. The stove proved a great convenience to the raiders. The coals in its ashes were easily fired. Only the outer shell of the building remained.[13]

Presided over by County Judge William Cloyd, Taylor County magistrates met after the fire.

> At a Special Term of the Taylor County Court held near the ruins of the Court in Campbellsville on Monday the 26th day of December 1864.
>
> It appearing to the Court that the Court House and clerk's offices in Taylor county had been burned on the 25th of December 1864 by the Soldiers under the Command of General Lyon of the Army of the so called Confederate States of America, It is therefore ordered by the court that the Clerk of this court and the clerk of the Taylor Circuit Court deposit such of the records, books and papers belonging to and pertaining to the respective offices, as were saved from said fire, in the brick house of John P. Davis on Main Street, on lot known as lot No. 11 and there safely keep the same until further order of this court, and it is further ordered that the lower room of said house adjoining the house of F.J. Hiestan be kept and used by said Circuit and Taylor County Court Clerks as the clerks offices of said courts respectively.[14]

On January 2, 1865, Judge Cloyd was authorized to take down, clean, and secure the brick in the walls of the former court house and clerks offices, "now standing."[15]

The committee made a fateful decision that has determined the way the Courthouse Square looks to this day. They decided to first build the Clerks' Office on the west end of the Courthouse Square, and then to later rebuild the Courthouse on the east end.[16]

Specifications were drawn up and the committee composed of A.F. Gowdy, Ben C. Hord, and R.S Montague was appointed to draw up the contracts for the offices of the circuit and county clerks and the courthouse. Robert Colvin was later added to the committee. The Clerks' Office Building, still standing on the square, featured an eight–foot-wide hall with equal size rooms for the Circuit Clerk on the south end and the County Clerk on the north end. The Federal-style building was designed with a Flemish bond brick pattern on its street side, a style that had been fashionable in the 1820s. It was begun in 1865 and finished in 1866.

Old Clerk's Office, 1865–1866

John P. Davis kept most of the records in his brick house, but the room attached to his house that the magistrates rented for a temporary courthouse must have been frame. The fee was for the room was $40 per year.[17]

A fire on the night of March 7, 1865, took out the room where the court was meeting on Main Street. It consumed law books, the county's tax assessment record books of the western district, and unnamed "other books." After this, the court was moved across North Columbia Avenue to the frame Baptist Church until the completion of the Clerks' Office building. There court was held until the Courthouse was finished the next year.[18]

The Courthouse was begun in 1866 and completed in 1867. It, too, was a one-story Federal-style brick building with shuttered windows. According to J.R. Smith, the first courthouse built in 1848 was more "commodious" than the second one that was built to replace it.[19]

Richard A. Sanders, II

Taylor County Courthouse Square 1890, showing courthouse built in 1866–1867

In 1873, the court appointed James M. Fidler to represent Taylor County in Washington "to present and claim from the United States Government rent for the use of the public property of said County used and occupied by the United States forces during the war which began in 1861." Fidler was to receive fifty per cent of the compensation, if any were awarded. Therefore, it is clear that the Courthouse was used by U.S. troops for some reason, whether as a hospital or a supply depot or both may never be known.[20]

Not until 1908 was a second story added to the courthouse. By 1910 a four-story clock tower was built on to the east side of the renovated 1867 courthouse. The 1867–1908 courthouse was razed in 1965 to allow the present contemporary-style building to be constructed.[21]

Aileen McKinley

Taylor County Courthouse 1910. The second floor addition to the 1867 courthouse is clearly shown in this photograph.

William Clarke Quantrill

Part Ten

Quantrill Threatens
February 1865

No Civil War commentary would be complete without a comment on Confederate guerrilla leader, William Clarke Quantrill. The closest he ever came to Taylor County was his visit to St. Mary's, New Market, and Bradfordsville in February 1865. The locals heard he was coming, the *Official Records* reported he was headed this way, and the fear that he inspired was equal to or surpassed the fear of Morgan. But it never materialized in Taylor County.

On February 8, Quantrill and about forty followers, descended upon St. Mary's in Marion County and waited for the train to arrive. While waiting, they entertained themselves with alcohol, but grew impatient. They departed for New Market where they captured a U.S. wagon train, its four guards, and killed three. They burned the wagons and shot the mules. Troops were sent from Lebanon and pursued Quantrill to Bradfordsville.

Most of the pursuers were from the Invalid Corps of the 13th Kentucky Cavalry, no match for the wily Quantrill gang. In the fight at a tollgate outside Bradfordsville, the four Federal prisoners from New Market were shot. Sue Munday's horse was killed, falling on him. With Quantrill's aid, he was able to free himself and escape. The guerrillas entered Bradfordsville on its Main Street [now Riverview], which, at that time, ran along the Rolling Fork River. They burned the Yowell Hotel, livery stable, and tavern, and the brick home of Dr. Joseph Rose, and took the horse from a doctor while he was tending to a patient.

The guerrillas rode on toward Hustonville and stopped at the Prior Prewitt's. They stole his horses, shot him, then drove the horses over his dead body. Union Captain J. Bridgewater, in hot pursuit, located Quantrill and his men about 2 A.M.

on February 9. The guerrillas fled, some barefoot, into the hills. Soon they moved on to Spencer County where Southern sympathizers protected them.[1]

On May 10, 1865, Quantrill and several of his followers were caught staying in a barn on the farm of James H. Wakefield near Taylorsville. Quantrill was shot trying to escape and fell face down in the mud. When he claimed to be a soldier from Missouri named Clark, his captor Edwin Terrell, a paid guerrilla-catcher, left him in Wakefield's house and rode off looking for Quantrill. His followers came to visit, one of the most infamous being Frank James. After he discovered Clark's real identity, Terrell returned to the Wakefield farm, placed the wounded Quantrill in a Conestoga wagon, took him to Louisville, turned him in to Federal authorities, and collected his bounty. Before his death on June 6, Quantrill converted to Catholicism and was buried in an unmarked grave in St. Mary's Catholic Cemetery in Louisville.

St. Mary's became St. John's. Quantrill's mother had a friend remove his skull and some bones and today, after a long journey through museums, the skull is interred in the 4th Street Cemetery of Dover, Ohio.[2]

An Uneasy Occupation until the End of the War

Stationed at Campbellsville during the months of January and February 1865 was Company A, 30th Kentucky Infantry. Replacing it, Company C, 54th Kentucky Infantry, under Capt. Dexter Gray, remained in Campbellsville during the months of March through June of 1865.

Finally peace came to this divided land!

Part 11

Stories and Legends

People and Places

Confederate Delegate

Dr. Daniel Price White, a slaveholder and a resident of the Whitewood section of Taylor-Green counties, was one of twelve justices of the peace appointed when Taylor County was formed out of Green in 1848. He was a member of the Kentucky House of Representatives 1857–59, 1859–61, a delegate to the Democrat National Convention in 1860 where he voted for Douglas, a delegate to the Provisional Confederate Government in Russellville in the fall of 1861, which voted to sever ties with the U. S. Government and declare Kentucky independent, and a delegate from the state to the Confederate Provisional Congress held in Richmond, Virginia, on February 18, 1862. The Kentucky Confederate government operated at Bowling Green until the Union army occupied the city and its officials fled the state.[1]

Black Agony

One of the human dilemmas of the institution of slavery was the arbitrary separation of Black family members from one another. Wallace Bottoms, a Black stone mason of much talent, was born in a log cabin in Taylor County on the George Stone farm. He was the grandson of Susan Chandler, who was reared on Joseph H. and Araminta Chandler's farm.

Susan Chandler had three sons—Tom, Stephen, and James. Tom was owned by tavern-keeper Ferdinand J. Hiestand, Stephen had three owners: county clerk Alfred F. Gowdy, merchant and sheriff Rezin H. Davis, and John Bottoms, who reared him and where he acquired his last name. Stephen was Wallace's father.

Susan was sold away from her husband to the South. Since James was a baby, he was sold with his mother.

Years went by. Susan's husband remarried with the understanding that if his first wife reappeared, he could return to her.

The war was over. The slaves were freed. To everyone's surprise, Stephen's mother and his brother, James, carefully worked their way back from the South to Taylor County.

Now, what was this man to do? Wallace's grand-father remembered his pledge. He dutifully left his second wife and returned to his first wife and son James. Thus is revealed part of the heartache in a society that permitted slavery.[2]

Aunt Mariah, Barr Tract Community

For as long as anyone can remember, there has been a road in Taylor County called Bear Tract. The name invokes mental images of a wilderness area replete with game, especially black bears, hunted by Indians and frontiersmen alike.

However, the name of the land was originally "D. Barr's Tract." It seems that a Virginia land owner freed his slaves in his will and gave each slave a portion of the property. As late as 1940, the land in the upper end of the road was Black-owned with many houses on its hillsides. There is also an African-American cemetery there.[3]

In one of these houses lived Aunt Mariah. A large stout lady, she was a free Black. She had worked hard and had purchased her husband's freedom. Whenever her husband would get out of line and disobey her, she'd say, "You'd better BE-HAVE or I'll put you back in my pocket." [that is, she would sell him and get her money back].[4]

Behind That Tree

The following story has been repeated over and over in the community. One day a stranger came to town on the train and walked from the station to Jim Tom Gowdy's livery stable at the corner of Main and Depot [now Central] Street. He asked for a horse and buggy to go out to the battlefield. Gowdy decided he would drive him out there himself. The stranger wanted to go to a spot in the road where a certain tree stood. When the stranger got there, he started to cry. Gowdy asked him, "What is the matter?" The stranger replied, "Behind that tree I shot my father and my brother."[5]

The story has various endings, but could it be true? The author believes that the story has been twisted through the years. Undoubtedly, relatives came to the battle site see the place where their kin were slain. The conversation may have been, "Behind that tree, I saw my father shot," or "I saw my brother shot."

There was not a father-son death in this battle. Migration patterns are such that it is highly unlikely for Morgan's men to have had a brother or father living in Michigan that happened to be in one of these five companies of Moore. However, both sides had brothers fighting in the battle, but fighting on the same side.

The "stranger" was likely a person from the Bluegrass. Several families from there sent more than one son to the war, such as the Cosbys, Tribbles, Currents, and Tevises. The Baldwins are the only ones who had a father and sons there, but only one of the sons was killed. The stranger story may be a myth.

Salem Church

The history of Salem Baptist Church, organized in 1861, states that soon after the church was erected, it was burned, some say, by Civil War soldiers. Since the church minutes are missing and few newspapers existed in this area during that time period, we only have oral tradition to support the story. Pleasant Hill Baptist was burned early in the war, but that was an unusual occurrence. It was seldom to soldiers' advantage to burn a building as sacred as a church, unless it contained supplies for the opposing side.

Salem Church is located on a very old road, called the old Greensburg dirt road, which left the Lebanon-Campbellsville Turnpike and ran to Sweeneyville down Fairview Road to the old, old Greensburg Road. It is certain that troops used it. Whether or not troops of either side burned the church, or if it were an accident, is another unanswered question.[6]

Saltpeter Cave, Green River Bluffs

Saltpeter Cave is located on the bluffs of Green River that surround Lemmons Bend. It is 300 yards south of the Confederate Monument, just below the campground. Its mouth is about ten yards wide and the shelter is large for about one hundred feet before it narrows.

Saltpeter, or potassium nitrate, is the ingredient that makes up to 75% of the mixture of "black gunpowder." It occurs in limestone caves when decaying animal and plant materials combine with oxygen.

Raymond Tye Faulkner, Jr., a former owner of the cave, recounts that he was told that saltpeter was removed from the cave during the Civil War, just as it was from Mammoth Cave, for the purpose of making gunpowder.[7]

Tales as told by J. Robert Sublett

Oh, to be a Soldier!

Daddy [William Henry Sublett] was 19 years old. Daddy wanted to go the Union Army so bad. He had forty fits a minute. But they wouldn't take him. Said he was too small or something.

Grandfather [James Allen Sublett] slipped around to one of Union captains. He told the captain, I wish you'd deputize Henry to take a load [of supplies]. They did. Well, the rain poured down on them from the day they left to the day they got back; said mud was knee-deep; wasn't no roads back then. Kept him five days and nights; said ticks and bugs like to eat him up in an old barn somewhere. That cooled him from going to the army.[8]

Caldwell's Rooster

The Northern troops got all of James Caldwell's chickens. One evening Grandmother, [Mrs. James Allen Sublett], was out there in the yard and three or four soldiers came riding down the road and one of them had an old Dominecker rooster under his arm. Said had spurs two inches long and not enough feathers to make a pin cushion out of. The old rooster was excited. The soldiers let the rooster loose at their house, and it ran around the yard like he was lost, and he was, so he stayed around here about two days.

Well, one day, the old rooster was out in the yard. Caldwell came riding by and exclaimed, "Well, my God Almighty, that looks like my rooster." James Allen explained to Caldwell that a soldier had given the rooster to his wife. Caldwell looked perplexed and Grandpappy said, "Well, you just get down and get that rooster." So Caldwell reached down, grabbed the rooster, and took him home.[9] James Caldwell was a neighbor of Sublett's, who lived at Willowdale. James Caldwell was later county judge.

Tales from the Old Stanford Road

Musters on Saturday Afternoon

Every county was required by law to have local Home Guards. Taylor County's are not listed in the Kentucky Adjutant General's Report, but may have been part of a neighboring county's guards. Rezin H. Davis, farmer, merchant, and sheriff of Taylor County from 1860–61, drilled the troops on the Old Stanford Road, now called Roberts Road. Too old to fight, he took it upon himself to train the troops in one of his meadows. Each Saturday afternoon, men came from all around to Roberts Road for "musters" to learn the rudiments of fighting. The men called him "Major Davis."[10]

One day early in the summer, the Rezin H. Davis family had just gathered in everything out of the garden, the first mess of beans and potatoes. Just before they were ready to eat, had everything of the table, six Southern soldiers burst into the room. They were on their way home, after having been paroled.

They ate everything that was on the table. This scene was witnessed by Rezin Davis's daughter, Malinda Davis Campbell, a young widow, and her son, Alfred Turner Campbell. A.T. Campbell became Taylor County Court Clerk in 1882 and served as such until his death in 1894.

Get a Yankee!

On another occasion, three of the grandchildren of Rezin H. Davis, Clay Davis, Reese Davis, and Turner Campbell, were sitting out on a rail fence with their pop guns watching the Yankee troops march by, going south, probably after the Battle of Perryville.

The Union captain walked over to the boys and asked what persuasion they were. Clay Davis, pre-school age, replied firmly, "We're Northern men." "Okay," said the Captain, and he shook hands with them.

But boys, being as they are, could not be satisfied until they had tried out their popguns on the captain. A roar arose from the men laughing at the boys taking aim at their commanding officer. Fortunately, the Yankee officer was a good sport about the matter!

Another time, Southern soldiers were coming by the house. Mrs. Wesley Davis had made some new blankets of wool and had them stacked in a chair, but hid the good ones by placing an old ragged quilt over the top. The men took everything else, but luckily, they missed the good warm blankets.[11]

A Tale from the Columbia Road

Henry Prescott had married Martha Robinson of Taylor County before the war broke out. He was working on an Ohio River boat, when the Northern draft began. Two Union soldiers came on board and made all the men on the ship draw from a can of beans. The beans were colored red and black. He drew the bean that placed him in the service. His wife returned to Taylor County with her four children to live with her father, Claiborne S. Robinson, at Hatcher until the war was over.

During the war, Henry came to Hatcher on furlough. Because there were so many Confederate soldiers around, Martha split the straw mattress in the middle, took his Union uniform and sewed it inside the mattress. Henry was able to return to his Ohio regiment safely, but he was later captured by the Confederates and placed in Libby Prison near Richmond. After the war, he returned to his wife in Taylor County, and they lived next door to the Robinsons, and raised a large family.

One of the ways the Prescott family was able to survive the war was that Claiborne Robinson had a contract with the U.S. Army to haul meal and corn on his wagon for a fee. Before he made the delivery to the troops, he would stop by the family home, pry the tops off the barrels, and take out enough of the meal for the family.

Birdell Prescott, the smallest child of Henry and Mary's, was born in April 1861 and she could remember sitting in the lap of Union soldiers who would stop by the house and get water as they marched by on the Columbia Turnpike.[12]

Story from Penitentiary Bend, Green County

Union troops occupying areas to suppress Rebel guerrilla attacks did not always receive rations in a timely fashion. Trains running to Lebanon might be delayed or the wagon trains might have difficulty getting over muddy roads. Therefore, even though it was not popular, Union cavalrymen went on foraging expeditions, just as the Rebels did, to feed their troops.

One day troops stopped by the farm of William Page and Elizabeth Bridgewater, who lived in a two-story frame house in Penitentiary Bend in Green County, near the Taylor County line. After scouting the premises, the Union Captain of the 13th Cavalry ordered a wagon to back up to the barn and load up. The scouts had found the pork hidden by the Bridgewater family in the hay. The soldiers confiscated all the sides of meat (bacon), all the hams except one, and took Mary Jemima "Mollie" Bridgewater's horse. Mollie, almost 15, stood watching her mare being taken away. After the war, Mollie married a former Union soldier, Jim Butler. He later admitted to his father-in-law that he was one of the troopers who had taken the meat and the horse.[13]

Georgia Beard

Mollie Bridgewater

William and Elizabeth Bridgewater

The father of William Page Bridgewater, Thomas Nathan, lived in Lemmons Bend of Taylor County. That may explain how William Page Bridgewater became the owner of a cannon shell, which was passed down to a descendant, Arbell Gupton Hall. It is said to have been fired at the Battle of Tebbs Bend.[14]

Sinking of the *Sultana*

Two brothers from Mannsville in Capt. Ed Penn's Company, 6th Kentucky Cavalry, James Wallace McDonald and Francis Marion McDonald, were captured at the Battle of Chickamauga and imprisoned in the infamous Confederate Prison at Andersonville, Georgia. When the war ended, the McDonald brothers, emaciated from lack of food and sick from being exposed to the weather with little protection from the elements, were freed and put on the steamship *Sultana* on the Mississippi River for the trip back to Kentucky. The *Sultana*, overcrowded with at least 2,146 Union men freed from Andersonville and Cahaba prison camps, 100 civilian passengers, Confederates going to northern prisons, 85 crew members, 21 military guards, and the pet alligator of the ship's crew, started its fateful journey up the river from Vicksburg on April 24, 1863.[15]

Major William F. Fidler, 6th Kentucky Cavalry, of Marion County was in charge of the prisoners, warning them not to shift the weight of the ship suddenly in that the ship's legal capacity was 376 passengers. It carried 76 life preservers, one yawl, and one metal lifeboat.

On April 27, 1863, at 2 A.M., when the ship was about eight miles north of Memphis, Tennessee, three of the four boilers of the ship exploded, killing many

The Sultana

instantly and setting the ship on fire. The noise sounded like a "hundred earthquakes" on the shore.

Fidler was one of its victims.[16] The survivors of the explosion, mostly sickly men, had to jump into the icy waters of a flooded Mississippi, which was three miles wide and attempt to swim to shore. Many soldiers had never learned to swim, but jumped into the water anyway.

A family story says that James said to his brother, "We'd better swim for it," as he jumped into the water. Many drowning men clung to James and he was pulled under, but he managed to return to the *Sultana*. He took off his clothes to better swim and he tore off two pieces from the ship to help him float in the water.

Francis remained on the deck, knowing that, in his weakened condition, he could not make it to the shore. When James looked back, Francis was kneeling on the blazing *Sultana* in prayer. James alternated swimming and resting on the board. Finally, he came to a tree to which he could cling, but he still could not touch the bottom of the river. He rested and swam to another tree from which he could touch the bottom, sitting in the tree while he watched the ship.

He was being bitten by mosquitoes, and he started swatting at them. Shaking, he fell out of the tree back into the water. He drifted into a log, on which another soldier was sitting. A man paddling a boat came along, picked them up, took them to his house, and gave them some clothes to wear. James was one of the 700 who survived, while Francis was one of over 1,800 who lost their lives on the ship.[17] In addition to Francis McDonald from Taylor County, Privates James Morris, William Wooley, S. W. Jones, and George Dabney, of Companies H and I, 6th Kentucky Cavalry, also died. Cpl. George W. Tucker, Co. I, 6th Kentucky Cavalry, survived.

The cause of the explosion was at first thought to be the work of Confederate sympathizers; however, a more credible cause seems to be a faulty patch put on one of the boilers while it was being repaired at Vicksburg.[18]

Pvt. William Wooley

Part Twelve

Taylor County Soldiers in the Civil War

This section of the book is, by its nature, incomplete. Since no one has ever made an organized effort to record the names of Taylor County's Civil War soldiers, names will be added as further research is conducted.

Number of Taylor County Men in Union Army, 1863

Number of Men from Fourth Congressional District of Kentucky Enlisted in the Union Army in 1863

Anderson 261	Larue 285	Spencer 91
Adair 541	Marion 735	Taylor 325
Bullitt 236	Meade 187	Washington 738
Green 440	Nelson 239	
Hardin 386	Shelby 469	

Source: G. Lee McClain, *Military History of Kentucky*, 197

The following sources were consulted in gathering the names of Taylor County soldiers:

Federal Troops: *The Report of Adjutant General of the State of Kentucky,* Miscellaneous Regimental Papers, such as Descriptive Rolls which state age, personal details, and residence of recruit at time of enrollment, held by the Kentucky Military Museum, Taylor County cemetery records; Union pension rolls. Ed Benningfield, author of "General Hobson's Thirteenth Kentucky Infantry," was most helpful for that regiment.

Confederate Troops: *The Report of the Adjutant General of the State of Kentucky*, Ed Porter Thompson, *History of the Orphan Brigade*, 659–666, 766, 768, and Taylor County cemetery

Beulah Campbell

John S. Durham,
10th Ky. Inf., USA

Nina Stiles

Samuel S. Allen,
13th Ky. Inf., USA

Taylor County Historical Society

Cpl. Elijah T. Stayton,
27th Ky. Inf., USA

Shirley Noel

Joel Noel,
6th Ky. Cav., USA

Bernice Mitchell

Sgt. Jeremiah A. Lindley,
110 Ohio Inf., USA

Steven L. Wright

John P. Gaines, CSA

records. The work of Geoffrey Walden, The "Greensburg Guards" and Steve Wright's work from WPA Veteran's Grave Registration Project were essential. Some Compiled Service Records held by the National Archives for both Union and Confederate soldiers were consulted.

Abbreviations: enr=enrolled; bur=buried; dis=discharged; des=deserted; capt=captured; d=died.

1st Kentucky Cavalry, Company B

RANK	LAST NAME	FIRST NAME	MI	AGE	RESIDENCE	MISC
Cpl.	Cox	Thomas		18	Marion Co, KY	5'8" blk eyes, dk hair, bur. Brookside Cem, Campbellsville
Pvt.	Eades	James	W.	17	Marion Co, KY	Born Taylor Co, 5'10" blk eyes, blk hair; farmer; enr in Casey Co.

1st Kentucky Cavalry, Company D

RANK	LAST NAME	FIRST NAME	MI	AGE	RESIDENCE	MISC
Pvt.	Carlile	James		22	Taylor Co., KY	6' blu eyes, lt hair, never mustered; left Camp D. Robinson Jan 15, 1862
Pvt.	Carson	Andrew		19	New Market, KY	5'8" blu eyes; lt hair, farmer
Pvt.	Cox	Alfred		22	Taylor Co., KY	5'10" blk eyes, dk hair, farmer
Pvt.	Craven	William		20	Taylor Co., KY	5'4" blk eyes, dk hair; farmer; enr Raywick
Pvt.	Dabney	William		35	Mannsville, KY	5'10" blk eyes, dk hair; farmer; des at Somerset May 10, 1863
Pvt.	Dabney	Calvin		29	Mannsville, KY	5'10" blk eyes, blk hair; farmer des at Somerset May 10, 1863
Pvt.	Davis	William	Joshua	24	Taylor Co., KY	5'9" blk eyes, dk hair; farmer; listed on Muster Roll only
Pvt.	Edwards	James	T.	25	Taylor Co., KY	4'2"dk eyes, dk hair, saddler
Pvt.	Farris	Joseph	A.	21	Taylor Co., KY	6' blk eyes, blk hair, farmer; died at home Dec.20, 1861; bur. Good Hope
Pvt.	Farris	Nathaniel	C.	19	Taylor Co., KY	6' dk hair; farmer
Pvt.	Gabheart	Stephen	T.	22	Taylor Co., KY	5'9" blu eyes, lt hair; farmer; med disab at Lebanon Oct. 29, 1862
Pvt.	Gaddis	Bluford			Taylor Co., KY	never mustered
Pvt.	Mann	James		35	Mannsville, KY	5'10" blue eyes, fair hr, farmer
Pvt.	Mason	John	W.	20	Taylor Co., KY	5'11" dk eyes, dk hair; blacksmith
Pvt.	Minor	Elijah		30	Mannsville, KY	5'10" blk eyes; dk hair; farmer
Pvt.	Murphy	Wesley		19	Mannsville, KY	6' blu eyes, lt. hair, farmer; died Dec. 11, 1861 near Somerset
Pvt.	Pickerel/Poole	James	H.	21	Taylor Co., KY	5'10" brn eyes, dk hair, farmer; 2nd bugler
Pvt.	Rivers	James	M.	20	Taylor Co., KY	5'9 farmer; died June 3/5 in hospital Columbia, TN
Pvt.	Roads [Rhodes]	John		18	Mannsville, KY	5'10" blu eyes, fair hair, farmer
Pvt.	Sanders	John	D.	25	Taylor Co., KY	5'9" brn eyes, blk hair; farmer
Pvt.	Shipp	William			Taylor Co., KY	Brn eyes, blk hair; killed at Saloma; bur Quisenberry Cem 1844–May31,1864
Pvt.	Williamson	W.	H.	28	Mannsville, KY	6' blk eyes, dk hair; med disab Murfreesboro, TN Aug.12/Oct. 20, 1862
Pvt.	Wood	Willis	A.	22	Mannsville, KY	5'9" blue eyes, lt hair; farmer

5th Kentucky Cavalry, Company G

RANK	LAST NAME	FIRST NAME	MI	AGE	RESIDENCE	MISC
Sgt.	Jennings	George	W.		Bur. Liberty Cem.	Enr Dec. 15, 1861 Gallatin, TN; dis May 3, 1865

6th Kentucky Cavalry, Company H

RANK	LAST NAME	FIRST NAME	MI	AGE	RESIDENCE	MISC
QuaMtr	Bridges	Charles		31	Marion Co., KY	Enr. Leb, Sept 15, 1862; resided Tay Co after war
Pvt.	Hash	W.	R.		bur. Hash Cem#2, TC	Enr Aug. 10, 1862, Lou; dis July 14, 1865 Edgefield, TN July 26, 1842–Feb 9, 1931
Pvt.	Morris	James			Taylor Co., KY	Enr Aug 10, 1862; cap Apr 6, 1865; killed on *Sultana* Apr 27, 1863

6th Kentucky Cavalry, Company I

RANK	LAST NAME	FIRST NAME	MI	AGE	RESIDENCE	MISC
Capt.	Penn	Edmund		29	Mannsville, KY	Later became Taylor County Judge; died Mar. 18, 1891
1Lt	Crandell	Samuel	W.	42		
1Lt.	Bright	Elijah		25	Mannsville, KY	
2Lt.	Richman/Richmond	Daniel	M.	36		
Pvt.	Grinstead	James	L.		Mannsville, KY	Transferred to 6th KY Veteran Cav.
Sgt.	Allison	Wilson			Mannsville, KY	Deserted at Shelbyville, TN July 1, 1863
Sgt.	Bright	William	T.	21	Mannsville, KY	Discharged, med disab, Calhoun, GA, Aug. 28, 1864
Sgt.	Rice	Joseph		21	Mannsville, KY	Died Nov. 15, 1862 Louisville
Sgt.	Adams	John		46	Mannsville, KY	Discharged, med disab, June 12, 1863
Sgt.	Butler	William	O	29	Plum Point, KY	Transferred to 6th KY Veteran Cav.
Sgt.Pvt	Cox	Squire	M.	38*	Lebanon, KY	Died Apr. 15, 1863 Nashville, diarrhea
Cpl.	Feather	Albert		23	Campbellsville, KY	Transferred to 6th KY Veteran Cav.
Sgt.	Cure	Hiram		19	Campbellsville, KY	
Sgt.	Smith	Jefferson		25	Mannsville, KY	
Cpl.	McAnnelly	John	H.	34	Mannsville, KY	Died Dec. 12, 1862 Louisville
Cpl.	Houk	James	W.	26	Sulphur Well, KY	Capt Sep. 21, 1863; died Richmond,VA, July 29, 1864
Cpl.	Buster	David	G.	37	Sulphur Well, KY	Discharged, med disab, Louisville Feb. 29, 1864
Cpl.	Hendrickson	John	C.	25	Plum Point, KY	Died Oct. 25, 1864 at home
Cpl.	Nunn	Richard	F.	20	Sulphur Well, KY	
Teamst	Burress	Alfred		18	Campbellsville, KY	Died Nov. 1, 1864 Louisville
Sgt.	Landers	James		20	Mannsville, KY	
Farrier	Johnson	William	H.	38	Mannsville, KY	
Farrier	Warren	Nathan			Mannsville, KY	Missing in action, Sep. 21, 1863; pow
Saddler	Williamson	David	M.	30	Mannsville, KY	Also Sgt; transferrd to 6th KY Veteran Cav.
Wagon	Cox	Nathan		23	Mannsville, KY	
Pvt.	Baldwin	Franklin		21	Mannsville, KY	Died June 23, 1863 Nashville
Pvt.	Bishop	Andrew	J.	18	Louisville, KY	Deserted at Wauhatchie, TN May 28, 1864
Pvt.	Brown	Samuel		21	Mannsville, KY	Missing in action, Sep. 21, 1863; pow
Pvt.	Carlile	James		22	Mannsville, KY	
Pvt.	Carlile	James				Missing in action Sep 21, 1863; pow
Pvt.	Colvin	William		20	Louisville, KY	Deserted at Louisville Nov. 22, 1862

Sgt.	Conner	Michael	26	Lebanon, KY	Transferred to Veteran Reserve Corps Jan.23, 1864
Pvt.	Cook	Thomas T.	18	Campbellsville, KY	
Pvt.	Cox	Andy B.	24	Mannsville, KY	Missing in action, Sep. 21, 1863; pow
Pvt.	Cox	Berry	19	Mannsville, KY	
Pvt.	Cox	Jacob	28	Mannsville, KY	Transferred to Veteran Reserve Corps
Pvt.	Cox	John	18	Mannsville, KY	Missing in action, Sep. 21, 1863; pow
Cpl.	Cox	Walker	20	Mannsville, KY	Deserted at Lebanon Feb. 22, 1863
Pvt.	Cox	William	34	Mannsville, KY	Missing in action, Sep. 21, 1863; saddler; pow
Sgt.	Crandell	William L.	18	Mannsville, KY	
Pvt.	Cummion/Cunnins	James	35	Louisville, KY	Deserted at Louisville Feb. 1, 1863
Pvt.	Dabney	John	24	Mannsville, KY	Died Apr. 7, 1863 Nashville
Pvt.	Dabney	Benjamin	18	Mannsville, KY	Missing in action, Sep. 21, 1863; pow
Pvt.	Dabney	George	19	Mannsville, KY	Capt Apr. 1, 1865; died on board the *Sultana* Apr. 27, 1865
Pvt.	Dawson	Charles	18	Louisville, KY	Missing in action, Sep. 21, 1863; pow
Cpl.	Diemer	Jacob	36	Louisville, KY	Deserted Sep. 20, 1862
Pvt.	Druin	William T.	22	Campbellsville, KY	Discharged, med disab, June 6, 1864
Pvt.	Edrington	Burwell	30	Mannsville, KY	Wagoner
Pvt.	Gaddis	Henry H.	35	Mannsville, KY	Missing in action, Sep. 21, 1863; pow
Pvt.	Garner	Henderson	19	Louisville, KY	Transferred to 6th KY Veteran Cav.
Pvt.	Garrett	William P.	24	Mannsville, KY	Deserted at Campbellsville Jan. 3, 1862/3
Pvt.	Hall	James T.		Louisville, KY	Lost on *Sultana*
Pvt.	Henrahan	John			Capt Sep. 21, 1863; exchangd died June 3, 1865
Pvt.	Herron	Washington M.	19	Sulphur Well, KY	
Pvt.	Herron	Robert	18	Sulphur Well, KY	Discharged, med disab, Louisville Feb. 8, 1864
Pvt.	Herron	Elijah B.	44	Mannsville, KY	Capt; died in prison Apr. 12, 1864
Sgt.	Herron	John Henry	35	Louisville, KY	Died Oct. 25, 1864 at home
Pvt.	Huddleston	Weldon	22	Mannsville, KY	Discharged Louisville
Pvt.	Huddleston	Henry L/T	23	Mannsville, KY	
Pvt.	Johnson	Charner	18	bur. Poplar Grove	Capt Apr. 1, 1865 near Centerville, AL; rel; hos Memphis
Pvt.	Johnson	Henry	18	Plum Point, KY	
Pvt.	Johnson	Silas	19	Louisville, KY	Deserted at Louisville Feb. 1, 1863
Pvt.	Jones	Abraham			Transferred to 6th KY Veteram Cav.
Pvt.	Jones	Frederick G.	41	Louisville, KY	Not listed in Adj. Gen. Report
Pvt.	Jones	Philip	40	Plum Point, KY	Not listed in Adj. Gen. Report
Cpl.	Jones	Stephen	18	Louisville, KY	Capt Apr. 6, 1865; rel; transferred to 6th KY Vet. Cav.
Pvt.	Keneda/Henida	Pierce	24	Louisville, KY	Discharged Evansville, IN, med disab, June 20, 1863
Pvt.	Kerr	James			Missing in action
Pvt.	Knopp	John H.	18	Sulphur Well, KY	
Pvt.	Landers	Isham	18	Mannsville, KY	Missing in action Sep. 21, 1863
Pvt.	Lawrence	John R.	45	Louisville, KY	Discharged, med disab, Nashville, June 10, 1863
Sgt.	Light	Henry	44	Plum Point, KY	Deserted Columbia Jan. 5, 1863
Pvt.	Lusk	Joel C.	18	Sulphur Well, KY	
Pvt.	Mallory/Moary	Charles R.	30	Louisville, KY	Capt Apr. 6, 1865; exch;died on *Sultana* Apr. 27, 1865
Pvt.	Mann	Benjamin F.	22	Mannsville, KY	
Pvt.	Mann	John	19	Mannsville, KY	One of the John Manns is buried at Spurlington Meth Ch.
Pvt.	Mann	John A.	18	Mannsville, KY	

Pvt.	McAdams	James	G.			
Pvt.	McDaniel	Joseph	W.	28	Mannsville, KY	Died at Lebanon Junction Jan. 15, 1864
Pvt.	McDonald	Francis	M.	22	Mannsville, KY	Capt Apr. 1, 1865; exchanged; died on *Sultana* Apr. 27,1865
Pvt.	McDonald	James	W.	20	Mannsville, KY	Capt Apr. 1, 1865; survived the sinking of the *Sultana*
Pvt.	Miller	Richard	A.	35	Plum Point, KY	Deserted at Louisville May 15, 1863
Pvt.	Minor	John	T.	18	Mannsville, KY	Died; accidental firing of gun; Dec. 21, 1864 Hopkinsvle
Pvt.	Monroe	James		20	Plum Point, KY	Missing in action Sep. 21, 1863; taken prisoner ; died.
Pvt.	Morris	Jesse		27	Mannsville, KY	Discharged Louisville
Pvt.	Noel	Joel		48	Mannsville, KY	Sick in Louisville since Nov. 27, 1864
Pvt.	Noel	Mark		38	Mannsville, KY	Not listed in Adj. Gen. Report
Pvt.	Parker	James				Transferred to 6th KY Veteram Cav.
Cpl.	Perry	Henry		19	Louisville, KY	Desertd Nov. 27, 1864; reported on duty at Nashville
Pvt.	Poor	Charles	W.			Transferred to 6th KY Veteram Cav.
Pvt.	Purvis	Joseph	M.	24	Lebanon, KY	Deserted at E-town Nov. 15, 1862; reported with Morgan
Pvt.	Rodes [Rhodes]	Abraham		18	Mannsville, KY	Capt near Centerville, Al Apr. 1, 1863; returnd May 1, 1865
Pvt.	Shipp	John		19	Campbellsville, KY	
Pvt.	Shipp	Thomas		18	Campbellsville, KY	Died Aug. 1, 1863 Winchester, TN
Pvt.	Shofner	Robert	H.	23	Campbellsville, KY	Deserted June 1, 1863 Campbellsville; farrier
Pvt.	Slinker	Joseph		18	Sulphur Well, KY	Transferred to 6th KY Veteran Cav.
Pvt.	Smith	George	W.	40	Plum Point, KY	Deserted June 1, 1863 Campbellsville
Pvt.	Spires	William	B.	20	Mannsville, KY	MIA Sep. 21, 1863; listed as Spiers Williamson in AGen Rept
Pvt.	Sweeney	Dennis				Deserted June 1, 1863, Campbellsville
Pvt.	Thomas	Elbert		24	Mannsville, KY	Deserted at Stanford, Oct 15, 1862
Pvt.	Tucker	George	W.	20	Mannsville, KY	Survived the *Sultana* explosion, then Cpl.
	Tucker	John				Transferred to 6th KY Veteram Cav.
Pvt.	Underwood	Charles/Chalen		18	Campbellsville, KY	Wagoner
	Warren	Nathan				Farrier; missing in action Sep. 21, 1863
Pvt.	Watson	Johnson		20	Plum Point, KY	Discharged Winchster, TN, med disab, July 15, 1863
Pvt.	Williams	John	F.	21	Mannsville, KY	Discharged Louisville, med disab, June 6, 1864
	Williams	Richard		18	Sulphur Well, KY	Discharged Oct. 18, 1864
2Lt.	Williams	James	H.	20	Plum Point, KY	Died at home Dec. 25, 1862
Sgt.	Williamson	James	M/E	18	Mannsville, KY	Died Dec. 25, 1862 at home
Pvt.	Williamson	Jacob		19	Mannsville, KY	Not listed in Adj. Gen. Report
Pvt.	Williamson	James	E.			
Sgt.	Williamson	Zachariah				Discharged, med disab, Louisville June 15, 1863
Cpl.	Williamson	David				Transferred to 6th KY Veteram Cav.
Pvt.	Wooldridge	Daniel	B.	40	Campbellsville, KY	Died Mar. 31, 1863 Nashville
Pvt.	Wooley	William		25	Mannsville, KY	Capt Apr. 1, 1865, exchanged; died on *Sultana* Apr. 27, 1865
Pvt.	Woolridge	Richard	T.	27	Campbellsville, KY	
Pvt.	Wright/White	Alfred	J.	44	Plum Point, KY	Discharged Nashville, TN, med disab, July 5, 1863

*Age at death; usually age is given at enlistment.

6th Kentucky Cavalry, Company L

RANK	LAST NAME	FIRST NAME	MI	AGE	RESIDENCE	MISC
Pvt.	Wheat	John	T.		born in Taylor Co., KY	Enr Feb 25, 1864, Lex; died at Park Barracks, Lou

The Sixth Kentucky Cavalry

The first five companies of this regiment were organized under Maj. Reuben Munday; Taylor County boys joined it in 1862, under the leadership of Col. D.J. Halisy of Manton and Capt. Ed Penn of Mannsville. Although many were unarmed, they pursued Morgan through Taylor County on the Christmas Raid. In 1863, under the leadership of Col. Louis Watkins, the men moved to TN and were stationed at Brentwood and Franklin, guarding Rosecrans' army and engaging the enemy at Franklin and Spring Hill. They moved across central TN and engaged in desperate fighting at Chickamauga. Heavy fighting against Pillow took place in Lafayette, GA. The regiment guarded the railroad around Resaca and then were sent to help stop the advance of Hood to Nashville. After fighting Gen. Lyon's advance at Hopkinsville, the regiment pursued the Confederates leaving Nashville.

13th Kentucky Cavalry, Company L

RANK	LAST NAME	FIRST NAME	MI	AGE	RESIDENCE	MISC
Pvt.	Monroe	Pleasant	S		Elkhorn, KY	Enr Oct. 10, 1863; dis Jan. 10, 1865 Cp Nelson; Lived in Adr Co after the war.

2nd Kentucky Infantry, Company B

RANK	LAST NAME	FIRST NAME	MI	AGE	RESIDENCE	MISC
Pvt.	Burge	Thomas	F.		Taylor Co., KY after war	Enr Jan. 19, 1861 Pendleton, O; dis June 19, 1864 Covington bur. Brookside, Sec.A Capt at Chickamauga; escaped from Richmond; returned to duty

3rd Kentucky Infantry, Company A

RANK	LAST NAME	FIRST NAME	MI	AGE	RESIDENCE	MISC
Pvt	Hubbard	John	W.	19	Taylor Co., KY Sch. Teacher	Enr Nov. 8, 1861; dis Sep. 30, 1862 Prom to Sgt Feb. 11, 1863; killed Nov. 25, 1863 Battle of Missionary Ridge, TN; buried there
Pvt.	Monroe	Daniel			Elkhorn, KY	Enr Sep 19, 1861; killed Kennesaw Mt, GA June 18, 1864

3rd Kentucky Infantry, Company I

RANK	LAST NAME	FIRST NAME	MI	AGE	RESIDENCE	MISC
1st Lt.	Murrah	William	D.		Elkhorn, KY	Enr Apr. 20, 1863 Murfreesboro;dis Oct. 13, 1864 Bur. Elkhorn Meth Ch Cem; Jan.14, 1836–Mar. 9, 1896

4th Kentucky Infantry, Company K

RANK	LAST NAME	FIRST NAME	MI	AGE	RESIDENCE	MISC
Pvt.	Benningfield	Randolph	R.		Taylor Co., KY	Enr Sep. 9, 1861; ill in hospital 1863

5th Kentucky Infantry, Company I

RANK	LAST NAME	FIRST NAME	MI	AGE	RESIDENCE	MISC
Pvt.	Robinson	William	P.		Taylor Co., KY	Enr Aug. 1, 1861Camp Joe Holt; disch because of wounds Sep. 30, 1863, Surg. Certificate; Bur. Bethel Pres Cem

10th Kentucky Infantry, Company B

RANK	LAST NAME	FIRST NAME	MI	AGE	RESIDENCE	MISC
2Lt.	Short	Jno.	P.	23	near New Market, KY	Name appears only in original Muster Roll
Pvt.	Clark	Royal	G.		Mannsville, KY	Died at Nashville May 26, 1864; widow Nancy
Cpl.	Durham	James	S.	36	Taylor Co., KY	At home near Saloma since Nov. 1, 1862, bur Saloma
Pvt.	Durham	John	S.		Taylor Co., KY	Transf to Vet. Reserve Corps
Cpl.	Lewellyn	Elisha	O/A	36	Taylor Co., KY	Cooper; mustered out Dec. 6, 1864 Louisville
Pvt.	Meadows	William		37	Taylor Co., KY	Mustered out Dec. 6, 1864 Louisville
Pvt.	Read/Reed	Philip	M.	18	Taylor Co., KY	Home near Mannsville sinc Apr. 1, 1862; then Murfreesboro

10th Kentucky Infantry, Company C

RANK	LAST NAME	FIRST NAME	MI	AGE	RESIDENCE	MISC
Pvt.	Allen	Samuel				Discharged Dec. 31, 1862 Nashville
Pvt.	Bright	William	D.	19	Taylor Co., KY	Mustered out Dec. 6, 1864
Pvt.	Feather	John	H.		Taylor Co., KY	Died at home Taylor County Apr. 17, 1862
Pvt.	Hunt	Reuben	W.		Taylor Co., KY	Disch Mar. 11, 1863 Lou; buried Good Hope Bapt. Ch.
Pvt.	Rodgers	Ben	O.	45	Taylor Co., KY	Discharged Mar. 11, 1863 Gallatin, TN
Pvt.	Rodgers	James		18	Taylor Co., KY	Died Nov. 28, 1861 at hospital Lebanon
Pvt.	Sapp	Peter		33	Taylor Co., KY	Died Mar. 28, 1862 at hospital Nashville
Pvt.	Spurling	James	H.		Taylor Co., KY	Mustered out Dec. 6, 1864; buried Elkhorn Meth. Ch.
Pvt.	Wise	Charles		22	Taylor Co., KY	Mustered out Dec. 6, 1864

10th Kentucky Infantry, Company H

RANK	LAST NAME	FIRST NAME	MI	AGE	RESIDENCE	MISC
Capt.	Pendleton	Buford	R.	30	Mannsville, KY	Resigned Nov. 16, 1862
Capt.	Shively	William	Thos.	31	Taylor Co., KY	Prom to Capt upon Pendleton's resignation
Sgt.	Wright	Thomas	R.	19	Taylor Co., KY	Discharged Sep. 17, 1862 Louisville; Brookside Cem, A Sec.
Sgt.	Shively	Stephen	M.	24	Taylor Co., KY	Mustered Out Dec. 6, 1864 Louisville
Sgt.	Shively	Joseph	H.	18	Taylor Co., KY	Mustered Out Dec. 6, 1864 Louisville
Cpl.	Newton	Elias		22	Taylor Co., KY	Died Mar. 15, 1862 Nashville

Cpl.	Rice	David	E.	19	Taylor Co., KY	Mustered Out Dec. 6, 1864 Louisville
Cpl.	Roots	William		35	Taylor Co., KY	Mustered Out Dec. 6, 1864 Louisville
Musician	Odewalt	Jacob		24	Taylor Co., KY	
Pvt.	Abell	Enoch		24	Marion Co., KY	Buried Gaddis Ridge Cem.
Pvt.	Brockman	James		19	Taylor Co., KY	Mustered Out Dec. 6, 1864 Louisville
Pvt.	Cabell	William	T.	22	Taylor Co., KY	Died Aug. 28, 1862 in Campbellsville, measles
Pvt.	Farmer	James		22	Taylor Co., KY	Discharged Mar. 12, 1863 Louisville
Pvt.	Farmer	John	F.	18	Taylor Co., KY	Discharged Mar. 31, 1863 Louisville
Pvt.	Farmer	Joseph		24	Taylor Co., KY	Only listed in the Muster Roll, not in Adj Gen Rept
Pvt.	Farmer	Moses		29	Taylor Co., KY	Mustered Out Dec. 6, 1864 Louisville
Pvt.	Farmer	Nathaniel		18	Taylor Co., KY	Mustered Out Dec. 6, 1864 Louisville
Pvt.	Farmer	Preston	P.	23	Taylor Co., KY	Discharged Nov. 12, 1862 Louisville
Pvt.	Farmer	Thomas		22	Taylor Co., KY	Deserted June 30, 1863 Lebanon
Pvt.	Farmer	William		19	Taylor Co., KY	Killed in a skirmish by enemy at Courtland, AL July 25,186?
Pvt.	Gunter	Henry		37	Taylor Co., KY	Discharged Dec. 15, 1862 Louisville
Pvt.	Harmon	Isaac		18	Taylor Co., KY	Discharged Jan. 18, 1864 Evansville, IN
Pvt.	Melton	David		18	Taylor Co., KY	Died Feb. 25, 1862 Crab Orchard
Pvt.	Newton	John	S	19	Taylor Co., KY	Discharged June 5, 1862 Gallatin, TN
Pvt.	Russell	Daniel	J.	26	Taylor Co., KY	Discharged Dec. 1, 1862 Louisville
Pvt.	Shively	David	A.	23	Taylor Co., KY	Mustered Out Dec. 6, 1864 Louisville
Pvt.	Shively	Samuel		20	Taylor Co., KY	Died Mar. 10, 1862 in Taylor County, typhoid fever
Pvt.	Sluder	James	H.	42	Taylor Co., KY	Mustered Out Dec. 6, 1864 Louisville
Pvt.	Sluder	John	M.	18	Taylor Co., KY	Discharged Oct. 16, 1863 of wounds
Pvt.	Smith	Johnson		40	Taylor Co., KY	Died Mar. 15, 1862 Taylor Co. of disease
Pvt.	Wise	John	R.	18	Taylor Co., KY	Died June 1862 on hospital boat
Pvt.	Wise	Samuel	T.	23	Taylor Co., KY	Supposed dead; Aug. 1862 left sick at Nashville
Pvt.	Wise	William		28	Taylor Co., KY	Discharged Dec. 20, 1862 Louisville
Pvt.	Wright	Ben		18	Taylor Co., KY	Died Mar. 10, 1862 Nashville
Pvt.	Wright	Samuel		23	Taylor Co., KY	Discharged Oct. 16, 1862 Nashville
Pvt.	Wright	Thomas		30	Taylor Co., KY	Mustered Out Dec. 6, 1864 Louisville

10th Kentucky Infantry

The 10th Infantry was organized at Lebanon under Col. John M. Harlan. The regiment marched to Mill Springs but saw no action. It returned to Louisville and traveled by steamboat to Nashville and then to the Battle of Shiloh. In July 1862 Company H was on duty at Courtland, AL, when they were surrounded by the enemy and captured. The regiment engaged Morgan's forces at Rolling Fork in December 1862 and returned to Nashville. Harlan resigned and William H. Hays replaced him. The men participated in many battles in TN and GA: Chickamauga, Missionary Ridge, Atlanta and Sherman's march to the sea.[1]

12th Kentucky Infantry, Company C

RANK	LAST NAME	FIRST NAME	MI	AGE	RESIDENCE	MISC
Pvt.	Rippetoe	Albert	W.		Bur Sanders-Murray Cem	Mustered in Jan. 30, 1862 at Camp Clio, KY

13th Kentucky Infantry, Company A

RANK	LAST NAME	FIRST NAME	MI	AGE	RESIDENCE	MISC
Pvt.	Nelson	Arnold		20	Taylor Co., KY	Enr Oct. 6, 1861; died Jan. 9, 1864 Knoxville
Pvt.	Oakes	William	D.	19	Taylor Co., KY	Enr Aug 14, 1863; dis Sep 6, 1865 Louisville
Pvt.	Romine	David	W.	24	Taylor Co., KY	Enr Sep. 28, 1861; dis Jan. 12, 1865 Lou; Good Hope Cem
Pvt.	Underwood	Jesse		18	Taylor Co., KY	Enr Aug. 14, 1863; died June 9, 1864 Nashville
Cpl.	Underwood	John		22	Taylor Co., KY	Enr Oct. 4, 1861; dis Jan. 12, 1865 Louisville

13th Kentucky Infantry, Company C

RANK	LAST NAME	FIRST NAME	MI	AGE	RESIDENCE	MISC
Pvt.	Breeding	John	H.		Knifley, KY	Enr Camp Andy Johnson, Cville; died 1924
Pvt.	Buckner	Aylette		18	Taylor Co., KY	Enr Sep. 23, 1861; dis Jan. 12, 1865 Louisville
Pvt.	Dudgeon	Thomas	J.	18	Campbellsville, KY	Enr Sep. 30, 1861; killed May 27, 1864 Dallas, GA
Cpl.	Forbis	James	S.	29	Campbellsville, KY	Enr Oct. 5, 1861; dis Apr. 23, 1863 Nashville.
Pvt.	Howard	Jones	S.	23	Campbellsville, KY	Enr Sep. 23, 1861; dis Jan. 12, 1865 Louisville
Cpl.	Lee	Joel	T.	18	Campbellsville, KY	Enr Sep. 27, 1861; dis Jan. 12, 1865 Louisville
Pvt.	May	Horace		18	Campbellsville, KY	Enr Sep. 30, 1861; dis Jan. 12, 1865 Lou; died Sep. 2, 1911
Pvt.	Pike	Elijah		20	Campbellsville, KY	Enr Oct. 6, 1861; dis 1863 Munfordville; died 1913 Flat Rock, IN
Sgt.	Romine	William	M/P.		Taylor Co., KY	Enr Oct 2, 1861; died Mar 1862 in Taylor Co., bur Gr Riv Mem
Pvt.	Skaggs	Jackson			Taylor Co., KY	Enr 1861 Camp Hobson; died 1862 Adr Co; bur Old Sand Lick
Pvt.	Smith	William	R.	38	Taylor Co., KY	Enr Nov. 6, 1861; dis Jan. 12, 1865 Louisville
Pvt.	Steger	Robert	B.	26	Campbellsville, KY	Enr Oct. 22, 1861; dis Jan. 12, 1865 Lou; died Mar. 24, 1913

13th Kentucky Infantry, Company E

RANK	LAST NAME	FIRST NAME	MI	AGE	RESIDENCE	MISC
Sgt.	Chaney	William	E.		Taylor Co., KY	Enr Oct. 20, 1861; dis Jan. 12, 1865 Lou, 5'9" dark hair & eyes
Cpl.	Chapman	G.	R.		Bur. Saloma Cem	Enr Sep. 30, 1861; dis Jan. 12, 1865 Lou (1837–1882)
Pvt.	Gaddie	Alfred	W.	20	Taylor Co., KY	Enr Oct. 20, 1861; died Apr. 28, 1862 Shiloh
Pvt.	Gaddie	William	J.	23	Taylor Co., KY	Enr Oct. 20, 1861; des Feb 14, 1862 Georgetown
Pvt.	Hall	Joseph	T.	18	Taylor Co., KY	Enr Oct. 3, 1861; dis Jan. 12, 1865 Louisville
Sgt.	Miller	James	T.	19	Taylor Co., KY	Enr Sep. 20, 1861; dis Jan. 12, 1865 Lou; died 1913; Bethel Cem

Pvt.	Morrison	William	J.	22	Taylor Co., KY	Enr Oct. 30, 1861; died Sep. 7, 1862 Nashville
Pvt.	Oakes	Daniel	G.	21	Taylor Co., KY	Enr Oct. 20, 1861; dis July 11, 1862 Louisville
Pvt.	Oakes	Henry		23	Taylor Co., KY	Enr Oct. 20, 1861; dis Jan. 12, 1865 Louisville
Pvt.	Oakes	William		27	Taylor Co., KY	Enr Oct. 20, 1861; dis Jan. 12, 1865 Louisville
Pvt.	Price	Henry	M.	25	Larue/Taylor Co., KY	Enr Nov. 9, 1861; dis Jan. 12, 1865 Lou;died Sep 30,1911
Pvt.	Shofner	William	E/C	18	Taylor Co., KY	Enr Sep. 30, 1861; dis Jan. 12, 1865 Lou; d. Dec.28, 1915 Cville
Pvt.	Underwood	William J.		18	Taylor Co., KY	Enr Nov. 4, 1861; des May, 1862 Corinth, MS
Pvt.	Wooldridge	William	E.	18	Taylor Co., KY	Enr Sep. 20, 1861; dis Jan. 12, 1865 Lou; d 1912 Shiloh Cem

13th Kentucky Infantry, Company F

RANK	LAST NAME	FIRST NAME	MI	AGE	RESIDENCE	MISC
Capt.	Duncan	John	P.	25	Munfordville, KY	Enr Nov. 15, 1861; dis Jan. 12, 1865 Lou; prom. Maj.
1st Lt.	Turner	Robert	H.	22	Taylor Co., KY	Enr Nov. 15, 1861; resigned May 10, 1863
2nd Lt.	Jones	Holland		20	Taylor Co., KY	Died Dec. 15, 1861; Jones Ck Cem
Sgt.	Butler	Champness	D.	25	Campbellsville, KY	Promoted to Capt. Mar. 25, 1863; killed June 27, 1864
Sgt.	Morris	Luther		29	Taylor Co., KY	Promoted to Orderly Sgt
Sgt.	Jones	Samuel	A.	23	Taylor Co., KY	Enr Dec. 27, 1861; res Feb. 21, 1863
Sgt.	Wilson	Thomas	N.	21	Taylor Co., KY	Enr Oct. 14, 1861; dis Jan. 12, 1865 Louisville
Sgt.	Martin	William	W.	18	Taylor Co., KY	Enr Oct. 14, 1861; dis Jan. 12, 1865; pro 4th Sgt.
Cpl.	Jones	Enoch	J.	24	Marion Co., KY	Enr Oct. 14, 1861; dis Jan. 12, 1865 Louisville
Cpl.	Hazard	John	H.	20	Taylor Co., KY	Promoted to 1st Sgt.; dis Jan. 12, 1865.
Cpl.	Morris	James	B.	23/5	Taylor Co., KY	Enr Oct. 20, 1861; prom 2nd Sgt; dis Jan. 12, 1865 Lou
Cpl.	Loyall	Jessie		34	Taylor Co., KY	Enr Oct. 14, 1861; disch; Surg. Certificate July 14, 1862
Cpl.	Smith	John	T.	23	Taylor Co., KY	Enr Oct. 14, 1861; dis Jan. 12, 1865 Louisville
Cpl.	Hackley	Francis		19	Campbellsville, KY	Enr Oct. 14, 1861; disch; Surg. Certificate June 10, 1862
Cpl.	Marshall	David	H.	25	Taylor Co., KY	Enr Nov. 5, 1861; disch June 21, 1862
Cpl.	Allen	Samuel	S.	26	Marion Co., KY	Capt. Dec. 14, 1863; died Belle Island
Music	Ratcliffe	Archibald		24	Taylor Co., KY	Enr Nov. 5, 1861;capt.Dec.14, 63;died Apr 3, 64 Andersonvle, GA
Music	Whitlock	Benj/Berry		25	Marion Co., KY	Enr Oct. 20, 1861; dis Jan 12, 1865 Louisville
Wagon	Nelson	James		45	Taylor Co., KY	Enr Oct. 20, 1861; dis Jan . 12, 1865 Louisville
Pvt.	Allen	James	B.	23	Taylor Co., KY	Died Nashville, TN Sept 5/10, 1862 remittent fever
Pvt.	Anderson	William	J.	27	Taylor Co., KY	Wounded at Shiloh Apr 7, 1862
Pvt.	Arvin	Joseph	H.	18	Taylor Co., KY	Enr Oct. 25, 1861; prom Cpl; dis Jan. 12, 1865 Lou.

Pvt.	Beard	John	A.	19	Taylor Co., KY	Enr Oct. 14, 1861; died Savannah, TN Apr. 10/11, 1862 fever
Pvt.	Biggs	Alfred	A.	25	Adair Co., KY	Transferred to Co. B
Pvt.	Bright	William	H.	20	Taylor Co., KY	Enr Oct. 25, 1861; dis Jan. 12, 1865 Louisville
Pvt.	Carlile	George	W.	24	Taylor Co., KY	Deserted Dec. 19, 1862 Munfordville
Pvt.	Cave	James		21	Taylor Co., KY	Disch; Surg. Certificate Mar. 24, 1863; d 1910; b Gr Co
Pvt.	Cave	Robert		27	Taylor Co., KY	Died Hart Co., KY Mar. 4/6, 1863 consumption
Pvt.	Childers	Thomas		28	Taylor Co., KY	Wounded at Shiloh Apr. 7, 1862; d 1912; b Gr Co
Pvt.	Chisham	John	S.	41	Taylor Co., KY	Enr Oct. 14, 1861; dis Jan. 12, 1865 Louisville
Pvt.	Chisham	Andrew		18	Taylor Co., KY	Disch; Surg. Certificate Feb. 15, 1863; b Gr Co
Pvt.	Cox	Nathan		20	Taylor Co., KY	Killed in action Resaca May 14, 1864
Pvt.	Coyle	Richard	W.	29	Taylor Co., KY	Died Bowling Green, KY Sept 5, 1862
Pvt.	DeWitt	Richard		21	Taylor Co., KY	Discharged; Surg. Certificate Jan. 21, 1863
Pvt.	DeWitt	William		19	Taylor Co., KY	Died Campbellsville Jan. 1, 1862 fever
Pvt.	Dezarn	William	F.	18	Taylor Co., KY	Discharged; Surg. Certificate Aug. 11, 1862
Pvt.	Druen	John	M.	20	Taylor Co., KY	Enr Oct. 14, 1861; dis Jan. 12, 1865 Louisville
Pvt.	Dye	Ben	T/F.	18	Taylor Co., KY	Died Shiloh, Apr. 27, 1862 consumption
Pvt.	Farris	Robert	H.	18	Taylor Co., KY	Enr. Nov. 5, 1861; dis Jan. 12, 1865 Lou; d 1919 Danvle, IL
Pvt.	Farris	Samuel	B/R.	33	Taylor Co., KY	Enr. Nov. 5, 1861; dis Jan. 12, 1865 Louisville
Pvt.	French	James		18	Marion Co., KY	Enr Oct. 25, 1861; dis Jan. 12, 1865 Lou; d 1921 Atilla
Pvt.	French	John		41	Marion Co., KY	Enr Nov. 2, 1861; dis Jan. 12, 1865 Louisville
Pvt.	French	Richard		33	Taylor Co., KY	Enr Oct. 25, 1861; dis Jan. 12, 1865 Louisville
Pvt.	French	William		25	Casey Co., KY	Des Danville, KY Oct. 10, 1862
Pvt.	Gill	James	L.	25	Taylor Co., KY	Discharged; Surg. Certificate Nov. 8, 1862
Pvt.	Graham	Edward		24	Taylor Co., KY	Discharged; Surg. Certificate Jan. 1863; d 1911 Feather Cem
Pvt.	Graham	Ezekial		27	Taylor Co., KY	Killed in action Shiloh Apr. 7, 1862
Pvt.	Harris	Jesse	F.	20	Taylor Co., KY	Des Danville, KY Oct. 10, 1862
Pvt.	Hash	Archibald		20	Taylor Co., KY	Enr Oct. 14, 1861; dis. Jan 12, 1865 Louisville
Pvt.	Hash	James		18	Taylor Co., KY	Enr Nov. 8, 1861;to Vet Reserve Corps; d 1922 Cville
Pvt.	Hash	Thomas		36	Taylor Co., KY	Discharged; Surg. Certificate Jan. 26, 1863
Pvt.	Hay	John	D.	38	Taylor Co., KY	Promoted to Cpl.; dis Jan. 12, 1865 Louisville
Pvt.	Hedgespeth	Holland		21	Taylor Co., KY	Enr Oct. 14, 1861; dis Jan. 12, 1865 Louisville
Pvt.	Hoskins	Woodruff		32	Campbellsville, KY	Discharged; Surg. Certificate Oct. 1862
Pvt.	Jones	Enoch		40	Larue Co., KY	Died Nashville, TN Aug. 2/26, 1863 intermittent fever
Pvt.	Mann	David	B.	18	Taylor Co., KY	Enr Oct. 28, 1861; dis Jan. 12, 1865 Lou; d 1909
Pvt.	Mann	John	G.	21	Taylor Co., KY	Enr Oct. 14, 1861; dis Jan. 12, 1865 Louisville

Pvt.	Mann	William		23	Taylor Co., KY	Enr Nov. 9, 1861; prom Sgt.; dis Jan. 12, 1865 Lou; d 1919 Speck
Pvt.	Martin	William	T.	37	Campbellsville, KY	Promoted to 2nd Lt.; resigned Dec. 4, 1863
Pvt.	Morris	David		26	Taylor Co., KY	Enr Oct. 25, 1861; dis Jan. 12, 1865 Louisville
Pvt.	Morris	George	W.	20	Taylor Co., KY	Died Taylor Co., KY Dec. 1, 1862
Pvt.	Morris	Holland		25	Taylor Co., KY	Enr Nov. 5, 1861; dis Jan. 12, 1865 Lou; d 1917
Pvt.	Morris	Thomas	R.	25	Taylor Co., KY	Died Camp Hobson December 1, 1862 fever
Pvt.	Morris	W.	F.	18	Taylor Co., KY	Enr Oct. 14, 1861; dis Jan. 12, 1865 Louisville
Pvt.	Nelson	John	T.	22	Taylor Co., KY	Enr Oct. 28, 1861; dis Jan. 12, 1865 Lou; d 1916 Stithtown
Pvt.	Parrott	Cyrus		18	Taylor Co., KY	Des Knoxville, TN Dec. 16, 1863; d July 30, 1915 Saloma
Pvt.	Parrott	George	W.	18	Taylor Co., KY	Enr Oct. 14, 1861; ill; d 1920 Taylor Co
Pvt.	Parrott	William	R.	20	Taylor Co., KY	Killed Shiloh Apr. 7, 1862
Pvt.	Price	Sylvester		18	Taylor Co., KY	Enr Nov. 5, 1861; dis Jan. 12, 1865 Lou; b Zion Sep, Maple
Pvt.	Ratliff	James	Archd	21	Taylor Co., KY	Discharged; Surg. Certificate July 12, 1862
Pvt.	Ratliff	William		41	Taylor Co., KY	Enr Oct. 14, 1861; des Jan. 12, 1865 Louisville
Pvt.	Redford	James	L.	38	Campbellsville, KY	Discharged; Surg. Certificate Jan. 20, 1863
Pvt.	Rice	George	A.	31	Campbellsville, KY	Enr. Oct. 14, 1861; dis Jan. 12, 1865 Louisville
Pvt.	Shipp	Easton		18	Taylor Co., KY	Enr. Oct. 28, 1861; dis Jan. 12, 1865 Lou; d May 8, 1913
Pvt.	Shipp	John	H.	19	Taylor Co., KY	Enr. Oct. 28, 1861; dis Jan. 12, 1865 Louisville
Pvt.	Smith	James	H.	27	Taylor Co., KY	Died Nashville, TN Sept 5, 1862 remittent fever
Pvt.	Smith	W.	B.	38	Taylor Co., KY	Transferred to Co. C.
Pvt.	Stains	John		37	Taylor Co., KY	Enr. Oct. 28, 1861; dis Jan. 12, 1865 Louisville
Pvt.	Sullivan	William		25	Taylor Co., KY	Disch; Surg. Certificate Jan. 6, 1863; d 1922 Willowtown
Pvt.	Underwood	Joshue		44	Marion Co., KY	Disch; Surg. Certificate Nov. 24, 1862
Pvt.	Whitlock	Woodson		18	Marion Co., KY	Died Aug. 25, 1864
Pvt.	Williams	Lafayette		21	Marion Co., KY	Enr Nov. 1, 1861; dis Jan. 12, 1865 Louisville
Pvt.	Wilson	James		23	Taylor Co., KY	Prom to 1st Sgt; dis Jan. 12, 1865 Lou; d Feb. 4, 1912
Pvt.	Wright	Samuel		25	Taylor Co., KY	Enr Nov. 5, 1861; died Taylor Co. July 4, 1862
Pvt.	Wright	William		24	Taylor Co., KY	Enr Oct. 20, 1861; des
Staff	Barbee	John	R.	34	Campbellsville, KY	Enr Jan. 7, 1863; resFeb. 5, 1864; chaplain

Most were enrolled in September and October 1861; discharged January 12, 1865 in Louisville

Often a family member took an ill soldier home without securing a Surg. Cert. and the soldier is listed as deserted in military records.

13th Kentucky Infantry, Company G

RANK	LAST NAME	FIRST NAME	MI	AGE	RESIDENCE	MISC
Cpl.	Allen	Joseph	M.	18	Taylor Co., KY	Enr Sep. 30, 1861; dis Jan. 12, 1865 Lou; died Sep. 10, 1923 Elkhorn
Pvt.	Chaney	Daniel		29	Taylor Co., KY	Enr Oct. 24, 1861; deserted on march Feb. 1862.
Pvt.	Despain	James	L.	32	Taylor Co., KY	Enr Nov. 1, 1861; dis May 8, 1862 Louisville
Pvt.	Graves	Francis	H.	28	Taylor Co., KY	Enr Oct. 21, 1861; dis Jan. 12, 1865 Lou; Saloma Cem
Pvt.	Maupin	Robert	M.	18	Taylor Co., KY	Enr Sep. 30, 1861; killed Nov. 14, 1863 Huff's Ferry, TN
Pvt.	Maupin	William	T.	18	Taylor Co., KY	Enr Sep. 30, 1861; dis Jan. 12, 1865 Lou; died Dec. 27, 1911 Maupin Cem
Pvt.	Nelson	Thomas	J.	32	Taylor Co., KY	Enr Oct. 1, 1861.
Pvt.	Wright	Charles		18	Taylor Co., KY	Enr Sep. 30, 1861; dis Jan. 12, 1865 Lou; died Mar. 15, 1910

13th Kentucky Infantry, Company H

RANK	LAST NAME	FIRST NAME	MI	AGE	RESIDENCE	MISC
Sgt.	Chaney	William	E.		Taylor Co., KY	Enr Oct. 20, 1861; dis Jan. 12, 1865 Lou, 5'9" dark hair & eyes
Pvt.	Purvis	Jesse		21	Taylor Co., KY	Enr Sep. 21, 1861; dis Jan. 12, 1865 Louisville
Sgt.	Warren	C.D.			bur. Poplar Grove Cem	Enr Oct. 1, 1861; discharge unclear

13th Kentucky Infantry

Col. E. H. Hobson of Greensburg raised the 13th Kentucky, assisted by his nephew, W.E. Hobson. Taylor County soldiers were sprinkled throughout the regiment, but principally served in Company F. Departing Green River Bridge, the regiment marched to Nashville to Shiloh, where it participated in heavy fighting on the morning of the second day. Led by Col. [E.H.] Hobson in a gallant charge," the 13th forced the Confederates to desert their guns. Maj. W.E. Hobson had his horse shot from under him. The 13th lost 8 killed and 41 wounded at Shiloh.

The regiment followed Buell's army to Perryville, but did not engage. It was brigaded with six other regiments and two batteries to defend Munfordville's great railroad bridge. Young Hobson took over the leadership of the regiment, when the elder Hobson was made a brigadier-general. The men marched to east Tennessee and participated in heavy fighting around Knoxville and were particularly valiant at Huff's Ferry. It moved south for the Atlanta campaign and fought at Resaca, Dallas, Cassville, Allatoona, Kennesaw, Jonesboro. It returned to Bowling Green and did guard duty the rest of the war. Gen. Julius White wrote of the regiment:

I have commanded during the war some sixty regiments of infantry, and among them all there was not one better, if as good, as the 13th Ky. Not only was that regiment wholly reliable during an engagement (for they were always as brave as the bravest), but in camp, on the march, on all occasions and everywhere, that regiment could be depended upon for the prompt performance of every duty. The country owes the 13th Ky. a heavy debt of gratitude for its lofty patriotism and unyielding courage and endurance.[2]

26th Kentucky Infantry, Company K

RANK	LAST NAME	FIRST NAME	MI	AGE	RESIDENCE	MISC
Pvt.	Warren	William	S.		Taylor Co., KY	Mustered in Sep.13, 1862 Munfordville; dis Mar 29, 1863 disabled. Bur.Union Sep Bap Ch. Had beeen in Co D, 33rd KY before consolidation

27th Kentucky Infantry, Company C

RANK	LAST NAME	FIRST NAME	MI	AGE	RESIDENCE	MISC
Cpl.	Stayton	Elijah	T.		Taylor Co.	Enr Oct. 12, 1861; dis Mar. 29, 1865 Louisville

27th Kentucky Infantry, Company E

RANK	LAST NAME	FIRST NAME	MI	AGE	RESIDENCE	MISC
Capt.	Robinson	John	R.	38	Campbellsville, KY	Resigned Mar. 6, 1864
1st Lt.	Rice	Benjamin	A.	26	Taylor Co., KY	Resigned Apr. 13, 1862
2nd Lt.	Waggener	Daniel	B.	20	Boyle Co., KY	Promoted to Adj.Jan. 21, 1862 & Resigned
Sgt.	Fisher	Thomas	T.	19	Taylor Co., KY	Promoted to Capt. July 21, 1864
Sgt.	Fisher	John	R.	21	Taylor Co., KY	Promoted to Capt.; killed July 20, 1864 at Atlanta
Sgt.	Culbertson	James		25	Hart Co., KY	Died Hardin Co., KY Dec. 23, 1861
Sgt.	Benningfield	John	S.	29	Taylor Co., KY	Reduced in rank Nov. 6, 1862
Sgt.	Rice	Randolph	W.	29	Adair Co., KY	Absent without leave
Cpl.	Smith	Ben	S.	45	Taylor Co., KY	Discharged June 13, 1862 St.Louis; Surg. Certificate
Cpl.	Poor	Dandridge		21	Hart Co., KY	Dead, place & date unknown
Cpl.	Colvin	William	A.	21	Taylor Co., KY	Reduced in rank Feb. 15, 1863
Cpl.	Harrison	William		19	Taylor Co., KY	Deserted
Cpl.	Jaggers	Hardy	U.	18	Hart Co., KY	Promoted to Sgt. Mar. 2, 1863
Cpl.	Poor	Charles	W.	18	Hart Co., KY	Discharged June 24, 1864 Louisville; Surg. Cert.
Cpl.	Kerr	Robert	L.	26	Taylor Co., KY	Reduced in rank May 14, 1862
Cpl.	Seay	John	S.	29	Hart Co., KY	Discharged Mar. 13, 1863 Woodsonville; Surg. Cert.
Music	Taylor	Charles		31	Taylor Co., KY	Promoted to Sgt.; wounded May 31, 1864
Music	Shively	Alexander		22	Taylor Co., KY	Promoted to 2nd Lt.; resigned May 1, 1862
Wagon	Durham	William	M	45	bur Good Hope	Enr Oct. 12, 1861; dis Mar. 29, 1865 Louisville

Pvt.	Avery	Andrew	J.	29	Taylor Co., KY	Died Mar. 2, 1862 at Grayson Springs/Corinth, MS
Pvt.	Bennett	Samuel	S.	18	Hart Co., KY	Died June 2, 1862 near Corinth, MS
Pvt.	Bennett	William		19	Hart Co., KY	Enr. Oct. 12, 1861; dis Mar. 29, 1865 Louisville
Pvt.	Benningfield	Fleming	S.	19	Taylor Co., KY	Promoted to Cpl. July 1863; disch Mar. 29, 1865 Lou
Pvt.	Boston	Julius	F.	19	Metcalfe Co., KY	Capt. July 15, 1864 near Atl; died in prison Aug. 1864
Pvt.	Bowles	Paul	C.	21	Taylor Co., KY	Enr Oct. 12, 1861; dis Mar. 29, 1865 Lou, bur Palestine
Pvt.	Cassedy	Joseph	S.	18	Metcalfe Co., KY	Enr. Oct. 12, 1861; dis Mar. 29, 1865 Louisville
Sgt.	Douglas	Ben	F.	24	Taylor Co., KY	Enr. Oct. 12, 1861; dis Mar. 29, 1865 Louisville
Pvt.	Durham	James		27	Taylor Co., KY	Enr. Oct. 12, 1861; dis Mar. 29, 1865 Louisville
Pvt.	Eaten	Thomas		45	Metcalfe Co., KY	Deserted Sept. 1862
Pvt.	Elkin	David		45	Larue Co., KY	Enr. Oct. 12, 1861; dis Mar. 29, 1865 Louisville
Pvt.	Estes	Robert	W.	43	Metcalfe Co., KY	Enr. Oct. 12, 1861; dis Mar. 29, 1865 Louisville
Pvt.	Gibson	David		27	Hart Co., KY	Enr. Oct. 12, 1861; dis Mar. 29, 1865 Louisville
Pvt.	Godby	George	W.	23	Casey Co., KY	Died Feb. 7, 1864 Elizabethtown
Pvt.	Green	George		25	Metcalfe Co., KY	Died Sept. 20, 1864 Metcalfe Co.
Pvt.	Green	William		20	Hart Co., KY	Enr. Oct. 12, 1861; dis Mar. 29, 1865 Louisville
Pvt.	Hall	May	M.	35	Metcalfe Co., KY	Promoted to Sgt. Apr. 15, 1862
Pvt.	Hall	W.	J.			Discharged July 15, 1862 Louisville; Surg. Cert.
Pvt.	Hamilton	J.	Z.		Born Taylor Co., KY	Lived in Green Co. after war.
Pvt.	Hodges	Samuel	S.	18	Hardin/Hart Co, KY	Discharged June 5, 1862 Louisville, Surg. Cert.
Pvt.	Horton	James	S/L	24	Green Co., KY	Enr. Oct. 12, 1861; dis Mar. 29, 1865 Louisville
Pvt.	Horton	Oscar	T.	28	Taylor Co., KY	Left sick in Taylor County Dec. 1861; dropped
Pvt.	Horton	William	T.	18	Green Co., KY	Enr. Oct. 12, 1861; dis Mar. 29, 1865 Louisville
Pvt.	Ireland	John		45	Hart Co., KY	Enr. Oct. 12, 1861; ill in hospital 1864
Pvt.	Jones	Andrew	J.	30	Metcalfe Co., KY	Enr. Oct. 12, 1861; dis Mar. 29, 1865 Louisville
Pvt.	Jones	George	W.	18	Hart Co., KY	Died Jan. 1, 1864 Knoxville, TN
Pvt.	Jones	William		45	Hart Co., KY	Enr Oct. 21, 1861; disch Oct. 15 1863 Surg Cert.
Pvt.	Kerr	William	C.	21	Taylor Co., KY	Absent without leave
Cpl.	Kirtley	William	H.	18	Hart Co., KY	Enr. Oct. 21, 1861
Pvt.	Lambert	William		25	Hart Co., KY	Enr. Oct. 21, 1861
Pvt.	Lobb	John	R.	18	Hart Co., KY	Enr. Oct. 21, 1861; dis Mar. 29, 1863 Louisville
Pvt.	Martin	John	J.	21	Metcalfe Co., KY	Absent without leave Jan. 1862
Pvt.	McCubbins	George	T.	20	Green Co., KY	Discharged
Pvt.	McCubbins	James	H.	36	Hart Co., KY	Died Jan. 5, 1863 Louisville
Pvt.	McCubbins	Samuel	B.	28	Hart Co., KY	Reduced rank from Cpl. Nov. 12, 1862
Pvt.	Mears	George	W.	27	Hart Co., KY	Worked on fortifications as penalty for AWOL

Pvt.	Michell	Martin	L.		Taylor Co., KY	Discharged Nov 25, 1862; Surg. Cert.
Pvt.	Middleton	Dudley	R.	26	Hart Co., KY	Died June 15, 1862 Hamburg, TN
Pvt.	Montgomery	Sylvester		30	Adair Co., KY	Discharged
Pvt.	Moore	William	J.	31	Taylor Co., KY	Died Sept 4, 1862 Huntsville, AL
Pvt.	Newcomb	John	G/S	38	Taylor Co., KY	Died Nov. 8, 1862 Louisville
Pvt.	Newcomb	Matt	T.	18	Taylor Co., KY	Died Feb. 9, 1862 Elizabethtown
Pvt.	Overstreet	James		24	Marion Co., KY	Died May 4, 1862 Shiloh
Pvt.	Overstreet	Resin	D.Sr	29	Taylor Co., KY	Promoted to Cpl. Mar. 1, 1864
Pvt.	Overstreet	Resin	D.Jr.	21	Marion Co., KY	Transferred; Hospital steward May 1, 1862
Pvt.	Phillips	Samuel	A.	22	Taylor Co., KY	Discharged 1862 Louisville, Surg. Cert.
Pvt.	Philpot	James	R/K	40	Green Co., KY	Discharged Jan. 25, 1863 Woodsonville; Surg.Cert
Pvt.	Pointer	James	H.	19	Metcalfe Co., KY	Deserted Jan. & died March 4, 1863
Pvt.	Pointer	William		39	Metcalfe Co., KY	Absent sick since Feb. 14, 1864
Pvt.	Prewitt	James	F.	19	Hart Co., KY	Died Dec. 15, 1862 Taylor Co.
Pvt.	Prewitt	Willis		39	Hart Co., KY	Enr Oct. 12, 1861; dis Mar. 29, 1865 Louisville
Pvt.	Puyear	William	L/T	18	Taylor Co., KY	Died July 1862 at Athens, AL
Pvt.	Reynolds	Daniel	T.	29	Hart Co., KY	Enr Oct. 12, 1861; dis Mar. 29, 1865 Louisville
Pvt.	Reynolds	Thomas	F.	29	Hart Co., KY	Enr Oct. 12, 1861; dis Mar. 29, 1865 Louisville
Pvt.	Richeson	James	M.	37	Taylor Co., KY	Died July 1862 Iuka, MS
Pvt.	Sexton	George	W.	21	Metcalfe Co., KY	Enr Oct. 12, 1861; dis Mar. 29, 1865 Louisville
Pvt.	Shipp	James	M.	22	Hart Co., KY	Died June 24, 1862 Corinth, MS
Pvt.	Skaggs	Alfred	S.	29	Hart Co., KY	Died Jan. 29, 1862 Elizabethtown
Pvt.	Skaggs	Bird	W.H.	21	Hart Co., KY	Died July 12, 1862 Louisville
Pvt.	Skaggs	James	V/F	22	Green Co., KY	Enr Oct. 12, 1861; dis Mar. 29, 1865 Louisville
Pvt.	Smith	Albert	G.	32	Taylor Co., KY	Enr Oct. 12, 1861; dis Mar. 29, 1865 Louisville
Pvt.	Smith	David	J.	41	Taylor Co., KY	Enr Oct. 12, 1861; dis Mar. 29, 1865 Louisville
Pvt.	Smith	John	R.	18	Taylor Co., KY	Enr Oct. 12, 1861; dis Mar. 29, 1865 Louisville
Pvt.	Smith	William	W.	27	Hart Co., KY	Died Jan. 14, 1865 Owensboro
Pvt.	Smith	William	H.	28	Taylor Co., KY	Pro. Cpl; capt.in TN; died Dec. 4, 1863 in prison
Pvt.	Sullivan	William	J.	28	Taylor Co., KY	Promoted to Cpl. Mar. 1, 1864
Pvt.	Taylor	Francis	M.	23	Taylor Co., KY	Promoted to Cpl. Mar. 1, 1864
Pvt.	Thorp	Rodolph	C.	18	Hart Co., KY	Discharged Oct. 15, 1862; Surg. Cert.; died Nville
Pvt.	Wallace	Gustavus		45	Metcalfe Co., KY	Deserted
Pvt.	Wetherson/spoon	Thomas	B.	18	Hart Co., KY	Enr Oct. 12, 1861; dis Mar. 29, 1865 Louisville
Pvt.	Wheat	Booker		45	Hart Co., KY	Discharged Oct. 15, 1862; Surg. Cert; Nashville
Pvt.	Wheat	George	W.	20	Hart Co., KY	Absent sick since Feb. 17, 1864
Pvt.	Whitley	John	W.	37	Taylor Co., KY	Died July 20, 1862 Huntsville, AL
Pvt.	Whitman	William		21	Hart Co., KY	Died Jan/July, 1862 Hart Co.
Pvt.	Willian	Robert	D.	19	Hart Co., KY	Promoted to 1st Lt. July 21, 1864
Pvt.	Wright	John, Jr.		45	Taylor Co., KY	Died at Grayson Springs Mar. 28, 1862
Maj.	Carlisle	James		Staff	Taylor Co., KY	Carlisle Cem, Meadow Ck, Nov 24,1836–Feb. 25, 1862

27th Kentucky Infantry

This regiment was organized by Gen. W.H. Ward of Greensburg, assisted by his son—Lt. Col. John H. Ward and Maj. James Carlisle, and had only nine companies, with Company E chiefly composed of Taylor County men. The regiment spent the winter of 1861–1862 around Leitchfield and arrived at Shiloh after the battle and assisted in removing the dead. From there they marched to Iuka and Rienzi, MS, then to AL and back to Kentucky with Gen. Crittenden's force to Perryville, but only engaged in skirmishing as the main battle was to their left. They marched to Gallatin and then to Stones River and back to Munfordville. In September 1863, the troops were mounted and joined Burnside in TN, with Col. John Ward commanding the regiment. They were in heavy fighting around Knoxville. From there the 27th went to Cumberland Gap to Mt. Sterling and back to GA for fierce battles around Atlanta.[3]

34th Kentucky Infantry, Company G

RANK	LAST NAME	FIRST NAME	MI	AGE	RESIDENCE	MISC
Pvt.	Carlile	Nathan	W.		Bur. Good Hope Cem	Enr 1st in July 2, 1862 in Co L, 5th KY Cav; dis May 31, 1865. Tombstone says Co G, 34th KY Inf.

37th Kentucky Vol. Mtd. Infantry, Company E

RANK	LAST NAME	FIRST NAME	MI	AGE	RESIDENCE	MISC
Pvt.	Graham	Green	B.		Taylor Co., KY	Mustered in June 26, 1863; out Dec. 29, 1864; bur Good Hope
Pvt.	Helton	Thomas			Taylor Co., KY	Mustered out Dec. 29, 1864;buried Zion Sep. Bapt.Church
Pvt.	Nelson	James			Taylor Co., KY	Mustered out Dec. 29, 1864;buried Nelson Cem.; 1845–1921
Pvt.	Perkins	John			Taylor Co., KY	Mustered in Aug. 20, 1863; out Dec. 29, 1864; bur Pop Grove
Cpl.	Read	James	H.		Taylor Co., KY	Mustered out Dec. 29, 1864;buried Brookside Cem; 1849–1926
Pvt.	Sanders	H.	E.	39	Taylor Co., KY	
Pvt.	Sanders	Robert	B.		Taylor Co., KY	Mustered out Dec. 29, 1864; buried Sanders Cem.

37th Kentucky Vol. Mtd Infantry, Company K

RANK	LAST NAME	FIRST NAME	MI	AGE	RESIDENCE	MISC
Sgt.	Ratliff	Reubin		45	Taylor Co., KY	
Sgt.	Shumake	Asa		22	Campbellsville, KY	
Pvt.	Clark	James E.			Taylor Co., KY	On detached service; not in 37th list in Adj Gen Rept
Pvt.	Dabney	Calvin		31	Taylor Co., KY	On detached service; transf to 4th KY Inf
Pvt.	Dabney	William		35	Taylor Co., KY	On detached service; transf to 4th KY Inf
Pvt.	Edwards	George	W.	18	Taylor Co., KY	5'4 bro eyes; drk hair; carder; enr Leb May 23, 1863; buried Saloma

Pvt.	Farmer	John		Campbellsville, KY	5'6" blu eyes; lt hair; farmer; transf to 4th KY Inf
Pvt.	Fields	Alexander A.	22	Taylor Co., KY	Died at Glasgow, Mar. 8, 1864
Pvt.	Hicks	Jesse	20	Taylor Co., KY	Mustered out Louisville Feb. 1, 1865
Pvt.	Hicks	John	22	Taylor Co., KY	Mustered out Louisville Feb. 1, 1865
Pvt.	Meers	Hamilton	]19	Taylor Co., KY	Transf to 4th KY Inf
Pvt.	Spratt	Charles W.	36	Taylor Co., KY	Mustered out Louisville Feb. 1, 1865

37th Kentucky Mounted Infantry

Both Company E and K were mustered in Glasgow, Company E in October and Company K in December of 1863. Charles S. Hanson commanded the regiment until he was severely wounded in the Battle of Saltville, VA. This regiment was engaged in the battles of Glasgow, KY, Jackson County, TN, Saltville, VA, and Mt. Sterling, KY.

55th Kentucky Vol. Mtd. Infantry, Company E

RANK	LAST NAME	FIRST NAME	MI	AGE	RESIDENCE	MISC
Pvt.	Harmon	John			Taylor Co., KY	Enr Nov. 18, 1864; dis Sep. 19, 1865 Louisville 5'8", blue eyes, light hair, farmer, age 18

Provo Guard Louisville

RANK	LAST NAME	FIRST NAME	MI	AGE	RESIDENCE	MISC
Pvt.	Wayland	D.	R.		Taylor Co., KY	Mustered in Oct 19, 1861 Lou; dis Aug. 26, 1862 On stone says in Co D 34th KY Inf, but not in co. in Adj. Gen. Rept. Bur. Brookside Sec A.

Hall's Gap Battalion, Company B

RANK	LAST NAME	FIRST NAME	MI	AGE	RESIDENCE	MISC
Pvt.	Boution	Marion			Bur Robinson Ck Cem	Enr Mar 14, 1865 Stanford; dis July 27, 1865 Merrimac

Kentucky Light Artillery, 1st Regiment

RANK	LAST NAME	FIRST NAME	MI	AGE	RESIDENCE	MISC
Cpl.	Loy	Eli			Liberty Bapt Ch Cem	Enr Jan. 1, 1864 Chattanooga; dis Nov. 15, 1865 Louisville (1835–1917)

1st Kentucky Light Artillery, Battery B

RANK	LAST NAME	FIRST NAME	MI	AGE	RESIDENCE	MISC
Cpl.	Sublett	John	Green		Taylor Co., KY	Enr Sep. 17, 1861; mustered in at Camp Dick Robinson; out Nov. 16, 1864 Louisville; buried Liberty Cem, Columbia Road.

12th Ohio Infantry, Company K

RANK	LAST NAME	FIRST NAME	MI	AGE	RESIDENCE	MISC
1st Lt.	Wise	John			Campbellsville, KY after the war	Enr Nov. 8, 1861; dis Sep. 30, 1862 5'11" tall, black hair, brown eyes; duty at Flat Top Mt, WVA. On force march became ill & discharged. Occ: Express agent. Died Mar. 12, 1900; bur Hiestand-Chandler Cem

69th Ohio Infantry, Company B

RANK	LAST NAME	FIRST NAME	MI	AGE	RESIDENCE	MISC
Pvt.	Harloff	George				Bur. Saloma Cemetery

110th Ohio Infantry, Company A

RANK	LAST NAME	FIRST NAME	MI	AGE	RESIDENCE	MISC
Sgt.	Lindley	Jeremiah A.			Campbellsville, KY	wounded at So. Mountain, bullet remained lodged after the war in shoulder until death; witnessed Lee's surrender buried in Hiestand-Chandler Cemetery.

126th Ohio Infantry, Company H

RANK	LAST NAME	FIRST NAME	MI	AGE	RESIDENCE	MISC
Pvt.	Prescott	Henry			Taylor Co., KY	Bur. Liberty Cem, Columbia Road.

Squirrel Hunters Regiment of Ohio

James I. Gilmore, honorably discharged by Gov. Tod, Sept 1862; bur Hiestand Cem.

U.S. Colored Troops

Campbell, Button, was a teamster

King, George, indexed on page 028 of Adj. Gen. Report, II, Co A, 107th US Col Inf, but name not on page, buried in Pleasant Union Cemetery.

Lively, Jeff, ancestor of Georgia Scott. He ran away from his master and joined the Federal Army. He took his pension from the army and bought land where she lives on Drake Street and the land out on Broadway.[4]

Mayes, George, died Nov 7, 1930, buried in Miller Cemetery.[5]

Peterson, Henry, Pvt., Co. A, 108th U.S.C.Inf., enrolled Aug. 17, 1864, Louisville; buried in Pleasant Union Baptist Church Cemetery.

Turner, Matt, listed in Co. I, 5th U.S. Cld. Cav. on tombstone, buried at Pleasant Union Baptist Church Cemetery.

Thurman, Frank, Co. F, 107th U.S.C. Inf., enrolled July 14, 1864 in Lebanon, KY; farrier for the Union army; married Lou and they lived in a log house, formerly a slave house, on the Will Henry Cowherd farm. Lou would say, "I put the first clothes on your daddy, Henry Colby, [born 1872], and I put the first clothes on you, Bob Henry." Thurman is buried in Pleasant Union Cemetery.[6]

Williams, William A. Buried in Jones-Taylor Cemetery (1848–1941).

Home Guards

Because the returning Rebels from the war were banding together to kill Home Guards, the 100th Regiment of the Kentucky Militia had difficulty keeping officers. **Col. W.H. Ratcliffe** resigned on December 8, 1863, because he had moved his business to Louisville; **Lt. Col. L. McClellan** declined promotion and resigned three days later. **R.E. Jeter** became Colonel February 7, 1864 because Ratcliffe and McClellan resigned. **Frank M.Chandler** then became Lt.Colonel on March 8, 1864.[7]

Small Bits and Pieces:

Capt. Champness D. Butler, 13th Ky. Inf, was killed in action June 27, 1864. Left widow, Sallie, and brothers, Oliver and Thomas P., according to Governor Bramlette Papers, Box 19, f 413, d133, KDLA.

Capt. Thomas T. Fisher, 27th Ky. Inf. When he and Captain Robinson would get together, they would have heated discussions about the way things happened in the war. He was the father of Stella Fisher.[8]

James B. Morris, 13th Ky. Inf, was discharged from the Union army. His grandson, James "Jimmy" Morris, was discharged from the US army following WWII exactly 100 years later.[9]

Pvt. Henry Oaks, near Mac, fought at Lookout Mountain.

Thomas J. Nelson lost an arm in the Civil War and was exempt from the county levy May 7, 1866, according to Taylor Co Order Bk 2, 417.

Pvt. Cyrus Parrott, 13th Ky. Inf. According to author's interview with Fred Parrott, July 29, 1976, Fred said his grandfather remembered eating sorghum molasses rations, eating off land, being thirsty, running out of anything to eat.

Capt. John R. Robinson, 27th Ky. Inf. When Henry Robinson was four years old, his mother put him behind her on a horse and they rode to Munfordville to see Captain Robinson. After the war he opened the Taylor Academy at Lebanon Avenue which operated from 1886–1891. [old Dr. M.M. Hall property, Paul Moore in 2004.] His white frame home sat on 520 Central Avenue where the Baptist Church is located. It is said that, after the war, he had a high fence around his yard and would not go out at night for fear of retribution from some of his enemies. Robinson Avenue is named for him. An attorney, Robinson's portrait hung behind the judge's bench in the 1867–1965 courthouse. A large land-owner, most of his holdings were located between Campbellsville and Spurlington. He was the father of Henry S. Robinson, an attorney, and Bettie Robinson, a teacher at RCA and BCI.[10]

Pvt. William S. Warren, 26th Ky. Inf, was shot and crippled by Capt. W. S. Edwards' men in the fall of 1862. By March of 1864, he was an asst. wagon master under Gen. W. T. Ward, according to AG, I, 230.

Confederate Soldiers:

Adair, A. Monroe, Co. D, 6th Inf, Orphan Brigade; 2nd Lt. Nov. 19, 1861. Fought at Shiloh, resigned May 2, 1862. Died at Col. John A. Adair's, Canmer, KY, March 22, 1892. He was a brother to the wife of Union Gen. E.H. Hobson and served as county attorney for Taylor County.

Allen, Joel P., Co. B, Waller's Brigade. Buried Griffin Cemetery, Ebenezer Road, (1838–1932).

Bell, James "Jim", Co. D, 6th Inf, Orphan Brigade. He came to Will Henry Cowherd to go fight in the Rebel army and Will Henry gave him a horse. He enlisted October 15, 1861, in Col. J. H. Lewis' Regiment at Cave City. Fought at Rocky Face Ridge, Resaca, Dallas, Peachtree Creek, and was wounded on July 22, 1864 at Intrenchment Creek near Atlanta. After the war, he was paroled at Washington, GA, and walked home. He returned with a silver dime, a bandana handkerchief, a hickory cane, and a pocketful of worthless Confederate money. He worked for Cowherd and then bought the old Thurman farm on Taylor-Green line from Cowherd, and became a successful farmer. When he applied for a pension, he stated that he suffered from chronic rheumatism in left arm and shoulder and could no longer work. He is buried on top of a hill in the Cowherd Cemetery (1840–1917) on the Bob Henry Cowherd farm, now the Dr. Colby Cowherd farm, in the Bengal community.[11] Tombstone says born 1840; deposition of the pension says May 17, 1839. Bell Pension application 3435, Roll No 993923.

Bailey, Wilson, Co. C, 7th Ky. Cav.

Barlow, Thomas B., Co. F, 4th Inf, Orphan Brigade. Fought at Shiloh, Vicksburg, and Stones River where he was captured, but exchanged; fought at Chickamauga where he was killed Sept. 20, 1863.

Chapell, Martin C.

Collins, John L., Co. C, 7th Cav, Morgan's Men, buried Collins Cemetery (1843–1920), old Woody Mitchell farm, Lebanon Road.

Collins, Richard S., Co. C, 7th Cav, Morgan's Men, buried Richerson Family Cemetery (1845–1920), old J.D. Warren farm, now off Northern Bypass.

Cowherd, Theodore, Co. F, 4th Inf, Orphan Brigade. Fought at Shiloh, Baton Rouge, Stones River, Jackson, Chickamauga, Missionary Ridge, Rocky Face Gap, Resaca, Dallas, Peachtree, Intrenchment, and Utoy Creeks. He was severely wounded at Shiloh, slightly at Resaca, and lost right arm July 22, 1864 at Intrenchment Creek. Buried in Cave Hill Cemetery (1844–1920), Louisville.

Cowherd, Thomas, son of James Cowherd.

Cox, Charles T., Co. C, 7th Cav, Morgan's Men, wounded and captured at Shiloh; became Taylor County Court Clerk; buried Brookside Cemetery (1837–1913), left widow, Mattie Jeter Cox.

Cox, Frederick C., Co. C, 7th Cav, Morgan's Men, buried Mt. Zion Cemetery (1853–1927), Acton Community.

Croudus, John P., Co. F, 4th Inf, Orphan Brigade. Was discharged on disability because of disease, April 1862.

Durham, J.E., Co. C, 7th Ky. Cav, Morgan's Men, buried Brookside Cemetery (1839–1905).

Durham, Robert P., Co. F, 4th Inf, Orphan Brigade, Cpl. Fought at Shiloh; was discharged on disability because of disease, July 1862.

Durham, William F., Co. F, 4th Inf, Orphan Brigade, deserted at Corinth.

Ferguson, F. Columbus.

Gaines, John P., Co. C, 7th Ky. Cav, aged 19 when killed by bushwhackers at Breeding; Oct. 22, 1862. His father took a wagon to bring him home. Bur. Gaines Cemetery on Meadow Creek.

Haselwood, William H., born 1841, Co D, 6th Inf, surrendered at Washington, Ga., was with Bell. Address Coakley, Ky. buried Brookside.

Hall, Ambrose J., Co. F, 4th Inf, Orphan Brigade; prom to 3rd Sgt. Sept 11, 1864. Fought at Shiloh, Vicksburg, Chickamauga, Missionary Ridge, Rocky Face Gap, Resaca, Dallas, Peachtree, Intrenchment, and Utoy creeks; at Jonesboro, he was wounded Sept. 1, 1864. Bur. Vance Cem, Green Co. (1840–1916).

Hill, Armstrong, buried Peterson Family Cemetery (1835–1901).

Johnson, C.H., Co. F, 4th Inf, Orphan Brigade. Wounded at Stones River; died of disease at Beech Grove May 3, 1863.

Johnson, Jesse, Co. F, 4th Inf, Orphan Brigade. Fought at Baton Rouge; left 2nd wife, widow Synthia Gaddie Johnson. Bur. Brookside Cem.

Johnston, Charles Henry, Co. F, 4th Inf, Orphan Brigade. Wounded at Murfreesboro. Died at Beech Grove, TN May 3, 1863.

Johnston, George E., Co. F, 4th Inf, Orphan Brigade; prom. Sgt. Apr. 1, 1863. Fought at Stones River, Jackson, Chickamauga, Missionary Ridge, Rocky Face Gap, Resaca, Dallas, Peachtree, Intrenchment and Utoy Creeks, and Jonesboro. Before the war, he was deputy sheriff and after the war sheriff in the 1870s. Bur. Floydsburg Cem, Crestview, KY.

Latimer, William D., Co. F, 4th Inf, Orphan Brigade. Wounded at Shiloh, died of disease at Grenada, MS Sept. 10, 1862.

Ledbetter, James M., mustered in Capt. David Hutcheson's Co. D in spring of

1862, O.P. Hamilton's Battalion, then transferred to Col. Dick Morgan's 14th Ky. Cav., Gen. Morgan's Men, was captured at Greeneville, TN; taken from the prison near Knoxville to a prison in Chattanooga, to Nashville, then back to Atlanta for exchange. When the Yankees came, the barracks were cleared, and he was put on train whose engine got off the track; he escaped and stayed with a Rebel friend, waiting to join another Confederate force. Born in Overton Co., TN, but lived at Hatcher in Taylor Co. after the war; buried in Liberty Cem, Columbia Road (1836–1916). Pension application no. 3447.

Marshall, Brady, son of Robert Marshall.

Marshall, T. Frank, son of Col. Billy Marshall, bur. Marshall Cemetery, (1836–1918).

Marshall, Samuel E., Co. F, 4th Inf, Orphan Brigade. Fought at Baton Rouge, ill health kept him out of ranks, continued at teamster. Bur in Oak Hill Cem, Whitewright, TX (1838–1911).

Millsap, left wife Martha.

Parsons, Robert C. buried Parsons Family Cemetery.

Pettus, Thomas T., Co. F, 4th Inf, Orphan Brigade. Died of disease at Burnsville, MS Apr. 10, 1862.

Pettus, William F., Co. F, 4th Inf, Orphan Brigade; prom. Cpl. Dec. 17, 1862. Fought at Stones River, Jackson, Chickamauga, Missionary Ridge, Rocky Face Gap, Resaca, Dallas, Peachtree and Intrenchment Creeks. Mortually wounded at Utoy Creek Aug. 6, 1864.

Scott, John B., Co. F, 4th Regt, Orphan Brigade. Fought at Shiloh where wounded and captured; exchanged; fought at Stones River, Jackson, Chickamauga, Missionary Ridge, Rocky Face Gap, and Resaca where he was severely wounded May 14, 1864. Died May 17, 1864. Bur in Oakland Cem, Atlanta.

Skaggs, Benjamin O., Co. I, 2nd Ark Inf. Buried Poplar Grove Cemetery, off 210 (1833–1914).

Smith, Daniel Lunksford, Co. F, 4th Inf, Orphan Brigade. Wounded at the battle of Shiloh, Apr. 6, 1862. Born 1841, Summersville, KY. His coat and discharge were donated to the Hiestand House Museum.

Smith, Frank M., Co. E, 6th Ky. Cav, ruddy complexion, brown hair, grey eyes, 5'10" tall, captured Buffington Island, O July 19, 1863; sent to Camp Chase, then to Ft Delaware.

Smith, Holman H., Co. D, 6th Regt., Orphan Brigade, Cpl. Fought at Baton Rouge, Stones River, Jackson, Rocky Face Ridge, Resaca, Dallas, and creeks around Atlanta; wounded at Jonesboro Sept 1, 1864. Born 1845, Summersville, KY.

Smith, R.H., Dr., Co. B, 2nd Ky. Inf. Buried Saloma Cemetery (1838–1904).

Thompson, A.H., Co. F, 4th Inf, Orphan Brigade; prom to Cpl. Dec. 19, 1862.

Fought at Shiloh, Vicksburg, Stones River, Jackson, and Chickamauga where he was killed Sept. 20, 1863.

Webster, Richard Archibald, Co. C, 7th Cav, 2nd Lt, Morgan's Men, buried Brookside Cemetery (1826–1911);also listed in Co E, 6th Ky. Cav.

After the war, he and his wife lived at the end of Main St.; when there was a fire, he would stand at the corner of Main and Columbia and shoot off a pistol to alert the townspeople.[13]

Willock, Hartwell T., Co. F, 4th Inf, Orphan Brigade. Fought at Shiloh, Vicksburg, Stones River, Jackson, Chickamauga, Missionary Ridge, Rocky Face Gap, and Resaca where he was wounded May 14, 1864.

Williams, James, Co. A, 5th Inf., buried Brookside Cem. (1838–1912).

Williams, J.H., may be same as above, left widow Sallie Blakey Williams.

Confederate Veterans from Taylor and Green Counties taken at the June 1905 Louisville Reunion.
Row I: Dr. Benjamin Scott, George E. Johnston, Theodore Cowherd, unknown.
Row II: James Bell, unknown, A.J. Hall, Holman H. Smith, possibly Daniel Lunksford Smith.

Appendices

Appendix A

Taylor County Statistics (1860–1865)

ITEM	1860	1861	1862	1863	1864	1865
White males over 21	1,224	1,261	1,259	1,231	1,254	1,207
Total slaves over 16	715	759	753	798	788	634
Total children 6 to 18	1,792	1,845	1,922	1,895	1,921	2,008
Total studs, jacks, bulls	34	26	16	12	6	9
Total tavern licenses	5	4	3	3	1	1
Free whites, blind						
Free whites, deaf and dumb	3	3	3	1	1	2
Total hogs	8,786	4,378	8,574	10,610	6,680	3,541
Pounds tobacco	1,254,765	535,850	498,239	907,403	1,400,905	983,546
Pounds of hemp	362		919			
Tons of hay	339	730	717	946	534	402
Bushels of corn	396,665	221,640	411,081	288,428	209,150	154,905
Bushels of wheat	22,354	14,006	39,408	26,989	22,533	16,253
Bushels of barley						
Enrolled Militia		496	934	898	908	790
Free Negroes	129	21	103	120	100	91
Total number of slaves	1,597	1,654	1,656	1,716	1,705	1,472
Value of all slaves	$758,090	$651,825	$494,626	$500,955	$394,845	$122,425
Number of town lots	109	106	117	96	115	108
Value of town lots	$39,217	$41,480	$40,610	$37,895	$40,640	$38,285

Value of carriages	$8,100	$8,735	$5,618	$5,390	$5,195	$3,970
Number of stores	17	14	12	13	14	11
Number of slaveowners	288				326	
Number of cattle	5,751	5,361	5,171	5,147	4,535	3,744
Number of horses and mares	2,646	1,743	2,745	2,492	2,504	2,227
Number of mules	301	340	442	364	246	187

Note from author: In 1860, the free Black and slave owner statistics were left blank by the reporter. The author added the number of free Blacks and slave owners from the 1860 Census. It appears that only an estimate of free Blacks was made for the following years.
Sources: Annual Reports, *Auditor of Public Accounts of the State of Kentucky*, Frankfort, Ky. and 1860 Slave Census.

APPENDIX B

Election Returns, U.S. House of Representatives 1861, 1863

Taylor County was in the Fourth Congressional District during the Civil War. Between 1861 and 1863 the makeup of the district changed dramatically. This is the first and last time Taylor County had a native, Aaron Harding, elected to either house of the U.S. Congress.

JUNE 20, 1861	AARON HARDING, UNION	A.G.TALBOTT, STATES RIGHTS
Cumberland	782	82
Clinton	554	49
Wayne	772	393
Russell	709	103
Pulaski	1847	516
Lincoln	1020	295
Boyle	772	313
Taylor	852	91
Green	812	323
Adair	1065	272
Casey	1154	32
TOTALS	10,339	2,469

AUGUST 3, 1863	AARON HARDING, UNION	WILLIAM J. HEADY
Meade	317	192
Adair	1006	13
Hardin	1059	605
Bullitt	455	165
Larue	885	137
Marion	1105	141

Washington	1090	119
Nelson	441	202
Spencer	216	382
Taylor	794	15
Green	824	29
Shelby	816	433
Anderson	431	67
Casey	996	8
TOTALS	10,435	2,508

Source: G. Glenn Clift, *Kentucky Votes, 1792–1894*, unpublished manuscript, 93, 94, 102, Special Collections and Archives, Kentucky Historical Society

APPENDIX C

Soldiers Listed as Dying of Disease in Campbellsville, Taylor County, Green River Bridge, and Camp Ward, late fall 1861–early 1862

Nm = Were enrolled, but never mustered in; cause of illness, age, and home town are listed, when stated. Occasionally a soldier's record will categorize him as "deserted" when, in reality, he is in a military hospital, sent home ill, or detached for another duty.

4th Ky Infantry

Pvt. Thos. B Thoroughman	Oct. 31, 1861
Pvt. Henry C. Means	Feb. 9, 1862

10th Ky Infantry

Pvt. Marion A. Slayton	Jan. 3, 1862
Pvt. John H. Feather	Apr. 17, 1862
Pvt. William T. Cabell	Aug. 28, 1862
Pvt. Samuel Shively	Mar. 10, 1862
Pvt. Johnson Smith	Mar. 10, 1862
Pvt. Jesse M. Ceaver	Jan. 8, 1862
Pvt. John Peters	Jan. 8, 1862

13th Ky Infantry

Sgt. Samuel M. Lile	Feb. 13, 1862, typhoid
2Lt. Holland Jones	Dec. 15, 1861, nm, typhoid*
Pvt. Geo. R. Erwin	Feb. 14, 1862, typhoid
Pvt. Mansfield Erwin	Feb. 13, 1862
Pvt. Robert Erwin	Feb. 14, 1862
Pvt. Berry Holt	Jan. 2, 1862
Pvt. Wm. P. Romine	Mar. 20, 1862
Cpl. Jesse G. Leftwich	Dec. 7, 1861
Pvt. Charles W. Davis	Nov. 26, 1861
Pvt. James S. Kelly	Dec. 21, 1861
Pvt. Charles R. Oldham	Dec. 13, 1861
Pvt. Ellis Wigginton	Nov. 22, 1861, age 18, Alabama

Pvt. James T. Wilson	Dec. 15, 1861
Pvt. William DeWitt	Jan. 1, 1862
Pvt. Thomas R. Morris	Jan. 1, 1862
Pvt. Geo. W. Morris	Dec. 1, 1862
Pvt. Edward L. Eckel	Jan. 1862
Pvt. Oliver P. Epperson	Jan. 2, 1862
Pvt. William G. Workman	Jan. 27, 1862, measl, 21, GrCo
Pvt. Geo.E. Golden	Jan. 1, 1862
Pvt. Wm. M. Nance	Jan. 1862
Pvt. Price E. Cook	Dec. 31, 1861,18, Campbellsburg
Pvt. Francis M. Head	Dec. 31, 1861
Pvt. Francis Stone	Dec. 31, 1861, 18, LaGrange
Pvt. Michael Suttles	Jan. 1, 1862, 19, Oldham Co
Pvt. John Hicks	Dec. 1, 1863 nm
Pvt. John I. Pedigo	Nov. 16, 1861 nm
Pvt. Madison Wade	Dec. 1, 1861 nm
Pvt. Thos. J. Huffmary	Dec. 19, 1861 nm
Pvt. Walter H. Word	Dec. 18, 1861 nm, 18, Metc Co.
Pvt. James Witty	Dec. 18, 1861 nm, 18, Metc Co
Pvt. Ishbrow Slinker	Jan. 1862, 32, Green Co
Pvt. Richard W. Hudgen	Feb. 13, 1862, typhoid
Pvt. Samuel Wright	July 4, 1862
Pvt. Isham Slinker	Jan. 1862, 22, Green Co
Pvt. Tully A. Slinker	Jan. 28, 1862, 31, Green Co.
Pvt. Joel Epperson	Jan. 17, 1863
Pvt. William A. Hazle	Jan. 1862

Greensburg also reported many deaths in 13th Ky Infantry.

*Jones is listed on a Casualty Sheet with two death dates, Dec. 15, 1861 and Dec. 27, 1861. Died at Camp Andy Johnson, Ky.

21st Ky Infantry

Capt.William C. Edwards	Co H "Beginning of war" *
Cpl. Joseph P. Lane	Feb 15, 1862 of measles
Pvt. Coleman P. Hedgepeth	Jan 9, 1862 of measles
Cpl. Henry C. Read	Jan 19, 1862
Cpl. John G. Patten	Jan 20, 1862
Pvt. Morris H. Griffin	Jan 25, 1862
Pvt. John H. Spikman	Feb 14, 1862, consumption
Pvt. Wm T. Jones	Dec 30, 1861 nm, measles

*Capt. Wm. C. Edwards raised a company. His brother, Cyrus, described his brother's fate in the book, *Cyrus Edwards Stories of Early Days,* 331–332:

> He was at Campbellsville in camp, where many were in training, when typhoid fever became epidemic. My father went up to see him and reported him very sick; I went the next day, reaching there in the late afternoon, and William died that night.

> I had to leave in the night to come home and tell the family, arrange about the grave, and get someone to go back with me for the body. I went back to Campbellsville in a few hours and returned for the burial, all the time fearful that the Southern soldiers near our home might not let us through. I had made two trips each way—a long journey then—in three days, and had brought my brother's remains safely home for burial, and I wasn't yet sixteen years old."

Cyrus kept his brother's portrait on the wall near his bed. He said about William: "I have seen and been intimate with many well educated men in my day, but he was by far the best educated man . . . that I ever knew."

27th Ky Infantry

Pvt. Junius C. Bryant	Dec 16, 1861 nm
Pvt. John Ross	Oct 18, 1861 nm

Several in Co C were sent home sick from Campbellsville and never mustered in. Many of the 27th died in Columbia of measles and typhoid fever.

3rd Ky Infantry

About thirty died in Columbia of typhoid fever or measles.

9th Ky Infantry

Many died in Columbia of measles and pneumonia Dec–Feb 1862.

Sources: Kentucky Adjutant General's Report and Muster Rolls of selected regiments.

APPENDIX D

Casualties of the 13th Kentucky Infantry at the Battle of Shiloh/Pittsburg Landing, Tennessee

On February 14, 1862, the regiment left Greensburg to go south. After marching 300 miles, it arrived at Pittsburg Landing, Tennessee to see action the first day in the Battle of Shiloh. The hard-fought battle lasted two days, April 7–8, 1862. Some died after the battle, having laid in the mud and rain, surrounded by dead men and horses, without tents for more than a week.

Company A, organized at Greensburg, mustered in at Camp Hobson-Green River Bridge, Dec. 30, 1861.

Pvt. Henry Moran, killed April 7, 1862

Company D, organized at Campbellsville, Nov. 14, 1861, mustered into service Dec.

30, 1861, at Camp Hobson-Green River Bridge.
Pvt. John R. Keltner, slightly wounded
Pvt. James O. Peers, died on battlefield Apr. 24, 1862
Pvt. Bartemus Bragg, died at Camp Shiloh May 2, 1862
Cpl. James R. Nichols, wounded
Pvt. John F. Dulin, killed in battle, Apr. 7, 1862
Pvt. James Spencer, killed in battle, Apr. 7, 1862
Pvt. Hiram Newberry, mortally wounded and died, Apr. 23, 1862.
Pvt. Thomas Y. Nichols, wounded Apr. 7, 1862
Pvt. Amos Eskew, wounded Apr. 7, 1862

Company E, organized at Campbellsville, Nov. 12, 1861, mustered into service Dec. 31, 1861, at Camp Hobson-Green River Bridge
Pvt. R. T. Chapman, wounded Apr. 7, 1862
Pvt. R. B. Holland, wounded Apr. 7, 1862
Pvt. Alfred W. Gaddie, died on field, Apr. 28, 1862
Pvt. James W. Morgan, mortally wounded, died Apr. 14, 1862
Pvt. Peter W. Strader, died on field Apr. 11, 1862

Company F, organized at Campbellsville, Fall 1861, mustered into service Dec. 30, 1861, at Camp Hobson-Green River Bridge.
Pvt. Ezekiah Graham, died Apr. 7, 1862
Pvt. William R. Parrott, died Apr. 7, 1862
Pvt. Benjamin F. Dye, died of wounds, Apr. 27, 1862

Company G, organized Fall 1861, mustered into service Dec. 31, 1861, at Camp Hobson-Green River Bridge
2Lt. Thomas A. Low, killed Apr. 7, 1862
Cpl. Hugh B. Moore, killed Apr. 7, 1862

APPENDIX E

Col. Orlando H. Moore's Report to Lt.Col. Geo B. Drake, Asst. Adjt. General, Lexington, Ky.

HEADQUARTERS 25TH MICHIGAN INFANTRY,
Battle-Field Of Tebb's Bend, Green River, Ky.
July 4th, 1863.

COLONEL: I have the honor to report that I have had a fight with the Rebel General, John Morgan.

I did not move my command from where it was encamped, on the north side of the river, until Morgan's advance had entered Columbia. I then moved forward to occupy the ground I had previously selected, and had the night before prepared for the fight, which was one and a half miles in advance, on the Columbia road, south side of the river. I did not at any time occupy the stockade, which was far in my rear, but gave battle on the narrows entering the bend.

I engaged the enemy's force this morning at 3 o'clock; early in the engagement he opened on our breastworks with a battery, and after firing a shot, disabling two of my men, he sent a flag of truce with the following dispatch:

> HEADQUARTERS MORGAN'S DIVISION,
> IN FIELD IN FRONT GREEN RIVER STOCKADE,
> JULY 4th, 1863.
>
> To the Officer Commanding the Federal Forces at Stockade near Green River Bridge, Ky.,
>
> SIR: In the name of the Confederate States government, I demand an immediate and unconditional surrender of the entire force under your command, together with the stockade.
>
> I am, very respectfully, sir,
> JOHN H. MORGAN,
> Commanding Division Cavalry, C.S.A.

I sent a reply to Gen. John Morgan that the Fourth day of July was no day for me to entertain such a proposition. After receiving the reply, he opened fire with his artillery and musketry. My force, which occupied the open field, were withdrawn to the woods where they engaged the enemy with a determination not to be defeated. The battle raged for three and a half (3½) hours when the enemy retreated with a loss of over fifty (50) killed and two hundred (200) wounded. Among the killed were Colonel Chenault, Major Brent, another major and five (5) captains, and six (6) lieutenants, as near as can be estimated.

The conflict was fierce and bloody. At times the enemy occupied one side of the fallen timber, while my men held the other, in almost a hand to hand fight. The enemy's force consisted of the greater part of Morgan's division. My force was a fraction of my regiment, consisting of two hundred (200) men, who fought gallantly. I cannot say too much in their praise.

Our loss was six (6) killed and twenty-three (23) wounded.

After the battle, I received, under a flag of truce, a dispatch asking permission to bury their dead, which request I granted, proposing to deliver them in front of our lines.

The detachment of forty men, under command of Lieut. M.A. Hogan, 8th Michigan Infantry, held the river at the ford, near the bridge, and repulsed a cavalry charge made by the enemy in a very creditable and gallant manner.

The gallantry of my officers and men in the action was such that I cannot individualize; they all did their duty nobly, and the wounded were treated with the greatest care and attention by Asst. Surgeon J.N. Gregg of my regiment, whose fine abilities as a surgeon are highly appreciated.

I am, Colonel, very respectfully,
Your obedient servant,
ORLANDO H. MOORE
Colonel 25th Mich. Inf.

Author's note: When the records were being compiled in the 1870s, officers were given the opportunity to read their reports before they were placed in the *Official Records of the War of the Rebellion*. Colonel Moore circled the next to last paragraph concerning M.A. Hogan and wrote in the margin "This is inaccurate."

Source: Original copy, *National Archives*, copy in Atkinson-Griffin House Museum, Green River Lake Park

APPENDIX F

Union Dead, Wounded, and Captured at the Battle of Tebbs Bend

25TH MICHIGAN INFANTRY (USA), recruited from southwest Michigan

<u>Company D:</u>

Killed

3rd Cpl. Roswell Beebe, Marcellus. Enlisted in Co. D, as Cpl., Aug. 11, 1862 at Lockport, for 3 years, age 25. Mustered Sept. 11, 1862. Killed in action at Tebbs Bend, Ky., July 4, 1863. Born Kalamazoo, Mich. Farmer; blue eyes, light hair, 5'11". Buried National Cemetery, Lebanon, Ky., Grave No. 311. Left wife Catherine

Poorman, Albert R. b. May 8, 1861 & Amanda J. b. Apr. 7, 1863. Bro. Gideon.

Pvt. Southard Perrin, Park. Enlisted in Co. D, Aug. 8, 1862 at Lockport, for 3 years, age 20. Mustered Sept. 11, 1862. Killed in action at Tebbs Bend, Ky., July 4, 1863. Born Sherman, Mich. Farmer; black hair, black eyes, 5'9" tall. Buried National Cemetery, Lebanon.

6th Cpl. Morgan Wallace, Leonidas. Enlisted in Co. D, Aug. 11, 1862, at Colon, for 3 years, age 27. Mustered Sept.11, 1862. Cpl. May 1, 1863. Killed in action at Tebbs Bend, Ky., July 4, 1863. Buried in National Cemetery, Lebanon, Ky., Grave No. 313. Born Onondaga, NY. Farmer; blue eyes, light hair, 5'10" tall.

Wounded

Pvt. Bruce Beebe, Marcellus. Enlisted in Co. D, Aug. 11, 1862 at Lockport, for 3 years, age 21. Mustered Sept. 11, 1862. Wounded in action at Tebbs Bend, Ky., July 4, 1863. Cpl. June 1, 1863. Mustered out at Salisbury, N.C. June 24, 1865. Born Huron, O. Farmer; black eyes, black hair, 5'10" tall.

Pvt. Henry Beebe, Flowerfield. Enlisted in Co. D, Aug. 22, 1862 at Lockport, for 3 years, age 17. Mustered Sept.11, 1862. Died Aug. 22, 1863 at Lockport, Mich. of wounds received in action at Tebbs Bend, Ky., July 4, 1863. Another record in National Archives states that he died Sept. 30, 1863 in US Hospital, Campbellsville. Born Marcellus, Mich. Farmer; blue eyes, light hair, 6' tall.

1st Sgt. Harvey C. Lambert, Lockport. Enlisted in Co. D, Aug. 11, 1862, at Lockport, for 3 years, age 25. Mustered Sept. 11, 1862. Wounded in action at Tebbs Bend, Ky., July 4, 1863. Sent to Louisville Military Hosp. No. 12; Discharged to accept promotion Apr. 10, 1864. Commissioned 2nd Lt. Feb. 23, 1864. Mustered Apr. 11, 1864. Commanding Co. A from Oct. 1, 1864 to Jan. 1865. Commissioned 1st Lt. Jan. 1, 1865. Mustered May 1, 1865. Commanding Co. A, from Jan. 1, to Mar. 4, 1865. Mustered out at Salisbury, N.C., June 24, 1865. Born Orange, N.Y. Mason; blue eyes, light hair, 5'9" tall. Residence at end of war, Marcellus, Mich.

Pvt. Gillespie M. Parsons, Schoolcraft. Enlisted in Co. D, Aug. 14, 1862 at Schoolcraft, for 3 years, age 19. Mustered Sept. 11, 1862. Wounded in action at Tebbs Bend, Ky., July 4, 1863. Discharged at Louisville, Ky., June 10, 1865. Born Whitmansville, Mich. Farmer; gray eyes, brown hair, 6' tall.

Pvt. Samuel Stecker, Park. Enlisted in Co. D, Nov. 29, 1862 at Lockport, for 3 years, age 21. Mustered Dec. 16, 1862. Joined regt. at Louisville, Ky., Dec. 24, 1862. Disch. Madison, Ind., March 12, 1864 on account of wounds received in action at Tebbs Bend, Ky. July 4, 1863. Born Northampton, Pa. Farmer; blue eyes, brown hair, 5'4" tall.

Pvt. Jonathan Walburt, Sherwood. Enlisted in Co. D, Aug. 12, 1862, at Colon for 3 years, age 18. Mustered Sept. 11, 1862. Wounded in action at Tebbs Bend, Ky., July 4, 1863. Sick at Detroit, Mich. Born Sherwood, Mich. Farmer; blue eyes, dark hair, 5'8" tall.

Cpl. Simon Young, Marcellus. Enlisted in Co. D, Aug. 11, 1862 at Lockport, for 3 years, age 28. Mustered Sept. 11, 1862. Wounded in action at Tebbs Bend, Ky., July 4, 1863. Transferred to Invalid Corps, Feb. 15, 1864. Discharged at Clifton Barracks, D.C., Apr. 11, 1864, from wounds. Born Huron, O. Farmer; blue eyes, brown hair, 5'10" tall.

Company E

Wounded

Pvt. Richard W. Baxter, Charleston. Enlisted in Co. E, Aug. 7, 1862 at Charleston for 3 years, age 23. Mustered Sept. 11, 1862. Wounded in action at Tebbs Bend, Ky., July 4, 1863. Cpl.; Sgt. March 1, 1865. Mustered out at Salisbury, N.C. June 24, 1865. Born Livingston Co, N.Y. Farmer; gray eyes, brown hair, 5'10" tall.

Sgt. Joseph Gault, Comstock. Enlisted in Co. E, Aug. 11, 1862, at Comstock for 3 years, age 37. Mustered Sept. 11, 1862. Sent to Louisville Military Hosp. Discharged at Madison, Ind., Dec. 7, 1863, on account of wounds received at Tebbs Bend, Ky., July 4, 1863. Born Monroe Co, N.Y.; Farmer; blue eyes, brown hair, 5'7" tall. Died July 25, 1896. Buried at Galesburg, Mich.

Pvt. George W. Hicks, Enlisted in Co. E, Aug. 11, 1862, at Comstock, for 3 years, age 21. Mustered Sept. 11, 1862. According to Dirk Van Raalte letter of August 3, 1863, he was nursed by Capt. Rod Jeter and his wife in their home in Campbellsville "and cared for him as if he were their own child. The family wept when he died." Died July 20/22,* 1863 at Campbellsville, on account of wounds from a shell received in action at Tebbs Bend, Ky., July 4, 1863. Buried in Campbellsville, Ky., possibly in Jeter Lot, Brookside Cemetery. His widow was not notified of his death until November. Memorial Mkr. in Oak Ridge Cemetery, Marshall, Mich. Left wife Charlotte Harris Hicks, 18-month-old son Wm. Samuel. Born Monroe Co, N.Y. Apr. 5, 1842, where his parents lived in a trappers' cabin on Braddock Bay, outside Rochester. George and new wife came to Michigan to take advantage of free land. Farmer; blue eyes, dark hair, 5'10" tall. He enlisted on August 11, 1862, in Comstock, Michigan. His widow later married Perry Gunn.

Pvt. Thomas A. Preston, Comstock. Enlisted in Co. E, Aug. 6, 1862, at Comstock for 3 years, age 31. Mustered Sept. 11, 1862. Wounded in action at Tebbs Bend, Ky., July 4, 1863. Sgt. Aug. 1, 1864. Mustered out at Salisbury, N.C. June 24, 1865. Born Darlington, Canada West. Painter; black eyes, black hair, 5'8" tall. Residence at end of war, St. Clair, Mich.

Pvt. Orin D. White, Charleston. Enlisted in Co. E, Aug. 18, 1862, at Charleston, for 3 years, age 18. Mustered Sept. 11, 1862. Wounded in action at Tebbs Bend, Ky., July 4, 1863. Transferred to Invalid Corps Feb. 15, 1864. Discharged at Philadelphia, Penn., Sept. 14, 1865, from 105th company, Second Battalion, Veteran Reserve Corps. Born Kalamazoo Co, Mich. Farmer; grey eyes, brown hair, 5'5" tall. Residence at end of war, Spring Lake, Mich.

Company F

Killed

2nd Cpl. Peter G. Cuddeback, Enlisted in Co. F, as Cpl., Aug. 13, 1862, at Niles, for 3 years, age 28. Mustered Sept. 11, 1862. Born Susquehanna Co, Pa. Farmer; blue eyes, dark hair, 5'9" tall. Died July 5, 1863 at Tebbs Bend, Ky., of wounds received in action July 4, 1863. Buried in National Cemetery, Lebanon, Ky. Grave No. 349. Left wife Margaret who resided at Dowagiac, two children, Ada b. Jan 19, 1860, Jacob b. June 15, 1861.

Wounded

8th Cpl. George Bement, Adamsville. Enlisted in Co. F, Aug. 13, 1862 at Adamsville, for 3 years, age 20. Mustered Sept. 11, 1862. Wounded in action at Tebbs Bend, Ky., July 4, 1863. Sgt. Aug. 31, 1864. Taken prisoner at Cedar Bluff, Ala., Oct. 26, 1864. Discharged at Detroit May 18, 1865. Residence at end of war, Adamsville, Mich.

3rd Sgt. Henry Bond, Niles. Enlisted in Co. F, Aug. 11, 1862 at Niles, for 3 years, age 22. Mustered Sept. 11, 1862. Wounded in action at Tebbs Bend, Ky., July 4, 1863. Discharged to accept promotion Dec. 12, 1864. Commissioned 2nd Lt. Nov. 2, 1864. Mustered Dec. 13, 1864. Commissioned 1st Lt. May 8, 1865. Mustered May 25, 1865. Mustered out at Salisbury, N.C. June 24, 1865.

1st Cpl. Henry Garmon, Adamsville. Enlisted in Co. F, Aug. 13, 1862 at Niles, for 3 years, age 21. Mustered Sept. 11, 1862. Discharged Dec. 7, 1863, on account of wounds received at Tebbs Bend, Ky., July 4, 1863. Residence at end of war, Union, Mich.

Pvt. Arbuth M. Nott, Niles. Enlisted in Co. F, Aug. 9, 1862 at Berien, for 3 years, age 31. Mustered Sept. 11, 1862. Discharged at Louisville, Ky., on account of wounds received in action at Tebbs Bend, Ky. July 4, 1863; arm amputated by Confederate surgeon during battle; then returned to Union forces.

2nd Sgt. Irving Paddock, Three Oaks. Enlisted in Co. F, Aug. 14, 1862 at New Buffalo, for 3 years, age 32. Mustered Sept. 11, 1862. Wounded in action at Tebbs Bend, Ky., July 4, 1863. 1st Sgt. Discharged to accept promotion Dec. 12, 1864. Commissioned 2nd Lt. Nov. 1, 1864. Commissioned 1st Lt. Nov. 2, 1864. Mustered Dec. 13, 1864. Commissioned Capt. May 8, 1865. Mustered May 25, 1865. Mustered out at Salisbury, N.C. June 24, 1865.

Pvt. Isaac Smith, Three Oaks. Enlisted in Co. F, Aug. 18, 1862 at Three Oaks, for 3 years, age 28. Mustered Sept. 11, 1862. Wounded in action at Tebbs Bend, Ky., July 4, 1863. Transferred to Invalid Corps Feb. 15, 1864. Discharged at Burnside Barracks, Indianapolis, Ind. July 5, 1865, from Co. G, 5th Regt., Veteran Reserve Corps.

Pvt. Marcus Tuttle, Berien. Enlisted in Co. F, Aug. 13, 1862 at Niles, for 3 years, age 25. Mustered Sept.11, 1862. Wounded in action at Tebbs Bend, Ky., July 4, 1863.

Transferred to Invalid Corps Feb. 4, 1864. Discharged at Jackson, Mich. July 17, 1865, 2nd Regt., Veteran Reserve Corps.

2nd Lt. Arthur M. Twombly, Niles. Entered service in Co. F; commissioned Aug. 10, 1862. Mustered Sept. 11, 1862. Wounded in action at Tebbs Bend, Ky., July 4, 1863. Acting Assistant Commissary Subsistence, 1st Brigade, 2nd Division, 23rd Army Corps from Mar. to July, 1864. Discharged on account of disability Sept. 18, 1864; was in California in 1865; was crippled for life at Tebbs Bend with wound below the knee; son of R.T. Twombly.

7th Cpl. Julius C. Webb, Niles. Enlisted in Co. F, Aug. 14, 1862 at Niles, for 3 years, age 19. Mustered Sept. 11, 1862. Cpl. Sept. 10, 1862. Wounded in action at Tebbs Bend, Ky., July 4, 1863. 1st Sgt. Jan. 1, 1865. Mustered out at Salisbury, N.C. June 4, 1865.

Pvt. Thomas Woods, Niles. Enlisted in Co. F, Aug. 14, 1862 at Niles, for 3 years, age 25. Mustered Sept. 11, 1862. Wounded in action at Tebbs Bend, Ky., July 4, 1863. Transferred to Invalid Corps Dec. 15, 1863.

Company I

Killed

Pvt. Pieter Verschure, Holland. Enlisted in Co. I, Aug. 14, 1862 at Adamsville, for 3 years, age 18. Mustered Sept. 23, 1862. Killed in action by a piece of shell at Tebbs Bend, Ky., July 4, 1863. Buried in National Cemetery, Lebanon, Ky., Grave No. 347. Born Dec. 27, 1843 in Holland, Europe. Tanner. Left parents Andries & Pieternella Verschure and brothers and sisters: Adrian, John, Dingenis, Cornelius, Wilhemina.

Wounded

Pvt. Jan Veen, Zeeland. Enlisted in Co. I, Aug. 22, 1862 at Zeeland, for 3 years, age 22. Mustered Sept. 23, 1862. [shown as wounded slightly in regimental record] Mustered out at Salisbury, N.C. June 24, 1865.

Company K

Killed

4th Sgt. James L. Slater, Weesaw. Enlisted in Co. K, Aug. 12, 1862 at Weesaw, for 3 years, age 25. Mustered Sept. 22, 1862. Sgt. Feb. 5, 1863. Killed in action at Tebbs Bend, Ky., July 4, 1863. Lawyer, hazel eyes, black hair, 5'10" tall. Buried at National Cemetery, Lebanon, Ky., Grave No. 314. Left a wife, Mary.

Wounded

Pvt. Hiram Dunham, Royalton. Enlisted in Co. K, Aug. 5, 1862 at Royalton, for 3 years, age 27. Mustered Sept. 22, 1862. [shown as wounded in regimental records] In Louisville Military Hospital. Transferred to Veteran Reserve Corps Apr. 10, 1864.

Died of illness soon after battle

1st Sgt. Henry G. Phillips, Climax. Enlisted in Co. E, Aug. 8, 1862, at Climax, for 3 years, age 32. Mustered Sept. ll, 1862, as 1st Sgt. After battle at Tebbs Bend became so ill with chronic diarrhea was emaciated. Discharged on Surgeon's certificate of disability at Louisville, Ky., Sept 14, 1863. Born Oswego, NY. Marble manufacturer and farmer. Died in Gen. Hosp., Indianapolis on way home, Sept. 21, 1863. Left wife Mary Wheeler, sons: Henry F. b. Apr 2, 1853, Frederick b Feb 7 1855. Blue eyes, light hair, 5'6" tall.

Captured

1st Sgt. Norris H. Merrill, Buchanan. Enlisted in Co. K, July 22, 1862, for 3 years, age 21. Mustered Sept. 22, 1862. Captured July 4, 1863 at Tebbs Bend, Ky.; paroled by Col. Basil Duke in Campbellsville, Ky.; exchanged; wounded by gunshot in battle near Atlanta; left forearm amputated. Commissioned 2nd Lt. Jan.1, 1864. Discharged Nov. 3, 1864, on account of wounds. Born Ohio. Farmer, hazel eyes, dark hair, 5'6" tall.

*Records in National Archives list both dates.

Source: Aaron T. Bliss, *Record of Service of Michigan Volunteers in the CIVIL WAR 1861–1865* (Kalamazoo: Ihling Bros. & Everard, n.d.); Compiled Service Records, Descriptive Books & Military Pension Records, National Archives.

APPENDIX G

Confederate Dead, Wounded, and Captured at the Battle of Tebbs Bend-Green River Bridge

The Union troops referred to the engagement as the Battle of Tebbs Bend. However, the Confederates called it Battle of Green River or Battle of Green River Bridge in their records. If known to the author, the county of residence follows the name.

Confederate regimental records are often unavailable. The last muster rolls for Morgan's men are in the spring of 1863. Confederate cavalry regiments were often reorganized. The 5th Kentucky Cavalry, which served with Buford's Brigade, was transferred to Morgan's command. The 7th Kentucky, known throughout the war as the 3rd, contained elements of Grigsby's 6th Kentucky during the Tebbs Bend engagement. The 11th Kentucky Cavalry was first known as the 7th. When men were captured, it is understandable that they sometimes gave erroneous information to Federal prison authorities as to the number of their regiments.

Smith's 5th Kentucky Cavalry, CSA

Killed

Pvt. A. J. Boggess, Anderson Co., Ky. Enlisted in Co. F, Sept. 2, 1862 at Lexington. Killed at Green River Bridge, July 4, 1863. His name is listed on the Confederate Monument, Anderson County Courthouse, Lawrenceburg.

Major Thomas Young Brent, Jr., Bourbon Co., Ky. Enlisted Sept. 2, 1862 at Lexington. When the 5th Ky. Cav. was transferred to Morgan's Command, the Adj. Gen. reports that he was promoted to Lt. Colonel. Killed by a minie ball in the heart at Green River Bridge, July 4, 1863. Born in Paris, Ky., December 29, 1835, son of Hugh Innes Brent and Margaret Chambers. Married Mary A. Moore, of Forest Retreat. Children were Mary Chilton who married Charles Wm. Dabney, pres. of U. of Cincinnati, and Margaret Thomas, born after her father's death, who married Joseph Adkins of Lexington. After his death, his body was placed on an oxcart and returned to the Bluegrass. His grave is in Fayette Co. between Mt.Horeb & Huffman Mill Road. His stone reads: Major Thomas Y. Brent, 29 Dec 1835–4 July 1863, Killed at Green River Bridge.

2nd Lt. Thomas Jefferson Current, Bourbon Co., Ky. Enlisted in Co. C, Sept. 2, 1862 at Lexington. Elected 2 Lt. May 23, 1863. Killed at Green River Bridge July 4, 1863. Born Mar. 16, 1829 at Ruddles Milll in Bourbon Co., son of Jesse and Ingabur Mason Current. Married Martha Thomas July 4, 1853. She died Jan. 6, 1862. When he died, he left three living children who were raised by his mother and two aunts, George Hamilton b. 1856, Mollie b. 1859, and Martha Ellen, b. 1860. His first child Nancy d. in 1860. His daughter Ellen married Allen M. Kiser, who fought under Morgan. He was one of four brothers in Confederate service and two were wounded in the war. His father, Jesse was deaf and was killed while crossing the road to his farm by Union soldiers when he did not stop when they ordered him to "Halt."

2nd Lt. James H. "Jim" Ferguson. Enlisted in Co. A, Sept. 2, 1862 in Woodford Co., Ky. Killed at Green River Bridge, July 4, 1863.

Pvt. Brockenbury "Judge" Fisher, Scott Co., Ky. Enlisted in Co I, Sept. 2, 1862 at Georgetown, Ky. Killed at Green River Bridge, July 4, 1863.

Pvt. James Addison Headley, Fayette Co., Ky. Enlisted in Co. A, Sept. 2, 1862 at Versailles, Woodford Co., Ky. Killed at Green River Bridge, July 4, 1863. Son of Samuel and Mary Lamme Headley who owned Manchester Farm on Rice Road behind Keeneland Race Track; grandson of James and Jane Patterson Headley.

Pvt. James Hockensmith. Listed in Company H, Anderson Co., Ky. Killed at Green River Bridge, July 4, 1863. May be the son of Henry and Margaret McConnell Hockensmith of Franklin County.

Pvt. Alexander Hockersmith, Anderson Co., Ky. Enlisted in Co. F, Sept. 2, 1862 at Lexington. Killed at Green River Bridge, July 4, 1863. Name is listed on the Confederate Monument, Anderson County Courthouse, Lawrenceburg.

1st Lt. George W. Holloway, Scott Co., Ky. Enlisted in Co. B, Sept. 2, 1862 at

Lexington. Fought at London, Mt. Sterling, Snow Hill, Greasy Creek and was killed at Green River Bridge, July 4, 1863. Born in Franklin Co. July 8, 1834, son of John Y. and Martha Davenport Holloway; brother of Capt. L.D. Holloway, CSA, AG; [CVA of Ky says he enlisted at Stamping Ground, Scott Co, in Aug., 1862.]

Pvt. S. T. Johnson. Listed in Co. B which was recruited from Scott Co., Ky. Killed at Green River Bridge, July 4, 1863.

Pvt. Samuel Miles, Jr., Millville, Franklin Co., Ky. Enlisted in Co. A, Sept. 2, 1862 in Woodford Co. Killed at Green River Bridge, July 4, 1863. Son of Samuel and Elizabeth Hawkins Miles.

Pvt. Dennis F. O'Nan, Franklin Co., Ky. Temporarily assigned to Co. A, 5th Ky. Killed at Green River Bridge, July 4, 1863. Born Feb. 7, 1841, son of William Brewer and Jane Steel O'Nan, grandson of Dennis O'Nan and Lydia Brewer.

3rd Sgt. Weston Threlkeld, Scott Co. Enlisted in Co. B, Sept. 2, 1862 at Lexington. Killed at Green River Bridge, July 4, 1863.

5th Kentucky Cavalry, CSA

Wounded

3rd Cpl. George W. Agee. Enlisted in Co. G, Sept. 2, 1862 in Lexington, Ky. Wounded at Green River Bridge, July 4, 1863. Continued raid and was taken prisoner at Cheshire, Ohio July 20, 1863. Sent to Camp Chase July 26, 1863. Received at Camp Douglas Aug. 22, 1863. Transferred to Pt. Lookout Mar. 2, 1865. Was 18 in 1860 census, resident in Cordovia area, Grant Co., Ky.

Capt. Joseph Marshall Bowmar, Woodford Co., Ky. Enlisted in Co. A, Sept. 2, 1862, elected 1st Lt.; appted Regimental Adj, May 1863. Wounded "left on the field" and taken prisoner at Green River Bridge, July 4, 1863. Sent to Louisville Military Prison Sept. 25, 1863. At Camp Chase by March 1864 where Sec. of War refused to consider his case. Transferred to Ohio Penitentiary, Columbus and to Ft. Delaware Mar. 25, 1864. Sent to City Point for exchange Mar. 7, 1865. Born in Woodford Co., son of Co. Clerk Herman and Eleline Tunis Bowmar. Grandson of Major Herman Bowmar of the American Revolution. At end of Civil War, Bowmar migrated to Missouri.

2nd Lt. James H. Ferguson, Scott Co., Ky. Enlisted in Company B, Sept. 2, 1862 in Scott Co. and was elected 3rd Lt. Fought at Perryville, Murfreesboro, Milton, Snow Hill, Greasy Creek. Was severely wounded "left on the field" and taken prisoner at Green River Bridge, July 4, 1863. Sent to Louisville Military Prison Aug. 6, 1863. Transferred to Columbus, Ohio Aug. 10, 1863. Forwarded to Johnson Island Oct. 19, 1863, then to Pt. Lookout for exchange Feb. 16, 1865. Born in Georgetown, Scott Co., May 11, 1835. He died at his home near Stamping Ground, Ky., July 31, 1871.

Pvt. Thomas Gormley. Enlisted in Co. A, Sept. 2, 1862 in Woodford Co., Ky. 3rd Sgt. in some records. Wounded in the leg at Green River Bridge, July 4, 1863 and left behind. He pulled himself up on his horse and rode to a farm, where a woman attended him as he lay in the barn. The woman was afraid if she did not attend him, Morgan would come back and burn her house down. He was eventually taken prisoner at Green River. Sent to Louisville Military Prison July 27, 1863. Received at Camp Morton Aug. 10, 1863. Transferred to Camp Douglas Aug. 22, 1863. Transferred to Pt. Lookout for exchange Mar. 2, 1865. Admitted to Chimborazo Hosp #1, Richmond Mar. 4, 1865; transferred to Hosp #2 and right leg treated. Furloughed 60 days Mar. 10, 1865. Born in 1833 in Ireland and migrated to America in 1850. Employed as a plantation overseer. Married Alice Haney from Kentucky. After the war, he had a pronounced limp all his life and carried a cane. He moved to Kansas where he owned several farms near Atchison.

Capt. Martin Van Gudgell, Anderson Co., Ky. Enlisted in Co. H, Sept. 2, 1862 in Lexington. Promoted to Capt., Mar. 23, 1865; acted as Captain of company after death of Capt. Jordon. "Left on the field severely wounded" at Green River Bridge, July 4, 1863. Sent to Louisville Military Prison, July 30, 1863, and to Columbus/Camp Chase Aug. 9, 1863. Paroled at Johnson Island; forwarded to Pt. Lookout for exchange Mar. 14, 1865.

Cpl. Robert Jones. Enlisted in Co. B, Sept. 2, 1862 in Scott Co., Ky. Severely wounded and taken prisoner at Green River Bridge, July 4, 1863. Sent to Louisville Military Prison Aug. 6, 1863. Transferred to Camp Morton Aug. 9, 1863 and sent to Camp Douglas Aug. 17, 1863.

Pvt. John R. Moreland. Enlisted in Co. C, Sept. 2, 1862 in Lexington, Ky. Severely wounded and left on the field, unfit for further service. Died at Confederate Soldiers' Home at Pewee Valley, Ky., Nov. 27, 1907; buried in Paris, Ky.

Pvt. Norton Stoughton, probably from Woodford Co., Ky. Listed in Co. A. Wounded at Green River Bridge, July 4, 1863.

Pvt. Thomas Jefferson Williamson, from Woodford Co., Ky. Enlisted in Co. A, Sept. 2, 1862 in Woodford Co. Wounded at Green River Bridge, July 4, 1863, but was able to continue with the troops. Captured at Buffington Island by Wolford, July 19, 1863. Transferred to Camp Morton July 23, 1863. On the rolls of Camp Douglas Aug. 22, 1863 and released there Feb. 2, 1865 by taking the oath of allegiance. Later resided in Anderson Co., was 5'9" tall, had dark hair, blue eyes.

Captured

Pvt. James R. Jones, Franklin Co., Ky. Enlisted in Co. B. Taken prisoner at Green River Bridge, July 4, 1863. Sent to Camp Douglas Aug. 11/22, 1863. Paroled there and forwarded to Pt. Lookout Feb. 21, 1865 for exchange. Admitted to hospital Feb. 28, 1865 in Richmond, Va. Sent to Camp Lee, Va. Mar. 1, 1865. Took oath of allegiance May 20, 1865.

Pvt. James A. Orr, Midway, Woodford Co., Ky. Enlisted in Co. A, Sept. 2, 1862 in Woodford Co. Taken prisoner at Green River Bridge, July 4, 1863. Sent to Louisville Military Prison Aug. 6, 1863 and to Camp Morton Aug. 9, 1863. Received at Camp Douglas Aug. 22, 1863. Paroled there and transferred for exchange to Pt. Lookout Mar. 2, 1865. Took the oath of allegiance in Chattanooga May 12, 1865. Born 1834, died 1921. Was buried with wife Susan and infant children in Versailles Cemetery. Was 5'3", had dark hair, hazel eyes. At Camp Chase: Burke's Journal, Aug. 2, 1863, said, "Parson James A. Orr ... delivered a good sermon to us in the open air under one of the shade trees." Burke Aug. 20, 1863: "In the evening Parson Orr held forth in the square and a good many of our boys attended." Burke Oct. 2, 1863: "Religious papers were distributed to the congregation and parson James Orr had a lot of books which he wished to put in a library to be drawn out by members of a religious society that he was about to form. The object of this society was to improve the morals of the camp."

Grigsby's 6th Kentucky Cavalry, CSA

Captured

Pvt. Philip S. Beswick, Mercer Co., Ky. Enlisted in Co. G, Aug. 10, 1862, in Lexington. Taken prisoner at Green River Bridge July 11, 1863. Sent to Louisville Military Prison July 16, 1863. Transferred to Camp Morton Aug. 9, 1863 and received there Aug. 10, 1863. Forwarded to Camp Douglas Aug. 22, 1863. Died in prison Sept. 10, 1864 of acute dysentery. Body sent to Danville for burial in Nield or "French" Graveyard on Quirk's Run Road, Boyle Co. Born Mar. 11, 1833.

Pvt. Michelberry Stephens. Listed in Co. A. Taken prisoner at Green River, July 4, 1863. Received at Louisville Military Prison Aug. 11, 1863. Discharged on Aug. 17, 1863 on order of General Boyle. Enlisted in Federal Army Aug. 17, 1863.

Pvt. William H. Tevis. Enlisted in Co. A, Sept. 8, 1862, at Stanford. Taken prisoner at Green River Bridge, July 4, 1863. Released on taking the oath of allegiance.

Gano's 7th Kentucky Cavalry, CSA

Known as 3rd Kentucky Cavalry during most of the war.

Killed

Capt. Robert H. Cowan, Danville, Ky, Centre College Graduate, Class of 54. Enlisted in Co. I, Aug. 20, 1861 at Danville. Company surrendered at Ft. Donelson. He was exchanged at Vicksburg, Mississippi. Returned to service. Killed at Green River Bridge, July 4, 1863. His brother James "Jim" was wounded, but still "took charge" of his body.

2nd Cpl. Henry Goodloe, Madison Co., Ky. Enlisted in Co. I, Aug. 20, 1861 at Danville. Killed at Green River Bridge, July 4, 1863. Son of Henry and Emily Duncan Goodloe; grandson of pioneer William and Susannah Woods Goodloe; related to wife of Governor Owsley.

Pvt. Jesse N. Hatcher. Enlisted in Co. C, Sept. 23, 1862, in Taylor Co. Killed at Green River Bridge, July 4, 1863.

1st Cpl. John Hudson, Hartsville, Tenn. Enlisted in Co. K, Aug. 21, 1862, in Hartsville. Killed at Green River Bridge, July 4, 1863.

1st Lt. Charles N. Kirtley, Hartsville, Tenn. Enlisted in Co. K, Aug. 21/22 at Hartsville. Appointed 1st Lt. Sept. 10, 1862. Killed at Green River Bridge, July 4, 1863.

2nd Sgt. J. "Duck" Nelson, Gradyville, Adair Co., Ky. Enlisted in Co. C, Sept. 17, 1862 in Taylor County. Killed at Green River Bridge, July 4, 1863.

Pvt. Joshua W. Turner. Enlisted in Co. D, Sept. 12, 1862 in Lexington. Transferred to Byrne's Battery. Killed at Green River Bridge, July 4, 1863.

Pvt. John Wood. Enlisted in Co. D, Sept. 12, 1862 in Lexington. Served as a wagon guard. Killed at Green River Bridge, July 4, 1863.

Wounded

Pvt. Henry Clay Buford, Lincoln Co., Ky. Enlisted in Co. F, Sept. 9, 1862 in Lexington, Ky. Wounded and taken prisoner at Green River Bridge, July 4, 1863. Sent to USA Post Hospital, Somerset on July 7, 1863, with gunshot wound in right thigh. Transferred to General Hospital, Camp Nelson Nov. 5, 1863. Sent to Louisville Military Prison Nov. 20, 1863. Transferred to Camp Morton Nov. 25, 1863. Forwarded to Ft. Delaware Mar. 19, 1864. Exchanged in Varina, Va., Sept. 22, 1864. Admitted to Chimborazo Hosp #3, Richmond, Sept. 22, 1864. Furloughed Oct. 1, 1864, probably re-enlisted. Surrendered at Augusta, Ga. May 20, 1865. Took the oath of allegiance, Nashville, May 29, 1865. Was 5'11" tall, had sandy hair, blue eyes.

Pvt. James "Jim" C. Cowan, Lincoln Co., Ky. Enlisted in Co I, Sept. 1, 1862, in Danville. Wounded at Green River Bridge, July 4, 1863. Taken prisoner by Col. O. H. Moore while in hospital July 6, 1863. Sent to McLean Barracks July 27/28, 1863. Received at Camp Chase Sept. 6, 1863. Sent to Rock Island Jan. 14, 1864. Transferred for exchange to City Point Mar. 2, 1865. Exchanged Mar. 9, 1865. Surrendered Augusta, Ga. May 9, 1865. Took the oath of allegiance May 16, 1865; paroled May 20, 1865. Was 6' tall, had dark hair, hazel eyes. Brother Robert was killed at Green River and Jim took charge of his body.

Pvt. J. C. McQueery. Enlisted in Co. D, 1st Ky. Cav., Sept. 2, 1862 in Lexington, Ky. Transferred to Morgan's Command, no company listed. Wounded at Green River Bridge, July 4, 1863, and "left on the field for dead." Turned up alive after the war in Arkansas.

Author's note: There is a James Clayton McQueery in Lancaster Cemetery, with 3rd Ky Cav, CSA, after the name. He was a native of Estill Co.; married Tecora West; was a minister. Possibly he went to Arkansas and returned to Garrard County.

Captured

Pvt. John Canter, Franklin Co., Ky. Enlisted in Co. K, Aug. 21, 1862 in Hartsville, Tenn. Taken prisoner at Green River Bridge, July 4, 1863. Sent to Louisville Military Prison Sept. 17, 1863. Transferred to Camp Douglas Aug./Sept. 1863. Paroled at Camp Douglas. Forwarded to Pt. Lookout for exchange Feb. 1865. Admitted to hospital Feb. 28, 1865 in Richmond, Va. Sent to Camp Lee, Va. Mar. 1, 1865. Took the oath of allegiance May 20, 1865.

Pvt. E.A. Hansbrough, Listed in Co. C, taken prisoner at Green River Bridge, July 4, 1863. Sent to Louisville Military Prison Aug. 6, 1863. Sent to Camp Morton Aug. 9, 1863. No further record.

Pvt. Gabriel B. Jennings, Garrard Co., Ky. Enlisted in Co. E, Sept. 15, 1862 in Lancaster. Taken prisoner at Green River Bridge, July 4, 1863. Sent to Kemper Barracks, Cincinnati July 20, 1863. Sent to Camp Chase. Received at Camp Douglas Aug 22/24, 1863 where paroled. Forwarded to Pt. Lookout for exchange Feb. 20, 1865. Surrendered at Decatur, Ala. May 16, 1865. Took the oath of allegiance May 18, 1865. Was 5'9" tall, had dark hair, hazel eyes.

Pvt. J. H. Jennings, Garrard Co., Ky. Enlisted in Co. E, Sept. 15, 1863, in Lancaster. Taken prisoner at Green River Bridge July 4, 1863. Sent to Louisville Military Prison Aug. 19, 1863. Transferred to Camp Chase Sept. 9, 1863 and received there Sept. 10, 1863. Sent to Rock Island Jan. 22, 1864. [This may be the James H. Jennings who was killed or died from wounds-See Hist. of Garrard Co, 154.]

Pvt. John A. Jennings, Garrard Co., Ky. Enlisted in Co. E, Sept. 15, 1862, in Lancaster. Taken Prisoner at Green River Bridge, July 4, 1863. Sent to Kemper Barracks, then Camp Chase July 20, 1863. Forwarded to Camp Douglas Aug 22/24, 1863 where he died of smallox Nov. 29, 1864. Buried near Camp Douglas.

Pvt. John R. Jordon. Giles Co., Tenn. Enlisted in Co. C, Sept. 23, 1863 in Pulaski, Giles Co. Taken prisoner at Green River Bridge, July 4, 1863. Sent to Louisville Military Prison July 27, 1863. Transferred to Camp Morton Aug. 9, 1863 and received there Aug. 20, 1863. On Aug. 18, 1864 was transferrred to Camp Douglas where he died of smallpox June 30, 1864. Buried near Camp Douglas.

3rd Sgt. John H. Kastenbine. Enlisted in Co. K, Sept. 10, 1862 in Lexington. Promoted to 3rd Sgt. Nov. 1, 1862. Taken prisoner at Green River Bridge, July 4, 1863. Sent to Louisville Military Prison July 12, 1863. Transferred to Camp Morton July 29, 1863. Forwarded to Camp Douglas and on roll Sept. 1, 1863. Exchanged. Was forwarded to General Hospital #13, Richmond Aug. 28, 1864. Died of typhoid fever Sept. 21, 1864.

Pvt. Joseph F. Scott, Harrison Co., Ky. Enlisted in Co. E, Sept. 15, 1863 in Oxford, Scott Co. Taken prisoner at Green River Bridge, July 4, 1863. Sent to Kemper Barracks, Camp Chase July 20, 1863. Transferred to Camp Douglas Aug. 22/24, 1863. Took the oath of allegiance at Camp Douglas and was released Feb. 3, 1865. Was 5'6" tall, had black hair, gray eyes.

Surgeon Edwin M. Sheppard, Collin Co., Tx. Taken prisoner at Green River Bridge, July 4, 1863. Sent to Louisville Military Prison Aug. 21, 1863. Discharged to Cincinnati Aug. 24, 1863. Forwarded to Ft. Delaware and paroled Aug. 27, 1863. Sent to Ft. McHenry for exchange at City Point Nov. 24, 1863. Re-enlisted in Louisville June 29, 1864. Captured at Cynthiana June 12, 1864. Surrendered Newton, N.C., Apr. 19, 1865. Took the oath of allegiance at Nashville May 14, 1865. Was 5'9" tall, had dark hair, hazel eyes.

Cluke's 8th Kentucky Cavalry, CSA

Captured

Pvt. Frederick Cook, possibly Montgomery Co, Ky. Enlisted in Co. I, Sept. 10, 1862 in Mt. Sterling. Taken prisoner in Campbellsville, July 5, 1863. Sent to Louisville Military Prison July 30, 1863. Transferred to Camp Morton Aug. 9, 1863 and received there Aug. 10, 1863. Forwarded to Camp Douglas Aug 18, 1863. Transferred to Pt. Lookout for exchange Feb. 24, 1865. Took the oath of allegiance May 30, 1865.

Pvt. Stephen Masterson, possibly Washington Co., Ky. Enlisted in Co. K, Sept. 10, 1862 in Springfield. Taken prisoner at Green River Bridge, July 4, 1863. Sent to Louisville Military Prison Aug. 6, 1863. Transferred to Camp Morton Aug. 9, 1863. Forwarded to Camp Douglas Aug. 18, 1863 and received there Aug. 22, 1863. Transferred to Pt. Lookout for exchange Mar. 2, 1865.

Johnson's 10th Kentucky Cavalry

Captured

Surgeon J. F. Keiser. Enlisted Aug. 15, 1862 in Clarksville, Tenn. Taken prisoner at Battle of Green River Bridge, July 4, 1863. Sent to Louisville Military Prison Sept. 1, 1863. On roll of prisoners at Cincinnati Sept. 4, 1863. On roll of prisoners at Ft. McHenry Sept. 12, 1863. Sent to City Point for exchange Nov. 21, 1863. [also on rolls of 5th and 6th Ky. Cav.]

Chenault's 11th Kentucky Cavalry, CSA

Killed

2nd Lt. William W. Baldwin, Clark Co., Ky. Enlisted in Co. A, Sept. 10, 1862 in Richmond. Killed at Green River Bridge, July 4, 1863. His father, William Baldwin, Sr., & two brothers, Samuel and John, all fought at Green River. Tombstone in Winchester Cemetery reads: William W. Baldwin, Lt, Ky Cav CSA, killed July 4, 1863, Green River Bridge, age 35 yrs, 8 mos, 5 days. Was a merchant. Widow married Lt. Rodney Haggard of 11th Kentucky.

Col. David Waller Chenault, near Foxtown, Madison Co., Ky. Enlisted Sept. 10, 1862 at Richmond, Ky., and recruited the 11th Kentucky Cavalry from Madison, Clark, and Estill counties at a barbeque in a grove on Big Hill Pike near Woodlawn, Richmond. Was commissioned colonel. Fought at Hartsville, Glasgow, Bacon Creek, Nolin's Creek, Muldraugh's Hill, Rolling Fork, Greasy Creek, Monticello. Killed at Green River Bridge, July 4, 1863. His body was returned to Madison County by oxcart; was first buried in the Chenault Family Cemetery; later reinterred in the Samuel Phelps lot, Richmond Cemetery. Born Feb. 5, 1825 in Madison Co., son of Anderson and Emily Cameron Chenault. Planter-farmer. Member of Tates Creek Baptist Church. Married Ann Tabitha Phelps. Served in Mexican War as subaltern in Stone's Co., Humphrey Marshall's 1st Regt., Ky. Vol. Cav. "Perhaps no more popular man ever lived in the county." In Compiled Service

Records and Adjutant General's Report, the reports incorrectly say: Killed at Bacon Creek [Bonnieville] July 4, 1863.

Pvt. Austin Dunn "Ausey" Cosby, Madison Co., Ky. Enlisted in Co. B, Sept. 10, 1862 at Richmond. Mortally wounded at Green River Bridge and died July 9, 1863. Born Dec. 15, 1836, son of Wingfield and Amanda Hudson Cosby. Memorial stone in Cosby Cemetery overlooking Kentucky River on Jacks Creek Pike, Fayette Co., Ky. One of four brothers on Great Raid. A brother, Oliver, stayed behind to care for Ausey before his death. Brother James was captured in Ohio and Oliver escaped into West Virginia.

Pvt. John Cosby, Madison Co., Ky. Enlisted in Co. B, Sept. 10, 1862 at Richmond. Killed at Green River Bridge, July 4, 1863. Born Sept. 9, 1840, son of Wingfield and Amanda Hudson Cosby. Memorial stone in Cosby Cemetery overlooking Kentucky River on Jacks Creek Pike, Fayette Co., Ky. One of four brothers on Great Raid. Brother A.D. Cosby was mortally wounded at Green River. Brother James was captured in Ohio and Oliver escaped into West Virginia.

Capt. Alexander H. Tribble, Madison Co., Ky. Enlisted in Co. K, 2nd Kentucky Cavalry, July 25, 1862 in Livingston, Tenn., as 1st Lt. Enlisted in Co. B, 11th Ky., Sept. 10, 1862, in Richmond. Elected Lt. and fought at Glasgow, Snow Hill, Marrowbone, Edgefield, Woodbury, Shiloh, Liberty, Milton, Gallatin; promoted to Capt. Achieved fame on Christmas Raid in a skirmish near New Market with Federal Capt. Halisy. He saw action at Bacon Creek, Nolin's Creek, Muldraugh's Hill, Rolling Fork, Monticello. Killed at Green River Bridge, July 4, 1863. Born in Madison Co., son of Dudley and Matilda Tevis Tribble. Brother James P. also wounded at Green River. Brother Dudley Tribble was wounded later on the Great Raid.

1st Lt. Frank A. West. Enlisted in Co. H, Sept. 10, 1862 in Bourbon Co., Ky. Killed at Green River Bridge, July 4, 1863.

Wounded

Pvt. James Polk Tribble, Madison Co., Ky. Enlisted in Co. B, Sept. 10, 1862 in Richmond, Ky. In battles of Hartsville, Elizabethtown, Muldraugh's Hill, Rolling Fork, Lebanon, Greasy Creek, Monticello, and severely wounded at Green River Bridge, July 4, 1863. Nursed back to health by Southern sympathizer, Joel Smith of Cane Valley, which enabled him to escape time in a Northern prison. Tribble named a child Joel Smith for the man who cared for him. Born in Richmond, Ky., son of Dudley and Matilda Tevis Tribble. Married Alice Phelps after the war and they were the parents of four children. He died in Richmond Jan. 18, 1893. Brother Alexander killed at Green River; brother Dudley wounded later on the Great Raid.

Captured

2nd Lt. Edmund Baxter, Madison Co., Ky. Enlisted in Co. B as farrier. Taken prisoner and sent to Louisville Military Prison. Transferred to Vicksburg, Miss. for exchange Nov. 15, 1862. Paroled Jan. 11, 1863. Was promoted to 2 Lt. July 1863. Taken prisoner again at Green River Bridge, July 4, 1863. Sent to Louisville Military Prison. In 1870 census he was 30, a farmer with wife Mary and daughter Hattie.

Pvt. John E. Benson. Enlisted in Co. A, Oct. 18, 1861, in 1st Ky. Mted Rifles at Prestonsburg, Ky. His horse was killed in a skirmish at Pikeville on Nov. 9, 1861 and was paid $75 from CSA treasury for the horse. In Sept. 1862 enlisted in Co H, 11th Ky. Cav. Captured at Green River Bridge, July 4, 1863. Sent to Louisville Military Prison, July 20, 1863. Transferred to Camp Morton Aug. 9, 1863. Recd at Camp Douglas Aug. 22, 1863. Transferred to Pt. Lookout for exchange Feb. 24, 1865. Recd at Wayside Hospital, Richmond, Mar. 2, 1865.
Born Dec. 29, 1842 in Harrison Co., son of James and Nancy Hunt Benson. Married Cansada Hunt in 1867 and they had four children. In 1888 he married Elizabeth Marshall and had seven children. In 1912 he applied for a pension. Died on Aug. 5, 1918 in Robertson Co. Buried in Republican Christian Church Cemetery in Harrison Co.

Pvt. James C. Browning, Bracken Co., Ky. Enlisted in Co. H Sept. 10, 1862, at Mt. Sterling. Taken prisoner at Green River Bridge, July 4, 1863. Sent to Louisville Military Prison July 20, 1863. Sent to Camp Morton Aug. 9, 1863. Forwarded to Camp Douglas Aug. 22, 1863. Released Jan. 18, 1865, after taking the oath of allegiance. Was 5'8" tall, dark hair, grey eyes.

Pvt. James Wesley Huguely, Madison Co., Ky. Enlisted in Co. B, Sept. 10, 1862 at Richmond. Taken prisoner at Green River Bridge, July 4, 1863. Sent to Louisville Military Prison July 20, 1863. Sent to Camp Morton Sept. 9, 1863. Forwarded to Camp Douglas Aug. 17, 1863. Escaped from there Dec. 2, 1863. Family story is that he was made to return to prison for the remainder of the war after which he walked back home. Family met him with horses in Mt. Sterling. Born in Madison Co. as one of 11 children of Jacob and Florine White Huguely. Married Mary Baxter and had one daughter, Hattie. Died Nov. 7, 1907. Was 5'8" tall, black eyes, black hair. Huguely had a sister, Harriet, who married another of Morgan's men, Andrew Mitchell McCord who was captured in Indiana on the Great Raid.

Pvt. Squire Huguely, Madison Co., Ky. Enlisted in Company B, Sept. 10, 1862, in Richmond, Ky. Taken prisoner at Green River Bridge, July 4, 1863. Sent to Louisville Military Prison, Aug. 6, 1863. Sent to Camp Morton Aug. 9, 1863. Transferred to Camp Douglas Aug. 22, 1863. Forwarded to Pt. Lookout Feb. 24, 1865. Took oath of allegiance. Walked back home and family met him with horses at Mt. Sterling. Born in Madison Co., one of 11 children, son of Jacob and Florine White Huguely. In 1870 census was age 27, farmer, wife Fannie, children Everett and Betsy.

Pvt. John M. Judd. Enlisted in Co. H, Sept. 10, 1862, in Mt. Sterling, Ky. Taken prisoner at Green River Bridge, July 4, 1863. Sent to Louisville Military Prison July 20, 1863. Sent to Camp Morton Aug. 9, 1863, forwarded to Camp Douglas. Transferred to Pt. Lookout, Md.

Cpl. John Ryan, Augusta, Ky. Enlisted in Co. H, Sept. 10, 1862 in Bracken Co. in the 8th Regt, but other records place him in 7th Cav. Taken prisoner at Green River Bridge, July 4, 1863. Sent to Louisville Military Prison July 27, 1863. Transferred to Camp Morton Aug. 9, 1863. Forwarded to Camp Douglas Aug. 17, 1863. Deserted to take oath of allegiance Dec. 15, 1863 and Feb. 1865 said "wished to remain North;" discharged May 16, 1865.

2nd Lt. James H. Tevis, Madison Co., Ky. Enlisted in Co. F, Sept. 10, 1862, at Richmond. Fought at Hartsville, Glasgow, Bacon Creek, Nolin's Creek, Elizabethtown, Muldraugh's Hill, Rolling Fork, Lebanon, Greasy Creek, Monticello, captured at Green River Bridge, July 4, 1863. Exchanged. Re-enlisted, with command in 1865. Released after taking the oath of allegiance. Born near Richmond, Mar. 1, 1837. Died at his home near Richmond, Mar. 9, 1895. [There is another James Tevis, Private, Co. B.]

4th Sgt. Squire Turner Tevis, Madison Co., Ky. Enlisted in Co. B, Sept. 10, 1862 at Richmond. Taken prisoner at Green River Bridge, July 4, 1863. Sent to Louisville Military Prison Aug. 19, 1863. Discharged to Camp Morton Aug. 28, 1863. Record indicates forwarding to Ft. Delaware Mar. 19, 1864, but he escaped from Ft. Douglas to Canada. Was on St. Albans Raid, Vt., in 1864. Son of Cyrus C. and Elizabeth Stone Tevis.

5th Sgt. Milton H. Vivian. Enlisted in Co. C, Sept. 5, 1862, in Clark Co., Ky. Taken prisoner at Green River Bridge, July 4, 1863. Sent to Louisville Military Prison, July 27, 1863. Transferred to Camp Morton, Aug. 9, 1863. Sick in hospital. Released from Camp Morton upon taking the oath of allegiance Feb. 14, 1865.

Pvt. W. S. Young, Wayne Co., Ky. Listed in Co. K. Taken prisoner at Green River Bridge, July 4, 1863. Sent to Louisville Military Prison. Released upon taking oath of allegiance. Re-enlisted. Surrendered in Washington, Ga., May 9, 1865. Took oath of allegiance, May 22, 1865. Was 5'10" tall, had brown hair, blue eyes.

Richard Morgan's 14th Kentucky Cavalry

Captured

Pvt. Samuel Geoghegan, Lexington. Enlisted in Co. D, 3rd Reg. Inf (Mted), July 5, 1861, at Camp Boone. Transferred to Co. D, 14th Ky. Cav. Taken prisoner in Campbellsville, July 5, 1863. Sent to Louisville Military Prison, July 12, 1863. Transferred to Camp Morton July 29, 1863. Forwarded to Camp Douglas Aug. 18, 1863. Transferred to Pt. Lookout for exchange Mar. 2, 1865. Took the oath of allegiance.

Surgeon W. B. Anderson. Taken prisoner at Green River Bridge, July 4, 1863. Sent to Louisville Military Prison. Transferred to Cincinnati for exchange Aug. 24, 1863. Released Oct 19, 1863 on order of General Jeremiah Boyle.

Ward's 9th Tennessee Cavalry

Wounded

1st Sgt. John W. Branham, Sumner Co, Tenn.; wounded in the wrist at Green River Bridge, Ky., July 4, 1863. Continued with troops. Captured at Buffington Island, Ohio. Sent to Camp Douglas.

Note: Upon learning that no one knew the names of the men buried in the mass grave at the

Confederate Cemetery at Tebbs Bend-Green River Bridge, the author researched the records for their names. Because the work was attempted so long after the battle, errors may appear. The record is still incomplete, particularly for the members of Byrne's artillery who were wounded or killed. If these names are located, probably out of state, please contact the author.

Sources: Compiled Service Records and Louisville Military Prison Records, National Archives; Kentucky Adjutant General's Report, CSA, 2 vols.; Confederate Veteran Association Yearbooks, D. Howard Smith Papers, Bluegrass county histories and Family Files, Kentucky Historical Society; Bluegrass county libraries; interviews with James Chenault, Gypsie Cosby Jones, Betsy McCord Amster, and James Neale of Madison County, Patty Biddle of Bourbon County, Rick Johnston of Scott County, Sam Flora of Fayette County, Geoff Bedford and Carl Reed of Clark County, Steve Menefee of Mercer County; Kathy Vockery of Garrard County; selected cemetery records in Boyle, Bourbon, Clark, Fayette, Lincoln, Madison, Scott, and Woodford counties.

Men probably captured at Green River Bridge:

Pvt. James P. Norman, Co. F, 7th Ky. Cav., was listed at captured at Columbia, July 4; sent to Louisville Military Prison, then to Camp Douglas where he contracted typhoid fever and died Nov. 27, 1864. [He may have given Columbia as to the location where he was captured because it was the last town through which the troops passed.]

Pvt. James M. Tuttle, Co. E, 7th Ky. Cav., was listed as captured at Columbia, July 4; sent to Louisville Military Prison, then to Camp Douglas; transferred to Pt. Lookout.

APPENDIX H

Letter of David Waller Chenault to his Brother
Dr. Robert C. Chenault, Richmond, Ky.

Intercepted by the Federal Army and Placed in Chenault's Military Record at the End of the War.

Albany, Ky. March the 11th '63

Brother

I write you as I have written to Puss [Ann Tabitha Phelps, D.W. Chenault's wife] several times lately. We have been here for seven weeks and leave this point tomorrow for Monticello. The health of the command is much better than for several weeks. We have lost three men by death since our arrival here. The disease of which they died was inflammation of the brain and spine. Their names are **G.H. Carter** of

Clarke, **Ed. Railsback** of Clarke and **Jas. Shaw**, son of old Hen. Shaw's. All that take it die. These boys died while I was gone to Richmond. My regt. is filling up daily. I suppose that we have recruited fifty men since we came out of Ky in December.

I suppose you saw some of the Regt. with Cluke parts of two or three companies went in with him [Col. Roy Cluke's Raid, men of the 11th KY, recruited from Wayne and Clinton counties]. I have as good or a better regt. of men than is in our brigade. We have the confidence of the Genl, and when anything dangerous is to be done, Chenault's regt. is called out. If the rear is to be protected on a march, we have our full share to perform. In our retreat from the state this winter [Christmas Raid] after pushing around Lebanon Ky. where there was a very superior Yankee force, we were on the rear. A report went up the lines that there was firing in the rear. Genl. Morgan rode back until he met Col. Breckinridge, "Who is on the rear today?" said Morgan. "Chenault's regt.," was the reply. "Then all will be right," was the answer and he rode back to the head of the column. I write this to show you that we have a reputation at headquarters.

My health is very good. The boys from our county are all well, at this time we have had the measles in camp, and several have had them very severely but are now well. The Cosby boys, John and Oliver, both had them but are well. T.B. Shearer also, but well. Jos. Davis has been very sick but is up and well again. Wm. & I[Isham] Fox* are perfectly fat. Jas. Cosby and A.D.[Ausey] Cosby weigh fifty pounds more than they ever did. Charley Stone is well and fat. Alex. Pence and Alex. Russell both got in safe and are well. Jake White is well. Dud[ley] Tribble well. Capt. [Cabell] Chenault has been sick but all right again. Pur White** well again and one of the best soldiers in camp. Ed Baxter and James and Squire Hugely got in safe and are all very well. Tom Fowler is well, in fact, all are well. Maj. McCreary is at Monticello with forty men selecting a camp-ground. Col. Tucker is very well and received a letter from his wife a few days since. **I saw a young Mr. Gregg from Madison County that had been at our friend on the Creek** a few days ago and was happy to **hear from home**. I have received two letters from Puss since I have been in the south. The last one dated 25th of Dec.

Was very much grieved to hear that she had been sick but hope she is now entirely well. My love to her and all the friends. Tif, [Anderson Tiffin Chenault, his brother] I wrote to her to come out south. If she has not started when you receive this, I think she had best stay with you all at home as I am satisfied that we will be moving soon and all the time for several months, and perhaps she would be as far from me down here as at home. While nothing on earth would afford me as much pleasure as to see Puss, I think this best at present. Tif, I think that you had better see my creditors and have my land sold, and let you and Dave Chenault (if Tom Chenault and George Phelps won't) buy it.[D.A. Chenault was his brother.]

I have a great deal to tell you when I get home that I can't write. We hear from Madison every week. Tell these poor insignificant creatures that have deserted that I hope the feds will get them, and this, that they will be captured and shot as they deserve to be. Tell Skip Parke that the boys are looking for him or expect to hear of him laying out. We think that Tom Fox & George Phelps and Joe, Tom, John Deatherage, and Will Crutcher did exactly right in staying at home as their advice and council has been of great benefit in Ky. Write to me soon. Give me all the news.

Direct your letter to J.D. Burton, Burkesville, have mine in an envelope inside of the one directed to him, and all will be right. We have a very wet time here, now the waters are very high and roads bad. We scout all up and down the Cumberland for miles daily. I could write to you for a whole day but must close as the bearer of this will be off in a moment. My love to Sisters and families, to Sam & Robt's family. Tell little Emma howdy. Tell Laura to be a good girl. Remember me to all the little negroes and old ones too. Abe & Charley are both well and want to hear from home and come home.

Your brother in haste,

D. W. Chenault, Col.

*Isham Fox carried Chenault's body off the battlefield at Tebbs Bend.
**Chenault appears to write Pur; there is a Durrett White on Muster Rolls
Source: National Archives, Microcopy No. 319, Roll No. 59, D. W. Chenault 46449964.
Author inserted punctuation and paragraphs to enhance clarity.

APPENDIX I

Letter of Mary Christie, Cane Valley, Ky. to Her Brother, Lt. N.R. Christie, 3rd Ky. Vol. Infantry, 3rd Brigade, 21st Army Corps

[Excerpt]

July, Friday morning the 17, 1863

Brother Norman,

It looks as that there is a generl Stir everwher and thire is no rest for a pore solder. I receved a letter from Kit the other day dated the 3 of this month. he had cot up with his reg. [regiment] he left home on the 30 of last month and I was very unesey about him for he was complaining when he left home but he States in his letter he was improving. his reg was eight mils this Side of Birksville Ky at the date of his letter. But I hav hird Since that thay ar at Cave Sitty [City]...

Well Norman I gess you hav hird of Morgan giving us another visit. he past throw on the 4 of July and done a grat deele of devilment in this Section of country. He done worse than he did when he past throw [through] last summer.

He taken every thing that he cold and distroied a grat dell of propty but thay did not come this road no ferther than Stephen Humphress. Thay taken too of his horses and wold hav taken all he had but he had some of them hid. Our men Stood them a fight at Columbia but thire was too many of them for what few union men was thire. Thir was abot one hundred solders at Green Rever Bridge. Thay fit like will cats and it is unknown how meny of the rebls thay kelled for thay taken a grat meny of them off with them and thay throwed a grate meny in the river. it is reported that thire was 23 ded rebles found on the ground and Severl wounded and but one of our men got klled. well I will quit that Subject and talk about Something I know more about fore I never like to talk on Subjects I do know eny thing about but thay tell me Morgan did pass throw [through] this Section of country and the report come that he was coming this road twenty times and all the skeedling [skedaddling] you never Saw the like but Some of them was Skird a hept [heap] worse than thay was hirt.

Your Sister mary
Plese excuse my bad writing and I will do beter
Every thing is quiet at home.

Source: Copy given to author by Norman Christie, Campbellsville, Ky.

APPENDIX J

Letter of Henry G. Phillips, 25th Michigan, to his sister, July 14th, 1863

> the Battle commenst about Sunrise in the Morn[ing] and lasted 3 hours and a half and it was [one of] the hardest fought Battles of the ware considring the ods in numbers the Rebel force was about Eight thousand and ours Two hundred but we had the advantage in position. they had Artilery and we had none. they drove our men out of the intreenchments the first charge and then we fought them in the Woods the rest of the time and our Boys fought like Tigars for the ground was strued with dead Rebels. it seemed as though every shot of ours toled for in tht 3 hours and a half . . . we killed 100 and wouuded 200 . . . of them and then thre hole Division took to there heales and Run as thou the Deval was after them.

Note: Henry Phillips, a farmer before the war, was 5'6", with light hair and blue eyes; died of illness soon after this battle.
Source: Letter donated to the Taylor County Historical Society by Phillips' descendants.

APPENDIX K

BRIDGE BUILDING CREW AT GREEN RIVER BRIDGE
Under Command of Lt. Michael A. Hogan, Co. G, 8th Michigan

From the 8th Michigan:

Lt. Thomas Campbell, Co. I; Cpl. James Hollenbach, Cpl. Henry Cally, William B. Calf, Thomas Clark, Mark Cline, Henry Lech, William Morton, Mike Nobles, William Weller, John Trumboe, W. Glesen, W. A. Newberry, Pvt. Malvenus Colby.

From the 79th New York:

John M. Olin, John Carr, H. Black, James Deleringle, James Mitchell, William Dernitt, Charles Crumford, John Spence, Isaac Douglass, Edward Harney, Thomas Lord, Wm. Coyle, Henry Bloomfield, Daniel McLaulin, Robert Cousey, Thomas Booth, Edmond J. Mathews, John D. Nogles, Robert Wolcot, John McIntyre, John Martin, D.M. Donald, E. D. Carty, A. J. Carigan, Henry Cook, Joseph Grimshaw, William Bennett of Co. D.

Civilians

Thomas Pearson, John Dudly, John Trombly, E. F. Crabtree, Elisha Mayher, John

Vining, John W. Johnson, James Hagan, Lewis Dumas, Augustus Dumas, C. C. Babcock, Charles Anderson.

Sources: Compiled Service Records, National Archives; *Louisville Journal*, October 29, 1863, gives a list of the men at that date; "From the Eighth Infantry," *Detroit Free Press,* August 8, 1863, lists civilians; letter of William Bennett to James Lorimer, Aug. 5, 1863, Gary Gardner Collection, Hodgenville, Ky. Some of the names have unconventional spelling, but the author listed the names as they appeared in the paper.

APPENDIX L

LABORATORY ANALYSIS OF THE STAINS ON THE FLOOR OF THE ATKINSON-GRIFFIN HOUSE

WOLTMAN RESEARCH
302 Arthur Avenue
Holland, Michigan 49423

17 October 1988

Ms. Betty M. Gorin
112 Kensington Way
Campbellsville, Ky. 42718

Dear Ms. Gorin,

Supported by laboratory analysis appended hereto, I confirm the stains which appear on the floors of the Atkinson-Griffin house, Campbellsville, Kentucky, used as a Confederate hospital after the battle of Tebbs Bend, 4 July 1863, to have originated from blood.

Sincerely,

Harold A. Woltman

(My credentials are: MS, Chemistry, member of American Chemical Society and New York Academy of Sciences.)

Six samples consisting of scrapings from the floors were taken, July 4, 1988. Five were from different areas bearing stain, the sixth from a "clear" area to be used as a control. Two types of test were given, a chemical and a microscopic, as detailed below.

Blood is a complex mixture containing a large number of cells, called red corpuscles. Red corpuscles are quite fragile and may begin decomposition once the blood is removed from the body, the degree of corpuscle deterioration is dependent on ambient conditions. Under an optimal environment, red cells have been recognized under the microscope after considerably greater periods than 125 years. Red Corpuscles derive their color from a large amount of an iron bearing pigment called hemoglobin. In event every constituent of blood should completely decay, the elemental iron would remain and respond to chemical tests.

Chemical Test for Iron: Samples from all stains and the control area were suspended in distilled water overnight (ca 20mg/5ml) and the next morning subjected to centrifugation to remove insoluble debris. Each sample was divided in two portions, one of which was tested with salicylic acid for ferric iron and the other with potassium ferricyanide for ferrous or reduced iron, normally present in blood. Every sample was strongly positive for ferrous iron while giving a faint indication for the ferric form. The control was negative for both forms.

The quantity of ferrous iron found in all stain samples is indicative of a hemoglobin residue and thereby justifies our opinion that the stains occurring on the Atkinson-Griffin house at Campbellsville, Kentucky are blood residues.

APPENDIX M

Poetry particular to Battle of Tebbs Bend

Immediately after the battle, a soldier of the 25th Michigan wrote a poem dedicated to Colonel Moore and the 25th Michigan Infantry appearing in a pamphlet published in Louisville by John P. Morton in 1863. The pamphlet contained Moore's Official Report and a list of the casualties. A copy of the pamphlet can be located in the Filson Historical Society, Louisville, Kentucky.

"Honor to Whom Honor is Due"

INTRODUCTION

Kind friends accept this tribute of the heart;
Accept this offering of the soldier's pen,
Tough unadorned by any grace of art,
'Tis most befitting to heroic men.
Like the rude mountain and the ruder glen,
Where all the scenes of which we speak transpired,
Thus let our thoughts flow on, unchecked, and when
To civil life we have again retired,
By such unstudied truths our hearts will be inspired.

Upon Green river's rocky shore,
The brave and gallant Col. Moore
With his heroic little band,
Achieved a victory truly grand,
And on our native land's birth day
Won honors which can ne'er decay.

'Tis not my purpose to prolong
Their memories by my humble song,
Nor will I try in simple verse,
Their names, their actions, to
rehearse,
For soon shall abler pens than mine
Record them in historic line,
And while of every human heart
True gratitude shall form a part,
It will not need the poet's pen
To bring to mind those noble men!

My purpose is but to entrwine
A comrade's wreath round mem'ry's
shrine,
With willing hand and heart to raise
A fitting meed of honest praise.
[mead]
*They met, they fought, and conquered
too,*
John Morgan with his rebel crew.

Bright dawned our nation's birth day
morn,
But war had "twanged it trumpet
horn,"
And ere the glorious sun arose,
"In dubious strife they darkly close,"
A flag of truce the foeman bore,
And asked the gallant Col. Moore
Tamely to yield to his demand,
Surrendering his little band.

The Col. quietly replied
"Your Chief's demand must be denied.
On such a day for truth and right
I am determined, sir, to fight."

The rebel to his post retired,
With rage and disappointment fired,
"But the stern joy which warriors feel
In foeman worthy of their steel,"
The robber chieftain's heart pos-
sessed,
And nobly he the truth confessed.—
For soon before our deadly fire
We forced the rebels to retire
In a precipitate retreat.
In short, the victory was complete.

But alas! There comes the bitter
thought,
How dearly was the victory bought.
Six of those heroes nobly died
And now lie sleeping side by side.
Beneath a shady grove they sleep,
And naught can wake their slumbers
deep;
Their comrades gently laid them
there,
And fixed their graves with pious
care.

Their names, the day on which they
fell,
Those little head-boards truly tell;
Those heroes ne'er will be forgot,
Though "no bright marble marks the
spot."
Within our hearts their names shall
live,
New strength and courage they shall
give,
And oft in after years will tell
How brave they fought, how nobly
fell.

The wounded, too, deserve our care,
And should our tenderest feelings
share;
May Heaven their valued lives prolong,
And may they soon be well and
strong.

Kind friends weep not for those who
fell;

Be this your comfort, "*It is well!*"
Well that they died in such a way,
Well that they died on such a day,
And be assured with you we feel
That grief which time can never heal;
Be sure the wounded, too, shall share
Our kind regards and earnest prayer.

To thee, dear Colonel, well we know
A debt of gratitude we owe;
And trust that while with us you stay,
We will that sacred debt repay.
Thy *happiness* our hearts shall cheer,
Thy sorrows ever bring a tear.

Thus hand in hand through good or
ill,
The Twenty-Fifth are with you still;
And may we soon again unite
Beneath that starry flag to fight.

POEM *written and delivered by* Col. O. H. Moore's daughter, Mrs. Jesse Moore Loveridge, *at the* Annual Reunion *of the* 25th Michigan *in* Marcellus, October 6–7, 1897.

For the first time in our history,
Since the great battle and noise
We now have the privilege of enter-
taining
The Twenty-fifth Michigan boys;
A privilege that we deem an honor,
And it fills our hearts with pride,
To look again into your faces—
Ye boys so brave, true and tried.

Thirty-five years have passed away,
So well remembered by you,
When the Twenty-fifth Michigan
boys encamped
In the park at Kalamazoo—
And twenty-five of those dear com-
rades,
Were Marcellus boys that we knew;
Bravely going forth to battle,
To fight for the cause so true.

There they drilled for the coming
battle,
And the orders that soon would
come
To take away from loved ones,
And leave the dear old home—
Leave sweethearts, sisters, mothers,
wives,
And children you loved so well;
Perhaps never again to see them—
None but God alone could tell.

Three long years to fight for freedom,
The land you loved to save,
From the galling chains of slavery,
And the crimes of men depraved
And when in October, of '62,
You left for Dixie's Land,
Your hearts beat high with loyalty,
For Country, God and Man!

And when in December, at West Point,
Colonel Moore gave the false alarm,
He praised you for your promptness-
Every man sprang to arms.
In your first skirmish at Munfordville,
With Morgan and his raiders: then
You came out victorious,
Without the loss of a man.

And in '63, July the fourth—
Near Green River, at Tebb's Bend,
One of the greatest battles occurred,
Ever known to men.
Where Colonel Moore was stationed
With less than two hundred men—
Scouts brought news of Morgan's
advance
In full force, upon the Bend.

Morgan with three thousand strong,
Of rebel men in gray,
Marching on to that little band,
Onward to the deadly fray.
No help within thirty miles was
near—
Colonel Moore might have retreated,
From patriotic motives he chose to
fight,
And with cheers from his men he was
greeted,

Scarcely could they hope to live,
That terrible story to tell—
Of the battle against three thousand
strong,
And the many men that fell;
So, all night long those men did work
With pick and with spade,
Throwing up entrenchments,
Until a barricade was made

Of fell trees, and rifle pits dug—
As you so well know,
To stand between your bosoms
And the bullets of the rebel fore;
Without one work of murmuring,
Those brave Michigan boys, you see,
Were ready to meet that terrible foe,
Though numerous they proved to be.

There was little sleep in camp that
night,
As the men in trenches lay,
Thinking of home, children and
wives,
And the future—of the coming day;
Memory was busy with days long fled,
And anxious thoughts for the morn;
Who could tell how many there
Would put on a martyr's crown.

The next day was July the Fourth,—
That thought alone made them
brave,
Filling their hearts with patriotic
pride
To fight, their country to save.
When at the gray of early dawn,
The rebels on your pickets did fire
You returned the shots with spirit,
And their hearts were filled with ire.

And when a shell came with hideous
shrick,
Wounding two men as they lead,
Not a hand trembled, not a heart fal-
tered
For the flag they fought and bled.
Then Morgan sent a flag of truce,
Demanding your surrender
The answer given by Colonel Moore
You boys so well remember—

"Present my compliments to Morgan,
And tell him my reply—
The Fourth of July is no day to sur-
render;
We'll fight for our country or die."
Then renewed was the conflict,
The enemy their artillery played,
Plunging shell into your earthworks,
But not a man was dismayed.

"Now, my brave men," says Colonel
Moore,
"Rise up and take good aim,
Pick those gunners from the battery
side"
As one gun they boom'd forth again,
And those gunners fell as one man;
Fell in their manhood and pride
Into Green River—a hundred feet
below,
And their hearts' blood crimsoned
the tide.

And now the foe with hideous yell,
Came charging across the field,
In face of a fire that moved them
down;
But yet they did not yield.
Almost a hand-to-hand struggle!
Like rain fell shot and shell,

Brave Harvey Lambert was
wounded—
The Lieutenant you loved so well.

And Roswell and Henry Beebe—
That day their lives did yield,
And their heart's blood stained to
crimson
The grass of that battle-field.
They fought and died for their
country—
The land you love, to save,
And on Green River's grassy banks
They lie in their lonely graves.

And Bruce Beebe, their cousin, was
wounded,
Yet lives the story to tell.
Of that great and terrible battle,
And the men who fought so well;
And Simon Young, a comrade—
Was wounded on that day;
But so after the war has gone to rest,
And sweetly passed away.

Surrounded by the enemy,
To you 'twas life or death;
No surrender without a struggle,
You would fight with your latest
breath;
But God, the Father was with you—
As with Joshua of old,
He gave you strength and courage,
Ye men! so brave, true and bold.

The battle was long and bloody;
Charge after charge you defeated—
After four long hours of fighting,
The rebel foe retreated:
Leaving their killed and wounded
Which outnumbered your little band,
Of the Twenty-fifth Michigan boys—
Who bravely held their stand.

And when the smoke had cleared
away,
Leaving the air so free,
The reaction made you sick at
heart—
That bloody sight to see.
And ever to you will memory bring
That dark and dismal day—
Of Green River, and that deadly fight,
Until you pass away.

[Eighteen more verses, spelling corrected] Almost everything is accurately described except that not every cannoneer fell into Green River. And the number of Confederate dead and wounded did not outnumber the Michigan troops present.

Source: Archives, Holland Museum, Holland, Michigan. One newspaper reported that it was delivered by Rose Loveridge.

APPENDIX N

Moore's Court Martial Charges; overturned on appeal

GENERAL ORDERS, No. 7.

DEPARTMENT OF THE OHIO.
ASSISTANT ADJUTANT GENERAL'S OFFICE,
Lexington, Ky., February 2, 1864.

At a General Court-martial which convened at Louisville, Kentucky, December 21, 1863, pursuant to Special Orders, No. 299, from Headquarters District of Kentucky, and 1st Division, 23d Army Corps, of date December 7, 1863, and of which Colonel S. D. BRUCE, 20th Regiment Kentucky Volunteers, is President, was arraigned and tried—

Colonel *O. H. Moore*, 25th Regiment Michigan Volunteer Infantry.

CHARGE 1ST.

"Neglect of duty to the prejudice of good order and military discipline."

Specification—"In this; that he, Colonel *O. H. Moore*, 25th Regiment Michigan Volunteer Infantry, did, on or about the night of the 28th day of June, 1863, when almost in the face of the enemy, and anticipating an attack from them, leave his camp at or near Tibbs' Bend, Kentucky, so poorly guarded that two persons approaching at midnight traversed the entire camp without meeting a sentinel or guard of any kind."

CHARGE 2D.

"Disobeying the lawful commands of his superior officer."

Specification—"In this; that he, Colonel *O. H. Moore*, 25th Regiment Michigan Volunteer Infantry, did visit the city of Louisville, Kentucky, on or about the 3d day of November, 1863, and, having neglected to register his name at the office of the Post Commandant, as directed by General Order, No. 33, of June 21, 1863, from Headquarters District of Kentucky, did, when ordered, on or about the 5th day of November, 1863, by Colonel Marc Mundy, commanding Post at Louisville, to report to his, the said Colonel Mundy's office, and comply with the said order, positively and wilfully refuse to obey the order. This at Louisville, Kentucky, on or about the said 5th day of November, 1863."

CHARGE 3D.

"Conduct to the prejudice of good order and military discipline."

Specification—"In this; that he, Colonel *O. H. Moore*, 25th Regiment Michigan Volunteer Infantry, having neglected to comply with General Order, No. 33, 1863, Headquarters District of Kentucky, upon visiting the city of Louisville, Kentucky, on or about the 3d day of November, 1863, and having been ordered by Colonel Marc Mundy, Post Commandant of said city, to report at his office, in compliance with said order, did, while in the office of the Provost Marshal of Louisville, and upon seeing Colonel Mundy and another officer approaching or pass-

2

ing said office of the Provost Marshal, appear at the door and say to the officer who accompanied Colonel Mundy, 'Here I am; and if either you or Colonel Mundy want me, you can find me either here or at my boarding house. I am an officer and a gentleman, and I will be treated as such;' or words to that effect. And, further, in this: that when, a short time thereafter, an officer visited the Provost Marshal's office, with positive orders for the said Colonel *Moore* to report to Colonel Mundy's office, he, the said Colonel *Moore*, did tell the officer bearing the order that if he attempted to take him he would do it at his peril, and did ask one of the officers who was in the Provost Marshal's office at the time, if he had a pistol, intending thereby to intimidate the said officer in the execution of his duty. This at the office of the Provost Marshal, in the city of Louisville, Kentucky, on or about the 5th day of November, 1863."

CHARGE 4TH.

"*Disrespect to his superior officers, and conduct unbecoming an officer and a gentleman.*"

Specification—"In this; that he, Colonel *O. H. Moore*, 25th Regiment Michigan Volunteer Infantry, did publicly say, in the office of the Provost Marshal of the city of Louisville, Kentucky, on or about the 5th day of November, 1863, that 'Colonel Mundy and General Boyle were both damned fools, and did not know their business as officers,' or words to that effect; and did further say: 'If I have to report to Colonel Mundy I will slap him in the mouth. That damned Colonel Mundy has incarcerated me once before in Barracks No. 1; he had no right to do it, and will be damned if he can do it again,' or words to that effect. And did tell the officer who brought him an order to report to Colonel Mundy, the post commandant, in compliance with a general order to that effect, from the Headquarters of the District of Kentucky, to say to Colonel Mundy that if he (Colonel *Moore*) did report he would make it a personal matter by slapping his (Colonel Mundy's) mouth, or words to that effect. All this, to the detriment of subordination and the great scandal of the service, at Louisville, Kentucky, on or about the 5th day of November, 1863."

CHARGE 5TH.

"*Conduct unbecoming an officer and gentleman.*"

Specification—"In this; that he, Colonel *O. H. Moore* 25th Michigan Regiment Volunteer Infantry, while Provost Marshal of the city of Louisville, Kentucky, and intrusted with the peace and good order thereof, did, on or about the 11th day of December, 1862, visit the Louisville Theater, in the said city of Louisville, in a state of intoxication, and did, by his boisterous talking and ungentlemanly conduct generally, annoy the ladies and

3

gentlemen sitting near him, and did afterward, under the influence of his intoxication, go to sleep in the said theater. All this to the disgrace of himself and the scandal of the service."

Specification 2d—" In this; that he, Colonel *O. H. Moore*, 25th Regiment Michigan Volunteer Infantry, did, on or about the evening of the 3d day of December, 1863, appear at the Louisville Theater, in the city of Louisville, Kentucky, in a state of intoxication, and did, by his loud talking and ungentlemanly behavior, make himself conspicuous to an unseemly degree, attracting the attention of the policeman of the theater, and annoying that part of the audience which was near him. This to the disgrace of himself and the discredit of the service."

To which charges and specifications the accused pleaded—

"*Not Guilty.*"

FINDING AND SENTENCE.

The Court, after mature deliberation on the evidence adduced, finds the accused as follows:

Of the *Specification*, 1st CHARGE, "*Guilty.*"

Of the 1st CHARGE, "*Guilty.*"

Of the *Specification*, 2d CHARGE, "*Guilty.*"

Of the 2d CHARGE, "*Guilty.*"

Of the *Specification*, 3d CHARGE, "*Guilty.*"

Of the 3d CHARGE, "*Guilty.*"

Of the *Specification*, 4th CHARGE, "*Guilty.*"

Of the 4th CHARGE, "*Guilty.*"

Of the 1st *Specification*, 5th CHARGE, "*Guilty,*" excepting the following words, to-wit: "while Provost Marshal of the city of Louisville, Kentucky, and instrusted with the peace and good order thereof."

Of the 2d *Specification*, 5th CHARGE, "*Not Guilty.*"

Of the 5th CHARGE, "*Guilty.*"

And does therefore, sentence him, Colonel *O. H. Moore*, 25th Regiment Michigan Volunteer Infantry, "*To be dismissed the service of the United States.*"

Proceedings, findings, and sentence disapproved, for the following reasons:

1st. The first charge and specification are not supported by the proof.

2d. The gist of the specification under the second charge is, that Captain Burleigh, 8th Regiment Kentucky Volunteer Infantry, acting under the orders of Colonel Marc Mundy, Post Commander, Louisville, Kentucky, requested or ordered Colonel *Moore* to report at Col-

4

onel Mundy's office. This Colonel *Moore* declined to do, without a written order to that effect. Colonel *Moore* had a right to demand this written order.

3d. Possibly the proof under the specification of the third charge may warrant the findings of the Court as to that charge and specification; but the whole transaction, both on the part of Captain Burleigh, acting under the orders of Colonel Marc Mundy, and of the accused, Colonel *Moore*, was in bad taste and frivolous in the extreme.

4th. The 4th charge is improperly drawn. It sets forth and contains two distinct offenses, and is fatally defective.

5th. The proof under the 1st specification of the 5th charge does not support the specification, but is at variance with it. The Court, therefore, erred in its finding under this charge.

6th The record shows that Lieutenant Colonel B. F. Orcutt, 25th Regiment Michigan Volunteer Infantry, the same regiment of which the accused is Colonel, was a member of and sat on the Court for the trial of Colonel *Moore*. This was a grievous error, and is in direct voilation of General Order No. 160, Headquarters Department of the Ohio, of 1863, which says: "No officer should be detailed as a member who would be benefitted by the dismissal or loss of rank of the accused."

7th. The record shows that the charges were held and allowed to accumulate against the accused.

The first offense in the order of time was the 11th of December, 1862, the last the 3d of December, 1863; the intervening offenses are given as June 28 and November 25, 1863.

Colonel *O. H. Moore*, 25th Regiment Michigan Volunteer Infantry, is released from arrest, and will at once assume command of his regiment.

BY COMMAND OF MAJOR GENERAL FOSTER:

W. P. ANDERSON,
Assistant Adjutant General.

OFFICIAL: W P Anderson
A. A. G.

Source: National Archives

APPENDIX O

Casualties at the Battle of Lebanon, July 5, 1863

Federal Casualties, 20th Kentucky Infantry: all privates, unless noted

Co. A—**Napoleon B. DeCourcy/devary,** wounded slightly in hip.

Co. B—**Sgt. Joseph Slaughter**, died after being knocked in head with a musket on way to Springfield and run over by artillery; **Joseph Houghton**, killed on way to Springfield by skull being broken by gun muzzle. [*Louisville Journal* report-cannot find in AGR]

Co. C—**Eugene McCarty**, mortally wounded in chest and right arm, died July 7; Thomas Lynott, wounded severely in right arm; **Sgt. John W. Foster**, wounded severely in left hand; **Henry C. Ball**, wounded severely in face & left shoulder.

Co. D—**Sgt. Peter Daniel**, killed; **Jos. Presley Matthews**, wounded slightly in face; **James Butler**, wounded severely in left leg; **Anderson Somers**.

Co. F—**Jesse Edwards**, killed; **Bellfield Marshall**, wounded severely in right arm and forearm.

Co G—**Josiah Groves**; **Richard P. Hayden**, wounded slightly in left shoulder.

Co. H—**Sgt. Wm. H. Yates**, wounded slightly in left arm; **R.P. Halstead**, wounded slightly in left shoulder.

Co. I—**Sam Ferguson** died, in Springfield of exhaustion; **Sgt. Joseph Bailey**, wounded severely in right forearm; **John Barlow**, wounded slightly in left leg.

Co. K—**Cpl. John House**, killed; **Jabez S. Gifford**, wounded slightly in right leg; **Adolphus Cooley**, wounded slightly in right thigh.

Total: 3 killed and 16 wounded at the battle; two died on way to Springfield.

Sources: Adjustant General's Report, 20th Kentucky Infantry; *Senour, Morgan and His Captors*, 114; *Louisville Journal*, July 14, 1863.

Confederate Casualties, Morgan's Men:

Confederate Killed:

Elliot, Pvt., Logan Co.

Franklin, 2nd Sgt. M.C., Co. F, 2nd Ky. Cav., from Tennessee

Gardner, 2nd Lt. Pat H., Quirk's Scouts

Hayden, Pvt. James, Grant Co.

Health, Pvt., Pulaski Co.

Kinman, Pvt. Hader, Co. G, 6th Ky. Cav.

Moore, Pvt. J.V., No. Middletown, Bourbon Co.

Moore, Pvt. Richard F., Co. D, 8th Ky Cav., Bourbon Co.

Morgan, 1st Lt. Tom, Co. A., 2nd Ky. Cav., Lexington

Reed, Sgt. William H., Co. E, 5th Ky Cav.

Richardson, Pvt. David, Mercer Co.

Smith, Pvt. David B. of Alabama

Worsham, Pvt. Richard, Co. B, 2nd Ky Cav. and then with Quirk's Scouts, born 1839, of Lexington, Ky.

And others unknown to the author.

Confederate Wounded:

Brown, John T., Co. D, 2nd Ky Cav., fracture of lower jaw*

Brown, Lt. S.J., Co. C, 6th Ky Cav. compound fracture of right arm*

Carlton, James, Co. F, 5th Ky Cav., left thigh,* from Anderson Co.

Clarke, Peter, Co. D, 6th Ky Cav., severe wound in right shoulder*

Crine, John F., Co. B, 3rd Ky Cav., dangerously in neck and shoulder*

Crow, F.M., Co. B, 3rd Ky Cav., dangerously in head

Davis, Thos., Co. C, 6th Ky Cav., severe wounded in leg, since dead

Eastham, Vincent, Co. B, 8th Ky Cav., sev. wounds, shou,chest; died*

Ferguson, H.B., Co. H, 6th Ky Cav.* [AGR report differs]

Franklin, Sgt. M.C., Co. F, 2nd Ky Cav., flesh wound of right thigh; died according to KAG, page 567.*

Franks, Capt. Tom B., Co. I, 2nd Ky Cav., flesh wound of left thigh*

Hawkins, E.O., Co. F, 5th Ky Cav., slightly in left cheek*

Hodges, Sgt. Daniel, Co. C, 3rd Ky Cav., flesh wound of right leg*

Johnson, James, Co. B, 3rd Tn. Cav., severe wound, r.leg, since dead

Johnson, James C., Co A, 5th Ky. Cav., from Woodford Co.

Jones, G.W., Co. B, 5th Ky Cav., flesh wound of back*

Jones, Sgt. W. R., Co. B., 2nd Cav., slight wound buttocks*

Jouett, J.L., Co. G, 6th Ky Cav., slight wound in wrist and hip

Logwood, Thomas S., Co. B, 2nd Ky Cav., wound in neck*

Lusby, Sgt. David, Co. A, 6th Ky Cav., compound fracture, left femur*

McClone, Robert, Co. severe wound in abdomen, since dead

Michael,—, Co. G, 3rd Ky Cav., flesh wound of right ankle

Ragar, Lt. J.J., Co. B, 9th Tn Cav., severe wound in chest *

Singleton, Lt. John, Co. D, 6th Ky Cav., flesh wound of right thigh; died later of wounds

Turball, C.A., Co. B, flesh wound of thigh

Witherspoon, Lt. James F., Co. H, 5th Ky. Cav., shot in arm

Louisville Military Prison Records list the following Confederates as captured July 5 or soon thereafter at Lebanon:

Adams, James L., Co. C, 2nd Ky Cav.

Adams, William

Barlow, Joseph F,. Co. C, 2nd Ky Cav.

Campbell, Richard W., Co. H, 2nd Ky Cav.

Davis, William, Co. C, 6th Ky Cav.

Evans, Polk, Co. C, 2nd Ky Cav.

Head, J.S., Commissary Sgt, 2nd Ky Cav.

Hinton, Bloom F., Co. E, 5th Ky Cav.

Hughes, Alvin Sgt., Co. C, 6th Ky. Cav.

Holland, T/F.W., Asst. Surg, 2nd Ky Cav.

Keating, Robert, Byrne's Battery, sent to Camp Douglas; escaped by digging out of dungeon

Jones, J.B., Co. D, 3rd Ky Cav.

Lawrence, D.S., Co. I, 3rd Ky Cav.

Meador, Thos. E., Co. E, 2nd Ky Cav.

Nell W.W., Co. K, 2nd Ky Cav.

Surber, Andrew B., Co. B, 6th Ky Cav.

Teal, David Wittenberger, bugler, Byrne Battery; capt. July 11, sent to Camp Morton; transferred to Camp Douglas, escaped by digging out of dungeon Oct 1863.

Sources: *Louisville Journal*, July 15, 1863; Smith, *D. Howard Smith*; AGReport, Confederate, 2 vols. An asterisk indicates that the name is also in the Louisville Military Prison records as having been captured at Lebanon on July 5, 1863.

APPENDIX P

Letter of Maria I. Knott of Lebanon to Samuel C. Knott, Her Son

Lebanon Ky August 5th /62 [1863]

Dear Sam,

Yours of the 8th of July has been received but owing to the indisposition of Sallie [her daughter-in-law] I have defered answering till now. She was taken sick with typhoid fever about the first of July, did not take her bed til after the battle here, she has been pretty low but is now mending, if no relapse. It will soon be so I can leave her, and then I will write to all the rest of the children—My health is still good, am not so fleshy as I was but still carry weight enough to tire me very soon. P [Proctor] is in tolerable health but mighty blue, has fallen off till he looks like little P[Proctor] again. When Morgan was here the 5th of July his [Proctor's] and Hill's office was burnt which has been a considerable blow to them.[1]

I suppose you have heard long since that there has been a battle here, and Lebanon partly burned—Well is it ever so—on the fifth of July John Morgan with a force of several thousand, some say 10 thousand men[2] made an attack on Col [Charles S.] Hanson with some three or four hundred stationed here. The fight lasted several hours, but not many killed on either side. Hanson fought from the depot, and some private houses; was promised reinforcements soon in the day, but failed to get them, was ordered to hold the town till they got here, but could not; his help was three or four miles of town; heard the contest going on but would not come to his aid, until to save the town he surrendered.[3]

The rebs burned some six or seven private dwellings besides the depot, Clerks office, jail, several law offices, commission houses etc. The private residences were Christopher Beeler, Judge[L.H.] Noble's, Widow Able's, Doct [J.C.]Maxwell's, Doct [Ben] Spaldings, and Mr.[J.S.] Braddock's, the superintendant of the female school.[4] He [Braddock] thinks there was more property destroyed by the rebs in Lebanon that day than has been destroyed by the feds since the war commenced. Well, he cant see very well no how, perhaps not enough to read the accounts of the wholesale destruction of towns and property too, by the feds in different states, but that[they] did not take his so it was all right—I heard one of Woffords [Colonel Frank Wolford, 1st Ky Cav, USA] men say a day or two after the fight that it was all right for said how we have destroyed fifty times as much for them in east Tennessee but Mr. Braddock was not there to see it, so concluded the feds were too clever to destroy property or burn houses—

Morgan in his raid through here took off all the good horses they could get leaving some farmers almost without. They left a good many broke down horses in their places but uncle Abe's servants are gathering them up. [The Federal authorities] wont let those who lost their horses keep them. this I think is entirely wrong—now and then through the intercession of someone they will allow a poor widow to keep one of the broke downs to try to finish her crop with—We have a great many troops here at this time ranging around pilfering and annoying the citizens—they go in gangs of some five or six to a place, call for something to eat and while food is being prepared for them, part of the gang will slip out and steal potatoes till their meal is ready, then go and eat, leave without saying [thanks], pay much less ... for what they got, and when they start off they carry several sacks of potatoes with them—They are playing a cheap game at stealing where ever they chance to be encamped. They are principally free state troops that we are blest with at this time Michiganders, Ohio, and Illinoians—The regiment that fought Morgan was the twentieth Ky but they didnt number over four hundred if that.

Well the election is over, if election it could be called, people had to vote just as the military saw fit or not at all, consequently a small vote was polled. Bramlette the administration man was elected governor, so were the other candidates that were elected not much credit Ky remaining Union when she cant help herself.

What is to be the next piece of tyranny is in the future, but it dont take a prophet now to predict—Yesterday was the day set apart for Thanksgiving and praise for recent victories, but I doubt whether it was generally observed—at any rate not about here.

Note: This letter is from the Knott Collection, Kentucky Library, Western Kentucky University. At the end of the Civil War, J. Proctor

Knott served six terms in the U.S. Congress; was governor of Kentucky from 1883–1887. A Kentucky Historic Highway Marker #1341 was placed at the J. Proctor Knott home site in Marion County from which these letters were written. Maria Knott died in 1864 and is buried in Ryder Cemetery, Lebanon, alongside her husband, Joseph. P. Knott.

APPENDIX Q

Death of Tom Morgan

Letter from Charlton Morgan in prison to his mother, Henrietta Morgan

Cincinnati July 24,'63

Dear Ma—

Misfortune upon misfortune has attended us during this tour...I know of no one who has had such a succession of disastrous misfortunes to befall them as I have suffered during this war. I understand we are to be held indefinitely, as the cartel of Exchange is now broken and must be renewed before our exchange can be effected.

Please inform me what disposition was made of poor Tom's body and whether it was removed to Lexington. The Medical Inspector of Rosecrantz's [sic] Army whom I captured and unconditionally released, promised to obtain permission for Tom's remains to be moved to Lexington. How sad, sad to think of one so young and promising to be so suddenly cut off! The death of Tom has forever clouded my heart, and each hour makes one more sensibly feel his loss, and I can but Exclaim, "Oh God! How inscrutable art thy laws." A few moments before his death, I was listening to him while he sang one of his favorite songs. (the lone grave by the glen) He is now in a better world, where sin and sorrow is not known, God has chosen him as one of his flock. Though a sinner, I daily kneel in prayer to God to pardon the transgression of my Brother, and in his great goodness & mercy receive him as one of his fold. Well, can it be said of Tom, "None knew him but to love him. None named him but to praise."*

Your devoted Son

Charlton

Love to Aunt Bettie [slave that the children loved]

*Literary allusion from *On the Death of Joseph Rodman Drake* by Fitz-Greene Halleck

Source: Hunt-Morgan Papers, Box 16, Folder 10, Special Collections, University of Kentucky Library.

APPENDIX R

Letter from Gen. Basil Duke to Henrietta Morgan, after John Hunt Morgan's Death

Jonesboro, Tenn

Sept 17th 1864

My Dear Mother,

I presume that ere this, you have heard of the sad occurrence of last Sunday.

We have sustained a great loss and a most painful affliction, and I find my own sorrow even easier to bear than the thought of how grievous will be yours. I have not heard from Mattie since she has learned of his death, and I almost fear to hear. He was buried at Abingdon yesterday at 4 o'clock.

When I left Abingdon last Sunday night Henrietta [his wife] and the children were all well; Key was with them and was in excellent health, as was also Dick who left this place on Monday. Calvin was in Richmond.

George Hunt is here with me, he sends you much love and desires me to say how much he sympathises (sic) with you in your sad bereavement.

I send this letter by flag of truce, and have had time to write only this briefly and hastily.

Accept my Dear Mother my heart felt condolence and believe me, ever

Your affectionate Son

Basil W. Duke

Note: Basil Duke was the son-in-law of Henrietta Morgan, married to Henrietta, her daughter. Key, Dick, and Calvin were her surviving sons. Mattie was the pregnant wife of J.H. Morgan.

Source: Morgan-Duke Papers, Filson Historical Society, Louisville, Ky.

APPENDIX S

Civil Wars Letters of Sgt. John Wesley Hubbard

John W. Hubbard, born in Taylor County, was the second child of ten children of Walker T. and Rachel Watson Hubbard. The family lived in the Soule's Chapel community. Born in 1842, at age 19, he volunteered for the Union Army and enlisted in Company A, 3rd Kentucky Infantry, for three years. He was promoted to corporal and then appointed sergeant on February 11, 1863.

Hubbard, 5'6½" tall, was fair complexioned with blue eyes and light hair. John, a school teacher, and the neighboring Steger family were great friends. He visited them the night before he left for the army. They all sang around an old pump organ and had prayer. After enlisting, he became ill in the winter of 1861, as so many others.

★ ★ ★

From hospital room in a private home
Danville, Boyle County

December 6, 1861

Dear Father and Mother,

… I am still so weak that I can merly [sic] stagger across the room. I do not know whether I am gaining my strength at all or not. I have night sweats.… Start [after me] the 17th… without fail. I think I will probably be able by that time to be conveyed home…

John W. Hubbard

No date

Dear Brother [Joseph Johnson Hubbard, born 1839]

...We are near Nashville, Tennessee on the Murfreesboro Railroad. The newsboys are out here by daylight of a morning although it is three miles from town...

John W. Hubbard

Camp Decherd Station

August 3, 1862

Dear Father and Mother,

... I learned that there is a great stir in Kentucky about the raising of more troops. There may be a draft through there pretty soon. Tell brother Jo to suffer himself to be drafted before he comes into the service for if he will take a brother's warning that cares for him and his family, he will keep out of it just as long as he can for [I] know he could never have went through the hardships and exposure that I have been through since I left Kentucky and live. I learned that there was some horses impressed by the Pennsylvanians.[9th Pa. Cav.] I do not know but what they took Pa's, but I hope not. I will be 20 years old in a few days.... I am now a man and a hardened soldier.... I feel as if I stood in need more of a father's love and care and a kind mother's prayers than I ever did before. Colonel Bramlette* has resigned and gone home and Scott is our colonel. Write to me and I can receive your letter in three days....

Your affectionate son until death

John W. Hubbard

*Bramlette became a candidate for elective office and won the Governorship of Kentucky in 1864.

Written to Thomas Johnston
Camp near Murfreesboro, Tenn.

February 1, 1863

Dear Friend,

... I have some important news to write. I suppose you have heard of the great battle of Murfreesboro.... The army moved from camp near Nashville December 26th. I had an attack of pleurisy a few days before and I was sent back to Nashville by surgeon Owens. Our army moved upon the rebels at Lavern [Lavergne and] skirmished with them and drove them from every position until within four miles of Murfreesboro where they were in position for battle. Our line of battle was formed Tuesday the 30th of December 1862[Battle of Stones River]. The next day the battle began our division held the right center where the attack was fiercest ... the rebels was sheltered by the thickest grove of cedars you ever saw. Our regiment went into the fight with 299 men with 60 rounds of cartridges. They began about 9 o'clock Wednesday morning the 31st. In about thirty minutes Colonel [Samuel] McKee fell shot in the head. George W. James was shot in the side and died in a little while. He belonged to our company. Jasper Adams wounded in the hip severely. John Jones was shot in the ankle with a large ball. James Gibson was hit in the forehead with a piece of bombshell which fortunately did not fracture his skull. All belonging to our company. Several others of our company got slightly wounded. Our Lieutenant Ben Powell commanded our company. He was hit by a bullet on the shin and slightly wounded. There was 117 killed and wounded which was over one third of our regiment but the good of it is, Tom, that while Ohio and other regiments run, the Kentucky boys never yielded an inch of ground. [Rest of letter missing]

Note: John Jones later died of wounds. Gibson was killed later at Missionary Ridge.

Written to Robert T. Steger, Company C, 13th Ky Infantry
Camp near Murfreesboro, Tenn.

March 7, 1863

Dear Friend:

... It has rained almost every other day for about a month which you must know has rendered camp a most uncomfortable place and more than that, our duty is very hard. We have to go on picket every fourth day. We have to go on foraging expeditions once a week which was more laborious duty. I regret very much Pa loosing his mare and horse but it seems as the war was touching and injuring almost every [one] more or less in Kentucky. I don't know when this is to end, Bob, if I thought our neighborhood would escape with what it has left I would rest perfectly easy. Bob, I would be so glad to see you. It seems as if the 3rd and 13th was doomed to keep separated for the war. I would be glad if we could get to come to Kentucky...Give my respects to all my friends in Company C....

Your best friend,

John Wesley Hubbard

P.S. Direct to Company A, 3rd Regt, Ky Vols, Haskills Brigade, Woods Division, Army of the Cumberland, in the care of Major Bullitt, to follow.

Written to William Johnston

Camp near Murfreesboro, Tenn.

March 19, 1863

Dear Old Friend,

...I guess we will march from here soon. We are ordered to leave our tents and most camp equipment behind. I do not know how we will make it without tents, but we have gum blankets with eyes in them so that we can tie several together and make a good shelter in time of a hard rain. I guess we will move on the rebels [Bragg's army] which are reported to be at Tullahoma a distance of about forty miles and you may look for a hard battle sometime this spring...Our whole corps was reviewed by General Rosecrans yesterday...

Your ever true friend,

J.W. Hubbard

Camp Murfreesboro, Tennessee

May 1, 1863

Dear Mother and Father,

... Yesterday was the day set apart by the President for Thanksgiving Day. We had preaching twice yesterday.... I guess you all are done planting corn by this time. Am glad to hear that you sold your tobacco as well as you did. Your best hogshead just lacked fifty cents coming up to my guess. If you had it in Louisville a week or two sooner it would have sold two or three dollars more on the hundred.... Tell Sally Bet* to be a good girl. Bring her up well Mother and for what is a woman without a refined and intellectual mind. I want you to give the boys all chance of education you can for it is worth more to them than gold. I see fellows here that would give me any price to teach them to write but not the opportunity. Since I was promoted to sergeant I have a great more to see to. I received a letter from Bob Steger yesterday dated two days ago. He is still in the hospital. I get letters frequently from Trav Miller.... Give my love to my old friend Joe Miller. Also to William Johnston and family. Tell Mary** howdy for me. Tell Isum** I would be glad to be at home to thin some of his tobacco....

Your affectionate son

Wesley Hubbard

*Sister, Sarah Elizabeth Hubbard, born 1852. **Mary and Isum were slaves. Mary is buried in the Hubbard Cemetery, off Lone Valley Road.

In Fort Dunlap near Chattanooga

September 26, 1863

My Dear Father and Mother,

It affords me much pleasure that I find an opportunity at this time to write to you in answer to yours wrote the 10th of September. . . . I happened to be somewhat low-spirited at that time. . . . I guess you have not yet heard of the battle fought Saturday and Sunday between here and Gordons Mill. There was some fighting Friday evening but the general battle began on Saturday morning and raged all day. Our brigade held a position near the mill but we were attacked on about two o'clock

P.M. We moved on the left where the battle raged. Our army whipped the rebels back some Saturday. It took us some time to find the line of battle. In fact we did not become regularly engaged that day although we got several killed and wounded. We lay on the line all night until near day when we moved a little to the rear and on the left of our line.

We got our breakfast. It was not the intention of our army to fight on Sunday without we were attacked. We moved on the line about 8 o'clock A.M. The rebels attacked our left as soon as we got on the line. Our brigade moved on the rebels. Our company was in front as skirmishers. We were attacked by the rebels in an open field while the rebel sharpshooters were under cover of bushes and tress. The fire was so hot we were obliged to get behind stumps…I saw we could not stand it any longer where we was so told the boys to rush forward to the woods and drive the rascals out. We pushed forward and run them back but we had not more than got to the wood when we had to retreat from grapeshot. We had run right on a battery. We got back and moved on to the left where our men was giving away. They ran through us, tangled up our regiment so that we were forced to fall back about a mile where we took position on a hill. This was about 11 A.M. and our brigade held this point against about twenty thousand until night. When they had driven back our flanks and we were forced to retreat… back to Chattanooga. We are well fortified here and I hope we can hold them back. We can see thousands of their campfires burning of a night.

You may think [it] strange that the rebels whipped us back but they outnumbered us two to one. General Longstreet is here from Lee's Virginia Army. I saw a good many of his men wounded. Johnston is here with a great many troops of his army. For every man of ours, the rebels have two. We have been looking for reinforcements from Burnside's but as yet we can hear nothing of them. We have lost thousands of our men killed wounded and prisoners. We have also killed wounded and taken thousands of the rebels. I will give you a list of the killed and wounded in our company. Thomas Hood killed. Wm. F. Anderson killed. James Long wounded in the side. Lt. Bradshaw in the hip and no doubt dead by this time. Bird Harvey wounded, his leg broke. Jack Ferguson in the leg. Aron R. Pike in the leg. Jim Curry in the thigh. Wm. T. Jones in the hand. James Shelton in the leg. Jim Powell slightly in the leg. Mother, I feel thankful to my Maker that I was spared. I fought so hard as hard as a man could for I had almost rather die than to be whipped back…. My love to all my family. Tell Pa he need not buy me a horse…

I remain your son.

J.W. Hubbard

Note: One month after the above letter was written, Sgt. John Wesley Hubbard was killed in action, suffering wounds in the abdomen, in the Battle of Missionary Ridge, November 25, 1863, and is buried in the National Cemetery there.

Source: Compiled Service Records, NA. The letters were owned by Herman Hubbard and were copied by the author, July 12, 1976, and slight punctuation has been added for clarity. Hubbard was the son of Owen, who was the son of William Lawrence, who was the youngest son of Walker T. Hubbard. Herman Hubbard owned the log home, built in 1855, of his ancestor, Walker T. Hubbard, until it was completely destroyed by a tornado in 1973. These Civil War letters were saved only because they were stored in a bank lockbox.

Acknowledgements

The author gratefully acknowledges the following people, some of whom are now deceased, who contributed to this work through their personal stories.

Arms, David W., Burkesville, Ky.
Badgett, J. Chester, Campbellsville, Ky.
Baker, Walter, Glasgow, Ky.
Barbee, Joe, Columbia, Ky.
Beard, Georgia, Campbellsville, Ky.
Bishop, Don, Campbellsville, Ky.
Black, Dorothy Bridgwater, Houston, Tex.
Blakeman, Chester and Ina, Campbellsville, Ky.
Blakeman, Henry, Campbellsville, Ky.
Bledsoe, Evelyn Steger Freund, Forest City, Mo.
Bottoms, Wallace, Campbellsville, Ky.
Bridgewater, David, Cane Valley, Ky.
Bridgwater, Elizabeth, Louisville, Ky.
Brockman, Jesse and Sarah, Campbellsville, Ky.
Brown, Raymond and Anita, Campbellsville, Ky.
Buchanan, Henry Allen, Campbellsville, Ky.
Burress, Raymond, Campbellsville, Ky.
Cahill, Lora, Attica, Ohio
Caldwell, Jack, Campbellsville, Ky.
Caldwell, Jimmy, Campbellsville, Ky.
Campbell, Beulah, Campbellsville, Ky.
Campbell, Jeff H., Sr., Campbellsville, Ky.
Carrico, Billy Ray, Springfield, Ky.
Carter, Mary Louise Hiestand, Campbellsville, Ky.
Chambers, Peggy Atkinson, Campbellsville, Ky.
Chandler, Shelby, Campbellsville, Ky.
Chowning, John, Campbellsville, Ky.
Collier, Martha Revis, Mobile, Ala.
Colvin, Evelyn Smith, Campbellsville, Ky.
Cook, Grafton and Barbara, Niles, Mich.
Cowherd, Robert H. and Ina, Campbellsville, Ky.
Curtis, Ann Heskamp, Columbia, Ky.
Davenport, Frances, Campbellsville, Ky.
Ellis, Kelly, Pellyton, Ky.
Elmore, Don, Somerset, Ky.
Faulkner, Fred, Sr., Campbellsville, Ky.
Faulkner, Mrs. Fred, Sr., Campbellsville, Ky.
Faulkner, Raymond Tye, Jr., Campbellsville, Ky.
Feather, Catherine Turner, Campbellsville, Ky.
Feather, Gary and Lori, Green County, Ky.
Fisher, Stella, Campbellsville, Ky.
Flowers, Randy, Columbia, Ky.
Fouser, Nancy, Georgetown, Ky.
Foust, Pam Hurt, Columbia, Ky.
Friend, Woodrow W., Nicholasville, Ky.
Fudge, Homer Brown, Breeding, Ky.
Gaddie, Elsie, Campbellsville, Ky.
Gilmore, Harley, Campbellsville, Ky.
Gilpin, Deborah, Campbellsville, Ky.
Hall, Arbell Gupton, Campbellsville, Ky.
Hall, Lyman S., Campbellsville, Ky.
Hamilton, Elizabeth Bridgwater, Louisville, Ky.
Harding, L. Fuller, Campbellsville, Ky.
Hayes, Nash, Lebanon, Ky.
Hazard, Murrell, Campbellsville and Lexington, Ky.
Hensley, Keith, Monroe, Ky.

Hubbard, Edna, Columbia, Ky.
Hubbard, Herman, Campbellsville, Ky.
Huber, Charles, Campbellsville, Ky.
Humphress, Jolly, Campbellsville, Ky.
Humphress, Keith, Campbellsville, Ky.
Hurt, Gladys Thurman, Burkesville, Ky.
Hutchison, Lois Hubbard, Columbia, Ky.
Jackson, Lorena, Cane Valley, Ky.
Jeffries, Thomas, Campbellsville, Ky.
Jeter, Gracie, Campbellsville, Ky.
Johnson, Paul, Sr., Campbellsville, Ky.
Jones, Gypsie Cosby, Richmond, Ky.
Karel, John, St. Louis, Mo.
Keene, Richard, Burkesville, Ky.
Kelly, Arthur, Springfield, Ky.
Kendall, Jimmy, Campbellsville, Ky.
Kerr, Billy Joe, Campbellsville, Ky.
Kerr, John, Campbellsville, Ky.
Kessler, Janet Caffee, Campbellsville, Ky.
Kirtley, Diana Farris, Washington, D.C.
Kolbenschlag, Vonnie, Columbia, Ky.
Larimore, Laura, Campbellsville, Ky.
Lee, Barilla, Campbellsville, Ky.
Lewis, Doug and Alta, Burkesville, Ky.
Lewis, Margaret Trotter, Campbellsville, Ky.
Martin, M. Douglas, Campbellsville, Ky.
Martin, Martha Barnes, Columbia, Ky.
McGeehan, Albert, Holland, Mich.
McKinley, Aileen, Campbellsville, Ky.
McKinley, Virginia Buchanan,
Campbellsville, Ky.
Mershon, W. A., Campbellsville, Ky.
Money, Bonnie, Louisville, Ky.
Moore, Sam, Sr., Greensburg, Ky.
Morris, James "Jimmy" and Margarite,
Campbellsville, Ky.
Murley, Magdalene, Burkesville, Ky.
Neal, James, Richmond, Ky.
Newcomb, Jerry, Finley, Ky.
Nunn, Shellie Kendall, Campbellsville, Ky.
Osborne, Gary, Campbellsville, Ky.
Parrott, R. Towler and Ann Tandy,
Campbellsville, Ky.
Perkins, Ray, Greensburg, Ky.
Phillips, Robert and Suzanne Sublett,
Campbellsville, Ky.
Price, Elizabeth, Campbellsville, Ky.
Quinn, E. W., Campbellsville, Ky.
Ratcliffe, Ritchie, Burkesville, Ky.
Reid, Celesta, Campbellsville, Ky.
Reynolds, Jewell Lemmons,
Campbellsville, Ky.
Risen, Clay, Campbellsville, Ky.
Roland, Charles P., Lexington, Ky.
Russell, Harold, Campbellsville, Ky.
Sanders, Richard Allen, II,
Campbellsville, Ky.
Sapp, Danny, Jessietown, Ky.
Sapp, Samuel, Campbellsville, Ky.
Scott, Georgia, Campbellsville, Ky.
Settle, Carol, Campbellsville, Ky.
Simmons, Barbara Durham, Greensburg, Ky.
Skidmore, Richard, Hanover, Ind.
Smith, E. B., Campbellsville, Ky.
Smith, Howard, Campbellsville, Ky.
Smith, Margaret Wood, Campbellsville, Ky.
Smith, Randolph, Burkesville, Ky.
Smith, Tim, Shiloh Battlefield, Tenn.
Sparks, Marilyn, Breeding, Ky
Steger, Gladys, Sharon, Pa.
Stewart, Margaret, Campbellsville, Ky.
Stivers, Sue, Columbia, Ky.
Stone, Dora, Cane Valley, Ky.
Sublett, James Robert, Campbellsville, Ky.
Sublett, Loneta, Coburg, Ky.
Sublett, Richard, Campbellsville, Ky.
Thomas, Shelby, Greensburg, Ky.
Trotter, George, LaGrange, Ky.
Turner, Henry R., Garrison, N.Y.
Walters, Clara, Campbellsville, Ky.
Ward, Terry, Lebanon, Ky.
Warren, Harlan, Campbellsville, Ky.
Webster, Barbara DeWitt, Campbellsville, Ky.
Webster, Robert, Campbellsville, Ky.
Whitehouse, Alice Thurman McElroy,
Lebanon, Ky.
Whitlock, Debbie, Campbellsville, Ky.
Wilcoxson, Frank, Campbellsville, Ky.
Wilkerson, Janice, Campbellsville, Ky.
Williams, Russell and Betty,
Campbellsville, Ky.
Wright, Barbara, Campbellsville, Ky.
Wright, Steven L., Elizabethtown, Ky.
Yates, Terry, Campbellsville, Ky.

Notes

Abbreviations used in the Notes

AGR,USA	*Report of the Adjutant General of the State of Kentucky*. 2 vols. 1861–66.
AGR,CSA	*Report of the Adjutant General of the State of Kentucky: Confederate Kentucky Volunteers*. 2 vols.1861–65.
CC	Calvin College, Grand Rapids, Mich.
CSRecord	Compiled Service Record
FHS	Filson Historical Society, Louisville, Ky.
HHT	Holland Historical Trust Collection of the Joint Archives of Holland, Hope College, Holland, Mich.
IHS	Indiana Historical Society, Indianapolis, Ind.
ISA	Indiana State Archives, Indianapolis, Ind.
KDLA	Kentucky Department of Libraries and Archives, Frankfort, Ky.
KHS	Kentucky Historical Society, Frankfort, Ky.
KL-WKU	Kentucky Library, Western Kentucky University, Bowling Green, Ky.
MRRL	Military Records Research Library, Frankfort, Ky.
NA	National Archives and Records Administration, Washington, D.C.
OHS	Ohio Historical Society, Columbus, Ohio
OR	*The War of the Rebellion: A Compilation of the Official Records of the Union and Confederate Armies*. 128 vols. 1880–1901.
ORN	*Official Records of the Union and Confederate Navies in the War of the Rebellion*. 30 vols.
OR Supp	*Supplement to the Official Records of the Union and Confederate Armies*. Part I-Reports. 12 vols. Part II-Record of Events. 78 vols.
RG	Record Group

SHC	Southern Historical Collection, Manuscripts Department, Wilson Library, University of North Carolina, Chapel Hill.
SHSW	State Historical Society of Wisconsin, Madison, Wis.
UKL	University of Kentucky Library, Lexington, Ky.
USAMHI	United States Army Military History Institute, Carlisle Barracks, Pa.

Location of Manuscript Collections Mentioned in the Notes:

Blair Papers, Burton Historical Collection, Detroit Public Library, Detroit, Mich.

Bramlette Papers, Kentucky Department of Libraries and Archives, Frankfort, Ky.

Hathaway Papers, University of Kentucky Library, Lexington, Ky.

Hines Papers, University of Kentucky Library, Lexington, Ky.

Holland Papers, University of Kentucky Library, Lexington, Ky.

Hunt-Morgan Papers, University of Kentucky Library, Lexington, Ky.

Knott Papers, Kentucky Library, Western Kentucky University, Bowling Green, Ky.

Moerdyk Papers, Hope College, Holland, Mich.

Moore Papers, Kalamazoo Valley Museum, Kalamazoo, Mich.

Slayton Papers, Bentley Historical Library, Ann Arbor, Mich.

Smith Papers, Kentucky Historical Society, Frankfort, Ky.

Todd Papers, Bentley Historical Library, University of Michigan, Ann Arbor, Mich.

Woodruff Papers, Bentley Historical Library, Ann Arbor, Mich.

Van Lente Papers, Holland Historical Trust Collection of the Joint Archives of Holland, Hope College, Holland, Mich.

Van Raalte Papers, Calvin College, Grand Rapids, Mich.

Van Raalte Papers, Holland Historical Trust Collection of the Joint Archives of Holland, Hope College, Holland, Mich.

Notes

Prologue

1. Ulysses S. Grant, *Personal Memoirs* (New York: Modern Library), 1999, 590. Punctuation added.
2. *Nashville Dispatch*, November 27, 1863 carried story from *Louisville Journal*.
3. Basil W. Duke, *History of Morgan's Cavalry*, (Cincinnati: Miami Printing, 1867), 29; James A. Ramage, *Rebel Raider: The Life of General John Hunt Morgan* (Lexington: University Press of Kentucky, 1986), 1.
4. Col. Thomas F. Berry, *Four Years with Morgan and Forrest* (Oklahoma City: Harlow-Rattliff, 1914), 196.
5. Duke, *History of Morgan's Cavalry*, 29–30.
6. J. Soul Smith, *Cincinnati News-Journal*, reprinted in *Courier-Journal*, July 1883.

PART ONE: Campbellsville, Kentucky *1860*, pp. 1–11

1. *Central Kentucky Researcher*, Winter, 1983, 2, and Spring, 1996, 12. Other old soldiers who gathered at Chandler's, often in the mornings, were Robert Kerr, Bill Shofner, Jack Duffy, Boney Thomas, Andy Lair, and Andy Carson.
2. Taylor County Order Book 2, 291; Order Book 3, 411. John Carpenter and William Scott, Jr., *Kentucky Courthouses*, 36, reported that the courthouse was a log building. However, Taylor County Order Book 2, 308, 372 indicates that it was brick. In 1864 a plank fence with gates was erected around the yard of the courthouse square. No photo of the 1848 courthouse is known to exist.
3. *Lebanon Weekly Standard*, November 27, 1872, cited hereafter as *Lebanon Standard*. The paper said that these buildings were erected by the founders of Campbellsville fifty or sixty years ago. In 1809 Andrew Campbell began operating a grist mill on Buckhorn Creek and by 1814 was selling town lots. In 1817 the Kentucky legislature recognized the establishment of a town. One cistern was located at the old Caulk Hardware Building, 117 E. Main, and another at Mitchell's Men Wear, 221 E. Main.
4. The Gowdy House, located at 315 Logan Street, Campbellsville, was called "Heritage Hall." The Wayne Hoskins home, located on the summit of the hill at the foot of Court Street, was purchased by Dr. Samuel Bass and later became the Buchanan Collegiate Institute. James Campbell's home is mentioned in Tresenrider v. Shuttleworth, Taylor County Circuit Court Records, 1853–54. The Davis home, Taylor County Order Book 2, 305; the Haselwood home in Gowdy v. Haselwood, Taylor Circuit Bundle 40, 1857.
5. Shelby Chandler, interview with author, 1983. Second North Street became Broadway.
6. Velmer Aaron, *Historical Sketch of the Campbellsville Methodist Church* (Campbellsville, Ky.: Star Printing, 1940), 31; Margaret Stewart, interview with author, June 3, 2004; Gowdy v. Haselwood, Taylor Circuit Bundle 40, 1857; "Taylor County Jottings," *Lebanon Standard*, May 10, 1876. The town cemetery referred to is now known as Brookside Cemetery.

7. For a photograph of the old school, see 1995 Taylor County Historic Calendar; for Andrew Campbell records, see Green County Deed Books and Tray of Inventories, Appraisals, & Mills; Green County Circuit Court Suit #5786; Green County Deed Book 17, 72, gives the death date of Andrew Campbell as 1819; source for site of grave of Andrew Campbell, Jeff H. Campbell, Sr. interview with author, 1998. For 1816 voting precinct, see Acts of Gen. Assembly, Chapter CCXCIV.

8. William R. Plum, *The Military Telegraph during the Civil War in the United States.* 2 vols; reprint, 2 vols in 1 (New York: Arno Press, 1974), 191; *Lebanon Post*, March 7, 1855. The ice house fronted on First St. and barns for horses were to the west of the tavern. Inventory of Redman, Taylor County Inventory Settlements and Sales Bill Book 4, 95–111. Bob Henry Cowherd said the tavern had a spacious dining room. To keep flies away, fans of split newspapers were pulled by a string over the food table. According to Pitman Lodge Minutes, June 24, 1850, the Masons regularly ate dinner there.

9. L&N v. Atkinson, Taylor County Circuit Bundle 29; for fees, see Taylor County Order Book 2, 207, July 6, 1863; U.S. Census Office, Taylor County Slaves, (1860); Taylor County Circuit Court Case, Redman v. Hiestand Heirs, Bundle 24, January 26, 1857, cleared title to Town Lot #31, the tannery lot. Tax information from Joe DeSpain, Speech, Taylor County Historical Society, April 19, 2005.

10. U.S. Census Office, *Seventh Census (1850)*, Taylor County; Betty Gorin, "History of the Post Office at Campbellsville, Kentucky, 1817–1985," n.p. According to House Journals, Frankfort, Ky., 1862, 1863, F.J. Hiestand remained town marshal.

11. Taylor County Order Book 2, 172, 181, 188, 202, 211, 233, 261, 274, 284.

12. U.S. Census Office, *Eighth Census (1860)*, Taylor County, 260–61, compiled and published by the Taylor County Historical Society, 1988, hereafter cited as Taylor County 1860 Census. The federal census lists 129 as the total for free blacks; however, the author counted only 97. Kentucky's population included 19.5 % enslaved people.

13. Robert Lee Nesbitt, *Early Taylor County History* (Campbellsville: *News-Journal*, 1941), 10.

14. Ibid.; Lewis Collins, *History of Kentucky*, II (Covington: Collins & Co., 1874), 265; Miscellaneous Book in possession of William Michael Hall.

15. "The Seat of War in Kentucky," *Louisville Daily Journal*, September 27, 1861. Hereafter cited as *Louisville Journal.*

16. C. A. Johnston, "Lebanon As I Have Known It," typed copy, Lebanon Public Library, n.d. The old Lebanon Road is 289 today and the road through Saloma is Hwy 744. Market St. in Lebanon became Proctor Knott.

17. Taylor County Order Book 2, 169.

18. Taylor County Circuit Court Case, Wallace v. Griffin, Bundle 230, 1874–1881, is one of the many examples of A.F. Gowdy loans.

19. Betty Gorin, "Men Who Rendered Service in the American Revolution from Taylor County," (Campbellsville, Ky.: Hayes Printing, 1978) n.p.; "Aaron Harding," *Biographical Dictionary of American Congress, 1774–1961* (U.S. Government Printing Office, 1961), 1005; *Louisville Journal,* May 9, 29, 1861; May 11, August 22, 1863; Taylor County Deed Book 1, 465–67. In 1873 the Chandlers built on E. Main, where Lyon-Dewitt Funeral Home is today.

20. Jasper B. Shannon and Ruth McQuown, *Presidential Politics in Kentucky 1824–1948* (Lexington: Bureau of Government Records, 1950), 21, 24, 29.

21. Ibid., 32, 36; Lowell H. Harrison, *Lincoln of Kentucky* (Lexington: University Press of Kentucky, 2000), 117–19.

22. Shannon and McQuown, *Presidential Politics,* 38, 40–41. According to Fuller Harding of Campbellsville, his great-grandfather Abraham Harding, who was a cousin of U.S. Representative Aaron Harding, John Feather, and W.T. Hubbard were three of the men who voted for Lincoln in 1861. Feather had two sons in the Union army, one of whom died. Hubbard had a son, Wesley, in the Union army who was killed at the Battle of Missionary Ridge. R.Jeter wrote to General Hobson that "there would not be a man in our country" to enroll Black troops. Congressman Harding said it was "nothing but robbery." John David Smith, "Recruitment of Negro Soldiers in Kentucky, 1863–1865," *Register of the Kentucky Historical Society* 72 (October 1974), 376, 378.

23. John E. Kleber, ed., *The Kentucky Encyclopedia* (Lexington: University Press of Kentucky, 1992), 429.

24. According to J.F. McElroy, "History of Lebanon," the present road, Hwy 289, (old US68) over Muldraugh's Hill was completed in 1837. For subscriptions to state and national newspapers, see estate settlements in the Taylor County Court 1848–1860.

25. Members of the Battery, *History of Battery M, First Regiment, Illinois Light Artillery* (Princeton, Ill.: Mercer & Dear, 1892), 119, hereafter cited as *Battery M, First Illinois Artillery*; T. B. Brooks to Maj. J. H. Simpson, Chief Engineer, Dept. of the Ohio, May 12, 1863, RG 393, Pt. 1, E. 3541, NA.

26. For James Sanders House, see records of the National Register of Historic Places; for Sanders Tavern, see Green County Minute Book, 1794–1800; for Tandy house, R. Towler Parrott, interview with author, June 20, 1976.

27. OR(ser.1)7: 116–17; F. Senour, *Morgan and His Captors* (Cincinnati: C.F. Vent & Co., 1865), 55; Map by Lt. H. Topping, 1st Ohio Cavalry. From Summersville, it goes to Gabe, across Green River at old Vaughn's Ferry, down Salem Road across Little Barren to Hwy 677. At the 6 mile marker on 677 there is an old hand dug well topped with rock in a field about 30 feet from road that was on the Lexington Pike. Horses were exchanged there. It continued through Monroe probably to Three Springs to connect eventually to 1295 to Cave City, James Dishman to author, April 18, 2005.

28. Quote is from *History, Battery M, First Illinois Artillery*, 27–28. Early settler-merchant Benoni Hotckhiss, ancestor of Henry R. Turner, made the trip to New Orleans and brought back a pair of diamond earrings for his wife. Henry R. Turner to author, 1970. G.W. Redman House is located on 107 Rose Street, Campbellsville; the Caldwell Home, built in 1854–55, is located on the Columbia Road and owned by Rufus Hansford in 2004. The Tate House, built 1803, is located on the Homeplace on Green River. James A. Sublett's log home, built in 1849, is located on Tebbs Bend Road.

29. For the Taylor County Militia List of 1862 see the *Central Kentucky Researcher*, Spring, Summer, Fall, Winter, 1992, original list at Kentucky History Military Museum, Frankfort, Ky. The Militia List of 1864 listed eight "expatriates" which may indicate how few Taylor Countians served in the southern forces. See AGR, CSA, I, 692, for record of R.A. Webster, a Confederate.

30. "Military Affairs in the Interior," *Louisville Journal*, September 27, 1861; Thomas W. Westerfield, ed., "Rodophil Jeter," *Kentucky Genealogy*, 5: 163–64. Rodophil Jeter,

CSRecords, NA. According to Aileen Wilson McKinley, interview with author, July 25, 2000, Jeter's son-in-law, Pvt. Charles T. Cox, Co. F, 4th Ky. Infantry, CSA, was wounded and captured at Shiloh, April 7, 1862. Cox's daughter, Bess Cox Terhune, would say about her father, "He was shot through and through at Shiloh." Confederate Cox returned to Campbellsville after the war and lived at 514 Lebanon Avenue, next door to his Union father-in-law at 516 Lebanon Ave.

31. *Louisville Journal*, May 9, 1861; for Taylor County settlers in the Rev. War, see Gorin, "Service in American Revolution."

32. Merton Coulter, *Civil War and Readjustment* (Chapel Hill: University of North Carolina Press, 1926), 101–05; Ronald R. Alexander, "Central Kentucky During the Civil War, 1861–1865" (Ph.D. diss., University of Kentucky, 1976), 84–85, 92, 95–96. For more on Frank Wolford 's colorful life, see Hambleton Tapp, "Incidents in the Life of Frank Wolford, Colonel of the First Kentucky Union Cavalry," *Filson Club History Quarterly* 10 (1936), 82–99. After his controversial speech against the policies of the Lincoln administration, Burbridge relieved him of his command. His men wrote a letter to Lincoln, protesting his treatment. Letter appeared in *Louisville Journal*, April 13, 1864.

33. Ramage, *Rebel Raider*, 30–32, 40, said that her illness was probably from an infected blood clot in her leg. After years of suffering and failed treatments, Rebecca's leg was amputated in January 1861 and she subsequently died. Lexington Cemetery Records, Bruce Family Plot.

PART TWO: Morgan Held Captive at Pleasant Hill *September 1861*, pp. 12–31

1. Coulter, *Civil War and Readjustment*, 67, 70, 72–73; *Cincinnati Gazette*, May 30, 1861. For a detailed study of the beginning of the Civil War in Kentucky, see Harrison, *Lincoln of Kentucky*, 139–54.

2. OR(ser. 1)7:117; Letter from Memphis, August 10, 1861, Hunt- Morgan Papers, UKL. A Lt. Short appears in a muster-in roll from New Market. No male named Short appears in the Taylor County 1860 Census.

3. OR(ser.1)7:117; *Louisville Journal*, October 17, 1861, and May 25, 1863 ran a story about Neville's career. He was subsequently appointed Deputy US Marshal and Inspector of Customs.

4. Alexander, "Central Kentucky," 89–99; Ramage, *Rebel Raider*, 45 ; William A. Perrin, *History of Fayette County, Kentucky* (Chicago: O.L. Baskin, 1882), 646.

5. Ramage, *Rebel Raider*, 50; Thomas D. Clark, *The Kentucky* (New York: Farrar & Rinehart, 1942), 299; Ky. Highway Marker, #1235 Morgan Inducted—CSA. Morgan did not have enough horses with his group of soldiers to form a cavalry regiment. Capt. Ed Byrne of Mississippi furnished Morgan with a sufficient number of cavalry horses, thereby creating a lasting friendship between Byrne and Morgan. See Diary of John Joyne, FHS.

6. OR(ser. 1)4: 307; Thomas Speed, *Union Regiments of Kentucky* (Louisville: *Courier-Journal* Job Printing Co., 1897), 552; Kate P. Evans, ed., *A Collection of Green County History* (Greensburg, Ky.: Green County Library, 1976), 78.

7. Muster In Rolls, 13th Kentucky Infantry, USA, NA.

8. The campsite was partially covered by Campbellsville City Lake in the 1950s. William H. Perrin, *History of Kentucky*, 4th ed., 1887, 730; Shelby Thomas, Greensburg, Civil War letter from Camp Andy Johnson in which the soldier writes that "we are on the old Fairground." Lebanon Avenue was Old US Highway 68, now 289. Margaret Wood Smith, granddaughter of J.R. Smith, interview with author, March 2000.

9. "Military Affairs in the Interior," *Louisville Journal*, September 27, 1861.

10. "Campbellsville, Ky., October 28, 1861," *Louisville Journal*, October 30, 1861.

11. Muster In Rolls, 21st Kentucky Infantry, USA, NA. There is only one Sarah Campbell, head of household, in the Taylor County 1860 Census. She is aged 72, born in Virginia, widow of Adam. Adam's plantation was on the south side of Greensburg Road, called West Main in 2004.

12. L. Fuller Harding, as told to him by his father, lawyer-historian Abel Harding, interview with author, March 2000.

13. "Campbellsville, Oct. 28, 1861," *Louisville Journal*, October 30, 1861.

14. "Letter from Camp Johnson" dated September 30, 1861, *Louisville Journal*, October 4, 1861.

15. Letter to the Editor from Campbellsville, *Louisville Journal*, October 30, 1861.

16. Westerfield, *Kentucky Genealogy*, 5: 164; AGR, USA, I, 859; R.E. Jeter, CSRecord, NA; Evans, *Collection of Green County History*, 86, 89.

17. 13th Kentucky and 27th Kentucky Loose Papers, KHS.

18. Ibid.

19. Petition of Underwood and Sprowles, September 1863, Governor Bramlette Papers, Box 8, f153, KDLA.

20. Map of L&N in Kentucky, *Louisville Journal*, September 27, 1861.

21. Kenneth W. Noe, ed., *A Southern Boy in Blue: Memoir of Marcus Woodcock* (Knoxville: University of Tennessee Press, 1996), 26.

22. Ibid., 26–28.

23. Ibid., 24, 29. Hambleton Tapp and James C. Klotter, ed., *The Civil War and John W. Tuttle* (Frankfort: Kentucky Historical Society, 1980), 52, 65 gives more detail about measles at Camp Dick Robinson and the typhoid epidemic at Columbia. In one company of the 3rd Kentucky Infantry there were over 200 cases of typhoid and 39 deaths. "All the vacant houses about the place [Columbia] were filled to overflowing by the sick and a place had to be found for many in the families of the citizens." Illness continued to plague the camps throughout the war. Maj. John Connally wrote home from Munfordville in November 1862 that he had typhoid fever and had lost 60 pounds. Most of men in his regiment, 123rd Ill Infantry, had had the measles and many died. Paul M. Angle, ed. *Three Years in the Army of the Cumberland* (Bloomington: Indiana University Press, 1959), 30.

24. 13th Ky File, MRRL. Lebanon was much affected by sickness, also. The mother of Kentucky Governor Proctor Knott, Maria Knott, wrote in her diary in Lebanon in 1861: Dec 26th I scarcely ever leave home now since so many soldiers have come in our midst, not even to church for some weeks for fear of the small pox, which has

been in town and vicinity—the basement of the P. [Presbyterian] Church is now used for a hospital for one of the regiments here—Several vacant houses in town are also occupied for hospitals—Knott Papers, KL-WKU.

25. Taylor County Deed Book 1, 410. The Trustees purchased Lot #46 from John P. Campbell, son of Adam Campbell.

26. MRRL. The citizens who made the appraisal were William Marrs, William Dearen, and James Blandford. The trustees of the church were F.M. Lewis, John Shreve, and Eastin Sanders.

27. Ibid.; Aaron, *Campbellsville Methodist Church*, 33.

28. MRRL; for Johnston's Mexican War service, see Pitman Lodge #124 Minute book, 1847–1854, copy in Hiestand House Museum, original owned by Dr. Richard Allen Sanders, III, Birmingham, Ala.

29. Stella Fisher, interview with author, July 29, 1976. During the war, T.T. Fisher (1842–1901) lost the index finger of his left hand and had his arm shattered. He married Lydia Davis and ran a large general store at Palestine. Every three months when their checks arrived, Civil War pensioners would come buy their supplies from him, tie the supplies to the saddles of their horses or mules, and lead them home. Fisher is buried at Palestine Church Cemetery.

30. AGR. The regiments that were polled were the 4th, Ky., 10th Ky., 13th Ky., 21st Ky., and the 27th Ky. infantries. It included deaths in Campbellsville, Taylor County, Green River Bridge/Camp, and Camp Ward in Taylor County in November and December of 1861; *Campbellsville News-Journal, 50th Edition,* August 4, 1960, sec 5, 1.

31. *Louisville Journal*, March 7, 24, 1862; Taylor County 1860 Census, 122.

32. Adalaide P. Butler, widow of Capt. John S. Butler, 13th Kentucky Infantry, Pension Application, NA, states that John Butler was placed in the Mayes hospital. Future Lt. Gov. J.R. Hindman of Columbia, Ky., lay ill in the Botts home; Pension Application, NA, of Rodophil Jeter, says that Camp Lizzie Mayes was 10 miles from Pleasant Hill Church.

33. Harry Forrest Lupold, ed., "A Union Surgeon Views the War from Kentucky, 1862," *Register of the Kentucky Historical Society* 72 (July, 1974), 274.

34. *Louisville Journal*, March 7, 1862.

35. E.S. Chandler to Mrs. Hobson, October 31, 1861, Hobson Papers, KHS Microfilm #68.

36. A. Monroe Adair, 2nd Lt, Co D, 6th Ky Inf, CSA, enlisted November 19, 1861; James W. Moss, Capt, Co A, 2nd Ky Inf, CSA, enlisted July 5, 1861.

37. "Excitement at Camp Andy Johnson," *Louisville Journal*, October 19, 1861; "From Greensburg," *Louisville Journal,* October 22, 1861; "Affairs at Greensburg," *Louisville Journal*, October 23, 1861.

38. "Genl Ward's Retreat from Greensburg," *Louisville Journal*, November 4, 1861.

39. OR(ser.1)4: 312; *Louisville Journal*, October 25, 1861. Speed, *Union Regiments*, 554f wrote that before being mustered in, some 32 men of the 27th left Greensburg October 10, 1861, on a scout into Hart County. They were met by about 50 Rebels who fired on them, leaving 1 killed, 1 mortally wounded, 6 wounded. This exchange

of fire, called the Cy Huthinson affair, probably confirmed Ward's desire for better training of his troops.

40. *Louisville Journal*, November 4, 1861.

41. OR(ser.1)4:492, T.C. Hindman and Lt. D. G. White, October 31, 1861.

42. "Gen. Ward's Retreat From Greensburg," *Louisville Journal*, November 4, 1861; "General W.R. Ward's Brigade," *Louisville Journal*, November 6, 1861.

43. OR(ser. I) 4:325.

44. Ibid., 489, 507, 537–38.

45. Bramlette Papers, Box 17, f 374, doc. 411, KDLA. Home Guards Josiah B. Skaggs and Wm. C. Thompson were charged with breach of peace for arresting spies at a sale. Brig. Gen. W.T. Ward wrote that Shofner and Lively were rebels and that the arrest of these rebels "deserves praise rather than censure, a reward instead of a fine." Home Guards James Edwards, Joe Brack Skaggs, and William S. Warren testified concerning the situation on Brush Creek. The guerrillas had murdered Curly Bill Thompson and were coming for Edwards, causing Edwards to flee to Indiana until the end of the war to save his life. The guards had received no pay, but all had been hunted down and their property destroyed.

46. "Baptist Minister's Letter Writes of Civil War Days," n.d.

47. Mrs. L. L. Pumphrey, "Old Times," *Central Kentucky Researcher,* Spring, 1996, 6.

48. *Louisville Journal*, October 30, 1861. In 2004 the Thurman farm was owned by Russell Skaggs, 6888 Bengal Road. Thurman, who once owned over fifty slaves, was one of many Kentuckians who were both slaveowners and loyal to the Union. Thurman died in 1866, Green County Circuit Case #383, May 21, 1867.

59. E. H. Hobson to John W. Barrett, November 5, 1861, Green County Historical Society, Greensburg, Ky.

50. Elizabeth Price, interview with author, September 25, 2004.

51. OR(ser. 1) 4: 481–82; William Lewis v. D.M. Williams, Taylor County Circuit Court Bundle #72. In Williams Account Book, he wrote a poem: "Come all ye sons of freedom and join our band, We are going to fight the enemy and drive them from our land … The South is our wagon and we all take a ride, Secession is our watch word, our rights we all demand, And to defend our fireside, We will pledge our heart and hand, Jeff Davis is our President with Heaven by his side." Spelling corrected. Letter from Ray Perkins, Greensburg, Ky., to author, 2003. The old D.M. Williams farm is owned by Gary and Lori Feather, 4416 Summersville Road, in 2004.

52. OR(ser.1)7:503. According to Record of Events cards, NA, Company E, under Capt. William B. Carroll, was posted at Lebanon during November and December 1861.

53. OR(ser.1)4:327, W.T.Sherman to W.T.Ward, November 2, 1861. General Sherman appointed a number of commissioners to hear cases concerning disloyalty; one was assigned to Campbellsville.

54. OR(ser.1)4:489.

55. OR(ser. I)52(1): 197, Special Orders 85, November 6, 1861, Ward is directed to "return to Campbellsville and resume command of his brigade." Evans, *Collection of*

Green County History, 78; Perrin, *History of Kentucky*, 730; War Department, Adjutant General's Office, List of Military Posts, 46. This area of Green River was where, in the early 1800s, over two billion passenger pigeons lived and where rare fish and mussels flourish today. Alexander Wilson and Charles L. Bonaparte, *American Ornithology*, II (London: Cassell Petter & Galpin, c1870), 200–204; Neltze Blanchan, *Birds That Hunt and Are Hunted* (Garden City, N.Y.: Doubleday, 1920), 294.

56. Shelby Thomas, interview with author, Campbellsville, Ky., January 2002; 13th Kentucky Muster-In Rolls & Record of Events Cards, NA. The Sublett farm was the camp site of the 2nd Michigan from April-May, 1863; the 12th Rhode Island June-early July, 1863; and many other regiments before the war was over. Record of Events Cards, NA. According to J. Robert Sublett, interview with author, July 15, 1976, at one time his 11-acre bottom was full of minie balls. "One year you'd go down and break ground, you'll turn your bullets up... and the next year you'll turn them under...The bullets are just as white as paper."

57. "From Kentucky: Incidents of Camp Life," *Detroit Free Press*, November 4, 1863; Capt. Rodophil Jeter and 100 men were left guarding the bridge until February 28, 1862, after other members of the 13th Kentucky Infantry had departed the site. Jeter Pension Records, NA; OR(ser. 1)52(1): 205.

58. C.C. Briant, *6th Regiment, Indiana Volunteer Infantry* (Indianapolis: William B. Burford, 1891), 143, describes building a stockade.

59. Logan's Cross Roads is called Nancy today. It is a village located near Somerset in Pulaski County, Ky.

60. OR(ser. 1)7:927; Kenneth A. Hafendorfer, *Mill Springs* (Louisville: KH Press, 2001), 102, 132.

61. 14th Ohio Infantry, Record of Events Cards, NA.

62. Hafendorfer, *Mill Springs*, 131, quoting Capt. Judson Bishop, Co A, 2nd Minnesota.

63. Ibid., 130; Samuel Thompson Diary, SHSW; Thomas M. Small Diary, IHS.

64. Kenneth Carley, "The Second Minnesota in the West," *Minnesota History*, June 1963, 260–01.

65. Hafendorfer, *Mill Springs*, 131 as cited in Judson Bishop, *Mill Springs Campaign*, 1890.

66. Ibid., 132; description of Campbellsville from John W. Switzer, 10th Ind., Co D, to Sister Mollie, January 3, 1862, W.H. Smith Memorial Library, IHS. This camp would be on the old Columbia Road, Ky. Hwy 3183, in the area of Amazon.com.

67. Hafendorfer, *Mill Springs*, 132; *Louisville Journal*, January 18, 1862.

68. James H. Price Diary, USAMHI. Spelling corrected.

69. OR(ser.1)7:927, George Thomas to D.C. Buell, January 1, 1862. Thomas reported that he was encamped near Campbellsville and is sending back regimental teams for "a load of subsistence," retaining four teams per regiment. He said that would enable him to have 100,000 rations in Columbia in two days.

70. William Bircher, *A Drummer-Boy's Diary* (St. Paul: St. Paul Book Company, 1889), 17. It is common for a northern traveler in the south to make these comments. Southerners were viewed as indolent, uneducated, clannish, leisure-loving, musical, prone to drinking and gambling, violent at times, not prone to commerce or improv-

ing his houses, but good horsemen and hunters, preferring herding as opposed to "hard farming." Grady McWhiney, in *Cracker Culture*, maintains that the southern culture reflected the Celtic tradition of the Irish, Scots, Welsh while the northern states reflected cultural characteristics of settlers from southwest England. The English tradition included good education, industriousness, steady habits, love of commerce and profit.

71. James Birney Shaw, *History of the Tenth Regiment Indiana Volunteer Infantry* (Lafayette, Ind., 1912), 19, 137.

72. Small Diary. Spelling corrected.

PART THREE: Morgan's Pleasant Hill Raid *January 31, 1862, pp. 32–47*

1. Plum, *Military Telegraph*, 188–189, 264. Fuller was a relative of the poet, John Greenleaf Whittier.

2. According to "The Released Telegraph Builders," *Louisville Journal*, March 7, 1862, the men on this mission were privates Benjamin Drake, Peter Adams, Matthew Johnson-son of the Hon. Andy Johnson, A.M. Hutchinson, James Smith-formerly the clerk of the Galt House, Leibel West, Rison, Thompson, and one other. (AGR, I, CSA, 542–548) According to Keith Hensley, April 18, 2005, the old Lee's Ferry Road crossed Green and Little Barren rivers above Defrice on 677 in Hart County on the Keith Fancher Farm (old Cartmill) into Green County. This old road ran across Taylor County to the top of Muldraugh Hill near Finley.

3. Ibid.

4. According to Harlan Warren, born 1915, Big Pitman Creek can rise quickly and become very dangerous to cross. His father, Rusaw Warren, whose farm was west of the creek, used to drive a team of horses and haul supplies back and forth from Campbellsville to Mac and Pitman. On occasion, the creek would rise and Rusaw Warren and his team would stay in James Bell's barn, which was near the ford on the east side of the creek, for which he was charged 15 cents. The ford is to the north of the present concrete bridge over Big Pitman Creek and the road to the ford is still visible in 2005. Harlan Warren, interview with author, Campbellsville, July 16, 2000.

5. Gorin, "Service in American Revolution." The gravestone of his father, John Thurman, read: "Died in The Full Hope of Unfading Glory, A Revolutionary Soldier."

6. Robert Henry Cowherd, interview with author, Campbellsville, July 1, 1976. This house was near Saloma, on the present Piercey Hill farm, formerly the Lee Young home, now torn down; later Nelson lived in the federal-style brick on the Perkins farm, off Highway 210. John T. B. Nelson and his wife, Elizabeth, are buried in Gaddie Cemetery #5 on the hill above the farm; Ina Cowherd, interview with author, December 21, 2000 for information about the pitcher; John T.B. Nelson is listed as merchant in the Taylor County 1860 Census.

7. OR(ser. 1)7:116. This is the junction of Pleasant Hill Church Road and old US 68, now Ky. Hwy 289.

8. D.L. Druien, *A Brief History of Pleasant Hill Church*, 2–7. The minutes of the church reveal interest in regulating "general worldliness in the community," such as horse racing, playing marbles, and croquet on the Sabbath.

9. *OR*(ser. I)7:116.

10. Ibid., 116–17; Plum, *Military Telegraph,* 189–90; "Capture of Telegraphic Workmen," *Louisville Journal*, February 5, 1862. Sources differ on the number of horses taken.

11. "Released Telegraph Builders," *Louisville Journal*, March 7, 1862.

12. *Louisville Journal,* March 7, 1862. The Taylor County 1860 Census shows Tandy with five sons, one a 16-year–old son, James D. The son of Tandy must have escaped from Morgan's Men, his service record never appearing in the AGR. Morgan, in his Report in the OR states that he took "three horses that were used in carrying the mail." OR(ser.1)7:117.

13. R. Towler Parrott and his wife, Ann Tandy Parrott, interview with author, Campbellsville, Ky., June 20, 1976.

14. OR(ser. 1)7:116. In Morgan's Report, he calls his captives two soldiers, but John Feather was a civilian. Morgan does not report that he put Feather into the church before he set it afire. Senour, *Morgan and His Captors,* 53, also states, in error, that Feather was one of the Union men in the church and that he was one of the six Union men captured. Dr. James Ramage, Morgan historian, thinks it is unlikely that Morgan intended to burn Feather alive.

15. Ibid., 117.

16. Margarite Feather Morris, great-granddaughter of John Feather, interview with author, Campbellsville, June 28, 1976; Howard Smith, a John Feather descendant, interview with author, Campbellsville, 1960s; Dr. Lyman S. Hall, tape recording, interview with author, Campbellsville, March 31, 1979; Dorothy Bridgwater Black of Houston, Tex., interview with author, May 14, 2003; Catherine Turner Feather, written account, November 14, 1997; "Pleasant Hill Baptist Church Survives War," *Campbellsville News-Journal*, August 4, 1960. John H. Feather was in 10th Ky Inf, Co. C, died April 17, 1862 at home. A second son, Albert, joined the Union army, 6th Ky Cav, Co. I, in August, 1862. AGR, I, USA, 166, 811. John Feather lived to be 95 and was the father of 10 children. According to church minutes, Pleasant Hill Church was not rebuilt until 1867.

17. *Louisville Journal*, February 5, 1862; Robert E. McDowell, *City of Conflict—Civil War in Louisville, 1861–65* (Louisville, 1962), 147. According to *Confederate Military History*, 506, Courtland Prentice, Corbett's Battery, was killed at Augusta, Sept. 18, 1862. Clarence Prentice served as Major, 2nd Battalion Cav. and participated in the last Morgan Raid. AGR, CSA, II, 308.

18. Highway 744 follows the old route from Tandy's, now called Hobson on a Taylor County map, through Saloma to Highway 210. (The Hodgenville Road, 210, did not exist in 1862.) The Lexington to Nashville Road continued down Fallen Timber Road and crossed through the Cowherd fields to the Overbrook Road and down to Summersville in 1863. Earlier, during the days of Andrew Jackson, the road took a slightly different route through Jones Road.

19. OR(ser.1)7:117; "Released Telegraph Builders," *Louisville Journal*, March 7, 1862. David Montgomery received permit for ferry over Green River in 1848, in agreement between he and David Vance, copy in Green County Public Library.

20. "Released Telegraph Builders," *Louisville Journal*, March 7, 1862.

21. Plum, *Military Telegraph*, 190.

22. Ibid., 200.

23. G.W. Jouett to Julietta Starbuck, February 2, 1862; John William Morris to Julietta Starbuck, February 3, 1862; Indiana State Archives, Indianapolis, Ind. These two members of the 57th Ind. wrote letters to Starbuck, mentioning the burning of the meeting house and a bridge. They claimed that the 1st Ohio brought back 8–10 Rebel prisoners, and that later the 58th Ind. brought in five more. Neither Morgan's nor the Federal report on Jan.31 mention this, OR(ser.1)7:117.

24. Jeter Pension File, NA.

25. Tombstone of James Sanders, Sanders Cemetery, Taylor County, Ky.; Gorin, "Service in American Revolution;" Clay Hill, a National Register site, is located eight miles north of Campbellsville on 289, old Hwy 68.

26. Anne White Elliott, daughter of Cary Sanders White, Dayton, Ohio, letter to author, October 28, 1974; Cisely can be found on the List of Slaves of the Henry Sanders Estate in Taylor County Circuit Court Bundle 71, Saml M. Sanders v H.F. White, Wm. B. Carlisle, adm. of Henry Sanders, 1858. Cisely, age 38, valued at $500. Cary was married on the day of the battle of Perryville; therefore, this incident predates that event.

27. Ramage, *Rebel Raider*, 82–83; quote, 82.

28. India W.P. Logan, *Kelion Franklin Peddicord* (New York: Neale Publishing Co., 1908), 114.

29. AGR, USA, I, 871; Tim Smith, Shiloh National Battlefield Park, telephone interview with author, January 3, 2003.

30. Obituary, Elijah F. Tucker, *Green County Review*, Summer, 2000, 13. The old name for Arista is Richeson's Crossing. A train engineer named the crossing Arista after a movie theater in Lebanon.

31. Bob to Nannie, April 12, 1862, Gary Lanham Collection, Lebanon, Ky.

32. Dee Alexander Brown, *Bold Cavaliers: Morgan's 2nd Kentucky Cavalry Raiders* (Philadelphia: J.B. Lippincott Co., 1959), 54–57.

33. Ibid., 63, says that Black Bess was used by General Dumont and then sold to a civilian. After the war the original owner, Warren Viley, advertised for her return, to no avail.

34. John M. Porter Manuscript, KL-WKU, 25–26; George A. Ellsworth, "An Old Story Retold," *New Orleans Time-Democrat,* Yandell Scrapbook, FHS; Edward M. Coffman, "The Civil War Career of Thomas Henry Hines" (Master's thesis, University of Kentucky, 1955), 10. Hines was involved in many undercover activities for the Confederacy. He was sent to reconnoiter the Ohio River fords for the Ohio Raid, helped plan Morgan's escape from the Ohio State Prison, and was involved in the plot to free the Confederates at Camp Douglas. After the war, he became a justice on the Kentucky Supreme Court.

PART FOUR: Morgan's First Kentucky Raid *July 1862*, pp. 48–63

1. J.H. Thomas to Edward H. Hobson, July 11, 1862, KHS microfilm reel 68.

2. Again, Morgan used present-day 323, turned up Overbrook Road and continued over the old roadbed that goes into Fallen Timber Road; he crossed 210 where the road becomes known as 744 to Saloma.

3. Johnston, "Lebanon As I Have Known It," 4.

4. *Lebanon Kentuckian*, July 17, 1862.

5. Harold Russell Farm in 2004, 2970 Bengal Road. Once a showplace, its mantels and nicely carved woodwork still demonstrate the beauty that surrounded its owners. It was originally the Cliff Haselwood 800-acre farm; then Archibald Webster farm; Archibald died in 1849, according to Barbara DeWitt Webster.

6. R.Towler Parrott, interview with author, Campbellsville, Ky., June 20, 1976.

7. Senour, *Morgan and His Captors,* 55; Murrell Hazard, formerly of Campbellsville, Ky., interview with author, Lexington, Ky., March 2000. The "well lot" is lot #16, Plat of Saloma, 1871; Roger Blair Studio in 2004; road had been changed somewhat since plat was first made. The Durham Store was located on the south side of Highway 744 on the old Murrell Hazard property. The store was razed in 1939. Durham Store Ledger is located in the Kentucky Building, Western Kentucky University.

8. Taylor County Deed Book 5, 221. A cousin of James Samuel's, James Elijah "Lidge" Durham, aged 23, was riding in Rebel Captain William S. Edwards' regiment. Taylor County 1860 Census, 116. Obituary of J.E. Durham appears in *Larue County Herald*, August 10, 1905; buried in Brookside Cemetery, Campbellsville.

9. Samuel Durham, Mecklenburg Co., Va., Militia, James Durham, War of 1812 Cornstalk Militia-16th Regt, James Samuel Durham and son John Samuel Durham, Co B, 10th Ky Inf, CSRecords, NA.

10. Beulah Campbell, interview with author, Campbellsville, Ky., August 11, 2003. Lettie Durham Moore and Beulah C. Campbell, The Durhams (Campbellsville, Ky.: p. p.) 10–11.

11. Duke, *History of Morgan's Cavalry*, 179.

12. Stephen Z. Starr, *Colonel Grenfell's Wars* (Baton Rouge: Louisiana State University Press, 1971), 22–37, 53–57, 271, 320–26.

13. Thomas S. Cogley, *Seventh Indiana Cavalry*, 187–202.

14. Duke, *History of Morgan's Cavalry*, 186.

15. Morgan's Report to R.A. Alston, July 30, 1862, printed in *Kentucky Explorer*, November 1996; Jeffery C. Mauck, A *Proud Heritage: Lebanon and Marion County, Kentucky in the Civil War* (Marion County Economic Development & Kentucky Heritage Council, 1997), 16–17; Brown, *Bold Cavaliers*, 81; "Morgan's Raid on Lebanon," *Louisville Journal*, July 17, 1862. At least one shot went into the beams of the wood bridge; Coy Sapp, who lived at the bridge site, claimed that his father who lived there before him dug out the cannon ball, according to Terry Yates, interview with author, January 19, 2005.

16. "Morgan's Raid on Lebanon," *Louisville Journal*, July 17, 1862; Sally R. Ford, *Raids and Romance of Morgan and His Men* (New York: C.B. Richardson, 1864), 170–173.

17. Ibid.; OR(ser.1)16:767–68; *Marion County Quarterly*, Fall, 1992.

18. Ramage, *Rebel Raider*, 95–96.

19. For more detail on this raid, Bennett H. Young, *Confederate Wizards of the Saddle* (Boston: Chapple Publishing Co., 1914), 95–125. For detail on the battles of

Cynthiana, see William A. Penn, *Rattling Spurs and Broad-Brimmed Hats* (Midway, Ky.: Battle Grove Press, 1995).

20. Steve Wright, interview with author, Elizabethtown, Ky., August 12, 2003. Wright is compiling the History of the 6th Kentucky Cavalry, USA.

21. Hambleton Tapp, ed. "A Sketch of the Early Life and Service in the Confederate Army of Dr. John A. Lewis of Georgetown, Ky.," *Register of the Kentucky Historical Society* 75 (April, 1977), 126. Memoirs, John M. Porter, Confederate Collection, Tennessee State Library and Archives, 54. Today, the campsite in Adair County is said to be on the Burkesville Road (Hwy 61) in the area of the c1820 brick Thomas Stotts and Turk houses. Both carry stories about Morgan's Men camping in this area in hot, dry weather. N.B. Turk from Columbia served in Morgan's 2nd Ky. Cav. Jimmy Woody is the owner of the Turk house in 2004. Nancy Moran Fouser is the granddaughter of Raymond and Amanda Stotts Moran. Her great uncle, Creed Stotts, who was 16 years old in 1862, remembered that the family hid their silverware and built pens to hide their horses and that the soldiers camped by the creek. Nancy Fouser, interview with author, July 6, 2004; Joe Barbee, interview with author, Columbia, Ky., March 1997, had also heard these stories.

22. The house was on Town Lot #58, Ruth P. Burdette, "Early Columbia," 10–11; Vonnie Kolbenschlag, interview with author, Columbia, Ky., March 19, 1997.

23. Bob Henry Cowherd, interview with author, Campbellsville, Ky., July 1, 1976. The Cowherd house was much larger during the war. From the house which remains, four rooms, two up and two down, were torn away from the right side of the house and two rooms, one up and one down, torn away from the left side of the house. Slave houses and a tanyard have also been removed. OR(ser. 1)16(1):320–322 discusses Bragg's troops on the New Haven route.

24. Today the woods and fields are Graham Memorial Park. The Knott Home burned in 1902, but Highway Marker #1341 on Ky. Hwy 49 marks the site.

25. OR(ser. I) 16(1): 322–325.

26. Diary of Capt. James Biddle, 16th US Infantry, Burton Historical Collection, Detroit Public Library, Detroit, Mich.

27. Price Diary, 47–48.

28. Small Diary, October 13, November 11, 1862.

29. Judson W. Bishop, *Story of a Regiment:Second Regiment, Minnesota Veteran Volunteer Infantry* (St. Paul, Minn., 1890), 76.

30. Eastham Tarrant, *Wild Riders of the First Kentucky Brigade* (Louisville: R.H. Carothers, 1894), 126.

31. Mattie G. Tucker, "A Tribute to my Parents" (Campbellsville: Capital Printing Co., 1962), n.p.

32. George Thomas to H.W. Halleck Oct. 30, 1862, OR(ser.1)16(2):657.

33. John D. Inskeep Diary, October 29–31, 1862, OHS.

34. OR(ser.1)20(2):51.

35. *Louisville Journal*, September 4, 1862.

36. AGR, CSA, I, 696. Under Morgan, they became Co C, 3rd Ky. Cav. At some point, the 3rd Ky. became known as the 7th Ky. and was entered as such in the AGR.

37. Frank Wilcoxson, interview with author, February 18, 2004; Green County Deed Book 31, 18, records Richard and Daniel Miller dividing John Miller land on Trace Fork, 1882; Green County 1870 Census (printed), 50. The cave is on Miller Road, Ryan property in 2004.

38. AGR, USA, II, 230. Attack was in the fall of 1862. Petition of William S. Warren, October 1864, Bramlette Papers, Box 11, f 244, KDLA.

39. Taylor County Circuit Clerk Commonwealth Cases copied by Steve Wright; see Taylor County 1860 Census, 112 for Jeremiah and Emily Sanders. Emily Sanders, wife of Durham Sanders, was not involved. The list of men from Green and Taylor counties in Edwards' Company, later entered in the Adjutant General's Report, I, 694, as the 7th Ky., Co. C, were as follows: Capt. W.S. Edwards, Isaac Chaudoin, Andy Gumm, two sons of John Miller, two sons of John Roach, Seldon Renfro, two sons of Fell Cox, Wilson Bailey, Frank Smith, Richard A. Webster, Tom Cowherd-son of Jim Cowherd, Brady Marshall-son of Robert Marshall, Frank Marshall-son of Col. Billy Marshall, George Carpenter, Richard Darnell, James B. Durham, Newman Chelf, son of Jack Williams, and John Gaines. This list is verified by a newsclipping in Darnell's book. Only three of this list were implicated in the murder of Scott. News clippings in back of C.C. Darnell's book mark Edwards' men, book owned by the late Robert Webster.

40. "Southern Kentucky," *Louisville Journal*, October 8, 1862. Martin Cure is not listed in the Taylor County 1860 Census.

41. Lt. Lewis Johnson, 10th Ind. to Brig. Gen. George Thomas, December 17, 1861, OR(ser.1)7: 502–03.

PART FIVE: Morgan's Christmas Raid *December, 1862–1863*, pp. 64–97

1. Ramage, *Rebel Raider,* 134–35.

2. Hal Engerud, "Morgan's 1862 Christmas Raid through Kentucky," *Kentucky Progress Magazine*, December 1931, FHS.

3. John A. Wyeth, *With Sabre and Scalpel* (New York: Harper & Row, 1914), 178–179; Young, *Confederate Wizards*, 424, 433.

4. OR(ser.1)20(1): 153; *Louisville Journal*, December 27, 1862; Wyeth, *With Sabre and Scalpel*, 180–81.

5. The skirmishing around Munfordville and the engagement at Rolling Fork will be the only times when the 10th, 13th and the 27th Ky. Taylor County soldiers will fight against Morgan. When Tebbs Bend occurs, these regiments are not engaged there.

6. OR(ser.1)20(1): 134; Burke, Civil War Journal, December 25, 1862, USAMHI.

7. OR(ser.1)20(1):134.; Wyeth, *With Sabre and Scalpel,* 182–83.

8. Burke, Civil War Journal, December 27, 1862; *Louisville Journal*, December 29, 1862. The Federals were commanded by Lt. Col. Harry S. Smith, 91st Ill. For detail on Morgan's Christmas Raid, see Edwin C. Bearss, "General John Hunt Morgan's Second Kentucky Raid," *Register of the Kentucky Historical Society* 77 (1973, 1974) 4 parts and James D. Brewer, *The Raiders of 1862* (Westport, Conn.: Praeger, 1997).

9. OR(ser. 1)20(1): 156.

10. Burke, *Journal*, December 28, 1862. Spelling corrected. OR(ser. I)20(l):156, Morgan claimed that 700 prisoners, including 27 officers, were captured and a large amount of medical and quartermaster's stores were destroyed.

11. *Louisville Journal*, December 29, 1862.

12. Burke, Civil War Journal, 93.

13. Bearss, "Second Kentucky Raid," *Register of the Kentucky Historical Society* (October 1973), 428–29.; Brewer, *Raiders of 1862*, 163–69.

14. OR(ser.1)20(1):138–141. Harlan commanded the 4th Ky., 14th Ohio, 74th Ind., 10th Ind., 10th Ky., 13th Ky., 12th Ky. Cav., Battery C, 1st Ohio Lt. Artillery.

15. Quote is from Burke, Civil War Journal, December 29, 1862; J.M. Porter, "A Brief Account of What I Saw . . .," Don John Collection, KHS. Porter was in Co E, 9th Ky Cav.

16. OR(ser. 1)20(1):136, 140–41; Bearss, "Second Kentucky Raid," *Register of the Kentucky Historical Society* 71 (October 1973), 435.

17. Ramage, *Rebel Raider*, 147. Morgan wrote endearing letters to his new wife some of which are in the John Hunt Morgan Papers, Southern Historical Collection, University of North Carolina Library, Chapel Hill. Many believe his preoccupation with his new marriage took his mind away from his command.

18. Dixie Hibbs, *Nelson County: A Portrait of the Civil War* (Charleston, S.C.: Arcadia Publishing, 1999), 75; "John Morgan at Bardstown," *Louisville Journal*, January 8, 1863; Burke, Civil War Journal, December 30, 1862.

19. Wyeth, *With Sabre and Scalpel*, 188; Bearss, "Second Kentucky Raid," *Register of the Kentucky Historical Society 72* (January 1974), 20.

20. OR(ser.1)20(1):143; *Louisville Journal*, January 6, 1863; Burke, Civil War Journal, December 30, 1862. After the war, Edmund Penn was elected county judge of Taylor County; Col. Arthur L.Kelly, "Crowded Moment," (Springfield, Ky. p.p. 2003), 22–23. Fidler was killed in the *Sultana* disaster in the Mississippi River.

21. OR(ser. 1)20(1): 158; Bearss, "Second Kentucky Raid," *Register of the Kentucky Historical Society* 72 (January 1974), 20 estimated 6,000. Troops at Lebanon included Craddock's Brigade consisting of the 12th Ky., 16 Ky., and 7th Tenn. infantries; 6th & 9th Ky. cavalry, and Reid's Brigade. The *Louisville Journal* estimated 4,500 men.

22. Sam W. Boldrick to O.W. Baylor, August 28, 1939, John Hunt Morgan File, KHS, says that Morgan took the old Elizabethtown Pike out of Springfield which went in the direction of Loretto. He then cut across the country passing through St. Mary's and crossed the Rolling Fork two miles below New Market and over Muldraugh's Hill one mile west of Finley. According to author's interview with Billy Ray Carrico, Springfield, Ky., June 13, 2004, the old Elizabethtown Pike turned west south of Springfield at Booker Branch Road, then turned down Reservoir Road where it terminates at the reservoir. It crossed Servant Run and 429 where it becomes known as Old Elizabethtown Road. Rawlins information is cited in Kelly, "Crowded Moment," 23–24.

23. Davis, *Partisan Rangers*, 133–34; James Bennett McCreary, "The Journal of My Soldier

Life," *Register of the Kentucky Historical Society* 33 (April, 1935) and (July, 1935) December 30, 1862, cited hereafter as McCreary, Journal. The valley where the Confederates built fires is on Ky Hwy 55, north of Lebanon, 200 yards north of the Cartwright's Station Highway Marker. Lebanon's defenses were placed on a high escarpment south of the Cartwright's Creek Highway Marker on the Springfield Road.

24. Wyeth, *With Sabre and Scalpel*, 189.

25. McCreary, Journal, December 30, 1862.

26. Young, *Confederate Wizards*, 44.

27. John Allan Wyeth, "Morgan's Christmas Raid, 1862–63," 153.

28. McCreary, Journal, December 30, 1862.

29. Burke, Civil War Journal, December 30, 1862.

30. OR(ser. 1)20(1):144; *Louisville Journal*, January 3, 1863. Some have thought that Morgan had no wagons on this raid. However, wagons and wagon trains are mentioned in diaries and newspapers.

31. OR(ser.1)20(1): 144–45.

32. John B. Castleman, *Active Service* (Louisville: *Courier-Journal* Job Printing Co., 1917), 109; Wyeth's version, Morgan's Christmas Raid, 154, adds a private to the group and his name appears in "Reminiscences of the Conflicts of the Sixties," *Lexington-Herald*, April 24, 1904.

33. Ibid. Castleman and Wyeth differ on which Federal first rode into the stream. C.C. Curry, Co E, 8th Ky. Cav., in Confederate Veteran Records, Clark County Library, claimed to be one of Morgan's rear guard who witnessed the event "in a small branch or creek." Steve Wright notes that Curry was not present.

34. OR(ser.1)20(1): 136, 157–58. Closely quoted from Wyeth, Morgan's Christmas Raid, 156. Steve Wright, unpublished manuscript on the Sixth Kentucky Cavalry, states that the gunfight took place in a lagoon which leads to the river next to P. Shewmaker farm, which is the old Bowman-Buckman place, while leads to the river, on Shewmaker Road, northwest of Phillips Ford, in Marion County. Interview with author, Elizabethtown, Ky., August 12, 2003. Some claim Halisy fell into the lagoon, or stream, others say his body was flung there. The lagoon would fill up with water in the winter and appear to be a river. When people from the neighborhood would pass over the spot after dark, they would say to each other, "Watch out or Halisy will get you." *Marion County Historical Society Bulletin*, VIII(2), 1998.

35. Wyeth, 156; "Latest From Morgan," *Louisville Democrat*, January 3, 1863; *Louisville Journal*, January 6, 1863. Halisy was buried in St. Rose Priory, Washington County. George Eastin was a participant in a failed plot in 1863 to free Confederate prisoners from Camp Douglas, a Federal prison near Chicago. Eastin wore Halisy's sword until the Great Raid crossing of the Ohio River. He hid it in a log, fearing certain capture, reported his brother-in-law, John B. Castleman, *Active Service*, 109. He was captured on the Great Raid, and, fearing retribution, used an assumed name. He escaped to Canada from Camp Douglas. There he read law under exiled Gen. John C. Breckinridge. After the war, he practiced law in Louisville and became a member of the Kentucky Court of Appeals. Eastin wrote his version of the affair in 1882, Southern Historical Papers 10, 513–518.

36. OR(ser.1)20(1):145; *Louisville Journal*, January 9, 1863 reported that the Rebels had cut a "new road" up Muldraugh's Hill. The road they used preceded the present "Turkeyfoot" curves of the Old Lebanon Road. The Old Hill Hollow Road, also called the Old Stagecoach Road, is one that ran from Jessietown north through the Danny Sapp farm, St. Joe Road-Hwy 412, in Marion County. 3 miles west of the present road-Hwy 289 and straight up the steep bluffs of Muldraugh's Hill. The Stagecoach Road came out on the present day Finley Ridge Road in Taylor County one mile west of Finley on the Jerry Newcomb farm, across from the cell tower and baseball field of the Catholic Church. Morgan's scouts had located this old road and used it to fool their pursuers. They also used St. Matthews Old Cemetery Road, also called Dug Road. Author interviews with Danny Sapp, Jessietown, and Jerry Newcomb, Finley Ridge, June 13, 2004.

37. OR(ser.)20(1):157.

38. Samuel Sapp, interview with author, August 8, 1991.

39. Ann Tandy Parrott, interview with author, Campbellsville, Ky., June 20, 1976.

40. McCreary, Journal, December 31, 1862.

41. Burke, Civil War Journal, December 31, 1862.

42. *Louisville Democrat,* January 13, 1863.

43. OR(ser.1)20(1):158; Aaron, *Campbellsville Methodist Church*, 32.

44. Burke, Civil War Journal, December 31, 1862.

45. Margaret Trotter Lewis, Campbellsville, Ky., and George Trotter, LaGrange, Ky., interview with author, July 27, 2000. Marrs Cobbler Shop was located on Town Lot #65 on the northwest corner of Broadway and North Columbia (office of Dr. James R. Angel in 2005). The weather-boarded over log Marr House sits adjacent to Dr. Angel's office and faces Broadway. The front porch was removed when Broadway was widened in the early 1950s. This story was told to Margaret Lewis and George Trotter by Sophronia Trotter as told to her by her mother-in-law, Hattie Marrs Trotter, daughter of William. Years after the Civil War, the family discovered six coin silver table spoons taped to the back of a sugar chest that Nancy Smith Marrs, wife of William, had placed for safekeeping. Taylor County 1860 Census lists William Marrs, shoemaker.

46. Sam Moore, Sr. of Greensburg, Ky., interview with author, July 22, 1976; Duke, *History of Morgan's Cavalry*, 437.

47. Burke, Civil War Journal, January 1, 1863. The tanyard was probably Redman's.

48. Aaron, *Campbellsville Methodist Church*, 32–33. After the war, Colvin brought down the warehouse and reused the bricks in the building at 115 East Main Street; quote from McCreary, Journal, January 1, 1863.

49. Cunningham, Co A, 11th Ky. Cav, Account of the Christmas Raid into Kentucky, given to Mattie Morgan, Miscellaneous Material, Holland Papers, Box 2, UKL.

50. OR(ser.1)20(1): 144–45.

51. Ibid., 145; quote from *Battery M, First Illinois Artillery*, 32.

52. The farm on the bank of the Russell Creek, located on the Campbellsville Road, was owned by the Barbee family in 2004. The *Louisville Journal* called it Camp Reid instead of Camp Gilbert.

53. *Battery M, First Illinois. Artillery,* 28–29, last quote on 31–32.

54. Ibid., 32.

55. Ibid., 27–30. At junction of Hwy 68 & 426 is the Whistling Pig in 2004. The 1826 1½ story S. Robertson House, was later owned by Carters, who may have owned it during the Civil War. It was purchased by John Luther Collins in 1887, according to the *Lebanon Enterprise*, Sept. 18, 1958 and Dorothy Black, interview with author, April 20, 2005. The stone wall in front of the house along the highway still stands.

56. Ibid., 33. Sam Boldrick agrees the Yanks stopped for the night at New Market. Boldrick to Baylor, 1939, John Hunt Morgan File, KHS.

57. OR(ser.1)20(1): 145. Morgan had some Texas Rangers as members of his troops. Buttons from Texas uniforms have been found at Finley in the churchyard, according to Father Jack Caldwell, interview with author, May 2000.

58. *Battery M, First Illinois Artillery*, 33. Gewgaws are showy, but worthless trinkets.

59. Ann Heskamp Curtis e-mail to author; Frances Davenport, interview with author, January 6, 2003; some of original story appears in Norman Johnson, "Covered Wagons" (Campbellsville, Ky.: Gozder Printing, 1950s). N.A. Johnson was the son of W. W. Johnson, the latter appearing in Taylor County 1860 Census, 59. Elsie married George Romine, Martha married Merritt Martin. Nannie, born January 10, 1863 after the raiders departed, later married William Munday.

60. J.M.Porter, "Brief Account of What I Saw and Experienced during the War for Southern Independence," Don John Collection, KHS.

61. Green River Ford is called DeMosses Ford in old deeds. Through the years, the name was corrupted and it is usually misspelled in deeds.

62. McCreary, Journal, January 1, 1863. According to Leona Walling, *Campbellsville News-Journal*, May 16, 1963, James Allen Sublett was a Union forage agent. A Confederate officer said he should be hung, but he was so big—300 pounds, that they'd never get his feet off the ground.

63. Martha Barnes Martin, great-granddaughter of Barnes, May 16, 2004. He was enrolled at Somerset in the 11th Ky., CSA, when 15, pretended to be a deaf mute selling chickens and supplies to Union soldiers in Wolford's camps along the Cumberland. Muster In rolls for I & K regiments of the 11th, men from Wayne and Clinton counties, were lost. The source of watching the bridge burn is Mary Elizabeth Griffin, daughter of James Madison Griffin, as told to her granddaughter, Martha Barnes Martin.

64. James Robert Sublett, interview with author, July 15, 1976.

65. Story told by M.L. Howard, *Campbellsville News-Journal*, April 9, 1936. Pleas Howard lived across the road from the stockade. M.L. was 11 in the 1860 Taylor County Census (printed) in household of Pleas Howard.

66. James Robert Sublett, interview with author, July 15, 1976; Doug Martin, interview with author, January 2002.

67. The Louisville Military Prison records do not confirm the number of Rebel captured or wounded. Russell Williams believes that he has one of the six pounder shells that was fired. It landed in a field considerable distance from the bridge. The position of the Federal artillery was somewhere on the Tate farm, according to Mayme Walters and Henry A. Buchanan. A good position would be on the high hilltop between old

Dr. W.R. Mann property and the Carl Hall House, all owned at one time by the Tate family. Laura Larimore reported that her husband found a shell on their property, also. Larimore interview with author, March 13, 1997. G. T. Eubank, found a round shot in Green River down below old KOA/Cedarcrest Campground, 300 Campground Road, said Henry Blakeman, interview with author, Summer 2003. Richard Sublett, interview with author, February 1997, said that Jordon Bridgewater found a cannon ball lodged in a tree on the old Tate farm, now the Homeplace on Green River.

68. Lois Hubbard Hutchison and Edna Hubbard, Columbia, Ky., interview with author, March 5, 1990; James Robert Sublett, interview with author, 1976.

69. Basil W. Duke, *Reminiscences of General Basil W. Duke, C.S. A.* (Garden City, N.Y.: Doubleday, Page & Co., 1911), 124–26; *Louisville Journal*, January 8, 1863; *Nashville Daily Press*, July 4, 13, 1865. Ferguson declined to go on the Great Raid. Richard Morgan to JHM, May 4, 1863 indicated that Ferguson preferred to remain where he was "under the pretext of trying to capture Tinker Dave [Beatty] but in reality to steal Horses & Negroes & sell them." A transcript of the trial of the US Government v. Ferguson can be found in Thurman Sensing's *Champ Ferguson* (Vanderbilt University Press), 1970.

70. J.H. Morgan to Mattie, January 2, 1863, Morgan Collection, Southern Historical Collection, University of North Carolina, Chapel Hill, N.C.

71. *Louisville Daily Democrat*, January 13, 1863.

72. McCreary, Journal, January 2, 1863.

73. Tarrant, *Wild Riders*, 130–131.

74. OR Supp(2)21: 764, 801–802.

75. *Battery M, First Illinois Artillery*, 34–36.

76. *Louisville Journal*, December 29, 1862.

77. Ibid., December 1862.

78. *Akron (Ohio) Summit Beacon*, March 5, 1863, from Mrs. Johnson of Campbellsville, Ky., article from collection of Dr. Stuart Sprague, Morehead (Ky.) State University.

79. *Louisville Journal*, January 30, 1863, February 19, 1863, March 7, 1863.

80. Ramage, *Rebel Raider*, 147; Duke, *History of Morgan's Cavalry*, 342–43. Federal reports list more Confederates killed on this raid. Over 50 were captured around Lebanon and sent by train to Lexington, reported the *Louisville Journal*, January 5, 1863.

81. Wartime Diary of John Weathered, a personal unpublished account in the possession of Jack Masters.

82. Ramage, *Rebel Raider*, 145, 147.

83. OR(ser.1) 20 (2): 294.

84. F.D. Dickinson to Aunt, May 15, 1863, Columbia, Ky., FHS.

85. Herman Hubbard, interview with author, July 12, 1976.

86. "The Case of E.M. Durham," *Lebanon Standard & Times*, November 7, 1883. John Mayes, Taylor County 1860 Census, 59. Durham died November 5, 1883 and is buried at Bethlehem Cemetery, Washington County, Ky.

PART SIX: Morgan's Great Raid *July 1863*, pp. 98–259

Chapter One: January – June, 1863, pp. 99–106

1. Duke, *History of Morgan's Cavalry*, 407.

2. Ibid., 396.

3. Quote, Morgan to Mattie, March 21, 1863, Morgan Papers, SHC; quote from *Louisville Journal*, May 15, 1863; *Louisville Journal*, April 8, 1863 stated that "with continued loss in battle, disease, and desertion, this boasted body of gallant but deluded men is fast wasting away."

4. Dr. J. Chester Badgett, son of J.W. Badgett, Jr.,interview with author, Campbellsville, Ky., March 2004.

5. Young, *Confederate Wizards*, 193.

6. Duke, *History of Morgan's Cavalry*, 397–98, 400, 404–5; McCreary, Journal, January 30, 1863. J.D. Sprake, Diary, 1863–65, typed copy by Bennett H. Young, 1897, FHS, April 7–30, 1863. On May 25, 1863, he wrote that "his horse was getting fat and sleek as a mold."

7. McCreary, Journal, January-March entries. McCreary, 11th Ky Cavalry stated that he was quartered at Riley's in Albany on January 22, in Gen. Coffey's old tavern in Monticello on March 4, and at Dr. Hall's March 6.

8. OR(ser. 1)23(2):286.

9. Sprake, Diary, April 29, 1863.

10. Ibid.; March 18, April 12, 13, 14, 15, 17, 26, 27, May 17, 1863.

11. Cecil F. Holland, *Morgan and His Raiders: A Biography of the Confederate General* (New York: Macmillan, 1942), 121.

12. Sprake, Diary, April 7, 1863; McCreary, Journal, February 2, March 20, 1863.

13. D.W. Chenault to brother, Dr. R.C. Chenault March 1863, David Waller Chenault, CSRecord, NA.

14. Ramage, *Rebel Raider*, 155–156.

15. Brig. Gen. Mahlon Manson to Brig. Gen. Horatio Wright, April 11, 1863, RG 393, Pt. 1, E.3514, NA.

16. OR(ser.1)52 (1):265; quote from "Headquarters 11th Ky. Cavalry," *Louisville Journal*, May 8, 1863. Spelling corrected.

17. *Confederate Military History*, vol. 9 (Atlanta: Confederate Publishing Co., 1899), 301.

18. Thomas Thorpe Diary, French-Tipton Papers, VI, 75, Crabbe Library, Eastern Kentucky University, Richmond. Capt. James E. Cantrill of Bourbon County, Co. E, 5th Ky. Cav., later Lt. Governor of Ky., was severely wounded at Greasy Creek by the same shell that killed Lt. J. Wallace Graves, according to *Confederate Military History*, vol. 9, 306.

19. McCreary, Journal, June 23, 1863.

20. Letter, SHC; quote from McCreary, Journal, January 3, 1863; John David Smith and William Cooper, Jr., ed. *A Union Woman in Civil War Kentucky: The Diary of Frances Peter* (Lexington: University Press of Kentucky, 2000), 64.

21. Duke, *History of Morgan's Cavalry*, 407.

22. Ibid., 408, claims Burnside had 15, 000–30,000 men. U.S. Military Telegraphs, Rosecrans to Hartsuff, July 22, 1863 stated the following, based on Union intelligence: "Buckner had 3,000 scattered all over east Tenn., Bushrod Johnson had 1,500 more infantry at Loudon Bridge and Kingston, Pegram had 1,500 men with warn down horses, Bragg had not more than 20,000 at Chattanooga. Forest and Wheeler had 5,000."

23. Duke, *History of Morgan's Cavalry*, 408; E. B. Long, *The Civil War Day by Day: An Almanac 1861–1865* (DaCapo, 1971), 375.

24. Dr. James Ramage to Betty Gorin, correspondence, February 21, 2005, for the most part, directly quoted; Duke, *History of Morgan's Cavalry*, 409.

25. Ibid., 409–410; quote, 410; Basil Duke, "A Romance of Morgan's Rough Riders," *Century Magazine* (January 1891), 9; OR(ser. 1)23(1): 817–18.

26. Burke, Civil War Journal, May 29, 1863; Wayne R. Austerman, "Bluegrass Enfields: The Arms of Morgan's Raiders, *Men At Arms* (May/June 1993), 20. Morgan's revolvers were ivory-handled.

27. George D. Mosgrove, *Kentucky Cavaliers in Dixie* (Wilmington, N.C.: Broadfoot Publishing Co., 1987), 62.

Chapter Two: Taking the War to the North, pp. 107–134

1. Duke, "Romance," *Century*, 10.

2. Ibid.; Duke, *History of Morgan's Cavalry*, 410.

3. U.S. Army, Corps of Engineers Maps, Diane Coon Speech, Hiestand House Museum, Campbellsville, Ky., November 2, 2003.

4 OR(ser 1)23(1):705; see Ramage, *Rebel Raider*,158

5. Duke, *History of Morgan's Cavalry*, 411; Sydney K. Smith, *Life, Army Record and Public Service of D. Howard Smith* (Louisville: Bradley & Gilbert, 1890), 56–7.

6. A.R. Johnson to J.H.Morgan, December 25, 1863, Holland Papers.

7. Smith, *D. Howard Smith*, 56.

8. Alston letter, Holland Papers.

9. Holland, *Morgan and His Raiders*, 224; quote from Duke, *History of Morgan's Cavalry*, 415.

10. Duke, *History of Morgan's Cavalry*, 414.

11. John L. Blair, "Morgan's Ohio Raid," *Filson Club History Quarterly* 36 (July 1962), 251.

12. A.C. Quisenberry, "History of Morgan's Men," *Register of the Kentucky Historical Society* 15 (September 1917), 34; Richard C. Morgan to J. H. Morgan, Morgan Papers, SHC; Logan, *Peddicord*, 111–112; Burke, Civil War Journal, April 28, 29, May 14, 20, 24, 1863.

13. Holland, *Morgan and His Raiders*, 227.

14. Duke, "Romance," *Century*, 10.

15. Duke, *History of Morgan's Cavalry*, 412–14.

16. McCreary, Journal, June 6, 1863.

17. William J. Davis, ed., *The Partisan Rangers of the Confederate States Army* (Louisville: George G. Fetter Co., 1904), 142. Fielding Helm was a Texan, member of Dick Morgan's 14th Ky. Adam Johnson will rescue Helm from drowning in the Ohio River crossing a few days later, according to Sid Cunningham, *Richmond Enquirer*, July 31, 1863.

18. Today the Obey River forms Dale Hollow Lake. After the construction of the lake, some of the roads over which Morgan's Men rode are covered with water.

19. Burke, Civil War Journal, June 28, 29, 1863; Sprake, Diary, June 28, 1863.

20. Burke, Civil War Journal, June 29, 1863.

21. Sprake, Diary, July 1, 1863.

22. Burke, Civil War Journal, June 30, 1863; Sprake, Diary, July 2, 1863; Magdalene Murley of Burkesville, Ky., owner of the frame home with center hall, telephone interview with D.W. Arms, March 13, 1997, as relayed to author, maybe an old Anderson home.

23. Randolph Smith, interview with author, Burkesville, Ky., March 12, 1997. Hominy Creek flows into Marrowbone Creek. Andy Garmon lived across Marrowbone Creek from the camp during the Civil War. Garmon's son, Tommy, relayed the information to Homer Spears who told Smith in an interview on January 22, 1975. According to Spears, the main part of the camp was on the old Homer Blythe farm and officers were quartered in log houses on a ridge. The camp around Marrowbone changed hands during the war. In February 1863, it was Wolford's. Tarrant, 131; in the spring of 1863, Confederate detachments of Smith's 5th Ky., Johnson's 10th Ky., and Chenault's 11th Ky., operated around Marrowbone and Mud Camp, even capturing a mill and operating it for the Rebel army. In 1864, the 13th Ky. Cav. was there pursuing Confederate guerrillas, Champ Ferguson and Littleton T. Richardson. OR, Supp. II, 20: 22. Garmon, of Haggards's 5th Ky. Cav., was almost captured at his house here. He was home from the Union Army and Confederates surrounded the house. Using two pistols and running from window to window, he shouted commands to his "supposed" men, and somehow intimidated his foe to depart. The Garmon house became Miss Effie Wilson's home in 20th century.

24. Logan, *Peddicord,* 111.

25. Burke, Civil War Journal, July 1, 1863.

26. Logan, *Peddicord,* 111–112. The Glasgow Road is Hwy. 90.

27. Burke, Civil War Journal, July 1, 1863.

28. Kenneth Williams, Radford and Friends of the Cumberland Valley, 1986, 17, copy owned by Russell and Betty Williams. Caleb was one of five to vote for Lincoln in the election of 1864. A group of Rebel sympathizers came looking for him and he survived by hiding between two feather beds. However, his barns were set on fire, losing his tobacco crop in consecutive years.

29. Duke, *History of Morgan's Cavalry*, 414.

30. Randolph Smith, interview with author, Burkesville, Ky., March 12, 1997; Willard R. Jillson, *A Tour Down Stream* (Frankfort: Perry Publishing, 1959), 31; Richard Keene, descendant of the Thrashers, interview with author, Burkesville, Ky., March 12, 1997. A horse could swim across at Neeley's more easily in 1863 than in 2004. Wolf Creek Dam makes the water colder and run more swiftly, according to D.W. Arms. Jillson wrote that some also crossed at Bow's Ferry.

31. Clarence, Clayton, and Claude Rush's grandfather was a friend of Morgan's. Randolph Smith, interview with author, Burkesville, Ky., March 12, 1997.

32. William A. Milton, Journal, 5, FHS.

33. Duke, *History of Morgan's Cavalry*, 411.

34. Henry Lane Stone, "Morgan's Men, A Narrative of Personal Experience," Speech delivered before the George B. Eastin Camp, United Confederate Veterans, Louisville Free Public Library, April 8, 1919, 10–11. Stone had three brothers in the Federal army.

35. Wartime Diary of John Weathered.

36. Young, *Confederate Wizards*, 370–371.

37. Ibid., 371.

38. John W. Trowbridge, ed., Memorandum Book of Sgt. John W. Shely, Co F, 5th Kentucky Cavalry, 1998.

39. J.A. Yeager, "A Boy with Morgan," *Confederate Veteran* (17), 295.

40. Stone, Speech.

41. Burke, Civil War Journal, July 2, 1863; Alston, Diary, July 2, 1863; Duke, *History of Morgan's Cavalry*, 415.

42. Logan, *Peddicord*, 114.

43. Ibid., 115.

44. Ibid., 115–116, Alston, Diary, July 2, 1863; OR Supp (1)Reports(4): 206; Leeland Hathaway, Gen. Morgan's Ohio Raid, July 2, 1863, handwritten copy, Hunt-Morgan Papers, UKL.

45. Gladys Thurman Hurt, born 1914, interview with author, in her home across from Norris Branch, Cumberland County, March 12, 1997. She reported that the red brick Flemish bond house was built in 1822 by Garrad Williams; then the Thurmans, and later the Hurts occupied it. She said that when the porch was repaired, bullet holes were in the old wood, and that people have picked up bullets between the two hills in the Norris Branch Road area (in front and back of red brick house). She said her grandfather Thrasher fought for the Confederacy; her grandfather Hurt, for the Union.

46. *Regimental History of 22nd Indiana.*

47. Lorenzo D. Hockersmith, *Morgan's Escape* (Madisonville, Ky.: Glenn's Graphic Print, 1903), 16.

48. Davis, *Partisan Rangers*, 142; Duke, *History of Morgan's Cavalry*, 414.

49. Davis, *Partisan Rangers*, 143.

50. Sprake, Diary, July 2, 1863. It is reported that some of the 2nd Brigade also crossed the river at Salt Lick Bend.

51. McCreary, Journal, July 3, 1863.

52. Burke, Civil War Journal, July 2, 1863.

53. Keller, *Morgan's Raid*, 1, 27, citing Keen's Diary.

54. McCreary, Journal, July 2, 1863.

55. Doug and Alta Lewis owned the house in 1997. The Allen family may have owned it during the Civil War. Alvin Lewis purchased it in 1891. Doug and Alta Lewis, interview with author, Burkesville, Ky., March 1997.

56. Randolph Smith, interview with author, Burkesville, Ky., March 12, 1997.

57. Blair, "Morgan's Ohio Raid," 247.

58. Ezra J.Warner, *Generals in Blue* (Baton Rouge: Louisiana State University, 1964), 255.

59. Blair quoting H.C. Weaver, "Morgan Raid in Kentucky, Indiana, and Ohio, July 1863," Sketches of War History, 1861–1865, Ohio Commandery of MOLLUS, ed. W. H. Chamberlain, vol. 4 (Cincinnati: Robert H. Clarke Co., 1896), 281–184. U.S. Military Telegraphs, Henry Judah to Gen. Hartsuff, June 29, 1863, NA.

60. U.S. Military Telegraphs, Henry Judah to Gen. Hartsuff, June 29, 1863, NA.

61. U.S. Military Telegraphs, May 30–June 30, 1863, and particularly, Judah to Hartsuff, June 29, 1863. NA.

62. OR(ser. 1) 23(1): 639–640. Holloway was from Clark County and knew many in Morgan's Command, especially those in the 11th Ky. Cav., (CSA). His wife, Mary Elliott Williams, was the daughter of Con. Gen. John Stuart Williams. His wife's mother was Francis Cluke.

63. Ritchie Ratcliffe, interview with author, Campbellsville University Civil War Symposium, August 1997; John Chowning, interview with author, Campbellsville, Ky., February 19, 2004. Both Ratcliffe and Chowning are descendants of the Baker family in Cumberland County.

64. Burke, Civil War Journal, July 2, 1863.

65. Ratcliffe and Chowing interviews. Ratcliffe lived on the old Elliott Plantation; Chatlin Chowning's farm was the old Rowe plantation.

66. Quote from Burke, Civil War Journal, July 2, 1863; Hathaway, Gen. Morgan's Ohio Raid, July 2, 1863.

67. Burke, Civil War Journal, July 3, 1863.

68. Cpl. Charles W. Durling, 45th Ohio Infantry, Civil War Diary, July 3, 1863, Ohio Historical Society, Columbus, Ohio; Tarrant, *Wild Riders*, 86, 88, 174. In this detachment were Capt. J.B. Fishback, Co L, Lt. D.R. Carr, Co C, Lt. Warren Launne, Co D, and Lt. James S. Pankey, Co I of the 1st Ky. Cavalry.

69. Tarrant, *Wild Riders*, 174–175; quote from Hathaway, Gen. Morgan's Ohio Raid, July 3, 1863.

70. Hathaway, Gen. Morgan's Ohio Raid, July 3, 1863; Duke, *History of Morgan's Cavalry*, 419; Duke wrote a letter to Col. Richard Morgan in the spring of 1863 in which he proposed transferring Co A of Duke's 2nd Kentucky to Morgan's 14th Kentucky and making a company of scouts to be merged with Quirks Scouts under Col. R. Morgan. The letter said that "Cassell ought to be promoted and he cannot be made a field officer in my regt without raising another row . . . Quirk's company will be all the better too for some of his [Cassell's] discipline." The AGR, CSA, 540–541, shows Cassell wounded at Buffington Island, but he was wounded at Columbia. Writers differ as to where Cassell was wounded in Columbia: Hathaway says in the town; others, in the charge outside the town.

71. Burke, Civil War Journal, July 3, 1863.

72. Hathaway, Gen. Morgan's Ohio Raid, July 3, 1863.

73. Eastham, *Wild Riders*, 174.

74. Pam Hurt Foust, granddaughter of Judge Rollin Hurt, interview with author, March 30, 1997.

75. Eastham, *Wild Riders*, 175.

76. Judge Hershel Baker, "Morgan's Men," *Adair County News*, May 24, 1898. Judge Baker mentioned the Lt. Governor Hindman place as where a large group of Federals were positioned. That site is now Gate filling station and a blinking light is at the intersection of Hwy 80 and Hwy 61. Information from interviews by author with Vonnie Kolbenschlag, Columbia, Ky., March 1997 and Randy Flowers, February 22, 2004.

77. Burke, Civil War Journal, July 3, 1863.

78. Baker, "Morgan's Men."

79. Judge Walter Baker, descendant of Hershel Baker, Glasgow, Ky., interview with author, Campbellsville, Ky., 1999. Baker was in the Centre College Graduating Class of 1860.

80. Baker, "Morgan's Men."

81. Pam Hurt Foust, interview with author, March 30, 1997.

82. Civil War Collection, Dr. Thomas Jeffries, Campbellsville, Ky.; US Military Telegraph, AG Hamilton, 12th Ky. Cav. to Gen. (Mahlon) Manson in Columbia, Apr. 15, 1863: "We are quartered in the Court House out of rations but will subsist off citizens. Forage scarce. . . . This is a good stockade. . . . They (Rebels) are in this vicinity."

83. Keller, *Morgan's Raid,* quoting an Ohio cavalryman, 30.

84. Dora Stone, descendant of Frank Wolford, interview with author, Cane Valley, Ky., March 13, 1997.

85. Sources vary in regard to killed and wounded. Burke commented that the Yanks lost 4 killed, 4–6 wounded. Sprake said that the Federals lost 3 killed, 2 mortally wounded; D. Howard Smith said that the Rebel losses were 2 killed and 2 wounded. Weathered said that two Rebels from the advanced guard were killed "in driving them out of Columbia." Duke's *History*, 419, reports two of Major Webber's [2nd KY] men killed.

Smith, Weathered, and Duke may be referring to the same two Confederate casualties.

86. Lorena Jackson, interview with author, Cane Valley, Ky., March 13, 1997.

87. Sprake, Diary, July 3, 1863.

88. Robert A. Alston, Diary, July 3, 1863, printed in *Central Kentuckian*; reprinted in *Niles* (Mich.) *Republican*, August 8, 1863.

89. Logan, *Peddicord*, 117.

90. Tarrant, *Wild Riders*, 175; Richard Keene, interview with author, Burkesville, Ky., March 12, 1997. Keene directed the author to the cemetery on a high hill on his property on Hwy 90.

91. Joe Barbee, interview with author, Columbia, Ky., March 19, 1997. This block is on the right hand side of the square as one is heading down the Campbellsville Road.

92. Randy Flowers, interview with author, Columbia, Ky., February 22, 2004; Hood, CSRecords; Louisville Military Prison Records, NA. Prison record of Hood should read "Captured July 3, 1863" instead of "June 3, 1863." Creed was the son of Eliphalet and Calista Hood.

93. Diana Farris Kirtley, interview with author, December 31, 2003.

94. OR Supp(1)4: 227.

95. McCreary, Journal, July 3, 1863.

96. David Waller Chenault to Robert Chenault, March 1863, David Waller Chenault, CSRecords, NA. Punctuation added by author.

97. Burke, Civil War Journal, July 3, 1863.

98. "Greensburg Independent Bank 1818," typed copy, Green County Library, story from Mrs. Walton (Helen Cabell) Burress, who is the granddaughter of Flora McCorkle. Flora was 15 in the 1860 Green Co. Census.

99. Sally Rice born 1862, daughter of Frank and Nancy Page Rice, was living with her parents and grandfather, James Page, a blacksmith in Cane Valley. Even though she was little, she remembered the soldiers all her life. Randy Flowers, Columbia, Ky., telephone interview with author, February 4, 2004.

100. Mary Christie to brother, N.C. Christie, July 17, 1863; Jolly Humphress, interview with author, Campbellsville, Ky., February 2003; Keith Humphress, interview with author, May 8, 2004. Steven Humphress (1815–1896) married three times; is buried in Cane Valley Cemetery. His first wife, America Page, died in 1858. Sarah Fisher was his wife when the farm was raided.

101. Martha Revis Collier, Mobile, Ala., interview with author, May 2, 2004.

102. Loneta Sublett, interview with author, October 1999.

Chapter Three: Two Commanders: Morgan and Moore, pp. 135–155

1. Ramage, *Rebel Raider*, 12–13; Jessie Moore Loveridge, "The Story of the Moore Family," Paper delivered to the Michigan State Conference, Daughters of American Revolution, October 4, 1932, 13, copy located in the Cabinet Room, Kalamazoo

Public Library; Grafton H. Cook and Barbara Wood Cook, "Colonel Orlando Hurley Moore," unpublished manuscript, 3.

2. Ramage, *Rebel Raider*, 13–14. The house is on the west side of Tates Creek Road near Alumni Drive.

3. Loveridge, "Story of the Moore Family," 5, 13–14; *Holland City News*, January 3, 1885; Grafton Cook of Niles, Mich., interview with author, June 29, 1997; Cook and Cook, "Moore," 4.

4. Ramage, *Rebel Raider*, 14–15, 32–33, 40.

5. Ibid., 18, 36–38.

6. Edward J. Masselink, "Ky Occupied Strategic Spot," *Holland Evening Sentinel*, December 13, 1961. Grafton Cook, a Moore family member, is uncertain of this information because those stories were not passed to him.

7. Loveridge, "Story of the Moore Family," 4–5, 15; Cook and Cook, "Moore," 3.

8. Ramage, *Rebel Raider*, 21–22, 27–28. For more detail, see Ramage, "John Hunt Morgan and the Kentucky Cavalry Volunteers in the Mexican War," *Register of the Kentucky Historical Society* 81 (Autumn 1983), 343–365.

9. Ibid., 35–36, 42–43.

10. Colonel Orlando Hurley Moore, Copy of the Original Military Records, 1856–1865, FHS; Cook and Cook, "Moore," 5.

11. Quote is from Moore, Copy of Official Record, 2; Loveridge, "Story of the Moore Family," 15–16; "Colonel O. H. Moore," *Holland City News*, February 7, 1885.

12. Moore, Copy of Official Record, 2–4; Loveridge, "Story of the Moore Family," 14–15; Editorial and Gen. George O. Cress, "He Broke Up Plot," *Oakland Tribune*, March 26, 1939; "Ready to Strike Blow," *Benicia Pacific Republic*, undated, in Moore Collection, Kalamazoo Valley Museum; "[Lt.]Col. [L.A.]Nickerson Sends Interesting Document," *Benicia* [Cal.] *Herald-New Era,* undated; *Washington Chronicle* reprinted in the *Detroit Advertiser* Feb. 6, 1865, in Moore Collection, Kalamazoo Valley Museum; Charles P. Roland, *Albert Sidney Johnston* (Austin: University of Texas Press, 1964), 243–50. Quote from Charles P. Roland, interview with author, Campbellsville University Civil War Symposium, August 20, 1999.

13. Loveridge, Story of the Moore Family, 15–16; "Colonel O.H. Moore," *Holland City News*, February 7, 1885.

14. Loveridge, Story of the Moore Family, 25–26. The son, a graduate of Cleveland Homeopathic Hospital College, became a professor there as well as working as a microscopist at Cleveland Medical College. He died at age 26 of blood poisoning. During his short life, he is reported to have discovered the method of double staining blood corpuscles and had articles published in medical journals.

15. John Robertson, *Michigan in the Civil War* (Lansing: W.S. George & Co., 1882), 891.

16. *Kalamazoo Gazette,* April 27, 28, 1929.

17. *Holland City News*, February 7, 1885.

18. Benjamin Van Raalte to A.C. Van Raalte, Camp Jouett, November 21, 1862, Van Raalte

Papers, CC. John Wilterdink consistently made positive comments about Colonel Moore in his letters. See Albert H. McGeehan, ed., *My Country and Cross: Civil War Letters of John Anthony Wilterdink* (Dallas: Taylor Publishing, 1982), August 14, 1863, March 27, 1864.

19. Charles Woodruff to parents, November 2, 1862, Woodruff Papers. Abbreviations spelled out.

20. Nelson Ogden to Sister, Camp 25th Michigan, March 12, 1863, HHT.

21. Robertson, *Michigan in the War,* 451.

22. Ibid.; Harry W. Bush, "Campfire Tales," undated newspaper article, Civil War Scrapbook, Kalamazoo Public Library, Kalamazoo, Mich.; McGeehan, *Wilterdink*, September 30, 1862.

23. First quote from Dirk Van Raalte to father, December 14, 1862, Van Raalte Papers, CC; second quote from Benjamin Van Raalte to father, December 22, 1862, Van Raalte Papers, HHT. Dirk and Benjamin are brothers, sons of Rev. A. C. Van Raalte, minister of the Dutch church in Holland, Michigan.

24. Soldier's Journal, December 25, 1861, Slayton Papers.

25. McGeehan, *Wilterdink,* December 28, 1862.

26. Charles Woodruff to parents, December 25, 28, 1862, Woodruff Papers.

27. S. L. Demarest to Lt. Slayton, February 2, 1863, Slayton Papers.

28. Dirk Van Raalte to mother and father, February 1, 1863, Van Raalte Papers, CC; Benjamin Van Raalte to mother, March 9, 1863, Van Raalte Papers, HHT; Woodruff Papers, January 27, 1863.

29. *Louisville Journal*, April 7, 1863; Dirk Van Raalte to father and mother, February 28, 1863, Van Raalte Papers, CC; Moore's Defense, a pamphlet Moore had published, is the source for boarding house.

30. Col. Orlando H. Moore, Court Martial Proceedings, RG 153, Folder No.LL1323, December 1863, NA.

31. *Louisville Journal* records, 1863, show the dates of the play "Seven Sisters" to be from March 16–30. The main source is Joseph P. Hazelton, "Narratives of Spies, Scouts, and Detectives," *National Tribune*, 1899, which claimed that the incident happened when Moore was Provost Marshal of Louisville. However, his appointment was not made until April 7, 1863.

32. Cushman married Charles Dickinson in 1853; her second husband was Jerry Frye. NA, RG 94, 26, file 1202587, Pension application WC 362644; RG 393, Pt 2, 902, vol. 126, 186–8726; RG 110, 36; "Narratives of Spies," *National Tribune*, 100f; Marshall Myers, "Blood and Smoke-Pauline Cushman 'Scout of the Cumberlands,'" *Cannonade* 9, 1999; Joy Jackson, "The Deadlier of the Species," *Courier-Journal Magazine*, n.d.

33. John E. Kleber, ed. *Encyclopedia of Louisville* (Lexington, University Press of Kentucky, 2001), 194–95; Charles Woodruff to parents, October 14, 1862, Woodruff Papers; J.M. Daniel to Asa Slayton, April 11, 1863, Slayton Papers; *Louisville Journal*, May 16, 18, 1863. According to Coleman's *Famous Kentucky Duels*, James Jackson was a good friend of Basil Duke's uncle, William K. Duke, before the war. Jackson was W.K. Duke's second in a famous duel between Duke and Roger Hanson in 1848.

34. Dirk Van Raalte to father and mother, March 29, April 6, 1863, Van Raalte Papers, CC.

35. Charlie Woodruff to father, April 12, 1863, Woodruff Papers.

36. McDowell, *City of Conflict*, 141–142; Journal of a Soldier of the 25th Infantry, October 1, 1862, Slayton Papers.

37. Masselink, "Kentucky Occupied," December 13, 1961,15; McDowell, *City of Conflict*, 206–208.

38. "A Soldier Shot by the Guard," *Louisville Journal*, May 2, 1863.

39. *Louisville Journal*, April 16, 1863.

40. Dirk Van Raalte to parents, April 27, 1863, Van Raalte Papers, CC.

41. *Louisville Journal*, April 28, 1863.

42. Ibid., May 16, 1863.

43. Coulter, *Civil War and Readjustment*, 151–53, 157. Kentucky was later moved to the Department of the Cumberland, April 23, 1863, a department commanded by Hartsuff. See Frederick H. Dyer, A *Compedium of the War of the Rebellion*, I (Des Moines, IA: Dyer Publishing Co., 1908), 528.

44. Coulter, *Civil War and Readjustment*, 147, 153, 156, 160–62.

45. *Louisville Journal*, May 16, 1863.

46. "Slight Breeze," *Louisville Journal*, April 23, 1863; "Descent on a Gambling Hall," *Louisville Journal*, April 27, *Louisville Journal;* Quote from Coulter, *Civil War and Readjustment*, 164, fn Frank Moore, *Rebellion Record*, vol. 6, 67 (diary).

47. According to the *Louisville Journal*, May 8, 1863, 3,000 contrabands were picked up by a steamboat in the Vicksburg area and brought north.

48. Coulter, *Civil War and Readjustment*, 164.

49. *Louisville Journal*, May 2, 4, 7, 14, 1863.

50. Special Orders 111, Moore, CSRecord, NA; *Louisville Journal*, May 7, 1863.

51. Special Orders No. 111 Col. Marc Munday relieved Moore from Provost Marshal, May 5, 1863. There was more to irritate Boyle and Munday than the newspaper article concerning contraband. In part of Moore's explanation to Munday, he claimed he was acting as some kind of detective to reveal a Rebel maid. Special Orders No 107—revocation of Order 111—and 117 followed. Dirk Van Raalte to parents, May 1863, revealed the trips to Cincinnati by Boyle and Moore, Van Raalte Papers, CC; Chester Slayton to Asa, Apr 4, 1863, reveals an earlier trip to Cincinnati, Slayton Papers.

52. Special Orders 107, 117, Moore, CSRecord, NA; *Louisville Journal*, May 19, 1863.

53. *Louisville Journal*, June 10, 1863.

54. Ibid.

55. McGeehan, Wilterdink to family, July 14, 1863.

56. Special Orders 136, June 7, 1863, relieved him of Provost Marshal again and sent Moore to superintend the building of the Rolling Fork Bridge. That order was later changed to Green River Bridge. It included a provision that no Negro will be permitted to pass on the ferry or other boat except on their pass. They were to work on public works for Louisville or on the railroad. Moore, CSRecord, NA

57. George D. Wood to Asa and Chester Slayton, June 21, 1863, Slayton Papers.

58. Charlie Woodruff to father, June 16, 25, 1863, Woodruff Papers. Woodruff added that "Col. Moore had been making an ass of himself. Because he held Provost Marshal he undertook to control the 'Dist of Ky.' But in this he came in contact with Gen'l Boyle and of course failed."

59. McGeehan, *Wilterdink*, June 15,1863. Benjamin Travis says that they arrived on June 14.

60. Benjamin F. Travis, *The Story of the Twenty-fifth Michigan* (Kalamazoo: Kalamazoo Publishing, 1897), 321.

61. *Louisville Journal*, May 13, 1863.

62. Travis, *Twenty-fifth Michigan*, 79.

63. Dirk Van Raalte to parents, June 18, 1863, Van Raalte Papers, CC; Moore to Hartsuff, May 30, and Burnside to Hartsuff, U.S. Military Telegraphs, June 18, 1863, NA.

64. Dirk Van Raalte to parents, June 14, 1863, Van Raalte Papers, CC; McGeehan, *Wilterdink*, June 15, 1863.

65. In today's army, these are called pup tents. The tents housed two soldiers. Each soldier carried his half of the tent on a march, or it was placed with the baggage. When ever they camped the two pieces were tacked together over a ridge pole.

66. Slayton Papers; Janice Van Lente Catlin, ed., *Civil War Letters of Johannes Van Lente* (Okemos, Mich: Yankee Girl Publications, 1992), 8.

67. Dirk Van Raalte, June 22, 1863, Van Raalte Papers, CC.

68. William A. Beard, III, *History of the 79th New York Cameron Highlanders, 1859–1876* (Strawberry Plains, Tenn.: Strawberry Plains Press, 1996), 22.; William Todd, *Seventy-ninth Highlanders: New York Volunteers in the War of the Rebellion 1861–1865* (Albany, N.Y.: Brandow, Barton, 1886), 286.

69. *Diary of Captain Ralph Ely of the Eighth Michigan Infantry* (Mt. Pleasant, Mich.: Central Michigan University Press, 1965), 53.

70. Ibid., 53. Ely spells the name Johnson, but he also says, "near our camp." The 8th Michigan camp was located south of the bridge on a hill where the Robert and Suzanne Sublett Phillips' home is in 2005. The John and Mary Johnstons lived in a two-story log home across the road from the camp and one-half mile east on a valley farm in Tebbs Bend, owned by Steve and Sadie Cure in 2005. That is probably where Captain Fuller's wife was also boarding.

71. Ibid., 53.

72. Brooks to Maj. J. H. Simpson, Chief Engineer, Dept. of the Ohio, May 25, 1863, RG 393, Pt. 1, 3541, NA.

73. Ibid., 54.

74. R. Benton Griffith, Co. B, 8th Mich., to Lt. A. W. Slayton, July 28, 1863, Slayton Papers.

75. Record of Events Cards, 8th Michigan, NA; "From the Eighth Infantry," *Detroit Free Press,* August 8, 1863, lists names of the non-combatants. Todd, *Seventy-Ninth Highlanders*, 286; *Louisville Journal*, October 25, 1863 lists names of men under Lt. Michael Hogan.

76. Hanson to Hartsuff, Military Telegraphs, June 8, 1863, NA. Record of Events Cards, 11th Kentucky Cavalry; Hogan's Map of the Cavalry Camp, Moore's Court Martial Trial, NA.

Chapter Four: Moore Prepares for Morgan, pp. 156–179

1. Dirk Van Raalte to Ana Van Raalte, June 19, 1863, Van Raalte Papers, CC.

2. Moore Court Martial, contains General Order No. 5: All officers of the Twenty-third Army Corps appearing in Louisville, Ky., for any cause, . . . are required to register their names in the Assistant Adjutant General's office, at General Boyle's Head-Quarters, where they will receive . . . a certificate that they are absent from their posts or commands by proper and competent authority." It continued that if the order were violated, the officer would be returned to command in arrest. Later, it was revised and the number changed.

3. Col. Marc Munday to Major J.F. Faris, June 21, 1863, ordered the arrest of Moore; Moore Letter to Captain A.C. Semple asked that he be allowed to return to his regiment without a guard, June 21, 1863, O.H. Moore, CSRecord, NA, also J.S. Carlisle to Sister, June 25, 1863, Bentley Historical Library; Moore's Defense Argument, Moore Court Martial, NA. Orcutt matter is revealed on June 25, 1863, Letter from Charles Woodruff to father, Woodruff Papers.

4. McGeehan, *Wilterdink*, June 28, 1863; Dirk Van Raalte to mother, June 26, 1863, Van Raalte Papers, CC; Masselink, "Kentucky Occupied;" 17; Louisville Military Prison Records, NA.

5. Of the ten wagons in the train, seven were from the 12th Rhode Island and three from the 33rd Kentucky. 12th Rhode Island Record of Events Cards, NA, say departure was June 24; O.H. Moore to Drake, U.S. Military Telegraphs, June 28, 1863, NA; Hogan testimony, December 24, 1863, Moore Court Martial, NA; *Louisville Journal*, June 30, 1863.

6. Travis, *Twenty-fifth Michigan*, 79.

7. Ibid., 80.

8. A.C. Semple to D.B. Drake, June 28, 1863, 5 P.M., Military Telegraphs, NA.

9. McGeehan, *Wilterdink*, June 28, 1863.

10. The picket post north of Moore's camp was probably behind and to the east of Emerald Hill, where the old Columbia Turnpike forked. One fork led to Tate Landing and another to the ford over Green River at Roachville. The picket on the Columbia Turnpike was in the woods on the south side of the road in front of Russell Williams House; the third picket was behind the home and farm of Gregg Williams or Debbie Gabbert. Moore Court Martial, NA.

11. Moore Court Martial, NA. Because of some artifacts left by their men, it is known that the 12th Rhode Island was first camped north of the river on land across the road from Moore's camp; however, it appears from this testimony that they had moved their camp south of the river with Hogan. In Hogan's testimony, he used an incorrect date for the bridge being washed away. It is incomprehensible that Moore did not challenge Hogan's testimony on this point. The bridge situation may have colored other events, such as not showing enough pickets. Many of the 25th Michigan men were engaged in trying to recover the bridge and constructing a ferry.

12. Moore Court Martial, NA. The testimony calls Suddarth a postmaster, but this could have been Samuel G. Suddarth, who was Quarter Master General of Kentucky during the Civil War. Burdette, "Early Columbia," 30.

13. Duke, "Romance," *Century,* 12.

14. The "S" curve cut into the bank of earth at least 11 feet, according to Raymond Tye Faulkner, Jr., whose mother had an automobile accident in the curve years ago. The fill, used to straighten the curve about 1930, changed the terrain.

15. The west end of the cultivated field would be to the left side of the home of Russell Williams, 2078 Tebbs Bend Road; the main battleground between the two forces was the house and garden of Russell Williams.

16. Moore to Drake, US Telegraph, July 1, 1863, NA; L.A. Gratz at Somerset to Col A. V. Kautz at Jamestown, June 30, 1863, conveyed the message that he should seek forage around the country since no supplies could get through because the bridge over Green River was destroyed. OR(ser. 1) 52 (1): 382; *History of 12th Rhode Island,* 158, USAMHI.

17. G.S. McAlister Letter, Detroit Public Library; Charles W. Durling, Civil War Diary, July 3, 1863.

18. Green Keller, "Where Fell Col. Chenault and Morgan's Men," *Carlisle Mercury,* reprinted in Richmond paper, May 31, 1899. Keller was a private in Co.C, 5th Ky. Cav., CSA KAG, I, 642. Soldiers who were at Tebbs Bend used a variety of ways to describe the fortification. Basil Duke called it an earthwork with abates, formidable abates with heavy timber breastworks, large trees cut down; Hockersmith and Joe Tucker both used the word "stockade" to describe it; Adam Johnson called it a heavy earthwork around an abatis, and D. Howard Smith described it as a heavy abatis and in front, felled timber.

19. Clara Walters, granddaughter of the Burresses, to Mary Bertram, September 19, 1976, Oral History Project, Taylor County Library.

20. Raymond Tye Faulkner, Jr.,interview with author, Campbellsville, Ky., June 21, 1976, story told to him by his aunt Jessie Faulkner Dearen. Faulkner and Dearen are descendants of Johnstons.

21. Loneta Sublett, interview with author, Campbellsville & Coburg, October 1999. Sublett is a descendant of William Branch Sublett.

22. Leona Walling, "Battle of Green River," *New-Journal,* May 16, 1963. Walling's story came from Mrs. Bob Faulkner, daughter of Mary Johnston.

23. Lowell Harrison, "Basil Duke: Managing Man," *Civil War Times Illustrated* 21, January 1983, 37. Burnside termed Duke "managing man." A reporter called Duke the "brains of the raid."

24. Sprake, Diary, July 4, 1863; Allan Keller, *Morgan's Raid* (New York: Bobbs-Merrill, 1961), 33; Travis, *Twenty-fifth Michigan*, 93. "Seeing the elephant" refers to a soldier's first experience in combat.

25. Davis, *Partisan Rangers*, 141, quote on 281.

26. Ibid., 143. The dirt road is today's KY 3183.

27. Webster served in prison with one of the commanders on the field at Tebbs Bend, Col. D. Howard Smith. It seems that Smith left some money in a pair of pants that he gave Webster, but Webster never found it. D. Howard Smith Papers.

28. Hockensmith, *Morgan's Escape*, 16; Davis, *Partisan Rangers*, 143; Taylor County Cemetery Book; Gorin, "Service in American Revolution," n.p.; Paul Johnson, Sr., interview with author, Campbellsville, Ky., June 27, 1976.

29. Doug Martin, interview with author, January 1998. In 2004 Merritt Martin's bottomland is owned by descendant, M. Douglas Martin.

30. The nights of July 2, 3, 4, 1863, all had bright moonlight, according to Dr. Smith Powell, Berea College, physicist.

31. Doug Martin, interview with author, January 2003. In 2004, the log house was owned by Paul Voigt.

32. Gracie Jeter, granddaughter of Robert Fields Rucker, interview with author, November 24, 1998. In 2004, the farm where Morgan's Men crossed the river at Bailey's Ford was owned by Richard and Gracie Jeter; Charles and Betty Tucker own the land in 2004 where the log Rucker house was located in which the soldiers ate.

33. Jake Lemmons, interview with Don Elmore, June 1971. Jake Lemmons was the grandson of Jacob and Mary "Polly" Lemmons who were robbed. In 2004, this is the Rick Reynolds farm, according to Jewell Lemmons Reynolds, interview with author, May 2004.

34. Catlin, *Van Lente*, 55, Van Lente to family, July 12, 1863.

35. Ibid. The stockade site is owned by Suzanne and Robert Phillips in 2004.

36. Henry Allen Buchanan, as told to him by James Robert Sublett, interview with author, Campbellsville, Ky., January 15, 2002.

37. Masselink, "Dutch Boys Stood Firm," *Grand Rapids Valley Review* I (Fall 1979),17 did not give a source for his information. Living in Michigan, he may have gotten this from interviews or have had documents or letters not available to this writer. He reports that a Confederate got exaggerated information about the number of Moore's troops from an Indian. Since Indians had been gone from Kentucky for years before the war, he may have meant a slave.

38. In 2004 bullets are still in the ground around the house of David Tungate, 1126 Tebbs Bend Road, the house which is located west of the Phillips house.

39. OR(ser.1)23(1):645.

40. The stockade site was the Burress farm, which has been divided, one part owned by David Tungate and one part owned by Suzanne Sublett and Robert Phillips.

41. Billy Joe Kerr, interview with author, Campbellsville, Ky., June 22, 1999; Lucinda Kerr, Taylor County 1860 Census, 105.

42. Destin Tibbs witnessed a will in 1799, Green County Will Book 1, 2. Destin Tibbs owned at least 200 acres in Taylor County (then called Green) and 280 acres in Shenandoah and Culpeper counties, Virginia, according to Green County Deed Book 6, 437. Tibbs' children married into the Brents, Edrington, Tanner, Sublett, Lee, Roach, and Riffe families, whose descendants still inhabit the area today. In the Orlando Moore Papers, Kalamazoo Valley Museum, Kalamazoo, in an undated newspaper clipping entitled, "Colonel Orlando H. Moore," is written: The name of 'Tebb's Bend" was given by Colonel Moore himself, adopting the name of a pioneer settler of the place.

43. Raymond Tye Faulkner, Jr., interview with author, Campbellsville, Ky., June 21, 1976.

44. Quote from Travis, *Twenty-fifth Michigan, 83;* McGeehan, *Wilterdink*, July 11, 1863. Today, the current of the river has been changed by the water flow controlled by engineers of the Green River Dam. The sand bar has been washed away.

45. The Buchanan home, "Emerald Hill," was later owned by Sam Coppock, then by Dr. W. R. and Becky Mann, followed by Harold Wilkerson in 2004.

46. Catlin, Van Lente to father, mother, July 11, 1863.

47. Ronald J. Posthuma, "The Response of Michigan's Dutch Immigrants to the Civil War," Paper, November 19, 1973.

48. Catlin, *Van Lente, 56;* Benjamin Travis, "From the 25th Michigan," *Detroit Advertiser and Tribune*, July 22, 1863.

49. David Bridgewater of Cane Valley, Ky., telephone interview with author, March 13, 1997; Elizabeth Bridgwater of Louisville, Ky, telephone interview with author, March 13, 1997; Patrick Bridgewater, "Battle of Green River Bridge," *Louisville Dispatch*, July 9, 1898.

50. Sprake, *Diary*, July 3, 1863. His regiment did not even unsaddle. They camped ten miles up road from Columbia.

51. *National Tribune*, 1905; Messelink, 17; Sherman Dozier, Georgetown, Ky., unpublished manuscript.

52. Berry Craig, "The Big Bluff," *Kentucky Living,* January 1994, 19. A native of Henderson, Johnson escaped capture on the Great Raid; was made Brig. General. In 1864 at Grubbs Crossroads in Caldwell County, Ky., he was blinded by friendly fire. After the war, he returned to Texas and founded the town of Marble Falls; is buried in Austin, Tex. D. Howard Smith was elected State Auditor after the war. He died in 1899 and is buried in the Lexington Cemetery. *Lexington Transcript*, July 18, 1899.

53. Burke of Quirk's Scouts writes observations in his journal July 4, 1863 about events after the battle and is apparently the last group to leave Campbellsville in the evening. Chenault's regiment, which had served as the rearguard on so many occasions, was probably engaged in organizing the return of their colonel's body to Richmond and becoming accustomed to its new leadership.

54. Quote from Larry J. Daniels, *Cannoneers in Gray* (University of Alabama Press), 10; Ed Porter Thompson, *History of the Orphan Brigade* (Louisville: L.N. Thompson, 1898), 857–59.

55. Dozier, unpublished manuscript; Gypsie Cosby Jones, *Reflections in the Wind: Reliving a Memorable Era in Northern Madison County* (Richmond, Ky.: p.p., 1995), 110. Baxter information located in Winchester Public Library.

56. *Paris Citizen*, June 29, 1860, January 1, July 10, 1863, December 13, 1888; David M. French, Brent Family, typed copy, Alexandria, Virginia, 1977, Paris Library.

57. Taylor County 1850 (Slave) Census; farm was owned by the late E.L. "Buddy" Quinn and is located on the east side, KY 55. Jefferson Lee Atkinson became a physician and a founding trustee of Russell Creek Academy, now called Campbellsville University, and was the father of Dr. Burr Atkinson.

58. Richard Morgan wrote to JHM May 4, 1863, stating that "Johnson's Regt & this [14th] are without Enfield cartridges & I have directed him to get about 4 Boxes;" Davis, *Partisan Rangers*, 143.

59. Hockersmith, "Morgan's Escape," 16–17.

60. McGeehan, *Wilterdink*, July 14, 1863.

61. Andries died in 1870. A fire in 1871, destroyed the VerSchure home and Pieter's letters. His mother, Pieternella, received a pension in her son's name until her death in 1894. Pieter VerSchure, CSRecord, NA; Holland newspaper, 1894.

62. WWF Atkinson Survey shows log house, survey is located in Old Clerks' Office, Taylor County Historical Society. This farm is owned by Jessie and Sarah Brockman in 2005. The log house was near the road and stood directly in front of the present Brockman brick home. A log stable was located about one hundred yards to the north (left) of the Brockman house and away from the road, whereas the log house was located near the road. After the battle the stable was riveted with bullet holes, according to Raymond Burress, interview with author, February 1997.

63. Travis, *Twenty-fifth Michigan*, 85, says that this is the first position occupied by the Confederates.

64. The site of the rifle pit is owned by Raymond and Anita Keltner Brown in 2005. Travis writes that the length of the rifle pit trench was a bit shorter, but the trench had to be about this long to allow for 75 men plus the forward pickets.

65. Duke, *History of Morgan's Cavalry*, 415; Smith, *D. Howard Smith*, 57. This location of the artillery was the old Gardner farm, owned in 2005 by Carolyn Gardner Crenshaw.

Chapter Five: Confederate Attack at Tebbs Bend of Green River, pp. 180–205

1. "A Soldier's Journal," Grand Rapids, July 22, 1863; quote from Travis, *Twenty-fifth Michigan*, 85; McGeehan, *Wilterdink*, July 11, 1863; Dirk Van Raalte Letter to Parents, July 12, 1863, Van Raalte Papers, CC. The *Lebanon Central Kentuckian*, July 7, 1863, reported a half hour's cannonading before Hicks was injured. Duke, "Romance," *Century*, 13, said that round shot was fired, but Parrots do not fire round shot. George Hicks, CSRecord, NA.

2. John S.C. Abbott, "Heroic Deeds of Heroic Men," *Harpers Magazine* 31 (August, 1865), 287–297; *Louisville Journal*, July 12, 1863; Duke, *Reminiscences*, 363; Travis, *Twenty-fifth Michigan*, 87. Spencer Lansing in *History of Berrien and Van Buren Counties, 86, and* Moore's Report to Gov. Austin Blair, Detroit Public Library, include Duke, but Duke never indicated that he was present in his writings. According to the *Dictionary of Georgia Biography*, Alston was born in Macon, GA in 1832, schooled in SC, became an attorney, served one year in the Charleston Light Dragoons, and joined Morgan in Knoxville. After the war, he served in the GA legislature. According to Mariam Hood Tucker's pension application, Tucker was born in Boston, MA in 1825 and married his wife in Winchester, KY. Elliott was a Tennessean.

3. OR(ser.1)23(1): 646. Copied from original note, Bentley Historical Library, Ann Arbor, Mich.

4. Ibid.; *History of Berrien and Van Buren Counties*, 86; *Lebanon Central Kentuckian*, July 7, 1863; Colonel Tucker wrote that Moore was smiling.

5. *Lebanon Central Kentuckian*, July 7, 1863 repeated in a Three Rivers, Mich. Paper; Travis, *Twenty-fifth Michigan*, 87.

6. Travis, *Twenty-fifth Michigan*, 87; J.T.Tucker, "Fifty Exposed as the '"Six Hundred,'"*Confederate Veteran* 7 (1899), 364. Jessie Loveridge, the daughter of Colonel Moore, donated the *Harpers Magazine* about this encounter to the Kalamazoo Public Library. She placed an x by Elliott's name and wrote in Alston's name. The meaning is ambiguous. It may mean that Elliott was not in the delegation; however, by her notes it does indicate that Alston was carrying the message, not Elliott.

7. Dirk Van Raalte to parents, July 12, 1863, Van Raalte Papers, CC. This field lies between the dwellings of Jesse Brockman and Raymond Brown on Tebbs Bend Road, known in 1863 as the Campbellsville to Columbia Turnpike.

8. Jonathan T. Dorris, *Old Cane Springs: A Story of the War between the States in Madison County*, rev. ed. from original by John Cabell Chenault (Louisville: Standard Printing, 1936), 232; 25th Michigan Monthly Reports and Morgan's February Monthly Report (last one available), NA; AGR, CSA, II, 96 gives 500 efficient men for the 11th KY at the time of Chenault's death; Duke, "Romance," *Century*, 13, however, commented that no more than 600 were committed. The article in *Century* was written in 1891, years after the battle.

9. Pvt. Green Keller, 5th Ky. Cav., CSA, later editor of *Carlisle Mercury*, May 31, 1899.

10. Ibid.; OR(ser.1)23(1): 646; "Battle of Tebb's Bend," *Holland City News*, August 11, 1894.

11. Howard Smith, interview with author, 1970, as told to him by Woodson Lewis, Sr. The man was at the Ernest Rogers place.

12. Dirk Van Raalte to parents, July 12, 1863, Van Raalte Papers, CC.

13. Richard Akehurst, *World of Guns* (London: Hamlyn Publishing, 1972), 24; *Berrien and Van Buren County History*, 86; Charles Lanman, *Red Book of Michigan* (Detroit: E.B. Smith, 1871), 394. The maximum effective fire is 550 yards for the British-made Enfield.

14. Charles Woodruff to Father, July 15, 1863, Woodruff Papers.

15. Dirk Van Raalte to parents, July 12, 1863, Van Raalte Papers, CC; Travis, "From the Twenty-fifth Michigan," *Detroit Advertiser and Tribune*, July 22, 1863. Newt Thompson, a landowner in the 20th century is reported to have found cannon balls on his property in Tebbs Bend, according to Paul Johnson, Sr. interview with author, Sept. 30, 1987.

16. Travis, *Detroit Advertiser*, July 22, 1863; J.A. Turner, "Riding with Morgan," *Sprite & Bugle*, October 22, 1972, reprint of *Adair County News* July 29, 1903, 7; OR(ser. 1) 23(1):646.

17. Davis, *Partisan Rangers*, 143; Smith, *D. Howard Smith, 59.*

18. "Battle of Tebb's Bend," *Holland City News*, August 11. 1894.

19. N.H. Bowen, "The Brave Fourth of July Fight of a Michigan Regiment, 50 Years Ago," *Detroit Saturday Night*, July 5, 1913; Davis, *Partisan Rangers,143*; *Grand Rapids Daily*; *Holland News*, 1894.

20. Frick quote in Bush, "Campfire Tales;" Bowen, "Brave Fourth."

21. Travis, *Twenty-fifth Michigan*, 82–83. According to the *History of Berrien and Van Buren Counties*, 86, Company F was on the right side.

22. Keller, *Carlisle Mercury*, reprinted in Richmond paper, May 31, 1899; Duke, *History of Morgan's Cavalry*, 420–421.

23. Quote from Davis, *Partisan Rangers*, 143; "Battle of Tebb's Bend," *Holland City News*, August 11, 1894 reported that the artillerymen were attempting to plant the battery at a short range so as to attack the fortified abatis; supporting that is an account in A Soldier's Journal, *Grand Rapids Daily Telegraph*, July 22, 1863.

24. Davis, *Partisan Rangers*, 143. Author cannot explain why the troops were running low on ammunition. Morgan had gone back to McMinnville before the raid to get sufficient ammunition, so where was it?

25. James A. Ramage, "A Military Genius and Tactician Ahead of His Time," *Kentucky's Civil War, 1861–1865*, III (Ashland, Ky.: *Back Home in Kentucky*, 2004), 34.

26. Bowen, "Brave Fourth;" Dirk Van Raalte, Van Raalte Papers, CC July 12, 1863; Davis, *Partisan Rangers*, 143, claims there were only 400 men in both regiments that made the charge. In April a report of the regiments reported 800 in the two regiments. Report located at USMHI, Carlisle Barracks, Penn. Dirk Van Raalte was wounded in action near Atlanta, Aug. 26, 1864, resulting in the amputation of his right arm at the shoulder.

27. Davis, *Partisan Rangers*, 143. They probably came from where the John Kerr residence is in 2004.

28. Travis, *Twenty-fifth Michigan*, 82–83; also in Lanhan, *Redbook*, 394; information about not showing colors is in Blair Papers.

29. Duke, *History of Morgan's Cavalry*, 421; Smith, *D.Howard Smith*, 58; Turner, "Riding with Morgan," *Sprite and Bugle*, October 22, 1972.

30. Berry, *Four Years*, 216.

31. Bush, Campfire Tales.

32. Travis, *Twenty-fifth Michigan.*, 91.

33. Davis, *Partisan Rangers*, 143.

34. Duke, *History of Morgan's Cavalry*, 421.

35. Bowen, "Brave Fourth;" Abbott, "Heroic Deeds," *Harper's Magazine 21 (August 1865)*.

36. "Memorial To Honor the 25th Infantry To Be Erected in Kalamazoo," *Daily Reporter*, 1923, Moerdyk Papers. Quote Hurrah boys from Dirk Van Raalte to parent, July 12, 1863, Van Raalte Papers. Lion was described as a magnificent Kentucky thoroughbred; however, this is doubtful because this breed is usually too high strung to be calm in battle. He was most likely a saddlebred, Colonel Duke's favorite breed of cavalry horse.

37. Bowen, "Brave Fourth."

38. Travis, *Twenty-fifth Michigan*, 90.

39. Ibid., 95.

40. OR(ser.1)23(1):646.

41. Dirk Van Raalte to parents, July 12, Dirk to father July 23, Dirk to Mrs. AC Van Raalte, Aug 2, 1863, Van Raalte Papers, CC.

42. Henry G. Phillips to Sister, July 14, 1863, copy in Atkinson-Griffin House.

43. Mary Christie to brother, N.C. Christie, July 17, 1863, copy given to author by Norman Christie.

44. Smith, D. Howard Smith., "Corrections on History of Morgan's Cavalry," *Register of the Kentucky Historical Society* 52 (April 1954), 115.

45. Regiment's Compiled Service Records, KDLA.

46. *Confederate Veteran*, 1899, 364.

47. Mary Christie to N. C. Christie, July 17, 1863; Poem written for 25th Michigan Reunion, October 6–7, 1897, delivered by Jesse Moore Loveridge referred to the bodies in the river; Letter of C.H. Taylor, Co. D, 25th Michigan, Long Prairie, Minn., printed in "That Scrap on Green River," *National Tribune*, March 28, 1907.

48. Wartime Diary of John Weathered.

49. Bowen, "Brave Fourth."

50. D.W. Chenault to R.C. Chenault, March 11, 1863

51. Travis, *Twenty-fifth Michigan*,91–92; Catlin, *Van Lente*, July 11, 1863, 56.

52. Bowen, *Holland News*. Some member of Company I only spoke Dutch. The bugle calls were essential for them to be effective.

53. McGeehan, Wilterdink to parents, July 11, 1863.

54. Travis, *Twenty-fifth Michigan*, 92; quote from McGeehan, *Wilterdink*, July 11, 1863.

55. Quote is from Travis, *Twenty-fifth Michigan*, 91; Bowen, "Brave Fourth;" Muster-In Rolls, 25th Michigan, NA; *Confederate Veteran*, 27; Young, *Confederate Wizards*, 373; Keith Rozendal, Tribble Family II, (El Cajon, Ca. p.p., 1992), 163.

56. James B. McCreary, speech in Taylor County, June 11, 1914, said that three officers and many other men and horses had been shot and killed all around him at Green River Bridge; Young, *Confederate Veteran*, 27; Richmond *Climax*, August 23, 1911, version mistakenly lists Tribble's name as Terrell. In 1855, Steele, as Morgan, was engaged in a duel when he was a medical student at Transylvania, slightly wounding James Blackburn, a law student. Then they shook hands and returned to Lexington. Coleman, *Famous Kentucky Duels*, 145. Steele carried the flag of truce to George Rue, of the 9th Ky, when Morgan surrendered in Ohio. He later married the daughter of Robert J. Breckinridge, Union leader.

57. Lanman, *Redbook*, 89.

58. Story told by James Robert Sublett, interview with author, July 15, 1976. Sublett thought the officer was Chenault, but Chenault was killed instantly.

59. Jones, *Reflections in the Wind,* 66–67. Years later, in the 20th century, Jim Will Rice told Howard Smith, that when trees were cut from the woods on the bank where the fighting occurred, they always had minie balls in them. If the mills knew where the logs came from, they would discard them because it would ruin their saws.

60. CSRecords for brothers James, Austin Dunn, John and Oliver Cosby, and Peter Dozier, NA. The Oliver Wingfield Cosby Cemetery, Jacks Creek Pike, Fayette Co. is where daughter Anne Elizabeth Wilson was buried in 1864.

61. Jones, *Reflections in the Wind*, 67. Today Isham Fox and Colonel Chenault are buried in Richmond, Ky., Cemetery.

62. Travis, *Twenty-fifth Michigan*, 92.

63. Smith, *D. Howard Smith*, 59.

64. Travis, *Twenty-fifth Michigan*, 92. The 25th Michigan cut up the flag of truce and divided it among the men, according to Van Lente.

65. McGeehan, *Wilterdink*, July 11, 1863.

66. Travis, *Twenty-fifth Michigan*, 99; quote from Colonel Moore's report to Gov. Austin Blair, Detroit Public Library.

67. Original note is located in Bentley Historical Library, Ann Arbor, Mich.

68. Young, *Confederate Wizards*, 374.

69. Flora E. Simmons, *Complete Account of the John Morgan Raid Through Kentucky, Indiana, and Ohio* (Flora Simmons, 1863), 80.

70. Hathaway, Gen. Morgan's Ohio Raid, July 4, 1863.

71. McCreary, Journal, July 4, 1863.

72. Travis, *Twenty-fifth Michigan*, 93.

73. OR(ser.1)23(1)646 is Moore's Official Report, NA. Travis' comment, *Twenty-fifth Michigan*, 99.

74. U.S. Military Telegraphs, Moore to Hartsuff, July 16, 1863, NA.

75. OR(ser.1) 23 (1): 646–7.

76. Ibid., 768–69.

77. Ibid., 647.

78. Journal of the House of Representatives of the Commonwealth of Kentucky (Frankfort: Commonwealth Office, 1863), 388.

79. Travis, *Twenty-fifth Michigan*, 95.

80. Correspondence of James Ramage to author, February 21, 2005.

81. Hockersmith, "Morgan's Escape," 17.

82. McGeehan, *Wilterdink,* July 11, 14, 1863; Catlin, Van Lente, October 23, 1863..
83. *Holland City News*, August 11, 1894; "Tebbs Bend," *National Tribune*, February 28, 1889.

Chapter Six: Aftermath of the Battle, pp. 206–224

1. Glady Hord Steger, widow of Charles Steger, (1891–1965), who was the son of John Steger (1851–1918), interview with author, March 20, 1973 and July 20, 1976. John Steger was the youngest son of Mackiness Goode Steger, who lived directly across from the Henry Hubbard farm on the Lone Valley Road on the bank of today's Green River Reservoir. When the name was still visible, Gladys Steger remembered the name on the sword as John C. Cook. That name does not appear in the AGR for one of Morgan's men nor in 25th Michigan records. At Camp Douglas, a Confederate soldier by the name of John Cook is in the cemetery there. Will Henry Sublett went to the battlefield, too, and picked up a bayonet and rosettes from bridles of Morgan's horses, according to Sapp Sublett Howard in a story by Leona Walling, *Campbellsville News-Journal*, May 16, 1963.
2. Shellie Kendall Nunn, typed copy of family story given to author, September 25, 2004. The pitcher was passed down to the daughter of Willie Smith, Hallie Smith Phillips, to Faith True Phillips Kendall, grandmother of Shellie Kendall Nunn. Joel Smith and family are buried in a cemetery on C.R. Jones Road, two miles west of Cane Valley, Ky. Jimmy Kendall, Shellie's father also interviewed Jakie Smith, another Smith descendant, April 20, 2005. A forerunner of the International Silver Co., Meriden Britannia Co. was based in CT, and William W. Lyman was one of its organizers. Britannia was a silver white alloy composed largely of tin hardened with copper, according to Rainwater's *Encyclopedia of American Silver Manufacturers,* 108.
3. James Neal, interview with author, Richmond, KY, ca 1995. Joel Smith is in the Adair County census, living in the Coburg-Cane Valley area, not far from the battlefield.
4. P.H. Burns, Knightstown, Ind., *Home Journal*, 1900.
5. "That Scrap on Green River," *National Tribune*, March 28, 1907.
6. James Robert Sublett quoting Will Henry Sublett, interview with author, July 15, 1976. Travis, *Twenty-fifth Michigan*, 102.
7. James Robert Sublett, interview with author, July 15, 1976; Bridgewater, "Battle of Green River Bridge," *Louisville Dispatch*, July 9, 1898. Billy Joe Kerr said that his uncle showed him exactly where the Confederates were first buried. Kerr, interview with author, June 22, 1999. Today it is near a large cedar tree about 20 feet west of the right of way across the road from the rifle pit.
8. Duke, *History of Morgan's Cavalry*, 423.
9. Ibid.; Alston, Journal, July 4, 1863.
10. Catlin, *Van Lente*, 56.
11. Travis, *Twenty-fifth Michigan,* 92.
12. Charlie Woodruff to Father, July 15, 1863, Woodruff Papers.

13. Travis, *Twenty-fifth Michigan*, 103.

14. Beginning in May 1863 the training camps for 20,000 volunteers for 12 months service in the Second Military District of Kentucky- composed of Russell, Cumberland, Clinton, Monroe, Metcalfe, Barren, Allen, Simpson, Warren, Adair, Todd, Logan, Hart, Meade, Hardin, Bullitt, Larue, Marion, Washington, Nelson, Spencer, Taylor, Green, Shelby, Anderson counties-were located at Russellville and Lebanon. *Louisville Journal*, May 29, 1863.

15. "Honor to Whom Honor Is Due," Filson Club. See Appendix H.

16. Morgan Wallace, CSRecord, NA. Capitalization and punctuation changed by author for clarity.

17. Keller, 35. This is also reported in Senour, *Morgan and His Captors*, as coming from the *Louisville Journal*. However, Lizzie is not mentioned in letters home that the author has examined. Charles Woodruff does mention "Frank Martin," who was with the 8th MI in the Louisville office. She was small, auburn haired, with large blue eyes, and she was a Canadian, who claimed to have fought at Fredericksburg. Wulf Van Appledoorn wrote that there was a female in Louisville who was wounded in Murfreesboro and General Rosecrans discharged her. When she arrived in Bowling Green, she re-enlisted in a Federal cavalry regiment where she served 10 months. She came to Louisville with prisoners, accompanied by her Captain. Her age was given as 18, but her name was not mentioned in this letter. Apeldoorn to H.Van Lente, May 11, 1863, Hein Van Lente Papers.

18. James Robert Sublett, interview with author, July 15, 1976. J. Robert was the son of William Henry Sublett. Will Henry was a gun trader and it was traded away. A pair of Chenault's spurs stayed in the family log house with other "curiosities" for years. The way that Sublett told the story she was a Rebel "Johnny girl" accompanying the Confederates, instead of a Federal. No diary of any Morgan Raider mentions a girl; therefore, the author thinks it was Lizzie. She was probably staying a Sublett's after she was run out of the Federal camp across the road.

19. Travis, *Twenty-fifth Michigan*, 201, 322; *New York Herald*, December 28, 1863, reported her to be a member of the 11th KY Cavalry, who were camped across from the Green River Stockade, south of Green River, from May 24 to June 20, 1863. Moore's 25 Mich. were camped north of the river; therefore, the news report concerning the 11th KY connection was probably erroneous. Prutzman, loved and respected by the regiment, was killed by grapeshot passing through his body at Resaca, Ga. in 1864.

20. E.W. Quinn, quoting John Griffin, interview with author, Campbellsville, Ky., June 27, 1976.

21. Lorena Jackson, interview with author, Cane Valley, Ky. March 19, 1997. When Mary Elizabeth Griffin Tupman was older, she said she scrubbed the floors of the upstairs bedroom where the soldiers were carried to try to get up the bloodstains, to no avail.

22. Fred Faulkner, Sr., interview with author, Campbellsville, Ky., ca 1968.

23. A plaque listing the names of the donors to the project of moving the house to the corps site, many of whom were descendants of the Atkinson-Griffin family, is located

inside the Atkinson-Griffin House. Dr. Sanders spent many hours of volunteer time preparing the house for transfer to the Green River Park site. The Corps of Engineers restored the house. The house passed out of the Griffin family to E.L Davis and then to his daughter Bonnie and her husband, E.W. Quinn. For a verification of the bloodstains, read chemist Harold Woltman's Report in the Appendix.

24. Allan M. Trout, "Greetings," *Louisville Courier-Journal*, n.d.; Taylor County 1860 Census (printed), 60. The log house was located where the Tailwater Recreation Area of Green River Dam is today. F.H. Buchanan purchased the log house from J.M. Wilkerson's son, Ivan, dismantled it, and made a camp of Green River. Janice Wilkerson, interview with author, January 2003.

25. Burke, Civil War Journal, July 4, 1863.

26. Burke, Civil War Journal, July 4, 1863; Debbie Whitlock, granddaughter of Garland Martin, Campbellsville, interview with author, 1999; Gracie Jeter, interview with author, November 24, 1998. The brush broom, used to sweep away leaves, was made of dogwood branches wired together. The Tebbs Bend Battlefield Association now owns the shell.

27. Burke, Civil War Journal, July 4, 1863.

28. Paul Johnson, Sr., interview with author, Campbellsville, Ky., June 27, 1976 and September 30, 1987; Merritt Martin, Taylor County 1860 Census, 106. Martin had been plowing by the moonlight in order to keep his horses from being taken.

29. Norris Merrill, CSRecords, NA; Travis, *Twenty-fifth Michigan*, 101–102, 263.

30. Laura Larimore, interview with author, March 13, 1997.

31. Jimmy Caldwell, descendant of James Caldwell, interview with author, February 2003.

32. Virginia Buchanan McKinley, interview with author, Campbellsville, Ky., June 28, 1972. The brick walls of the house were 18 inches thick. Two stairways led to the rooms upstairs and a third stairway led to the upstairs over one of the ells. The parlor had carved mantels and door facings. The door leading into the parlor had a fan-shaped transom with side-lights. Slave houses were in the yard. The house was destroyed by fire.

33. Thomas Campbell, Co. I, 8th Michigan Infantry, CSRecord, NA.

34. *Louisville Journal*, July 3, 1863.

35. "The Hon. Aaron Harding," *Louisville Journal*, July 18, 1863.

36. Will of Jacob Hiestand, Taylor Co. Will Book 1, 5; G. Glenn Clift, *Biographical Directory of the Kentucky General Assembly*, unpublished manuscript, 1960s, Kentucky Historical Society, says that Chandler was a member of the General Assembly as representative from 1861–65 and a member of the senate from 1865–69.

37. Harley Gilmore, as told to him by Bruce Hiestand, interview with author, Campbellsville, Ky., March 12, 1981; Mary Louise Hiestand Carter, interview with author, Campbellsville, KY, 2002. Joseph H. and Araminta Chandler are the grandparents of Eugene Siler, Sr., candidate for governor on the Republican ticket in 1950.

38. The house was called "Heritage Hall," built in the 1850s. Sarah was well-connected, the daughter of wealthy merchant, Benoni Hotchkiss, and the granddaughter of Adam Campbell, who had inherited from his brother, Andrew, many of the town lots. The house is located on 315 Logan Street, owned by Mrs. P.C. Clark in 2004. A.F. Gowdy and his wife are buried behind the house on a knoll in the Gowdy Cemetery which fronts on South Central Avenue. Town spring, on south side of S. Court, is noted in *Campbellsville News-Journal*, July 28, 1938.

39. Chester and Ina Blakeman, interview with author, Campbellsville, Ky., July 8, December 31, 2002. Chester Blakeman is a descendant of William Linsey Miskell. The lot was thought to be 104 East Main Street, where Green River Graphics was until 2005.

40. Evelyn Smith Colvin, interview with author, Campbellsville, Ky., 2002 and E.B. Smith, interview with author, Campbellsville, KY, October 17, 2003. The farm is located on Palestine Road and is owned by Walter Ray Rafferty, a descendant in 2003.

41. Janet Caffee Kessler, interview with author, Campbellsville, Ky., June 10, 2004. Before 1879, the name for Arista was Richeson's Crossing. The Richeson farm was once owned by pioneer Mark Lively; in the 20th century, it was known as the Paul Holt farm.

42. L. Fuller Harding, interview with author, Campbellsville, Ky., June 30, 2004. Jane Colvin married Abel Harding, and they were the grandparents of Fuller Harding. Troops on both sides are described as "filthy" because the dust from the dirt roads covered their uniforms and faces.

43. Mrs. D.R.Green nee Ellen Browning letter to *Lebanon Enterprise* April 14, 1911; in the OR(ser.1)23(1):634, Burmside called the Morgan's trip a "detour" to Lebanon.

44. Burke, Civil War Journal, July 4, 1863.

45. William C. Davis to Miss Frank Cunningham, November 23, 1863, FHS.

46. Alston, Journal, July 4, 1863.

47. Duke, *History of Morgan's Cavalry*, 424–25.

48. "A Tasteful Tour of Historic Homes Lebanon/Marion County," 95–96.

49. Hathaway Papers, 40.

50. Martha Buford Jones Diary, FHS.

Chapter Seven: From Lebanon to the Ohio, pp. 225–244

1. Duke, *History of Morgan's Cavalry*, 425. Bricken Hill is East of Hatfield Inn.

2. Ibid., OR(ser. 1)23(1): 647–48; Smith, *D. Howard Smith*, 61; Mosgrove, *Kentucky Cavaliers in Dixie*, 209 for description of Hanson.

3. Terry Ward, "John Hunt Morgan: a portrait of the man who burned Lebanon," *Lebanon Enterprise*(Summer 1991), 14. L.A. Spalding sold to the Koburt family. According to Nash Hayes, June 13, 2004, the outer defensive line was about where

Walnut St. turns off Main St. There were only two homes on that end of Main Street at the time of battle. The rest of the land was a corn field and an orchard.

4. Hathaway Papers, 41–42.; *Lebanon Central Kentuckian*, July 9, 1863. According to Nash Hayes, the ploughed field may have been where Pickerill Motors lot is today.

5. Robert P. Ashley, *Rebel Raiders: A Story of the St. Albans Raid* (Philadelphia: Winston, 1956), 22–24.

6. Woodrow W. Friend, descendant of Ben House, interview with author, Richmond, Ky., May 21, 2004. Ben House's watch is still in the family. The boys are buried in the House-Reynolds Cemetery, off Kissing Ridge, Jessamine County, Ky. When Ben House died in 1918, he still had a deep sunken place in his neck.

7. OR(ser. 1) 23(1): 648–49.

8. Logan, *Peddicord*; quote from Hathaway, Gen. Morgan's Ohio Raid.

9. John T. Moore, "Varied War Experiences," *Confederate Veteran* (17) 1909, 213.

10. Smith, *D. Howard Smith*, 61–62; Duke, *History of Morgan's Cavalry*, 425–6; John T. Moore, "Varied War Experiences," *Confederate Veteran* XVII, 213.

11. Smith, *D. Howard Smith*, 63.

12. Duke, *History of Morgan's Cavalry*, 426.

13. Rose Cleland Grundy, PeWee Valley, to Sam Boldrick, Lebanon, January 9, 1939, copy in possession of Nash Hayes. Tom was laid out in the front south room.

14. Ramage says that Charleton grabbed the whiskers 164–165; *Lebanon Central Kentuckian*, July 9, 1863, reported that John Morgan grabbed Hanson's whiskers; last quote, Keller, *Morgan's Raid*, 42.

15. Hathaway Papers, 43; Alston, Diary, July 5, 1863; Smith, *D.Howard Smith*, 62–63.

16. Johnson, Lebanon; Charlton Morgan to Henrietta, July 24, 1863, Hunt-Morgan Papers, Box 16, Folder 10, UKL.

17. *Louisville Journal*, July 9, 1863. The Clerks' Offices were located where Attorney John Smith formerly practiced. Some of the homes set afire were those of Dr. Ben Spalding, Dr. J C. Maxwell, L.H. Noble, J.S. Braddock, and Mrs. Abell, most all on the north side of town, all Unionists. Mrs. Beeler's caught fire from its proximity to the depot. The *Louisville Journal* carried stories about Lebanon for days, July 6, 8, 9, 13, 14, 15, 16.

18. OR(ser.1)23(1): 647–651; *Louisville Journal*, July 14–15, 1863. [*Central Kentuckian* said Hanson had no artillery] Smith lists the 24-pounder Union gun as captured. What role it played in the battle is a mystery, because accounts of the battle seldom mention it.

19. Burke, Civil War Journal, July 5, 1863.

20. Ward, "John Hunt Morgan," 15; Alston, Diary; Woodrow Friend, interview with author, May 21, 2004.

21. *Louisville Journal*, July 24, 1863.

22. Brown, *Bold Cavaliers*, 184–85. They are buried in Cave Hill Cemetery, Louisville.

23. Woodrow W. Friend interview with author, May 21, 2004

24. Mrs. Clay to James B. Clay, July 9, Hunt-Morgan Papers, UKL.

25. Peter Diary, 139.

26. OR(ser. 1)23:633–34.

27. John Karel, interview with author, Campbellsville College Civil War Institute, July 1997. Karel, of Ste. Genevieve, Missouri, is a descendant of Mary Emeline, one of Campbell's eleven children. Campbell is a descendant of the Campbell family who founded Campbellsville. Samuel J. and Mary Campbell are buried together in the church at Stithton, now part of Fort Knox.

28. Brown, 188; Quote from Deatherage to Hardaway, February 17, 1930, FHS, spelling corrected.

29. OR(ser.1)23(1):639.

30. Ibid., 640, 656. Josephine Hutcherson said she had two grandfathers who were well-to-do before the Civil War. One was ferryman, Fielding Vaughn. He was awakened all during the night by soldiers, north and south, forcing him to transport them across the river. After the war, he was poor, was left "without a chicken." Her other grandfather would entertain the officers, both north and south, at his home for dinner, making sure his cattle and horses remained safe. After the war, he remained wealthy. Hutcherson to Barbara Simmons who relayed it to author, September 21, 2004. Vaughn was granted permit to a operate ferry beginning in 1846, according to Ruth Perkins, Green County Public Library.

31. Lowell Harrison, "John Hunt Morgan Pursued," *Filson Club Quarterly* 48 (1974), 134–35. Spelling corrected.

32. ORN(ser.1)25: 238–246, 254–255. For a detailed account of the Battle of Buffington Island, see Lester V. Horwitz, *The Longest Raid of the Civil War* (Cincinnati: Farmcourt Publishing, 1999), 207–246,

33. ORN(ser.1)25: 244.

34. Ellsworth to Charlton Morgan, August 12, 1893, reported in Paris *Western Citizen*, August 22, 1896. The article reported the town of Bellevue, Ohio; however, the place this occurred was Reedsville, Ohio, and the escaping men reached the shore near Belleville, W. Va., according to James Ramage.

35. Smith, *D. Howard Smith*, 40.

36. Horwitz, *Longest Raid*, 313.

37. Ibid., 318.

38. Ibid., 321–324.

39. Ibid., 330. According to a speech by Wolford delivered in Lexington, June 3, 1914, reprinted in the *Campbellsville New-Journal*, June 25, 1914, Morgan and Burbick were sitting on old boxes in front of a store in Salineville where Gen. Morgan was writing the terms of surrender. He wanted to be allow the men to keep their horses and the officers to keep their firearms, and that all should be paroled and allowed to return to Southern lines within ten days.

40. Ibid., 332–334. Numbers vary from 330–400 as to how many surrendered here. OR, Rue's report, says 336; Shackelford reports about 400. Basil Duke says 364.

41. *Cincinnati Commercial*, July 28, 1863.

42. Travis, *Twenty-fifth Michigan*, 97. Indiana and Ohio set up a Claims Commission to reimburse citizens for their losses during the Morgan Raid. Therefore, extensive records are available in those states, whereas in Kentucky, the citizen losses were, for the most part, unrecorded and not reimbursed.

Chapter Eight: Subsequent Events at Tebbs Bend, pp. 243–259

1. *Detroit Free Press*, August 4, 1863.

2. *Louisville Journal*, September 8, 1863. The flag is clearly over large in the Civil War painting of Henry on the book jacket.

3. Harry, "Incidents of Camp Life," *Detroit Free Press*, November 4, 1863.

4. "From the Twenty-Fifth Michigan: A Monument to be Erected for the Fallen Heroes," *Detroit Free Press*, October 12, 1863.

5. "It Should Not Longer be Neglected," *Adair County News*, June 14, 1911; "Mills Point to Big Sandy," *Louisville Times*, November 15, 1938.

6. Bridgewater, "Battle of Green River Bridge," *Louisville Dispatch*, July 9, 1898.

7. In Ralph W. Widener, Jr., *Confederate Memorials*, 95, the date for the monument is listed as 1867. According to the *Lebanon Weekly Standard*, April 17, May 22, 1872, the men were still in a mass grave without a monument in May. Plans were being made, however, for a granite monument.

8. "The Coming Reunion," *Adair County News*, April 26, 1911; Mrs. Fred Faulkner, Sr., interview with author, June 8, 1980. The planners of the celebration, Dr. J.H. Grady, Dr. E. A. Waggener, and J.W. Thompson, and most of the people on the program were people from Adair County. Entire program is listed in *Adair County News*, May 24, 1911. Quote from "At the Monument," *Adair County News*, June 7, 1911.

9. Taylor County Deed Book 41, 255 and 84, 494. Richard Sublett and his father mowed the cemetery for years. Raymond Brown and John Kerr mow it today.

10. Tebbs Bend Battleground, Historic American Buildings Survey Inventory Form, 1970, Margaret E. Tucker, recorder, May 25, 1940.

11. The Watsons, Dan and his son, Mike, Eddie Krug, and David Hensley volunteered to make major repairs and to lengthen the stone wall. Ed Gabehart, of Gabehart Lumber Company, donated the mortar.

12. The fund raising campaign within the community was called "Adopt a Soldier." Banks, civic clubs, and individuals donated funds for individual memorial tombstones for the soldiers buried at Tebbs Bend. The list of donors appears at the Atkinson-Griffin House. Robert Phillips and Glen Stephens volunteered their time to build up the entrance posts to the cemetery.

13. Marker was dedicated July 3, 1988. Gary Osborne, Gordon Smith, and the author designed the first driving tour and brochure.

14. Todd Family Papers. The time he was present in Louisville away from his post at Tebbs Bend concerned the birth of the second baby. When he sought permission to testify at a later time in Crandell's court martial, it was because he needed to get his ill wife home to Michigan. In 1867, his three-hour absence from duty because of his daughter's illness resulted in a second court martial trail.

15. Edward Henry to A.C. Semple, July 20, 1863; Brig. Gen. J.T. Boyle to Maj.J.H. Simpson, Chief of Engineers, Dept of the Ohio, July 25, 1863; Special Order 286, Hdqrters Dept of Ohio, Burnside to Maj. Simpson; A.C. Semple to Maj. Simpson, Nov. 16, 1863; Special Orders, Dec. 8, 1863, J.H. Simpson to A.C. Semple, in Edward Henry, CSRecord, NA. Henry was unable to return until after Jan. 2, 1864. RG 393, Pt. 1, 3540, NA.

16. Robert A. Powell, "Kentucky's Covered Bridges and Water Mills," 28. The bridge at Green River was similar to the present standing covered bridge over Beech Fork of Chaplin River on Mt. Zion Road, Ky 458, Washington County, Ky, according to Bonnie Money, engineer, interview with author, February 16, 2004. Bridge's length is given in Robt. B. Griffith, 8th Mich to Lt. A.W. Slayton, May 18, 1863, Slayton Papers.

17. Richmond, Ky., newspaper, 1880s, is attached to the back of the frame of the painting. It relates the story of the provenance of the work. At the time of the newspaper article, the painting was in the home of Mrs. America Chandler; Alice Thurman McElroy Whitehouse, interview with author, July 4, 2000; 1860 Marion County Census, Elizabeth Chandler, 16, is in the household of John W. Chandler; 1880 Marion County Census, Mrs. America Chandler, keeper of boarding house where painting was viewed by the writer of the newspaper article.

18. Lt. M. A. Hogan, CSRecord, NA; Pension Application 72521, of Mary Elizabeth Lake Hogan, widow. Death date is February 2, 1864, according to court martial records. Pension application says Feb. 1; *Louisville Journal*, dated Feb 4 indicates death date as Feb. 2; AG of Michigan states Feb. 9; *Louisville Journal*, February 6, 1864, says the body was returned to MI.

19. Samuel M. Crandell, CSRecords, NA. Crandell was a lieutenant in the 8th Ky Cav, USA then mustered into 13th KY Cav. on December 23, 1863 in Columbia, Ky. as a captain.

20. Crandell Court Martial, Record Group 153, File No. LL2260, Folder 1, February 1, 1864, NA; *Louisville Journal*, February 4, 6, 10, 27, March 2, 1864.

21. Pension Application 72521, NA, of Mary Elizabeth Lake Hogan, widow of M.A. Hogan. She and Hogan were married in Cleveland, Ohio, and the children were listed as Frank, Irene, and Martha, all living in Detroit.

22. Moore, CSRecord, NA. The amended order was Special Order No. 165. Proof it was Crandell's Court Martial is found in Moore's letter to Senator Jacob, June 5, 1864. Col. C.D. Pennebaker, the presiding officer, did not find it offensive, Capt W.R. Hardy did, however. Hardy reported the incident to Burbridge.

23. McGeehan, *Wilterdink*, Letter from Mossy Creek, Tenn., March 27, 1864.

24. Special Orders 248, War Department.

25. Quote from newspaper article in Moore Collection, Kalamazoo Valley Museum; flag story in Bell letter, Moore, CSRecords.

26. Letters in Moore, CSRecord, NA. Bravery at Fort Anderson chronicled in Van Lente letter to father, mother, April 2, 1865, in Catlin, *Van Lente*, 125. Van Lente said that Moore almost lost his life, but "the Lord saved him again." Quote from action at Franklin, "Colonel Moore," *E. Saginaw Courier*, December 14, 1864;

27. Cook and Cook, "Moore," 34; Moore Court Martial, Record Group 153, File No. OO-2345, July 20, 1867, NA.

28. Edgar I. Stewart, *Custer's Luck* (London: University of Oklahoma Press, 1955), 221–227, 482; James Donahue, "Surrender He Didn't On Fourth of July," *Kalamazoo Gazette,* July 5, 1970; Carrie J. Crouch, "In Old Indian Territory Days," *National Republic,* November 1923, 7; Cook and Cook, Moore, 30.

29. *Coldwater Republican*, November 29, 1881; "Funeral of Col. O. H. Moore," *Tulare Weekly Register* sent to *Coldwater Republican*, November 21, 1890; photograph of grave in Tulare made by cemetery secretary to author.

30. Edward Masselink, "The Dutch Boys Stood Firm," *Grand River Valley Review*, I, Fall, 1979, 20 quoting from Lewis Beeson, *The Dutch Churches in Michigan during the Civil War* (Lansing: 1965).

PART SEVEN: Morgan's Escape *November 1863,* pp. 260–267

1. Dave Roth, "John Hunt Morgan's Escape from the Ohio Penitentiary," *Blue and Gray Magazine* 12 (1994–1995), 10f.

2. Ramage, *Rebel Raider*, 195.

3. Caroline T. Cunningham, "How General John H. Morgan Escaped," Hunt-Morgan Papers, Box 16, f12, UKL.

4. Ben Johnson, Bardstown, son of William Johnson, to Cecil Holland, June 20, 1937, Holland Papers, Box 1, UKL.

5. Thomas Henry Hines, *Southern Bivouac*, June 1885; Hibbs, 92.

6. According to Steven Wright, Elizabethtown, interview with author, February 16, 2005, McCormick lived off Hwy 84 and is buried in Beech Grove Methodist Church Cemetery.

7. Thomas Henry Hines, "The Escape," *Century* Magazine, 32. Clay Risen, Mac-Pitman Road, interview with author, February 26, 2005, reports that his deed mentions the

Old Greensburg-Bardstown Turnpike as his boundary on the north side. It ran between the Snow Hill Cemetery and old Snow Hill School. This could have been the route Morgan used; Hibbs, *Nelson County*, 92.

8. The provenance of the book is from C. C. Darnell to W.W. Webster to Robert Webster. Robert Webster, interview with author, October 1986. The message is written in ink on page 363 of Duke's book.

9. Barbara Durham Simmons, descendant of R.A. Taylor, Jr., interview with author, September 21, 2004. This story is supported by an article in the *Filson Club History Quarterly* 64 (April 1990), 274. The Cox house was owned by Brooks Edwards in 2004. The Taylor house has been torn down. Notebook of Barbara Durham, interviews with her mother, Flossie Durham, ca 1966.

10. Jillson, *Tour Down Stream*, 71.

11. Horwitz, *Longest Raid*, 365–366.

12. Louisville Military Prison Rolls, NA; Taylor County 1860 Census, 7.

13. Louisville Military Prison Rolls, NA. Taylor County 1860 Census, 16.

14. OR(ser.1)31(2): 338.

15. Albert Castel, "Morgan's Last Raid," *Blue & Gray Magazine* 6, no. 2, 43.

16. Many versions of the death of Morgan exist.

17. Kentucky, Indiana, and Ohio are marking the Great Raid Trail with interpretive wayside signs. Other raids are marked in Kentucky. Call the Kentucky or the Indiana Departments of Tourism for brochures.

PART EIGHT: After Morgan: Confederate Guerrillas *November 20, 1864*, pp. 268–275

1. US v. H.C. Magruder, Record Group 153, File No. MM2958, NA; Henry C. Magruder, *Three Years in the Saddle* (Louisville: Maj. Cyrus J. Wilson, 1865, reprt, Utica, KY: McDowell Publications, n.d.), 3–15; AGR, CSA, I, 560, execution date 1865, not 1863 as stated there.

2. US v. H.C. Magruder. After the Campbellsville incident, the gang robbed a bank in Springfield on December 3, 1864. A witness described his physical appearance. People in Bloomfield testified as to his clothes.

3. McElroy, "History of Lebanon," 22.

4. Magruder, *Three Years*, 34. "That night we came up through Bush [Brush] Creek to Williams' on the Lebanon and Greensburg road…"

5. "Particulars of the Guerilla Raid on Campbellsville, Ky," *Louisville Journal*, November 29, 1864. Williams was recruited from Adair County and death date listed as November 27, 1863 in the AGR. Sol Thompson was a native of Marion Co.; his brother, John P., was an attorney, in Co K, Cluke's 8th Ky., captured near Brandenburg, and sentenced to be hung.

6. Ibid.; "Guerillas at Campbellsville," *Louisville Journal*, November 28, 1864; Magruder, *Three Years*, 40. In his confession, Magruder claims that they killed one and wounded three. The newspaper only reported Blankenship killed in Campbellsville and another seriously wounded. The records of the 13th Kentucky Cavalry do not reflect another death. However, the OR(ser. 1)45(1): 981, J.W. Weatherford to Capt. J.S. Butler, November 11, 1864, reported that the guerrillas killed and wounded five men.

7. Even though he used the name Henry C. Magruder when he wrote his confession, a family member says that his name was William Henry Magruder. That may account for his name, "Billy Magruder." Thomas Shelby Watson, *The Silent Riders* (Louisville: Beechmont Press, 1971), 43. Jeter had assumed the leadership of the 100th Militia as colonel by 1864.

8. "Particulars of Guerilla Raid," *Louisville Journal*, November 28, 1864. According to Magruder's court martial, when the gang robbed the bank in Springfield in January 1865, Magruder commanded everybody to stay still and not move or they would be shot. Then one of the guerrillas gathered the citizens in one spot, while the other members spread out over town. They ordered the bank official to open the vault. When insufficient funds fell out, Captain Magruder rubbed his pistol across Hugh McElroy's forehead, "Now g-damn you, tell me where the balance of the money is or I will blow your brains out." After the gang killed Thornton Lee, robbed several others, and took some silver church chalices, they departed town. They probably used the same technique here in Campbellsville.

9. Aileen McKinley, interview with author, Campbellsville, Ky., July 23, 2000. The Chandler home was at 301 East Main; in 2004 the offices of Wise, Lee, and Buckner occupy the lot. When the baby grew up, he changed his name to Morgan J. Chandler and became the editor of the local newspaper. A member of the battery may have been John Green Sublett who had just been mustered out.

10. Ibid., AGR,CSA, I, 358, 506.

11. Magruder, *Three Years*, 53.

12. *Louisville Daily Union Press*, November 30, 1864.

13. Ibid., 56; OR(ser.1)49(1): 673–77,683–84, 694, 698; John Sickles, *The Legends of Sue Munday and One Armed Berry* (Merrillville, Indiana: Heritage Press, 1999), 45. Numbers vary concerning the number killed here from 3 to 27, the number of wagons said to be up to 20.

14. Edward E. Leslie, *The Devil Knows How to Ride: William Clarke Quantrill* (New York: Random House, 1996), 362–63; Watson, *Silent Riders*, 41–43.

15. US v. H.C. Magruder, NA; *Louisville Journal*, October 21, 1865. His stone is in Magruder Cemetery, Hwy 61, south of Lebanon Junction, KY. He was indicted on only those counts that could directly be penned to him personally, as opposed to those of members of the gang. He was not brought to trial on the murders in Taylor County.

16. Hobson Papers, Green County Historical Society. Greensburg.

17. *Louisville Journal*, October 24, 1863.

18. Hobson Papers, Green County Historical Society, Greensburg.

19. Petition of William Wallace of Green County, June 6, 1864, Governor Bramlette Papers, Box 10, f 223.

20. Petitions of J. Young and John Lampkin, Bramlette Papers, Box 15, f 328, 330; Harding and Short Case, Bramlette Papers, Box 13, 17, f 253, 276, 283, 368.

21. Mrs. Robert T. (Elsie) Gaddie, interview with author, June 30, 1976. Robert T. Gaddie is the son of S.S. Gaddie, who was the son of John G. Gaddie.

PART NINE: Lyon Visits Taylor County *December 25, 1864*, pp. 276–285

1. OR(ser.1)45(1): 804–06; Hall Allen, *Center of Conflict* (Paducah: *Paducah Sun-Democrat*, 1961), 146.

2. "Rebel Operations at Burkesville," *Louisville Journal*, January 9, 1865.

3. *Biographical Register of Officers and Graduates of U.S. Military Academy*, II (Boston: Houghton Mifflin, 1891), 653.

4. Geoffrey C. Ward, *The Civil War* (London: Bodley Head), 345.

5. OR(ser.1)45(1): 805; B.L. Roberson, "The Courthouse Burnin'est General," *Tennessee Historical Quarterly* 23 (December 1964), 372–378. To read more detail about this raid, see "Memoirs of Hylan B. Lyon," ed. Edward M. Coffman, *Tennessee Historical Quarterly* 18 (March 1959), 35–53.

6. "Movements of Rebel Gen. Lyon," *Nashville Daily Press*, December 29, 1864. Spelling corrected.

7. Bob Henry Cowherd, interview with author, Campbellsville, Ky., July 1, 1976, as told to him by Henry Robinson; Aaron, *Campbellsville Methodist Church*, 17.

8. "Lyon at Campbellsville," *Louisville Daily Union Press*, December 29, 1864. This report said that he burned Green River Bridge, but no report of it appears in the Official Records. The paper also said that he threatened to burn Columbia, but the troops "were pressed too hard to accomplish it."

9. J. W. Wells, *History of Cumberland County* (Louisville: Standard Printing, 1947), 67–68.

10. "Rebel Operations in Burkesville," *Louisville Journal*, January 9, 1865.

11. *Biographical Register*, 653; "Gen. H.B. Lyon," *Confederate Veteran*, 560–61; Ezra J. Warner, *Generals In Gray: Lives of the Confederate Commanders* (Baton Rouge: Louisiana State University, 1959), 197.

12. Richard H. Collins, *History of Kentucky*, II (Covington, Ky.: Collins & Co., 1874), 726; Hall Allen, "Civil War Rough on Courthouses," *Louisville Courier-Journal*, August 25, 1963; Hall Allen, *Center of Conflict*, 148. A *Campbellsville News-Journal* article August 19, 1937, indicates that there was Federal opposition in Campbellsville. The author can find no evidence to support this.

13. Taylor County Order Book 2, October 3, 1863, 291.

14. Taylor County Order Book 2, 305–06. The address of Lot 11 is 217 East Main Street, Scott's Store in 2004.
15. Ibid., 308.
16. Ibid., 371.
17. Ibid., 306.
18. Ibid., 334, 335, 356, 371,375. The frame Baptist Church building occupied Lot 46, site of the 1889 brick Gothic revival Baptist Church, served as the Taylor County Library during the latter years of the 20th century. The fire probably spread to Ferdinand Hiestand's business next door, which confirms a story told the author by Gladys Hord Steger about Hiestand losing his boarding house-tavern in a fire during the Civil War. Hiestand was a "Peace Democrat," naming a child, Clement Laird Vallandigham Hiestand after the northern Copperhead Ohio Senator. The child became known as Dr. C.V. Hiestand in the twentieth century.
19. Aaron, *Campbellsville Methodist Church,* 17.
20. Taylor County Order Book 3, 469–70.
21. Ibid., 23, 135–137, 159, 173–175.

PART TEN: Quantrill Threatens *February* 1865, pp. 286–288

1. OR(ser. 1)49(1):35–36; *Nashville Daily Press*, February 11, 1865; "Quantrill's Trail from New Market to Danville," Bradfordsville Historical Society Brochure; Leslie, *Quantrill*, 355–7.
2. Leslie, *Quantrill*, 364–369, 436.

PART ELEVEN: Stories and Legends, pp. 289–297

1. Harrison, *Lincoln of Kentucky*, 151. White (1813–1890) is buried in White Cemetery, in Whitewood section of Green County. White sources are Taylor County Order Book 1, 1; Richard Collins, *History of Kentucky*, I, 84, 346,364, 369; II, 295.
2. Wallace Bottoms, interview with author, May 15, 1970. Many of the tailored field stone homes, foundations and retaining walls in evidence in Taylor County today reflect the handiwork of Wallace Bottoms. He worked for other stone masons, other times by himself. Some of the public buildings which foundations he helped lay are the Campbellsville Baptist Church, Christian Church, First Methodist Church, the addition to the Bethel First Presbyterian Church, the Lyon-Beard Garage, the Merchant's Hotel, the wall along Buckhorn Creek, and the Campbellsville City School, his own house on Baptist Street. He started working in mortar with Jim Denny. Bottoms became so proficient in stone cutting that spectators found it interesting to watch him, round-ball hammer in hand, tap a huge piece of stone at a certain point that only a master perceives, and chip the rock into exactly the shape he desired. Buck Mikel was also a very good stone mason. He may have helped Mikel also.

3. Taylor County Deed Book 2, 312.

4. Story came from Howard Smith, interview with author, 1970. Son of Herbert and Addie Feather Smith, Howard was reared on Bear Tract Road. Mrs. Celesta Reid also related the story of Barr's land and it is verified by deed books.

5. Clara Walters, interview at Taylor County Library for Oral History Project. Howard Smith to author, 1970; Dr. Robert Ingram, *News-Journal,* July 25, 1974.

6. "Salem Baptist has homecoming services Sunday," *Central Kentucky News-Journal,* October 2, 2003.

7. Interview with author, June 21, 1976.

8. James Robert Sublett, interview with author, July 17, 1976.

9. Ibid. Willowdale is owned by Rufus Hansford. A descendant of Caldwell is James Caldwell of Campbellsville.

10. Celesta Reid, interview with author, June 20, 1976. Celesta was the daughter of Lucy Davis and John V. Davidson. Lucy Davis was the daughter of Wesley Davis and Nancy Phillips, Wesley Davis was the son of Rezin H. Davis and Mary R. Johnston. Rezin H. Davis was the son of Rezin Davis and Ann Webb. This Rezin was the son of Rezin Davis and Nancy Phillips who were married in Frederick Co, Md., March 15, 1782. The original farm of Rezin Davis, the immigrant to Taylor County before 1800, is where the Taylor County Airport is located today.

11. Ibid.

12. Evelyn Steger Freund Bledsoe, interview with author, February 22, 2004. Henry Prescott family is listed in Taylor County 1860 printed Census, 103 and in 1870 Census, 77.

13. Georgia Beard, interview with author, January 28, 2003. The story was told by the grandson of William Page Bridgewater, Jim Bridgewater, to Georgia Beard. Butler and Mollie are buried at Penitentiary Bend Cemetery. Mollie was born Sep. 6, 1848-died Dec. 17, 1913. James "Jim" Butler has a Union grave marker with the words, Co K, 13 Ky Cav.

14. Arbell Gupton Hall, interview with the author, summer, 2004. The shell, 3½ inches in diameter with three rings around it, was passed from William Page Bridgewater to his daughter, Lola, who married Thomas Virgil Gupton, to Arbell. Bridgewater relationships provided by Georgia Beard, Campbellsville, and Martha Houk, Green County.

15. Jerry O. Potter, *The Sultana Tragedy* (Gretna; Pelican Publishing, 1997), 70.

16. Ibid., 74, 80, 81, 95.

17. Stephen B. Humphress, "The Sinking of the Sultana," *Kentucky Heritage* (Fall-Winter Issue, 1981), 8–9. Stephen interviewed his great uncle, Dr. L. R. McDonald; McDonald Pension certificate 155569.

18. Potter, *Sultana*, 153–155.

PART TWELVE: Taylor County Soldiers in the Civil War, pp. 299–323

1. Speed, *Union Regiments of Kentucky*, 169–174.
2. Ibid., *Union Regiments of Kentucky*, 407–411, Hobson quote from 408; White quote from 410.
3. Ibid., *Union Regiments of Kentucky*, 552–560.
4. Georgia Scott, interview with author, Summer 2002, Campbellsville, KY.
5. *Campbellsville News-Journal*, November 13, 1930.
6. Ibid.
7. Guerrilla File, Kentucky Military History Museum.
8. Howard Smith, interview with author, 1970.
9. James "Jimmy" Morris interview with author, June 27, 1976. Jimmy Morris was the son of A. Chester Morris, who was the son of James B. Morris.
10. Bob Henry Cowherd, interview with author, July 1, 1976, Campbellsville, KY; Fuller Harding, interview with author, Campbellsville, Ky., July 4, 1976; Howard Smith, interview with author, 1970. Smith heard that during the war, Robinson had had someone court-martialed and shot for going to sleep on picket duty.
11. Bob Henry Cowherd, interview with author, July 1, 1976, Campbellsvillle, KY.
12. Story from Aileen McKinley to author.

APPENDICES, pp. 324–376

1. According to Johnston in "Lebanon As I Have Known It," after Proctor and Sallie Knott returned to Lebanon from Missouri in late 1862, he went into law practice with C.S. Hill, who became a leading attorney in Lebanon. After the war, Proctor resumed his political career in Kentucky.
2. According to James Ramage in a 1997 speech at the Hiestand House Museum, part of the Morgan legend was the exaggerated reports of his troop strength. The *Central Kentuckian*, July 9, 1863, stated that 5,000 troops were on the Great Raid, when in reality the raid began in Tennessee with 2,460 soldiers.
3. Colonel David's Michigan troops.
4. Knott, *History*, 46.

Index

Y

Z

TRAVIS
OF TEBBS BI
PUI

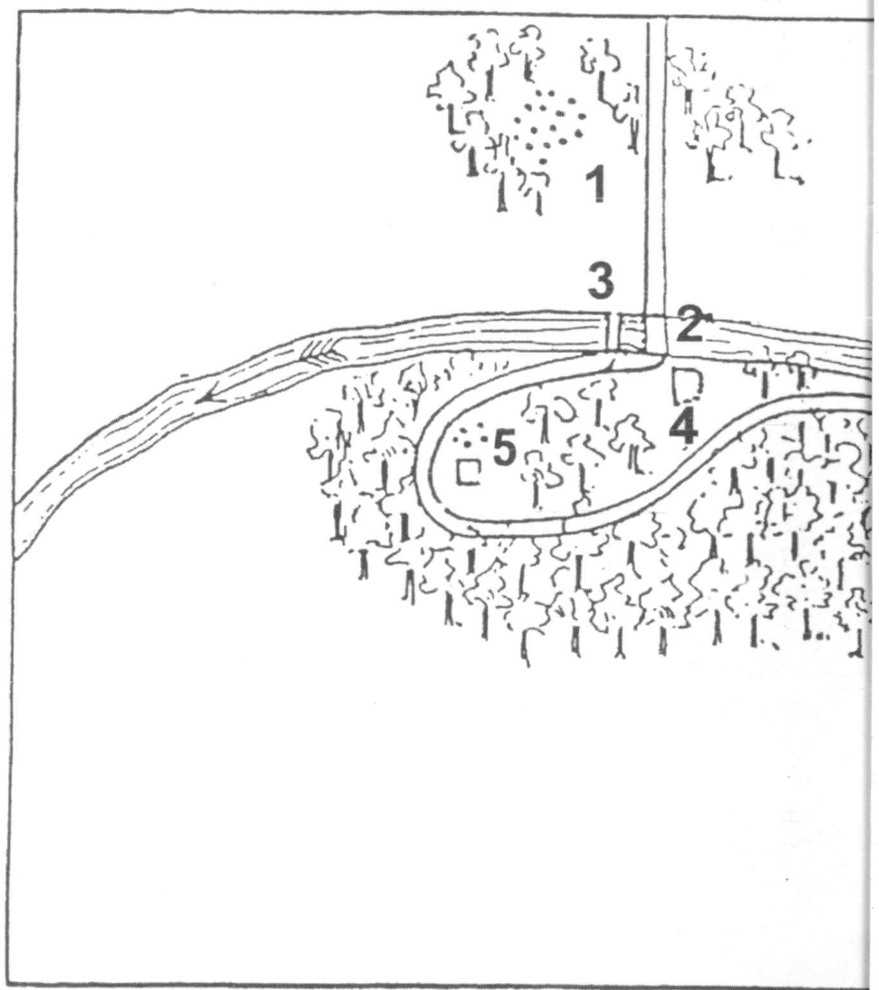

1 - First camp north of the river. 2 - Bridge. 3 - Fo
7 - Outer works. 8 - Barriers. 9 - Rebel artillery
log building seized by the rebel skirmishers to beg